SCOTLAND

BED & BREAKFAST

ACCOMMODATION

Friendly, economical bed-and-breakfasting is one of the best ways you can choose to get to know Scotland – and the Scots. It's a great combination – good food, comfortable bedrooms, a holiday atmosphere – and all in the setting of a family home, where the owner's touch makes all the difference. Much more personal than a hotel, a bed and breakfast adds up to superb value.

There's a wide and varied range of bed and breakfasts to choose from, around the country. Welcoming doors are opened in country cottages, superior suites, city drawing rooms, farmhouse kitchens, warm with baking, even in mansions with trout streams in the grounds.

A bed and breakfast is perfect for a short break – a weekend in the country, or a theatre stop in Edinburgh or Glasgow. It's the perfect place to stop on a touring holiday to take in the history and scenery that make Scotland famous. It's the ideal place to unwind after a day's business or travel – always relaxing, never too grand for comfort.

Start making your choices now. Just reading this book will put you in the holiday mood – and once you get here, we don't think you'll be disappointed !

Where to Stay...?

Over 1100 answers to the age-old question!

Revised annually, this is the most comprehensive guide to bed and breakfast establishments in Scotland.

Every property in the guide has been graded and classified by Scottish Tourist Board inspectors. See page vi for details of this reliable quality assessment scheme.

How to find accommodation

This book split into eight areas of Scotland:

South of Scotland

Edinburgh City, Coast & Countryside

Greater Glasgow & Clyde Valley

West Highlands & Islands, Loch Lomond, Stirling and Trossachs

Perthshire, Angus & Dundee and the Kingdom of Fife

Grampian Highlands and the North-East Coast

The Highlands & Skye

Outer Islands

The map on page 1 shows these areas. Within each area section you will find accommodation listed alphabetically by location. Alternatively there is an index at the back of this book listing alphabetically all accommodation locations in Scotland. There is also an alphabetical list of all the establishments in this book.

Learn to use the symbols in each entry - they contain a mine of information! There is a key on the back flap. You can use them to check on facilities from four-poster beds to swimming pools, from babysitting services to access for disabled visitors. Naturally, it is always advisable to confirm with the establishment that a particular facility is still available.

Prices in the guide are quoted per person and represent the minimum and maximum charges expected to apply to most rooms in the establishment. They include VAT at the appropriate rate and service charges where applicable.

The prices of accommodation, services and facilities are supplied to us by the operators and were, to the best of our knowledge, correct at the time of going to press. However, prices can change at any time during the lifetime of the publication, and you should check again when you book.

Bookings can be made direct to the establishment, through a travel agent, or through a local Tourist Information Centre.

Remember, when you accept accommodation by telephone or in writing, you are entering a legally binding contract which must be fulfilled on both sides. Should you fail to take up accommodation, you may not only forfeit any deposit already paid, but may also have to compensate the establishment if the accommodation cannot be re-let.

QUALITY HOLIDAY ACCOMMODATION

To ensure you find the right place to stay, we have visited nearly 10,000 individual establishments.

Every year, Scottish Tourist Board inspectors travel the country, staying in hotels, guest houses and bed and breakfasts and visiting self catering holiday homes, to assess them for the standards expected by visitors to our country and ensure your needs are met.

Using our Grading and Classification Scheme they assess all the important factors that contribute to the comforts of your accommodation and highlight the range of facilities and services offered.

GRADING for QUALITY of facilities and services

DELUXE	An overall EXCELLENT quality standard
HIGHLY COMMENDED	An overall VERY GOOD quality standard
COMMENDED	An overall GOOD quality standard
APPROVED	An overall ACCEPTABLE quality standard

Quality grades are awarded by the Scottish Tourist Board inspectors only after they have slept in the beds, sampled meals and talked to staff. They are based on a wide ranging assessment of quality and service aspects, including the warmth of welcome, atmosphere and efficiency of service, as well as the quality of furnishings, fittings and decor. Each establishment is assessed on its own merits, irrespective of the range of facilities on offer.

CROWN CLASSIFICATION for RANGE of facilities and services

When you book a hotel, guest house or bed and breakfast with the following crown classification you will receive at least the facilities and services indicated.

NOTE: Each level includes all the facilities and equipment listed underneath.

👑👑👑👑👑	All bedrooms with full ensuite facilities. Restaurant serving breakfast, lunch and dinner. Night porter and room service. 24 hour lounge service.
👑👑👑👑	Evening meal, choice of dishes and selection of wine. Colour TV, radio and telephone in bedrooms. Laundry services, toiletries. Quiet seating area.
👑👑👑	Evening meal. Hairdryer. Shoe cleaning equipment. Ironing facilities and tea and coffee making facilities.
👑👑	Colour TV. Early morning tea. Minimum of 20% bedrooms with ensuite/private facilities.
👑	Your own bedroom key. Shared lounge area. Washbasins in bedrooms or in private bathrooms.
LISTED	Clean and comfortable accommodation. Cooked or continental breakfast. Adequate heating at no extra charge. Clean towels and fresh soap. Bedding clean and in sound condition. Hot water with no extra charge for baths or showers.

Classification covers the range of facilities and services offered, from LISTED to 5 CROWNS. More crowns mean more facilities.

For full details of the scheme contact The Quality Assurance Department, Visitor Services Division, Scottish Tourist Board, Thistle House, Beechwood Park North, Inverness IV2 3ED. Telephone: (01463) 716996.

Over 4,000 hotels, guest houses and bed & breakfasts have been inspected by the Scottish Tourist Board, and they are to be found in all parts of Scotland.

Look out for this distinctive sign of Quality Assured Accommodation

vii

POUR UTILISER CE LIVRE

Où loger?

Plus de 1100 réponses à l'éternelle question!

Ce livre révisé chaque année est le guide le plus complet des Bed & Breakfasts en Ecosse.

Chaque établissement dans ce guide a été noté et classé par les inspecteurs du Scottish Tourist Board. Reportez-vous à la page x pour plus de détails sur ce système fiable d'évaluation de la qualité.

Comment trouver où loger

Ce livre est divisé en huit parties, chacune consacrée à une région écossaise:

Le sud de l'Ecosse
Edimbourg - ville, littoral et campagne
Le Greater Glasgow et la vallée de la Clyde
Les West Highlands et leurs îles, le Loch Lomond, Stirling et les Trossachs
Le Perthshire, l'Angus & Dundee et le royaume de Fife
Les Grampian Highlands et le littoral nord-est
Les Highlands et Skye
Les îles extérieures

La carte de la page 1 montre ces régions. Dans la section correspondant à chaque région, vous trouverez une liste des possibilités d'hébergement, classées géographiquement par ordre alphabétique. Vous pouvez aussi utiliser l'index à la fin de ce livre, qui répertorie par ordre alphabétique tous les lieux offrant des possibilités d'hébergement en Ecosse. Il y a aussi une liste alphabétique de tous les établissements apparaissant dans ce livre.

Familiarisez-vous avec les symboles dans chaque annonce. Ce sont des mines d'informations! La légende se trouve sur la dernière page de couverture. Vous pouvez les utiliser pour vérifier quels sont les aménagements proposés, des lits à baldaquin aux piscines, et des services de

garde d'enfants à l'accès pour les visiteurs handicapés. Evidemment, il est toujours conseillé de vérifier auprès de l'établissement qu'un aménagement particulier est toujours disponible.

Les prix dans ce guide s'entendent par personne et représentent le prix minimum et le prix maximum auxquels s'attendre dans la plupart des chambres de l'établissement. La TVA au taux approprié et le service (le cas échéant) sont compris.

Les prix de l'hébergement, du service et des aménagements nous ont été fournis

par les organisateurs et étaient, à notre connaissance, corrects au moment d'imprimer. Cependant, les prix sont susceptibles de changer à tout moment pendant la durée de vie de la publication et il est donc bon de les revérifier au moment de réserver.

Les réservations peuvent être effectuées directement auprès de l'établissement, par l'intermédiaire d'une agence de voyages ou d'un Tourist Information Centre local.

Souvenez-vous qu'accepter une chambre par téléphone ou par écrit revient à passer un contrat légal qui lie les deux parties et doit être exécuté par celles-ci. Si vous ne prenez pas la chambre, vous risquez non seulement de perdre les arrhes éventuellement versées, mais aussi de devoir indemniser l'établissement s'il ne peut relouer la chambre.

UN HÉBERGEMENT DE QUALITÉ

Pour que vous soyez sûr de trouver l'hébergement qui vous convient, nous avons inspecté près de 10000 établissements différents.

Chaque année les inspecteurs de l'Office de Tourisme écossais sillonnent le pays, séjournent dans les hôtels, les pensions et les B&B et inspectent les locations meublées pour les évaluer en fonction des niveaux de qualité auxquels peuvent s'attendre les touristes en vacances en Ecosse, et pour s'assurer qu'ils répondent à vos besoins.

En appliquant notre Système de Classement et de Classification, ils évaluent tous les facteurs importants qui contribuent au confort de l'hébergement et mettent en relief la gamme d'aménagements et de prestations de service offerte.

CLASSEMENT en fonction de la QUALITÉ des aménagements et prestations de service

DELUXE	EXCELLENT niveau global de qualité.
HIGHLY COMMENDED	TRÈS BON niveau global de qualité.
COMMENDED	BON niveau global de qualité.
APPROVED	Niveau global de qualité ACCEPTABLE.

Les inspecteurs de l'Office de Tourisme écossais n'attribuent ces mentions qu'après avoir dormi dans les lits, goûté aux repas et bavardé avec le personnel. Ces mentions reposent sur une évaluation générale de la qualité et des prestations de service - dont la chaleur de l'accueil, l'ambiance et la compétence du service, ainsi que la qualité de l'ameublement, des installations et du décor. Chaque établissement est évalué selon ses propres mérites, quelle que soit la gamme d'équipements offerte.

CLASSIFICATION PAR COURONNES en fonction de la GAMME d'aménagements et de prestations de service

Si vous réservez une chambre dans un hôtel, une pension ou un B&B ayant reçu une des classifications suivantes, vous bénéficierez au moins des aménagements et des prestations de service indiqués.

NB: Chaque niveau comprend tous les aménagements et installations des niveaux précédents.

👑👑👑👑👑	Salle de bains dans toutes les chambres. Restaurant servant petit déjeuner, déjeuner et dîner. Portier de nuit et service à l'étage. Service au salon 24h sur 24.
👑👑👑👑	Dîner, choix de plats et carte des vins. TV couleurs, radio et téléphone dans les chambres. Service de blanchisserie, produits de toilette. Coin salon tranquille.
👑👑👑	Dîner. Sèche-cheveux. Nécessaire de cirage de chaussurs. Possibilité de repassage et nécessaire pour préparer des boissons chaudes.
👑👑	TV couleur. Thé servi au réveil. 20% des chambres, au moins, ont une salle de bains attenante/privée.
👑	Chambres fermant à clef. Salon commun. Lavabos dans chambres ou dans salles de bains privées.
LISTED	Hébergement propre et confortable. Petit déjeuner à l'anglaise ou continental. Chauffage suffisant sans supplément. Serviettes propres et savon neuf. Literie propre et en bon état. Eau chaude sans supplément pour bains et douches.

Chaque niveau de classification, de LISTED (Répertorié) à 5 COURONNES, est attribué en fonction de la gamme d'aménagements et de prestations de service offerte. Plus il y a de couronnes plus la gamme d'aménagements et de prestations de service est importante.

Pour recevoir des informations complètes sur ce système contactez The Quality Assurance Department, Visitor Services Division, Scottish Tourist Board, Thistle House, Beechwood Park North, Inverness IV2 3ED. Téléphone: (01463) 716996.

Plus de 4000 établissements hôteliers partout en Ecosse ont été inspectés par l'Office du Tourisme écossais.

Recherchez ce signe caractéristique d'un hébergement de qualité garantie

Unterkunftsmöglichkeiten...

Über 1100 Angebote, aus denen Sie auswählen können!

Hierbei handelt es sich um den umfassendsten Führer zu "Bed & Breakfast"-Unterkünften in Schottland; dieser wird jedes Jahr überarbeitet.

Jede Unterkunft in diesem Führer wurde von Inspektoren des Scottish Tourist Board gradiert und klassifiziert. Einzelheiten zu diesem zuverlässigen Qualitätssicherungs-schema auf Seite xiv.

Unterkunftssuche

Dieses Buch ist in acht Gegenden Schottlands unterteilt:

Der Süden Schottlands
Edinburgh - Stadt, Küste & Land
Greater Glasgow & Clyde-Tal
Die westlichen Highlands & Inseln, Loch Lomond, Stirling und Trossachs
Perthshire, Angus & Dundee und das Königreich von Fife
Die Grampian Highlands und die Nordostküste
Die Highlands & Skye
Die äußeren Inseln

Die Karte auf Seite 1 zeigt diese Gegenden. Innerhalb jedes Gebiets-abschnittes finden Sie Unterkünfte, die in alphabetischer Reihenfolge nach Ort aufgeführt sind. Daneben befindet sich am Ende dieses Buches eine alphabetische Auflistung aller Unterkunftsorte in Schottland sowie eine alphabetische Auflistung aller Einrichtungen.

Machen Sie sich mit den Symbolen in jedem Eintrag vertraut, denn sie enthalten eine Vielzahl von Informationen! Auf der Rückenklappe finden Sie eine Zeichen-erklärung. Sie können damit die jeweiligen Einrichtungen überprüfen, angefangen von Himmelbetten zu Swimmingpools, von Babysitterdiensten bis Zugangs-möglichkeiten für Behinderte. Es ist

Veranstaltern mitgeteilt und waren nach unserer Kenntnis korrekt zum Zeitpunkt der Drucklegung. Die Preise können sich jedoch jederzeit nach Veröffentlichung ändern, und Sie sollten sich daher bei der Buchung nochmals erkundigen.

Buchungen können direkt bei der Unterkunft, über ein Reisebüro oder über ein Tourist Information Centre vor Ort vorgenommen werden.

Bitte beachten Sie, daß Sie bei telefonischer oder schriftlicher Unterkunftsannahme einen rechtsgültigen Vertrag eingehen, der von beiden Parteien zu erfüllen ist. Bei Nicht-anspruchnahme der Unterkunft verfällt unter Umständen nicht nur eine bereits getätigte Anzahlung, sondern ist auch Schadenersatz zu leisten, falls eine anderweitige Vermietung der Unterkunft nicht möglich ist.

natürlich immer ratsam, sich von einer Unterkunft die Verfügbarkeit einer bestimmten Einrichtung bestätigen zu lassen.

Die Preise in diesem Führer gelten pro Person und stellen die Mindest- bzw. Höchstbeträge dar, mit denen man für die meisten Zimmer in dieser Unterkunft rechnen muß. Die Preise enthalten ggf. Bedienung und Mehrwertsteuer zum jeweils geltenden Tarif.

Die Preise für Unterbringung, Leistungen und Einrichtungen werden uns von den

Um zu gewährleisten, daß Sie die richtige Unterbringungsmöglichkeit finden, haben wir nahezu 10.000 individuelle Unterkünfte besucht.

Jedes Jahr reisen Prüfer des Scottish Tourist Board durch Schottland und wohnen in Hotels, Pensionen sowie "Bed & Breakfast"-Unterkünften und besuchen Ferienwohnungen für Selbstversorger, um diese auf deren Standards, die von Besuchern unseres Landes erwartet werden, hin zu beurteilen und um zu gewährleisten, daß Ihre Anforderungen erfüllt werden.

Anhand unseres Gradierungs- und Klassifikationsschemas bewerten unsere Prüfer alle wichtigen Faktoren, die zum Komfort Ihrer Unterkunft beitragen, und heben die Auswahl an Einrichtungen und den angebotenen Service hervor.

QUALITÄTSGRADIERUNG von Einrichtungen und Leistungen

DELUXE	Ein insgesamt AUSGEZEICHNETER Qualitätsstandard.
HIGHLY COMMENDED	Ein insgesamt SEHR GUTER Qualitätsstandard.
COMMENDED	Ein insgesamt GUTER Qualitätsstandard.
APPROVED	Ein insgesamt ANGEMESSENER Qualitätsstandard.

Qualitätsgradierungen werden von den Prüfern des Scottish Tourist Board erst verliehen, nachdem sie in den Unterkünften übernachtet, gegessen und sich mit dem Personal unterhalten haben. Diese Gradierungen basieren auf eine umfassende Bewertung von Qualität und Leistungen, wie z.B. ein herzliches Willkommen, Atmosphäre und effizienter Service sowie die Qualität von Möbeln, Einrichtung und Ausstattung. Jede Unterkunft wird nach ihren eigenen Leistungen beurteilt, unabhängig von der angebotenen Auswahl an Einrichtungen.

KRONENKLASSIFIKATION für ANGEBOTENE Einrichtungen und Service

Wenn Sie ein Hotel, eine Pension oder eine "Bed & Breakfast"- Unterkunft mit folgender Klassifikation buchen, werden Sie mindestens die angegebenen Einrichtungen und Leistungen vorfinden.

HINWEIS: Jede Stufe enthält alle Einrichtungen und Ausstattung der vorherigen Stufen.

👑 👑 👑 👑 👑	Alle Zimmer mit eigenem Bad. Restaurant, in dem Frühstück, Mittag– und Abendessen serviert werden. Nachtportier und Zimmerservice. 24-stündiger Service in der Lounge.
👑 👑 👑 👑	Abendessen, Menüwahl und Auswahl an Weinen. Farbfernsehen, Radio und Telefon in Zimmern. Wäschedienst, Toilettenartikel. Ruhiger Sitzbereich.
👑 👑 👑	Abendessen. Fön. Schuhputzzeug. Bügelmöglichkeiten und Vorrichtungen zur Tee-/Kaffeebereitung.
👑 👑	Farbfernsehen. Tee vor dem Frühstück. Mindestens 20% der Zimmer mit eigenem Bad.
👑	Eigener Zimmerschlüssel. Gemeinschaftlicher Lounge-Bereich. Zimmer mit Waschbecken oder eigenem Bad.
LISTED	Saubere und bequeme Unterkunft. Warmes oder kontinentales Frühstück. Angemessene Heizung ohne Aufpreis. Saubere Handtücher und frische Seife. Bettwäsche sauber und in gutem Zustand. Heißes Wasser ohne Aufpreis für Bäder oder Duschbäder.

Die Klassifikation gibt den Umfang der angebotenen Einrichtungen und Leistungen an. Die Klassifikationen reichen von LISTED bis zu 5 KRONEN. Mehr Kronen bedeuten mehr Einrichtungen.

Für ausführliche Einzelheiten zu diesem Schema wenden Sie sich bitte an: The Quality Assurance Department, Visitor Services Division, Scottish Tourist Board, Thistle House, Beechwood Park North, Inverness IV2 3ED. Tel.: (01463) 716996.

Über 4000 Hotels, Pensionen und "Bed & Breakfast"–Unterkünfte in allen Landesteilen Schottlands wurden vom Scottish Tourist Board überprüft.

Achten Sie auf dieses unverwechselbare
Zeichen für Qualitätsunterkünfte

VISITOR ATTRACTION QUALITY ASSURANCE

In the same way that you want to be sure of the standard of accommodation you choose to stay in while on holiday in Scotland, you also want to be sure you make the most of your time.

The Scottish Tourist Board has introduced a quality assurance scheme for Visitor Attractions which provides valuable information on the quality of such attractions as castles, museums, gardens, nature reserves, leisure centres and much more.

The Scottish Tourist Board awards provide you with an assurance that an attraction has been independently verified by one of our inspectors, who has assessed the condition and standard of facilities and services provided.

The three Quality grades are;

acceptable quality standard

good quality standard

very good quality standard

The Scottish Tourist Board Quality Assurance Scheme for Visitor Attractions is integrated with our Accommodation Scheme so you can follow the STB quality trail night and day.

THE BENEFITS OF QUALITY ASSURANCE

Scottish Tourist Board Quality Assurance answers two very important questions for you as a visitor.

Question: – How do you know what standards I can expect to find as I travel around Scotland?

Answer: Quality – The Scottish Tourist Board inspects all types of accommodation, holiday parks and visitor attractions throughout Scotland. We view each place in the same way as you the visitor would, giving an appropriate award to show the standard you can expect to find. The awards given range from an acceptable standard to a very high standard.

Question: – How can I be sure of finding the standard I want?

Answer: Assurance – Using this book and every other Scottish Tourist Board guide, you have the assurance that every type of accommodation, holiday park and visitor attraction has been inspected.

In addition to the entries in our guide, many more of these visitor facilities have been inspected throughout Scotland.

So if you want to find the answer to these two important questions, look for these signs of Quality Assurance.

SCOTLAND WELCOMES VISITORS WITH DISABILITIES

We want visitors with a disability to get around Scotland and enjoy its attractions, secure in the knowledge that comfortable, suitable accommodation is waiting at the end of the day. Obviously, you need to know in advance just what kind of access and facilities will be available in the accommodation you choose.

Along with the quality grading and classification scheme that applies to all establishments in Scottish Tourist Board guides, we operate a national accessibility scheme. Through it, we can identify and promote places that meet the needs of visitors with a disability.

The three categories of accessibility – drawn up in close consultation with specialist organisations – are:

 Unassisted wheelchair access for residents

 Assisted wheelchair access for residents

 Access for residents with mobility difficulties

Look out for these symbols in establishments, in advertising and brochures. They assure you that entrances, ramps, passageways, doors, restaurant facilities, bathrooms and toilets, as well as kitchens in self- catering properties, have been inspected. Write or telephone for details of the standards in each category – address on page vii.

For more information about travel, accommodation and organisations to help you, write (or ask at a Tourist Information Centre) for the Scottish Tourist Board booklet "Practical Information for Visitors with Disabilities."

Useful advice and information can also be obtained from:

Disability Scotland
Information Department
Princes House
5 Shandwick Place
EDINBURGH EH2 4RG
Tel: (0131) 229 8632
Fax: (0131) 229 5168

Holiday Care Service
2nd Floor
Imperial Buildings
Victoria Road
Horley, Surrey RH6 7PZ
Tel: (01293) 774535
Fax: (01293) 784647

Welcome Host

You can be sure of a warm welcome where you see the Welcome Host sign displayed.

Welcome Host is one of the most exciting and far reaching customer programmes ever developed for the tourism industry. The aim of Welcome Host is to raise the standards of hospitality offered to you during your stay. You will see the Welcome Host badge being worn by a wide variety of people in Scotland (people who have taken part in STB's Welcome Host training programme and have given a personal commitment to providing quality service

during your stay). In many organisations you will also see the Welcome Host certificate, displaying an organisation's commitment to the provision of this quality service.

Welcome Hosts are everywhere, from Shetland to Coldstream and from Peterhead to Stornoway and all places in between.

Scotland is famous for its warm welcome and Welcome Hosts will ensure you receive first class service throughout your stay. Look out for the Welcome sign.

From Scotland's natural larder comes a wealth of fine flavours.

The sea yields crab and lobster, mussels and oysters, haddock and herring to be eaten fresh or smoked. From the lochs and rivers come salmon and trout.

Scotch beef and lamb, venison and game are of prime quality, often adventurously combined with local vegetables or with wild fruits such as redcurrants and brambles. Raspberries and strawberries are cultivated to add their sweetness to trifles and shortcakes, and to the home-made jams that are an essential part of Scottish afternoon tea.

The Scots have a sweet tooth, and love all kinds of baking – rich, crisp shortbread, scones, fruit cakes and gingerbreads. Crumbly oatcakes make the ideal partner for Scottish cheeses, which continue to develop from their ancient farming origins into new – and very successful – styles.

And in over a hundred distilleries, barley, yeast and pure spring water come together miraculously to create malt whisky – the water of life.

Many Scottish hotels and restaurants pride themselves on the use they make of these superb natural ingredients – over 300 are members of the Taste of Scotland Scheme which encourages the highest culinary standards, use of Scottish produce, and a warm welcome to visitors. Look for the Stockpot symbol at establishments, or write to Taste of Scotland for a copy of their guide.

In Shops: £6.99
By Post: UK   £7.99
           Europe £8.00
           US   £10.00

Taste of Scotland Scheme
33 Melville Street
EDINBURGH
EH3 7JF
Tel: (0131) 220 1900
Fax: (0131) 220 6102

Scotland has some of the finest food products in the world.

Our seafood, beef, lamb, venison, vegetables and soft fruit are renowned for their high quality. These fine indigenous raw materials and a wide assortment of international food products are skillfully combined by cooks and chefs into the vast range of cuisine available in Scotland.

As you travel throughout the country you will find an excellent standard of cooking in all sorts of establishments from restaurants with imaginative menus to tea rooms with simple wholesome home-baking.

You will find some of these culinary gems by reading of their reputation in newspapers and magazines, from advice given by Tourist Information Centre staff or by using your own instinct to discover them yourself.

The Scottish Tourist Board has recognised that it would be helpful for you, the visitor, to have some assurance of the standards of food available in every different type of eating establishment; and indeed to be able to find a consistent standard of food in every place you choose to eat.

We recently launched a new initiative called The Natural Cooking of Scotland, which is a long-term plan to encourage all eating places to follow the lead of those who are best in their field and to provide catering of a consistently good standard. We are also working to introduce a food quality assurance scheme similar to our accommodation scheme which lets you know in advance what standards of food you can expect in each establishment.

The Natural Cooking of Scotland initiative is a partnership between the Scottish Tourist Board and prominent food and tourism industry representatives. So, we have harnessed the skills of chefs, the experience of restaurateurs and the expertise of catering trainers to develop this long term initiative.

Whilst you will appreciate the good experiences you will find in eating your way around Scotland this year, the Natural Cooking of Scotland will ensure that the profile of our fine Scottish cooking is even greater in future years.

SCOTLAND: FACTFILE

Getting around

Scotland is a small country and travel is easy. There are direct air links with UK cities, with Europe and North America. There is also an internal air network bringing the islands of the North and West within easy reach.

Scotland's rail network not only includes excellent cross-border InterCity services but also a good internal network. All major towns are linked by rail and there are also links to the western seaboard at Mallaig and Kyle of Lochalsh (for ferry connections to Skye and the Western Isles) and to Inverness, Thurso and Wick for ferries to Orkney and Shetland.

All the usual discount cards are valid but there are also ScotRail Rovers (multi journey tickets allowing you to save on rail fares) and the Freedom of Scotland Travelpass, a combined rail and ferry pass allowing unlimited travel on ferry services to the islands and all of the rail network. In addition Travelpass also offers discounts on bus services and some air services.

InterCity services are available from all major centres, for example: Birmingham, Carlisle, Crewe, Manchester, Newcastle, Penzance, Peterborough, Preston, Plymouth, York and many others.

There are frequent InterCity departures from Kings Cross and Euston stations to Edinburgh and Glasgow. The journey time from Kings Cross to Edinburgh is around 4 hours and from Euston to Glasgow around 5 hours.

Coach connections include express services to Scotland from all over the UK; local bus companies in Scotland offer explorer tickets and discount cards. Postbuses (normally minibuses) take passengers on over 130 rural routes throughout Scotland.

Ferries to and around the islands are regular and reliable, most ferries carry vehicles, although some travelling to smaller islands convey only passengers.

Contact the Information Department, Scottish Tourist Board, PO Box 705, Edinburgh EH4 3EU, or any Tourist Information Centre, for details of travel and transport.

Many visitors choose to see Scotland by road – distances are short and driving on the quiet roads of the Highlands is a new and different experience. In remoter areas, some roads are still single track, and passing places must be used. When vehicles approach from different directions, the car nearest to a passing place must stop in or opposite it. Please do not use passing places to park in!

Speed limits on Scottish roads:
Dual carriageways 70mph/112kph;
single carriageways 60mph/96kph;
built-up areas 30mph/48kph.

The driver and front-seat passenger in
a car must wear seatbelts; rear seatbelts,
if fitted, must be used. Small children
and babies must at all times be restrained
in a child seat or carrier.

Opening times

Public holidays: Christmas and New Year's
Day are holidays in Scotland, taken by
almost everyone. Scottish banks, and
many offices, will close in 1996 on 1 and
2 January, 5 and 8 April, 6 and 27 May,
26 August, 25 and 26 December. Scottish
towns also take Spring and Autumn
holidays which may vary from place
to place, but are usually on a Monday.

Banking hours: In general, banks open
Monday to Friday, 0930 to 1600, with
some closing later on a Thursday. Banks
in cities, particularly in or near the main
shopping centres, may be open at
weekends. Cash machines in hundreds
of branches allow you to withdraw cash
outside banking hours, using the
appropriate cards.

Pubs and restaurants: Licensing laws in
Scotland generally allow bars to service
alcoholic drinks between 1100 and 1430,
and from 1700 to 2300, Monday to
Saturday. Most are also licensed to open
on Sundays; some open in the afternoon,
or later at night. Hotel bars have the same
hours as pubs except for Sunday, when
they open 1230 to 1430, and 1830 to
2300. Residents in hotels may have drinks
served at any time.

Telephone codes

If you are calling from abroad, first dial
your own country's international access
code (usually 00, but do please check).
Next, dial the UK code, 44, then the area
code except for the first 0, then the
remainder of the number as normal.

Quarantine regulations

If you are coming to Scotland from
overseas, please do not attempt to bring
your pet on holiday with you. British
quarantine regulations are stringently
enforced, and anyone attempting to
contravene them will incur severe penalties
as well as the loss of the animal.

South of Scotland

Until Feb 8
Pride & Passion
The National Burns Exhibition
Collection of manuscripts, paintings, artefacts, imagery and sound. Museum Dept. Dick Institute, Kilmarnock
Tel: 01563 526401

23 May - 1 June
Dumfries & Galloway Arts Festival
Ten day festival embracing all the arts. Throughout Dumfries & Galloway Tel/Fax 01387 260447

17 - 20 July
1997 Open Golf Championship Premier golfing tournament, attracting the world's finest golfers.
Royal Troon, Ayrshire Royal & Ancient Golf Club of St Andrews Tel 01334 472112

25 July
Langholm Common Riding
A ceremonial procession through the town, followed by Highland dancing and sports. Langholm, Dumfriesshire
Mr J B Hill Tel 01387 380428

16 - 17 Aug*
Scottish Championship Horse Trials
Thirlestane Castle, Lauder, Berwickshire Mr T Hogarth
Tel 01896 860242

Edinburgh – City, Coast & Countryside

22 March - 6 Apr
Edinburgh International Science Festival
The world's largest international science festival.
Various venues
Mr S Mitchell Tel 0131 220 3977

26 May - 1 June
Scottish International Children's Festival
Theatre, music, dance, mime and puppetry.
Ms Katie Stuart Tel 0131 554 6297

1 - 23 Aug
Edinburgh Military Tattoo
Unique blend of music, ceremony and entertainment, on the castle esplanade. Edinburgh Castle,
Tattoo Office Tel 0131 225 1188

10 - 30 Aug
Edinburgh International Festival
International festival of theatre, music, dance and opera.
EIF Box Office Tel 0131 226 4001

31 Dec
Edinburgh's Hogmanay
Major end of year celebrations, culminating in a massive Hogmany spectacular. Various venues, Edinburgh and Lothians Tourist Board
Tel 0131 557 1700

Greater Glasgow & Clyde Valley

16 Jan - 2 Feb*
Celtic Connections
Much acclaimed Celtic Festival with music from around the Celtic world. Glasgow Royal Concert Hall
Tel 0141 353 4137

1 - 24 May*
Mayfest Glasgow's annual festival of popular arts and entertainment. Ms Sally Fletcher Tel 0141 552 6612

27 June - 6 July
11th Glasgow International Jazz Festival
The largest and widest ranging Jazz Festival in the UK.
Various venues, Glasgow Tel 0141 552 3572

16 Aug
World Pipe Band Championships
Glasgow Mr J M Hutchieson Tel 0141 221 5414

17 Oct*
The Massed Bands of the Royal Air Force Concert Tour
Royal Concert Hall, Glasgow Ms H Standfast
Tel 01285 713300 Fax 01285 713456/714268

West Highlands and Islands, Loch Lomond, Stirling & Trossachs

28 Mar - 8 Dec
William Wallace 700th Anniversary
Exhibition
Exhibition interpreting the life, myth and enormous legacy of William Wallace. Smith Art Gallery & Museum, Stirling Tel 01786 471917

26 Apr
Fiddlers Rally
OBAN Ms Mary Pollock Tel 01631 710488

24 – 25 May
Loch Fyne Food Fair
A feast of West Coast sea food and demonstrations
Loch Fyne, Argyll Mrs V Sumsion, Tel: 01499 600217

1 - 8 Aug
Tennents West Highland Yachting Week
Yacht racing. Crinan/ Oban/ Tobermory Miss J L Heap
Tel/Fax 01631 563309

12 - 13 Sept
Battle of Stirling Bridge – Theatre Event
Two evening extravaganza with a large scale open air
theatre event
Stirling Ken Gill Tel 01786 443122

Perthshire, Angus & Dundee and the Kingdom of Fife

3 - 9 Mar*
Glenshee Snow Fun Week
Skiing competitions, races, fun & Apres Ski. Glenshee,
Perthshire Tel 01575 582213

2 May - 11 Oct
Pitlochry Festival Theatre
Six plays in six days, plus Sunday concerts and fringe
events. Pitlochry Perthshire Tel 01796 472680

21 May - 2 June*
Perth Festival of the Arts
Festival of music, drama & visual arts.
Perth, Mrs Liz Dewar (Festival Box Office)
Tel 01738 621031

5 - 7 June
The Scottish Rally
This rally forms a round of the European, UK &
Scottish Rally Championships. Perth
Mr J Lord Tel 0141 204 4999

13 Sept
RAF Leuchars Battle of Britain Airshow
Scotland's largest International Airshow with over 100
aircraft on display. Leuchars, Fife Tel 01334 839000

Grampian Highlands, Aberdeen and the North East Coast

1 Jan
Stonehaven Fireball Ceremony
On first stroke of midlight fireballs are carried through
the High Street swung above the heads of the carriers.
At the end of the ceremony the embers are thrown into
the harbour Contact: Aberdeenshire Council,
Stonehaven Tel: 01569 762001

16 - 18 May
Buchan Heritage Festival
13th Annual Festival of music, song and verse held in
Strichen. Contact: Mrs E Mundie, Tel: 01771 653761

12 – 15 July
Cutty Sark Tall Ships Race
Tall ships from around the world will muster in
Aberdeen for five days of celebrations, culminating
with a spectacular Parade of Sail as the vessels begin
the race across the North Sea to Tronheim.
Lynn Oxley, Grampian Enterprise Tel 01224 252150

9 - 18 Oct*
Aberdeen Alternative Festival
Music, drama, dance and more from all over the world.
Aberdeen Tel: 01224 635822

Nov & Dec
Christmas Shopping Festival
Seasonal entertainment based around Aberdeen's
Union Street which is closed off to traffic for Sunday
shopping.
Contact: Aberdeen & Grampian Tourist Board
Tel: 01224 632727

The Highlands and Skye

22 - 1 Mar
Inverness Music Festival
1997 marks the festival's 75th anniversary.
Inverness Ms E Davis Tel 01463 233902

21 - 23 Mar
Cairngorm Snow Festival
Fun event with Skiing competitions, races.
Aviemore Ms Tanya Adams Tel 01479 861261

23 May - 7 June
The Second Annual Highland Festival
From Argyll to Aviemore, from Benbecula to Bettyhill
and from the Cuillins to Cromarty – events and venues
throughout the Highlands and Islands.
The Highland Festival Tel 01463 719000

10 - 17 Oct
Royal National Mod ~ Inverness
Annual competitive Gaelic Music Festival with
supporting fringe events. An Comunn Gaidhealach Tel
01463 231226

8 Nov
Dunvegan Castle Fireworks Spectacular
Spectacular lochside fireworks display. Dunvegan
Castle, Isle of Skye Macleod Estates Tel 01470 521206

Outer Islands

28 January
Up Helly Aa
Traditional Viking Fire Festival. Lerwick, Shetland
Tourist Information Centre Tel 01595 693434

3 - 7 Apr *
Shetland Folk Festival
Various venues, Shetland Folk Festival Office
Tel 01595 694757

22 - 25 May
Orkney Traditional Folk Festival
Various Venues, Orkney
Mr J Mowat Tel 01856 850773

20 - 25 June
St Magnus Festival
A compact six day festival encompassing music, drama,
poetry and the visual arts.
Kirkwall / Stromness, Orkney
Mrs D Rushbrook Tel 01856 872952

6 – 18 July*
Feis Bharraigh (Barra Festival)
Festival of gaelic, song, dance and drama.
Isle of Barra, Western Isles
Feis Secretary Tel 01871 810667

* Provisional Dates

SCOTLAND'S TOURIST AREAS

1. South of Scotland

2. Edinburgh – City, Coast & Countryside

3. Greater Glasgow and Clyde Valley

4. West Highlands and Islands,
   Loch Lomond, Stirling and Trossachs

5. Perthshire, Angus & Dundee
   and the Kingdom of Fife

6. Grampian Highlands, Aberdeen
   and the North East Coast

7. The Highlands and Skye

8. Outer Islands

Area Tourist Boards
Scotland is split into eight tourist areas.
You will find accommodation listed
alphabetically by location within each
of these areas. There are indices at the
back of this book which may also aid you.

MAPS

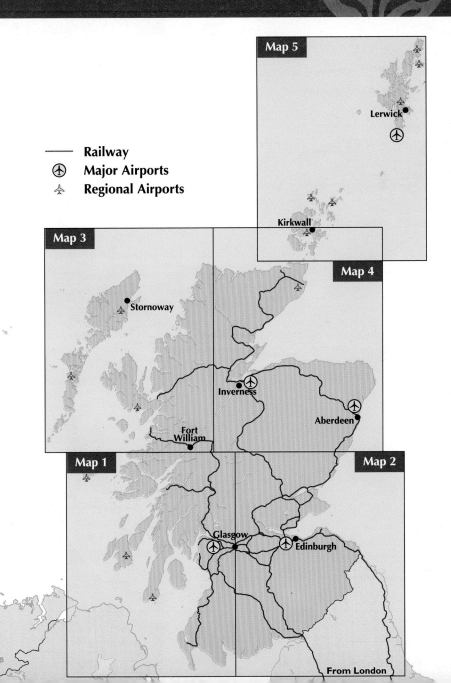

Railway

Major Airports

Regional Airports

Map 5

Lerwick

Kirkwall

Map 3

Stornoway

Map 4

Inverness

Aberdeen

Fort William

Map 1

Map 2

Glasgow

Edinburgh

From London

MAP 1

A B C D E F G H

1 COLL Arinagour · Strontian · Glencoe · Ballachulish · Duror · Kinl Rann · Tobermory · Dervaig

Isle of Tiree · Scarinish · Lawer

2 TIREE · Lochaline · Fishnish · Appin · Benderloch · Connel · Oban · Killin · St Fill

MULL · Craignure · Kinlochspelve · Dalmally · Kilchrenan · Crianlarich · Balquhidder

3 Fionnphort · Bunessan · Inveraray · St Catherines · Lochgoilhead · Tarbet · Arrochar · Port of Menteith · Aberfoyle · Strathyre · Callan · Thornhil

Craobh Haven · Ardfern · Minard · Luss · Balmaha · Kipp

4 COLONSAY · Scalasaig · Isle of Colonsay · JURA · Crinan · Ardrishaig · Drymen · Arden · Balloch · Milngav · Bearsde

5 ISLAY · Port Askaig · Ballygrant · Feolin · Tarbert · Rhubodach · Portavadie · Dunoon · Colintraive · Greenock · Wemyss Bay · Clydebank · Paisley · GLASGO · Port Charlotte · Kennacraig · Rothesay · Ascog · Largs · Kilbarchan · Johnstone · Lochwinnoch · Helensburgh · Cardross · Dumbarton

6 Port Ellen · Ardminish · Claonaig · Cumbrae · Fairlie · Beith · Uplawmoor · Eaglesha · Tayinloan · BUTE · CUMBRAE · Kilwinning · Fenwick · Darvel · Muasdale · Ardrossan · Stevenston · Kilmarnock

7 ATLANTIC · ARRAN · Brodick · Irvine · Galston · Mauchlin · Carradale · Shiskine · Troon · Prestwick · OCEAN · Blackwaterfoot · Corriecravie · Whiting Bay · Ayr · Campbeltown · Dunure

8 Maybole · Girvan

9 Barrhill · New Gallowa · Ballantrae

10 Cairnryan · Newton Stewart · Gatehouse of Fleet · Stranraer · Glenluce · Wigtown · Larne · Portpatrick

11 Luce Bay

12 BELFAST · To Liverpool · To Douglas, Isle of Man

Car ferries and terminals:

Brodick ---- Rothesay

Scale 1:1 300 000

0   10   20 miles

© Bartholomew, 1996

These maps are for "Bed & Breakfast" locations only. For route planning and touring please use a current road atlas.

MAP 2

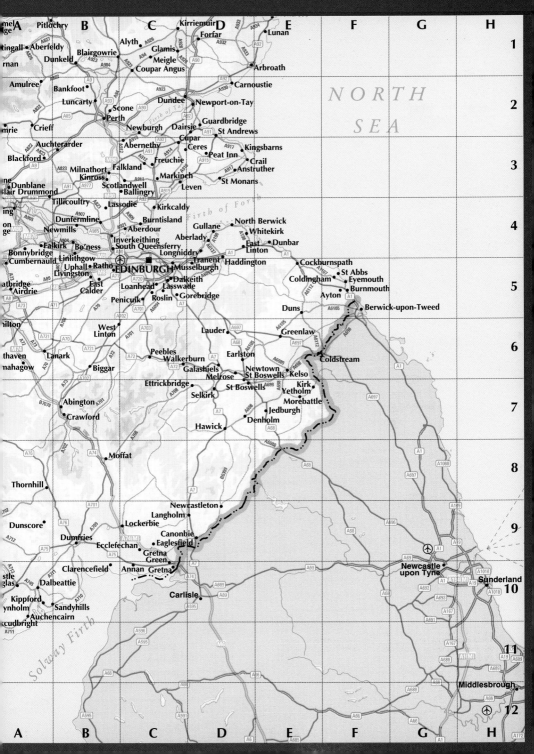

MAP 3

These maps are for "Bed & Breakfast" locations only. For route planning and touring please use a current road atlas.

MAP 3 MAP 4

OUTER HEBRIDES

LEWIS
Back
Callanish Stornoway Aignish
Achmore

Kinlochbervie
Scourie
Kylesk
Lochinver

HARRIS Tarbert

Ullapool

Leverburgh

The Minch

Aultbea Laide
Dundonnell
Poolewe
Gairloch
Badachro
Loch Maree

Berneray
Otternish
Sollas
Lochmaddy
NORTH
UIST
Grimsay
Torlum
Liniclate BENBECULA

Kilmuir
Uig Staffin
Treaslane Kensaleyre
Glendale Bernisdale
Dunvegan

Diabaig
Shieldaig Torridon
Kinlochewe

Portree
RAASAY
Raasay
Sconser
SKYE Broadford
Luib

Kishorn Strathcarron
Lochcarron
Plockton
Stromeferry
Kyle of Balmacara
Lochalsh Dornie
Glenelg

Cann

SOUTH
UIST

Lochboisdale

Ludag
Eriskay

CANNA

Kylerhea
Ord
Elgol Isleornsay
Teangue
Armadale
Ardvasar

Glenshiel

Invergarr

BARRA
Castlebay

RUM

EIGG

Mallaig
Morar
Arisaig

Loch Morar

Loch
Lochy

Spe
Brid
Corpach
Fort William

MUCK

Ardnamurchan Acharacle
Kilchoan

Onich Kinlochleven

MAP 4

MAP 5

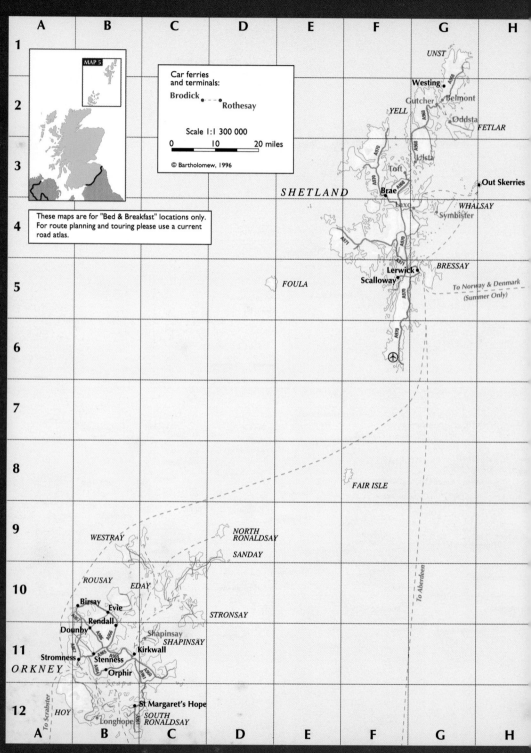

MAP 5

Car ferries
and terminals:

Brodick •----• Rothesay

Scale 1:1 300 000

0   10   20 miles

© Bartholomew, 1996

These maps are for "Bed & Breakfast" locations only.
For route planning and touring please use a current
road atlas.

UNST

Westing •

Gutcher • **Belmont**

YELL • **Oddsta**

FETLAR

Ulsta

Toft • **Out Skerries**

SHETLAND   **Brae** •

Lexo *WHALSAY*

Symbister

BRESSAY

Lerwick •

Scalloway •

FOULA

To Norway & Denmark
(Summer Only)

To Aberdeen

FAIR ISLE

WESTRAY

*NORTH
RONALDSAY*

SANDAY

ROUSAY

EDAY

STRONSAY

Birsay •

Evie •

Rendall •

Dounby •

Shapinsay

Kirkwall •

SHAPINSAY

Stromness •

Stenness •

Orphir •

ORKNEY

To Scrabster

HOY

St Margaret's Hope •

Longhope • *SOUTH
RONALDSAY*

SCOTLAND

BED & BREAKFAST - ACCOMMODATION

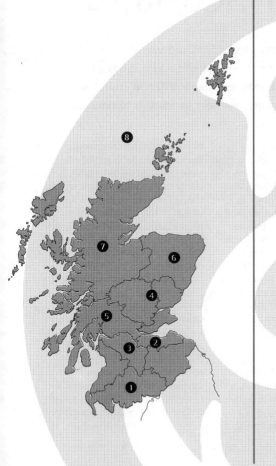

South of Scotland

The South of Scotland is the first part of Scotland you encounter by road or rail after you cross the Border. Right away, it has all the subtle characteristics which make Scotland different from the rest of the UK, from different names for beer to Scottish banknotes!

First impressions can be of a surprisingly wild area, though the river valleys of the Scottish Borders with their woodlands and farms soon give a softer appearance. However, if it is ruggedness you want, then head west for Galloway, where, at places like the Galloway Forest Park there is quintessentially 'Scottish' scenery of lochs and steep-sided hills. Or head for the island of Arran, often called Scotland in miniature because it too has these characteristics of rocky hillslopes as well as a softer and gentler side.

South of Scotland towns are very distinctive. The typical Galloway townscape of wide streets and pastel painted frontages is highly attractive (Kirkcudbright, for example, has a long tradition of attracting artists).

In the Scottish Borders, places like Melrose or Kelso are full of personality and they also offer plenty to do: visiting abbeys or stately homes or museums will take up lots of time. Another distinct feature is the wealth of attractions in Ayrshire, along the Clyde coast. This makes a superb family holiday destination, with places like the Magnum Leisure Centre at Irvine, Loudoun Castle Park (featuring Scotland's largest carousel!) near Galston, Kelburn Country Park near Largs, Wonderwest World at Ayr and lots more places all great for children. Also consider the options of the ferry connections to the Cumbraes (excellent for cycling) or to Arran, with its wealth of walking, cycling and other outdoor pursuits.

The thriving town of Peebles on the River Tweed. Ancient royal burgh and site of a hunting lodge of the early Scottish Kings.

Other highlights and 'must sees' of
the area include the Border abbeys,
for example, Dryburgh in its
beautifully secluded setting or
Jedburgh, where a visitor centre
tells the story of the part played
by the great abbeys in Borders life.
The abbeys are open to visitors all
year. There is a great choice of
stately homes and castles: for
example, Brodick Castle on Arran
(superb gardens, too), Culzean Castle
near Ayr (magnificent country park)
or Floors Castle (the largest inhabited
house in Scotland) – though these
are just the start of a long list.

Out of the ordinary visitor attractions
include the Scottish Museum of Lead
Mining at Wanlockhead, Mill on the
Fleet at Gatehouse-of-Fleet and the
Scottish Maritime Museum at Irvine.
All these provide entertainment and
an insight into other facets of
Scottish life.

South of Scotland

You can walk the Southern Upland Way from west to east,
all 212 miles if time permits, go mountain biking in the forests,
go angling in our rivers – there are activities galore here.

You can enjoy this area at any time of year – it is easy to reach and there is plenty going on from the Common Ridings in the Borders in summer, to the spectacular winter flights of wild geese at places like Caerlaverock National Nature Reserve near Dumfries. For town or country breaks this area is ideal at any time of year.

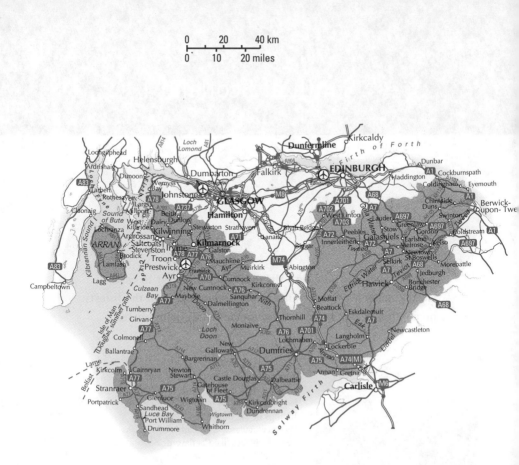

AREA TOURIST BOARD ADDRESSES

1 AYRSHIRE AND ARRAN
  TOURIST BOARD
  Burns House
  Burns Statue Square
  AYR
  KA7 1UP
  Tel: 01292 262555
  Fax: 01292 269555

2 DUMFRIES AND
  GALLOWAY TOURIST
  BOARD
  Campbell House
  Bankend Road
  DUMFRIES
  DG1 4TH
  Tel: 01387 250434
  Fax: 01387 250462

3 SCOTTISH BORDERS
  TOURIST BOARD
  Tourist Information
  Centre
  Murray's Green
  Jedburgh
  TD8 6BE
  Tel: 01835 863435/
           863688
  Fax: 01835 864099

TOURIST INFORMATION CENTRES IN SCOTLAND

AYRSHIRE & ARRAN TOURIST BOARD

AYR ✉
Burns House
Burns Statue Square
Tel: (01292) 288688
Jan-Dec

BRODICK ♿ ✉
The Pier
Isle of Arran
KA27 8AU
Tel: (01770) 302140/302401
Jan-Dec

GIRVAN
Bridge Street
Tel: (01465) 714950
April-Oct

IRVINE
New Street
Tel: (01294) 313886
Jan-Dec

KILMARNOCK ♿ ✉
62 Bank Street
KA1 1ER
Tel: (01563) 539090
Jan-Dec

LARGS ✉
Promenade, KA30 8BG
Tel: (01475) 673765
Jan-Dec

MILLPORT ♿
28 Stuart Street
Isle of Cumbrae
Tel: (01475) 530753
Easter-Oct

TROON
Municipal Buildings
South Beach
Tel: (01292) 317696
Easter-Sept

DUMFRIES & GALLOWAY TOURIST BOARD

CASTLE DOUGLAS
Markethill Car Park
Tel: (01556) 502611
Easter-Oct

DALBEATTIE
Town Hall
Tel: (01556) 610117
Easter-Sep

DUMFRIES ✉
Whitesands
DG1 4TH
Tel: (01387) 253862
Jan-Dec

GATEHOUSE OF FLEET
Car Park
Tel: (01557) 814212
Easter-Oct

GRETNA ♿ ✉
Gateway to Scotland
M74 Service Area
DG16 5HQ
Tel: (01461) 338500
Jan-Dec

GRETNA GREEN
Old Blacksmith's Shop
Tel: (01461) 337834
Easter-Oct

KIRKCUDBRIGHT ♿
Harbour Square
Tel: (01557) 330494
Easter-Oct

LANGHOLM
High Street
Tel: (01387) 380976
Easter-Sept

MOFFAT
Churchgate
Tel: (01683) 220620
Easter-Oct

NEWTON STEWART
Dashwood Square
Tel: (01671) 402431
Easter-Oct

SANQUHAR ♿
Tolbooth, High Street
Tel: (01659) 50185
Easter-early Oct

STRANRAER
1 Bridge Street
Tel: (01776) 702595
Easter-Oct

SCOTTISH BORDERS TOURIST BOARD

COLDSTREAM ♿
High Street
Tel: (01890) 882607
April-Oct

EYEMOUTH ♿
Auld Kirk
Manse Road
Tel: (018907) 50678
April-Oct

GALASHIELS ♿
St Johns Street
Tel: (01896) 755551
April-Oct

HAWICK ♿
Drumlanrig's Tower
Tel: (01450) 372547
April-Oct

JEDBURGH ♿ ✉
Murray's Green
TD8 6BE
Tel: (01835) 863435/863688
Jan-Dec

KELSO
Town House
The Square
Tel: (01573) 223464
April-Oct

MELROSE ♿
Abbey House
Tel: (01896) 822555
April-Oct

PEEBLES ♿
High Street
Tel: (01721) 720138
Jan-Dec

SELKIRK ♿
Halliwell's House
Tel: (01750) 20054
April-Oct

✉   Accept written enquiries
♿   Disabled access

SOUTH OF SCOTLAND

by ANNAN Dumfriesshire Mrs Forrest Hurkledale Farm, Cummertrees Annan Dumfriesshire DG12 5QA Tel: (Cummertrees) 01461 700228	Map 2 C10	COMMENDED 🏆🏆	1 Twin 2 Double	2 En Suite fac 1 Priv. NOT ensuite	B&B per person from £17.00 Double	Open Jan-Dec Dinner 1800-1900 B&B + Eve. Meal from £26.00
			Traditional farmhouse on extensive mixed farm at village outskirts, with panoramic views across the Solway Firth to England.			

ISLE OF ARRAN

BLACKWATERFOOT, Isle of Arran Mrs Sherwood Morvern House Blackwaterfoot Isle of Arran KA27 8EU Tel: (Shiskine) 01770 860254	Map 1 E7	APPROVED 🏆🏆	1 Twin 2 Double	1 En Suite fac 1 Pub Bath/Show	B&B per person £15.50-£17.50 Single £15.00-£18.50 Double	Open Jan-Dec Dinner from 1830 B&B + Eve. Meal from £25.00
			Former bank house now a family home in the heart of the village. Accommodation on first floor.			
BRODICK, Isle of Arran	Map 1 F7					
Allandale Guest House Brodick Isle of Arran KA27 8BJ Tel: (Brodick) 01770 302278		COMMENDED 🏆🏆🏆	1 Single 2 Twin 1 Double 2 Family	5 En Suite fac 1 Priv. NOT ensuite 1 Pub Bath/Show	B&B per person £17.00-£22.00 Single £17.00-£22.00 Double	Open Jan-Oct Dinner 1900-1930 B&B + Eve. Meal £26.00-£32.00
			Comfortable guest house in south-facing position on the edge of Brodick, only a few minutes' walk from the ferry. Some annexe accommodation.			
Carrick Lodge Brodick Isle of Arran KA27 8BH Tel: (Brodick) 01770 302550 Fax: 01770 302550		COMMENDED 🏆🏆🏆	1 Single 2 Twin 2 Double 1 Family	5 En Suite fac 1 Priv. NOT ensuite	B&B per person £18.00-£22.00 Single £18.00-£22.00 Double Room only per person £15.00-£19.00	Open Feb-Oct Dinner from 1900 B&B + Eve. Meal £30.00-£34.00
			Sandstone-built, former manse in its own gardens. Panoramic views over Brodick Bay from sitting room. Convenient for ferry terminal.			

Glen Cloy Farmhouse

Glen Cloy, Brodick, Isle of Arran KA27 8DA
Telephone: 01770 302351

Glen Cloy Farmhouse is a beautiful sandstone house set in its own grounds in a quiet glen close to Brodick. Golf, castle and mountains nearby. All the rooms are tastefully furnished and a log fire burns warmly. We grow most of our own vegetables and use quality local produce.

Glen Cloy Farmhouse Brodick Isle of Arran KA27 8DA Tel: (Brodick) 01770 302351		COMMENDED 🏆🏆	1 Single 2 Twin 2 Double	2 En Suite fac 1 Pub Bath/Show	B&B per person £20.00-£23.00 Single £20.00-£25.00 Double	Open Mar-Nov Dinner 1900-1930 B&B + Eve. Meal £32.50-£38.00
			Farmhouse set in peaceful glen with views of hills and sea. Within easy reach of Brodick ferry. Chef/proprietor uses fresh, homegrown produce. Taste of Scotland.			
Rosa Burn Lodge Brodick Isle of Arran KA27 8DP Tel: (Brodick) 01770 302383		COMMENDED 🏆	2 Twin 1 Double Suite avail	3 En Suite fac 1 Pub Bath/Show	B&B per person £25.00-£36.00 Single £19.00-£24.00 Double	Open Mar-Oct Dinner 1830-1900 B&B + Eve. Meal £31.00-£48.00
			Set amidst 2 acres (0.8ha) of gardens and woodlands on the river bank. Relaxing and informal atmosphere with easy access to the hills.			

VAT is shown at 17.5%: changes in this rate may affect prices. Prices shown are for guidance only. Please send SAE with each enquiry.

SOUTH OF SCOTLAND

CORRIECRAVIE, Isle of Arran

Map 1 E7

Mrs Adamson
Rosebank, Corriecravie
Kilmory
Isle of Arran
KA27 8PD
Tel: (Sliddery) 01770 870228

COMMENDED
👑👑

1 Single
1 Twin
1 Family

1 En Suite fac
1 Pub Bath/Show

B&B per person
£15.00-£17.00 Single
£15.00-£17.00 Double

Open Jan-Nov

Traditional farmhouse with warm welcome, home baking and open fires.
Views over sea to Mull of Kintyre and Ireland.

LOCHRANZA, Isle of Arran

Map 1 E6

Kincardine Lodge Guest House
Lochranza
Isle of Arran
KA27 8HL
Tel: (Lochranza) 01770 830267

APPROVED
👑👑

2 Twin
2 Double
2 Family

3 En Suite fac
1 Pub Bath/Show

B&B per person
£18.00-£20.00 Single
£18.00-£20.00 Double

Open Mar-Oct
Dinner 1830-1900
B&B + Eve. Meal
£26.00-£28.00

Facing a sea loch, with panoramic views of the castle, its mountain backdrop and
the coasts of Kintyre and Bute.

SHISKINE, Isle of Arran

Map 1 E7

C J E & E P Mills
Road End Christian
Guest House
Shiskine
Isle of Arran
Tel: (Shiskine) 01770 860448

COMMENDED
👑

1 Double
1 Family

1 Limited ensuite
2 Pub Bath/Show

B&B per person
£15.00-£18.00 Double

Open Jan-Dec
Dinner 1800-2100
B&B + Eve. Meal
£23.00-£26.00

A small Christian guest house on the west coast of Arran. Superb view of the Shiskine valley.

WHITING BAY, Isle of Arran

Map 1 F7

View Bank House
Golf Course Road
Whiting Bay
Isle of Arran
KA27 8QT
Tel: (Whiting Bay)
01770 700326

COMMENDED
👑👑

1 Single
1 Twin
3 Double
2 Family

4 En Suite fac
2 Pub Bath/Show

B&B per person
£18.00-£22.00 Single
£18.00-£22.00 Double

Open Jan-Nov
Dinner from 1800

Converted farmhouse with warm, friendly welcome and home cooking.
Lovely sea views and a large lawned garden. Private parking.
Ground-floor ensuite available.

**AUCHENCAIRN,
by Castle Douglas
Kirkcudbrightshire**

Map 2 A10

Mrs F M Cannon
Collin Hill
Auchencairn, by Castle Douglas
Kirkcudbrightshire
DG7 1QN
Tel: (Auchencairn)
01556 640242

HIGHLY
COMMENDED
👑👑

1 Double
1 Family

2 En Suite fac

B&B per person
£17.50-£18.50 Double

Open Feb-Nov

Tastefully furnished house with spectacular views over the Solway Firth to the
Cumbrian Hills. Half-a-mile to village and sea.

Mrs E Hendry
Rascarrel Cottage
Auchencairn, by Castle Douglas
Kirkcudbrightshire
DG7 1RJ
Tel: (Auchencairn)
01556 640214

HIGHLY
COMMENDED
👑👑

2 Twin
1 Double

2 En Suite fac
1 Pub Bath/Show

B&B per person
£16.00-£18.50 Double

Open Mar-Oct

Attractive cottage with open rural and sea views. Coastal and forest walks nearby.
Only 2 miles (3 kms) from village where good meals are available.

Details of Grading and Classification are on page vi.

Key to symbols is on back flap.

AYR

AYR	Map 1 G7						
Mrs W Campbell Ferguslea, 98 New Road Ayr Ayrshire KA8 8JG Tel: (Ayr) 01292 268551		COMMENDED 👑👑	1 Single 2 Twin	1 Priv. NOT ensuite 1 Pub Bath/Show	B&B per person £13.00-£15.00 Single £13.00-£15.00 Double Room only per person £10.00-£13.00	Open Jan-Dec	
			Traditional Scottish hospitality in comfortable family home, within 10 minutes' walk of town centre and all amenities.				
The Chimney's 14 Queens Terrace Ayr KA7 1DU Tel: (Ayr) 01292 263912		COMMENDED Listed	1 Twin 1 Double 3 Family	3 Pub Bath/Show	B&B per person from £18.00 Single from £16.00 Double	Open Jan-Dec	
			Family run guest house in quiet residential street close to seafront, short walk from town centre and all amenities.				
Craggallan Guest House 8 Queen's Terrace Ayr KA7 1DU Tel: (Ayr) 01292 264998		COMMENDED 👑👑	1 Single 1 Twin 2 Double 2 Family	2 En Suite fac 2 Pub Bath/Show	B&B per person £16.00-£18.00 Single £16.00-£22.00 Double	Open Jan-Dec Dinner 1730-1800	
			Small family guest house close to seafront, shops, harbour and public swimming pool.				
Dargil Guest House 7 Queen's Terrace Ayr KA7 1DU Tel: (Ayr) 01292 261955		COMMENDED 👑👑	1 Twin 2 Double 1 Family	3 En Suite fac 2 Pub Bath/Show	B&B per person £18.00-£20.00 Single £18.00-£20.00 Double	Open Jan-Dec Dinner 1700-1730	
			Small, friendly guest house with sea front location. Only a few minutes' walk from the town centre. Private parking.				
Eglinton Guest House 23 Eglinton Terrace Ayr KA7 1JJ Tel: (Ayr) 01292 264623		COMMENDED 👑	2 Single 1 Twin 1 Double 2 Family	2 En Suite fac 2 Pub Bath/Show	B&B per person £15.00-£20.00 Single £14.00-£18.00 Double	Open Jan-Dec Dinner from 1800 B&B + Eve. Meal £22.00-£25.00	
			Victorian terraced house in residential area overlooking tennis courts. A short walk from the sea, yet convenient for town centre and swimming pool.				
Mrs T Filippi Coilbank Villa 32 Castlehill Road Ayr KA7 2HZ Tel: (Ayr) 01292 262936		COMMENDED Listed	1 Single 2 Twin	2 Pub Bath/Show	B&B per person £17.50-£18.00 Single £15.50-£16.00 Double	Open Apr-Sep	
			Stone-built Victorian townhouse with large garden, convenient for town centre and beach. Near railway station.				
Mrs Ann Gambles Jacmar, 23 Dalblair Road Ayr KA7 1UF Tel: (Ayr) 01292 264798		COMMENDED Listed	2 Single 1 Twin 1 Double	2 Pub Bath/Show	B&B per person from £16.00 Single from £16.00 Double	Open Jan-Dec	
			Friendly hosted town centre accommodation. A favourite with golfers worldwide.				
Mrs Agnes Gemmell Dunduff Farm, Dunure Ayr Ayrshire KA7 4LH Tel: (Dunure) 01292 500225 Fax: 01292 500222		HIGHLY COMMENDED 👑👑	1 Twin 2 Double	2 En Suite fac 1 Priv. NOT ensuite	B&B per person £25.00-£28.00 Single £20.00-£22.50 Double	Open Mar-Nov	
			17th century farmhouse on working farm in elevated position 5 miles (8kms) south of Ayr, with fine views over Firth of Clyde to Arran. Private trout loch.				

Glenmore Guest House 35 Bellevue Crescent Ayr Ayrshire KA7 2DP Tel: (Ayr) 01292 269830 Fax: 01292 269830	COMMENDED	1 Single 1 Twin 1 Double 2 Family	5 En Suite fac	B&B per person £18.00-£25.00 Single £18.00-£25.00 Double	Open Jan-Dec Dinner 1700-1830 B&B + Eve. Meal from £28.00	
		Victorian, terraced house in broad, leafy, quiet street. Ground-floor room. Central for town, beach and golf.				
Heston 19 Castlehill Road Ayr Ayrshire KA7 2HX Tel: (Ayr) 01292 288188	HIGHLY COMMENDED	1 Twin 1 Double	1 Pub Bath/Show	B&B per person £18.00-£25.00 Single £15.00-£25.00 Double	Open Jan-Dec	
		Centrally located semi-detached sandstone villa convenient for railway station and shops. Ideal centre for touring Burns Country.				
Iona Guest House 27 St Leonards Road Ayr KA7 2PS Tel: (Ayr) 01292 269541 Fax: 01292 269541	COMMENDED	2 Single 1 Twin 1 Double	2 En Suite fac 1 Pub Bath/Show	B&B per person £14.00-£18.00 Single £14.00-£18.00 Double	Open Jan-Nov Dinner 1830-1930 B&B + Eve. Meal £20.00-£26.00	
		Traditional family home in residential area, ideally situated for both the business and holiday traveller.				
Charles & Ann Johnston Chaz-Ann, 17 Park Circus Ayr KA7 2DJ Tel: (Ayr) 01292 611215 Fax: 01292 285491	COMMENDED	2 Twin 1 Family	3 En Suite fac	B&B per person £21.00-£25.00 Single £16.00-£20.00 Double	Open Jan-Dec	
		Relaxed, family welcome at this Victorian terraced villa. Quiet residential area 5 minutes' walk from town centre and beach.				
Mrs J B Mair Laggan, 42 Craigie Road Ayr KA8 0EZ Tel: (Ayr) 01292 264947	COMMENDED	1 Double 1 Family	1 Pub Bath/Show	B&B per person £16.50-£17.50 Single £16.50-£17.50 Double	Open Apr-Sep	
		Semi-detached villa in residential area, close to racecourse, woodland, riverside walks and public parks. 15 minutes' walk from town centre and its amenities.				
Mrs Wilson Deanbank, 44 Ashgrove Street Ayr KA7 3BG Tel: (Ayr) 01292 263745	HIGHLY COMMENDED	1 Double 1 Family	1 Pub Bath/Show	B&B per person from £17.00 Single from £17.00 Double	Open Jan-Dec	
		Friendly, semi-detached home with many additional comforts. In a quiet residential situation, yet convenient for town centre, golf courses and Burns country.				
AYTON, by Eyemouth **Berwickshire** Mrs Riach Ayton Mains Farm House Ayton Berwickshire TD14 5RE Tel: (Ayton) 018907 81336	Map 2 F5 COMMENDED Listed	2 Single 1 Twin 1 Double	2 Pub Bath/Show	B&B per person £15.00-£16.00 Single £14.00-£15.00 Double Room only per person £11.00-£12.00	Open Apr-Oct	
		On the main Eyemouth to Ayton road, this traditional farmhouse built in 1840 has delightful gardens. A non-smoking house.				
Mrs Stevens Springbank Cottage, Beanburn Ayton Berwickshire TD14 5QZ Tel: (Ayton) 018907 81263	COMMENDED Listed	1 Twin 1 Family	1 Pub Bath/Show	B&B per person £15.00-£20.00 Double	Open Jan-Dec	
		Victorian cottage set in attractive gardens in peaceful village convenient for A1. Ideal centre for touring Borders. Close to coastal Nature Reserve.				

Key to symbols is on back flap.

SOUTH OF SCOTLAND

BALLANTRAE **Ayrshire** Mrs Drummond Ardstinchar Cottage Main Street Ballantrae Ayrshire KA26 0NA Tel: (Ballantrae) 01465 831343	Map 1 F9	COMMENDED ♛	1 Twin 2 Double	1 Pub Bath/Show	B&B per person £15.00-£20.00 Single from £15.00 Double	Open Jan-Dec	

Comfortable accommodation in family home,
within 20 minutes' drive from Irish ferries.

Mrs Georgina McKinley Laggan Farm Ballantrae, Girvan Ayrshire KA26 0JZ Tel: (Ballantrae) 01465 831402		COMMENDED ♛♛	1 Double 1 Family	1 En Suite fac 1 Pub Bath/Show	B&B per person £14.00-£18.00 Single £14.00-£18.00 Double	Open May-Oct Dinner 1700-1900 B&B + Eve. Meal £22.00-£26.00	

Family run dairy farm 0.5 miles (1km) south of Ballantrae on the Ayrshire coast.
Woodland walks, fishing by arrangement.

Mrs J Sloan The Haven, 75 Main Street Ballantrae Ayrshire KA26 0NA Tel: (Ballantrae) 01465 831306		COMMENDED ♛♛	1 Twin 1 Family	2 Priv. NOT ensuite	B&B per person from £17.00 Double	Open Jan-Dec	

Comfortable characteristic bungalow in elevated private position overlooking
Ballantrae Bay. A varied choice of traditional Scottish breakfast fayre.

BARRHILL **Ayrshire** Mrs Hughes Blair Farm Barrhill, Girvan Ayrshire KA26 0RD Tel: (Barrhill) 01465 821247	Map 1 G9	COMMENDED ♛♛	1 Twin 2 Double	1 En Suite fac 1 Pub Bath/Show	B&B per person £15.00-£18.00 Single £15.00-£18.00 Double	Open Easter-Oct Dinner 1700-1800 B&B + Eve. Meal £23.00-£26.00	

Comfortable traditional farmhouse, convenient for Glen Trool Country Park and
Ayrshire coast. Fishing available.

BEITH **Ayrshire**	Map 1 G6

SHOTTS FARM
BEITH, AYRSHIRE KA15 1LB
TELEPHONE: 01505 502273

Comfortable friendly accommodation is offered on this 160-acre dairy farm, one
mile from the A736, well situated to visit golf courses, country parks and leisure
centre. Also ideal for the ferry to Arran or Millport and for many good shopping
centres all around.

Mrs Gillan Shotts Farm Barrmill, Beith Ayrshire KA15 1LB Tel: (Beith) 01505 502273		COMMENDED Listed	1 Double 1 Family	2 Pub Bath/Show	B&B per person from £12.00 Single from £12.00 Double	Open Jan-Dec Dinner 1830-2230	

Family run farmhouse accommodation on a 160-acre (65ha) dairy farm.
Ideal base for Burns country, Arran and cultural Glasgow.

BURNHOUSE, by Beith **Ayrshire** Manor Farm Burnhouse, by Beith Ayrshire KA15 1LJ Tel: (Stewarton) 01560 484006	Map 1 G6	COMMENDED	1 Single 3 Twin 3 Double 2 Family	6 En Suite fac 1 Priv. NOT ensuite 2 Pub Bath/Show	B&B per person £17.00-£35.00 Single £15.00-£25.00 Double	Open Jan-Dec Dinner 1700-1930

Family run hotel, peacefully situated in own gardens, within easy reach of city and countryside. Ideal venue for weddings.

BURNMOUTH, Eyemouth **Berwickshire** Mr & Mrs R Goff Greystonelees Farm House Burnmouth Berwickshire TD14 5SZ Tel: (Ayton) 018907 81709	Map 2 F5	COMMENDED	1 Single 1 Twin 1 Double	2 En Suite fac 1 Pub Bath/Show	B&B per person £18.00-£25.00 Single £18.00-£19.00 Double	Open Jan-Dec Dinner 1800-2000

Georgian farmhouse in quiet countryside 200 yards (183m) from A1. Good walking country. St Abbs Head 5 miles (8kms), Eyemouth 2 miles (3kms), home baking. No children under 5.

CANONBIE **Dumfriesshire** Mr & Mrs Carruthers Watchknowe, Watchhill Road Canonbie Dumfriesshire DG14 0TA Tel: (Canonbie) 01387 371805	Map 2 D9	COMMENDED	1 Double 1 Family	2 Priv. NOT ensuite	B&B per person to £17.00 Double	Open Apr-Sep

Renovated 1930s bungalow set in 1 acre (0.4ha) of secluded garden. Open views of rolling countryside.

CAPPERCLEUCH **Selkirkshire** Fiona Paterson The White House St Mary's Loch Selkirk Tel: (Cappercleuch) 01750 42246	Map 2 C7	APPROVED Listed	1 Twin	1 Priv. NOT ensuite 1 Pub Bath/Show	B&B per person from £25.00 Single from £15.00 Double Room only per person from £13.00	Open Mar-Dec excl Xmas Dinner 1800-2000 B&B + Eve. Meal from £22.00

Detached house in peaceful and relaxing location overlooking the beautiful St Mary's Loch. Home cooking.

CASTLE DOUGLAS **Kirkcudbrightshire** Balmaghie House Balmaghie Deer Park Castle Douglas Kirkcudbrightshire DG7 2PB Tel: (Castle Douglas) 01556 670234	Map 2 A10	COMMENDED	2 Family	2 Priv. NOT ensuite	B&B per person £15.00-£17.50 Single £14.00-£17.50 Double	Open Jan-Dec Dinner 1750-2050 B&B + Eve. Meal £21.50-£25.00

Traditional mansion house in extensive woodland setting. Excellent home cooking with local produce.

Mrs McBride Airds Farm Crossmichael by Castle Douglas Kirkcudbrightshire DG7 3BG Tel: (Crossmichael) 01556 670418		COMMENDED	1 Single 1 Twin 1 Double 1 Family	2 En Suite fac 1 Pub Bath/Show	B&B per person £14.50-£17.50 Single £14.50-£17.50 Double	Open Mar-Nov

On mixed livestock farm in quiet rural location, with excellent views to Loch Ken. 4 miles (6kms) from Castle Douglas.

CASTLE DOUGLAS – COCKBURNSPATH

CASTLE DOUGLAS continued **Kirkcudbrightshire** Mrs A Muir Milton Park Farm Castle Douglas Kirkcudbrightshire DG7 3JJ Tel: (Haugh-of-Urr) 01556 660212	**Map 2** A10	**COMMENDED** ♔	1 Twin 2 Double	2 Pub Bath/Show	B&B per person £16.00-£18.00 Single £16.00-£18.00 Double	Open Apr-Oct	

Well-appointed farmhouse overlooking a large lawn and down the Urr valley.
Free trout and salmon fishing on River Urr. Home baking.

CRAIGADAM

CASTLE DOUGLAS, KIRKCUDBRIGHTSHIRE DG7 3HU
Telephone: 01556 650233   Fax: 01556 650233

Eighteenth-century farmhouse with panoramic views of surrounding countryside. An ideal base for golf, walking, fishing. Come home in the evening to comfort, super food and good Scottish hospitality. We specialise in local produce including venison, pheasant, salmon. All rooms are ensuite.

Mrs C Pickup Craigadam Castle Douglas Kirkcudbrightshire DG7 3HU Tel: (Kirkpatrick Durham) 01556 650233 Fax: 01556 650233	**COMMENDED** ♔♔♔	2 Twin 1 Double	3 En Suite fac	B&B per person £20.00 Single £20.00 Double	Open Jan-Dec Dinner 1800-2030 B&B + Eve. Meal £32.00

Working farm, with private trout loch and extensive stalking, driven and rough shooting. Specialising in fresh local produce, venison, pheasant, salmon etc.

Rose Cottage Guest House Gelston, by Castle Douglas Kirkcudbrightshire DG7 1SH Tel: (Castle Douglas) 01556 502513	**COMMENDED** ♔♔	3 Twin 2 Double	1 En Suite fac 2 Pub Bath/Show	B&B per person £16.00 Single £16.00-£18.50 Double	Open Jan-Dec

Friendly welcome in personally run guest house situated in quiet village.
Ideal for walkers and birdwatchers. Some accommodation in annexe.

Mrs C Smith Ingleston Farm Castle Douglas Kirkcudbrightshire DG7 1SW Tel: (Castle Douglas) 01556 502936	**COMMENDED** ♔♔	1 Twin 1 Double	2 En Suite fac	B&B per person £18.00 Single £18.00 Double Room only per person £14.00	Open Apr-Oct Dinner from 1830 B&B + Eve. Meal £27.00

Charming old farmhouse, rich in history, spacious bedrooms with own bathrooms.
Outstanding rural views, lovely walking country.

CLARENCEFIELD, by Dumfries **Dumfriesshire** Mr Pearson Farmer's Inn, Main Street Clarencefield Dumfriesshire DG1 4NF Tel: (Dumfries) 01387 870675	**Map 2** B10	**APPROVED** ♔♔ ⋀	3 Family	3 En Suite fac	B&B per person from £20.00 Single from £18.00 Double	Open Jan-Dec Dinner 1900-2100 B&B + Eve. Meal from £20.00

Late 17th century coaching inn in peaceful village. Convenient for the coast.
Well-equipped motel style bedrooms to rear. Disabled facilities.

COCKBURNSPATH **Berwickshire** Mrs B M Russell Townhead Farm Cockburnspath Tel: (Innerwick) 01368 830465	**Map 2** E5	**COMMENDED** Listed	2 Double	2 Pub Bath/Show	B&B per person £14.00-£16.00 Double	Open Apr-Oct

Warm welcome at this family farmhouse set high above the sea.
Sandy beaches nearby. Edinburgh only 38 miles (61kms).

SOUTH OF SCOTLAND

COLDINGHAM **Berwickshire** Cul-Na-Sithe Coldingham Bay . Berwickshire TD14 5PA Tel: (Coldingham) 018907 71565	Map 2 F5	**HIGHLY COMMENDED** ⚜ ⚜ ⚜	1 Twin 2 Double	3 En Suite fac	B&B per person £18.50-£22.00 Double	Open Feb-Nov Dinner 1900-2100
			Friendly, family run guest house overlooking Coldingham Sands with superb sea views. Open log fire in lounge. French and German spoken. Good home cooking.			

by COLDSTREAM **Berwickshire**	Map 2 E6	

HOMEBANK HOUSE
Near Birgham Village, by Coldstream, Berwickshire TD12 4ND
Tel: 01890 830285
Country house with spectacular views of the River Tweed and hills beyond. A warm welcome to a peaceful and comfortable home surrounded by gardens and lawns. Ample, secure and private parking. Good food, home cooking. On A698 situated half-a-mile from the A697 Newcastle-Edinburgh road.

Mrs Forrester Homebank House Nr Birgham Village Coldstream Berwickshire TD12 4ND Tel: (Birgham) 01890 830285		**COMMENDED** ⚜ ⚜	1 Twin 1 Double	2 Priv. NOT ensuite 2 Pub Bath/Show	B&B per person £20.00-£25.00 Double	Open Apr-Oct Dinner 1800-2000 B&B + Eve. Meal £32.50-£35.00
			Elegant country home set in beautiful gardens convenient for touring the Scottish Borders and Northumbria.			
DALBEATTIE **Dumfriesshire** Briardale House Haugh Road Dalbeattie Kirkcudbrightshire DG5 4AR Tel: (Dalbeattie) 01556 611468/ 0850 267251 (mobile)	Map 2 A10	**DELUXE** ⚜ ⚜ ⚜	1 Twin 2 Double	3 En Suite fac	B&B per person £19.50 Double	Open Jan-Oct Dinner 1800-1900 B&B + Eve. Meal £31.00
			Detached Victorian villa retaining many original features in residential area on the outskirts of town. Excellent food, no licence, no corkage.			
DARVEL **Ayrshire** Scoretulloch House Darvel Ayrshire KA17 0LR Tel: (Darvel) 01560 323331 Fax: 01560 323331	Map 1 H6	**HIGHLY COMMENDED** ⚜ ⚜ ⚜	1 Twin 1 Double	2 En Suite fac	B&B per person from £32.50 Single from £22.50 Double	Open Jan-Dec excl Xmas Dinner 1800-1950 B&B + Eve. Meal £35.00-£45.00
			In tranquil gardens, the superbly restored 16th-century millhouse, nestles on the fringe of the grouse moor, gazing out over the wooded valley. Peace, wildlife, photography, good food.			
DENHOLM **Roxburghshire** Mr Douglas Newlands The Fox and Hounds Inn Main Street Denholm Roxburghshire TD9 8NU Tel: (Denholm) 01450 870247 Fax: 01450 870500	Map 2 D7	**COMMENDED** ⚜	1 Single 1 Double 1 Family	3 En Suite fac 1 Pub Bath/Show	B&B per person £18.00-£20.00 Single £18.00-£20.00 Double Room only per person from £15.00	Open Jan-Dec Dinner 1800-2100 B&B + Eve. Meal £25.00-£30.00
			Family run inn situated in pretty village overlooking the green. Enclosed beer garden and children's play area. A wide selection of Real Ales available.			

DUMFRIES – by DUMFRIES

DUMFRIES

Map 2 B9

Mrs Conaghan Glencairn Villa, 45 Rae Street Dumfries DG1 1JD Tel: (Dumfries) 01387 262467	**COMMENDED** Listed	2 Single 1 Double 1 Family	2 En Suite fac 1 Pub Bath/Show	B&B per person £15.00-£17.00 Single £17.50-£19.00 Double Room only per person £12.50-£16.50	Open Jan-Dec

Comfortable 19th century home within walking distance of town centre.
Close to railway station and library.

Dalston House Laurieknowe Dumfries DG2 7AH Tel: (Dumfries) 01387 254422 Fax: 01387 254422	**COMMENDED**	2 Single 3 Twin 7 Double 4 Family	16 En Suite fac 1 Pub Bath/Show	B&B per person £45.00-£55.00 Single £27.50-£32.50 Double	Open Jan-Dec Dinner 1800-2100 B&B + Eve. Meal £43.50-£65.00

Family run establishment close to town centre and all amenities.
Varied menu with accent on fresh produce. Special breaks off-season.
Ground-floor accommodation available.

Glenaldor House 5 Victoria Terrace Dumfries DG1 1NL Tel: (Dumfries) 01387 264248	**COMMENDED** Listed	1 Twin 1 Double 2 Family	2 En Suite fac 1 Pub Bath/Show	B&B per person £16.00-£20.00 Single £16.00-£20.00 Double Room only per person £14.00-£18.00	Open Jan-Dec

Elegant Victorian terraced house within a few minutes' walk of the town centre.

Laurelbank Guest House 7 Laurieknowe Dumfries DG2 7AH Tel: (Dumfries) 01387 269388	**COMMENDED**	2 Twin 1 Double 1 Family	3 Limited ensuite 1 Pub Bath/Show	B&B per person from £24.00 Single £17.00-£18.00 Double	Open Feb-Nov

Elevated sandstone villa, a short walk to River Nith, town centre and Bus Station.
Golf, swimming and Ice Bowl 3 minutes away. Secure private car park at rear.

Mrs C A Murphy Orchard House 298 Annan Road Dumfries DG1 3JE Tel: (Dumfries) 01387 255099	**HIGHLY COMMENDED**	1 Twin 1 Double 1 Family	3 En Suite fac	B&B per person £25.00 Single £18.50 Double	Open Jan-Dec

On the outskirts of the town, converted stable block offering spacious
annexe accommodation with extensive parking.

by DUMFRIES

Map 2 B9

Mrs Hood Kirk House Farm Beeswing, by Dumfries Dumfriesshire DG2 8JF Tel: (Kirkgunzeon) 01387 248249 Fax: 01387 760209	**COMMENDED**	1 Twin 1 Double	2 En Suite fac	B&B per person £20.00 Single £16.00 Double	Open Jan-Dec

Working dairy farm in quiet village with fine views. Sauna available for guests' use.

Mr Ireson Smithy House Torthorwald, by Dumfries Dumfriesshire DG1 3PT Tel: (Collin) 01387 750518	**APPROVED** Listed	1 Twin 1 Double 1 Family	1 En Suite fac 2 Pub Bath/Show	B&B per person £14.00-£17.50 Double Room only per person £10.00-£15.00	Open Jan-Dec Dinner 1800-2000 B&B + Eve. Meal £22.50-£26.00

Converted village smithy with annexe accommodation available.
3 miles (5km) from busy shopping town of Dumfries and local amenities.

VAT is shown at 17.5%: changes in this rate may affect prices. Prices shown are for guidance only. Please send SAE with each enquiry.

Mrs C M Schooling Locharthur House Beeswing, by Dumfries Dumfriesshire DG2 8JG Tel: (Dumfries) 01387 760235		COMMENDED	1 Twin 1 Family	1 En Suite fac 1 Pub Bath/Show	B&B per person £16.00-£19.00 Single £16.00-£18.00 Double Room only per person £15.00-£17.00	Open Jan-Dec Dinner 1800-2000 B&B + Eve. Meal £23.00-£26.00	

Late Georgian house set in 3 acres (1.2ha) of grounds with access off A711.
Excellent views of countryside. Home baking and cooking. Good base for touring.

DUNS **Berwickshire** Mrs Hannay St Albans, Clouds Duns Berwickshire TD11 3BB Tel: (Duns) 01361 883285/ 0589 683799 (mobile)	Map 2 E5	HIGHLY COMMENDED	1 Twin 1 Double	1 Priv. NOT ensuite 1 Pub Bath/Show	B&B per person £17.50-£19.50 Single £16.00-£18.50 Double	Open Jan-Dec	

Pleasant Georgian house with secluded south-facing garden. Magnificent view
over small town to Cheviot Hills. Peaceful location yet close to town centre.

Mrs Alison Landale Cranshaws House Cranshaws Farm Duns Berwickshire TD11 3SJ Tel: (Longformacus) 01361 890242 Fax: 01361 890295		COMMENDED	2 Twin 1 Double	1 En Suite fac 2 Priv. NOT ensuite 2 Pub Bath/Show	B&B per person £17.50-£20.00 Single £17.50-£20.00 Double Room only per person from £15.00	Open Jan-Dec Dinner 1700-2200 B&B + Eve. Meal from £30.00	

Country-house on a working hill-farm. Tranquil setting, stunning
views and lovely walks. Duns 10 miles (16 kms), Edinburgh 30 miles (48 kms).

DUNSCORE, by Dumfries **Dumfriesshire** Mrs Zan Kirk Low Kirkbride Auldgirth Dumfriesshire DG2 0SP Tel: (Dunscore) 01387 820258	Map 2 A9	COMMENDED Listed	1 Twin 1 Double	2 Pub Bath/Show	B&B per person £15.00-£17.00 Single £15.00-£17.00 Double	Open Jan-Dec Dinner 1800-2100 B&B + Eve. Meal £25.00-£27.00	

Traditional farmhouse in country location with abundant wildlife, 2 miles (3 kms)
from Dunscore. Specialising in super breakfasts and tasty homebaking.

DUNURE **Ayrshire** Mrs L Wilcox Fisherton Farm Dunure Ayrshire KA7 4LF Tel: (Dunure) 01292 500223	Map 1 G7	COMMENDED	2 Twin	1 Pub Bath/Show	B&B per person £15.00-£17.50 Single £15.00 Double	Open Mar-Nov	

Traditional stone-built farmhouse on working mixed farm, with extensive sea
views to Arran. 5 miles (8kms) from Ayr. Ground-floor accommodation available.

EAGLESFIELD, by Lockerbie **Dumfriesshire** Mr & Mrs Mason Douglas House, The Courtyard Eaglesfield, by Lockerbie Dumfriesshire DG11 3PQ Tel: (Kirtlebridge) 01461 500215	Map 2 C9	COMMENDED Listed	1 Twin 2 Double	3 En Suite fac	B&B per person £17.50-£21.00 Single £15.00-£17.00 Double Room only per person £13.00-£15.00	Open Jan-Dec Dinner 1900-2100 B&B + Eve. Meal £30.00-£35.00	

Spacious single-storey accommodation in converted outbuildings
overlooking courtyard adjacent to restaurant, bar and car park.

EARLSTON **Berwickshire** Colin MacDonald Ardross, Melrose Road Earlston Berwickshire Tel: (Earlston) 01896 848007 Fax: 01896 848007	Map 2 D6	COMMENDED Listed	1 Single 1 Twin 1 Double	1 Priv. NOT ensuite 2 Pub Bath/Show	B&B per person £16.00 Single £16.00 Double	Open Jan-Dec Dinner 1800-2200	

Comfortable accommodation in large bungalow. Central heating and log fire.
Private parking. Ideal for all Borders attractions. Private bathroom available.

Details of Grading and Classification are on page vi. | **Key to symbols is on back flap.** | 17

SOUTH OF SCOTLAND

EARLSTON continued **Berwickshire** Mrs Susan Sillar Birkhill, Birkenside Earlston Berwickshire TD4 6AR Tel: (Earlston) 01896 849307 Fax: 01896 848206	Map 2 D6	HIGHLY COMMENDED	2 Twin 1 Double	2 En Suite fac 1 Priv. NOT ensuite	B&B per person £35.00 Single £29.50 Double	Open Jan-Dec Dinner 1930-2130 B&B + Eve. Meal £47.00-£50.00	

Elegant white Georgian house set in 12 acres (4.8ha) of woodland and gardens. Good home cooking. Ideal base from which to enjoy the Scottish Borders and Edinburgh. Parking.

Mr and Mrs J Todd Melvaig, Lauder Road Earlston Berwickshire TD4 6EE Tel: (Earlston) 01896 849303 Fax: 01896 849303		COMMENDED	1 Twin 1 Double 1 Family	1 En Suite fac 1 Pub Bath/Show	B&B per person £16.00-£20.00 Double	Open Feb-Dec	

A warm welcome at this comfortable personally run Bed and Breakfast. Ideal for touring the Borders. Off road parking.

ECCLEFECHAN **Dumfriesshire**	Map 2 C9

Carlyle House
Main Street, Ecclefechan, Lockerbie DG11 3DG
Telephone: 01576 300322
18th-century house situated in centre of village, ideally placed for exploring the Borders and Dumfries and Galloway. Home cooking, ample parking.

Mrs M Martin Carlyle House Ecclefechan Dumfriesshire DG11 3DG Tel: (Ecclefechan) 01576 300322		APPROVED Listed	1 Single 1 Twin 1 Family	2 Pub Bath/Show	B&B per person £12.50 Single £12.50 Double	Open Jan-Dec, excl Xmas & New Year Dinner 1800-2000 B&B + Eve. Meal £18.00	

Comfortable family accommodation convenient for A74. Children and pets welcome. Opposite Carlyle's birthplace.

ETTRICKBRIDGE, by Selkirk **Selkirkshire** Mrs S Nixon Oakwood Farm Ettrickbridge, Selkirk Selkirkshire TD7 5HJ Tel: (Selkirk) 01750 52245	Map 2 D7	COMMENDED Listed	1 Twin 1 Double	1 Pub Bath/Show	B&B per person £13.00-£15.00 Single	Open Jan-Dec	

Large spacious farmhouse in quiet rural location on mixed farm 4 miles (7kms) from Selkirk.

EYEMOUTH **Berwickshire** Mrs McGovern Ebba House, Upper Houndlaw Eyemouth Berwickshire TD14 5BU Tel: (Eyemouth) 018907 50350	Map 2 F5	COMMENDED Listed	1 Single 1 Twin 1 Double	2 Pub Bath/Show	B&B per person from £15.00 Single from £15.00 Double	Open Jan-Dec Dinner 1730-1830 B&B + Eve. Meal £23.00-£25.00	

Centrally located terraced house in quiet street. Short walk to beach, harbour and shops. Friendly welcome, home cooking.

Mrs J MacKay Hillcrest, Coldingham Road Eyemouth Berwickshire TD14 5AN Tel: (Eyemouth) 018907 50463		COMMENDED Listed	1 Twin 1 Double	1 Pub Bath/Show	B&B per person from £15.00 Double	Open Jan-Dec	

Pleasantly situated with own garden in residential area of coastal town. Ideal for touring. Off-street parking.

by EYEMOUTH **Berwickshire** Mrs E Blades Houndwood Reston Berwickshire TD14 5TP Tel: (Reston) 01361 850262	Map 2 F5	**APPROVED** Listed	1 Twin 1 Double 1 Family	2 En Suite fac 1 Limited ensuite 1 Pub Bath/Show	B&B per person £14.00-£18.00 Single £14.00-£18.00 Double Room only per person £12.00-£16.00	Open Jan-Dec Dinner 1800-2200 B&B + Eve. Meal £22.00-£26.00	

Former manse set in extensive grounds, close to the A1.
Ideal for touring the Scottish Borders.

FAIRLIE **Ayrshire** Mrs Gardner Mon Abri, 12 Main Road Fairlie Ayrshire KA29 0DP Tel: (Fairlie) 01475 568241	Map 1 G6	**COMMENDED** ♛	1 Single 1 Twin 1 Family	1 Pub Bath/Show	B&B per person £15.00-£17.00 Single £15.00-£17.00 Double	Open Jan-Dec Dinner from 1800	

Detached bungalow on main tourist route, overlooking the Firth of Clyde.
45 minutes by road from Glasgow. Personally run, evening meals available.

FENWICK, by Kilmarnock **Ayrshire** Mr & Mrs T Dick Langside Cottage Fenwick Ayrshire KA3 6AL Tel: (Fenwick) 01560 600884 Fax: 0141 424 1054	Map 1 H6	**COMMENDED** ♛ ♛	2 Twin 1 Double	1 En Suite fac 2 Priv. NOT ensuite	B&B per person £16.00-£22.00 Single £16.00-£20.00 Double	Open Jan-Dec Dinner 1900-2000 B&B + Eve. Meal £22.00-£28.00	

Situated in Fenwick, halfway between Glasgow and the Ayrshire Coast
with its golf courses, Burns Country and sandy beaches.

GALASHIELS **Selkirkshire** Mrs S Field Ettrickvale 33 Abbotsford Road Galashiels Selkirkshire TD1 3HW Tel: (Galashiels) 01896 755224	Map 2 D6	**COMMENDED** ♛	1 Single 2 Twin	2 Pub Bath/Show	B&B per person from £16.00 Single from £14.00 Double	Open Jan-Dec Dinner 1800-2000 B&B + Eve. Meal from £20.00	

Comfortable semi-detached bungalow with garden on A7, on outskirts of town
but only a short walk from local amenities. All accommodation on ground floor.
Evening meals by arrangement.

Mrs Murray Binniemyre House Abbotsford Road Galashiels Tel: (Galashiels) 01896 757137 Fax: 01896 757137		**COMMENDED** ♛ ♛ ♛	1 Single 1 Double 3 Family	3 En Suite fac 2 Priv. NOT ensuite	B&B per person £25.00-£30.00 Single £25.00-£30.00 Double Room only per person £20.00-£25.00	Open Jan-Dec Dinner 1800-2000	

A Victorian detached house recently refurbished
set in its own grounds on the edge of town.

Mrs A M Platt Wakefield Bank 9 Abbotsford Road Galashiels Selkirkshire TD1 3DP Tel: (Galashiels) 01896 752641		**HIGHLY** **COMMENDED** ♛ ♛	1 Twin 2 Double	1 Priv. NOT ensuite 2 Pub Bath/Show	B&B per person from £16.50 Double	Open Apr-Oct Dinner from 1800 B&B + Eve. Meal from £26.50	

Elegant house c.1840, retaining fine original features. Private garaging, easy access
to town centre. A non-smoking house. Awarded top B&B by "Discover Britain".

Bill & Sheila Salkeld Williamhope, Old Peel Galashiels Selkirkshire Tel: (Clovenfords) 0189685 243		**COMMENDED** ♛ ♛	1 Twin 1 Double	1 En Suite fac 1 Priv. NOT ensuite	B&B per person £16.50-£18.50 Double	Open Jan-Dec Dinner 1800-1930 B&B + Eve. Meal £26.00-£28.00	

Peace and tranquility surround you in this former farmhouse deep in the
Peeblesshire hills. Good home cooking and warm hospitality.

Details of Grading and Classification are on page vi.

SOUTH OF SCOTLAND

GALASHIELS continued **Selkirkshire** Mr & Mrs W Warner Monorene, 23 Stirling Street Galashiels Selkirkshire TD1 1BY Tel: (Galashiels) 01896 753073	**Map 2** D6	COMMENDED ♕	2 Single 3 Twin 1 Double 1 Family	2 Pub Bath/Show	B&B per person £16.50 Single £16.50 Double	Open Jan-Dec Dinner 1800-1900 B&B + Eve. Meal £22.50	
Friendly family house conveniently situated for shops and transport. Ideal for bus services to tour Border area.							
Mrs Gwen Young Glenellwyn, 89 Melrose Road Galashiels TD1 2BX Tel: (Galashiels) 01896 752964		COMMENDED Listed	2 Single 1 Family	1 Pub Bath/Show	B&B per person to £15.00 Single to £15.00 Double Room only per person to £10.00	Open Jan-Dec excl Xmas	
Family house on edge of Galashiels. Convenient for all areas of the Scottish Borders.							
by GALASHIELS **Selkirkshire** Mrs Sheila Bergius Over Langshaw Farm Langshaw, by Galashiels Selkirkshire TD1 2PE Tel: (Blainslie) 01896 860244	**Map 2** D6	COMMENDED ♕	1 Double 1 Family	1 En Suite fac 1 Priv. NOT ensuite	B&B per person £18.00-£20.00 Double	Open Jan-Dec	
Traditional farmhouse on mixed working farm on 500 acres (200ha), 4 miles (6kms) from Galashiels with spectacular views of surrounding countryside.							
GALSTON **Ayrshire** Mrs J Bone Auchencloigh Farm Galston Ayrshire KA4 8NP Tel: (Galston) 01563 820567	**Map 1** H6	COMMENDED Listed	2 Twin 1 Double	1 Pub Bath/Show	B&B per person from £16.00 Double	Open Jan-Dec excl Xmas/New Year Dinner from 1830 B&B + Eve. Meal from £25.00	
Spacious 18th century farmhouse amidst large gardens on 240-acre (97ha) farm. Non-smokers only please.							
by GATEHOUSE OF FLEET **Kirkcudbrightshire** Girthon Kirk Guest House Sandgreen Road by Gatehouse of Fleet Kirkcudbrightshire DG7 2DW Tel: (Gatehouse) 01557 814352	**Map 1** H10	COMMENDED ♕♕	1 Twin 2 Double	2 En Suite fac 1 Priv. NOT ensuite	B&B per person £20.00-£24.00 Double	Open Mar-Sep Dinner from 1830 B&B + Eve. Meal £30.00-£34.00	
Lovely country house in idyllic rural setting. Fine home cooking. All rooms with private facilities. 0.5 miles (1 km) off A75 on Sandgreen Road.							
GIRVAN **Ayrshire** Glendrissaig Guest House Newton Stewart Road by Girvan Ayrshire KA26 0HJ Tel: (Girvan) 01465 714631	**Map 1** F8	HIGHLY COMMENDED ♕♕♕	1 Twin 1 Double 1 Family	2 En Suite fac 1 Priv. NOT ensuite 1 Pub Bath/Show	B&B per person from £19.00 Single £18.00-£22.00 Double	Open Apr-Oct Dinner 1800-1900	
Modern detached house in elevated position with excellent outlook towards Mull of Kintyre. Organic produce when available used in vegetarian meals.							
Mrs L Hogarth St Oswalds 5 Golf Course Road Girvan Ayrshire KA26 9HW Tel: (Girvan) 01465 713786		COMMENDED ♕♕	1 Twin 1 Double	1 En Suite fac 1 Priv. NOT ensuite	B&B per person £16.00-£20.00 Double	Open Jan-Dec	
Semi-detached Victorian seaside villa. Close to beach and harbour and short walk to municipal golf course.							

VAT is shown at 17.5%: changes in this rate may affect prices. Prices shown are for guidance only. Please send SAE with each enquiry.

Mrs Isobel Kyle Hawkhill Farm Old Dailly, by Girvan Ayrshire KA26 9RD Tel: (Old Dailly) 01465 871232	**HIGHLY COMMENDED** 👑👑	1 Twin 2 Double	1 En Suite fac 1 Priv. NOT ensuite 1 Pub Bath/Show	B&B per person £18.00-£20.00 Double	Open Easter-Oct	
		Large traditional farmhouse on mixed farm, 3 miles (5 kms) from Girvan. **Friendly, informal atmosphere, home-baking and cooking using fresh produce.**				
Thistleneuk Guest House 19 Louisa Drive Girvan Ayrshire KA26 9AH Tel: (Girvan) 01465 712137	**COMMENDED** 👑👑👑	1 Single 2 Twin 2 Double 2 Family	7 En Suite fac	B&B per person £19.00-£20.00 Single £19.00-£20.00 Double	Open Apr-Oct Dinner from 1800 B&B + Eve. Meal £26.00-£27.00	
		19th century terraced house on seafront overlooking Ailsa Craig. **Within easy walking distance of town centre.**				

by GIRVAN **Ayrshire**	Map 1 F8

Glengennet Farm

Barr, by Girvan, Ayrshire KA26 9TY
Telephone: 01465 861220

Victorian shooting lodge on hill farm, lovely views over Stinchar Valley and neighbouring Galloway Forest Park. Has ensuite bedrooms with tea trays. Near conservation village with 2 hotels for evening meals. Good base for Glentrool, Burns Country, Culzean Castle, Ayrshire coast.

Contact Mrs V. Dunlop for a brochure.

Mrs V Dunlop Glengennet Farm Barr, by Girvan Ayrshire KA26 9TY Tel: (Barr) 01465 861220	**HIGHLY COMMENDED** 👑👑	1 Twin 1 Double	2 En Suite fac	B&B per person from £18.50 Double	Open Apr-Oct	
		Former shooting lodge set on hillside overlooking Stinchar Valley, **1.5 miles (3kms) from Barr, a conservation village.**				
Mrs M Whiteford Maxwelston Farm Dailly, by Girvan Ayrshire KA26 9RH Tel: (Dailly) 01465 811210	**HIGHLY COMMENDED** 👑	1 Twin 1 Family	2 Pub Bath/Show	B&B per person from £16.50 Single from £15.00 Double	Open Mar-Oct Dinner 1830-1930	
		18th century Listed farmhouse on working sheep and beef farm, **5 miles (8kms) inland from Girvan. New golf course adjacent to farm.**				

GLENLUCE **Wigtownshire**	Map 1 G10					
Mrs C Marshall Grayhill Farm Glenluce Wigtownshire DG8 0NS Tel: (Glenluce) 01581 300400	**COMMENDED** 👑	1 Twin 1 Double	1 Pub Bath/Show	B&B per person £16.00-£17.00 Single £15.00-£16.00 Double	Open Apr-Oct	
		Friendly, family welcome on a traditional farm on outskirts of village. **Centrally situated for touring and leisure pursuits. Convenient for Irish ferries.**				
Rowantree Guest House 38 Main Street Glenluce DG8 0PS Tel: (Glenluce) 01581 300244	**COMMENDED** 👑👑 ♿	1 Twin 2 Double 2 Family	2 En Suite fac 2 Limited ensuite 1 Priv. NOT ensuite 1 Pub Bath/Show	B&B per person £15.00-£18.00 Single £12.00-£16.00 Double Room only per person £10.00-£13.00	Open Jan-Dec Dinner 1830-2000 B&B + Eve. Meal £19.00-£23.00	
		Family run house, popular with fishers, golfers, tourists and ferry passengers. **In village 15 minutes from Stranraer. Disabled facilities**				

SOUTH OF SCOTLAND

GLENLUCE continued **Wigtownshire** Mrs M Stewart Bankfield Farm Glenluce Wigtownshire DG8 0JF Tel: (Glenluce) 01581 300281	Map 1 G10	COMMENDED	1 Twin 1 Double 1 Family	2 En Suite fac 1 Priv. NOT ensuite 1 Pub Bath/Show	B&B per person from £16.00 Single from £16.00 Double	Open Apr-Oct

Farmhouse on 370-acre (150ha) working farm conveniently situated between the village and the main A75 tourist route. 5 minutes' walk into village.

GREENLAW, by Duns **Berwickshire** Bridgend House 36 West High Street Greenlaw Berwickshire TD10 6XA Tel: (Greenlaw) 01361 810270 Fax: 01361 810270	Map 2 F6	COMMENDED	2 Twin 2 Family	3 En Suite fac 1 Priv. NOT ensuite	B&B per person £16.00-£18.00 Double	Open Jan-Dec Dinner 1900-2000 B&B + Eve. Meal from £24.00

Built in 1816 with riverside trout fishing. On scenic Borders A697
Newcastle to Edinburgh road. Edinburgh 38 miles.

GRETNA **Dumfriesshire** Mrs Donabie The Beeches, Loanwath Road Gretna Dumfriesshire DG16 5EP Tel: (Gretna) 01461 337448	Map 2 C10	COMMENDED	1 Twin 1 Family	2 En Suite fac	B&B per person £17.50-£18.00 Double	Open Feb-Nov

Former farmhouse overlooking the Solway and Lakeland hills.
A non-smoking house with homely and peaceful atmosphere, ensuite facilities.

GRETNA GREEN **Dumfriesshire** Kathleen M Smith The Mill, Grahamshill Kirkpatrick Fleming Gretna Green Dumfriesshire DG11 3BQ Tel: (Kirkpatrick Fleming) 01461 800344/800603	Map 2 C10	COMMENDED Listed	2 Single 2 Twin 12 Double 8 Family	24 En Suite fac	B&B per person £26.00-£28.00 Single £20.00-£22.00 Double	Open Jan-Dec Dinner 1800-2200

Converted farm steading. Stone-built chalet accommodation just off the M74.
Fully licensed bar restaurant. Continental breakfast only.

HAWICK **Roxburghshire** Mrs Sandra Allan Hillview, 4 Weensland Road Hawick Roxburghshire TD9 9NP Tel: (Hawick) 01450 374100	Map 2 D7	COMMENDED Listed	1 Single 1 Twin 1 Double	1 Pub Bath/Show	B&B per person to £16.00 Single from £14.00 Double Room only per person to £10.00	Open Jan-Dec Dinner 1700-1800 B&B + Eve. Meal £20.00-£23.00

Comfortable, terraced house on main tourist route near town centre.
Public car park opposite. Near leisure centre.

Ellistrin
6 Fenwick Park, Hawick, Borders TD9 9PA
Telephone: (01450) 374216

Situated on the outskirts of the knitwear town of Hawick, this family house enjoys an elevated position with a lovely view. Three bedrooms all ensuite. All local amenities within easy walking distance. An attractive base for touring the lovely Borders countryside or walking in the Borders hills.

Mrs E Smith Ellistrin, 6 Fenwick Park Hawick Roxburghshire TD9 9PA Tel: (Hawick) 01450 374216		COMMENDED	1 Twin 2 Double	3 En Suite fac 1 Pub Bath/Show	B&B per person £17.00 Single £17.00 Double	Open Apr-Oct

Comfortable Victorian villa within spacious grounds in an elevated position
overlooking Hawick. All rooms ensuite. Meals available. Private parking.

Mrs Telfer		**COMMENDED**	1 Twin	2 Pub Bath/Show	B&B per person	Open Apr-Oct	
Craig-Ian, 6 Weensland Road			2 Double		from £15.00 Single		
Hawick					from £14.00 Double		
Roxburghshire							
TD9 9NP							
Tel: (Hawick) 01450 373506			**Large Victorian terraced house, set above main A698 tourist route and close to centre of historic Borders town.**				

by HAWICK	Map 2						
Roxburghshire	D7						
Mrs S Shell		**COMMENDED**	1 Twin	2 En Suite fac	B&B per person	Open Jan-Dec	
Wiltonburn Farm		Listed	1 Double	1 Priv. NOT ensuite	£16.00-£18.00 Single		
Hawick			1 Family	1 Pub Bath/Show	£16.00-£18.00 Double		
Roxburghshire							
TD9 7LL							
Tel: (Hawick) 01450 372414			**A friendly welcome at this comfortable farmhouse, in a sheltered valley, under 2 miles (3kms) from Hawick. Designer knitwear showroom in converted barn.**				

IRVINE	Map 1						
Ayrshire	G6						
Mr J Daunt		**APPROVED**	3 Single	2 En Suite fac	B&B per person	Open Jan-Dec	
The Conifers			1 Twin	1 Priv. NOT ensuite	£15.00-£20.00 Single		
40 Kilwinning Road			1 Double		£15.00-£17.50 Double		
Irvine			1 Family		Room only per person		
Ayrshire					£12.50		
KA12 8RY							
Tel: (Irvine) 01294 278070			**Bungalow with large well-maintained garden, convenient for town centre. Ample off-street parking in safe location. All rooms can be let as singles.**				

JEDBURGH	Map 2						
Roxburghshire	E7						
Mrs S Fordham		**APPROVED**	1 Single	1 Pub Bath/Show	B&B per person	Open Jan-Dec	
Primrose Leisure		Listed	1 Double		from £15.50 Single		
2 Old Hall Cottages					from £15.50 Double		
Western Ulster Road							
Jedburgh							
Roxburghshire							
TD8 6TF							
Tel: (Jedburgh) 01835 864551			**Former farmhouse set in peaceful surroundings just a mile from Jedburgh. Ideal for fishing, golfing, walking and riding.**				

Select your holiday accommodation with confidence,

use The Scottish Tourist Board's
Grading and Classification Scheme

SOUTH OF SCOTLAND

JEDBURGH continued Roxburghshire	Map 2 E7

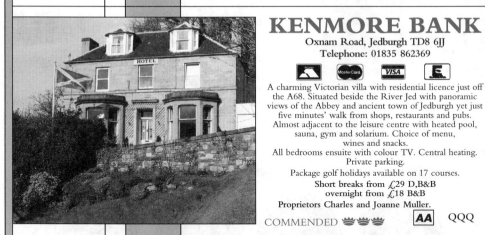

FROYLEHURST
The Friars, Jedburgh TD8 6BN
Telephone: 01835 862477

An impressive Grade 'B' Listed Victorian Town-house dated 1894, retaining original fireplaces, stained glass windows, cornices and tiled vestibule. Offering spacious and comfortable guest rooms and residents' lounge. Enjoying an elevated position in a large secluded garden in a quiet residential area with ample private off-street parking, yet only 2 minutes from town centre. All bedrooms have wash basins, shaver points, tea/coffee-making facilities, colour TV and radio. Full Scottish breakfast. This is a family home, and guests are made welcome by the owner.

Further details are available from Mrs H Irvine.
AA Selected QQQQ

Mrs H Irvine Froylehurst, The Friars Jedburgh Roxburghshire TD8 6BN Tel: (Jedburgh) 01835 862477 Fax: 01835 862477	HIGHLY COMMENDED 👑	1 Twin 2 Double 1 Family	2 Pub Bath/Show	B&B per person £15.00-£17.00 Double	Open Mar-Nov

Detached Victorian house (retaining many original features) with large garden and private parking. Spacious rooms. Overlooking town, 2 minutes' walk from the centre.

KENMORE BANK
Oxnam Road, Jedburgh TD8 6JJ
Telephone: 01835 862369

A charming Victorian villa with residential licence just off the A68. Situated beside the River Jed with panoramic views of the Abbey and ancient town of Jedburgh yet just five minutes' walk from shops, restaurants and pubs. Almost adjacent to the leisure centre with heated pool, sauna, gym and solarium. Choice of menu, wines and snacks.
All bedrooms ensuite with colour TV. Central heating. Private parking.
Package golf holidays available on 17 courses.
Short breaks from £29 D,B&B
overnight from £18 B&B
Proprietors Charles and Joanne Muller.

COMMENDED 👑👑👑 **AA** QQQ

Kenmore Bank Guest House Oxnam Road Jedburgh Roxburghshire TD8 6JJ Tel: (Jedburgh) 01835 862369	COMMENDED 👑👑👑	2 Twin 2 Double 2 Family	6 En Suite fac	B&B per person £25.00-£42.00 Single £18.00-£22.00 Double Room only per person £18.00-£21.00	Open Jan-Dec Dinner 1830-1930 B&B + Eve. Meal £40.00-£57.00

Friendly, relaxing family run hotel with residential licence and good home cooking. Splendid views of the Abbey. Excellent base for touring the Borders.

SOUTH OF SCOTLAND

THE SPINNEY GUEST HOUSE

Langlee, Jedburgh, Roxburghshire TD8 6PB
Telephone: 01835 863525   Fax: 01835 863525

Attractive house set in extensive garden with quality accommodation and friendly welcome. Private bathrooms and ample parking. Two miles south of Jedburgh on A68.

Spinney Guest House The Spinney, Langlee Jedburgh Roxburghshire TD8 6PB Tel: (Jedburgh) 01835 863525 Fax: 01835 863525	**DELUXE** 👑👑	1 Twin 2 Double	2 En Suite fac 1 Priv. NOT ensuite	B&B per person £19.00-£21.00 Double	Open Mar-Nov

A warm welcome at this attractive house with large pleasant garden lying just off main A68. All rooms have private facilities. Ample parking.

Willow Court The Friars Jedburgh Roxburghshire TD8 6BN Tel: (Jedburgh) 01835 863702 Fax: 01835 864601	**HIGHLY COMMENDED** 👑👑	1 Twin 2 Double 1 Family	3 En Suite fac 1 Priv. NOT ensuite	B&B per person £23.00-£32.00 Single £15.00-£20.00 Double Room only per person £12.00-£17.00	Open Jan-Dec

Set in 2 acres of garden above the town with excellent views. Peaceful setting, yet close to all amenities. Most accommodation on the ground floor.

by JEDBURGH **Roxburghshire** Mrs Hensens Ancrum Craig Ancrum, Jedburgh Roxburghshire TD8 6UN Tel: (Ancrum) 01835 830280	Map 2 E7 **COMMENDED** 👑👑	1 Twin 2 Double	3 En Suite fac	B&B per person £27.00-£34.00 Single £18.00-£23.00 Double	Open Mar-Oct

Country house with many authentic 19th century features. Large garden and magnificent views of surrounding countryside. Private bathrooms. Open fire. All rooms ensuite.

Mrs McNeill Millheugh Jedburgh Roxburghshire TD8 6RA Tel: (Jedburgh) 01835 862208	**HIGHLY COMMENDED** Listed	1 Single 1 Twin 1 Double	1 Pub Bath/Show	B&B per person £15.00-£16.00 Single £15.00-£16.00 Double	Open May-Oct

Non-smokers welcomed to this charming farmhouse to which guests regularly return. Jedburgh 3.5 miles (6kms), Kelso 10 miles (16kms).

Mrs Whittaker Hundalee House Jedburgh Roxburghshire TD8 6PA Tel: (Jedburgh) 01835 863011 Fax: 01835 863011	**DELUXE** 👑👑	1 Twin 2 Double 1 Family	3 En Suite fac 1 Pub Bath/Show	B&B per person £25.00-£35.00 Single £16.50-£20.00 Double	Open Mar-Oct

Extensively refurbished country house 1 mile (2 kms) south of Jedburgh. Excellent views of Cheviot Hills. One bedroom with a 4-poster bed. Ideal touring base.

KELSO **Roxburghshire** Barbara Chapman Wooden House Kelso Roxburghshire TD5 8HG Tel: (Kelso) 01573 224204 Fax: 01573 225976	Map 2 E6 **HIGHLY COMMENDED** 👑👑	2 Twin 1 Double	3 En Suite fac	B&B per person £20.00-£22.50 Double	Open May-Sep

A beautiful Georgian castellated house standing in 11 acres (4.5ha) of mature gardens, overlooking the River Tweed. 0.5 miles (1km) from Kelso.

KELSO – by KELSO

KELSO continued Roxburghshire Ms Hawkins Wester House 155 Roxburgh Street Kelso Roxburghshire Tel: (Kelso) 01573 225479	Map 2 E6	COMMENDED Listed	1 Single 1 En Suite fac 1 Double 2 Pub Bath/Show 1 Family	B&B per person £12.00-£13.00 Single £15.00-£18.50 Double	Open Jan-Dec

Comfortably furnished 16th century townhouse. Warm welcome and friendly atmosphere. A few minutes' walk from town centre and Floors Castle.

ABBEY BANK

The Knowes, Kelso, Roxburghshire TD5 7BH
Telephone/Fax: 01573 226550

"Abbey Bank" is a Highly Commended, historic, walled house with luxurious continental furniture and features and beautiful garden. Ideally located for touring, fishing and shopping; only three minutes' walk away from the Abbey ruins, the River Tweed and the town centre. Dogs may be accepted. Special breaks available. **NO SMOKING**

Miss W Hess Abbey Bank, The Knowes Kelso Roxburghshire TD5 7BH Tel: (Kelso) 01573 226550 Fax: 01573 226550		HIGHLY COMMENDED Listed	2 Single 3 En Suite fac 1 Twin 1 Priv. NOT ensuite 3 Double 1 Pub Bath/Show	B&B per person £18.50-£36.00 Single £18.50-£26.00 Double Room only per person £13.50-£31.00	Open Jan-Dec

Elegant 1820 townhouse with character, providing comfortable accommodation and a friendly welcome. 3 min walk to the Abbey, Town Centre and Tweed. Ideal touring base.

Mrs Isobel Liddle 5 Station Road Kelso Roxburghshire TD5 8DQ Tel: (Kelso) 01573 224647		COMMENDED Listed	1 Single 1 Pub Bath/Show 1 Twin	B&B per person £14.00 Single £14.00 Double	Open Jan-Dec

Friendly family home on the outskirts of Kelso. Sunny garden with terrace. Home baking.

Mrs Jan McDonald Craignethan House Jedburgh Road Kelso Roxburghshire TD5 8AZ Tel: (Kelso) 01573 224818		COMMENDED Listed	1 Twin 2 Pub Bath/Show 2 Double	B&B per person £16.50 Single £16.50 Double	Open Jan-Dec

Delightful detached house overlooking the town centre with panoramic views of Floors Castle and surrounding countryside. Ground-floor bedroom. Off-road parking.

Mr D Watson Clashdale, 26 Inchmead Drive Kelso Roxburghshire TD5 7LW Tel: (Kelso) 01573 223405		COMMENDED Listed	1 Single 1 Pub Bath/Show 1 Double	B&B per person £14.00 Single £14.00 Double	Open Jan-Dec

Comfortable, double glazed, centrally heated accommodation in a quiet cul-de-sac. 5 minutes from town centre. Tea on arrival and evening cuppa.

by KELSO Roxburghshire Mrs D M Playfair Morebattle Tofts Kelso Roxburghshire TD5 8AD Tel: (Morebattle) 01573 440364 Fax: 01573 420750	Map 2 E6	COMMENDED	1 Twin 2 En Suite fac 2 Double 1 Priv. NOT ensuite	B&B per person £16.00 Single £17.00 Double	Open Apr-Oct Dinner 1830-2000 B&B + Eve. Meal £27.00-£28.00

Elegant 18th century farmhouse set in idyllic location beside the Kalewater. Ideal base for touring, walking, fishing and golf.

SOUTH OF SCOTLAND

Mrs B Smith Whitehill Farm Nenthorn, by Kelso Roxburghshire TD5 7RZ Tel: (Stichill) 01573 470203 Fax: 01573 470203		HIGHLY COMMENDED	2 Single 2 Twin	1 En Suite fac 1 Pub Bath/Show	B&B per person to £17.00 Single to £18.00 Double	Open Jan-Dec Dinner 1900-2000 B&B + Eve. Meal £31.00-£32.00	
			18th century farmhouse with superb views on mixed farm. Ideally placed for touring the Borders region and just off the Kelso/Edinburgh road. Real cooking, fresh food.				
KILMARNOCK **Ayrshire** Eriskay Guest House 2 Dean Terrace Kilmarnock Ayrshire KA3 1RJ Tel: (Kilmarnock) 01563 532061/05851 09971	Map 1 G6	APPROVED	2 Single 1 Twin 3 Double 1 Family	3 En Suite fac 2 Pub Bath/Show	B&B per person £16.00-£22.00 Single £15.00-£18.00 Double	Open Jan-Dec	
			Detached villa conveniently situated on main bus route and close to Dean Park and Castle. Enclosed secure car park.				
Mrs A Grant 177 Dundonald Road Kilmarnock Ayrshire KA2 0AB Tel: (Kilmarnock) 01563 522733		COMMENDED	2 Twin 1 Double	1 En Suite fac 1 Pub Bath/Show	B&B per person from £18.00 Single from £14.00 Double	Open May-Oct	
			Modern detached home with attractive enclosed patio and garden on town outskirts. Golf and good touring base. Under 30 miles (48kms) from Glasgow.				
Mrs Mary Howie Hillhouse Farm Grassyards Road Kilmarnock Ayrshire KA3 6HG Tel: (Kilmarnock) 01563 523370		COMMENDED	1 Twin 2 Family	1 En Suite fac 2 Pub Bath/Show	B&B per person £17.00-£20.00 Single £15.00-£17.00 Double	Open Jan-Dec	
			Working dairy farm 500 acres (200ha), with fine views of Ayrshire countryside situated about 2 miles (4 kms) east of Kilmarnock.				
Mrs M Love Muirhouse Farm Gatehead, by Kilmarnock Ayrshire KA2 0BT Tel: (Kilmarnock) 01563 523975		COMMENDED	1 Twin 1 Double 1 Family	2 En Suite fac 1 Priv. NOT ensuite	B&B per person £16.00-£18.00 Single £16.00-£18.00 Double	Open Jan-Dec Dinner 1800-1900	
			Large family farmhouse on 170-acre (69ha) dairy farm 2 miles (3kms) from Kilmarnock. Quiet rural position.				
Mrs C Turner Tamarind, 24 Arran Avenue Kilmarnock Ayrshire KA3 1TP Tel: (Kilmarnock) 01563 571788 Fax: 01563 571787		COMMENDED	1 Single 2 Twin 1 Family	4 En Suite fac	B&B per person £20.00-£25.00 Single £15.00-£20.00 Double	Open Jan-Dec	
			Ranch-style bungalow with small heated swimming pool in residential area. Convenient base for touring.				
by KILMARNOCK **Ayrshire** Mrs L Howie Muirhouse Farm Symington, by Kilmarnock Ayrshire KA1 5PA Tel: (Symington) 01563 830218	Map 1 G6	COMMENDED	1 Twin 1 Double	1 Pub Bath/Show	B&B per person from £16.00 Double Room only per person from £11.00	Open Jan-Dec	
			Traditional farmhouse peacefully situated and convenient for A77. Provides a good base for touring Ayrshire coast, golfing, fishing, walking etc.				

Details of Grading and Classification are on page vi.   Key to symbols is on back flap.   27

KILWINNING – LANGHOLM

KILWINNING
Ayrshire
Mrs C Harris
Woodburn Cottage, Woodwynd
Kilwinning
Ayrshire
Tel: (Kilwinning) 01294 551657/
0589 494567 (mobile)
Fax: 01294 558297

Map 1
G6

COMMENDED
Listed

1 Single   1 Pub Bath/Show
2 Twin

B&B per person
£16.00-£18.00 Single
£16.00-£18.00 Double

Open Jan-Dec

Attractive cottage in its own grounds – a little bit of countryside in the centre of Kilwinning.

KIPPFORD, by Dalbeattie
Kirkcudbrightshire
Mrs Janet M McKinnon
Brookside
Kippford, by Dalbeattie
Kirkcudbrightshire
DG5 4LL
Tel: (Kippford) 01556 620240

Map 2
A10

HIGHLY COMMENDED

1 Twin   1 En Suite fac
1 Double   1 Priv. NOT ensuite

B&B per person
to £25.00 Single
£17.50-£19.50 Double

Open Mar-Oct

Quiet location in the village set in beautiful gardens with brook and pond.
Comfortable accommodation. Private parking.

Mrs J Muir
Rosemount, On the Sea Front
Kippford, by Dalbeattie
Kirkcudbrightshire
DG5 4LN
Tel: (Kippford) 01556 620214

COMMENDED

2 Twin   3 En Suite fac
2 Double   2 Priv. NOT ensuite
1 Family   2 Pub Bath/Show

B&B per person
from £20.00 Single
from £17.00 Double

Open Feb-Nov
Dinner from 1900
B&B + Eve. Meal
from £27.00

Small friendly guest house on the Urr Estuary offering a superb view and
spectacular sunsets. Smoking and non-smoking lounges.

KIRKCUDBRIGHT

Gladstone House
48 High Street
Kirkcudbright
DG6 4JX
Tel: (Kirkcudbright)
01557 331734
Fax: 01557 331734

Map 2
A10

HIGHLY COMMENDED

3 Double   3 En Suite fac

B&B per person
£25.00-£34.00 Single
£24.00-£28.00 Double

Open Jan-Dec

Elegance and comfort in sympathetically restored Georgian townhouse
in a quiet corner of the old town. Secret garden.

KIRK YETHOLM
Roxburghshire
E M Sinfield
Spring Valley, The Green
Kirk Yetholm
Roxburghshire
TD5 8PQ
Tel: (Yetholm) 01573 420253

Map 2
E7

COMMENDED

1 Twin   2 Priv. NOT ensuite
1 Double

B&B per person
£16.00-£19.00 Double
Room only per person
from £14.00

Open Jan-Dec

Peacefully located in the conservation village of Kirk Yetholm at the end of the
Pennine Way. Charming 18th-century home with attractive views.

LANGHOLM
Dumfriesshire
The Reivers Rest
81 High Street
Langholm
Dumfriesshire
DG13 0DJ
Tel: (Langholm) 01387 381343

Map 2
C9

COMMENDED
Listed

1 Twin   1 En Suite fac
2 Double   2 Pub Bath/Show
1 Family

B&B per person
£20.00-£25.00 Single
£15.00-£23.00 Double

Open Jan-Dec
Dinner 1800-2100

Family run inn, in the heart of small Borders town offering bar meals,
real ale and an à la carte menu using fresh local produce whenever possible.

Scotland for Golf . . .

Find out more about golf in Scotland. There's more to it than
just the championship courses so get in touch with us now for
information on the hidden gems of Scotland.

Write to: Information Unit, Scottish Tourist Board,
23 Ravelston Terrace, Edinburgh EH4 3EU
or call: 0131-332 2433

LARGS **Ayrshire** Mr S Henderson Glendarroch, 24 Irvine Road Largs Ayrshire KA30 8HW Tel: (Largs) 01475 676305	**Map 1** F5	COMMENDED 👑	2 Family	2 En Suite fac	B&B per person £18.00-£22.00 Single £15.00-£19.50 Double Room only per person £16.50-£18.50	Open Jan-Dec

Red sandstone house with off-road parking within 5 minutes' walking distance of all amenities. Friendly welcome assured.

Lilac Holm Guest House 14 Noddleburn Road Off Barr Crescent Largs Ayrshire KA30 8PY Tel: (Largs) 01475 672020	COMMENDED 👑	2 Single 2 Twin 3 Double 1 Family	2 Pub Bath/Show	B&B per person from £16.00 Single from £16.00 Double	Open Jan-Dec

Built in 1935, in quiet residential area overlooking the Noddle Burn. Personal attention of owners.

Elizabeth Mackey St Leonards, 9 Irvine Road Largs Ayrshire KA30 8JP Tel: (Largs) 01475 673318	COMMENDED 👑	1 Twin 1 Double 1 Family	1 En Suite fac 1 Pub Bath/Show	B&B per person £16.00-£21.00 Single £15.00-£21.00 Double	Open Jan-Dec

Elegant villa with off-street parking, short walk away from town centre, restaurants and the beach front.

Mrs M L Russell Rutland Guest House 22 Charles Street Largs Ayrshire KA30 8HJ Tel: (Largs) 01475 675642	COMMENDED 👑 👑	1 Single 1 Twin 1 Family	3 Priv. NOT ensuite 2 Pub Bath/Show	B&B per person £14.00-£16.00 Single £14.00-£15.00 Double Room only per person £11.00-£12.00	Open Jan-Dec

1930s terraced house in quiet residential area near the promenade. An easy 5 minutes' walk to the town centre.

Tigh-na-Ligh Guest House 104 Brisbane Road Largs Ayrshire KA30 8NN Tel: (Largs) 01475 673975	COMMENDED 👑 👑 👑	2 Twin 2 Double 1 Family	4 En Suite fac 1 Priv. NOT ensuite	B&B per person from £22.00 Double	Open Jan-Dec Dinner from 1800

Red sandstone house in quiet residential area, close to local amenities and convenient for touring Firth of Clyde area and Burns Country.

Mrs M Watson South Whittlieburn Farm Brisbane Glen Largs Ayrshire KA30 8SN Tel: (Largs) 01475 675881	HIGHLY COMMENDED 👑 👑	1 Twin 1 Double 1 Family	2 En Suite fac 2 Pub Bath/Show	B&B per person from £16.50 Single from £16.50 Double	Open Jan-Dec

Working 150-acre (61ha) sheep farm, warm friendly atmosphere, comfortable rooms. Beautiful quiet location only 5 minutes by car from the centre of Largs.

Details of Grading and Classification are on page vi. | Key to symbols is on back flap. |

LARGS continued Ayrshire	Map 1 F5

WHIN PARK

16 Douglas Street, Largs, Ayrshire KA30 8PS
Telephone: 01475 673437
Personally managed by Mrs Henderson and situated close to the
seafront in an attractive area of Largs. It is convenient for access to
the islands of the Clyde and to Argyll, and within easy reach of many
other scenic areas of West Scotland and Glasgow International Airport.
AA selected QQQQ.

Whin-Park Guest House 16 Douglas Street Largs Ayrshire KA30 8PS Tel: (Largs) 01475 673437	HIGHLY COMMENDED 👑👑	1 Single 1 Twin 1 Double 1 Family	4 En Suite fac 1 Pub Bath/Show	B&B per person • from £23.00 Single from £23.00 Double	Open Jan-Dec

Warm, comfortable and relaxing atmosphere, near seafront and swimming pool.

LAUDER Berwickshire Mr P Gilardi The Grange, 6 Edinburgh Road Lauder Berwickshire TD2 6TW Tel: (Lauder) 01578 722649	Map 2 D6 COMMENDED 👑	2 Twin 1 Double	1 Pub Bath/Show	B&B per person £14.00-£18.00 Single £14.00-£16.00 Double	Open Jan-Dec

Detached house standing in large garden with lovely views of surrounding countryside.
A non-smoking house. Ideal location for all of Borders and Edinburgh.

Redpath House Bed & Breakfast

25 East High Street, Lauder, Berwickshire TD2 6SS
Telephone: 01578 718795

We provide quality accommodation in a lovely burgh town in the heart
of the Scottish Borders. Redpath House is ideally situated for walking,
cycling, fishing, golf and has many historical castles and gardens on its
doorstep. Lauder is on the A68 and Edinburgh is just 40 minutes away.

Miss Henderson Redpath House 25 East High Street Lauder Berwickshire TD2 6SS Tel: (Lauder) 01578 718795	COMMENDED Listed	1 Twin 1 Double 1 Family	2 Pub Bath/Show	B&B per person £15.00-£25.00 Single £15.00-£20.00 Double Room only per person from £15.00	Open Jan-Dec

Bright and sunny family home on A68 within easy reach of Edinburgh and
the Border towns. On Southern Upland Way. Private parking.

LOCKERBIE Dumfriesshire Mrs C Hislop Carik Cottage Waterbeck, Lockerbie Dumfriesshire DG11 3EU Tel: (Waterbeck) 01461 600652	Map 2 C9 HIGHLY COMMENDED Listed	1 Twin 2 Double	1 En Suite fac 1 Pub Bath/Show	B&B per person £16.00-£24.00 Single £15.00-£19.00 Double Room only per person £13.00-£17.00	Open Jan-Nov Dinner 1900-2000 B&B + Eve. Meal £21.00-£26.00

Tastefully converted cottage in peaceful rural setting yet only 3 miles (5kms)
from the A74. Ideal for touring the Border countryside.

NETHER BORELAND FARM
BORELAND, LOCKERBIE, DUMFRIESSHIRE DG11 2LL
Telephone/Fax: 01576 610248

Welcome to quality accommodation in our spacious, comfortable farmhouse 7 miles from M74. In peaceful, friendly surroundings, choose your breakfast from a varied menu to include free-range eggs and home-made preserves. Large bedrooms with ensuite or private bathroom. TV, tea trays, hairdryers and clock/radios.
Brochure available.

Mrs M Rae Nether Boreland Farm Boreland, Lockerbie Dumfriesshire DG11 2LL Tel: (Boreland) 01576 610248 Fax: 01576 610248 ·	HIGHLY COMMENDED	1 Twin 2 Double	2 En Suite fac 1 Priv. NOT ensuite	B&B per person £19.00-£21.00 Double	Open Mar-Nov	
		Stone-built farmhouse situated beside B723, in centre of small village. Excellent views of surrounding hill country.				
Rosehill Guest House Mr & Mrs R A Callander Carlisle Road Lockerbie Dumfriesshire DG11 2DR Tel: (Lockerbie) 01576 202378	COMMENDED	1 Single 1 Twin 1 Double 2 Family	2 En Suite fac 3 Pub Bath/Show	B&B per person £18.00-£20.00 Single £18.00-£20.00 Double	Open Jan-Dec	
		Family guest house in residential area, 5 minutes' walk from town centre. Ample car parking.				
by LOCKERBIE **Dumfriesshire** Mrs M M Fletcher Glengower Eaglesfield, by Lockerbie Dumfriesshire DG11 3LT Tel: (Kirtlebridge) 01461 500253	Map 2 C9 COMMENDED	1 Single 1 Twin 1 Double 1 Family	1 En Suite fac 1 Priv. NOT ensuite 2 Pub Bath/Show	B&B per person £14.00-£15.00 Single £14.00-£15.00 Double	Open Mar-Oct	
		Spacious, modern villa in rural location, yet convenient for A74. Ground-floor accommodation available. Families welcome.				
LONGFORMACUS **Berwickshire** Mrs M Amos Eildon Cottage Longformacus Berwickshire TD11 3PB Tel: (Longformacus) 01361 890230	Map 2 F5 COMMENDED	2 Family	2 En Suite fac	B&B per person £16.00-£18.00 Single £16.00-£18.00 Double	Open Jan-Dec Dinner 1800-2000 B&B + Eve. Meal £26.00-£28.00	
		Charming cottage in lovely gardens in quiet Borders village, yet within easy reach of East Lothian golf courses. On Southern Upland Way.				
MAUCHLINE **Ayrshire** Mrs L Smith Dykefield Farm Mauchline Ayrshire KA5 6EY Tel: (Mauchline) 01290 553170	Map 1 H7 APPROVED Listed	2 Family	1 Pub Bath/Show	B&B per person £10.00 Single £10.00 Double Room only per person £8.00	Open Jan-Dec	
		Working farm, 2 miles (3kms) from Mauchline in the centre of Burns Country. Home baking.				

SOUTH OF SCOTLAND

MAYBOLE
Ayrshire

Map 1
G8

HOMELEA

62 Culzean Road, Maybole, Ayrshire KA19 8AH
Tel: 01655 882736   Fax: 01655 883557

Attractive Victorian family home. Large walled garden,
tea/coffee, home baking on arrival. Burns Country,
Galloway Forest, Turnberry, nearby.
Culzean Castle four miles.

No smoking.

Mrs J McKellar Homelea, 62 Culzean Road Maybole Ayrshire KA19 8AH Tel: (Maybole) 01655 882736 Fax: 01655 883557	**COMMENDED** Listed	1 Double 1 Family	2 Pub Bath/Show	B&B per person from £16.00 Single from £15.00 Double Room only per person from £12.00	Open Mar-Oct

Victorian family villa on B7023, 4 miles (6kms) north of Culzean Castle.
Ideal centre for touring Burns Country.

MELROSE Roxburghshire Mrs M Aitken The Gables, Darnick Melrose Roxburghshire TD6 9AL Tel: (Melrose) 01896 822479	Map 2 D6 **COMMENDED**	1 Single 1 Twin 1 Double	1 Pub Bath/Show	B&B per person £16.00 Single to £16.00 Double	Open Jan-Dec Dinner 1800-1930 B&B + Eve. Meal from £24.00

Georgian villa in centre of quiet village, 1 mile (2kms) from Melrose.
Ideal base for touring the Borders. Good home cooking.

Mrs J Bennet Collingwood, Waverley Road Melrose Roxburghshire TD6 9AA Tel: (Melrose) 01896 822670	**COMMENDED**	1 Twin 1 Double	2 En Suite fac	B&B per person £21.00 Double	Open Jan-Dec

Detached Victorian house on outskirts of Melrose with enclosed garden and
good parking. A friendly home within walking distance of River Tweed.

Dunfermline House Guest House Buccleuch Street Melrose Roxburghshire TD6 9LB Tel: (Melrose) 01896 822148 Fax: 01896 822148	**HIGHLY COMMENDED**	1 Single 2 Twin 2 Double	4 En Suite fac 1 Priv. NOT ensuite	B&B per person £21.00-£22.00 Single £21.00-£22.00 Double	Open Jan-Dec

Comfortable family home overlooking Melrose Abbey. Ideal base for touring
Scott country and Edinburgh. No smoking.

Mrs Christine Edmond Schoolhouse, Huntly Road Melrose Roxburghshire TD6 9SB Tel: (Melrose) 01896 823621	**COMMENDED** Listed	2 Twin 1 Double	1 Pub Bath/Show	B&B per person £15.00 Double	Open Apr-Oct

Red sandstone detached house with open outlook over the park to town and Eildon Hills.
A few minutes' walk from town and riverside.

Mrs M Graham Braidwood, Buccleuch Street Melrose Roxburghshire TD6 9LD Tel: (Melrose) 01896 822488	**HIGHLY COMMENDED**	1 Single 1 Twin 1 Double	1 En Suite fac 1 Pub Bath/Show	B&B per person £17.00 Single £17.00-£20.00 Double	Open Jan-Dec

Friendly welcome in attractive Listed townhouse only a stones throw
from Melrose Abbey and Priorwood Gardens. Home baking.

Mrs E Haldane Priory View, 15 Priors Walk Melrose Roxburghshire TD6 9RB Tel: (Melrose) 01896 822087		HIGHLY COMMENDED	1 Twin 2 Double	1 Pub Bath/Show	B&B per person £16.00 Double	Open Jan-Dec Dinner 1800-2000

Situated in quiet residential area with views to Abbey,
and a short distance from the centre of Melrose.

Mrs L A Paterson Fiorlin, Abbey Street Melrose Roxburghshire TD6 9PX Tel: (Melrose) 01896 822984		COMMENDED	1 Double 1 Family	2 En Suite fac	B&B per person £20.00-£21.00 Double	Open Jan-Dec

Detached house of character set in quiet residential area with private parking.
Convenient for town centre and restaurants, ideal touring base.

Mrs P Schofield Torwood Lodge High Cross Avenue Melrose Roxburghshire TD6 9SU Tel: (Melrose) 01896 822220		COMMENDED	1 Twin 2 Double	3 En Suite fac	B&B per person £21.00-£22.00 Double	Open Jan-Dec

Large comfortable Victorian family house in attractive location. Easy walking
distance to town, River Tweed and Eildon Hills. All ensuite facilities.

MOFFAT **Dumfriesshire** Mr & Mrs D A Armstrong Boleskine, 4 Well Road Moffat Dumfriesshire DG10 9AS Tel: (Moffat) 01683 220601	Map 2 B8	HIGHLY COMMENDED	1 Single 1 Twin 2 Double	2 En Suite fac 1 Pub Bath/Show	B&B per person £15.00 Single £15.00-£17.50 Double	Open Jan-Dec

A large Victorian house, built in 1886. Close to the town centre
it offers comfortable spacious accommodation.

Burnock Water
Haywood Road, Moffat DG10 9BU
Telephone: 01683 221329

Comfortable Victorian house in peaceful scenic location, yet only ½ mile
from town centre. Ensuite facilities. Ground-floor bedroom.
All bedrooms have central heating, colour TV, tea/coffee tray.
Secluded garden and ample parking. Fire certificate.
Less mobile grading. Warm welcome. *Brochure available.*

David Barclay Burnock Water, Haywood Road Moffat Dumfriesshire DG10 9BU Tel: (Moffat) 01683 221329		COMMENDED	1 Twin 2 Double 2 Family	3 En Suite fac 1 Pub Bath/Show	B&B per person £17.00-£19.00 Single £15.00-£17.00 Double	Open Jan-Dec

Personally run c.1845 large house, in own grounds and secluded garden.
Approx. ½ mile (1 km) to High Street. Private parking.

Barnhill Springs Country Guest House Moffat Dumfriesshire DG10 9QS Tel: (Moffat) 01683 220580		COMMENDED	2 Twin 2 Double 1 Family	1 Priv. NOT ensuite 2 Pub Bath/Show	B&B per person £19.00-£20.00 Single £19.00-£20.00 Double	Open Jan-Dec Dinner from 1830 B&B + Eve. Meal £31.50-£32.50

Early Victorian country house, ideally situated for walking the Southern Upland Way.
Access from A74 via south-bound slip road at Moffat junction.

Mrs Eileen Baty Thai-Ville, 3 Dundanion Place Moffat Dumfriesshire DG10 9GD Tel: (Moffat) 01683 220922		DELUXE	2 Twin	2 En Suite fac	B&B per person £17.00 Double	Open Mar-Nov

Modern bungalow with individual style, in quiet residential area, close to town centre.
Warm and friendly welcome, ensuite rooms. Ground-floor accommodation.

MOFFAT

	Map 2 B8						
MOFFAT continued **Dumfriesshire** Gilbert House Beechgrove Moffat Dumfriesshire DG10 9RS Tel: (Moffat) 01683 220050		HIGHLY COMMENDED	1 Single 1 Twin 2 Double 2 Family	5 En Suite fac 1 Limited ensuite	B&B per person £17.00-£20.00 Single £17.00-£20.00 Double	Open Jan-Dec Dinner from 1830 B&B + Eve. Meal £27.00-£30.00	

Spacious family run guest house in residential area, 5 minutes' walk from the centre of Moffat. Emphasis on good food. Ideal base for touring.

Mrs Gourlay Fernhill, Grange Road Moffat Dumfriesshire DG10 9HT Tel: (Moffat) 01683 220077	DELUXE	1 Twin 1 Double	2 En Suite fac	B&B per person from £16.50 Double	Open Apr-Sep	

A warm welcome assured with lots of care, attention and personal touches in this quietly situated house. Delightful garden. A few minutes' walk from town centre.

Hartfell House Hartfell Crescent Moffat Dumfriesshire DG10 9AL Tel: (Moffat) 01683 220153	HIGHLY COMMENDED	2 Single 2 Twin 3 Double 2 Family	5 En Suite fac 1 Priv. NOT ensuite 2 Pub Bath/Show	B&B per person £18.00-£25.00 Single £15.00-£21.50 Double	Open Mar-Nov Dinner at 1900 B&B + Eve. Meal £26.00-£36.00	

Family run, in rural setting, within walking distance of the town centre. Large, well-maintained garden and fine views.

Mrs Jackson Woodhead Farm Moffat Dumfriesshire DG10 9LU Tel: (Moffat) 01683 220225	HIGHLY COMMENDED	2 Twin 1 Double	3 En Suite fac	B&B per person to £25.00 Single to £24.00 Double	Open Jan-Dec Dinner 1900-2000 B&B + Eve. Meal to £36.50	

Luxuriously furnished farmhouse situated on 220-acre (89ha) working stock farm with commanding panoramic views of the surrounding countryside. All ensuite.

Craigie Lodge

Ballplay Road, Moffat DG10 9JU

Telephone: 01683 221037

A true Scottish welcome awaits you in this beautiful Victorian Home offering quality food and accommodation. Situated on outskirts of Moffat yet only 10 minutes' walk from centre. Off-road parking and large garden for guests' enjoyment. Ground-floor ensuite room available, also separate self-catering cottage.

Mrs Jappy Craigie Lodge, Ballplay Road Moffat Dumfriesshire DG10 9JU Tel: (Moffat) 01683 221037	HIGHLY COMMENDED	1 Twin 1 Double 1 Family	3 En Suite fac	B&B per person to £25.00 Single £16.00-£18.00 Double	Open Jan-Dec, ex Xmas/New Year Dinner from 1830 B&B + Eve. Meal £26.00-£35.00	

Large Victorian family house set in mature ½ acre (0.2ha) garden. All rooms private facilities. Ground-floor accommodation available. Reduced rates 3 days.

Evelyn Lindsay Alba House, 20 Beechgrove Moffat Dumfriesshire DG10 9RS Tel: (Moffat) 01683 220418	DELUXE	1 Twin 1 Double 1 Family	3 En Suite fac	B&B per person from £20.00 Double	Open Apr-Oct	

A delightful old house c.1730 with beamed dining room, inglenook and colourful garden. Warm and friendly welcome. Quietly set within walking distance of town.

Joan & John Marchington Seamore House Academy Road, Moffat Dumfriesshire DG10 9HW Tel: (Moffat) 01683 220404 Fax: 01683 220404	COMMENDED	1 Single 1 Twin 2 Double 2 Family	2 En Suite fac 2 Pub Bath/Show	B&B per person £13.00-£20.00 Single £15.00-£17.50 Double	Open Jan-Dec Dinner 1830-1930 B&B + Eve. Meal £20.00-£24.50

Comfortable family run guest house in centre of Moffat. Children and pets welcome.
Good centre for touring.

Mrs K Miller Broomlands Farm Beattock, Moffat Dumfriesshire DG10 9PQ Tel: (Beattock) 01683 300320 Fax: 01683 300320	HIGHLY COMMENDED	1 Single 1 Twin 1 Double	3 En Suite fac	B&B per person £20.00 Single £18.00-£19.00 Double	Open Apr-Oct

Farmhouse on a working 200-acre (81ha) mixed farm. Convenient to A74
and 2 miles (3kms) from Moffat. Self-catering cottage available.

Rockhill Guest House 14 Beech Grove Moffat Dumfriesshire DG10 9RS Tel: (Moffat) 01683 220283	COMMENDED	2 Single 1 Twin 3 Double 4 Family	5 En Suite fac 2 Pub Bath/Show	B&B per person £16.00-£20.00 Single £16.00-£20.00 Double	Open Jan-Nov Dinner from 1830 B&B + Eve. Meal £24.00-£28.00

Victorian house overlooking bowling green and park, in quiet area close
to town centre. Open outlook to hills. Own private carpark, ensuite rooms.

Merkland House

Buccleuch Place, Moffat, Dumfriesshire DG10 9AN
Telephone: 01683 220957

An elegant Victorian house situated in 2½ acres of quiet woodland
gardens, close to Moffat town centre, offering ensuite accommodation.
A comfortable residents' lounge with open fire, ample parking and a
varied breakfast menu also catering for vegetarians.
Relaxing aromatherapy sessions can also be arranged to enhance your stay.

Mr A Tavener Merkland House Buccleuch Place Moffat Dumfriesshire DG10 9AN Tel: (Moffat) 01683 220957	COMMENDED	1 Single 2 Double 2 Family	4 En Suite fac 1 Priv. NOT ensuite 1 Pub Bath/Show	B&B per person £15.00-£18.00 Single £15.00-£18.00 Double	Open Jan-Dec

19th century detached villa in 2½ acres (1ha) of gardens situated in quiet
residential area, yet only 5 minutes' walk from town centre.

Mrs G T Walker Springbank, Beechgrove Moffat Dumfriesshire DG10 9RS Tel: (Moffat) 01683 220070	HIGHLY COMMENDED	1 Twin 1 Double	1 Priv. NOT ensuite 2 Pub Bath/Show	B&B per person from £15.00 Double	Open Apr-Oct

Early 19th century detached house in quiet residential area. Home baking
a speciality. Private parking and colourful garden.

Mrs Ruth Watson Hazel Bank, Academy Road Moffat Dumfriesshire DG10 9HP Tel: (Moffat) 01683 220294	COMMENDED	1 Single 1 Twin 1 Double	1 En Suite fac 2 Pub Bath/Show	B&B per person £20.00-£25.00 Single £15.00-£17.50 Double	Open Jan-Dec

Family home, centrally situated 2 minutes from town centre.
Good base for touring. Ground-floor ensuite available.

Details of Grading and Classification are on page vi. | Key to symbols is on back flap. | 35

SOUTH OF SCOTLAND

NEWCASTLETON Roxburghshire Mrs Linda Stenhouse Borders Honey Farm Newcastleton Roxburghshire TD9 0SG Tel: (Liddlesdale) 013873 76737 Fax: 013873 76737	Map 2 D9	COMMENDED	1 Single 1 Twin 1 Double	1 En Suite fac 1 Priv. NOT ensuite	B&B per person to £20.00 Single to £20.00 Double	Open Jan-Dec Dinner 1930-2030 B&B + Eve. Meal £28.00-£35.00	

Peaceful house of real character nestling at the foot of the forest and Larriston Fells.
Lovely walking country.

by NEW GALLOWAY Kirkcudbrightshire	Map 1 H9						

HIGH PARK FARM

Balmaclellan, New Galloway, Castle Douglas DG7 3PT
Telephone: 01644 420298

HIGH PARK is a comfortable stone-built farmhouse built in 1838. The 171-acre dairy, sheep and stock rearing farm is situated by Loch Ken on the A713 amidst Galloway's beautiful scenery within easy reach of hills and coast. Good food guaranteed. All bedrooms have washbasins, shaver points, tea/coffee facilities. Pets welcome.
Commended �   **Brochure: Mrs Jessie E. Shaw at above address**

Mrs J Shaw High Park Balmaclellan Kirkcudbrightshire DG7 3PT Tel: (New Galloway) 01644 420298		COMMENDED	1 Twin 2 Double	1 Pub Bath/Show	B&B per person £14.00-£15.00 Single £14.00-£15.00 Double	Open Apr-Oct Dinner from 1900 B&B + Eve. Meal £22.00-£23.00	

Early 19th century farmhouse on working dairy and sheep farm, situated by
Loch Ken off A713, amidst beautiful Galloway scenery.

KALMAR

Balmaclellan, Nr New Galloway, Castle Douglas DG7 3QE
Telephone: 01644 420685   Fax: 01644 420244

New, purpose-built, centrally heated, all rooms ensuite.
Set amidst beautiful Galloway countryside with mountain views – central for all activities of the area.
After dinner, enjoy the ambience of our large residents' lounge with leather furniture and log-burning stove.
One suite on the ground floor.   *Off-road parking.*

Wallace & Doreen Wood 'Kalmar' Balmaclellan Kirkcudbrightshire DG7 3QE Tel: (Balmaclellan) 01644 420685 Fax: 01644 420244		HIGHLY COMMENDED	1 Twin 1 Family	2 En Suite fac	B&B per person from £23.50 Single from £18.50 Double	Open Jan-Dec Dinner 1830-2000 B&B + Eve. Meal £26.50-£31.50	

Recently built, village home, set amidst beautiful Galloway countryside.
Full office facilities available. Home cooking. Ground-floor accommodation.

WELCOME

Whenever you are in Scotland, you can be sure of a warm welcome at your nearest Tourist Information Centre.
For guide books, maps, souvenirs, our Centres provide a service second to none – many now offer bureau-de-change facilities. And, of course, Tourist Information Centres offer free, expert advice on what to see and do, route-planning and accommodation for everyone – visitors and residents alike!

VAT is shown at 17.5%: changes in this rate may affect prices. Prices shown are for guidance only. Please send SAE with each enquiry.

NEWTON STEWART **Wigtownshire** Mrs P Adams Clugston Farm Newton Stewart Wigtownshire DG8 9BH Tel: (Kirkcowan) 01671 830338	Map 1 G10	COMMENDED	1 Twin 2 Double	2 Pub Bath/Show	B&B per person £15.00-£16.00 Single £14.00-£16.00 Double Room only per person from £10.00	Open Apr-Oct Dinner from 1800 B&B + Eve. Meal £20.00-£22.00	

About 5 miles (8kms) off the A75. Near the sea, hillwalking and easy access to 3 golf courses. Two ground-floor rooms.

Flower Bank Guest House Minnigaff Newton Stewart Wigtownshire DG8 6PJ Tel: (Newton Stewart) 01671 402629		COMMENDED	1 Twin 4 Double 1 Family	3 En Suite fac 1 Priv. NOT ensuite 2 Pub Bath/Show	B&B per person from £20.00 Single £16.00-£19.50 Double	Open Jan-Dec Dinner from 1830 B&B + Eve. Meal £24.00-£27.50	

Detached 18th century house set in 1 acre (0.4ha) of grounds on banks of River Cree. Quiet peaceful location 0.5 miles (1km) from town centre.

Mrs M Hewitson Auchenleck Farm Newton Stewart Wigtownshire DG8 7AA Tel: (Newton Stewart) 01671 402035		COMMENDED	1 Twin 2 Double	1 En Suite fac 2 Priv. NOT ensuite	B&B per person from £18.50 Double	Open Easter-Oct	

Turretted former shooting lodge on working sheep-farm. Set within Glen Trool National Park. Ideally situated for fishing, cycling, walking and touring.

Mrs E Imrie Rowallan House, Corbsie Road Newton Stewart DG8 6JB Tel: (Newton Stewart) 01671 402520		COMMENDED	1 Single 2 Twin 2 Double	5 En Suite fac	B&B per person to £22.00 Single to £22.00 Double Room only per person to £16.00	Open Jan-Dec	

Personally run Victorian country house with large garden in quiet residential area. Ideal stopover for Irish ferries and Sea Cat.

Mr S A Rankin Cree Villa, Creebridge Newton Stewart Wigtownshire DG8 6NR Tel: (Newton Stewart) 01671 403914		COMMENDED	1 Twin 2 Double	2 En Suite fac 1 Priv. NOT ensuite 3 Pub Bath/Show	B&B per person £17.00 Single £16.00-£18.00 Double Room only per person £15.00-£17.00	Open Jan-Dec	

Cheerful home situated on riverside with garden and private parking. Ideally located for fishing, cycling and touring.

NEWTOWN ST BOSWELLS **Roxburghshire** Mrs Margaret Clyde West Mount, Langlands Place Newtown St Boswells Roxburghshire TD6 0RY Tel: (Newtown St Boswells) 01835 822077	Map 2 D7	APPROVED Listed	1 Single 1 Double	1 Pub Bath/Show	B&B per person £12.50 Single £12.50 Double	Open Jan-Dec exc Xmas Dinner 1700-2000	

Victorian townhouse, just off A68. Centrally situated for touring the Borders Abbeys and all attractions.

PEEBLES Mrs D Davidson Hillside, 44 Edinburgh Road Peebles EH45 8EB Tel: (Peebles) 01721 729817	Map 2 C6	COMMENDED Listed	1 Double 1 Family	1 En Suite fac 1 Pub Bath/Show	B&B per person £15.00-£17.00 Double	Open Jan-Dec exc Xmas/New Year	

Detached house with delightful gardens situated on the outskirts of the town – ideal as a touring base.

PEEBLES

PEEBLES continued	Map 2 C6							
Mrs Fawcett Woodlands, Venlaw Farm Road Peebles Tel: (Peebles) 01721 729882		HIGHLY COMMENDED 👑👑	1 Twin 2 Double	2 En Suite fac 1 Priv. NOT ensuite 1 Pub Bath/Show	B&B per person £16.00-£20.00 Single from £16.00 Double	Open Apr-Nov		
Modern detached house in peaceful walled garden setting. Ample parking. Totally secluded, yet only 1 mile (2kms) from town centre.								
Mrs Haydock Winkston Farmhouse Peebles EH45 8PH Tel: (Peebles) 01721 721264		HIGHLY COMMENDED 👑👑	1 Twin 2 Double	1 En Suite fac 2 Pub Bath/Show	B&B per person £15.50-£18.00 Double	Open Apr-Oct		
'B' Listed Georgian farmhouse of historical interest, in own grounds. Friendly family atmosphere. On main bus route, 21 miles (34kms) from Edinburgh.								
Evelyn Inglis Robingarth, 46 Edinburgh Road Peebles EH45 8EB Tel: (Peebles) 01721 720226		COMMENDED Listed	1 Twin 1 Double	1 En Suite fac 1 Priv. NOT ensuite	B&B per person £17.00 Double	Open Jan-Dec		
Personally run, stone-built bungalow offering comfortable accommodation. 0.5 miles (1 km) to town facilities. Ideal touring base.								
Mr & Mrs C Lane Lindores, Old Town Peebles EH45 8JE Tel: (Peebles) 01721 720441		COMMENDED 👑👑👑	1 Twin 1 Double 2 Family	2 En Suite fac 1 Pub Bath/Show	B&B per person £18.00-£28.00 Single £15.00-£18.00 Double	Open Jan-Dec Dinner 1830-2000 B&B + Eve. Meal £22.00-£25.00		
Stone-built late Victorian townhouse near edge of town, situated on main A72 tourist route. Convenient for touring the Borders and Edinburgh. Private parking.								
Mrs Jacqueline Lockett 3 Dukehaugh Peebles EH45 9DN Tel: (Peebles) 01721 720017		COMMENDED Listed	1 Double 1 Family	1 En Suite fac 1 Priv. NOT ensuite 1 Pub Bath/Show	B&B per person £16.00-£17.50 Double	Open Jan-Dec		
Modern family home quietly set in residential area, easy walking distance of town centre. Off-street parking.								
Mrs E McTeir Colliedean 4 Elibank Road, Eddleston Peebles EH45 8QL Tel: (Eddleston) 01721 730281		COMMENDED Listed	1 Twin 1 Double	1 Pub Bath/Show	B&B per person £17.50 Single £15.00 Double	Open Apr-Oct		
Quietly situated in small village on main bus route to Edinburgh and Borders towns. Homely and friendly atmosphere. Good restaurant within walking distance.								
Mrs Muir Whitestone House Innerleithen Road Peebles EH45 8BD Tel: (Peebles) 01721 720337		COMMENDED 👑	1 Twin 1 Double 1 Family	2 Pub Bath/Show	B&B per person £16.00-£18.00 Single £15.50-£16.00 Double	Open Jan-Dec		
Personally run Victorian house with fine views to surrounding hills. Ideal touring base for fishing and walking. Parking.								
Mrs Jean Kenyon Phillips Drummore, Venlaw High Road Peebles EH45 8RL Tel: (Peebles) 01721 720336 Fax: 01721 723004		COMMENDED 👑	1 Twin 1 Double	1 Pub Bath/Show	B&B per person from £16.00 Double	Open Apr-Sep		
Hillside house in quiet cul-de-sac off the A703. Ideally situated for visiting Edinburgh and the Borders.								

by PEEBLES	Map 2 C6	COMMENDED	1 Twin 2 Double	3 En Suite fac 1 Pub Bath/Show	B&B per person £18.00 Double	Open May-Sep
Mrs R Smith Chapel Hill Farm Peebles EH45 8PQ Tel: (Peebles) 01721 720188						

Farmhouse c.1695 on working farm offering warm welcome and ample parking. Peaceful rural setting yet only 1 mile (2kms) from Peebles. All rooms ensuite.

		COMMENDED Listed	1 Twin 2 Double	2 Priv. NOT ensuite 2 Pub Bath/Show	B&B per person £16.00-£18.00 Single £15.00-£17.00 Double Room only per person £15.00-£17.00	Open Mar-Nov
Mrs A Waddell Lyne Farmhouse, Lyne Farm Peebles EH45 8NR Tel: (Kirkton Manor) 01721 740255						

Victorian farmhouse on mixed farm with magnificent views over Stobo Valley. 4 miles (6kms) west of Peebles on A72. 23 miles (32kms) from Edinburgh.

PORTPATRICK Wigtownshire	Map 1 F10	COMMENDED	2 Twin 4 Double 1 Family	6 En Suite fac 1 Pub Bath/Show	B&B per person £16.00-£28.00 Single £16.00-£20.00 Double	Open Jan-Dec Dinner 1800-1900 B&B + Eve. Meal £25.00-£36.50
Carlton Guest House South Crescent Portpatrick Wigtownshire DG9 8JR Tel: (Portpatrick) 01776 810253						

Comfortable, family run guest house on the seafront, with superb views over the Irish Sea. Fresh local produce.

PRESTWICK Ayrshire	Map 1 G7	COMMENDED	1 Single 1 Twin 1 Double	1 En Suite fac 1 Pub Bath/Show	B&B per person £14.00-£15.00 Single £14.00-£18.00 Double	Open Jan-Dec
Mrs Reeve 28 Monkton Road Prestwick Ayrshire KA9 1AR Tel: (Prestwick) 01292 478816						

Semi-detached, Victorian villa in residential area, with easy access to airport, railway station and local amenities.

ST ABBS Berwickshire	Map 2 F5	HIGHLY COMMENDED	1 Single 1 Twin 1 Double 1 Family	4 En Suite fac 1 Pub Bath/Show	B&B per person from £23.00 Single from £23.00 Double	Open Easter-Oct Dinner 1900-1930 B&B + Eve.Meal from £38.00
Castle Rock Guest House Murrayfield St Abbs Berwickshire TD14 5PP Tel: (Coldingham) 01890 771715 Fax: 01890 771520						

Good food and comfort plus sea views from all rooms are features of this attractive clifftop house. Close to nature reserve and 3 miles (5kms) from A1.

		HIGHLY COMMENDED Listed	1 Twin 1 Family	1 En Suite fac 1 Pub Bath/Show	B&B per person £14.50-£17.00 Single £14.50-£17.00 Double	Open Jan-Dec
Wilma Wilson 7 Murrayfield St Abbs Berwickshire TD14 5PP Tel: (Coldingham) 01890 771468						

Former fisherman's cottage, in quiet village, close to beach, harbour and nature reserve. One room ensuite.

SOUTH OF SCOTLAND

| by ST ABBS
Berwickshire
Westwood House Guesthouse
The Old Coaching Inn
Houndwood (Nr Grantshouse)
Eyemouth
Berwickshire
TD14 5TP
Tel: (Grantshouse)
01361 850232
Fax: 01361 850333 | Map 2
F5 | COMMENDED
👑👑👑
♿ | 1 Single
2 Twin
1 Double
2 Family | 6 En Suite fac | B&B per person
from £20.00 Single
from £20.00 Double | Open Jan-Dec
Dinner 1830-2030 | |

Old coaching inn set back from A1. Local Eyemouth seafood a speciality.
Flower arranging, computing and art courses available.

| ST BOSWELLS
Roxburghshire
Mrs A M Tyrer
Whitehouse
St Boswells
Roxburghshire
TD6 0ED
Tel: (St Boswells)
01573 460343
Fax: 01573 460361 | Map 2
D7 | HIGHLY
COMMENDED
👑👑 | 2 Twin
1 Double | 1 En Suite fac
1 Priv. NOT ensuite
1 Pub Bath/Show | B&B per person
£23.00-£25.00 Single
£18.00-£20.00 Double | Open Jan-Dec
Dinner 1830-2000
B&B + Eve. Meal
from £32.00 | |

Large comfortable farmhouse, with warm and friendly atmosphere,
situated amidst rolling Border countryside. 4 miles (6kms) from St Boswells.

| SANDYHILLS, by Dalbeattie
Kirkcudbrightshire
Craigbittern House
Sandyhills, by Dalbeattie
Kirkcudbrightshire
DG5 4NZ
Tel: (Southwick) 01387 780247 | Map 2
B10 | HIGHLY
COMMENDED
👑👑 | 1 Twin
3 Double
1 Family | 2 En Suite fac
3 Pub Bath/Show | B&B per person
£30.00-£40.00 Single
£20.00-£25.00 Double | Open Jan-Dec
Dinner 1830-1900
B&B + Eve. Meal
£29.50-£34.00 | |

Granite-built Victorian house with large garden and superb views
over Solway Firth. Home cooking using fresh local ingredients.

| SELKIRK | Map 2
D7 | | | | | | |

ENDLER

Victoria Crescent, Selkirk, Selkirkshire TD7 5DE
Telephone: 01750 21305

30 miles south of Edinburgh in the Border Country, this comfortable home set in its own ground, gives peace and tranquillity. A homely, welcoming atmosphere and a true Scottish breakfast has made many visitors regular guests. Beautiful scenery, fishing, golfing, riding, many historic homes and abbeys make this region a tourist attraction.

| Marie Bowers
Endler, Victoria Crescent
Selkirk
TD7 5DE
Tel: (Selkirk) 01750 21305 | | COMMENDED
Listed | 1 Twin
1 Double | 1 Pub Bath/Show | B&B per person
from £18.00 Single
from £15.00 Double | Open Apr-Oct | |

Modern bungalow in quiet location, 5 minutes' walk from town centre.
Views across Selkirk from the garden. German spoken.

| Mrs P Dickson
Sunnybrae House
75 Tower Street
Selkirk
TD7 4LS
Tel: (Selkirk) 01750 21156 | | COMMENDED
👑👑👑 | 1 Twin
1 Double | 2 En Suite fac | B&B per person
to £20.00 Single
to £20.00 Double | Open Jan-Dec
Dinner 1800-2000
B&B + Eve. Meal
to £34.00 | |

Two suites (own private bathroom and sitting room). Home cooking using
local produce. Ideal for touring the Borders and Edinburgh. Private parking.

| Mrs D J Hannah
Hillholm, 36 Hillside Terrace
Selkirk
TD7 4ND
Tel: (Selkirk) 01750 21293 | | COMMENDED
👑👑 | 2 Twin
1 Double | 2 En Suite fac
1 Priv. NOT ensuite
1 Pub Bath/Show | B&B per person
from £20.00 Single
from £15.00 Double | Open Mar-Dec
Dinner from 1800 | |

Elegant semi-detached Victorian house on outskirts of Selkirk.
Small interesting garden with rockery and Alpine plants. Ideal base for touring.

			Accommodation			
Mrs Lindores Dinsburn, 1 Shawpark Road Selkirk TD7 4DS Tel: (Selkirk) 01750 20375		COMMENDED	1 Twin 1 Double 1 Family	2 En Suite fac 1 Priv. NOT ensuite 1 Pub Bath/Show	B&B per person from £16.00 Single from £16.00 Double	Open Jan-Dec Dinner from 1800 B&B + Eve. Meal from £24.00
			Semi-detached, sandstone Victorian house in residential area on east side of town centre. Next to bowling green.			
Mrs J F MacKenzie Ivybank, Hillside Terrace Selkirk TD7 2LT Tel: (Selkirk) 01750 21270 Fax: 01750 21270		COMMENDED	1 Twin 1 Double	1 Pub Bath/Show	B&B per person £16.00 Single £15.00 Double Room only per person £10.00	Open Feb-Nov
			Set back from A7 with fine views over the hills beyond. Private off-street parking.			
Mrs S M Todd 34 Hillside Terrace Selkirk TD7 4ND Tel: (Selkirk) 01750 20792		COMMENDED	2 Twin 1 Double	1 Priv. NOT ensuite 2 Pub Bath/Show	B&B per person £15.00 Double	Open Mar-Oct
			Family run house in a small, historic border town. An ideal centre for touring and hillwalking.			
STEVENSTON **Ayrshire** Mrs J Thomson Lochraigs Farm Stevenston Ayrshire KA20 4LB Tel: (Stevenston) 01294 465288	Map 1 G6	COMMENDED Listed	1 Single 1 Twin 1 Double	1 Pub Bath/Show	B&B per person £15.00-£16.00 Single £15.00-£16.00 Double	Open Jan-Dec
			Working beef and cattle farm on outskirts of town. Some views. Central for the north and south Ayrshire coast.			
STRANRAER **Wigtownshire** Mrs Black Glen Otter, Leswalt Road Stranraer Wigtownshire DG9 0EP Tel: (Stranraer) 01776 703199	Map 1 F10	COMMENDED	1 Twin 1 Double 1 Family	2 En Suite fac 1 Priv. NOT ensuite	B&B per person £17.00-£25.00 Single £17.00-£20.00 Double	Open Jan-Dec
			A warm and friendly welcome awaits you at this B&B with private parking in residential area. Within easy access of ferry terminals.			
Mrs M Downes Rankins Close 25/27 Dalrymple Street Stranraer Wigtownshire DG9 7ET Tel: (Stranraer) 01776 702632		COMMENDED Listed	1 Twin 1 Double 1 Family	1 En Suite fac 2 Pub Bath/Show	B&B per person £15.00-£25.00 Single £15.00-£18.00 Double	Open Jan-Dec
			Terraced house, family run, central location. Close to ferry terminals.			
Mrs N Farroll Hawthorn Cottage Stoneykirk Road Stranraer Wigtownshire DG9 7BT Tel: (Stranraer) 01776 702032		COMMENDED	1 Twin 2 Double	2 En Suite fac 1 Pub Bath/Show	B&B per person £15.00-£19.00 Double	Open Jan-Dec
			Two-storey cottage in residential area, personally run. Convenient for town centre and ferries. Private parking. Non-smoking.			
Fernlea Guest House Fernlea, Lewis Street Stranraer Wigtownshire DG9 7AQ Tel: (Stranraer) 01776 703037		COMMENDED	1 Twin 2 Double	2 En Suite fac 1 Pub Bath/Show	B&B per person £16.00-£19.00 Double Room only per person £14.00-£17.00	Open Jan-Dec Dinner 1800-1900 B&B + Eve. Meal £24.50-£27.50
			Personally run, with friendly atmosphere. Close to town centre, Stranraer and Cairnryan ferries. Fully double-glazed and private parking. Non-smoking.			

SOUTH OF SCOTLAND

STRANRAER continued **Wigtownshire** Mrs O M Kelly Windyridge Villa 5 Royal Crescent Stranraer DG9 8HB Tel: (Stranraer) 01776 889900	Map 1 F10	HIGHLY COMMENDED 👑👑	1 Twin 2 Double	3 En Suite fac	B&B per person £20.00-£25.00 Single £18.00-£20.00 Double	Open Jan-Dec

A very warm welcome awaits you at this family home overlooking the Garden of Friendship and Loch Ryan. Few minutes from Irish ferry terminals. Lock-up garage available.

Mrs McDonald Auld Ayre, 4 Park Lane Stranraer Wigtownshire DG9 0DS Tel: (Stranraer) 01776 704500		COMMENDED 👑👑👑	1 Twin 1 Double 1 Family	3 En Suite fac	B&B per person £18.00-£25.00 Single £15.00-£17.00 Double Room only per person £12.50-£15.00	Open Jan-Dec Dinner 1700-1830

Large detached house in quiet residential area close to seafront, ferry and town centre. Own parking.

Mr & Mrs Whitworth Kildrochet House Stranraer Wigtownshire DG9 9BB Tel: (Lochans) 01776 820216		HIGHLY COMMENDED 👑👑👑	2 Twin 1 Double	2 En Suite fac 1 Priv. NOT ensuite	B&B per person £26.00-£27.00 Single £23.00-£24.00 Double	Open Jan-Dec Dinner at 1930 B&B + Eve. Meal £36.00-£40.00

18th century Adam Dower House set in peaceful 6 acres (2.4ha) of gardens, pasture and woodlands with open views over Rhinns of Galloway. Non-smoking. Home cooking.

THORNHILL **Dumfriesshire** Mrs Dorothy Hill Drumcruilton Thornhill Dumfriesshire DG3 5BG Tel: (Thornhill) 01848 500210	Map 2 A8	HIGHLY COMMENDED 👑👑	1 Twin 2 Double	1 En Suite fac 2 Priv. NOT ensuite 1 Pub Bath/Show	B&B per person £20.00-£25.00 Single £19.00-£22.00 Double	Open May-Nov Dinner 1830-1930 B&B + Eve. Meal £32.00-£38.00

Refurbished country farmhouse set on working stock farm with excellent views of Lowther Hills. Fishing, shooting, deer stalking can be arranged.

TROON **Ayrshire** Advie Lodge 2 Bentinck Drive Troon Ayrshire KA10 6HX Tel: (Troon) 01292 313635	Map 1 G7	COMMENDED 👑👑	1 Single 1 Twin 2 Double	2 En Suite fac 2 Priv. NOT ensuite 1 Pub Bath/Show	B&B per person £20.00-£25.00 Single £20.00-£25.00 Double	Open Jan-Dec

A warm welcome awaits you in this 19th century house. Centrally situated for beach, shops, marina and golf courses. Private parking. Ground-floor accommodation.

Mrs L Devine 5 St Meddans Street Troon Ayrshire KA10 6JU Tel: (Troon) 01292 311423 Fax: 01292 311423		COMMENDED 👑👑	2 Twin 1 Double	2 En Suite fac 1 Priv. NOT ensuite	B&B per person from £16.00 Single from £16.00 Double	Open Jan-Dec

Stone-built house, centrally located near to beach and golf courses. All rooms with private facilities.

Mrs Norma McLardy 116 Bentinck Drive Troon Ayrshire KA10 6ZB Tel: (Troon) 01292 314100 Fax: 01292 317231		HIGHLY COMMENDED 👑👑👑	1 Single 3 Twin	3 En Suite fac 1 Priv. NOT ensuite	B&B per person from £27.50 Single from £22.50 Double	Open Jan-Dec

Secluded elegant villa with extensive oak panelling. Golfing trips arranged. Minutes from Royal Troon.

Tigh Dearg 31 Victoria Drive Troon Ayrshire KA10 6JF Tel: (Troon) 01292 311552 Fax: 01292 311552		APPROVED 👑	1 Single 1 Twin 1 Family	2 Pub Bath/Show	B&B per person £15.00-£25.00 Single £15.00-£25.00 Double	Open Jan-Dec
Red sandstone villa handy for beach, golf, train and Prestwick Airport.						

Mrs M Tweedie The Cherries, 50 Ottoline Drive Troon Ayrshire KA10 7AW Tel: (Troon) 01292 313312		COMMENDED 👑 👑	1 Single 1 Twin 1 Family	1 En Suite fac 2 Pub Bath/Show	B&B per person from £17.00 Single from £17.00 Double Room only per person from £14.00	Open Jan-Dec
Warm welcome in family home. Quiet residential area backing onto golf course.						

TWYNHOLM **Kirkcudbrightshire** Mrs M McMorran Miefield Farm Twynholm Kirkcudbrightshire DG6 4PS Tel: (Twynholm) 01557 860254	Map 2 A10	COMMENDED Listed	2 Family	1 Pub Bath/Show	B&B per person £13.50-£14.00 Single £13.50-£14.00 Double	Open Apr-Oct Dinner from 1730 B&B + Eve. Meal £18.50-£19.00
Working sheep and beef farm at the head of a quiet glen. See sheep dogs and shepherds at work.						

Mrs L Robson Glencroft Twynholm Kirkcudbrightshire DG6 4NT Tel: (Twynholm) 01557 860252		COMMENDED 👑	1 Single 1 Double 1 Family	2 Pub Bath/Show	B&B per person £14.00-£15.00 Single £14.00-£15.00 Double	Open Apr-Oct Dinner from 1730 B&B + Eve. Meal £19.50-£20.50
Modernised, 18th century former farmhouse with extensive garden and fine countryside views. 0.25 mile (0.5km) from A75. A non-smoking home.						

WALKERBURN **Peeblesshire** Mrs A Barbour Willowbank, 13 High Cottages Walkerburn Peeblesshire EH43 6AZ Tel: (Walkerburn) 01896 870252	Map 2 C6	COMMENDED Listed	2 Twin 1 Double	2 Pub Bath/Show	B&B per person £16.00-£18.00 Single £15.00-£17.00 Double	Open Jan-Dec Dinner 1830-1900 B&B + Eve. Meal £23.00-£25.00
Personally run, stone-built semi-detached villa, situated on main tourist route through the Borders. Outstanding views of surrounding countryside.						

WEST LINTON **Peeblesshire** Mrs Cottam Rowallan, Mountain Cross West Linton Peeblesshire EH46 7DF Tel: (West Linton) 01968 660329	Map 2 B6	COMMENDED 👑	1 Double 1 Family	2 Pub Bath/Show	B&B per person from £15.00 Double	Open May-Oct
A warm welcome at modern house on A701, about half an hour's drive from Edinburgh. Fine views over the valley. Well situated for touring Borders and Peebles.						

Mrs Joyce Muir Jerviswood, Linton Bank Drive West Linton Peeblesshire EH46 7DT Tel: (West Linton) 01968 660429		COMMENDED Listed	2 Twin 1 Double	1 Pub Bath/Show	B&B per person £18.00-£19.00 Single £15.00-£16.00 Double	Open Jan-Dec
Comfortable modern house set in attractive gardens in picturesque historic village. Only half hour's drive from Edinburgh.						

SOUTH OF SCOTLAND

WEST LINTON continued
Peeblesshire
Mrs R M Rose
Millview, Blyth Bridge
West Linton
Peebleshire
EH46 7DG
Tel: (Peebles) 01721 752206
Fax: 01721 752622

Map 2
B6

COMMENDED
Listed

1 Single	2 En Suite fac	B&B per person	Open Jan-Dec
1 Twin	1 Priv. NOT ensuite	£14.00 Single	
1 Family	1 Pub Bath/Show	£16.00 Double	

Spacious modern family home set back from main route to Edinburgh (20 miles) (32kms) with lovely hill views to rear.

WIGTOWN

Mr & Mrs W B Cairns
Glaisnock House
20 South Main Street
Wigtown
DG8 9EH
Tel: (Wigtown) 01988 402249

Map 1
H10

COMMENDED

1 Twin	2 En Suite fac	B&B per person	Open Jan-Dec
2 Family	1 Limited ensuite	£15.50-£16.50 Single	Dinner 1800-2030
	1 Pub Bath/Show	£15.50-£16.50 Double	B&B + Eve. Meal
			£23.00-£24.00

Family run guest house with restaurant in the heart of the town.

YETHOLM, by Kelso
Roxburghshire
Mrs Gail Brooker
Bluntys Mill
Yetholm
Roxburghshire
TD5 8PG
Tel: (Yetholm) 01573 420288

Map 2
E7

COMMENDED

1 Twin	1 En Suite fac	B&B per person	Open Jan-Dec
		£16.00-£18.00 Single	Dinner 1800-2030
		from £16.00 Double	

Peaceful ground-floor accommodation in family home set in 6 acres (2.4ha) of pasture. In picturesque conservation village right at the end of the Pennine Way.

Edinburgh – City, Coast and Countryside

Who could ever tire of Edinburgh and the hills, beaches, castles and golf courses in the Lothian countryside around it?? With a city skyline every bit as spectacular as the postcards suggest, Scotland's capital is simply outstanding.

Though it reaches near capacity during the annual Edinburgh International Festival in late August, when the great accommodation choice outside the city is at its most valuable, Edinburgh remains the liveliest of places all year round.

Its castle is one of the most famous symbols of Scotland. Though there is much to see here it is only one of a whole range of historic attractions stretching down the Royal Mile, the heart of the Old Town of Edinburgh. Between the castle and the Palace of Holyroodhouse are museums such as Huntly House or the unique Museum of Childhood, historic properties such as John Knox House or Gladstone's Land and attractions such as the Scotch Whisky Heritage Centre. There is also a whole range of historic

details to be explored – and excellent shopping and plenty of places to eat as well. The same is true of the towns of the Lothians: attractive Georgian architecture in places like Haddington, or superb giftwares such as crystal glassware from Penicuik.

As a major cultural centre, Edinburgh is well supplied with galleries and important collections: the National Gallery of Scotland is simply unmissable for any art lover, while the Fruitmarket Gallery and the City Art Centre ring the changes with their stimulating exhibition programme. The Gallery of Modern Art extends the cultural options further, as do a range of smaller commercial galleries.

The fine Georgian streets of Edinburgh's New Town, with their cobbles and grand facades, add much to the city ambience.

The fine Georgian streets of Edinburgh's New Town, with their cobbles and grand facades, add much to the city ambience. The period settings of the National Trust for Scotland's Georgian House in Charlotte Square re-create life the New Town in the time of its first occupants. Only a little further afield, the city's Royal Botanic Garden features the largest rhododendron collection in the world, and many other horticultural delights besides – worth a visit at any season. As a relaxing green space in the bustling city, 'the Botanics' also offer fine views south, over the city rooftops to the Pentland Hills. These rolling hills are a reminder that an essential part of the Edinburgh experience is really outside the city, in the attractive Lothians countryside which surrounds it.

Edinburgh –
City, Coast and Countryside

You can get to grips with the Lothians countryside at high-level places like the Pentland Hills, or sea-level sites like the John Muir Country Park, near the handsome little resort of Dunbar.

However, there is plenty more to see: Tantallon Castle on its dramatic coastal headland setting, Linlithgow Palace, birthplace of Mary, Queen of Scots, Hopetoun House for sheer opulence and style. Explore the attractive red-roofed villages out in the wooded countryside below the Lammermuir Hills, discover Scotland's finest mediaeval stone carving at Rosslyn Chapel by the village of Roslin, or experience a day in the life of a miner at the Scottish Mining Museum at Newtongrange. Remember, too, that the coastline and countryside of the Lothians is all so easy to reach from the city. Combine city and countryside for the total experience.

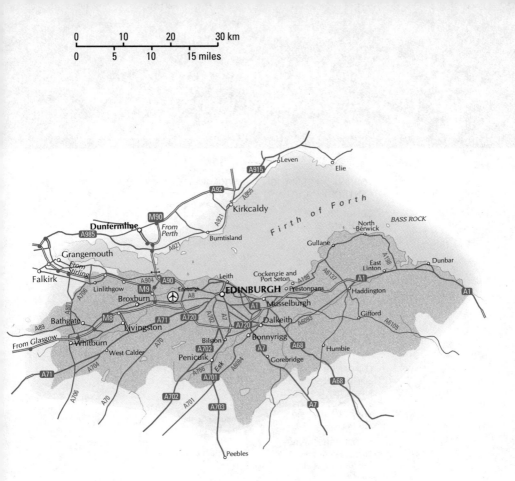

Edinburgh – City, Coast and Countryside

TOURIST INFORMATION CENTRES IN SCOTLAND

EDINBURGH & LOTHIANS TOURIST BOARD

DALKEITH
The Library
White Hart Street
Tel: (0131) 660 6818
Easter - September

DUNBAR &
143 High Street
Tel: (01368) 863353
Jan-Dec

EDINBURGH &
Edinburgh & Scotland
Information Centre
3 Princes Street, EH2 2QP
Tel: (0131) 557 1700
Jan-Dec

EDINBURGH AIRPORT &
Tourist Information Desk
Tel: (0131) 333 2167
Jan-Dec

LINLITHGOW &
Burgh Halls
The Cross, EH49 7EJ
Tel: (01506) 844600
Jan-Dec

NEWTONGRANGE
Scottish Mining Museum
Lady Victoria Colliery
Tel: (0131) 663 4262
April-Oct

NORTH BERWICK
Quality Street
Tel: (01620) 892197
Jan-Dec

OLDCRAIGHALL &
Granada Service Area (A1)
Musselburgh
Tel: (0131) 653 6172
Jan-Dec

PENCRAIG
A1 by East Linton
Tel: (01620) 860063
Jan-Dec

PENICUIK
Edinburgh Crystal
Visitor Centre
Eastfield
Tel: (01968) 673846
May-Oct

 Accept written enquiries
& Disabled access

50

ABERLADY
East Lothian
Mrs A Dyer, The Sidings
Aberlady Station
Haddington Road
Aberlady
East Lothian
EH32 0PZ
Tel: (Aberlady) 01875 870666

Map 2
D4

COMMENDED
Listed

1 Twin 1 En Suite fac

B&B per person
from £20.00 Single
from £17.50 Double
Room only per person
from £15.00

Open Jan-Dec

Detached modern bungalow on edge of caravan park, approximately ½ mile (1km) from village. Continental breakfast only. Chalet accommodation also available.

DALKEITH
Midlothian
Mrs M Blair
'Woodcot' 22 Bonnyrigg Road
Eskbank, Dalkeith
Midlothian
EH22 3EZ
Tel: 0131 663 2628

Map 2
C5

APPROVED
Listed

2 Family 1 Pub Bath/Show

B&B per person
£15.00-£17.00 Single
£15.00-£17.00 Double

Open Jan-Dec

Family home with convenient access to city. Ideal base for touring Lothians. Parking. Adjacent to bus stop.

by DALKEITH
Midlothian
Mrs Dorothy Stevenson
1 Hadfast Road
Cousland, by Dalkeith
Midlothian
EH22 2NU
Tel: 0131 663 1294

Map 2
C5

COMMENDED
Listed

1 Twin 2 En Suite fac
2 Double 1 Priv. NOT ensuite

B&B per person
£17.00-£23.00 Single
£14.00-£17.00 Double
Room only per person
£11.00-£14.00

Open Mar-Oct

Modern house with paddock and horses in quiet village, 2 miles (3kms) from Dalkeith, approximately 9 miles (14kms) from Edinburgh with views of Pentlands. All rooms with private facilities.

DUNBAR
East Lothian
Cruachan Guest House
East Links Road
Dunbar
East Lothian
EH42 1LT
Tel: (Dunbar) 01368 863006

Map 2
E4

COMMENDED

1 Single 1 Limited ensuite
1 Twin 2 Pub Bath/Show
2 Family

B&B per person
£15.00-£16.00 Single
£15.00-£16.00 Double
B&B + Eve. Meal
from £23.00

Open Jan-Dec
Dinner 1800-1830

Victorian semi-detached house with character and rear walled garden with direct access to sandy beach. Ideal for touring, golfing and local amenities.

Mrs Gardner
Muirfield, 40 Belhaven Road
Dunbar
East Lothian
EH42 1NF
Tel: (Dunbar) 01368 862289

COMMENDED

2 Twin 2 En Suite fac
1 Double 1 Pub Bath/Show

B&B per person
£15.00-£20.00 Double

Open Mar-Oct

Victorian house close to town centre, beach and John Muir Country Park. Comfortably furnished with off-street parking.

St Helen's Guest House
Queens Road
Dunbar
East Lothian
EH42 1LN
Tel: (Dunbar) 01368 863716

COMMENDED

1 Single 2 En Suite fac
4 Twin 2 Pub Bath/Show
1 Double
1 Family

B&B per person
from £17.00 Single
£16.00-£19.00 Double

Open Mar-Oct

Victorian red sandstone house situated in quiet area of Dunbar. Few minutes' walk from beach and golf course. Friendly welcome.

Springfield Guest House
Belhaven Road
Dunbar
East Lothian
EH42 1NH
Tel: (Dunbar) 01368 862502

COMMENDED

1 Single 1 Priv. NOT ensuite
1 Twin 2 Pub Bath/Show
1 Double
2 Family

B&B per person
£16.00-£17.50 Single
£15.00-£16.50 Double
Room only per person
£14.00-£15.00

Open Jan-Nov
Dinner at 1800
B&B + Eve. Meal
£26.50-£27.50

An elegant 19th century villa with attractive garden. Family run with home cooking. Ideal base for golf and touring.

EDINBURGH – CITY, COAST AND COUNTRYSIDE

Details of Grading and Classification are on page vi. | Key to symbols is on back flap. | 51

EDINBURGH – CITY, COAST AND COUNTRYSIDE

| EAST CALDER | Map 2 |
| West Lothian | B5 |

Near EDINBURGH
OVERSHIEL FARM, EAST CALDER
Telephone: 01506 880469 Fax: 01506 883006

PEACEFUL COUNTRY SETTING, 6 MILES WEST OF EDINBURGH. EASY ACCESS INTO CITY CENTRE BY CAR, BUS OR TRAIN (STATION 1.5 MILES). ALL ROOMS HAVE COLOUR TV PLUS TEA/COFFEE-MAKING FACILITIES. SAFE PARKING.

Mrs Jan Dick Overshiel Farm East Calder West Lothian EH53 0HT Tel: (Mid Calder) 01506 880469 Fax: 01506 883006	COMMENDED	2 Twin 1 Double	2 En Suite fac 2 Pub Bath/Show	B&B per person £20.00-£27.00 Single £16.00-£20.00 Double	Open Jan-Dec

Stone-built farmhouse. Set in large garden and surrounded by arable farmland. 5 miles (8kms) from Edinburgh Airport. Easy access to M8 and M9.

Mrs Lorna Scott Whitecroft, 7 Raw Holdings East Calder West Lothian EH53 0ET Tel: (Mid Calder) 01506 882494	COMMENDED	1 Twin 2 Double	3 En Suite fac 31 Pub Bath/Show	B&B per person £20.00 Double	Open Jan-Dec

Family bungalow on 5-acre (2ha) smallholding adjacent to Almondell Country Park. On main bus route to Edinburgh (20 mins). Private parking. Ground-floor accommodation.

| EAST LINTON | Map 2 |
| East Lothian | D4 |

Kippielaw Farmhouse
East Linton, East Lothian EH41 4PY   Tel/Fax: 01620 860368

Comfortable, welcoming, tastefully restored 18th century farmhouse with stunning views òver East Lothian countryside. Pleasant local walks to Traprain Law, Hailes Castle and East Linton village. The attractions of Edinburgh are only 30 minutes away. Relax and enjoy candlelit dinners in our log-fired dining room overlooking attractive gardens and courtyard.

Mrs E Campbell Kippielaw Farmhouse East Linton East Lothian EH41 4PY Tel: (East Linton) 01620 860368	HIGHLY COMMENDED Listed	2 Twin 1 Double	2 Pub Bath/Show	B&B per person from £20.00 Single £18.00-£20.00 Double	Open Jan-Dec Dinner 1930-2000 B&B + Eve. Meal £34.00-£38.00

17th century farmhouse overlooking open farmland to the coast. 25 miles (40kms) from Edinburgh. Interesting garden. Imaginative candlelit dinners.

Book your accommodation anywhere in Scotland the easy way – through your nearest Tourist Information Centre.

A booking fee of £2.75 is charged, and you will be asked for a small deposit.

Local bookings are usually free, or a small fee will be charged.

Kiloran House

East Linton, East Lothian EH40 3AY Tel: 01620 860410

Victorian house close to A1. Enjoy the benefits of countryside, coast and Edinburgh city. Half-hour drive or train journey to Princes Street and Castle. Short drive to coast and all golf courses. Large garden. Children welcome. Pets by arrangement. **NO SMOKING THROUGHOUT**

Mrs M Henderson Kiloran House East Linton East Lothian EH40 3AY Tel: (East Linton) 01620 860410	HIGHLY COMMENDED	2 Double 1 Family	2 En Suite fac 1 Pub Bath/Show	B&B per person £18.00-£25.00 Single £18.00-£25.00 Double	Open Jan-Dec	

A Victorian house of great character, furnished to a high standard. Relaxed and friendly atmosphere. Non-smoking house.

Miss E Jeffrey The Red House, 2 The Square East Linton East Lothian EH40 3AD Tel: (East Linton) 01620 860347	COMMENDED	1 Single 2 Double	1 En Suite fac 1 Priv. NOT ensuite 1 Pub Bath/Show	B&B per person £17.00-£25.00 Single £17.00-£20.00 Double	Open Jan-Dec Dinner 1900-2130 B&B + Eve. Meal £25.00-£30.00	

Traditional house with private gardens in the centre of this attractive village. Ideal for touring National Trust properties. Creative interior environment, private bathrooms.

EDINBURGH Aaron Guest House 16 Hartington Gardens Edinburgh EH10 4LD Tel: 0131 229 6459 Fax: 0131 228 5807	Map 2 C5	COMMENDED Listed	1 Single 3 Twin 2 Double 5 Family	9 En Suite fac 1 Limited ensuite 1 Priv. NOT ensuite	B&B per person £20.00-£32.00 Single £20.00-£32.00 Double	Open Jan-Dec

Former Victorian manse, in quiet cul-de-sac, private parking. 10 minutes' walk from city centre. Ground-floor accommodation available. No smoking.

Abbotthead House 40 Minto Street Edinburgh EH9 2BR Tel: 0131 668 1658	COMMENDED	3 Twin 2 Double 3 Family	6 En Suite fac 2 Limited ensuite 1 Pub Bath/Show	B&B per person £16.00-£25.00 Double	Open Jan-Dec	

Personally run guest house. Centrally located to main city routes and all attractions.

Abcorn Guest House

4 Mayfield Gardens, Edinburgh EH9 2BU
Tel: 0131 667 6548 Fax: 0131 667 9969

The Abcorn is a family run guest house in a detached Victorian villa, near to the city centre, with a private car park. All our rooms are ensuite and also have colour TV and tea/coffee-making facilities.

Abcorn Guest House 4 Mayfield Gardens Edinburgh EH9 2BU Tel: 0131 667 6548 Fax: 0131 667 9969	COMMENDED	1 Single 2 Twin 2 Double 2 Family	7 En Suite fac	B&B per person £23.00-£30.00 Single £23.00-£30.00 Double	Open Jan-Dec	

Detached Victorian stone villa with private parking on main route to city centre.

EDINBURGH – CITY, COAST AND COUNTRYSIDE

Details of Grading and Classification are on page vi. | Key to symbols is on back flap. |

EDINBURGH continued	Map 2 C5						
Abingdon Lodge 24 Cammo Crescent Edinburgh EH4 8DZ Tel: 0131 339 4994		HIGHLY COMMENDED	1 Single 1 Twin 1 Double 1 Family	1 En Suite fac 2 Limited ensuite 2 Pub Bath/Show	B&B per person £16.00–£26.00 Single £16.00–£28.00 Double Room only per person £15.00–£25.00	Open Jan-Dec	

Victorian family mansion house designed by Sir Robert Lorimer. Gardens, billiard room, satellite TV. Airport 3 miles (5kms). City centre 4 miles (6.4kms).

| Acorn Guest House 70 Pilrig Street Edinburgh EH6 5AS Tel: 0131 554 2187 | COMMENDED | 1 Twin 1 Double 3 Family | 1 En Suite fac 2 Pub Bath/Show | B&B per person £15.00–£22.50 Double | Open Jan-Dec | |

Terraced house on bus route to and from city centre.

| Acorn Lodge Guest House 26 Pilrig Street Edinburgh EH6 5AJ Tel: 0131 555 1557 Fax: 0131 555 4475 | COMMENDED | 1 Single 2 Twin 3 Double 1 Family | 7 En Suite fac | B&B per person £22.50–£45.00 Single £22.50–£45.00 Double | Open Jan-Dec Dinner 1900-2100 B&B + Eve. Meal £32.50–£55.00 | |

Recently refurbished and renovated Georgian Town House. Unrestricted parking. Ideal location for all amenities.

ADAM GUEST HOUSE

2 HARTINGTON GARDENS, EDINBURGH EH10 4LD
Telephone: 0131 229 8664   Fax: 0131 229 9743

ADAM HOUSE is a Victorian terraced, non-smoking guest house situated in a quiet cul-de-sac only 15 minutes' walk from the city centre. We are close to bus routes, shops, theatres and restaurants. Our bedrooms are bright and comfortable with colour television and hot drinks facilities.
We look forward to welcoming you.

| Adam Guest House 2 Hartington Gardens Edinburgh EH10 4LD Tel: 0131 229 8664 Fax: 0131 229 9743 | COMMENDED Listed | 1 Single 1 Twin 1 Double 2 Family | 1 En Suite fac 1 Priv. NOT ensuite 2 Pub Bath/Show | B&B per person £17.00–£22.00 Single £17.00–£27.00 Double Room only per person £15.00–£20.00 | Open Jan-Dec | |

Family run Victorian terraced house in quiet cul-de-sac. Easy access to city centre by bus. Unrestricted parking. Non-smoking.

| A-Haven in Edinburgh 180 Ferry Road Edinburgh EH6 4NS Tel: 0131 554 6559 Fax: 0131 554 5252 | COMMENDED | 2 Single 4 Twin 3 Double 2 Family | 11 En Suite fac | B&B per person £25.00–£49.00 Single £24.00–£40.00 Double | Open Jan-Dec Dinner 1830-1930 | |

Family run city centre guest house with private parking and main bus routes. Scottish welcome and hospitality.

| Airlie Guest House 29 Minto Street Edinburgh EH9 1SB Tel: 0131 667 3562 Fax: 0131 662 1399 | COMMENDED | 2 Single 3 Twin 5 Double 2 Family | 7 En Suite fac 1 Priv. NOT ensuite 2 Pub Bath/Show | B&B per person £18.00–£30.00 Single £15.00–£30.00 Double | Open Jan-Dec | |

Formerly two terraced houses, some rooms featuring plaster cornicing. On bus route with easy access to city centre. Off-road parking.

Alness Guest House 27 Pilrig Street Edinburgh EH6 5AN Tel: 0131 554 1187	COMMENDED	1 Single 1 Twin 2 Double 4 Family	3 Pub Bath/Show	B&B per person £17.00-£20.00 Single £16.00-£20.00 Double	Open Jan-Dec

Friendly, family run guest house. On main bus route,
1 mile (2kms) from Princes Street and Castle.

An Fuaran Guest House 35 Seaview Terrace, Joppa Edinburgh EH15 2HE Tel: 0131 669 8119	COMMENDED	2 Twin 1 Double 1 Family	4 En Suite fac	B&B per person £18.00-£25.00 Single £16.50-£22.00 Double	Open Jan-Dec

Victorian house overlooking the Firth of Forth, 4 miles (6 kms) from Edinburgh
city centre. Regular bus service. Evening meal by arrangement.

Ardgarth Guest House 1 St Mary's Place, Portobello Edinburgh EH15 2QF Tel: 0131 669 3021 Fax: 0131 669 3021	COMMENDED	3 Single 2 Twin 3 Double 2 Family	2 En Suite fac 3 Pub Bath/Show	B&B per person £15.00-£22.00 Single £15.00-£22.00 Double	Open Jan-Dec Dinner 1800-2000 B&B + Eve. Meal £20.00-£32.00

Comfortable accommodation in friendly guest house. Close to sea.
Special diets catered for, full ensuite disabled facilities. French spoken.

Aries Guest House 5 Upper Gilmore Place Edinburgh EH3 9NW Tel: 0131 229 4669	APPROVED Listed	1 Twin 2 Double 1 Family	1 Limited ensuite 2 Pub Bath/Show	B&B per person £13.00-£25.00 Single £13.00-£22.00 Double	Open Jan-Dec

Terraced house in quiet street, but with easy access to city centre.
Ground-floor rooms available.

Mrs Armstrong 481 Queensferry Road Edinburgh EH4 7ND Tel: 0131 336 5595	COMMENDED Listed	1 Twin 1 Double	2 En Suite fac	B&B per person £20.00-£25.00 Double Room only per person £18.00-£23.00	Open Apr-Oct

Family house on busy road, easy access to all routes.
Excellent bus service to city centre. Non-smoking house. All ensuite.

Ashdene House 23 Fountainhall Road Edinburgh EH9 2LN Tel: 0131 667 6026	HIGHLY COMMENDED	1 Twin 2 Double 2 Family	4 En Suite fac 1 Priv. NOT ensuite	B&B per person £20.00-£28.00 Double	Open Jan-Dec

Edwardian town house retaining many features, in quiet residential conservation area.
Convenient for bus route to city centre (10 minutes). Non-smoking establishment.

Ashlyn Guest House 42 Inverleith Row Edinburgh EH3 5PY Tel: 0131 552 2954	HIGHLY COMMENDED	2 Single 2 Twin 3 Double 1 Family	5 En Suite fac 1 Priv. NOT ensuite 3 Pub Bath/Show	B&B per person £18.00-£25.00 Single £20.00-£30.00 Double Room only per person £19.00-£29.00	Open Jan-Dec

Georgian Listed building in residential area of city. Approximately 1.5m (2.5kms)
on main bus route to centre with street parking.

Details of Grading and Classification are on page vi.

Key to symbols is on back flap.

EDINBURGH – CITY, COAST AND COUNTRYSIDE

EDINBURGH continued	Map 2 C5						
Ashwood Guest House
20 Minto Street
Edinburgh
EH9 1RQ
Tel: 0131 667 8024	COMMENDED
Listed	1 Twin
1 Double
2 Family	2 En Suite fac
1 Limited ensuite
1 Pub Bath/Show	B&B per person
£17.00-£28.00 Double	Open Jan-Dec		

Small, friendly guest house, ideally situated close to the city centre and tourist attractions. Private parking, ensuite rooms.

| Assegai B&B
27 Quality Street
Edinburgh
EH4 5BP
Tel: 0131 467 4551 | COMMENDED
Listed | 2 Family | 2 Priv. NOT ensuite
1 Pub Bath/Show | B&B per person
£12.50-£17.50 Double | Open Apr-Oct | | |

Stone-built villa, easy access to city centre. Close to local amenities and transport to city.

| Auld Reekie Guest House
16 Mayfield Gardens
Edinburgh
EH9 2BZ
Tel: 0131 667 6177
Fax: 0131 662 0033 | COMMENDED | 1 Single
1 Twin
2 Double
3 Family | 7 En Suite fac | B&B per person
£20.00-£32.00 Single
£18.00-£30.00 Double | Open Jan-Dec | | |

Family run stone built house on south side of city centre. On main bus route to Princes Street.

CENTRAL EDINBURGH

AVERON GUEST HOUSE

44 Gilmore Place, Edinburgh EH3 9NQ

Built in 1770 as a farmhouse, charming, centrally situated Georgian period house offers a high standard of accommodation at favourable terms.

- Full cooked breakfast -
- All credit cards accepted -
- 10 minutes' walk to Princes Street and Castle -
- STB Approved • AA Listed -
- Private car park -

Tel: 0131-229 9932

| Averon Guest House
44 Gilmore Place
Edinburgh
EH3 9NQ
Tel: 0131 229 9932 | APPROVED | 1 Single
3 Twin
4 Double
2 Family | 3 Pub Bath/Show | B&B per person
£16.00-£25.00 Single
£14.00-£22.00 Double | Open Jan-Dec | | |

Central location with private car park to rear. 10 minutes' walk to Princes Street and Castle. Near King's Theatre and Conference Centre.

| Mr P Ayres
21 Mayfield Road, Newington
Edinburgh
EH9 2NQ
Tel: 0131 667 8435 | COMMENDED | 1 Twin
1 Double | 1 En Suite fac
1 Priv. NOT ensuite | B&B per person
£20.00-£27.50 Double | Open May-Sep | | |

Warm welcome assured in traditionally furnished Victorian family home. 1 mile (2 kms) to city centre.

Mrs Helen Baird
'Arisaig', 64 Glasgow Road, Edinburgh EH12 8LN
Telephone: 0131 334 2610

Warm Scottish welcome awaits you here at this highly commended private home with lovely gardens. The bedrooms are kept to a very high standard with tea/coffee-making facilities and delicious breakfast. Good local restaurants. Three miles from City Centre. Parking spaces. Good bus service. All private facilities. Lounge with TV.

Mrs H Baird Arisaig, 64 Glasgow Road Edinburgh EH12 8LN Tel: 0131 334 2610	**HIGHLY COMMENDED**	1 Twin 1 Double	2 En Suite fac	B&B per person £25.00-£30.00 Single £20.00-£23.00 Double	Open Apr-Sep

Personally run comfortable and friendly accommodation in detached dormer bungalow. Good bus service to town centre, approximately 3 miles (5 kms).

Balquhidder Guest House 94 Pilrig Street Edinburgh EH6 5AY Tel: 0131 554 3377	**COMMENDED**	1 Single 2 Twin 2 Double 1 Family	5 En Suite fac 1 Limited ensuite 1 Pub Bath/Show	B&B per person £18.00-£30.00 Single £18.00-£24.00 Double	Open Jan-Dec

Detached house in its own grounds overlooking public park and on bus routes to the city centre.

Mrs E Banigan Elliston, 5 Viewforth Terrace Edinburgh EH10 4LH Tel: 0131 229 6698	**APPROVED Listed**	2 Single 1 Twin	1 Pub Bath/Show	B&B per person £18.00-£20.00 Single £16.00-£18.00 Double	Open Apr-Sep

Victorian villa approx 2 miles (3kms) from Princes Street. In quiet residential location. Close to bus routes.

Belford Guest House
13 Blacket Avenue, Edinburgh EH9 1RR
Telephone: 0131 667 2422

Small and friendly family run guest house in quiet tree-lined avenue 1 mile from the city centre. Buses run from either end of the avenue to all attractions in the city. *Private parking.*

Belford Guest House 13 Blacket Avenue Edinburgh EH9 1RR Tel: 0131 667 2422	**COMMENDED**	3 Twin 4 Family	2 Pub Bath/Show	B&B per person £20.00-£24.00 Single £20.00-£22.00 Double	Open Jan-Dec

Family run guest house in quiet road just off main A68/A7. Conveniently situated for main tourist attractions and town centre.

Muriel Bell Bell's House, 18 Moat Place Edinburgh EH14 1PP Tel: 0131 538 3437	**COMMENDED Listed**	4 Twin 1 Double 1 Family	2 Pub Bath/Show	B&B per person £15.00-£20.00 Single £15.00-£20.00 Double Room only per person £13.00-£18.00	Open Apr-Oct

Traditional terraced house with stylish modern decor yet retaining many original features. Additional guests' kitchen available. On main bus route to city centre.

EDINBURGH – CITY, COAST AND COUNTRYSIDE

EDINBURGH continued	Map 2 C5

Ben-Craig House

3 Craigmillar Park, Edinburgh EH16 5PG
Telephone: 0131 667 2593

Edinburgh's newest guest house, completely refurbished with your comfort in mind. Walking distance to Princes Street. Large well-appointed bedrooms all with ensuite facilities. Bus service to most areas of town. Private parking.

See inside front cover

Ben-Craig House 3 Craigmillar Park Edinburgh EH16 5PG Tel: 0131 667 2593	HIGHLY COMMENDED	1 Twin 2 Double 1 Family	4 En Suite fac	B&B per person £19.00-£34.00 Double	Open Jan-Dec

Traditional, detached, stone Victorian townhouse with quiet gardens. On main route for city centre.

Mrs P Birnie Casa Buzzo, 8 Kilmaurs Road Edinburgh EH16 5DA Tel: 0131 667 8998	COMMENDED	1 Twin 1 Double 2 Family	2 Pub Bath/Show	B&B per person £14.00-£16.00 Double	Open May-Sep

A terraced property, conveniently situated for bus routes to the town centre and visitor attractions. Unrestricted parking. Non-smoking house.

MRS BARBARA BLOWS
FAIRHOLME

13 Moston Terrace, Edinburgh EH9 2DE
Telephone: 0131 667 8645

Set in a quiet terrace adjoining major bus routes, under the personal supervision of the owners, this spacious family home offers Victorian elegance to your stay.

Mrs B Blows Fairholme, 13 Moston Terrace Edinburgh EH9 2DE Tel: 0131 667 8645	COMMENDED Listed	1 Single 1 Twin 1 Double	2 Pub Bath/Show	B&B per person £13.00-£20.00 Single £12.00-£20.00 Double	Open Apr-Oct Dinner 1800-1900 B&B + Eve. Meal £16.50-£24.50

Comfortable, elegant period home, friendly ambience. Convenient for city centre.

Book your accommodation anywhere in Scotland the easy way – through your nearest Tourist Information Centre.

A booking fee of £2.75 is charged, and you will be asked for a small deposit.

Local bookings are usually free, or a small fee will be charged.

BONNINGTON GUEST HOUSE

202 Ferry Road, Edinburgh EH6 4NW
Telephone: 0131 554 7610

A comfortable early Victorian house (built 1840), personally run, where a friendly and warm welcome awaits guests. Situated in residential area of town on main bus routes. Private car parking.
For further details contact Eileen and David Watt, Proprietors.

Bonnington Guest House 202 Ferry Road Edinburgh EH6 4NW Tel: 0131 554 7610	HIGHLY COMMENDED	1 Twin 2 Double 3 Family	3 En Suite fac 1 Priv. NOT ensuite 1 Pub Bath/Show	B&B per person £22.00-£30.00 Double	Open Jan-Dec	

Early Victorian Listed building with private parking on the north side of the city, convenient bus routes to centre.

Mrs Maria Boyle Villa Maria 6a Mayfield Gardens Edinburgh EH9 2BU Tel: 0131 667 7730	COMMENDED Listed	1 Double 1 Family	1 Pub Bath/Show	B&B per person £15.00-£19.00 Double	Open Apr-Oct	

Victorian house on main road, but with quiet rooms. 5 minutes on bus route to city centre and all attractions. Private parking.

Brae Guest House 119 Willowbrae Road Edinburgh EH8 7HN Tel: 0131 661 0170	COMMENDED	1 Single 1 Twin 1 Double 1 Family	3 En Suite fac 1 Priv. NOT ensuite	B&B per person £17.00-£25.00 Single £17.00-£28.00 Double	Open Jan-Dec	

Friendly, family run guest house on bus route to city centre.
10 minutes' walk from Meadowbank Stadium and Holyrood Palace.

Brig O'Doon Guest House 262 Ferry Road Edinburgh EH5 3AN Tel: 0131 552 3953	COMMENDED Listed	3 Twin 1 Double 2 Family	3 Pub Bath/Show	B&B per person £25.00-£27.00 Single £18.50-£22.50 Double	Open Jan-Dec	

Stone-built terraced house on north side of city centre, overlooking playing fields with fine views to castle. Bus route to city centre.

Ms C Brown Kilmorie House 83 Colinton Road Edinburgh Lothian EH10 5DF Tel: 0131 313 1939	COMMENDED Listed	1 Single 1 Twin 1 Double 2 Family	3 Pub Bath/Show	B&B per person £18.00-£20.00 Single £18.00-£20.00 Double	Open Apr-Oct, Xmas/New Year	

Townhouse built c.1850 retaining the original character of the property.

Bruntsfield Guest House 55 Leamington Terrace Edinburgh EH10 4JS Tel: 0131 228 6458 Fax: 0131 228 6458	COMMENDED Listed	2 Single 2 Twin 2 Double 1 Family	1 En Suite fac 2 Pub Bath/Show	B&B per person £18.00-£26.00 Single £18.00-£28.00 Double	Open Jan-Dec	

Situated in residential area close to main bus route to city centre.
No residents' lounge but TV in all bedrooms.

EDINBURGH – CITY, COAST AND COUNTRYSIDE

EDINBURGH – CITY, COAST AND COUNTRYSIDE

EDINBURGH continued	Map 2 C5

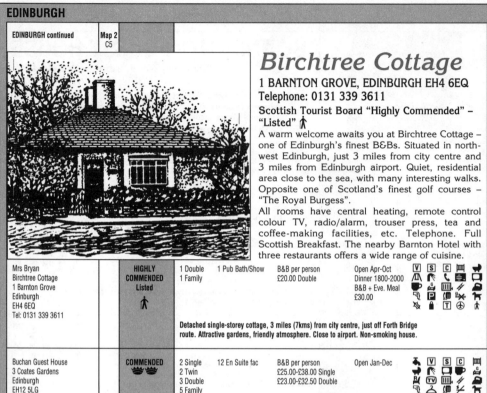

Birchtree Cottage

1 BARNTON GROVE, EDINBURGH EH4 6EQ
Telephone: 0131 339 3611

Scottish Tourist Board "Highly Commended" – "Listed" 🏃

A warm welcome awaits you at Birchtree Cottage – one of Edinburgh's finest B&Bs. Situated in north-west Edinburgh, just 3 miles from city centre and 3 miles from Edinburgh airport. Quiet, residential area close to the sea, with many interesting walks. Opposite one of Scotland's finest golf courses – "The Royal Burgess".

All rooms have central heating, remote control colour TV, radio/alarm, trouser press, tea and coffee-making facilities, etc. Telephone. Full Scottish Breakfast. The nearby Barnton Hotel with three restaurants offers a wide range of cuisine.

Mrs Bryan Birchtree Cottage 1 Barnton Grove Edinburgh EH4 6EQ Tel: 0131 339 3611	HIGHLY COMMENDED Listed 🏃	1 Double 1 Family	1 Pub Bath/Show	B&B per person £20.00 Double	Open Apr-Oct Dinner 1800-2000 B&B + Eve. Meal £30.00	

Detached single-storey cottage, 3 miles (7kms) from city centre, just off Forth Bridge route. Attractive gardens, friendly atmosphere. Close to airport. Non-smoking house.

Buchan Guest House 3 Coates Gardens Edinburgh EH12 5LG Tel: 0131 337 1045 Fax: 0131 538 7055	COMMENDED 👑👑	2 Single 2 Twin 3 Double 5 Family	12 En Suite fac	B&B per person £25.00-£38.00 Single £23.00-£32.50 Double	Open Jan-Dec	

Comfortable former merchant's house. Centrally situated for Princes Street and close to Haymarket Station.

BUCHANAN GUEST HOUSE

97 Joppa Road, Edinburgh EH15 2HB
Telephone: 0131 657 4117

A warm welcome is extended to all visitors by Margaret and Stewart Buchanan at their personally run Victorian guest house with panoramic view overlooking Firth of Forth. The bedrooms are well equipped with every comfort in mind and full Scottish breakfast is provided. Conveniently located. Frequent bus service to city centre and en-route to main golf courses. Businessmen welcome. FREE UNRESTRICTED PARKING.

Buchanan Guest House 97 Joppa Road Edinburgh EH15 2HB Tel: 0131 657 4117	COMMENDED 👑👑	2 Twin 1 Double 1 Family	1 En Suite fac 2 Pub Bath/Show	B&B per person £17.00-£22.50 Double	Open Jan-Dec	

Comfortable personally run guest house, on major bus route to city centre. Unrestricted parking. Front views overlooking sea.

BURNS B&B

Tel: 0131 229 1669
Fax: 0131 229 9225

67 Gilmore Place, Edinburgh EH3 9NU

Popular homely B&B accommodation in city centre close to
Princes Street, Castle, tourist attractions, theatres, EICC,
restaurants etc. Comfortable rooms (all ensuite).
Good breakfasts. Some parking. Non-smoking. No pets.
Access at all times with your own keys.
Write, telephone or fax Mrs Burns.

Mrs M Burns 67 Gilmore Place Edinburgh EH3 9NU Tel: 0131 229 1669 Fax: 0131 229 9225	COMMENDED ♕♕	1 Twin 2 Double	3 En Suite fac	B&B per person £20.00-£27.00 Double	Open Apr-Oct

Victorian terraced house close to city centre, tourist attractions,
King's Theatre and local restaurants. All ensuite. Non-smoking.

Mrs E C Cahill 1 Silverknowes Brae Edinburgh EH4 5PH Tel: 0131 312 7266	COMMENDED Listed	1 Single 1 Twin	2 Pub Bath/Show	B&B per person £17.00-£18.00 Single £16.00-£17.00 Double	Open May-Dec Dinner 1900-2000 B&B + Eve. Meal from £25.00

Detached villa in quiet residential area within 1 mile (2kms) from Cramond foreshore.
Conveniently placed for public transport to city centre.

Mrs Cairns 28 Cammo Road Edinburgh EH4 8AP Tel: 0131 339 3613	HIGHLY COMMENDED Listed	2 Double	1 Pub Bath/Show	B&B per person £20.00-£25.00 Single £18.00-£22.00 Double	Open Apr-Oct

Family home in quiet residential area with easy access to Queensferry Road and
airport. Ideal base for touring Edinburgh and surrounding countryside.

CAMERON TOLL GUEST HOUSE

299 DALKEITH ROAD, EDINBURGH EH16 5JX
Telephone: 0131 667 2950   Fax: 0131 662 1987

Our friendly family-run Guest House has
11 bedrooms with own shower and toilet, colour TV
and tea/coffee facilities. The spacious lounge offers
comfort and plenty of tourist information. We are
ideally situated on the A7 (close to the University and
Commonwealth Pool) handy for exploring city and
countryside. We have private parking and frequent
bus services, only 10 minutes' drive from the City
Centre. We can help arrange activities, local tours
and bagpiping from our resident piper. We offer a
varied Scottish breakfast and evening meals.
Picnic lunches and special diets by arrangement.
Contact Andrew and Mary Deans.

Cameron Toll Guest House 299 Dalkeith Road Edinburgh EH16 5JX Tel: 0131 667 2950 Fax: 0131 662 1987	COMMENDED ♕♕♕	3 Single 2 Twin 3 Double 3 Family	10 En Suite fac 1 Priv. NOT ensuite	B&B per person £25.00-£33.00 Single £19.00-£29.00 Double Room only per person £18.00-£28.00	Open Jan-Dec Dinner 1800-1830 B&B + Eve. Meal £27.00-£41.00

Family run guest house with some private parking. Conveniently located on A7
with frequent bus service to city centre. Close to Commonwealth Pool.

EDINBURGH – CITY, COAST AND COUNTRYSIDE

EDINBURGH – CITY, COAST AND COUNTRYSIDE

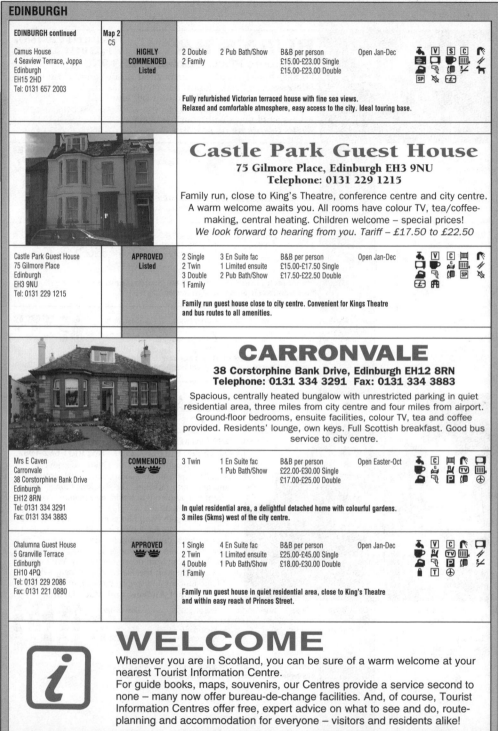

EDINBURGH continued	Map 2 C5						
Camus House 4 Seaview Terrace, Joppa Edinburgh EH15 2HD Tel: 0131 657 2003		HIGHLY COMMENDED Listed	2 Double 2 Family	2 Pub Bath/Show	B&B per person £15.00-£23.00 Single £15.00-£23.00 Double	Open Jan-Dec	

Fully refurbished Victorian terraced house with fine sea views. Relaxed and comfortable atmosphere, easy access to the city. Ideal touring base.

Castle Park Guest House
75 Gilmore Place, Edinburgh EH3 9NU
Telephone: 0131 229 1215

Family run, close to King's Theatre, conference centre and city centre. A warm welcome awaits you. All rooms have colour TV, tea/coffee-making, central heating. Children welcome – special prices! *We look forward to hearing from you. Tariff – £17.50 to £22.50*

Castle Park Guest House 75 Gilmore Place Edinburgh EH3 9NU Tel: 0131 229 1215	APPROVED Listed	2 Single 2 Twin 3 Double 1 Family	3 En Suite fac 1 Limited ensuite 2 Pub Bath/Show	B&B per person £15.00-£17.50 Single £17.50-£22.50 Double	Open Jan-Dec

Family run guest house close to city centre. Convenient for Kings Theatre and bus routes to all amenities.

CARRONVALE
38 Corstorphine Bank Drive, Edinburgh EH12 8RN
Telephone: 0131 334 3291 Fax: 0131 334 3883

Spacious, centrally heated bungalow with unrestricted parking in quiet residential area, three miles from city centre and four miles from airport. Ground-floor bedrooms, ensuite facilities, colour TV, tea and coffee provided. Residents' lounge, own keys. Full Scottish breakfast. Good bus service to city centre.

Mrs E Caven Carronvale 38 Corstorphine Bank Drive Edinburgh EH12 8RN Tel: 0131 334 3291 Fax: 0131 334 3883	COMMENDED	3 Twin	1 En Suite fac 1 Pub Bath/Show	B&B per person £22.00-£30.00 Single £17.00-£25.00 Double	Open Easter-Oct

In quiet residential area, a delightful detached home with colourful gardens. 3 miles (5kms) west of the city centre.

Chalumna Guest House 5 Granville Terrace Edinburgh EH10 4PQ Tel: 0131 229 2086 Fax: 0131 221 0880	APPROVED	1 Single 2 Twin 4 Double 1 Family	4 En Suite fac 1 Limited ensuite 1 Pub Bath/Show	B&B per person £25.00-£45.00 Single £18.00-£30.00 Double	Open Jan-Dec

Family run guest house in quiet residential area, close to King's Theatre and within easy reach of Princes Street.

WELCOME

Whenever you are in Scotland, you can be sure of a warm welcome at your nearest Tourist Information Centre.

For guide books, maps, souvenirs, our Centres provide a service second to none – many now offer bureau-de-change facilities. And, of course, Tourist Information Centres offer free, expert advice on what to see and do, route-planning and accommodation for everyone – visitors and residents alike!

Charleston House Guest House 38 Minto Street Edinburgh EH9 2BS Tel: 0131 667 6589	COMMENDED Listed	1 Twin 1 Double 2 Family	2 Pub Bath/Show	B&B per person £18.00-£25.00 Single £16.00-£24.00 Double Room only per person £15.00-£23.00	Open Jan-Dec

Traditionally furnished Georgian family home – 1826, ½ mile from city centre.

Mrs Judy Cheng 2 St Catherine's Gardens Edinburgh EH12 7AS Tel: 0131 334 6159	COMMENDED	2 Twin 1 Double 1 Family	2 Pub Bath/Show	B&B per person £20.00-£23.00 Double	Open Apr-Oct

Close to Edinburgh Zoo. On major bus route to city centre.
Chinese breakfast available. No smoking.

Clarin Guest House 4 East Mayfield Edinburgh EH9 1SD Tel: 0131 667 2433 Fax: 0131 667 2433	COMMENDED	1 Twin 3 Double 3 Family	4 Limited ensuite 3 Pub Bath/Show	B&B per person £16.50-£20.00 Single £33.00-£40.00 Double	Open Jan-Dec

Personally run guest house close to main bus routes to city centre.
Tea-making facilities and televisions in bedrooms.

Mrs Margaret Clark Sakura House 18 West Preston Street Edinburgh EH8 9PU Tel: 0131 668 1204	APPROVED Listed	3 Family	2 En Suite fac 1 Limited ensuite 2 Pub Bath/Show	B&B per person £14.00-£22.00 Double	Open Apr-Sep

Victorian house in central location, close to castle and shopping centre.
Continental breakfast only.

Classic House

50 Mayfield Road, Edinburgh EH9 2NH
Telephone: 0131 667 5847   Fax: 0131 662 1016

A warm welcome awaits you at this elegant Victorian house. Frequent bus
service to all major attractions. All rooms with private/ensuite shower
rooms, TV, central heating, hospitality tray. Relaxed and comfortable
atmosphere at this totally non-smoking guest house.
STB Commended   **AA QQQQ**

Classic House 50 Mayfield Road Edinburgh EH9 2NH Tel: 0131 667 5847 Fax: 0131 662 1016	COMMENDED	1 Single 1 Twin 1 Double 1 Family	3 En Suite fac 1 Priv. NOT ensuite 1 Pub Bath/Show	B&B per person £18.00-£45.00 Single £20.00-£30.00 Double	Open Jan-Dec

Friendly welcome at this family home, recently refurbished to a high standard.
Short bus ride from city centre. Non-smoking.

Claymore Guest House 68 Pilrig Street Edinburgh EH6 5AS Tel: 0131 554 2500 Fax: 0131 554 2500	COMMENDED	2 Twin 2 Double 2 Family	3 En Suite fac 1 Priv. NOT ensuite 1 Pub Bath/Show	B&B per person £16.00-£25.50 Single £16.00-£25.50 Double	Open Jan-Dec

Red sandstone Victorian terraced villa, a former manse, situated close
to the city centre and on the main bus routes.

Commonwealth Guest House 96 Dalkeith Road Edinburgh Midlothian EH16 5HA Tel: 0131 668 1680 Fax: 0131 668 1680	COMMENDED	1 Single 2 Twin 2 Double 1 Family	6 En Suite fac	B&B per person £25.00-£30.00 Single £23.00-£30.00 Double Room only per person £23.00-£30.00	Open Jan-Dec

Family run, stone-built house, all bedrooms with ensuite facilities. Situated on south
side of city centre, close to Royal Commonwealth swimming pool and Edinburgh
University residences.

| EDINBURGH continued | Map 2 C5 |

Braid Hills Cottage
20 Jordan Lane, Edinburgh EH10 4QZ
Telephone: 0131 447 3650

This early 19th-century detached cottage is in a quiet corner near the centre of Edinburgh. There is a large garden, parking spaces and several bus routes to the City Centre. Appointments can be made for a variety of complementary therapies. Vegetarian breakfasts are a speciality. Families are welcome.

| Lynn Cooper 20 Jordan Lane Edinburgh EH10 4QZ Tel: 0131 447 3650 | APPROVED Listed | 1 Single 1 Twin 1 Double 1 Family | 1 En Suite fac 1 Pub Bath/Show | B&B per person £20.00-£25.00 Single £18.00-£25.00 Double Room only per person £15.00-£22.00 | Open Apr-Oct |

Stone-built 19th century single-storey house with large garden in quiet location. Convenient bus routes to city centre.

| Corstorphine Guest House 188 St Johns Road Edinburgh EH12 8SG Tel: 0131 539 4237 Fax: 0131 539 4945 | HIGHLY COMMENDED | 1 Single 1 Twin 1 Double 1 Family | 2 En Suite fac 2 Priv. NOT ensuite 2 Pub Bath/Show | B&B per person £22.00-£30.00 Single £20.00-£28.00 Double | Open Jan-Dec |

Pleasant Victorian house providing a warm welcome and excellent facilities. Close to city centre and airport. Off-street parking.

| Mrs M Coutts Meadowplace House 1 Meadowplace Road Edinburgh EH12 7TZ Tel: 0131 334 8459 | APPROVED Listed | 1 Single 1 Twin 1 Family | 2 Pub Bath/Show | B&B per person £15.00 Single £12.00-£15.00 Double | Open Apr-Oct |

Comfortable, personally run B&B close to major bus routes to city centre and airport. Own parking. Ideal base for touring.

| Mrs A Cowan 85 Colinton Road Edinburgh EH10 5DF Tel: 0131 337 7575 | COMMENDED | 1 Double | 1 Pub Bath/Show | B&B per person £25.00-£32.00 Double Room only per person £21.00-£28.00 | Open Easter-Oct Dinner 1900-2000 B&B + Eve. Meal £45.00-£52.00 |

Elegant first-floor flat in quiet residential area. Walking distance of restaurants, shops and cinemas. Free parking.

Mrs Moira Conway
Crannoch But & Ben
467 QUEENSFERRY RD EDINBURGH EH4 7ND TEL: 0131 336 5688

STB Grade of Highly Commended and Classification of has been awarded to this outstanding family home. This bungalow has private facilities for all rooms and residents' lounge. Near Airport on A90 and three miles from city centre with excellent bus service and car parking.

All guests receive a warm welcome.

| Crannoch But & Ben 467 Queensferry Road Edinburgh EH4 7ND Tel: 0131 336 5688 | HIGHLY COMMENDED | 1 Twin 1 Family | 2 En Suite fac | B&B per person £22.00-£25.00 Double | Open Jan-Dec |

Detached bungalow with warm and friendly atmosphere, on Forth Road Bridge route, 3 miles (5kms) from city centre. Non-smoking house. Ensuite bathrooms, parking.

Cree House 77 Mayfield Road Edinburgh EH9 3AA Tel: 0131 667 2524 Fax: 0131 668 4455	COMMENDED Listed	2 Single 3 Twin 1 Double 1 Family	2 Limited ensuite 3 Pub Bath/Show	B&B per person £15.00-£25.00 Single £15.00-£25.00 Double	Open Jan-Dec

Friendly accommodation close to the University. Convenient for city centre and all tourist attractions.

Crion Guest House

33 Minto Street, Edinburgh EH9 2BT
Telephone: 0131 667 2708 Fax: 0131 662 1946

A warm friendly welcome awaits you at this family-run guest house. Fully refurbished with your comfort in mind offering outstanding Bed & Breakfast value. 3 ensuite rooms now available. Double ensuite prices from £18 to £32 max per person. Situated within 1½ miles of city centre on an excellent bus route near most tourist attractions, near University and Commonwealth Pool. For enquiries send SAE or telephone.

Crion Guest House 33 Minto Street Edinburgh EH9 2BT Tel: 0131 667 2708 Fax: 0131 662 1946	COMMENDED	1 Single 2 Twin 2 Double 1 Family	3 En Suite fac 3 Pub Bath/Show	B&B per person £19.00-£25.00 Single £18.00-£32.00 Double	Open Jan-Dec

Refurbished, friendly, family run guest house, close to Commonwealth Pool and University. On main bus route to city centre.

Mrs Doris Crook 2 Seton Place Edinburgh EH9 2JT Tel: 0131 667 6430	COMMENDED Listed	1 Twin 1 Family	2 Limited ensuite 1 Pub Bath/Show	B&B per person £18.00-£22.00 Single £18.00-£22.00 Double	Open Apr-Oct

Upper flatted villa at end of Georgian terrace in quiet residential area. Private parking and easy access to town centre.

Cruachan Guest House 53 Gilmore Place Edinburgh EH3 9NT Tel: 0131 229 6219 Fax: 0131 229 6219	COMMENDED	2 Single 1 Twin 1 Double 1 Family	1 En Suite fac 1 Limited ensuite 1 Pub Bath/Show	B&B per person £18.00-£26.00 Single £18.00-£26.00 Double Room only per person £16.00-£24.00	Open Jan-Dec

Comfortable family run accommodation close to city centre and major bus routes. Non-smoking house.

Daisy Park Guest House 41 Abercorn Terrace Joppa Edinburgh EH15 2DG Tel: 0131 669 2503 Fax: 0131 669 2503	COMMENDED	1 Single 1 Twin 1 Double 2 Family	3 En Suite fac 1 Pub Bath/Show	B&B per person £17.50-£25.00 Single £17.50-£25.00 Double	Open Jan-Dec

Family run, friendly guest house with comfortable rooms. On short bus route for city centre. Children welcome.

Dene Guest House 7 Eyre Place, off Dundas Street Edinburgh EH3 5ES Tel: 0131 556 2700 Fax: 0131 557 9876	APPROVED	3 Single 3 Twin 2 Double 2 Family	2 En Suite fac 2 Pub Bath/Show	B&B per person £19.50-£26.50 Single £19.50-£30.00 Double Room only per person £18.00-£28.50	Open Jan-Dec

Family run, centrally located guest house, close to Botanic Gardens. Georgian townhouse offering friendly service, relaxed atmosphere and hearty breakfast. Nearby restaurants, bars.

EDINBURGH – CITY, COAST AND COUNTRYSIDE

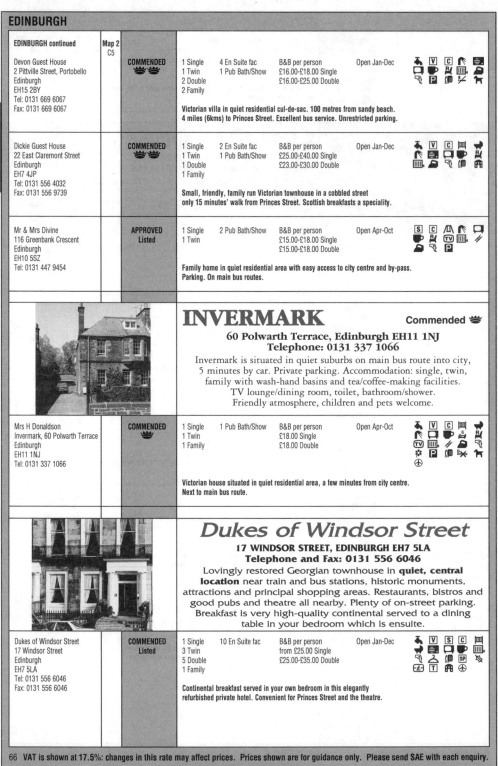

EDINBURGH

EDINBURGH – CITY, COAST AND COUNTRYSIDE

EDINBURGH continued							
Map 2 C5							

Devon Guest House
2 Pittville Street, Portobello
Edinburgh
EH15 2BY
Tel: 0131 669 6067
Fax: 0131 669 6067

COMMENDED 👑👑

1 Single · 4 En Suite fac
1 Twin · 1 Pub Bath/Show
2 Double
2 Family

B&B per person
£16.00-£18.00 Single
£16.00-£25.00 Double

Open Jan-Dec

Victorian villa in quiet residential cul-de-sac. 100 metres from sandy beach.
4 miles (6kms) to Princes Street. Excellent bus service. Unrestricted parking.

Dickie Guest House
22 East Claremont Street
Edinburgh
EH7 4JP
Tel: 0131 556 4032
Fax: 0131 556 9739

COMMENDED 👑👑

1 Single · 2 En Suite fac
1 Twin · 1 Pub Bath/Show
1 Double
1 Family

B&B per person
£25.00-£40.00 Single
£23.00-£30.00 Double

Open Jan-Dec

Small, friendly, family run Victorian townhouse in a cobbled street
only 15 minutes' walk from Princes Street. Scottish breakfasts a speciality.

Mr & Mrs Divine
116 Greenbank Crescent
Edinburgh
EH10 5SZ
Tel: 0131 447 9454

APPROVED
Listed

1 Single · 2 Pub Bath/Show
1 Twin

B&B per person
£15.00-£18.00 Single
£15.00-£18.00 Double

Open Apr-Oct

Family home in quiet residential area with easy access to city centre and by-pass.
Parking. On main bus routes.

INVERMARK

Commended 👑

60 Polwarth Terrace, Edinburgh EH11 1NJ
Telephone: 0131 337 1066

Invermark is situated in quiet suburbs on main bus route into city,
5 minutes by car. Private parking. Accommodation: single, twin,
family with wash-hand basins and tea/coffee-making facilities.
TV lounge/dining room, toilet, bathroom/shower.
Friendly atmosphere, children and pets welcome.

Mrs H Donaldson
Invermark, 60 Polwarth Terrace
Edinburgh
EH11 1NJ
Tel: 0131 337 1066

COMMENDED 👑

1 Single · 1 Pub Bath/Show
1 Twin
1 Family

B&B per person
£18.00 Single
£18.00 Double

Open Apr-Oct

Victorian house situated in quiet residential area, a few minutes from city centre.
Next to main bus route.

Dukes of Windsor Street

17 WINDSOR STREET, EDINBURGH EH7 5LA
Telephone and Fax: 0131 556 6046

Lovingly restored Georgian townhouse in **quiet, central
location** near train and bus stations, historic monuments,
attractions and principal shopping areas. Restaurants, bistros and
good pubs and theatre all nearby. Plenty of on-street parking.
Breakfast is very high-quality continental served to a dining
table in your bedroom which is ensuite.

Dukes of Windsor Street
17 Windsor Street
Edinburgh
EH7 5LA
Tel: 0131 556 6046
Fax: 0131 556 6046

COMMENDED
Listed

1 Single · 10 En Suite fac
3 Twin
5 Double
1 Family

B&B per person
from £25.00 Single
£25.00-£35.00 Double

Open Jan-Dec

Continental breakfast served in your own bedroom in this elegantly
refurbished private hotel. Convenient for Princes Street and the theatre.

---

66 VAT is shown at 17.5%: changes in this rate may affect prices. Prices shown are for guidance only. Please send SAE with each enquiry.

Dunard Guest House 16 Hartington Place Edinburgh EH10 4LE Tel: 0131 229 6848	APPROVED Listed	2 Single 2 Twin 1 Family	2 Pub Bath/Show	B&B per person £17.00-£22.50 Single £16.00-£20.00 Double	Open Jan-Dec	

Friendly guest house in residential area with easy access to city centre. Evening meal by arrangement.

Dunedin Guest House 8 Priestfield Road Edinburgh EH16 5HH Tel: 0131 668 1949	COMMENDED	1 Single 1 Twin 3 Double 2 Family	6 En Suite fac 1 Priv. NOT ensuite	B&B per person £19.00-£28.00 Single £19.00-£28.00 Double	Open Jan-Dec	

Friendly, family run guest house in residential area, close to Commonwealth Pool and bus route. 1.5 miles (2.5kms) from city centre. Parking available. Non-smoking.

Ecosse International
Commended
15 McDonald Road, Edinburgh EH7 4LX
Telephone: 0131 556 4967   Fax: 0131 556 7394

Central, luxury Guest House. Bedrooms with private bathrooms, one four-poster, TV, centrally heated, tea/coffee facilities, courtesy whisky in lounge and parking. Personally run by the owner – warm, friendly atmosphere. Central to Edinburgh Castle, Holyrood Palace, Botanic Gardens, galleries, museums and zoo. An ideal base for day trips to Loch Lomond, Gleneagles and Borders. No credit cards accepted. *(Smoking in lounge).*
A good night's sleep awaits you in our comfortable beds.

Ecosse International Guest House 15 McDonald Road Edinburgh EH7 4LX Tel: 0131 556 4967 Fax: 0131 556 7394	COMMENDED	2 Double 3 Family	5 En Suite fac	B&B per person £30.00-£45.00 Single £22.50-£28.50 Double	Open Jan-Dec Dinner 1800-2000	

Personally run with friendly atmosphere. Situated in residential area with easy access to city centre and station. Non-smoking bedrooms.

Edinburgh Thistle Guest House 10 East Hermitage Place Leith Links Edinburgh EH6 8AA Tel: 0131 554 8457/5864 Fax: 0131 554 5864	APPROVED Listed	1 Twin 1 Double 3 Family	2 En Suite fac 1 Pub Bath/Show	B&B per person £18.00-£25.00 Single £15.00-£20.00 Double Room only per person £13.00-£18.00	Open Jan-Dec Dinner 1800-1930	

Victorian, ex-sea merchant's house, overlooking park. Close to local amenities.

Ellesmere Guest House 11 Glengyle Terrace Edinburgh EH3 9LN Tel: 0131 229 4823 Fax: 0131 229 5285	HIGHLY COMMENDED	1 Single 2 Twin 2 Double 1 Family	6 En Suite fac	B&B per person £20.00-£30.00 Single £20.00-£30.00 Double	Open Jan-Dec	

Terraced house overlooking the Meadows. Quiet location within walking distance of Kings Theatre, Conference Centre and all amenities. Bus routes to city centre.

Mrs A Fairbairn The Knoll, 8 Glenlockhart Bank Edinburgh Midlothian EH14 1BL Tel: 0131 443 1710 Fax: 0131 443 1710	COMMENDED	1 Single 1 Twin 1 Double	1 Pub Bath/Show	B&B per person £20.00-£35.00 Single £20.00-£35.00 Double Room only per person £18.00-£30.00	Open Apr-Oct	

Personally run, elegant family house in quiet residential cul-de-sac. Approximately 4 miles (6 kms) from city centre, and approximately 5 miles (8kms) from airport. Non-smoking.

EDINBURGH – CITY, COAST AND COUNTRYSIDE

EDINBURGH – CITY, COAST AND COUNTRYSIDE

Ellesmere House

11 Glengyle Terrace,
EDINBURGH
EH3 9LN

Tel: 0131 229 4823   Fax: 0131 229 5285

"Your home away from home"

Ellesmere House is situated in an enviable location overlooking "Bruntsfield Links" in the centre of Edinburgh, within easy walking distance of most places of interest. The International Conference Centre, theatres and various good restaurants are very close by. Rooms are all ensuite and are tastefully furnished and decorated to a very high standard and many extras added with your comfort in mind. For honeymooners or that special anniversary there is a four-poster bed available. Start the day with our delicious full Scottish breakfast.
Prices from £20, all rooms ensuite. Excellent value and competitive prices.

Personally run by Cecilia & Tommy Leishman who extend a very warm welcome to all of their guests.

STB Highly Commended 👑👑 AA QQQQ "Selected"

VAT is shown at 17.5%: changes in this rate may affect prices.   Prices shown are for guidance only.   Please send SAE with each enquiry.

Falcon Crest

**70 South Trinity Road
Edinburgh EH5 3NX
Tel: 0131 552 5294**

A friendly welcome awaits at our family run guest house in a quiet residential Victorian terrace. Located between the Royal Botanic Gardens, Newhaven Harbour and Granton Marina. Ten minutes by frequent bus service from the city centre. Good road links. Private parking. *Evening meals and special diets by prior request.*

Falcon Crest Guest House 70 South Trinity Road Edinburgh EH5 3NX Tel: 0131 552 5294	APPROVED ♛	1 Single 2 Twin 2 Double 2 Family	2 En Suite fac 2 Pub Bath/Show	B&B per person £15.00-£22.00 Single £14.00-£20.00 Double Room only per person £12.00-£18.00	Open Jan-Dec Dinner 1730-1900 B&B + Eve. Meal £20.00-£28.00	
		Victorian terraced family home in attractive residential area, near main bus route to city centre.				
Mary & Ronald Finlay Pentland View 69 Glasgow Road Edinburgh EH12 8LL Tel: 0131 316 4712	COMMENDED Listed	1 Twin 1 Family	1 En Suite fac 1 Priv. NOT ensuite 1 Pub Bath/Show	B&B per person £20.00-£25.00 Single £15.00-£20.00 Double	Open Apr-Oct	
		Comfortable family home. Convenient for airport and all major routes. Private parking. Ground-floor accommodation. Ensuite available.				
Mrs Jane Forno 35 Newington Road Edinburgh EH9 1QR Tel: 0131 667 2839	COMMENDED Listed	1 Twin 1 Family	2 En Suite fac	B&B per person £16.00-£25.00 Double	Open Apr-Oct	
		Full of character, tastefully decorated garden flat. Conveniently located 20 minutes' walk from Princes Street. All rooms ensuite.				
Fountainhall Guest House 40 Fountainhall Road Edinburgh EH9 2LW Tel: 0131 667 2544	APPROVED ♛	1 Single 2 Twin 1 Double 3 Family	1 Limited ensuite 3 Pub Bath/Show	B&B per person £20.00-£24.00 Single Room only per person £18.00-£22.00	Open Jan-Dec	
		Victorian house in quiet residential area, 2 miles (3 kms) from city centre, with public transport nearby.				
Mr & Mrs G Fraser 7 Bellevue Place Edinburgh EH7 4BS Tel: 0131 556 5123 Fax: 0131 556 5123	COMMENDED Listed	1 Twin 1 Double 1 Family	1 Pub Bath/Show	B&B per person £17.00-£25.00 Single £17.00-£25.00 Double Room only per person £16.00-£23.00	Open Apr-Oct, Xmas/New Year	
		Personally run, refurbished terraced house. Approx 0.5 mile (1km) from East End and Princes Street.				
Galloway Guest House 22 Dean Park Crescent Edinburgh EH4 1PH Tel: 0131 332 3672	COMMENDED ♛♛♛	1 Single 3 Twin 3 Double 3 Family	6 En Suite fac 2 Pub Bath/Show	B&B per person £25.00-£45.00 Single £17.00-£25.00 Double	Open Jan-Dec	
		Friendly, family run guest house, beautifully restored and situated in a residential area of the city centre. Free street parking.				
Gifford House 103 Dalkeith Road Edinburgh EH16 5AJ Tel: 0131 667 4688	COMMENDED ♛♛	1 Single 1 Twin 2 Double 3 Family	7 En Suite fac	B&B per person £24.00-£45.00 Single £20.00-£40.00 Double Room only per person £17.00-£35.00	Open Jan-Dec	
		Situated on one of the main routes into Edinburgh. A well-appointed guest house with nearby bus service to city centre. Commonwealth Pool 300 metres.				

EDINBURGH – CITY, COAST AND COUNTRYSIDE

Details of Grading and Classification are on page vi.

Key to symbols is on back flap.

EDINBURGH

EDINBURGH continued	Map 2 C5						
Glenalmond Guest House 25 Mayfield Gardens Edinburgh EH9 2BX Tel: 0131 668 2392 Fax: 0131 668 2392		COMMENDED 👑👑	1 Twin 5 Double 1 Family	7 En Suite fac	B&B per person £20.00-£35.00 Single £18.00-£30.00 Double	Open Jan-Dec	
			Personally run guest house with private parking. On main bus routes to city centre.				
Glendale House 5 Lady Road Edinburgh EH16 5PA Tel: 0131 667 6588 Fax: 0131 667 6588		APPROVED 👑👑	2 Single 2 Twin 2 Double 2 Family	5 En Suite fac 1 Priv. NOT ensuite 3 Pub Bath/Show	B&B per person £20.00-£35.00 Single £20.00-£32.00 Double	Open Jan-Dec Dinner 1800-1900 B&B + Eve. Meal £27.00-£41.50	
			Refurbished property. Off-road parking. Situated opposite Cameron Toll. Frequent bus service to city centre.				
Glenerne Guest House 4 Hampton Terrace West Coates Edinburgh EH12 5JD Tel: 0131 337 1210 Fax: 0131 337 1210		COMMENDED 👑👑	1 Twin 2 Double	2 En Suite fac 1 Priv. NOT ensuite	B&B per person £30.00-£70.00 Single £27.50-£40.00 Double	Open Jan-Dec	
			Comfortable family home with off-street parking within walking distance of city centre. All rooms with private facilities.				
Glenesk Guest House 39 Liberton Brae Edinburgh EH16 6AG Tel: 0131 664 1529 Fax: 0131 664 1529		APPROVED Listed	2 Twin 1 Double 1 Family	1 Pub Bath/Show	B&B per person £15.00-£20.00 Double	Open Jan-Dec Dinner 1800-2000 B&B + Eve. Meal £22.50-£27.50	
			Personally run, small guest house. Convenient for bus route to city centre. Limited car parking available.				
Glenfield Guest House 21 West Mayfield Edinburgh EH9 1TQ Tel: 0131 662 9242 Fax: 0131 662 9232		COMMENDED 👑👑👑	2 Single 2 Twin 3 Double 5 Family	11 En Suite fac 1 Priv. NOT ensuite	B&B per person £23.00-£30.00 Single £23.00-£30.00 Double Room only per person £18.00-£25.00	Open Jan-Dec Dinner 1800-1900 B&B + Eve. Meal from £31.00	
			Tastefully restored, family run Georgian house. 1.5 miles (2.4kms) from city centre on main bus route.				
The Gorvic Guest House 14 Granville Terrace Edinburgh EH10 4PQ Tel: 0131 229 6565/229 0447		COMMENDED Listed	1 Twin 3 Double 4 Family	2 En Suite fac 3 Limited ensuite 2 Pub Bath/Show	B&B per person £22.00-£35.00 Single £18.00-£30.00 Double	Open Jan-Dec	
			Traditional Victorian terraced house within easy reach of Castle, Royal Mile and Princes Street. Convenient for local theatres, cinemas and restaurants.				
Mrs Alexia Graham 18 Moston Terrace Edinburgh EH9 2DE Tel: 0131 667 3466		HIGHLY COMMENDED Listed	2 Double	1 Pub Bath/Show	B&B per person £20.00-£25.00 Single £17.00-£24.00 Double	Open Apr-Oct	
			Traditionally furnished, elegant Victorian house in quiet, residential area. Convenient for main bus routes to city centre. Unrestricted parking.				

The Grange
2 MINTO STREET, EDINBURGH EH9 1RG
Telephone and Fax: 0131 667 2125

Family run guest house with warm eastern hospitality. One mile
from Princes Street. Frequent bus services. Comfortable rooms.
TV, central heating, H&C, tea/coffee facilities in all rooms.
Full ensuite facilities. Three family rooms. Walking distance to
Commonwealth Swimming Pool, Holyrood Park and Palace.
University and Royal College of Surgeons and Physicians nearby.

The Grange 2 Minto Street Edinburgh EH9 1RG Tel: 0131 667 2125 Fax: 0131 667 2125	APPROVED Listed	3 Twin 2 Double 3 Family	8 En Suite fac 1 Pub Bath/Show	B&B per person £20.00-£25.00 Single £17.00-£25.00 Double	Open Jan-Dec

Stone-built Georgian house on main A7. On bus route for the city centre
and all amenities.

Hermitage Guest House 16 East Hermitage Place Leith Links Edinburgh EH6 8AB Tel: 0131 555 4868	COMMENDED Listed	2 Twin 1 Double 2 Family	2 Pub Bath/Show	B&B per person £15.00-£20.00 Double	Open Jan-Dec

Victorian terraced villa overlooking park, offering a warm and friendly welcome.
Close to main bus route, 10 minutes from city centre.

Highfield Guest House 83 Mayfield Road Edinburgh EH9 3AE Tel: 0131 667 8717 Fax: 0131 668 3006	COMMENDED	1 Single 1 Twin 2 Double 1 Family	2 En Suite fac 1 Priv. NOT ensuite 1 Pub Bath/Show	B&B per person £15.00-£21.00 Single £15.00-£25.00 Double	Open Jan-Dec

Stone-built Victorian house offering friendly and comfortable accommodation
for non-smokers. 10 minutes from city centre on bus routes 46 and 42.

HIGHLAND PARK GUEST HOUSE
16 KILMAURS TERRACE, EDINBURGH EH16 5DR
Telephone: 0131 667 9204

Comfortable guest house situated in quiet street off
Dalkeith Road. Unrestricted parking and easy access to
City Centre. Near Holyrood Park, University and
Royal College of Surgeons.
All rooms TV, Tea/Coffee, Central Heating and H&C.

Highland Park Guest House 16 Kilmaurs Terrace Edinburgh EH16 5DR Tel: 0131 667 9204	COMMENDED	2 Single 2 Twin 2 Family	2 Pub Bath/Show	B&B per person £16.00-£21.00 Single £15.00-£21.00 Double	Open Jan-Dec

Victorian stone-built house retaining many original features in quiet residential
area. 1.5 miles (3kms) from city centre. On main bus routes.

Scottish TOURIST BOARD COMMENDED

FOR QUALITY GO GRADED

Details of Grading and Classification are on page vi.

Key to symbols is on back flap.

EDINBURGH continued	Map 2 C5

ELMVIEW

15 GLENGYLE TERRACE, EDINBURGH EH3 9LN
Telephone and Fax: 0131 228 1973

Conveniently situated in an elegant Victorian terrace 15 minutes' walk from *Edinburgh Castle* and *Princes Street*. **ELMVIEW** provides luxurious and peaceful rooms in the heart of Edinburgh.

Theatres, Universities and the *International Conference Centre* are close to hand as are some of Edinburgh's finest restaurants. You are ideally situated to explore Edinburgh on foot or by bus.

Three spacious ensuite rooms offer all the expected amenities and many thoughtful extras including direct-dial telephone and fridges.

Luxuriously equipped and furnished and maintained to a very high standard, **ELMVIEW** offers every modern comfort and convenience, yet retains its Victorian elegance.

AA QQQQQ Premier Selected   **Totally non-smoking**

Mrs Marny Hill Elmview, 15 Glengyle Terrace Edinburgh EH3 9LN Tel: 0131 228 1973 Fax: 0131 228 1973	DELUXE Listed	2 Twin 1 Double	3 En Suite fac	B&B per person £30.00-£35.00 Double	Open Apr-Oct

Comfortable Victorian terraced house in centre of Edinburgh with luxurious well-appointed rooms. 0.5 mile (1km) from Princes Street. Non-smoking.

HILLVIEW

22 Hillview, Queensferry Road, Blackhall, Edinburgh EH4 2AF
Telephone: 0131 343 2969

Elegant terraced house with easy access to historic Edinburgh 2 miles. Buses pass door. Establishment is completely non-smoking. Well furnished and good breakfast provided. Airport travel is four miles and city bypass nearby. Good centre for touring central Scotland, Trossachs, Fife, East Lothian and the Borders. Personal Scottish hospitality.

Hillview 22 Hillview Queensferry Road, Blackhall Edinburgh EH4 2AF Tel: 0131 343 2969	HIGHLY COMMENDED	2 Double 1 Family	2 En Suite fac 1 Priv. NOT ensuite	B&B per person £18.00-£26.00 Double	Open Jan-Dec

Elegant Edwardian terraced family home with easy access to the city centre.

EDINBURGH
Hopetoun Guest House

15 Mayfield Road, Edinburgh EH9 2NG   Tel: 0131 667 7691

Rhoda Mitchell is delighted to be included once again in the *Which? Books Good B&B Guide*. Hopetoun, now with private facilities, is 1½ miles south of Princes Street, in a stone-built Victorian terrace. With only three guest rooms, personal service and a warm, friendly welcome are assured. Parking.

AA QQ Recommended.   COMPLETELY NON-SMOKING

Hopetoun Guest House 15 Mayfield Road Edinburgh EH9 2NG Tel: 0131 667 7691	COMMENDED	1 Double 2 Family	1 En Suite fac 1 Priv. NOT ensuite 1 Pub Bath/Show	B&B per person £20.00-£30.00 Single £17.00-£30.00 Double	Open Jan-Dec

Completely non-smoking, small, friendly guest house on the south side of the city, 1.5 miles (2.5kms) from Princes Street.

House O'Hill Guest House 7 House O'Hill Terrace Blackhall, Edinburgh EH4 2AA Tel: 0131 332 3674 Fax: 0131 343 3446	COMMENDED 👑 👑	2 Twin 1 Double 2 Family	4 En Suite fac 1 Priv. NOT ensuite	B&B per person £25.00-£35.00 Single £17.00-£25.00 Double	Open Jan-Dec	
		Semi-detached house approx 1.5 miles (2.5kms) from West End. Convenient access to city via Queensferry Road. Parking.				
Mrs L Hume 13 Moat Street Edinburgh EH14 1PE Tel: 0131 443 8266	COMMENDED Listed	1 Twin 1 Family	1 Pub Bath/Show	B&B per person £14.00-£16.00 Single £13.00-£16.00 Double	Open Apr-Oct	
		Family house in quiet residential street. Close to main city centre bus routes.				
David & Theresa Ingram 24 Northumberland Street Edinburgh EH3 6LS Tel: 0131 556 8140 Fax: 0131 556 4423	HIGHLY COMMENDED Listed	3 Twin	2 En Suite fac 1 Limited ensuite	B&B per person £45.00 Single £35.00 Double	Open Jan-Dec	
		Georgian townhouse in heart of Edinburgh's New Town. Bedrooms with ensuite and private facilities. Fax available and individual telephones.				
International Guest House 37 Mayfield Gardens Edinburgh EH9 2BX Tel: 0131 667 2511/9833 Fax: 0131 667 1112	HIGHLY COMMENDED 👑 👑	3 Single 2 Twin 2 Double 1 Family	8 En Suite fac	B&B per person £19.00-£32.00 Single £19.00-£32.00 Double	Open Jan-Dec	
		Stone-built Victorian house in residential area with regular bus service to city centre. All rooms have private facilities. Some private parking.				
Ivy Guest House 7 Mayfield Gardens, Newington Edinburgh EH9 2AX Tel: 0131 667 3411	COMMENDED 👑 👑	2 Twin 3 Double 3 Family	6 En Suite fac 2 Priv. NOT ensuite	B&B per person £17.00-£45.00 Single £16.00-£28.00 Double Room only per person £16.00-£28.00	Open Jan-Dec	
		Victorian terraced house on convenient bus route for city centre. Recommended restaurants nearby. Handy for Commonwealth Pool. Private car-park.				
Joppa Rocks Guest House 99 Joppa Road Edinburgh EH15 2HB Tel: 0131 669 8695	COMMENDED 👑	1 Single 2 Twin 1 Family	1 En Suite fac 1 Priv. NOT ensuite 1 Pub Bath/Show	B&B per person £17.50-£18.50 Single £17.50-£18.50 Double	Open Jan-Dec	
		Situated 10 minutes' drive from Princes Street on major city centre route and easy access to city bypass. Seaviews and safe beaches close by.				
Joppa Turrets Guest House 1 Lower Joppa Edinburgh EH15 2ER Tel: 0131 669 5806 Fax: 0131 669 5190	COMMENDED 👑 👑	4 Double 1 Family	3 En Suite fac 1 Pub Bath/Show	B&B per person £15.00-£25.00 Single £14.00-£23.00 Double	Open Jan-Dec	
		Quiet and friendly, with fine sea views from every room. Close to sandy beach. Easy access to city centre. Unrestricted parking.				

EDINBURGH – CITY, COAST AND COUNTRYSIDE

BE SURE TO CHOOSE THE
SCOTTISH TOURIST BOARD'S
SIGN OF QUALITY

International Guest House

37 MAYFIELD GARDENS, EDINBURGH EH9 2BX

Telephone:
0131 667 2511

EDINBURGH

Fax:
0131 667 1112

SCOTTISH TOURIST BOARD. HIGHLY COMMENDED 👑👑. AA. QQQQ

"One of the best Guest Houses in town."

"International reputation for quality – service – comfort"

- Well-appointed bedrooms all with ensuite facilities
- Colour TVs, tea/coffee-making facilities
- Short distance from city centre

- Realistic rates from £19.00 Bed & Breakfast
- Own keys for all day access
- Warm and friendly atmosphere
- Some private parking

"All the comforts of home at a price you can afford"

VAT is shown at 17.5%: changes in this rate may affect prices. Prices shown are for guidance only. Please send SAE with each enquiry.

Kay

**30 Arboretum Place
Inverleith
Edinburgh EH3 5NZ
Telephone:
0131 332 7315**

Luxury modern home situated in a quiet residential area next to the Royal Botanic Gardens overlooking Inverleith Park. Within easy walking distance of city centre and tourist attractions. Private car parking available and near main bus routes.

Mr Andrew M Kay 30 Arboretum Place, Inverleith Edinburgh EH3 5NZ Tel: 0131 332 7315	COMMENDED Listed	3 Double	1 En Suite fac 1 Pub Bath/Show	B&B per person £16.00-£28.00 Double	Open Apr-Oct

**Modern house in quiet, residential area next to Royal Botanic Gardens.
Convenient for city centre. Private off-street parking.**

KENVIE GUEST HOUSE

16 Kilmaurs Road, Edinburgh EH16 5DA
Telephone/Fax: 0131 668 1964

Quiet and comfortable house situated in a residential area with easy access to City Centre on an excellent bus route. All rooms have tea and coffee-making facilities and TV. Central heating throughout.
A warm and friendly welcome is guaranteed.

Kenvie Guest House 16 Kilmaurs Road Edinburgh EH16 5DA Tel: 0131 668 1964 Fax: 0131 668 1964	COMMENDED	2 Twin 1 Double 2 Family	2 En Suite fac 2 Pub Bath/Show	B&B per person £19.00-£25.00 Single £18.00-£25.00 Double	Open Jan-Dec

**Personally run, situated in quiet residential area close to city centre
and on main bus routes.**

Kew Guest House 1 Kew Terrace, Murrayfield Edinburgh EH12 5JE Tel: 0131 313 0700 Fax: 0131 313 0747	HIGHLY COMMENDED	1 Single 1 Twin 2 Double 2 Family	6 En Suite fac	B&B per person £35.00-£36.00 Single £29.00-£32.50 Double	Open Jan-Dec

**Victorian terraced house situated on main Glasgow road 1 mile (2kms)
from West End with secure parking.**

Kilmaurs House 9 Kilmaurs Road Edinburgh EH16 5DA Tel: 0131 667 8315	COMMENDED	2 Twin 2 Double 1 Family	5 En Suite fac	B&B per person £23.00-£25.00 Single £21.00-£26.00 Double	Open Jan-Dec

**Family run guest house in quiet residential area close to Commonwealth Pool
and only ten minutes by bus from city centre.**

Kingsley Guest House 30 Craigmillar Park Edinburgh EH16 5PS Tel: 0131 667 8439 Fax: 0131 667 8439	COMMENDED	2 Twin 1 Double 3 Family	4 En Suite fac 1 Priv. NOT ensuite 2 Pub Bath/Show	B&B per person £20.00-£25.00 Single £16.00-£23.00 Double	Open Jan-Dec

**Friendly, comfortable and family run Victorian villa with own private car park.
Excellent bus service for all major attractions in the city.**

EDINBURGH – CITY, COAST AND COUNTRYSIDE

EDINBURGH – CITY, COAST AND COUNTRYSIDE

EDINBURGH continued	Map 2 C5						
Kingsview Guest House 28 Gilmore Place Edinburgh EH3 9NQ Tel: 0131 229 8004 Fax: 0131 229 8004	COMMENDED	1 Single 2 Twin 2 Double 4 Family	3 En Suite fac 1 Limited ensuite 1 Pub Bath/Show	B&B per person £19.00-£25.00 Single £16.00-£28.00 Double	Open Jan-Dec	
		Family run, city centre guest house conveniently situated near the Kings Theatre. Close to all main bus routes.					
Kingsway Guest House 5 East Mayfield Edinburgh EH9 1SD Tel: 0131 667 5029 Fax: 0131 662 4635	COMMENDED Listed	1 Single 2 Twin 2 Double 2 Family	1 En Suite fac 2 Pub Bath/Show	B&B per person £18.00-£25.00 Single £16.00-£25.00 Double	Open Jan-Dec	
		Family run guest house in Victorian terrace in quiet residential area near bus routes and 2 miles (3 kms) from Princes Street. Private parking.					

Kirkland Bed and Breakfast

6 Dean Park Crescent, Edinburgh EH4 1PN
Telephone: 0131 332 5017

Warm friendly Victorian house on two floors, only 10 minutes' walk from West End of Princes Street. Recently refurbished and offering interesting local shops and restaurants. Traditional Scottish breakfast is available and we are happy to cater for any special needs you may have.

Mrs M Kirkland Kirkland Bed & Breakfast 6 Dean Park Crescent Edinburgh EH4 1PN Tel: 0131 332 5017	COMMENDED Listed	1 Single 1 Twin 2 Double 1 Family	1 En Suite fac 2 Pub Bath/Show	B&B per person £16.00-£22.00 Single £15.00-£25.00 Double	Open Apr-Oct	
		Centrally situated terraced house with convenient access to city centre, West End and Queensferry Road.					
Kirklea Guest House 11 Harrison Road Edinburgh EH11 1EG Tel: 0131 337 1129 Fax: 0131 337 1129	COMMENDED	2 Single 1 Twin 2 Double 1 Family	1 En Suite fac 1 Limited ensuite 2 Pub Bath/Show	B&B per person £20.00-£25.00 Single £18.00-£25.00 Double	Open Jan-Dec	
		A family run guest house in Victorian terrace convenient for bus routes to city centre and all attractions. 1.25 miles (2kms) from Princes Street.					
Kirtle Guest House 8 Minto Street Edinburgh EH9 1RG Tel: 0131 667 2813 (office)/ 5353 (guests)	COMMENDED	3 Double 4 Family	4 En Suite fac 3 Limited ensuite 2 Pub Bath/Show	B&B per person £36.00-£48.00 Single £18.00-£24.00 Double	Open Jan-Dec	
		On main bus routes for city centre, 1 mile (2kms). Some private car parking available. Close to Commonwealth Pool.					
Lauderville Guest House 52 Mayfield Road Edinburgh EH9 2NH Tel: 0131 667 7788/4005 Fax: 0131 667 7788	HIGHLY COMMENDED	1 Twin 2 Double 1 Family	3 En Suite fac 1 Limited ensuite	B&B per person £20.00-£33.00 Double	Open Jan-Dec	
		The Marriots warmly welcome visitors to Edinburgh. Comfortable surroundings, substantial breakfasts. Centrally located for attractions.					

Lindsay Guest House 108 Polwarth Terrace Edinburgh EH11 1NN Tel: 0131 337 1580 Fax: 0131 337 9174	**COMMENDED** Listed	2 Single 3 Twin 2 Double 1 Family	3 En Suite fac 2 Pub Bath/Show	B&B per person £22.50-£35.00 Single £22.50-£27.50 Double	Open Jan-Dec
Semi-detached sandstone house in residential area on bus route to city centre. 1.5 miles (3 kms) from Princes Street. Car parking and TV in all bedrooms.					
Mrs Valerie Livingstone Ceol-na-Mara 50 Paisley Crescent Edinburgh EH8 7JQ Tel: 0131 661 6337	**COMMENDED** Listed	1 Twin 2 Double	1 Limited ensuite 1 Pub Bath/Show	B&B per person £16.00-£19.00 Double	Open Apr-Oct
Modern terraced villa in quiet area adjacent to Arthur's Seat, with fine views over Firth of Forth. Near main bus route to city centre. No smoking.					
Lorne Villa Guest House 9 East Mayfield Edinburgh EH9 1SD Tel: 0131 667 7159 Fax: 0131 667 7159	**COMMENDED** Listed	1 Single 2 Double 4 Family	3 En Suite fac 1 Priv. NOT ensuite 2 Pub Bath/Show	B&B per person £18.00-£28.00 Single £18.00-£28.00 Double	Open Jan-Dec
Personally run guest house conveniently situated for city centre bus route with off-street parking.					
Wilma Lusty 36 Barony Terrace Edinburgh EH12 8RE Tel: 0131 334 2259	**COMMENDED**	1 Twin 1 Family	1 En Suite fac 1 Priv. NOT ensuite 1 Pub Bath/Show	B&B per person £17.00-£22.00 Single £16.00-£22.00 Double Room only per person £15.00-£20.00	Open Apr-Oct
Detached bungalow in quiet residential area on west side of city. Convenient for airport, Edinburgh Zoo and bus routes to city centre. Unrestricted parking.					
Dorothy M G McKay 41 Corstorphine Bank Drive Edinburgh EH12 8RH Tel: 0131 334 4100	**COMMENDED** Listed	1 Twin 1 Double	1 Priv. NOT ensuite 2 Pub Bath/Show	B&B per person £16.00-£18.00 Single £15.00-£17.00 Double	Open Apr-Oct
Detached house in quiet residential area. About 3 miles (5kms) from city centre and 4 miles (6kms) from airport. 500 yards from bus stop.					
Mrs E M MacKinnon 5 Bangholm Terrace Edinburgh EH3 5QN Tel: 0131 552 3320	**COMMENDED** Listed	1 Twin 1 Double	1 Pub Bath/Show	B&B per person £30.00 Single £16.50-£17.50 Double	Open Apr-Oct Dinner 1800-1930
Personally run, comfortable family tenement home, close to Botanical Gardens. Convenient for city centre.					
Mrs S J McLennan Airdenair, 29 Kilmaurs Road Edinburgh EH16 5DB Tel: 0131 668 2336	**APPROVED**	2 Twin 1 Double	1 Pub Bath/Show	B&B per person £16.00-£20.00 Single £16.00-£18.00 Double	Open Apr-Oct
Double upper flatted villa. Quiet residential area on south side of city. Near Royal Commonwealth Pool and Holyrood Park. Good bus routes to centre.					

SCOTTISH TOURIST BOARD
QUALITY COMMENDATIONS ARE:

Deluxe – An EXCELLENT quality standard
Highly Commended – A VERY GOOD quality standard
Commended – A GOOD quality standard
Approved – An ADEQUATE quality standard

EDINBURGH continued	Map 2 C5						
Maple Leaf Guest House 23 Pilrig Street Edinburgh EH6 5AN Tel: 0131 554 7692 Fax: 0131 554 7692	COMMENDED	2 Single 2 Twin 2 Double 3 Family	5 En Suite fac 1 Limited ensuite 2 Pub Bath/Show	B&B per person from £20.00 Single from £16.00 Double	Open Jan-Dec Dinner 1800-1830 B&B + Eve. Meal from £27.50		

Georgian, terraced house, conveniently situated 5 minutes from town centre. A good Scottish welcome here. French spoken.

| Marrakech Guest House 30 London Street Edinburgh EH3 6NA Tel: 0131 556 4444/7293 Fax: 0131 557 3615 | COMMENDED | 2 Single 3 Twin 4 Double 2 Family | 9 En Suite fac 2 Pub Bath/Show | B&B per person £20.00-£30.00 Single £20.00-£30.00 Double | Open Jan-Dec Dinner 1800-2200 B&B + Eve. Meal £25.00-£40.00 | | |

Family run in New Town. Close to the city centre with its own restaurant serving North African cuisine and featuring many home-made specialities.

| Sheena M Marshall Sutherland House 16 Esslemont Road Edinburgh EH16 5PX Tel: 0131 667 6626/ 0831 185792 (mobile) Fax: 0131 667 6626 | COMMENDED | 2 Double 1 Family | 3 En Suite fac | B&B per person £28.50-£30.00 Single £25.00-£30.00 Double | Open Jan-Dec | | |

A Victorian stone-built house with some off-road parking. Fully refurbished to a high standard, all rooms have ensuite or private facilities. Main bus routes to city centre nearby.

The Meadows Guest House

Terraced flat in quiet location overlooking park. Spacious rooms with colour TV, hospitality trays. Most rooms ensuite. Scottish Tourist Board 1 Crown Commended. Amex, Mastercard, Access and Visa accepted. Very central so get metered car parking by day.

Jon Stuart, 17 Glengyle Terrace, Edinburgh EH3 9LN Telephone: 0131 229 9559 Fax: 0131 229 2226.

| The Meadows Guest House 17 Glengyle Terrace, Bruntsfield Edinburgh EH3 9LN Tel: 0131 229 9559 Fax: 0131 229 2226 | COMMENDED | 1 Single 1 Twin 1 Double 3 Family | 4 En Suite fac 1 Pub Bath/Show | B&B per person from £26.00 Single £26.00-£32.00 Double | Open Jan-Dec | | |

Quietly situated terraced house overlooking Bruntsfield Links. Convenient for theatre and shops. Family run.

| Mrs Elizabeth Melville 30 East Preston Street Edinburgh EH8 9QB Tel: 0131 668 1862 | COMMENDED Listed | 1 Single 1 Twin 1 Double | 1 Pub Bath/Show | B&B per person £15.00-£18.00 Single £15.00-£18.00 Double | Open Apr-Oct | | |

Ground-floor Victorian flat, 1 mile (2kms) from Princes Street and our city's historical attractions.

Scotland for Golf . . .

Find out more about golf in Scotland. There's more to it than just the championship courses so get in touch with us now for information on the hidden gems of Scotland.

Write to: **Information Unit, Scottish Tourist Board, 23 Ravelston Terrace, Edinburgh EH4 3EU or call: 0131-332 2433**

Menzies Guest House
33 Leamington Terrace, Edinburgh EH10 4JS
Telephone and Fax: 0131 229 4629

Small family run guest house situated in the heart of Edinburgh, 10 minutes' walk to Princes Street, Edinburgh Castle, King's Theatre and all main attractions. Central heating, colour TV, tea/coffee-making facilities. Some rooms ensuite. Friendly service and a warm welcome assured. Private parking. *Prices from £13.30 per person.*

Menzies Guest House 33 Leamington Terrace Edinburgh EH10 4JS Tel: 0131 229 4629 Fax: 0131 229 4629	APPROVED	1 Twin 4 Double 1 Family	2 En Suite fac 1 Limited ensuite 2 Pub Bath/Show	B&B per person £13.30-£27.00 Single £13.30-£27.00 Double	Open Jan-Dec

Situated in residential area near Bruntsfield Links and close to main bus route to city centre. Private parking. (Approx. ½ - 1 mile Princes Street and West End.)

Mrs F M Mickel Newington Cottage 15 Blacket Place Edinburgh EH9 1RJ Tel: 0131 668 1935 Fax: 0131 668 1935	DELUXE	2 Double	2 En Suite fac	B&B per person £50.00-£60.00 Single £40.00-£50.00 Double	Open Apr-Oct

Elegant Georgian cottage in unique conservation area. Very close to the city centre and main busy bus routes.

Mrs Maureen Miller 5 Dean Park Crescent Edinburgh EH4 1PN Tel: 0131 332 4620	COMMENDED Listed	1 Twin 2 Double	1 Pub Bath/Show	B&B per person £19.00-£25.00 Double	Open Jun-Sep

Completely refurbished, personally run Victorian terraced house. Approximately 1 mile (2kms) to West End, Princes Street and city centre.

Milton House 24 Duddingston Crescent Edinburgh EH15 3AT Tel: 0131 669 4072	COMMENDED	1 Twin 3 Double	2 En Suite fac 2 Pub Bath/Show	B&B per person £18.00-£22.00 Single £16.00-£20.00 Double	Open Jan-Dec

Friendly family atmosphere with off-street parking and easy access to the city centre. Adjacent to 9-hole golf course.

Mrs N Mitchell 19 Meadowplace Road Edinburgh EH12 7UJ Tel: 0131 334 8483	COMMENDED	1 Twin 1 Family	2 Pub Bath/Show	B&B per person £14.00-£16.00 Double	Open Apr-Oct

On the west side of the city, detached bungalow offering ground-floor accommodation and off-street parking.

Mrs Margaret Moore Moores, 44B Stevenson Drive Edinburgh EH11 3DJ Tel: 0131 443 9370	COMMENDED Listed	1 Single 1 Twin	2 En Suite fac	B&B per person £16.00-£18.00 Single £16.00-£18.00 Double	Open May-Sep

Comfortable, well furnished personally run bed and breakfast. Unrestricted parking. Close to major bus routes to city centre. Ensuite rooms.

EDINBURGH – CITY, COAST AND COUNTRYSIDE

EDINBURGH continued	Map 2 C5

Murrayfield Park Guest House

89 Corstorphine Road, Edinburgh EH12 5QE
Tel: 0131 337 5370   Fax: 0131 337 3772

A warm and friendly welcome awaits you at this extremely comfortable family run guest house, which is situated in a quiet residential area, close to local golf clubs, yet only five minutes to city centre by bus. Our rooms are tastefully decorated and have ensuite facilities, private car parking, central heating, TV and tea and coffee making facilities. According to our previous guests who have signed our visitors' book, everyone found us very comfortable and recommended us to their family and friends. Many have returned time and time again and Tom and Linda always look forward to seeing them.

AA LISTED QQQ   COMMENDED

Murrayfield Park Guest House 89 Corstorphine Road Murrayfield Edinburgh EH12 5QE Tel: 0131 337 5370 Fax: 0131 337 3772	COMMENDED	1 Single 4 Twin 1 Double	5 En Suite fac 1 Priv. NOT ensuite 1 Pub Bath/Show	B&B per person £20.00-£27.00 Single £22.00-£27.00 Double	Open Jan-Dec

5 minutes by bus from the city centre, this location is ideal for enjoying the attractions of Edinburgh. Near to airport. Private parking.

Newington Guest House 18 Newington Road Edinburgh EH9 1QS Tel: 0131 667 3356 Fax: 0131 667 8307	COMMENDED	1 Single 2 Twin 3 Double 2 Family	5 En Suite fac 3 Limited ensuite 1 Pub Bath/Show	B&B per person £26.00-£30.00 Single £20.00-£30.00 Double Room only per person £18.50-£28.50	Open Jan-Dec

Interestingly furnished Victorian house on main road into city from South. Easy access to centre. Most rooms double-glazed.

Parklands Guest House 20 Mayfield Gardens Edinburgh EH9 2BZ Tel: 0131 667 7184 Fax: 0131 667 2011	COMMENDED	2 Twin 3 Double 1 Family	5 En Suite fac 1 Priv. NOT ensuite	B&B per person £19.00-£28.00 Double Room only per person £17.00-£26.00	Open Jan-Dec

Look forward to a warm welcome at this late Victorian house with fine woodwork and ceilings, situated on the south side. On main bus routes to city centre.

Park View Villa Guest House 254 Ferry Road Edinburgh EH5 3AN Tel: 0131 552 3456	COMMENDED	2 Twin 2 Double 3 Family	4 En Suite fac 2 Pub Bath/Show	B&B per person £20.00-£36.00 Single £15.00-£20.00 Double	Open Jan-Dec

Victorian villa retaining original woodwork and enjoying panoramic views of the city skyline.

WELCOME

Whenever you are in Scotland, you can be sure of a warm welcome at your nearest Tourist Information Centre.

For guide books, maps, souvenirs, our Centres provide a service second to none – many now offer bureau-de-change facilities. And, of course, Tourist Information Centres offer free, expert advice on what to see and do, route-planning and accommodation for everyone – visitors and residents alike!

Pollock Halls of Residence
University of Edinburgh
18 Holyrood Park Road, Edinburgh EH16 5AY
Tel: 0131 667 0662   **Fax: 0131 662 9479**

Great value rooms in our properties within minutes of the Old Town and overlooking Holyrood Park. Excellent quality catering at nearby John McIntyre Centre. New en-suite as well as modern single rooms with wash basins only. *Send for our free colour brochure today.*

Pollock Halls of Residence 18 Holyrood Park Road Edinburgh EH16 5AY Tel: 0131 667 0662 Fax: 0131 662 9479	COMMENDED 👑👑👑	1153 Single 475 En Suite fac 122 Double 130 Pub Bath/Show	B&B per person £23.44-£46.00 Single £31.73-£33.00 Double	Open Mar-Oct, Jun Dinner 1800-1900 B&B + Eve. Meal £31.38-£53.93	
		On campus in Holyrood Park beside Arthur's Seat. Close to Royal Commonwealth Pool and well sited for city centre. Conference and meeting facilities.			
Mr & Mrs G Pretsell Colligan, 40 Drum Brae North Edinburgh EH4 8AZ Tel: 0131 339 6811	COMMENDED 👑	1 Twin 1 Pub Bath/Show 1 Double	B&B per person £20.00-£22.00 Single £16.00-£19.00 Double Room only per person £12.00-£14.00	Open Apr-Oct	
		Personally run Bed and Breakfast. Close to airport and main bus route to city centre. Off-road parking.			
Mrs M Rooney Edinburgh House 11 McDonald Road Edinburgh EH7 4LX Tel: 0131 556 3434	COMMENDED 👑👑👑	1 Twin 3 En Suite fac 1 Double 2 Pub Bath/Show 1 Family	B&B per person £20.00-£34.00 Double Room only per person £18.00-£30.00	Open Apr-Oct Dinner 1800-1900	
		Personally run tenement house, approximately 0.5 mile (0.8km) from Princes Street.			
Roselea House 11 Mayfield Road Edinburgh EH9 2NG Tel: 0131 667 6115 Fax: 0131 667 3556	HIGHLY COMMENDED 👑👑	1 Single 5 En Suite fac 2 Twin 2 Priv. NOT ensuite 3 Double 1 Family	B&B per person £27.00-£37.00 Single £22.00-£35.00 Double	Open Jan-Dec	
		A warm welcome at personally run guest house close to city centre on main bus route. Ideal touring base.			
Rosevale House 15 Kilmaurs Road Edinburgh EH16 5DA Tel: 0131 667 4781	APPROVED Listed	2 Twin 5 En Suite fac 2 Double 1 Family	B&B per person £18.00-£25.00 Single £18.00-£25.00 Double Room only per person £16.00-£22.00	Open Jan-Dec	
		In quiet residential area near Commonwealth Pool, with nearby transport connections to city centre. All rooms ensuite.			
Angela Ross 3a Clarence Street Edinburgh EH3 5AE Tel: 0131 557 9368	COMMENDED Listed	1 Twin 1 Pub Bath/Show 1 Double	B&B per person £13.00-£17.00 Single £13.00-£17.00 Double Room only per person £12.00-£17.00	Open Apr-Oct	
		Garden flat in Georgian terrace in New Town. Central location yet in quiet area.			
Mr & Mrs Ross 33 Silverknowes Crescent Edinburgh EH4 5JD Tel: 0131 336 5242	COMMENDED Listed	1 Twin 1 En Suite fac 1 Double 1 Pub Bath/Show	B&B per person £17.00-£18.00 Double	Open Jan-Dec	
		Friendly welcome at this Scandinavian-style bungalow in quiet residential area. Private parking. Non-smoking.			

EDINBURGH – CITY, COAST AND COUNTRYSIDE

EDINBURGH

EDINBURGH – CITY, COAST AND COUNTRYSIDE

EDINBURGH continued

Map 2 C5

Mrs M K Rothwell
The Limes, 4 Corbiehill Road
Edinburgh
EH4 5EF
Tel: 0131 336 2881

COMMENDED
Listed

2 Single
1 Family

1 Pub Bath/Show

B&B per person
£16.00–£26.00 Single
£16.00–£26.00 Double
Room only per person
£16.00–£26.00

Open Jan-Dec

Detached house set in pleasant garden in quiet residential area,
yet only 10 minutes' drive and next to bus routes to city centre. Parking.

ROWAN GUEST HOUSE

13 GLENORCHY TERRACE, EDINBURGH EH9 2DQ
Telephone and Fax: 0131 667 2463

Elegant Victorian house with comfortable well-equipped bedrooms in attractive, leafy area only ten minutes by bus from centre. Within easy reach of the Castle, Royal Mile, University and a selection of restaurants. Our breakfast, including traditional porridge and freshly baked scones, will keep you going until dinner! Parking.

Rowan Guest House
13 Glenorchy Terrace
Edinburgh
EH9 2DQ
Tel: 0131 667 2463
Fax: 0131 667 2463

COMMENDED

2 Single
2 Twin
3 Double
2 Family

2 En Suite fac
2 Pub Bath/Show

B&B per person
£19.00–£23.00 Single
£19.00–£26.00 Double

Open Jan-Dec

Victorian townhouse in quiet residential area with
easy access to city centre and all amenities.

Roxzannah
36 Minto Street
Edinburgh
EH9 2BS
Tel: 0131 667 8933

COMMENDED

1 Twin
1 Double
2 Family

4 En Suite fac

B&B per person
£25.00–£40.00 Single
£17.00–£26.00 Double
Room only per person
£14.00–£20.00

Open Jan-Dec

B Listed, Georgian villa, situated 5 minutes from city centre.
Ideal location for all amenities and attractions. Parking facility.

St Bernards Guest House
22 St Bernards Crescent
Edinburgh
EH4 1NS
Tel: 0131 332 2339
Fax: 0131 332 8842

COMMENDED

1 Single
4 Twin
3 Double

4 En Suite fac
2 Pub Bath/Show

B&B per person
£20.00–£30.00 Single
£20.00–£30.00 Double

Open Jan-Dec

Elegant terraced house in Georgian New Town area of the city.
Convenient for Princes Street. Many excellent restaurants within walking distance.

St Conans Guest House
30 Minto Street
Edinburgh
EH9 1SB
Tel: 0131 667 8393

APPROVED

2 Twin
3 Double
2 Family

5 En Suite fac
2 Pub Bath/Show

B&B per person
£18.00–£26.00 Single
£16.00–£25.00 Double

Open Jan-Dec

Spacious guest house on main A7, close to the city centre and all amenities.

St Margaret's Guest House
18 Craigmillar Park
Edinburgh
EH16 5PS
Tel: 0131 667 2202
Fax: 0131 667 2202

COMMENDED

3 Twin
3 Double
2 Family

4 En Suite fac
1 Priv. NOT ensuite
2 Pub Bath/Show

B&B per person
£20.00–£28.00 Single
£16.00–£26.00 Double

Open Jan-Dec

Well-appointed Victorian house with spacious lounge and thoughtfully decorated
bedrooms. Many additional features for guests' comfort. Private car park.

---

82   VAT is shown at 17.5%: changes in this rate may affect prices.   Prices shown are for guidance only.   Please send SAE with each enquiry.

"The Salisbury"

45 SALISBURY ROAD, EDINBURGH EH16 5AA
TELEPHONE/FAX: 0131 667 1264

Enjoy real Scottish hospitality in the comfort of this Georgian house, quietly situated yet only two minutes' walk from main bus routes to City Centre. Comfortable, centrally-heated bedrooms, all with private facilities, colour TV, tea/coffee-making etc. Convenient for bus/railway stations. Private car park.
We will be delighted to assist with arranging local tours and activities.
AA/RAC ACCLAIMED.
Contact: **Mr and Mrs William Wright.**

Salisbury Guest House 45 Salisbury Road Edinburgh EH16 5AA Tel: 0131 667 1264 Fax: 0131 667 1264	COMMENDED	2 Single 4 Twin 3 Double 3 Family	9 En Suite fac 3 Priv. NOT ensuite	B&B per person £24.00-£30.00 Single £20.00-£26.00 Double	Open Jan-Dec

Georgian Listed building in quiet conservation area, 1 mile (2kms) from city centre.
Ensuite and private facilities. Private car park. Non-smoking house.

'33 Colinton Road'

33 COLINTON ROAD, EDINBURGH EH10 5DR
Telephone: 0131 447 8080

'33 Colinton Road' is a Victorian terraced, 2 crown commended friendly family home. Conveniently situated for all amenities and within walking distance of the city centre. On major bus routes. All rooms non-smoking with private facilities. Diets catered for. Children welcome. Open March-October, other times by arrangement.

Mrs J Sandeman 33 Colinton Road Edinburgh EH10 5DR Tel: 0131 447 8080	COMMENDED	1 Single 1 Twin 1 Double	2 En Suite fac 1 Priv. NOT ensuite	B&B per person £30.00-£38.00 Single £22.00-£28.00 Double	Open May-Sep

Victorian terraced house within easy reach of city centre. Warm welcome
and relaxed family atmosphere. Unrestricted parking. Non-smoking.

Sandilands House

25 QUEENSFERRY ROAD, EDINBURGH EH4 3HB
Telephone: 0131 332 2057

Superbly situated only 5 minutes from city centre by bus for exploration of Scotland's capital. Furnished to a high standard with colour TVs, tea-making facilities, hair dryers, all rooms have ensuite facilities. Includes full Scottish breakfast. Special diets and evening meals on request. Near Murrayfield Rugby Stadium. Children under 12 years 1/2 price sharing parents' room. Car parking on-site. *Contact: Mrs Maureen Sandilands.*

Mrs Sandilands 25 Queensferry Road Edinburgh EH4 3HB Tel: 0131 332 2057 Fax: 0131 332 2057	COMMENDED	1 Twin 1 Double 1 Family	3 En Suite fac	B&B per person £25.00-£40.00 Single £19.00-£27.00 Double	Open Apr-Oct Dinner 1800-1900 B&B + Eve. Meal £29.00-£50.00

Personally run family house with convenient access to West End and City Centre.
Private parking.

EDINBURGH – CITY, COAST AND COUNTRYSIDE

EDINBURGH continued	Map 2 C5						
Shalimar Guest House 20 Newington Road Edinburgh EH9 1QS Tel: 0131 667 2827/0789	APPROVED	1 Single 3 Twin 2 Double 3 Family	5 En Suite fac 3 Limited ensuite 3 Pub Bath/Show	B&B per person £20.00-£22.50 Single £22.00-£22.50 Double	Open Jan-Dec		

Family run guest house under 1 mile (2 kms) from city centre.
Vegetarian breakfasts available.

Sharon Guest House
1 KILMAURS TERRACE, EDINBURGH EH16 5BZ
Tel: 0131 667 2002 Fax: 0131 316 4755

Quiet, semi-detached Victorian house in residential area just off A7 (pre-1992 A68) and only 5 minutes by public transport to city centre. Close to Commonwealth Swimming Pool and Royal College of Surgeons.

OFF-STREET PARKING with access all day.

House completely refurbished recently to a high standard. H&C, central heating, shaver point, tea/coffee facilities and colour TV in all rooms.

LARGE traditional Scottish breakfast.
Menu available and special diets catered for.
See symbols below for additional facilities.

| Sharon Guest House
1 Kilmaurs Terrace
Edinburgh
EH16 5BZ
Tel: 0131 667 2002
Fax: 0131 316 4755 | COMMENDED
Listed | 2 Single
1 Twin
3 Double
3 Family | 2 Pub Bath/Show | B&B per person
£16.00-£24.00 Single
£14.00-£22.00 Double | Open Jan-Dec | | |

Victorian house in residential area but near bus routes for city centre.

| Sherwood Guest House
42 Minto Street
Edinburgh
EH9 2BR
Tel: 0131 667 1200 | COMMENDED | 2 Twin
2 Double
2 Family | 5 En Suite fac
1 Priv. NOT ensuite | B&B per person
£18.00-£32.00 Double | Open Jan-Dec | | |

Stone-built Georgian terraced house in residential area of city.
On main bus route, 1.5 miles (2.5kms) to city centre. Limited parking.

Sibbet House
26 Northumberland Street, Edinburgh EH3 6LS
Telephone: 0131 556 1078 Fax: 0131 557 9445

Sibbet House is situated in the middle of Edinburgh's 18th century New Town and is an elegant, yet comfortable Georgian family home having guest facilities. However, the 20th Century has been admitted – with central heating, direct-dial telephones, cable TV and ensuite bathrooms. Shopping, restaurants nearby. Owner plays bagpipes. Parking available.

| Mrs Aurora Sibbet
Sibbet House
26 Northumberland Street
Edinburgh
EH3 6LS
Tel: 0131 556 1078
Fax: 0131 557 9445 | DELUXE | 1 Twin
2 Double
1 Family | 3 En Suite fac
1 Priv. NOT ensuite | B&B per person
£30.00-£40.00 Double | Open Apr-Oct
Dinner 1800-1930
B&B + Eve. Meal
£25.00 | | |

Georgian townhouse of considerable character built in 1809 and furnished
with antiques. Bagpipes played on request. 5 minutes' walk from Princes Street.

Mrs Anne K C Simpson The Birches 419 Queensferry Road Edinburgh EH4 7NB Tel: 0131 336 4790	**COMMENDED** Listed	1 Single 1 Twin 1 Double	2 Pub Bath/Show	B&B per person £18.00–£20.00 Single £18.00–£20.00 Double Room only per person £18.00–£20.00	Open Apr-Sep, Xmas/New Year	
		Spacious house on busy Queensferry Road with easy access to all routes and airport. Private parking.				

LANSDOWNE
Commended

1 Wester Coates Road, Edinburgh EH12 5LU
Telephone: 0131 337 5002 *Proprietor:* **Mrs R. Sinclair**

Pleasantly situated villa in attractive garden in a quiet residential area near West End of Princes Street. Very convenient for buses, stations, airport. Private parking. All rooms have wash-hand basins, electric blankets, radio and central heating – one room on ground floor. Spacious and comfortable guests' lounge.
You are assured of a warm welcome.

Mrs R Sinclair Lansdowne 1 Wester Coates Road Edinburgh EH12 5LU Tel: 0131 337 5002	**COMMENDED**	1 Single 1 Double 1 Family	2 Pub Bath/Show	B&B per person £18.00–£25.00 Single £18.00–£24.00 Double	Open Easter-Oct	
		Detached villa in pleasant garden setting in quiet residential area near west end of city. Close to main bus routes, convenient for station and airport.				
Six Mary's Place Guest House 6 Mary's Place Edinburgh EH4 1JD Tel: 0131 332 8965	**COMMENDED**	3 Single 2 Twin 3 Double	2 En Suite fac 2 Pub Bath/Show	B&B per person £25.00–£30.00 Single £25.00–£30.00 Double	Open 10 Jan-Dec Dinner 1800-2130 B&B + Eve. Meal £34.50–£39.50	
		Restored Georgian townhouse in central location offering vegetarian cuisine and a restful homely atmosphere.				
Mrs Elizabeth Smith 14 Lennel Avenue Edinburgh EH12 6DW Tel: 0131 337 1979	**HIGHLY COMMENDED** Listed	2 Twin 1 Double	2 Pub Bath/Show	B&B per person £25.00–£30.00 Single £18.00–£24.00 Double	Open Apr-Oct	
		Personally run, beautiful house, quietly situated in residential area. Approx. 1.5 miles (3 kms) to West End and Princes Street. Unrestricted parking.				
Mrs Sommerville 7 Kilmaurs Road Edinburgh EH16 5DA Tel: 0131 667 8636	**COMMENDED** Listed	1 Twin 2 Family	1 Pub Bath/Show	B&B per person £16.00–£18.00 Double	Open Apr-Oct	
		Family run guest house in quiet residential area. Convenient for bus routes to city centre. French spoken.				
Sonas Guest House 3 East Mayfield Edinburgh EH9 1SD Tel: 0131 667 2781 Fax: 0131 667 0454	**COMMENDED**	1 Single 2 Twin 4 Double 1 Family	8 En Suite fac	B&B per person £25.00–£45.00 Single £20.00–£32.50 Double	Open Jan-Dec	
		Terraced house situated on south side of city, with private parking. Convenient bus routes to centre and all amenities.				
Southdown Guest House 20 Craigmillar Park Edinburgh EH16 5PS Tel: 0131 667 2410	**COMMENDED**	2 Twin 2 Double 2 Family	4 En Suite fac 2 Limited ensuite 2 Pub Bath/Show	B&B per person £25.00–£40.00 Single £18.00–£29.50 Double	Open Jan-Nov incl New Year	
		Victorian terraced house in residential area on main A701 road, with many bus routes to city centre. Friendly and family run. Private car park. Satellite TV.				

Details of Grading and Classification are on page vi. Key to symbols is on back flap. 85

EDINBURGH – CITY, COAST AND COUNTRYSIDE

EDINBURGH – CITY, COAST AND COUNTRYSIDE

EDINBURGH continued	Map 2 C5						
A Stark 17 McDonald Road Edinburgh Midlothian EH7 4LX Tel: 0131 556 3709	COMMENDED	1 Twin 1 Double 1 Family	3 En Suite fac	B&B per person £19.00-£28.50 Double	Open Apr-Oct		
Centrally located, personally run, terraced house 0.5 mile (1 km) to Princes St. All ensuite. Unrestricted parking.							
Straven Guest House 3 Brunstane Road North Edinburgh EH15 2DL Tel: 0131 669 5580	COMMENDED	1 Single 1 Twin 2 Double 3 Family	7 En Suite fac 1 Pub Bath/Show	B&B per person £18.00-£32.00 Single £18.00-£30.00 Double	Open Jan-Dec		
Semi-detached Victorian villa in a quiet residential area just off the beach in Joppa. 3 miles (5kms) from Edinburgh city centre. Close to frequent bus service.							
Mrs Gloria Stuart 20 London Street Edinburgh EH3 6NA Tel: 0131 557 0216 Fax: 0131 556 6445	HIGHLY COMMENDED	1 Twin 1 Double	2 En Suite fac	B&B per person £25.00-£35.00 Double	Open Apr-Oct		
Centrally located in the heart of Edinburgh. Beautifully appointed house. Luxurious bedrooms all ensuite containing many thoughtful extras.							
Sylvern Guest House 22 West Mayfield Edinburgh EH9 1TQ Tel: 0131 667 1241	APPROVED Listed	1 Twin 3 Double 2 Family	4 En Suite fac 2 Pub Bath/Show	B&B per person £25.00-£35.00 Single £18.00-£24.00 Double	Open Jan-Dec		
Detached Victorian house in residential area. Private parking and convenient for main bus routes. Four rooms ensuite.							
Tania Guest House 19 Minto Street Edinburgh EH9 1RQ Tel: 0131 667 4144	APPROVED Listed	1 Single 1 Twin 1 Double 3 Family	1 En Suite fac 1 Pub Bath/Show	B&B per person £17.50-£25.00 Single £15.00-£25.00 Double	Open Jan-Dec		
Situated on main bus route, 10 minutes from city centre. Private parking.							
Tankard Guest House 40 East Claremont Street Edinburgh EH7 4JR Tel: 0131 556 4218 Fax: 0131 452 8630	APPROVED Listed	2 Twin 1 Double 3 Family	2 Pub Bath/Show	B&B per person £18.00-£25.00 Single £18.00-£25.00 Double Room only per person £15.00-£22.00	Open Jan-Dec		
Townhouse convenient for bus route to city centre and within walking distance of Playhouse Theatre.							
Andrea Targett-Adams 27 Heriot Row Edinburgh Midlothian EH3 6EN Tel: 0131 225 9474/220 1699 Fax: 0131 220 1699	DELUXE	1 Single 1 Twin 1 Double	3 En Suite fac	B&B per person £50.00-£55.00 Single £40.00-£45.00 Double Room only per person £40.00-£45.00	Open Apr-Oct		
An elegant Georgian house, a stone's throw from Princes Street. All rooms are luxuriously furnished with bathrooms ensuite.							

SCOTTISH TOURIST BOARD
QUALITY COMMENDATIONS ARE:

Deluxe – An EXCELLENT quality standard
Highly Commended – A VERY GOOD quality standard
Commended – A GOOD quality standard
Approved – An ADEQUATE quality standard

The Thirty-Nine Steps Guest House

62 South Trinity Road, Edinburgh EH5 3NX
Telephone: 0131 552 1349   Fax: 0131 552 7282

Victorian house quietly situated, close to city centre and Royal Botanic Gardens. All rooms tastefully decorated with colour TV, tea/coffee facilities and are fully ensuite. Traditional Scottish breakfast served. Easy access to main A9 road north. Bed and Breakfast ensuite from £18.50-£27.50. Parking. A warm and friendly welcome is assured from resident proprietors Shirley and Derek Mowat.

	Grade	Rooms	Facilities	Rates	Open	
The Thirty-Nine Steps Guest House 62 South Trinity Road Edinburgh EH5 3NX Tel: 0131 552 1349 Fax: 0131 552 7282	COMMENDED	1 Single 2 Twin 2 Double 2 Family	6 En Suite fac 1 Priv. NOT ensuite 1 Pub Bath/Show	B&B per person £23.50-£29.50 Single £18.50-£27.50 Double	Open Jan-Dec	
Victorian terraced house in quiet residential area. Convenient bus route for city centre. Unrestricted parking.						
Tiree Guest House 26 Craigmillar Park Edinburgh EH16 5PS Tel: 0131 667 7477 Fax: 0131 662 1608	COMMENDED Listed	1 Single 2 Twin 2 Double 1 Family	4 En Suite fac 1 Limited ensuite 2 Pub Bath/Show	B&B per person £16.00-£18.00 Single £18.00-£27.00 Double	Open Jan-Dec	
Victorian terraced house on bus route into city centre. Private parking. Close to shopping centre.						
Torivane Guest House 1 Morton Street Edinburgh EH15 2EW Tel: 0131 669 1648	COMMENDED	1 Single 1 Twin 1 Double	1 En Suite fac 1 Pub Bath/Show	B&B per person £15.00-£17.00 Single £15.00-£20.00 Double	Open Mar-Nov	
Stone-built house on main bus route to city centre. A one-minute walk to beach and seafront promenade.						
Mrs R C Torrance 15 Viewforth Terrace Edinburgh EH10 4LJ Tel: 0131 229 1776	COMMENDED Listed	3 Twin	1 Pub Bath/Show	B&B per person £17.00-£18.00 Double	Open May-Sep	
Comfortable, semi-detached Victorian villa, centrally situated in quiet area near Churchill and King's Theatre. Approximately 2 miles (3kms) to West End.						
J Toynbee 21 Dean Park Crescent Edinburgh EH4 1PH Tel: 0131 332 3096	COMMENDED	1 Single 1 Double 1 Family	3 En Suite fac	B&B per person £17.50-£21.00 Single £17.50-£21.00 Double Room only per person £15.00-£18.50	Open May-Sep	
Terraced Georgian house close to city centre. Within walking distance of shops, restaurants and cultural attractions.						
Mrs June Tulloch Da Homin 24 Summerside Street Edinburgh EH6 4NU Tel: 0131 554 8652 Fax: 0131 554 8652	COMMENDED Listed	1 Twin 2 Double	2 Pub Bath/Show	B&B per person £15.00-£18.00 Single £12.00-£18.00 Double Room only per person £11.00-£15.00	Open Apr-Oct	
Victorian house, north of city centre on excellent bus route. Parking. Friendly atmosphere. All welcome.						
Turret Guest House 8 Kilmaurs Terrace Edinburgh EH16 5DR Tel: 0131 667 6704 Fax: 0131 668 1368	HIGHLY COMMENDED	1 Single 2 Twin 2 Double 1 Family	4 En Suite fac 1 Priv. NOT ensuite 1 Pub Bath/Show	B&B per person £18.00-£28.00 Single £18.00-£28.00 Double	Open Jan-Dec	
Recently refurbished Victorian house in quiet residential area. Convenient for buses to city centre. Commonwealth Pool nearby.						

EDINBURGH – CITY, COAST AND COUNTRYSIDE

| EDINBURGH continued | Map 2 C5 | | | |

VILLA NINA House

Villa Nina House
39 LEAMINGTON TERRACE, EDINBURGH EH10 4JS
Telephone and Fax: 0131 229 2644
Very comfortable Victorian terraced house situated in a quiet residential part of the city yet only ten minutes' walk to Princes Street, Edinburgh Castle, theatres, shops and major attractions. Some rooms with private showers. TV in all rooms. Full cooked breakfast. Member of STB, GHA & AA.
Bed and Breakfast from £15 per person.

Villa Nina Guest House 39 Leamington Terrace Edinburgh EH10 4JS Tel: 0131 229 2644 Fax: 0131 229 2644	COMMENDED Listed	1 Twin 2 Double 1 Family	3 Limited ensuite 2 Pub Bath/Show	B&B per person £15.00-£20.00 Double	Open Jan-Dec

Terraced house. Approximately 1 mile (2 kms) from city centre.
Near Kings Theatre, the Castle and shops. Showers in bedrooms.

Mrs T Wawro 61 Cragcrook Avenue Edinburgh EH4 3PU Tel: (Edinburgh) 0131 336 3025	COMMENDED Listed	2 Twin	1 Limited ensuite	B&B per person £15.00-£18.00 Double	Open May-Sep

In quiet residential area, with views over open country,
yet within 10 minutes' drive from Princes Street.

Albion House
6 Templeland Road, Corstorphine, Edinburgh EH12 8RP
Telephone: 0131 539 0840
A friendly welcome along with daily complimentary home baking and biscuits awaits at our comfortable Edwardian family home. Non-smoking, situated three miles west of city centre with fast frequent bus service to town. Three miles from airport with easy access to main touring routes.

Mrs Wilson 6 Templeland Road Edinburgh EH12 8RP Tel: 0131 539 0840	HIGHLY COMMENDED Listed	1 Single 1 Twin 1 Double	1 En Suite fac 2 Priv. NOT ensuite 1 Pub Bath/Show	B&B per person £17.00-£19.00 Single £18.00-£22.00 Double	Open Apr-Oct

Semi-detached Edwardian sandstone house in peaceful location in west of city.
3 miles (5kms) from airport. Non-smoking house.

GOREBRIDGE **Midlothian** Mrs Cathie Nelson 18 Bellmains, Gorebridge EH23 4QD Tel: (Gorebridge) 01875 820252	Map 2 C5 COMMENDED 👑👑	1 Twin 1 Double	2 Pub Bath/Show	B&B per person £17.50-£20.00 Double	Open Apr-Sep

Private bungalow, well-appointed inside and out. Quiet residential area 10 miles
south of Edinburgh on the A7. Five minutes from both Borthwick Castle and
Dalhousie Castle.

GULLANE **East Lothian** Mrs I Knight Hopefield House, Main Street Gullane, East Lothian EH31 2DP Tel: (North Berwick) 01620 842191	Map 2 D4 COMMENDED 👑👑 🚶	3 Twin 1 Double	3 En Suite fac 1 Priv. NOT ensuite	B&B per person £19.00-£21.00 Single £19.00-£21.00 Double	Open Apr-Sep

Traditional 19th century stone-built farmhouse in centre of Gullane and golfing
countryside. 0.25 miles (0.5kms) from sandy beach and dunes. Private parking.

Mr & Mrs G Nisbet Faussett Hill House, Main Street Gullane, East Lothian EH31 2DR Tel: (Gullane) 01620 842396 Fax: 01620 842396	**HIGHLY COMMENDED**	2 Twin 1 Double	2 En Suite fac 1 Priv. NOT ensuite 1 Pub Bath/Show	B&B per person £26.00-£30.00 Single £20.00-£23.00 Double		Open Mar-Dec	

Detached Edwardian house with pleasant garden. Edinburgh 30 minutes by car. Sandy beaches and several golf courses nearby. Private parking.

HADDINGTON **East Lothian** Mrs S A Clark Fieldfare, Upper Bolton Farm Haddington East Lothian EH41 4HW Tel: (Gifford) 01620 810346	Map 2 D4 **COMMENDED**	1 Twin 1 Double 1 Family	1 Priv. NOT ensuite 2 Pub Bath/Show	B&B per person £18.00-£20.00 Single £17.00-£19.00 Double Room only per person £15.00-£17.00		Open Jan-Dec Dinner from 1800 B&B + Eve. Meal £17.00-£29.00	

Modernised Victorian farm cottage in peaceful rural situation yet only half an hour's drive from Edinburgh. Local produce when available.

Mrs C M D Gibson Carfrae, Garvald Haddington East Lothian EH41 4LP Tel: (Haddington) 01620 830242 Fax: 01620 830320	**HIGHLY COMMENDED**	1 Twin 2 Double	1 En Suite fac 1 Pub Bath/Show	B&B per person £18.00-£25.00 Single £18.00-£22.00 Double		Open May-Oct	

19th century Listed farmhouse with open aspect overlooking the walled garden. Furnished to a high standard. Edinburgh, the Borders and many golf courses within easy reach.

Mrs A Kinghorn 12 Traprain Terrace Haddington East Lothian EH41 3QD Tel: (Haddington) 01620 824635	**COMMENDED** Listed	2 Double	1 Pub Bath/Show	B&B per person £13.50-£14.00 Double		Open Jan-Dec	

Personally run B&B in quiet location, close to A1, Edinburgh 17 miles (27kms). Ideal for touring East Lothian.

The Plough Tavern Hotel

11 Court Street, Haddington, East Lothian EH41 3DS
Telephone: 01620 823326   Fax: 01875 852240

The Plough Tavern Hotel has been owned and managed by Allan and Alison Inglis since 1990 and has been completely refurbished during this period. The bedrooms are warm and comfortable with ensuite facilities, TV and tea/coffee tray. **The Plough** has an excellent reputation for its friendly atmosphere and good food both with locals and returning visitors. Located thirty minutes' drive from Edinburgh, in the centre of Haddington, county town of beautiful East Lothian, which hosts a variety of shops, sports facilities, golf courses and historic buildings. **The Plough** is an ideal base for all age groups.

The Plough Tavern 11 Court Street Haddington East Lothian EH41 3DS Tel: (Haddington) 01620 823326 Fax: 01875 852240	**COMMENDED**	2 Twin 2 Family	4 En Suite fac	B&B per person £20.00-£25.00 Single £20.00-£25.00 Double		Open Jan-Dec Dinner 1900-2100	

19th century traditional family run Inn. Comfortably furnished with good home cooking. Ideal base for golf. Edinburgh 17 miles (27kms).

EDINBURGH – CITY, COAST AND COUNTRYSIDE

EDINBURGH – CITY, COAST AND COUNTRYSIDE

HADDINGTON continued **East Lothian** Catherine Richards Schiehallion, 19 Church Street Haddington East Lothian EH41 3EX Tel: (Haddington) 01620 825663/ 0378 841931(mobile)	Map 2 D4	COMMENDED 👑👑	1 Twin 1 Double	1 Pub Bath/Show	B&B per person £19.00-£21.00 Double Room only per person £16.00-£18.00	Open Jan-Dec Dinner 1900-2100 B&B + Eve. Meal £25.00-£27.00	

Victorian terraced family home in historic county town.
Central location, 2 Old English sheepdogs in residence.

Mrs B Williams Eaglescairnie Mains Gifford, Haddington East Lothian EH41 4HN Tel: (Gifford) 01620 810491 Fax: 01620 810491		COMMENDED 👑👑	2 Single 1 Twin 1 Double	1 En Suite fac 1 Priv. NOT ensuite 2 Pub Bath/Show	B&B per person from £20.00 Single £18.00-£22.00 Double	Open Jan-Dec	

In quiet rural situation, on working mixed farm, large family house with
magnificent views of Fife and Lammermuirs. 4 miles (6kms) from Haddington.

LASSWADE **Midlothian** Mrs Ann O'Brien Droman House Lasswade Midlothian EH18 1HA Tel: 0131 663 9239	Map 2 C5	COMMENDED Listed	1 Single 2 Twin 1 Family	2 Pub Bath/Show	B&B per person from £15.00 Single from £15.00 Double	Open May-Oct	

Former Georgian manse in secluded setting. Informal and warm welcome assured.
Ample private parking.

LINLITHGOW **West Lothian**	Map 2 B4						

Belsyde Farm

Lanark Road, Linlithgow, West Lothian EH49 6QE
Telephone and Fax: 01506 842098

An 18thC farmhouse located in large, secluded gardens with
panoramic views over the Forth estuary. Golfing and fishing
available locally. All bedrooms have washbasin (hot and cold),
tea/coffee-making facilities, colour TV, central heating, 1 bedroom
ensuite. AA Listed. Located close to M8, M9 and M90 and to
Edinburgh airport. Open all year except Christmas.

Mrs A Hay Belsyde House/Farm Lanark Road Linlithgow West Lothian EH49 6QE Tel: (Linlithgow) 01506 842098 Fax: 01506 842098		COMMENDED 👑👑	2 Single 1 Double 1 Family	1 En Suite fac 2 Pub Bath/Show	B&B per person from £16.00 Single from £16.00 Double	Open Jan-Dec, exc Xmas	

Late 18th century house set on a 100-acre (40ha) sheep farm beside Union Canal.
Views over Forth over Forth Estuary and Ochil Hills. Easy access to M8, M9, M90
and Edinburgh Airport.

Use the Scottish Tourist Board's
Quality Commendations to select
the holiday accommodation which
is right for you!

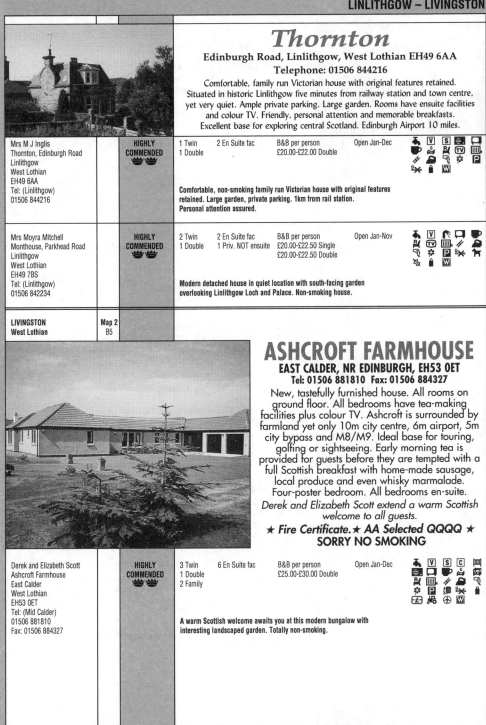

Thornton
Edinburgh Road, Linlithgow, West Lothian EH49 6AA
Telephone: 01506 844216
Comfortable, family run Victorian house with original features retained.
Situated in historic Linlithgow five minutes from railway station and town centre,
yet very quiet. Ample private parking. Large garden. Rooms have ensuite facilities
and colour TV. Friendly, personal attention and memorable breakfasts.
Excellent base for exploring central Scotland. Edinburgh Airport 10 miles.

Mrs M J Inglis Thornton, Edinburgh Road Linlithgow West Lothian EH49 6AA Tel: (Linlithgow) 01506 844216	**HIGHLY COMMENDED**	1 Twin 1 Double	2 En Suite fac	B&B per person £20.00-£22.00 Double	Open Jan-Dec

Comfortable, non-smoking family run Victorian house with original features
retained. Large garden, private parking. 1km from rail station.
Personal attention assured.

Mrs Moyra Mitchell Monthouse, Parkhead Road Linlithgow West Lothian EH49 7BS Tel: (Linlithgow) 01506 842234	**HIGHLY COMMENDED**	2 Twin 1 Double	2 En Suite fac 1 Priv. NOT ensuite	B&B per person £20.00-£22.50 Single £20.00-£22.50 Double	Open Jan-Nov

Modern detached house in quiet location with south-facing garden
overlooking Linlithgow Loch and Palace. Non-smoking house.

LIVINGSTON
West Lothian

Map 2
B5

ASHCROFT FARMHOUSE
EAST CALDER, NR EDINBURGH, EH53 0ET
Tel: 01506 881810 Fax: 01506 884327
New, tastefully furnished house. All rooms on
ground floor. All bedrooms have tea-making
facilities plus colour TV. Ashcroft is surrounded by
farmland yet only 10m city centre, 6m airport, 5m
city bypass and M8/M9. Ideal base for touring,
golfing or sightseeing. Early morning tea is
provided for guests before they are tempted with a
full Scottish breakfast with home-made sausage,
local produce and even whisky marmalade.
Four-poster bedroom. All bedrooms en-suite.
*Derek and Elizabeth Scott extend a warm Scottish
welcome to all guests.*
★ Fire Certificate.★ AA Selected QQQQ ★
SORRY NO SMOKING

Derek and Elizabeth Scott Ashcroft Farmhouse East Calder West Lothian EH53 0ET Tel: (Mid Calder) 01506 881810 Fax: 01506 884327	**HIGHLY COMMENDED**	3 Twin 1 Double 2 Family	6 En Suite fac	B&B per person £25.00-£30.00 Double	Open Jan-Dec

A warm Scottish welcome awaits you at this modern bungalow with
interesting landscaped garden. Totally non-smoking.

EDINBURGH – CITY, COAST AND COUNTRYSIDE

EDINBURGH – CITY, COAST AND COUNTRYSIDE

LOANHEAD Midlothian	Map 2 C5

Aaron Glen Guest House

7 Nivensknowe Road, Loanhead EH20 9AU
Telephone: 0131 440 1293   Fax: 0131 440 2155

Newly built family run guest house conveniently situated just off city bypass and minutes from city centre on main bus route. Tastefully decorated with all rooms ensuite, Sky TV, tea/coffee facilities, hairdryers, beautiful Scottish breakfast. Drinks served in licensed lounge with evening meals served on request. Monitored car park. Disabled facilities.

Aaron Glen Guest House 7 Nivensknowe Road Loanhead Midlothian EH20 9AU Tel: 0131 440 1293 Fax: 0131 440 2155	COMMENDED 🏵🏵🏵	1 Twin 1 Double 3 Family	5 En Suite fac	B&B per person £20.00-£30.00 Single £17.50-£25.00 Double	Open Jan-Dec Dinner 1700-2100

Modern purpose-built guest house with all rooms ensuite.
Convenient for Edinburgh city centre, on main bus route.

LONGNIDDRY East Lothian Mrs M Anderson 5 Stevenson Way Longniddry East Lothian EH32 0PF Tel: (Longniddry) 01875 853395	Map 2 D4 COMMENDED Listed	2 Double	1 Pub Bath/Show	B&B per person £10.00-£15.00 Single to £15.00 Double	Open May-Sep

Bungalow with small attractive garden in quiet residential area.
Easy road and rail access to Edinburgh. Ideal for East Lothian golf courses.

Mrs P Morrison 13 Glassel Park Road Longniddry East Lothian EH32 0NY Tel: (Longniddry) 01875 852333	COMMENDED Listed	1 Twin 1 Double	1 Priv. NOT ensuite 1 Pub Bath/Show	B&B per person from £15.00 Double	Open May-Sep

Friendly welcome at this B&B in quiet residential area. Close to golf courses.
Twenty minutes to Edinburgh by train.

MUSSELBURGH East Lothian	Map 2 C5

Mrs Elizabeth Aitken

COMMENDED 🏵

18 WOODSIDE GARDENS, MUSSELBURGH, EAST LOTHIAN EH21 7LJ
Telephone: 0131 665 3170/3344

Well-appointed bungalow within 6 miles of Edinburgh in quiet suburb with private parking. Excellent bus/train service to city. 2 minutes from oldest golf course in world and race course. Easy access to beaches and beautiful countryside.

All rooms hot and cold, colour TV and tea/coffee.   *Private parking.*

Mrs E Aitken 18 Woodside Gardens Musselburgh East Lothian EH21 7LJ Tel: 0131 665 3170/3344	COMMENDED 🏵	1 Twin 1 Double 1 Family	2 Pub Bath/Show	B&B per person from £16.00 Single from £16.00 Double	Open Jan-Dec

Detached bungalow in quiet residential area, close to Musselburgh Racecourse and golf course. Private parking.

Craigesk Guest House 10 Albert Terrace Musselburgh East Lothian EH21 7LR Tel: 0131 665 3344/3170	APPROVED ♛	2 Twin 2 Family	2 Pub Bath/Show	B&B per person from £16.00 Single from £16.00 Double	Open Jan-Dec
Victorian terraced house with private parking, overlooking golf and racecourse. Convenient bus route to city centre (20 minutes).					
Mrs C Douglas 5 Craighall Terrace Musselburgh East Lothian EH21 7PL Tel: 0131 665 4294	APPROVED Listed	1 Double 1 Family	1 Pub Bath/Show	B&B per person to £18.00 Single from £16.00 Double	Open May-Oct
Family bungalow with private parking in quiet residential area, close to seashore, golf course and race course.					

NORTH BERWICK
East Lothian — Map 2 D4

Mrs Fife Beehive Cottage, Kingston North Berwick East Lothian EH39 5JE Tel: (North Berwick) 01620 894785	COMMENDED ♛♛	1 Double	1 En Suite fac	B&B per person £16.00-£19.00 Double Room only per person £14.00-£17.00	Open Feb-Sep
200-year-old cottage with pantiled roof and garden with extensive views. 2 miles (3kms) drive to the sea. Home-produced honey. Ground-floor ensuite accommodation.					
Mrs S Gray Seabank, 12 Marine Parade North Berwick East Lothian EH39 4LD Tel: (North Berwick) 01620 892884 Fax: 01620 895561	COMMENDED Listed	1 Twin 4 Family	2 Pub Bath/Show	B&B per person £18.00-£20.00 Single £15.00-£18.00 Double	Open Jan-Dec
Stone-built house with sea views and adjoining sandy beach. Tennis courts behind. Off-road parking. 5 mins walk to town centre.					

The Studio
Grange Road, North Berwick EH39 4QT
Telephone: 01620 895150 Fax: 01620 895120

Newly refurbished and extended historic building, tastefully decorated and furnished, situated within a walled garden. Guests can enjoy a high degree of privacy in quiet rural surroundings yet convenient for North Berwick and railway station. Private sittingroom with television with French doors to garden. Regret no smoking. Parking available.

Mrs M Ramsay The Studio, Grange Road North Berwick East Lothian EH39 4QT Tel: (North Berwick) 01620 895150 Fax: 01620 895120	HIGHLY COMMENDED ♛♛	1 Double	1 Priv. NOT ensuite	B&B per person £20.00 Double	Open Jan-Dec
Attractive Listed building set in walled garden. Quiet peaceful location, private parking. Close to all amenities and local golf courses.					
Mrs G Scott The Glebe House, Law Road North Berwick East Lothian EH39 4PL Tel: (North Berwick) 01620 892608	HIGHLY COMMENDED Listed	1 Twin 2 Double	1 En Suite fac 2 Priv. NOT ensuite 1 Pub Bath/Show	B&B per person £17.50-£22.00 Double	Open Jan-Dec
Former Georgian manse (1780) furnished in period style and set in own grounds above North Berwick, with views of the sea and Berwick Law. Four-poster bed available.					

EDINBURGH – CITY, COAST AND COUNTRYSIDE

Details of Grading and Classification are on page vi. | Key to symbols is on back flap. |

NORTH BERWICK – by PENICUIK

	Map 2						
NORTH BERWICK continued **East Lothian** Mrs P Swanston Chestnut Lodge, 2A Ware Road North Berwick East Lothian EH39 4BN Tel: (North Berwick) 01620 894256 Fax: 01620 894256	D4	COMMENDED	2 Twin 1 Double	3 En Suite fac	B&B per person £18.00-£25.00 Single £14.00-£18.00 Double	Open Mar-Nov	

Modern well-appointed house in quiet location. Ground-floor ensuite. Public transport nearby. Edinburgh ½ hour. Ideal base for golfing. Private parking.

	Map 2						
PENICUIK **Midlothian** Mr & Mrs G Taylor Silverburn Steading Penicuik Midlothian EH26 9JL Tel: (Penicuik) 01968 678420	C5	COMMENDED	1 Twin 1 Double	2 En Suite fac 1 Pub Bath/Show	B&B per person £19.00-£20.00 Double	Open Jan-Dec	

Converted farm steading in a rural location on the main A702 Edinburgh road, offering personal attention. Ground floor ensuite accommodation.

by PENICUIK
Midlothian
Map 2
C5

Patieshill Farm

CARLOPS, PENICUIK EH26 9ND
Telephone: 01968 660551   Fax: 01968 661162

This is a working hill sheep and cattle farm. Set in the midst of the
Pentland Hills with panoramic views of the surrounding countryside yet
only 20 minutes' drive from the City of Edinburgh. A perfect centre for
touring Central Scotland.

A very warm and friendly welcome awaits visitors.

Mrs Janet Burke Patieshill Farm Carlops, by Penicuik Midlothian EH26 9ND Tel: (West Linton) 01968 660551 Fax: 01968 661162	COMMENDED	1 Twin 2 Double	3 En Suite fac	B&B per person £20.00-£24.00 Single £18.00-£20.00 Double	Open Jan-Dec	

Panoramic views from this hill farm just off A702 13 miles (21 kms) from Edinburgh. New guest wing with accommodation on ground-floor level.

R Marwick Walltower Farm Howgate, by Penicuik Midlothian EH26 8PY Tel: (Penicuik) 01968 672277	COMMENDED	1 Twin 1 Double 1 Family	1 En Suite fac 1 Pub Bath/Show	B&B per person £18.00-£25.00 Single £14.00-£20.00 Double	Open Jan-Dec	

Traditional farmhouse, with conservatory, set in mature garden. 10 miles (16kms) from Edinburgh and airport. Access to Borders. Non-smoking bedrooms.

RATHO Midlothian	Map 2 B5

Ratho Hall

51 Baird Road, Ratho, Midlothian EH28 8QY
Tel: 0131 335 3333   Fax: 0131 335 3035

Accommodation in a classical Georgian mansion set in 22 acres with a walled garden, tennis court and croquet lawn. Close to Edinburgh airport and 20 minutes away from the centre of Edinburgh. Ideal location for day tours to the Borders, Trossachs, Fife and Perthshire.

Mrs J Small Ratho Hall, 51 Baird Road Ratho Midlothian EH28 8QY Tel: 0131 335 3333 Fax: 0131 335 3035	HIGHLY COMMENDED	2 Twin 1 Double	2 En Suite fac 1 Priv. NOT ensuite	B&B per person £30.00-£50.00 Single £30.00-£40.00 Double Room only per person £25.00-£35.00	Open Apr-Oct Dinner 1900-2300 B&B + Eve. Meal £50.00-£60.00

A warm welcome awaits you at this classical Georgian house in extensive grounds with walks, tennis and croquet. Close to Ratho and 1 mile from Airport.

ROSLIN Midlothian Mrs Rae Stephen The Old Waterhouse Rosslyn Castle Roslin Midlothian EH25 9QB Tel: 0131 440 2318	Map 2 C5 / COMMENDED Listed	1 Double	1 En Suite fac	B&B per person £17.00-£20.00 Double	Open Apr-Sep

Recently converted waterhouse set in quiet and beautiful countryside with panoramic views of Pentland Hills, yet only 6 miles (10kms) from Edinburgh city centre.

SOUTH QUEENSFERRY West Lothian Priory Lodge The Loan South Queensferry West Lothian EH30 9NS Tel: 0131 331 4345 Fax: 0131 331 4345	Map 2 B4 / COMMENDED	1 Twin 1 Double 3 Family	4 En Suite fac	B&B per person £25.00 Single £20.00 Double	Open Jan-Dec

Traditional Scottish hospitality in friendly family run guest house, located in picturesque village of South Queensferry. Within easy walking distance of Forth Bridges. Ground-floor accommodation.

TRANENT East Lothian Mrs R Harrison Rosebank House 161 High Street Tranent East Lothian EH33 1LP Tel: (Tranent) 01875 610967	Map 2 D5 / COMMENDED	1 Twin 3 Double 1 Family	2 Pub Bath/Show	B&B per person £15.00-£17.00 Single £15.00-£16.00 Double	Open Jan-Dec

Stone-built house near centre of Tranent. 10 miles (16kms) to Edinburgh city centre with frequent bus service. Ideal base for golfing and touring East Lothian.

WELCOME

Whenever you are in Scotland, you can be sure of a warm welcome at your nearest Tourist Information Centre.

For guide books, maps, souvenirs, our Centres provide a service second to none – many now offer bureau-de-change facilities. And, of course, Tourist Information Centres offer free, expert advice on what to see and do, route-planning and accommodation for everyone – visitors and residents alike!

EDINBURGH – CITY, COAST AND COUNTRYSIDE

Details of Grading and Classification are on page vi.

Key to symbols is on back flap.

UPHALL West Lothian	Map 2 B5

Coille-Mhor House

20 Houston Mains Holdings, Uphall, West Lothian EH52 6PA
Telephone: 01506 854044   Fax: 01506 855118

Relax in our family run converted smallholding where everyone, including children and the disabled is made very welcome. All bedrooms on ground floor with ensuite, house speciality is good honest porridge laced with liqueur, herbal teas, seasonal fruit, Scottish breakfast, private parking. Central for Edinburgh, airport, motorways. Free brochure.

Coille-Mhor House
20 Houston Mains Holdings
Uphall
West Lothian
EH52 6PA
Tel: (Broxburn) 01506 854044
Fax: 01506 855118

COMMENDED

1 Twin 4 Double 1 Family	6 En Suite fac	B&B per person to £35.00 Single £23.00-£25.00 Double	Open Jan-Dec

Characteristically converted smallholding furnished to a high standard.
Close to Edinburgh, airport and Glasgow motorway. Private parking.

Your key to quality accommodation in Scotland:

Scottish TOURIST BOARD DELUXE

Scottish TOURIST BOARD HIGHLY COMMENDED

Scottish TOURIST BOARD COMMENDED

Scottish TOURIST BOARD APPROVED

The Scottish Tourist Board's
Grading and Classification Scheme

Welcome to...

Greater Glasgow
and Clyde Valley

For sheer excitement, Glasgow is one of the top UK destinations. For shopping choice, entertainment and culture, it should not be missed.

The legendary Glasgow friendliness is a bonus but first time visitors will be struck by the sheer panache of 'downtown' Glasgow. The magnificent Victorian architecture of the city centre further adds to the vibrancy. In short, Glasgow is where things happen, whatever time of year you visit.

For example, in 1996, Glasgow opened its new Gallery of Modern Art, right in the heart of the city in the former Stirling's Library, a handsome neoclassical building. Charles Rennie Mackintosh's 'House for an Art Lover', designed for a competition in 1901, was also completed, as a further addition to the several locations in the city where Mackintosh, its most famous architect, can be encountered. Other places include his peerless School of Art and also the Mackintosh House

at the Hunterian Art Gallery. On the subject of art collections, one of Britain's finest civic collections can be viewed at the Art Gallery and Museum at Kelvingrove. Then you can nip across the road to the Museum of Transport. East of the city-centre, close to the old heart of Glasgow around its magnificent cathedral, you will also find the unique St Mungo Museum taking its wide ranging foray through the world's religions (lots of artefacts and paintings). Another excursion which is a must is to see the magnificent Burrell Collection, the lifetime's hobby of a shipping magnate, now in the care of the city and housed in an inspiring sylvan setting in Pollok Park. With so much to see indoors, Glasgow is an especially good winter break destination.

97

Glasgow in the nineties is a city with a style all its own with a range of shops that ranks it one of the top three shopping cities in the U.K.

If all this cultural gallivanting sounds tiring, then take a break in one of the city's many pubs and eating places. You will certainly need to if you have been shopping along one of the many pedestrianised streets, such as Buchanan Street, or sampling the upmarket wares at Princes Square or the chic Italian Centre. Remember, though, that the city itself has no monopoly on cultural centres of excellence. For example, take a look at the Paisley Museum and Art Galleries, not only for the story of the renowned Paisley shawl with its distinct pattern, but for a major painting collection.

Greater Glasgow and Clyde Valley

Similarly, on no account overlook what the Clyde Valley can offer.

The River Clyde winds out of the grassy rounded hills then enters a rocky wooded gorge with such force that it this beautiful setting became the site for a textile mill village. New Lanark became a bold experiment in social welfare and worker care and its fame went round the world. Today it is a nominated World Heritage Site – but, even more importantly, a great day out for visitors with lots to see and do. Its sheltered location make it a particularly good late season place to visit (and its visitor centre opens all year round). In addition, the town of Biggar is also within easy reach, with a further choice of museums and places of interest. Between them, Glasgow and Clyde Valley offer an unrivalled range of things to see and do.

AREA TOURIST BOARD ADDRESSES

GREATER GLASGOW AND CLYDE VALLEY TOURIST BOARD
11 George Square
Glasgow
G2 1DY
Tel: 0141 204 4400
Fax: 0141 221 3524

Greater Glasgow and Clyde Valley

TOURIST INFORMATION CENTRES IN SCOTLAND

GREATER GLASGOW & CLYDE VALLEY TOURIST BOARD

ABINGTON &
Welcome Break Service Area
Junction 13, M74
Tel: (01864) 502436
Jan-Dec

BIGGAR
155 High Street
Tel: (01899) 22106
April-end Oct

COATBRIDGE &
The Time Capsule
Buchanan Street
Tel: (01236) 431133
April-end Oct

GLASGOW ✉
35 St Vincent Place
G1 2ER
Tel: (0141) 204 4400
Jan-Dec

GLASGOW AIRPORT
Tourist Information Desk
Tel: (0141) 848 4440
Jan-Dec

GOUROCK
Pierhead
Tel: (01475) 639467
April-Sept

HAMILTON &
Road Chef Services
(M74 Northbound)
Tel: (01698) 285590
Jan-Dec

LANARK & ✉
Horsemarket
Ladyacre Road, ML11 7LQ
Tel: (01555) 661661
Jan-Dec

PAISLEY
Town Hall, Abbey Close
Tel: (0141) 889 0711
April-mid-Nov

✉ Accept written enquiries
& Disabled access

 102

ABINGTON
Lanarkshire
Mrs C Craig
Townfoot
Roberton, by Abington
Lanarkshire
ML12 6RS
Tel: (Lamington)
01899 850655

Map 2
B7

COMMENDED
Listed

2 Twin
1 Family

1 En Suite fac
1 Pub Bath/Show

B&B per person
£14.00-£17.00 Single
£14.00-£17.00 Double

Open Jan-Dec

In a delightfully quiet position, set back from the main road, small and friendly
with comfortable rooms. Some annexe accommodation with ensuite facilities.

Mrs Mary Hodge
Craighead Farm
Abington, by Biggar
Lanarkshire
ML12 6SQ
Tel: (Crawford) 01864 502356
Fax: 01864 502356

COMMENDED

1 Twin
1 Double

2 Priv. NOT ensuite
2 Pub Bath/Show

B&B per person
£15.00-£17.00 Single
£15.00-£17.00 Double

Open May-Oct
Dinner 1800-1900
B&B + Eve. Meal
£23.50-£25.50

Stone built 18th century farmhouse, on working farm in peaceful rural location.
Friendly, relaxed atmosphere. Evening meals.

Mrs J Hyslop
Glentewing Farm
Crawfordjohn, by Abington
Lanarkshire
ML12 6ST
Tel: (Crawfordjohn)
01864 504221

HIGHLY
COMMENDED

1 Twin
1 Double

2 En Suite fac

B&B per person
£17.00-£19.00 Double

Open Jan-Dec
Dinner 1830-1930
B&B + Eve. Meal
£25.00-£27.00

Early 20th century farmhouse set in a glen with extensive view towards Tinto Hill.
Far from the madding crowd yet only 5 miles (8kms) from M74.
Home cooking a speciality.

AIRDRIE
Lanarkshire
Mrs E Hunter
Easter Glentore Farm
Slammanan Road
Greengairs, by Airdrie
Lanarkshire
ML6 7TJ
Tel: (Greengairs)
01236 830243

Map 2
A5

HIGHLY
COMMENDED

3 Double

1 En Suite fac
1 Pub Bath/Show

B&B per person
from £22.00 Single
from £18.00 Double

Open Jan-Dec
Dinner 1700-2000

Working stock rearing farm only 15 miles (24kms) from the centre of Glasgow.
Warm welcome, home cooking and homely atmosphere.

Rosslee Guest House
107 Forrest Street
Airdrie
Lanarkshire
ML6 7AR
Tel: (Airdrie) 01236 765865

COMMENDED

2 Single
3 Twin
1 Family

3 En Suite fac
2 Pub Bath/Show

B&B per person
£20.00-£25.00 Single
£20.00-£25.00 Double
Room only per person
£18.00-£23.00

Open Jan-Dec
Dinner 1730-1830
B&B + Eve. Meal
£27.50-£34.50

Former church manse, now family run guest house with comfortable rooms.
Central situation for Edinburgh or Glasgow.

BEARSDEN
Dunbartonshire
Kilmardinny Guest House
Milngavie Road
Bearsden, Glasgow
Dunbartonshire
G61 3DH
Tel: 0141 943 1310

Map 1
H5

COMMENDED
Listed

4 Single
1 Twin
3 Double

2 Pub Bath/Show

B&B per person
£16.00-£17.00 Single
£15.00-£16.00 Double

Open Jan-Dec

Personally run guest house in residential area. 6 miles (10 kms) from
Glasgow city centre. On main bus route. Close to railway station.

BIGGAR
Lanarkshire
Mr & Mrs P Brotherstone
Daleside, 165 High Street
Biggar
Lanarkshire
ML12 6DL
Tel: (Biggar) 01899 220097

Map 2
B6

COMMENDED
Listed

2 Twin
1 Double

1 Pub Bath/Show

B&B per person
£18.00-£20.00 Single
£16.00-£17.00 Double

Open Jan-Dec

Comfortable accommodation overlooking the wide tree-lined High Street
of this historic market town. Ideal centre for exploring southern Scotland.

GREATER GLASGOW AND CLYDE VALLEY

Details of Grading and Classification are on page vi.

Key to symbols is on back flap.

GREATER GLASGOW AND CLYDE VALLEY

BIGGAR continued
Lanarkshire
Mrs Margaret E Kirby
Walston Mansion Farmhouse
Walston, Carnwath
Lanarkshire
ML11 8NF
Tel: (Dunsyre) 01899 810338
Fax: 01899 810338

Map 2
B6

COMMENDED

1 Twin   2 En Suite fac
1 Double   2 Pub Bath/Show
1 Family

B&B per person
£13.50-£15.50 Single
£13.50-£15.50 Double

Open Jan-Dec
Dinner 1800-2000

19th century stone-built farmhouse situated in small village at south west end of Pentland Hills. 5 miles (8kms) from Biggar.

Mayfield House
Edinburgh Road
Biggar
Lanarkshire
ML12 6AT
Tel: (Biggar) 01899 220544

COMMENDED

2 Twin   3 En Suite fac
1 Double

B&B per person
from £19.00 Single
£16.00-£19.00 Double

Open Jan-Dec
Dinner 1730-2100
B&B + Eve. Meal
£22.00-£25.00

Typical Scottish Victorian villa on the outskirts of Biggar on main route to Edinburgh and the Borders.

LINDSAYLANDS HOUSE
BIGGAR, LANARKSHIRE ML12 6NR
TELEPHONE: 01899 220033/221221 FAX: 01899 221009

THIS LOVELY LISTED COUNTRY HOUSE IS SET IN ITS OWN GROUNDS SURROUNDED BY 94 ACRES OF ITS OWN FARMLAND. SITUATED OFF MAIN ROAD 1 MILE WEST OF BIGGAR. 3 LARGE BEDROOMS WITH PRIVATE FACILITIES, GUEST LOUNGE AND DINING ROOM. IDEAL BASE FOR TOURING GLASGOW, EDINBURGH, BORDERS OR JUST RELAXING.
PRICES FROM £23 PER PERSON, PER NIGHT.

Mrs M E Stott
Lindsaylands House
Biggar
Lanarkshire
Tel: (Biggar) 01899 220033/
221221
Fax: 01899 221009

HIGHLY COMMENDED

1 Twin   2 En Suite fac
2 Double   1 Priv. NOT ensuite

B&B per person
£26.00-£28.00 Single
£23.00-£25.00 Double

Open Mar-Nov
Dinner 1930-2030
B&B + Eve. Meal
£36.00-£41.00

Attractive country house, with lots of character, set in 6 acres (2.4ha) of garden, amidst lovely countryside. With views to Border Hills. Hard tennis court.

BRIDGE OF WEIR
Renfrewshire
Margaret Bryan
21 Bankend Road
Bridge of Weir
Renfrewshire
PA11 3EU
Tel: (Bridge of Weir)
01505 614414

Map 1
H5

HIGHLY COMMENDED

2 Twin   1 En Suite fac
1 Double   1 Pub Bath/Show

B&B per person
£20.00-£25.00 Double

Open Jan-Dec
Dinner 1830-2000
B&B + Eve. Meal
£32.00-£37.00

Victorian villa in commanding position, with open views to the Kirkpatrick Hills and Ben Lomond. 10 minutes from airport.

CLYDEBANK, Glasgow
Dunbartonshire
Mrs M Johnston
Tudor House, 10 Drumry Road
Clydebank, Glasgow
G81
Tel: 0141 941 3171

Map 1
H5

APPROVED

2 Single   2 Limited ensuite
2 Twin   2 Pub Bath/Show

B&B per person
£17.50-£20.00 Single
from £15.00 Double
Room only per person
£13.50-£15.00

Open Jan-Dec

Family guest house with cable TV in bedrooms. Situated in residential area. Convenient for the college, train station, shopping centre and business park.

COATBRIDGE **Lanarkshire** Mrs Barr Auchenlea 153 Langmuir Road Bargeddie, by Coatbridge Lanarkshire G69 7RT Tel: 0141 771 6870	Map 2 A5	COMMENDED 👑👑	1 Twin 1 Family	1 En Suite fac 1 Priv. NOT ensuite	B&B per person £18.00-£20.00 Single from £18.00 Double Room only per person from £16.00	Open Jan-Dec	

Comfortable accommodation in family home. Easy access to M8 and the North.
Close to train station.

CUMBERNAULD **Dunbartonshire** Mrs M Abercrombie 68 Lammermoor Drive Greenfaulds, Cumbernauld Dunbartonshire G67 4BE Tel: (Cumbernauld) 01236 721307	Map 2 A5	COMMENDED Listed	3 Twin	1 Pub Bath/Show	B&B per person £16.50 Single £16.50 Double	Open Jan-Dec	

Modern family home, centrally situated with easy access to
main roads to Glasgow, Stirling and Edinburgh.

EAGLESHAM **Renfrewshire** Mrs F Allison New Borland, Glasgow Road Eaglesham Renfrewshire G76 0DN Tel: (Eaglesham) 01355 302051	Map 1 H6	COMMENDED 👑👑	2 Single 2 Twin	1 Pub Bath/Show	B&B per person £20.00-£22.50 Single £18.50-£20.00 Double Room only per person £15.00-£20.00	Open Jan-Dec	

Detached modern house in quiet rural setting 0.25 miles (0.4kms) from the village.
Ample private parking.

GLASGOW Adelaide's Guest House 209 Bath Street Glasgow G2 4HZ Tel: 0141 248 4970 Fax: 0141 226 4247	Map 1 H5	COMMENDED 👑👑	1 Single 3 Twin 2 Double 2 Family	6 En Suite fac 1 Pub Bath/Show	Room only per person £10.00-£40.00	Open Jan-Dec	

Guest house with self-service eating facilities in redeveloped
Victorian church building, close to King's Theatre and city centre.

Mrs L Alexander 11 Attow Road Glasgow G43 Tel: 0141 632 1440/632 2788		COMMENDED Listed	1 Single 1 Double 1 Family	2 Pub Bath/Show	B&B per person £20.00 Single £20.00 Double	Open Jan-Dec	

Stone semi villa c.1910 in quiet residential area on southside of city.
Transport connections nearby.

Belgrave Guest House 2 Belgrave Terrace Gt Western Road Glasgow G12 8JD Tel: 0141 337 1850/1741 Fax: 0141 337 1741		COMMENDED 👑	3 Single 3 Twin 2 Double 3 Family	1 En Suite fac 1 Limited ensuite 1 Priv. NOT ensuite 3 Pub Bath/Show	B&B per person £20.00-£25.00 Single £17.00-£22.50 Double	Open Jan-Dec	

Refurbished guest house, under new management in West End.
Convenient for Botanic Gardens, other local attractions and amenities.

GREATER GLASGOW AND CLYDE VALLEY

Details of Grading and Classification are on page vi.

Key to symbols is on back flap.

105

GLASGOW continued Mrs A Bennett 107 Dowanhill Street Glasgow G12 9EQ Tel: 0141 337 1307	**Map 1** H5	COMMENDED Listed	2 Twin	1 En Suite fac 1 Pub Bath/Show	B&B per person £18.00-£22.00 Single £16.00-£18.50 Double	Open Jan-Dec

Early Edwardian terraced town-house in the West End.
Convenient for buses and underground to city centre.

Blair Villa 256 Wedderlea Drive Glasgow G52 2SB Tel: 0141 882 4803/6440		COMMENDED	2 Single 1 Twin 1 Double	1 Priv. NOT ensuite 2 Pub Bath/Show	B&B per person £20.00-£25.00 Single £20.00-£25.00 Double Room only per person £16.00-£18.00	Open Jan-Dec

Victorian detached house in quiet residential area, some 7 miles (11kms)
from city centre, but conveniently near motorway system to East and West.

John G Bristow 56 Dumbreck Road Glasgow G41 5NP Tel: 0141 427 0129		COMMENDED	1 Twin 1 Double	2 En Suite fac	B&B per person £20.00-£25.00 Single £17.00-£20.00 Double	Open Jan-Dec

Traditional Victorian semi-villa with full disabled facilities.
Easy access to M8. Convenient for Burrell Collection, city and touring.

FASGADH
135 Yokermill Road, Glasgow G13 4HL Tel: 0141 952 3334
We provide quality accommodation in a quiet location 20 minutes by
car to city centre, 20 minutes from Loch Lomondside. Short walk to
restaurants. Rooms have washbasins, TVs, radios, tea/coffee-making
facilities. Large garden play area. Private parking. Cot available.
Babysitting/listening service. No smoking. £16-£18 pp per night.
Open Jan-Dec.   **Commended**

June Brown Fasgadh, 135 Yokermill Road Glasgow G13 4HL Tel: 0141 952 3334		COMMENDED	1 Twin 1 Double	1 Pub Bath/Show	B&B per person £16.00-£18.00 Double Room only per person £10.00-£12.00	Open Jan-Dec

Traditional semi-villa c.1925 in quiet residential area with transport connections
nearby. Easy access to city centre, Loch Lomond and the North.

Margaret Bruce 24 Greenock Avenue Glasgow G44 5TS Tel: 0141 637 0608		HIGHLY COMMENDED	1 Single 2 Twin 1 Double	2 En Suite fac 2 Pub Bath/Show	B&B per person £17.50-£20.00 Single £18.00-£19.00 Double	Open Jan-Dec

Modern, architect designed villa, peacefully situated in residential area,
5 minutes from train station. Private parking.

Chez Nous Guest House 33 Hillhead Street Glasgow G12 Tel: 0141 334 2977		APPROVED	12 Single 4 Twin 8 Double 7 Family	14 En Suite fac 4 Limited ensuite 6 Pub Bath/Show	B&B per person £18.50-£25.00 Single £18.50-£25.00 Double	Open Jan-Dec

Situated in West End of city, close to University and Art Gallery.
Within easy reach of M8 and all amenities. Private parking.

Craigielea House 35 Westercraigs Glasgow G31 2HY Tel: 0141 554 3446		APPROVED Listed	2 Twin 1 Double 1 Family	1 Limited ensuite 1 Pub Bath/Show	B&B per person £17.00-£18.00 Single £14.00-£15.00 Double	Open Jan-Dec

Victorian semi-villa in East End of city, yet close to centre and all amenities.

HOLLY HOUSE
54 IBROX TERRACE, GLASGOW G51 2TB
Telephone: 0141 427 5609

Holly House, family owned, offers spacious rooms, ensuite, situated in an early Victorian tree-lined terrace in city centre south. Convenient amenities: *Burrell Gallery, Rennie Macintosh House, Ibrox Stadium, SECC* and five minutes to *Glasgow International Airport* makes your stay comfortable and warm welcome assured by resident owner.

Mr Peter Divers Holly House 54 Ibrox Terrace Glasgow G51 2TB Tel: 0141 427 5609	COMMENDED Listed	1 Double 1 Family	2 En Suite fac	B&B per person £20.00-£25.00 Single £18.00-£25.00 Double	Open Apr-Dec

Holly House offers spacious ensuite rooms within early Victorian tree-lined terrace, in city centre south. Convenient for all city centre amenities.

Kirkland House
42 St Vincent Crescent, Glasgow G3 8NG
Telephone and Fax: 0141 248 3458

City-centre guest house in *Glasgow's Little Chelsea* in the area known as Finnieston offers excellent rooms, most with ensuite facilities, full central heating, colour TV, tea and coffee makers.
The house is located within walking distance of the Scottish Exhibition Centre, Museum, Art Gallery and Kelvingrove Park. We are very convenient to all City Centre and West End facilities, also only ten minutes from Glasgow International Airport.
Our house is featured in the *Frommers Tour Guide*.
Being family owned you can be assured of a friendly welcome.
Contact Carole Divers for details.

Mrs C Divers Kirkland House 42 St Vincent Crescent Glasgow G3 8NG Tel: 0141 248 3458 Fax: 0141 248 3458	COMMENDED Listed	2 Single 1 Twin 1 Double 1 Family	3 En Suite fac 2 Limited ensuite	B&B per person £25.00-£35.00 Single £25.00-£27.00 Double	Open Jan-Dec

Ideally situated for city centre, S.E.C.C., University and Museums.
Easy access to M8. Continental breakfast served in bedrooms.

Mrs D Hallam Park House 13 Victoria Park Gardens South Glasgow G11 7BX Tel: 0141 339 1559 Fax: 0141 339 1559	HIGHLY COMMENDED	1 Twin 1 Double	1 En Suite fac 1 Priv. NOT ensuite	B&B per person £25.00-£30.00 Single £22.50-£27.50 Double	Open Apr-Sep Dinner 1800-2030 B&B + Eve. Meal £34.50-£42.50

Large Victorian townhouse in quiet residential area. Convenient for Clydeside Expressway to city centre. Ideal base for touring.

Hillview Guest House 18 Hillhead Street Glasgow G12 Tel: 0141 334 5585 Fax: 0141 353 3155	COMMENDED Listed	4 Single 2 Twin 2 Double 2 Family	3 Pub Bath/Show	B&B per person £21.00-£22.00 Single £18.00-£19.00 Double	Open Jan-Dec

Privately owned hotel situated close to Glasgow University and the Kelvin Hall Sports Arena. Convenient for city centre.

GREATER GLASGOW AND CLYDE VALLEY

GLASGOW continued	Map 1 H5						
Iona Guest House 39 Hillhead Street Glasgow G12 8PX Tel: 0141 334 2346 Fax: 0141 334 2346		COMMENDED	3 Single 2 Twin 2 Double 2 Family	3 Pub Bath/Show	B&B per person £20.00-£26.00 Single £16.00-£20.00 Double	Open Jan-Dec Dinner 1800-1900 B&B + Eve. Meal £24.00-£36.00	

Stone-built house in residential area in West End of city centre close to Glasgow University and Kelvingrove Park.

| Mrs L McAlpine
Avonbank, 132 Yokermill Road
Glasgow
G13 4HN
Tel: 0141 952 1637 | | COMMENDED
Listed | 1 Single
1 Twin
3 Family | 2 Pub Bath/Show | B&B per person
£20.00-£22.00 Single
£20.00-£22.00 Double
Room only per person
£18.00-£20.00 | Open Jan-Dec | |

Comfortable ground floor accommodation in traditional villa with transport connections nearby. Easy access to city centre, Loch Lomond and the North.

| Number Thirty Six
36 St Vincent Crescent
Glasgow
G3 8NG
Tel: 0141 248 2086 | | COMMENDED
Listed | 1 Twin
1 Double | 2 En Suite fac | B&B per person
£25.00-£35.00 Single
£25.00-£30.00 Double | Open Apr-Sep | |

Situated in Victorian terrace, convenient for the Exhibition Centre. Continental breakfast served in the comfort of your bedroom.

| Mrs Margaret Ogilvie
Lochgilvie, 117 Randolph Road
Glasgow
G11 7DS
Tel: 0141 357 1593 | | COMMENDED
Listed | 1 Single
1 Twin
1 Double | 2 Limited ensuite
2 Pub Bath/Show | B&B per person
£20.00-£25.00 Single
£18.00-£25.00 Double | Open Jan-Dec | |

Victorian townhouse in popular West End with bus and rail connections nearby. Easy access to A82 for Loch Lomond and Trossachs.

| Mrs A Paterson
16 Bogton Avenue
Glasgow
G44 3JJ
Tel: 0141 637 4402/
0589 534965 | | COMMENDED | 1 Single
1 Double | 1 Priv. NOT ensuite
2 Pub Bath/Show | B&B per person
£18.00 Single
£18.00 Double
Room only per person
£16.00 | Open Jan-Dec
Dinner 1800-1900 | |

Family home in quiet residential area, 200 yds (180m) from railway station with direct access to city centre by train or bus.

| Mrs J Sinclair
23 Dumbreck Road
Glasgow
G41 5LJ
Tel: 0141 427 1006 | | COMMENDED
Listed | 1 Single
1 Twin
1 Double | 2 Pub Bath/Show | B&B per person
£20.00 Single
£18.00-£20.00 Double | Open Apr-Sep
Dinner 1800-2100
B&B + Eve. Meal
£26.00-£30.00 | |

Spacious Victorian house close to Bellahouston Park and local amenities. On bus route to Burrell Collection. ¼ mile (0.4km) from exit 23 on M8.

| Symington Guest House
26 Circus Drive
Glasgow
G31 2JH
Tel: 0141 556 1431 | | COMMENDED
Listed | 1 Twin
1 Double
1 Family | 2 Pub Bath/Show | B&B per person
£14.00-£16.00 Single
£13.00-£15.00 Double | Open Jan-Dec
Dinner 1700-1900 | |

Victorian semi-villa in quiet residential area of East End, 10 minutes' walk from Cathedral and Royal Infirmary.

| The Town House
4 Hughenden Terrace
Glasgow
G12 9XR
Tel: 0141 357 0862
Fax: 0141 339 9605 | | **HIGHLY
COMMENDED**
👑👑👑 | 3 Twin
5 Double
2 Family | 10 En Suite fac | B&B per person
£52.00 Single
£31.00 Double | Open Jan-Dec
Dinner 1830-2000 | |
| Elegantly refurbished Victorian townhouse in quiet conservation area in Glasgow's West End. | | | | | | | |

| The Victorian House
212 Renfrew Street
Glasgow
G3
Tel: 0141 332 0129
Fax: 0141 353 3155 | | **COMMENDED**
👑👑 | 12 Single
12 Twin
12 Double
9 Family | 40 En Suite fac
4 Pub Bath/Show | B&B per person
£21.00-£25.00 Single
£18.00-£20.00 Double | Open Jan-Dec | |
| Terraced house in quiet location close to city centre. | | | | | | | |

| Mrs P Wells
21 West Avenue
Stepps
Glasgow
G33 6ES
Tel: 0141 779 1990
Fax: 0141 779 1990 | | **COMMENDED**
👑👑 | 1 Double
1 Family | 2 En Suite fac | B&B per person
£20.00-£22.00 Single
£20.00-£22.00 Double | Open Jan-Dec | |
| Family home in quiet residential area with easy access to motorway network and city centre. | | | | | | | |

| **GREENOCK**
Renfrewshire
Mrs V Nelis
Lindores, 61 Newark Street
Greenock
Renfrewshire
PA16 7TE
Tel: (Greenock) 01475 783075 | Map 1
G5 | **COMMENDED**
Listed | 1 Twin
1 Double
1 Family | 1 En Suite fac
3 Pub Bath/Show | B&B per person
£18.00-£25.00 Single
£17.50-£20.00 Double | Open Jan-Dec | |
| Comfortable accommodation in wing of 19th century mansion, ideally situated for Clyde Ferries and touring Argyll. 35 minutes' drive to Glasgow. | | | | | | | |

| **HAMILTON**
Lanarkshire
Mrs M Jones
5a Auchingramont Road
Hamilton
ML3 6JP
Tel: (Hamilton) 01698 285230 | Map 2
A6 | **COMMENDED**
Listed | 2 Single
2 Double
1 Family | 2 En Suite fac
1 Limited ensuite
2 Pub Bath/Show | B&B per person
£20.00-£30.00 Single
£20.00-£25.00 Double | Open Jan-Dec | |
| Scandinavian split-level villa, with private parking.
Ensuite accommodation available. | | | | | | | |

| **JOHNSTONE**
Renfrewshire
Mrs C Capper
Auchans Farm
Johnstone
Renfrewshire
PA6 7EE
Tel: (Johnstone) 01505 320131 | Map 1
G5 | **COMMENDED**
Listed | 1 Twin
1 Double
1 Family | 3 Priv. NOT ensuite
2 Pub Bath/Show | B&B per person
£15.00-£20.00 Single
£15.00-£20.00 Double | Open Jan-Dec | |
| Friendly welcome awaits on working farm, a few minutes away from motorway link and Glasgow Airport. Easy access to tourist routes. | | | | | | | |

GREATER GLASGOW AND CLYDE VALLEY

Details of Grading and Classification are on page vi. | Key to symbols is on back flap. | 109

| KILBARCHAN
Renfrewshire | Map 1
G5 | |

Gladstone Farmhouse

**Burntshields Road, Kilbarchan, by Johnstone,
Renfrewshire PA10 2PB   Telephone: 01505 702579**

The farmhouse is less than 10 minutes from Glasgow
Airport on a direct route. It is surrounded by beautiful, quiet
countryside and is ideally situated for touring the Ayrshire
coast, Loch Lomond and only 1 hour from Edinburgh.
*A warm welcome awaits you at our comfortable
300-year-old farmhouse.*

| Mrs Douglas
Gladstone Farmhouse
Kilbarchan, by Johnstone
Renfrewshire
PA10 2PB
Tel: (Kilbarchan) 01505 702579 | **COMMENDED**
Listed | 1 Twin
1 Double
1 Family | 1 En Suite fac
1 Pub Bath/Show | B&B per person
£15.00-£18.00 Single
£15.00-£18.00 Double
Room only per person
£12.00-£14.00 | Open Jan-Dec
Dinner 1800-1900 |

300-year-old farmhouse on working farm. 7 miles (11kms) from Airport.
Convenient for touring Ayrshire and Loch Lomond.

| LANARK | Map 2
A6 | |

Jerviswood Mains Farm

LANARK ML11 7RL   Telephone: 01555 663987

*Good hospitality is offered in this early 19th-century traditional farmhouse,
1 mile from Lanark on the A706, heading northwards. We are near a trout
and deer farm and provide good food in a relaxed atmosphere.
We combine old world charm with modern amenities.
The unique 1758 industrial village of New Lanark, now a World Heritage
Site, and many places of historical interest are nearby, equidistant between
Glasgow and Edinburgh. This is an excellent touring base.*

| Mrs M Findlater
Jerviswood Mains Farm
Lanark
ML11 7RL
Tel: (Lanark) 01555 663987 | **COMMENDED** | 1 Twin
2 Double | 2 Pub Bath/Show | B&B per person
£20.00-£25.00 Single
£17.00-£19.00 Double | Open Jan-Dec |

19th century stone-built farmhouse of considerable character,
1 mile (2 kms) North of historic market town.

| by LANARK

Mrs Faye Hamilton
Corehouse Home Farm
by Lanark
ML11 9TQ
Tel: (Lanark) 01555 661377 | Map 2
A6

COMMENDED | 1 Double
2 Family | 3 En Suite fac | B&B per person
£18.00-£20.00 Single
£16.00-£19.00 Double | Open Jan-Dec |

Warm family welcome on traditional mixed farm close to Falls of Clyde
and nature reserve. 3 miles (5km) from Lanark and Heritage Centre.
Ground floor accommodation.

| LESMAHAGOW
Lanarkshire
Mrs Hamilton
Hillview, 1 New Kayes
Auchenheath, by Lesmahagow
Lanarkshire
ML11 9XJ
Tel: (Lesmahagow)
01555 893908 | Map 2
A6

**HIGHLY
COMMENDED** | 1 Double
1 Family | 1 En Suite fac
1 Priv. NOT ensuite | B&B per person
£18.00-£20.00 Single
£17.00-£19.00 Double
Room only per person
£15.00-£17.00 | Open Jan-Dec |

Modern spacious family home with well-appointed rooms.
Landscaped garden. Secure parking. Easy access to all routes.

by LESMAHAGOW
Lanarkshire
Mrs I H McInally
Dykecroft Farm
Kirkmuirhill, near Lesmahagow
Lanarkshire
ML11 0JQ
Tel: (Lesmahagow)
01555 892226

Map

COMMENDED
Listed

1 Twin
2 Double

1 Pub Bath/Show

B&B per person
£17.00-£18.00 Single
£16.00-£17.00 Double

Open Jan-Dec

Modern farmhouse bungalow in rural situation 20 miles (32kms) South of Glasgow.
An hour's drive from Edinburgh, Stirling, Ayr and Loch Lomond.

LOCHWINNOCH
Renfrewshire
Mrs V McMeechan
Garnock Lodge
Boydstone Road
Loanhead, Lochwinnoch
Renfrewshire
PA12 4JT
Tel: (Beith) 01505 502161/
503680
Fax: 01505 503680

Map 1
G5

HIGHLY
COMMENDED

2 Twin
1 Double

2 En Suite fac
1 Priv. NOT ensuite
1 Pub Bath/Show

B&B per person
£15.00-£20.00 Double

Open Jan-Dec
Dinner 1800-2000
B&B + Eve. Meal
£21.00-£27.00

1940s extended bungalow in peaceful situation, yet central for airport and touring.

---

by LOCHWINNOCH
Renfrewshire
Mrs D Rothney
Springfield
Kerse, by Lochwinnoch
Renfrewshire
PA12 4DT
Tel: (Beith) 01505 503690

Map 1
G5

COMMENDED
Listed

1 Single
1 Twin
1 Double

1 Pub Bath/Show

B&B per person
£16.00 Single
£16.00 Double
Room only per person
£14.00

Open Jan-Dec
Dinner 1700-1930
B&B + Eve. Meal
£23.00

Detached house in rural setting, convenient for RSPB reserve, golf course
and watersports centre on local loch. Glasgow Airport 15 mins.

MILNGAVIE, Glasgow

J M & J G McColl
Westview
1 Dougalston Gardens South
Milngavie, Glasgow
G62 6HS
Tel: 0141 956 5973

Map 1
H5

COMMENDED

1 Twin
1 Double
1 Family

3 En Suite fac

B&B per person
to £20.00 Single
to £18.00 Double

Open Jan-Dec

Detached house in cul-de-sac, with private parking. Families welcome.

PAISLEY
Renfrewshire
Ardgowan Guest House
92 Renfrew Road
Paisley
Renfrewshire
PA3 4BJ
Tel: 0141 889 4763

Map 1
H5

COMMENDED
Listed

2 Single
2 Twin
2 Double
4 Family

2 Pub Bath/Show

B&B per person
£25.00-£27.50 Single
£20.00-£22.00 Double
Room only per person
£18.00-£25.50

Open Jan-Dec
Dinner 1830-2030

Victorian house close to airport yet quietly located with large garden.

Dryfesdale Guest House
37 Inchinnan Road
Paisley
Renfrewshire
PA3 2PR
Tel: 0141 889 7178

APPROVED
Listed

2 Twin
2 Double
2 Family

2 Pub Bath/Show

B&B per person
£18.00-£20.00 Single
£16.00-£18.00 Double

Open Jan-Dec
Dinner 1800-2000
B&B + Eve. Meal
£26.00-£28.00

Personally run and owned guest house 0.5 mile (1km) from Glasgow Airport
and M8 access. Close to Paisley and all facilities.

Greenlaw Guest House
12 Greenlaw Drive
Paisley
Renfrewshire
PA1
Tel: 0141 889 5359

APPROVED
Listed

3 Single
1 Twin
3 Family

3 Pub Bath/Show

B&B per person
£18.00-£20.00 Single
£15.00-£16.00 Double

Open Jan-Dec

Family run guest house, situated in quiet street, yet central for all
local amenities of town and near airport and main motorway.

Details of Grading and Classification are on page vi.

Key to symbols is on back flap.

GREATER GLASGOW AND CLYDE VALLEY

PAISLEY continued **Renfrewshire** Myfarrclan Guest House 146 Corsebar Road Paisley Renfrewshire PA2 9NA Tel: 0141 884 8285 Fax: 0141 884 8285	Map 1 H5	**DELUXE**	1 Twin 2 Double	2 En Suite fac 1 Priv. NOT ensuite	B&B per person £27.00-£40.00 Single £27.00-£32.00 Double Room only per person £20.00-£25.00	Open Jan-Dec Dinner 1900-2030 B&B + Eve. Meal £37.00-£45.00
Detached bungalow in residential area, convenient for Glasgow Airport. Non-smoking house.						
by PAISLEY **Renfrewshire** Ashburn Guest House Milliken Park Road Kilbarchan, by Paisley Renfrewshire PA10 2DB Tel: (Kilbarchan) 01505 705477 Fax: 01505 705477	Map 1 H5	**APPROVED**	1 Single 3 Twin 2 Family	2 En Suite fac 2 Pub Bath/Show	B&B per person £23.00-£27.00 Single £19.00-£25.00 Double Room only per person £17.00-£23.00	Open Jan-Dec Dinner 1800-2000
19th century house in an acre (0.4ha) of garden, 5 minutes from Glasgow Airport. 20 minutes to Glasgow city centre. 400 yds (365m) from railway station.						
STRATHAVEN **Lanarkshire** Mrs Goodwillie Haroldslea, 3 Kirkhill Road Strathaven Lanarkshire ML10 6HN Tel: (Strathaven) 01357 20617	Map 2 A6	**APPROVED** Listed	1 Double 1 Family	1 Priv. NOT ensuite 2 Pub Bath/Show	B&B per person £16.00-£17.00 Single £15.50-£16.00 Double	Open Jan-Dec
Detached bungalow in residential area 800 yds (730m) from village centre. Ground floor accommodation available.						
by STRATHAVEN **Lanarkshire** Mrs Anderson Kypemhor, West Type Farm by Strathaven Lanarkshire ML10 6PR Tel: (Strathaven) 01357 529831	Map 2 A6	**COMMENDED** Listed	1 Twin 1 Double	1 Pub Bath/Show	B&B per person £15.00-£18.00 Single £14.00-£17.00 Double Room only per person £14.00-£17.00	Open Jan-Dec Dinner 1700-2000 B&B + Eve. Meal from £20.00
Modern bungalow set in open countryside, with fine views and easy access to Clyde Valley. Good walking country.						
UPLAWMOOR **Renfrewshire** Mrs J MacLeod East Uplaw Farm Uplawmoor Renfrewshire G78 4DA Tel: (Uplawmoor) 01505 850383/850594 Fax: 01505 850383	Map 1 G6	**COMMENDED** Listed	1 Twin 1 Double 1 Family	1 En Suite fac 2 Pub Bath/Show	B&B per person £14.00-£16.00 Single £14.00-£16.00 Double Room only per person £11.00-£13.00	Open Jan-Dec Dinner 1800-2200 B&B + Eve. Meal £22.50-£25.00
Modern comfortable accommodation, convenient for Burns country on 320 acre (130ha) beef farm. Good farmhouse cooking, mainly fresh produce. Children welcome.						

VAT is shown at 17.5%: changes in this rate may affect prices. Prices shown are for guidance only. Please send SAE with each enquiry.

Welcome to...

West Highlands and Islands, Loch Lomond, Stirling and Trossachs

From the islands of Coll and Tiree, lying low out in the Hebridean sea to the west, to the green slopes of the Ochil Hills east of Stirling, this is a large chunk of Scotland straddling Highland and Lowland.

In the early days of tourism, the location of Loch Lomond and the Trossachs, a highly scenic area just beyond the Highland line, made them easy to reach. Visitors have been admiring the 'bonny banks' and the beauties of the Trossachs at all seasons since the dawning of the romantic age, two centuries ago. Today, these areas are still an excellent choice, particularly for off-peak holidays. Similarly, the west has its own old established resorts, at places like Oban, a railhead on the western seaboard and gateway to the islands.

Visitors come to the West Highlands at least partly for the scenic attractions: for the wildness of Breadalbane around Crianlarich; for the interplay of land and sea-loch that adds so much interest to the western seaboard; for the glorious views of islands from Knapdale or Kintyre. However, the area offers much more than simply scenery. As well as Oban, there are other towns with plenty to see and do. Inveraray on Loch Fyne offers a good range of attractions in and around it, including Inveraray Castle and Inveraray Jail. Dunoon, so easily accessible across the Clyde, is the gateway to the richly forested lands of Cowal.

Situated west of Gloom Hill and beside Burn of Sorrow and the Burn of Care, Castle Campbell was once known as Castle Gloom. However 'Castle Gloom' is a wholly inappropriate name when you see the spectacular views of the Dollar Glen and Pentland Hills.

As a gateway and an important route centre leading on to the Highlands, Stirling played a leading role in Scotland's story. Today its castle is just one of many attractions which range from the National Wallace Monument – find out the real story of Braveheart – to the Old Town Jail. Falkirk is another major town where, within easy reach, the Bo'ness and Kinneil Railway is the re-creation of a typical Scottish branch line in the days of steam.

There are plenty of surprises in store as well. East of Stirling, you will find Scotland's second largest textile area,

around the Hillfoots towns below the Ochil Hills – worth following up if you want to combine a late season break with some Christmas shopping. Follow the Mill Trail to look for the best of the wool and tweed bargains.

In the west, the mild climate grows some great gardens at places like Crarae on Loch Fyne or Arduaine south of Oban. A late spring trip here is a gardener's delight. Or discover a grand Gothic mansion, with breathtaking interiors of marble and stained glass, at Mount Stuart on the island in Bute.

Mull, with its spectacular scenery and tiny Iona, Cradle of Scottish Christianity, close by;

As well as Bute, whose main town Rothesay, has been a popular destination for generations, there is a great choice.

Mull, with its spectacular scenery and tiny Iona, Cradle of Scottish Christianity, close by; Islay and Jura as two contrasting places, one busy with distilling and farming, the other comparatively empty and wild. Lots more to choose from – just head for Oban and make your choice. Or go cruising on the Firth of Clyde or even on inland waters such as Loch Lomond, Loch Katrine or, to the west, Loch Awe.

Finally, however you choose, transport links are excellent, with motorways within minutes of Stirling Castle or simply one of the most scenic train journeys in Scotland taking you to Oban.

AREA TOURIST BOARD
ADDRESSES

ARGYLL, THE ISLES,
LOCH LOMOND,
STIRLING AND
TROSSACHS TOURIST
BOARD
7 Alexandra Place
DUNOON
Argyll
PA23 8AB
Tel: 01369 701000
Fax: 01369 706085

TOURIST INFORMATION CENTRES IN SCOTLAND

ARGYLL, THE ISLES, LOCH LOMOND, STIRLING & TROSSACHS TOURIST BOARD

ABERFOYLE &
Main Street
Tel: (01877) 382352
April-Oct

ALVA &
Mill Trail Visitor Centre
Tel: (01259) 769696
Jan-Dec

ARDGARTAN &
Arrochar
Tel: (01301) 702432
April-Oct

BALLOCH &
Balloch Road
Tel: (01389) 753533
April-Oct

BO'NESS
Seaview Car Park
Tel: (01506) 826626
April-Sept

BOWMORE
Isle of Islay
Tel: (01496) 810254
Jan-Dec

CALLANDER &
Rob Roy & Trossachs
Visitor Centre
Ancaster Square
Tel: (01877) 330342
Jan-Dec

CAMPBELTOWN ✉
Mackinnon House
The Pier
ARGYLL, PA28 6EF
Tel: (01586) 552056
Jan-Dec

CRAIGNURE
Isle of Mull
Tel: (01680) 812377
April-Oct

DRYMEN
Drymen Library
The Square
Tel: (01360) 660068
May-Sept

DUMBARTON
Milton
A82 Northbound
Tel: (01389) 742306
Jan-Dec

DUNBLANE &
Stirling Road
Tel: (01786) 824428
May-Sept

DUNOON ✉
7 Alexandra Parade
Argyll, PA23 8AB
Tel: (01369) 703785
Jan-Dec

FALKIRK & ✉
2-4 Glebe Street
Tel: (01324) 620244
Jan-Dec

HELENSBURGH &
The Clock Tower
Tel: (01436) 672642
April-Oct

INVERARAY
Front Street
Argyll
Tel: (01499) 302063
Jan-Dec

KILLIN &
Breadalbane Folklore Centre
Tel: (01567) 820254
March-Dec

KINCARDINE BRIDGE
Airth, by Falkirk
Tel: (01324) 831422
Easter-Sept

LOCHGILPHEAD
Lochnell Street, Argyll
Tel: (01546) 602344
April-Oct

OBAN & ✉
Argyll Square
Argyll, PA34 4AR
Tel: (01631) 563122
Jan-Dec

ROTHESAY ✉
15 Victoria Street
Isle of Bute, PA20 0AJ
Tel: (01700) 502151
Jan-Dec

STIRLING & ✉
Dumbarton Road, FK8 2LQ
Tel: (01786) 475019
Jan-Dec
Royal Burgh of Stirling Visitor Centre
Tel: (01786) 479901
Jan-Dec
Pirnhall Motorway Service Area
Junction 9 (M9)
Tel: (01786) 814111
April-Oct

TARBERT
Harbour Street, Argyll
Tel: (01880) 820429
April-Oct

TARBET-LOCH LOMOND
Main Street
Tel: (01301) 702260
April-Oct

TOBERMORY
Isle of Mull
Tel: (01688) 302182
Jan-Dec

TYNDRUM &
Main Street
Tel: (01838) 400246
April-Oct

ABERFOYLE Perthshire Mrs A Jennings The Bield, Trossachs Road Aberfoyle Perthshire FK8 3SX Tel: (Aberfoyle) 01877 382351	Map 1 H3	COMMENDED ♕♕	2 Double 1 Family	1 En Suite fac 1 Pub Bath/Show	B&B per person £15.00-£17.00 Double	Open Apr-Oct

Refurbished Edwardian sandstone villa set high up over village of Aberfoyle. Spectacular views yet only 2 minutes' walk from village.

Mrs Fiona Oldham Mayfield, Main Street Aberfoyle Perthshire FK8 3UQ Tel: (Aberfoyle) 01877 382845		COMMENDED Listed	1 Single 2 Double	3 En Suite fac 2 Pub Bath/Show	B&B per person £15.00-£17.00 Single £15.00-£17.00 Double	Open Jan-Dec

Large detached villa in central location. Ground-floor bedrooms all with private facilities offer combination of warm hospitality and relaxed atmosphere.

by ABERFOYLE Perthshire	Map 1 H3

Creag-Ard House B&B
MILTON, NEAR ABERFOYLE, STIRLING FK8 3TQ
Telephone: 01877 382297
Nestling in three acres of beautiful gardens, this lovely Victorian house enjoys some of the most magnificent scenery in Scotland. Overlooking *Loch Ard,* with long distance views to *Ben Lomond* and surrounded by tree-clad mountains. Own trout fishing and boat hire available. Secure car parking. Centrally situated for touring Scotland.

Andrew and Pauline Carter Creag-Ard House B&B Milton, near Aberfoyle Perthshire FK8 3TQ Tel: (Aberfoyle) 01877 382297		COMMENDED ♕♕	1 Single 2 Twin 3 Double 1 Family	4 En Suite fac 1 Pub Bath/Show	B&B per person £25.00-£60.00 Single £17.50-£30.00 Double	Open Jan-Dec

Detached Victorian house with superb views over Loch Ard and Ben Lomond beyond. Private fishing and boating. Most bedrooms ensuite.

by APPIN Argyll	Map 1 E1

LOCHSIDE COTTAGE
Fasnacloich, Appin, Argyll PA38 4BJ   Tel: 01631 730216
Enjoy the West Highlands and Islands. The tranquil setting of Lochside Cottage (wonderful walks from cottage garden), combined with the friendly atmosphere of the Broadbents' home, ensures a pleasant relaxing holiday away from the hurly burly of modern life. Comfortable, attractive bedrooms, sittingroom and delicious home cooking. Local information readily available.

Mrs Stella M Broadbent Lochside Cottage Fasnacloich, Appin Argyll PA38 4BJ Tel: (Oban) 01631 730216 Fax: 01631 730216		HIGHLY COMMENDED ♕♕♕	2 Twin 1 Double	2 En Suite fac 1 Priv. NOT ensuite	B&B per person £20.00-£24.00 Single £20.00-£24.00 Double	Open Jan-Dec Dinner from 1930 B&B + Eve. Meal £36.50-£40.50

Set in the beauty and the grandeur of the Highland Glen where the historic Campbell/Stewart rivalry inspired R.L. Stevenson's "Kidnapped".

ARDEN Dunbartonshire Mrs P McNair North Polnaberoch Arden, by Luss Dunbartonshire G83 8RQ Tel: (Arden) 01389 850615 Fax: 01389 850615	Map 1 G4	HIGHLY COMMENDED ♕♕	1 Double 1 Family	2 En Suite fac	B&B per person £21.00-£23.00 Double	Open Easter-Oct

In tranquil rural setting with large garden. Short distance from Loch Lomond, golf courses and country walks.

STIRLING & TROSSACHS

WEST HIGHLANDS & ISLANDS, LOCH LOMOND,

STIRLING & TROSSACHS

WEST HIGHLANDS & ISLANDS, LOCH LOMOND,

ARDFERN	Map 1
Argyll	E3

Lunga Estate

Ardfern, Argyll PA31 8QR
Telephone: 01852 500237 Fax 01852 500639

Lunga, a 17th century mansion overlooking Firth of Lorne and Sound of Jura, home to the MacDougalls for over 300 years, who offer comfortable rooms for B & B and self-catering flats or cottages. Join us for our famous candle-lit dinners and share the facilities of this beautiful 3,000-acre coastal estate.

C Lindsay-MacDougall of Lunga	APPROVED	1 Single	4 En Suite fac	B&B per person	Open Jan-Dec
Lunga	♛♛♛	1 Twin	1 Pub Bath/Show	£15.00-£19.00 Single	Dinner from 2000
Ardfern, by Lochgilphead		2 Double		£15.00-£19.00 Double	
Argyll				Room only per person	
PA31 8QR				£11.00-£15.00	
Tel: (Barbreck) 01852 500237					
Fax: 01852 500639					

18th century mansion house on 3,000-acre (1,214ha) estate. Riding, fishing, sailing and hillwalking available. Annexe accommodation.

ARDRISHAIG, by Lochgilphead	Map 1				
Argyll	E4				
Mrs Hamilton	COMMENDED	1 Twin	1 En Suite fac	B&B per person	Open Jan-Dec
Seaview, St Clair Road	♛	2 Double	2 Pub Bath/Show	£15.00-£18.00 Single	
Ardrishaig, by Lochgilphead				£15.00-£18.00 Double	
Argyll				Room only per person	
Tel: (Lochgilphead)				£10.00-£15.00	
01546 603300					

Traditional stone-built house set above the village with open views over the harbour and loch. Home bakes and friendly welcome.

HAWTHORN

**West Bank Road, Ardrishaig, Argyll PA30 8HG
Tel: 01546 603447**

Edwardian home beautifully situated on banks of Crinan Canal, in centre of village. Views over Loch Fyne and Isle of Arran. Ideal touring centre for mid Argyll and the Islands. No smoking, ensuite rooms with central heating, TV and hospitality trays. Breakfast in conservatory overlooking boats on the canal.

Rosemary McAllister	COMMENDED	1 Twin	2 En Suite fac	B&B per person	Open Jan-Dec
Hawthorn, Westbank Road	♛♛	2 Double	1 Pub Bath/Show	£15.00-£20.00 Single	
Ardrishaig				£15.00-£20.00 Double	
Argyll					
PA30 8HG					
Tel: (Lochgilphead)					
01546 603447					

Traditional stone-built family home overlooking the Crinan Canal. Ideal base for exploring scenic Argyll. Totally non-smoking.

Book your accommodation anywhere in Scotland the easy way – through your nearest Tourist Information Centre.

A booking fee of £2.75 is charged, and you will be asked for a small deposit.

Local bookings are usually free, or a small fee will be charged.

ARROCHAR Dunbartonshire	Map 1 G3

FERRY COTTAGE
ARROCHAR, DUNBARTONSHIRE G83 7AH
Tel: 01301 702428   Fax: 01301 702699

This 200-year-old house, fully refurbished by a local craftsman, is central for touring and all outdoor activities. Our scenic views across Loch Long and the Arrochar Alps are second to none. Bedroom facilities include tea/coffee, hairdryers, ensuites and firm beds to ensure a restful night. One features a "FOUR-POSTER WATER BED". Central heating throughout. Cosy lounge and PAY PHONE. For your peace of mind there is private parking and a Fire Certificate.
★ OPEN MOST OF THE YEAR.
★ Colour TV in all bedrooms.
5 minutes' drive from Loch Lomond.
NON-SMOKING ESTABLISHMENT!
Situated 1 mile south of Arrochar on the A814.

Mrs C Bennetton
Ferry Cottage
Ardmay, Arrochar
Dunbartonshire
G83 7AH
Tel: (Arrochar) 01301 702428
Fax: 01301 702699

COMMENDED 👑👑👑

1 Twin
1 Double
1 Family

3 En Suite fac

B&B per person
£20.00-£23.50 Double

Open Jan-Dec
Dinner at 1930
B&B + Eve. Meal
£31.00-£35.50

Refurbished 200-year-old house with attractive bedrooms and ensuite shower-rooms. Scenic views across Loch Long.

Mrs J R Hetherington
5 Admiralty Cottage
Arrochar
Dunbartonshire
G83 7AQ
Tel: (Arrochar) 01301 702427

APPROVED Listed

2 Twin
1 Double

1 Pub Bath/Show

B&B per person
£14.00-£16.00 Single
£12.00-£14.00 Double

Open Mar-Nov

Small, family house, situated by roadside, overlooking Loch Long. Ideal location for all outdoor activities.

Lochside Guest House
Arrochar
Dunbartonshire
G83 7AA
Tel: (Arrochar) 01301 702467
Fax: 01301 702467

APPROVED 👑👑

2 Single
1 Twin
3 Double
1 Family

3 En Suite fac
1 Priv. NOT ensuite
3 Pub Bath/Show

B&B per person
£17.50-£25.00 Single
£17.50-£22.00 Double

Open Jan-Dec
Dinner from 1830
B&B + Eve. Meal
£27.50-£32.00

Friendly atmosphere in this guest house on the shore of Loch Long with view across the loch to the Cobbler. Evening meals by arrangement.

BALLOCH Dunbartonshire	Map 1 G4

Mrs M Brown
6 McLean Crescent
Lomond Road Estate
Balloch
Dunbartonshire
G83 8HW
Tel: (Alexandria) 01389 752855

COMMENDED Listed

1 Twin
1 Double

1 Pub Bath/Show

B&B per person
£16.00-£17.00 Single
£15.50-£16.50 Double

Open Feb-Nov
Dinner from 1800
B&B + Eve. Meal
from £22.00

Modern family villa in quiet residential area, offering a warm and friendly welcome. 30 minute drive from Glasgow Airport.

Mrs M Cameron
Ballagan Farm
Balloch
Dunbartonshire
G83 8LY
Tel: (Balloch) 01389 752966

APPROVED Listed

1 Single
2 Double

2 Priv. NOT ensuite

B&B per person
to £19.00 Single
to £18.00 Double

Open Mar-Nov

Stone-built white-washed farm steading in lovely rural location. One mile (1.6kmd) from Balloch.

STIRLING & TROSSACHS

WEST HIGHLANDS & ISLANDS, LOCH LOMOND,

BALLOCH	Map 1						
BALLOCH **Dunbartonshire continued** Gowanlea Guest House Mrs M Campbell Drymen Road Balloch Dunbartonshire G83 8HS Tel: (Alexandria) 01389 752456 Fax: 01389 710543	G4	**HIGHLY COMMENDED**	1 Twin 2 Double	3 En Suite fac	B&B per person £17.00-£25.00 Single £16.00-£20.00 Double	Open Jan-Dec	
Situated in residential area of Balloch, close to world famous Loch Lomond. Friendly welcome, all rooms ensuite.							
Kinnoul Guest House Mrs Janice Elder Drymen Road, Balloch Dunbartonshire G83 8HS Tel: (Alexandria) 01389 721116		**COMMENDED**	1 Twin 2 Double 1 Family	3 En Suite fac 1 Priv.NOT ensuite	B&B per person £23.00-£26.00 Single £16.00-£19.00 Double	Open Jan-Dec Dinner from 1900 B&B + Eve.Meal £27.50-£30.50	
Real Scottish hospitality guaranteed. Spacious accommodation with ensuite and private facilities. Private parking.							
Mrs G McKinney Norwood, 58 Balloch Road Balloch Dunbartonshire G83 8LE Tel: (Alexandria) 01389 754304		**COMMENDED**	2 Twin 1 Double	2 En Suite fac 1 Pub Bath/Show	B&B per person £22.00 Single £14.00-£17.00 Double	Open Jan-Dec	
Comfortable, friendly welcome only 5 minutes from Loch Lomond. Convenient for station and bus terminus.							
Norwood Guest House Mrs C McGinty 60 Balloch Road Balloch Dunbartonshire G83 8RZ Tel: (Alexandria) 01389 750309		**COMMENDED**	2 Twin 3 Double	5 En Suite fac	B&B per person to £20.00 Single to £18.00 Double	Open Jan-Dec	
Centrally located overlooking Balloch Castle Country Park close to all local amenities.							
Mrs E Oultram Westville, Riverside Lane Balloch Dunbartonshire G83 8LF Tel: (Alexandria) 01389 752307		**COMMENDED**	1 Double 1 Family	1 Pub Bath/Show	B&B per person £17.00-£19.00 Single £17.00-£19.00 Double	Open Jan-Dec	
Mature bungalow, situated in quiet area of Balloch. Private parking. Overlooking the marina at River Leven. Ideal location for touring.							
Mr Thomas Patrick Woodvale, Drymen Road Balloch Dunbartonshire G83 8HT Tel: (Alexandria) 01389 755771		**APPROVED Listed**	2 Double 1 Family	3 En Suite fac	B&B per person £16.00-£18.00 Single £12.00-£17.00 Double Room only per person £10.00-£15.00	Open Jan-Dec Dinner 1730-1900	
Family home in centre of Balloch. Short walk to all amenities, ideal base for touring.							
Mrs Margo J Ross Glyndale, 6 McKenzie Drive Lomond Road Estate Balloch Dunbartonshire G83 8HL Tel: (Alexandria) 01389 758238		**COMMENDED Listed**	1 Twin 1 Double	1 Pub Bath/Show	B&B per person £14.50-£15.50 Double	Open Jan-Dec	
Modern family home in residential area, 10 minutes' walk from Loch Lomond, and 30-minute drive from Glasgow Airport.							
Mr C Tait 240 Main Street, Jamestown Balloch Dunbartonshire Tel: (Balloch) 01389 752473		**COMMENDED**	1 Family	1 En Suite fac	B&B per person £15.00 Double	Open Mar-Oct	
Self-contained, serviced flat in family home. Personal attention from your hosts. Ideal for touring Loch Lomond and the Trossachs.							

BALMAHA, by Drymen **Stirlingshire** Mrs K MacFadyen Dunleen, Milton of Buchanan Balmaha Stirlingshire G63 OJE Tel: (Balmaha) 01360 870274	Map 1 G4	**HIGHLY COMMENDED** ♛	1 Twin 1 Double	1 Pub Bath/Show	B&B per person £17.00-£18.00 Double	Open May-Oct	

Comfortable modern bungalow situated in a quiet spot
within easy reach of Loch Lomond. Friendly atmosphere.

Mrs F Macluskie Critreoch, Rowardennan Road Balmaha Stirlingshire G63 0AW Tel: (Balmaha) 01360 870309		**COMMENDED** ♛♛	1 Twin 2 Double	1 En Suite fac 2 Priv. NOT ensuite	B&B per person £17.00-£19.00 Double	Open Apr-Oct	

Friendly, family home in beautiful location, close to shore of Loch Lomond,
with magnificent views. Warm welcome assured.

BALQUHIDDER **Perthshire** Mrs Lesley Blain Calea Sona Balquhidder Perthshire FK19 8NY Tel: (Strathyre) 01877 384260 Fax: 01877 384260	Map 1 H2	**COMMENDED** ♛♛	1 Twin 1 Double	1 En Suite fac 1 Priv. NOT ensuite	B&B per person £21.00 Double	Open Jan-Dec	

Cottage, an interesting blend of old and new, peacefully
situated with superb views. Good walking area.

Craigruie Farmhouse

Craigruie Farm, Balquhidder, By Lochearnhead, Perthshire FK19 8PQ

Telephone: 01877 384262

Craigruie Farmhouse is set in the beautiful Braes of Balquhidder
overlooking Loch Voil. Enjoy personally organised sporting activities
including fishing, stalking and shooting on this family run hill farm.
Excellent traditional fayre in very comfortable surroundings.
Warm welcome to all.

Mrs Marshall Craigruie Farmhouse Balquhidder, by Lochearnhead Perthshire FK19 8PQ Tel: (Balquhidder) 01877 384262		**COMMENDED** **Listed**	1 Twin 2 Family	1 En Suite fac 1 Pub Bath/Show	B&B per person £21.00-£23.00 Single £18.00-£20.00 Double	Open Jan-Dec Dinner 1800-2130 B&B + Eve. Meal £26.00-£34.00	

Tastefully renovated farmhouse, overlooking Loch Voil, peacefully situated
2 miles (3 kms) from Balquhidder. Personally organised sporting and fishing.

BENDERLOCH, by Connel **Argyll** Mrs June Currie Hawthorn Benderloch, by Connel Argyll PA37 1QS Tel: (Ledaig) 01631 720452	Map 1 E2	**COMMENDED** ♛	1 Twin 1 Double	1 Pub Bath/Show	B&B per person £15.00 Single £14.00-£18.00 Double	Open Mar-Oct Dinner 1830-2000	

Bungalow in peaceful rural setting 9 miles (14 kms) from Oban,
and 5 minutes' walk from Tralee beach. Own restaurant adjacent.

BLAIR DRUMMOND **Perthshire** Mrs P Darby The Linns, Kirk Lane Blair Drummond, by Stirling Perthshire FK9 4AN Tel: (Doune) 01786 841679	Map 2 A3	**COMMENDED** ♛♛	1 Twin 2 Double	1 Priv. NOT ensuite 2 Pub Bath/Show	B&B per person £18.00-£20.00 Single £16.50-£19.00 Double	Open Apr-Sep	

19th century cottage with modern extension in rural setting. 4 miles (6.4kms)
from Stirling. Next to Safari Park.

Details of Grading and Classification are on page vi. | Key to symbols is on back flap. |

STIRLING & TROSSACHS

WEST HIGHLANDS & ISLANDS, LOCH LOMOND,

| BO'NESS
West Lothian
Hollywood House
25 Grahamsdyke Road
Bo'ness
West Lothian
EH51 9ED
Tel: (Bo'ness) 01506 823260 | Map 2
B4 | COMMENDED
👑👑 | 1 Single
1 Double
1 Family | 1 En Suite fac
2 Pub Bath/Show | B&B per person
£20.00-£25.00 Single
£20.00-£25.00 Double | Open Jan-Dec |

Victorian house with original architecture, set in attractive gardens, with extensive views over the Firth of Forth. Private parking.

| BRIG O'TURK | Map 1.
H3 |

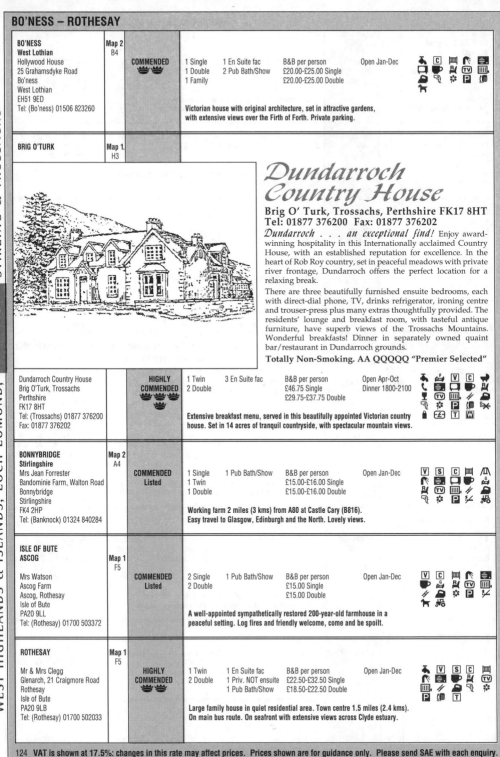

Dundarroch Country House

Brig O' Turk, Trossachs, Perthshire FK17 8HT
Tel: 01877 376200 Fax: 01877 376202

Dundarroch . . . an exceptional find! Enjoy award-winning hospitality in this Internationally acclaimed Country House, with an established reputation for excellence. In the heart of Rob Roy country, set in peaceful meadows with private river frontage, Dundarroch offers the perfect location for a relaxing break.

There are three beautifully furnished ensuite bedrooms, each with direct-dial phone, TV, drinks refrigerator, ironing centre and trouser-press plus many extras thoughtfully provided. The residents' lounge and breakfast room, with tasteful antique furniture, have superb views of the Trossachs Mountains. Wonderful breakfasts! Dinner in separately owned quaint bar/restaurant in Dundarroch grounds.

Totally Non-Smoking. AA QQQQQ "Premier Selected"

| Dundarroch Country House
Brig O'Turk, Trossachs
Perthshire
FK17 8HT
Tel: (Trossachs) 01877 376200
Fax: 01877 376202 | | HIGHLY
COMMENDED
👑👑👑 | 1 Twin
2 Double | 3 En Suite fac | B&B per person
£46.75 Single
£29.75-£37.75 Double | Open Apr-Oct
Dinner 1800-2100 |

Extensive breakfast menu, served in this beautifully appointed Victorian country house. Set in 14 acres of tranquil countryside, with spectacular mountain views.

| BONNYBRIDGE
Stirlingshire
Mrs Jean Forrester
Bandominie Farm, Walton Road
Bonnybridge
Stirlingshire
FK4 2HP
Tel: (Banknock) 01324 840284 | Map 2
A4 | COMMENDED
Listed | 1 Single
1 Twin
1 Double | 1 Pub Bath/Show | B&B per person
£15.00-£16.00 Single
£15.00-£16.00 Double | Open Jan-Dec |

Working farm 2 miles (3 kms) from A80 at Castle Cary (B816). Easy travel to Glasgow, Edinburgh and the North. Lovely views.

| ISLE OF BUTE
ASCOG
Mrs Watson
Ascog Farm
Ascog, Rothesay
Isle of Bute
PA20 9LL
Tel: (Rothesay) 01700 503372 | Map 1
F5 | COMMENDED
Listed | 2 Single
2 Double | 1 Pub Bath/Show | B&B per person
£15.00 Single
£15.00 Double | Open Jan-Dec |

A well-appointed sympathetically restored 200-year-old farmhouse in a peaceful setting. Log fires and friendly welcome, come and be spoilt.

| ROTHESAY
Mr & Mrs Clegg
Glenarch, 21 Craigmore Road
Rothesay
Isle of Bute
PA20 9LB
Tel: (Rothesay) 01700 502033 | Map 1
F5 | HIGHLY
COMMENDED
👑👑 | 1 Twin
2 Double | 1 En Suite fac
1 Priv. NOT ensuite
1 Pub Bath/Show | B&B per person
£22.50-£32.50 Single
£18.50-£22.50 Double | Open Jan-Dec |

Large family house in quiet residential area. Town centre 1.5 miles (2.4 kms). On main bus route. On seafront with extensive views across Clyde estuary.

CALLANDER Perthshire Abbotsford Lodge Stirling Road Callander Perthshire FK17 8DA Tel: (Callander) 01877 330066	Map 1 H3	COMMENDED	1 Single 4 Twin 5 Double 8 Family	10 En Suite fac 4 Pub Bath/Show	B&B per person £24.00-£29.00 Single £18.00-£23.00 Double	Open Jan-Dec Dinner from 1900 B&B + Eve. Meal £29.50-£35.00

Family run Victorian house in its own grounds with private parking, some ground-floor rooms. Close to town centre. Home cooking and baking.

Annfield Guest House North Church Street Callander Perthshire FK17 8EG Tel: (Callander) 01877 330204		COMMENDED	2 Twin 4 Double 1 Family	4 En Suite fac 2 Pub Bath/Show	B&B per person £17.00-£19.00 Double Room only per person £17.00-£19.00	Open Jan-Dec

Centrally situated in a quiet area of the town in close proximity to shops and restaurants. Stepping-stone to the Highlands.

Arden House Guest House Bracklinn Road Callander Perthshire FK17 8EQ Tel: (Callander) 01877 330235 Fax: 01877 330235		HIGHLY COMMENDED	1 Single 2 Twin 2 Double 1 Family	6 En Suite fac	B&B per person £20.00-£22.00 Single £20.00-£22.00 Double	Open Mar-Nov Dinner from 1900 B&B + Eve. Meal £30.00-£32.00

Family run, peacefully situated in its own grounds. Superb panoramic views to Ben Ledi and the Trossachs. A non-smoking house.

Craig Villa Guest House Craig Villa, Leny Road Callander Perthshire FK17 8AW Tel: (Callander) 01877 330871		COMMENDED	1 Twin 3 Double	4 En Suite fac	B&B per person £20.00-£22.00 Double	Open Apr-Nov

Stone-built villa in main street, 5 minutes' walk from shops and Rob Roy Centre. Own car park with easy access to ground-floor bedroom.

Mrs J Donald Trean Farm Callander Perthshire FK17 8AS Tel: (Callander) 01877 331160		COMMENDED	1 Twin 2 Double	2 En Suite fac 1 Pub Bath/Show	B&B per person £16.00-£19.00 Double	Open May-Oct

House situated on a 235-acre (95ha) working farm on the outskirts of Callander. Magnificent views of Ben Ledi.

East Mains Guest House
East Mains House, Bridgend
Callander FK17 8AG   Tel: 01877 330535

East Mains is a family run 18th-century guest house set in its own grounds, ideally situated to tour central Scotland. Offering a high standard of accommodation with impressive Georgian lounge (log fire). Most rooms have private facilities, colour TV and tea/coffee-making. Home cooking and private parking.

East Mains House Bridgend Callander FK17 8AG Tel: (Callander) 01877 330535 Fax: 01877 330535		COMMENDED	3 Double 2 Family	4 En Suite fac 1 Pub Bath/Show	B&B per person £24.00-£26.00 Single £17.00-£21.00 Double	Open Jan-Dec Dinner 1830-1930 B&B + Eve. Meal £27.00-£33.00

Fine, 18th century mansion house, with impressive lounge, situated in its own grounds. Close to town centre and River Teith.

STIRLING & TROSSACHS, LOCH LOMOND, WEST HIGHLANDS & ISLANDS

STIRLING & TROSSACHS

WEST HIGHLANDS & ISLANDS, LOCH LOMOND,

| CALLANDER continued | Map 1 |
| Perthshire | H3 |

INVERTROSSACHS COUNTRY HOUSE

Invertrossachs, by Callander, Perthshire FK17 8HG
Telephone: 01877 331126 Fax: 01877 331229

At this splendid lochside Edwardian Mansion we are pleased to offer a superior accommodation and breakfast service complemented with a discreet level of personal attention.

Our Loch Room with private bath, shower and wc is a large double or twin with commanding views over Loch Venachar. Our Victoria Suite in its own private wing sleeps up to 4 in a choice of bedrooms (double, small double and single) with private bath, shower and wc. Both Loch and Victoria have colour TV, d/dial phone, trouser press, hairdryers, video, CD and tea-making facilities. Prices include 5-course Scottish breakfast served in our conservatory. Optional dinner service available.

Leisurely walking, cycling, fishing on site. Golf/water sports close by. Ideal touring base for freedom, flexibility and a complete escape. – *Advance booking recommended.*
As featured in BBC's "Summer Holiday" 1995. Please quote EBB

Invertrossachs Country House
Invertrossachs, by Callander
Perthshire
FK17 8HG
Tel: (Callander) 01877 331126
Fax: 01877 331229

HIGHLY COMMENDED

1 Twin / 2 Double / Suite avail
3 En Suite fac / 1 Pub Bath/Show
B&B per person £35.00-£75.00 Single / £35.00-£60.00 Double
Open Jan-Dec

Edwardian mansion in its own 28 acres (11ha) of mature woodlands overlooking Loch Venachar. Quiet rural setting 4 miles (6 kms) up a private drive.

Mrs A Lochans
The Lochans, 5 Lubnaig Drive
Callander
Perthshire
FK17 8JT
Tel: (Callander) 01877 330627

COMMENDED

1 Twin / 1 Family
2 En Suite fac
B&B per person £21.00-£22.50 Single / £18.00-£19.50 Double
Open May-Oct / Dinner 1830-1930 / B&B + Eve. Meal £27.00-£28.50

Detached chalet bungalow in quiet residential area on south side of town, ½ mile (1 km) from town centre. Both bedrooms with ensuite facilities.

Mrs E MacKenzie
Lamorna, Ancaster Road
Callander
Perthshire
FK17 8EL
Tel: (Callander) 01877 330868

COMMENDED

1 Twin / 1 Double
1 Pub Bath/Show
B&B per person £15.50-£16.50 Double
Open Apr-Oct

Family run, detached bungalow in a quiet area. Comfortable rooms, warm, friendly atmosphere. Private parking.

Riverview House
Leny Road
Callander
Perthshire
FK17 8AL
Tel: (Callander) 01877 330635

COMMENDED

1 Single / 1 Twin / 3 Double
4 En Suite fac / 1 Limited ensuite / 1 Pub Bath/Show
B&B per person £19.00-£20.00 Single / £19.00-£20.00 Double
Open Apr-Nov / Dinner 1900-1915 / B&B + Eve. Meal from £31.00

19th century house situated back from the main route north out of Callander. All meals with choice of menu, using fresh produce in season.

Tulipan Lodge Guest House
Tulipan Crescent
Callander
Perthshire
FK17 8AR
Tel: (Callander) 01877 330572

COMMENDED

2 Twin / 3 Double
5 En Suite fac
B&B per person £28.00-£30.00 Single / £18.00-£20.00 Double
Open Apr-Oct / Dinner 1830-1900 / B&B + Eve. Meal £29.00-£31.00

Substantial stone villa on edge of village with level walking to shops and all amenities. Evening meals available.

The Priory Guest House

Bracklinn Road, Callander, Perthshire FK17 8EH
Telephone and Fax: 01877 330001

Former Victorian manse, refurbished to high standard. Spacious ensuite rooms, five rooms with central heating, TV, beverage tray, hairdryer. Interesting food. Cooked Breakfast Specials of The Priory change daily plus extensive buffet. Best of field and stream for dinner. Licensed. Private parking in quiet one-acre walled garden. Tour the Trossachs and much of Scotland.

Our ground-floor twin is suitable for those with mobility difficulties. King room available. Relax in large lounge with provided newspapers, magazines, books or sample fine malts or cocktails before or after a four-course meal with tea or coffee. Reduced rates for three or more days Dinner, Bed and Breakfast. Lovely, large family room.

Ms Karin A Warren, Mr Ian Wylie The Priory, Bracklinn Road Callander FK17 8EH Tel: 01877 330001 Fax: 01877 330001	**HIGHLY COMMENDED** 👑👑👑 🚶	1 Single 2 Twin 4 Double 1 Family	8 En Suite fac	B&B per person to £26.00 Single £24.00-£26.00 Double	Open Mar-Oct Dinner from 1900 B&B + Eve. Meal £36.00-£38.00	

Former Victorian manse within walled garden. Refurbished to a high standard. Daily changing menu with a refreshing difference. Ample private parking.

CAMPBELTOWN **Argyll** Mrs J. Scott-Dodd Rosemount, Low Askomil Campbeltown Argyll PA28 Tel: (Campbeltown) 01586 553552	Map 1 D7 **COMMENDED** 👑👑	1 Twin 2 Double 1 Family	4 En Suite fac	B&B per person from £21.00 Single from £19.00 Double	Open Jan-Dec	

Georgian B Listed home in elevated position with magnificent views over Campbeltown Loch and 10 minutes' walk from town centre. Annexe cottage suite.

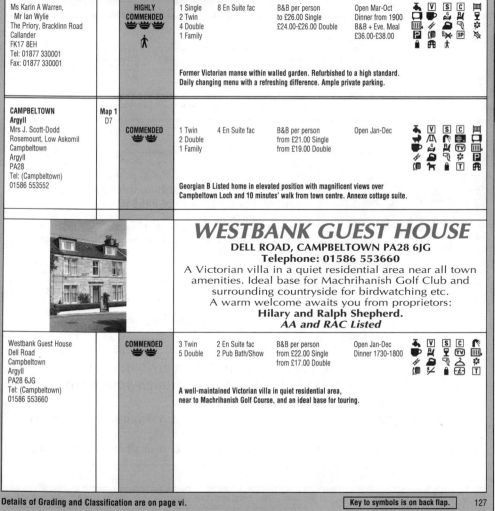

WESTBANK GUEST HOUSE

DELL ROAD, CAMPBELTOWN PA28 6JG
Telephone: 01586 553660
A Victorian villa in a quiet residential area near all town amenities. Ideal base for Machrihanish Golf Club and surrounding countryside for birdwatching etc.
A warm welcome awaits you from proprietors:
Hilary and Ralph Shepherd.
AA and RAC Listed

Westbank Guest House Dell Road Campbeltown Argyll PA28 6JG Tel: (Campbeltown) 01586 553660	**COMMENDED** 👑👑	3 Twin 5 Double	2 En Suite fac 2 Pub Bath/Show	B&B per person from £22.00 Single from £17.00 Double	Open Jan-Dec Dinner 1730-1800	

A well-maintained Victorian villa in quiet residential area, near to Machrihanish Golf Course, and an ideal base for touring.

STIRLING & TROSSACHS

WEST HIGHLANDS & ISLANDS, LOCH LOMOND,

STIRLING & TROSSACHS

WEST HIGHLANDS & ISLANDS, LOCH LOMOND,

CARDROSS Dunbartonshire	Map 1 G4			

Kirkton House
Darleith Road, Cardross G82 5EZ.
Tel: 01389 841951. Fax: 01389 841868.
A converted 18th century farmstead, in a tranquil country setting, with panoramic views of the Clyde, offering old world-charm and all modern amenities. In all the best guides, yet informal and unpretentious. Enjoy a cosy open fire on chilly evenings. Wine and dine by oil lamplight – extensive daily dinner menus.

Logis

Kirkton House Darleith Road Cardross Dunbartonshire G82 5EZ Tel: (Cardross) 01389 841951 Fax: 01389 841868	HIGHLY COMMENDED	2 Twin 4 Family	6 En Suite fac	B&B per person £37.50 Single £26.00-£30.00 Double

Open Jan-Dec
Dinner 1930-2030
B&B + Eve. Meal
£40.00-£55.50

Built around central courtyard in a quiet, elevated rural position commanding magnificent views of the River Clyde.

CARRADALE Argyll Mrs McCormick The Mains Farm Carradale Argyll PA28 6QG Tel: (Carradale) 01583 431216	Map 1 E6 COMMENDED Listed	1 Single 1 Double 1 Family	1 Pub Bath/Show	B&B per person from £14.00 Single from £14.00 Double

Open Apr-Oct
Dinner from 1800
B&B + Eve. Meal
from £19.50

Traditional farmhouse on working farm, on the outskirts of the village and a short walk from the beach. Panoramic views across to the Isle of Arran.

CARRON BRIDGE Stirlingshire	Map 2 A4			

Drum Farm
Carronbridge, Stirling, Stirlingshire FK6 5JL
Telephone and Fax: 01324 825518
Beautiful farmhouse situated in unspoilt countryside with views overlooking Carron Dam, just 15 minutes from Stirling and the M9 and M80, where you can start your tours around this beautiful part of Scotland.

Drum Farm Carronbridge Denny Stirlingshire Tel: (Denny) 01324 825518 Fax: 01324 825518	COMMENDED	1 Twin 1 Double	1 Pub Bath/Show	B&B per person £16.00-£18.50 Single £13.50-£17.00 Double

Open Jan-Dec
Dinner from 1800

Modernised 200-year-old farmhouse in quiet location with magnificent views. 7 miles (11 kms) from Stirling. Ideal for touring.

Book your accommodation anywhere in Scotland the easy way – through your nearest Tourist Information Centre.

A booking fee of £2.75 is charged, and you will be asked for a small deposit.

Local bookings are usually free, or a small fee will be charged.

COLONSAY, Isle of Argyll	Map 1 C4

SEAVIEW

Isle of Colonsay, Argyll PA61 7YN   Tel: 01951 200315

Situated in a quiet crofting community by the standing stones at Kilchattan looking over the Atlantic to Dhu Hertach Lighthouse. Comfort and good home cooking.

A warm welcome assured.

Mr & Mrs Lawson Seaview Colonsay, Isle of Argyll PA61 7YN Tel: (Colonsay) 01951 200315	COMMENDED Listed	2 Twin 1 Double	1 Pub Bath/Show	B&B per person £21.00 Single £21.00 Double	Open Apr-Oct Dinner at 1900

Traditional island hospitality on working croft. Comfortable rooms with interesting touches. Mrs Lawson a keen cook, and home baker.

CONNEL Argyll	Map 1 E2

ACH-NA-CRAIG

Grosvenor Crescent, Connel, Argyll PA37 1PQ
Telephone: 01631 710588

Ach-na-Craig is situated in a woodland glade with extensive private parking space in the picturesque village of Connel (5 miles from Oban). We offer warm comfortable accommodation with breakfast and evening meal (if required). Ground-floor bedrooms are centrally heated with en-suite shower room, colour TV and tea/coffee facilities.

Mrs N H Craig Ach-na-Craig Grosvenor Crescent Connel, by Oban Argyll Tel: (Connel) 01631 710588	COMMENDED	2 Twin 1 Double	3 En Suite fac	B&B per person £17.00-£18.00 Double	Open Jan-Dec Dinner 1830-2000 B&B + Eve. Meal from £24.50

Newly built family house in quiet village, 5 miles (8 kms) from Oban. Secure off-street parking. All rooms on ground floor and ensuite.

CRAOBH HAVEN by Lochgilphead Argyll	Map 1 E3

BUIDHE LODGE

Craobh Haven, by Lochgilphead, Argyll PA31 8UA
Telephone/Fax: 01852 500291

Beautiful Swiss-style lodge on perfect sealoch-side setting. Excellent home cooking, carefully selected wines. All six rooms ground level and ensuite. National Trust gardens, historic sites and trips nearby. Lodge featured in Which? Good Bed and Breakfast Guide.
Phone Nick or Simone for colour brochure. Let us spoil you!

Buidhe Lodge Eilean Buidhe Craobh Haven Argyll PA31 8UA Tel: (Barbreck) 01852 500291	COMMENDED	5 Twin 1 Double	6 En Suite fac	B&B per person £29.00-£34.00 Single £21.00-£26.00 Double	Open Jan-Dec Dinner 1930-2100 B&B + Eve. Meal £35.00-£40.00

Architect-designed, timber lodge, on unique island setting connected by causeway to village.

STIRLING & TROSSACHS

WEST HIGHLANDS & ISLANDS, LOCH LOMOND,

Details of Grading and Classification are on page vi.

Key to symbols is on back flap.

STIRLING & TROSSACHS

WEST HIGHLANDS & ISLANDS, LOCH LOMOND,

CRIANLARICH **Perthshire** Ewich House Crianlarich Perthshire FK20 8RU Tel: (Crianlarich) 01838 300300	Map 1 G2	COMMENDED 👑👑👑	1 Single 2 Twin 2 Double	5 En Suite fac 1 Pub Bath/Show	B&B per person £20.00-£30.00 Single £20.00-£30.00 Double Room only per person £20.00-£30.00	Open Jan-Dec Dinner 1930-2030 B&B + Eve. Meal £35.00-£45.00	

150-year-old stone-built farmhouse, completely renovated stonework, secluded setting with river and mountain views.

Glenardran Guest House Crianlarich Perthshire FK20 8QS Tel: (Crianlarich) 01838 300236		COMMENDED Listed	1 Single 2 Twin 3 Double	1 En Suite fac 1 Pub Bath/Show	B&B per person £17.50-£19.50 Single £17.50-£19.50 Double	Open Jan-Dec Dinner 1915-2000 B&B + Eve. Meal £28.00-£30.00	

Late Victorian house in centre of village. Excellent base for touring, walking or climbing. Non-smoking.

CRINAN, by Lochgilphead **Argyll**	Map 1 E4

Tigh-Na-Glaic

By Lochgilphead, Argyllshire PA31 8SW
Telephone: 01546 830245

Superbly situated in its own grounds with beautiful views over Loch Crinan and Duntrune Castle. An ideal base for touring, walking, fishing, boating and golfing. All rooms en-suite. T.V., Tea/Coffee facilities. There is ample car parking and a large garden for guests to enjoy.

Mrs Mairi Anderson Tigh Na Glaic Crinan, by Lochgilphead Argyll PA31 8SW Tel: (Crinan) 01546 830245 Fax: 01546 830243		COMMENDED 👑👑	1 Twin 1 Double	2 En Suite fac 1 Pub Bath/Show	B&B per person to £30.00 Single £18.00-£20.00 Double	Open Jan-Dec	

Country cottage in peaceful setting, overlooking Loch Crinan to Duntrune Castle. Ideal area for artists, photographers and walkers.

DALMALLY **Argyll** Mrs Borrett Cruachan Dalmally Argyll PA33 1AA Tel: (Dalmally) 01838 200496	Map 1 F2	COMMENDED 👑👑👑 ♿	2 Twin 1 Double	2 En Suite fac 1 Priv. NOT ensuite	B&B per person £18.00-£20.00 Single £15.00-£17.50 Double	Open Jan-Dec Dinner 1900-2000 B&B + Eve. Meal £26.00-£31.00	

Traditional stone villa with purpose-built accommodation for disabled guests. Multi-lingual proprietors offer friendly, informal atmosphere.

Craig Villa Guest House Dalmally Argyll PA33 1AX Tel: (Dalmally) 01838 200255		COMMENDED 👑👑👑	2 Twin 2 Double 2 Family	5 En Suite fac 1 Priv. NOT ensuite	B&B per person £19.00-£23.00 Double	Open Apr-Oct Dinner from 1900 B&B + Eve. Meal £30.00-£35.00	

Personally run guest house in own grounds amidst breathtaking scenery. Good touring base. Home cooking.

Mrs MacDougall Strathorchy Dalmally Argyll Tel: (Dalmally) 01838 200373 Fax: 01838 200373		COMMENDED 👑👑	2 Twin 2 Double	2 En Suite fac 1 Pub Bath/Show	B&B per person £15.00-£18.00 Single £15.00-£18.00 Double	Open Jan-Dec	

Recently built traditional style house in countryside setting beside No 1 tee on golf course. Good base for touring Argyll, the glens and islands.

PORTINNISHERRICH FARM
By Dalmally, Argyll PA33 1BW Tel: 01866 844202

Peaceful, picturesque working farm situated on Lochaweside. Ensuite bedrooms with loch views. Guests' lounge and diningroom, dinner available using local produce. Ideally positioned for famous gardens, forest walks, ornithology. Own jetty provides fishing, boating, sailing. Close to historic island castle. Pets in kennel or car. **Non-smoking establishment.**

R N & P B McKenzie Portinnisherrich Southeast Lochaweside by Dalmally Argyll Tel: (Lochavich) 01866 844202	COMMENDED ♛♛	2 Family	2 En Suite fac	B&B per person £17.50-£20.00 Double	Open Apr-Sep Dinner from 1900 B&B + Eve. Meal £32.00-£33.50

Working farm peacefully situated on Lochaweside. Ideally positioned for forest walks and bird-watching. Own jetty provides boating, fishing and sailing.

Orchy Bank Guest House Dalmally Argyll PA33 1AS Tel: (Dalmally) 01838 200370	COMMENDED Listed	2 Single 2 Twin 2 Double 2 Family	2 Pub Bath/Show	B&B per person £16.00-£18.00 Single £16.00-£18.00 Double	Open Jan-Dec Dinner 1900-2000 B&B + Eve. Meal £26.00-£28.00

Victorian house situated on the banks of the River Orchy and surrounded on 3 sides by mountains over 3000 feet. Fishing, golf, walking and bird-watching.

DOUNE **Perthshire** Mrs Joyce Anderson Inverardoch Mains Farm Doune (B824), Dunblane Perthshire FK15 9NZ Tel: (Dunblane) 01786 841268	Map 2 A3 COMMENDED ♛	1 Single 1 Double 1 Family	2 Limited ensuite 1 Pub Bath/Show	B&B per person £17.00-£18.00 Single £15.50-£16.50 Double	Open Apr-Oct

Traditional Victorian farmhouse on 200-acre (81ha) working farm. Originally main farm of 15th century Doune Castle.

Mrs L Butlin Glenardoch, Castle Road Doune FK16 6EA Tel: (Doune) 01786 841489	COMMENDED ♛♛	2 Double	2 En Suite fac	B&B per person £21.00-£26.00 Single £18.50-£21.50 Double	Open May-September

Interesting 18th century house by Doune Castle. Extensive riverside gardens. Quiet location. Excellent central touring base.

Mrs F J R Graham Mackeanston House Doune Perthshire Tel: (Doune) 01786 850213 Fax: 01786 850414	HIGHLY COMMENDED ♛♛♛	1 Twin 1 Double	2 En Suite fac	B&B per person £25.00-£35.00 Single £22.00-£26.50 Double	Open Jan-Dec Dinner from 1950 B&B + Eve. Meal £37.00-£41.50

Peaceful, comfortable old farmhouse with large garden. Enjoy open fires, home cooking with free-range eggs and home-made bread. Ensuite bathrooms.

DRYMEN **Stirlingshire** Mrs Julia Cross Easter Drumquhassle Farm Gartness Road Drymen Stirlingshire G63 0DN Tel: (Drymen) 01360 660893	Map 1 H4 COMMENDED ♛	1 Double 1 Family	1 En Suite fac 1 Priv. NOT ensuite	B&B per person £19.50 Single £16.50 Double	Open Jan-Dec Dinner 1800-2000 B&B + Eve. Meal £24.50-£27.50

Studio-type bedroom and accommodation in main house. Ideal base for touring Loch Lomond area. Quiet, rural location. Spectacular views. Come and be well fed.

STIRLING & TROSSACHS

WEST HIGHLANDS & ISLANDS, LOCH LOMOND,

STIRLING & TROSSACHS *(side margin)*

WEST HIGHLANDS & ISLANDS, LOCH LOMOND, *(side margin)*

DUNBLANE Perthshire	Map 2 A3

MOSSGIEL

DOUNE ROAD, DUNBLANE, PERTHSHIRE FK15 9ND
Telephone: 01786 824325

Situated in a country setting, **Mossgiel** offers guests a warm welcome, comfortable, well-equipped bedrooms – two ensuite and one private, large garden with safe off-road parking and a good Scottish breakfast. **Mossgiel** is located near the M9 Motorway and is an ideal base for touring *Loch Lomond* and *The Trossachs*.

Mrs Judy Bennett Mossgiel, Doune Road Dunblane Perthshire FK15 9ND Tel: (Dunblane) 01786 824325	COMMENDED	2 Twin 1 Double	2 En Suite fac 1 Priv. NOT ensuite	B&B per person £17.50-£18.00 Double	Open Apr-Oct

**Bungalow in beautiful rural setting, 1 mile (2 km) from Dunblane on A820.
Two ground-floor ensuite bedrooms.**

Mrs Elizabeth J Duncan Westwood, Doune Road Dunblane Perthshire FK15 9ND Tel: (Dunblane) 01786 822579	HIGHLY COMMENDED	1 Twin 2 Double	2 En Suite fac 1 Priv. NOT ensuite	B&B per person from £30.00 Single from £20.00 Double	Open Mar-Nov

**In rural and peaceful setting with attractive gardens. Conveniently near to A9/M9.
Relaxed and friendly atmosphere. Ground-floor room available.**

DUNOON Argyll	Map 1 F5

The Anchorage Shore Road, Ardnadam Dunoon Argyll PA23 8QG Tel: (Dunoon) 01369 705108 Fax: 01369 705108	HIGHLY COMMENDED	1 Twin 4 Double	5 En Suite fac	B&B per person £21.50-£30.00 Double	Open Jan-Dec Dinner 1800-2130 B&B + Eve. Meal £37.50-£45.00

**Stylish traditional stone villa c.1870 with magnificent open views over Holy Loch.
Easy access ferry terminal. High standard of service and accommodation.**

CLAYMORE

Wellington Street, Dunoon, Argyll PA23 7LA
Telephone: 01369 702658

Sample the warmth and hospitality of superior accommodation. Centrally located. All rooms tastefully furnished with ensuite facilities, tea/coffee, satellite TV, books, hairdryers etc. Renowned for good food, we can guarantee an enjoyable evening meal. Relax in our pleasant garden area or enjoy a leisurely walk along the nearby promenade.

Mrs Smith Claymore, Wellington Street Dunoon Argyll PA23 7LA Tel: (Dunoon) 01369 702658	COMMENDED	1 Twin 1 Double 1 Family	3 En Suite fac	B&B per person £16.00-£20.00 Double	Open Jan-Dec Dinner 1800-2000 B&B + Eve. Meal £25.00-£29.00

**Comfortable accommodation in family run villa within
a few minutes' walk of shops, ferry and promenade.**

STIRLING & TROSSACHS

WEST HIGHLANDS & ISLANDS, LOCH LOMOND,

FALKIRK
Stirlingshire
Mrs Mitchell
Darroch House, Camelon Road
Falkirk
Stirlingshire
FK1 5SQ
Tel: (Falkirk) 01324 623041
Fax: 01324 626288

Map 2
A4

HIGHLY COMMENDED

1 Twin 3 En Suite fac
2 Double

B&B per person
£45.00-£50.00 Single
£25.00-£30.00 Double

Open Jan-Dec
Dinner 1900-2100

Built in 1838. Family home. Well-proportioned, Victorian manor house, set in 9 acres (3.6ha) of garden and woodland in the heart of Falkirk.

Mrs S Taylor
Wester Carmuirs Farm
Larbert, by Falkirk
Stirlingshire
FK5 3NW
Tel: (Bonnybridge)
01324 812459

COMMENDED

2 Twin 2 Pub Bath/Show
1 Double

B&B per person
from £20.00 Single
from £18.00 Double

Open Jan-Oct

Family house on working arable and beef farm. Falkirk leisure centre 0.5 miles (1 km). Bonnybridge 1.5 miles (3kms). Good base for touring Central Scotland.

HELENSBURGH
Dunbartonshire
Bellfield Guest House
199 East Clyde Street
Helensburgh
Dunbartonshire
G84 7AJ
Tel: (Helensburgh)
01436 671628

Map 1
G4

COMMENDED

1 Single 3 En Suite fac
1 Twin 1 Priv. NOT ensuite
1 Double 1 Pub Bath/Show
1 Family

B&B per person
£16.00-£22.00 Single
£19.00-£25.00 Double
Room only per person
£15.00-£24.00

Open Jan-Dec
Dinner 1800-2200
B&B + Eve. Meal
£26.00-£36.00

A family run guest house. Friendly accommodation in "The Garden City of the Firth of Clyde". Ideal for touring.

Mrs E Blackwell
Longleat, 39 East Argyle Street
Helensburgh
Dunbartonshire
G84 7EN
Tel: (Helensburgh)
01436 672465

COMMENDED

1 Twin 1 Pub Bath/Show
2 Double

B&B per person
£17.00-£18.00 Single
£17.00-£18.00 Double

Open Jan-Dec

Magnificently situated family house in quiet residential area overlooking Firth of Clyde. Non-smoking.

Mrs Johnston
Lethamhill
20 West Dhuhill Drive
Helensburgh
Dunbartonshire
G84
Tel: (Helensburgh)
01436 676016

HIGHLY COMMENDED

2 Double 2 En Suite fac
1 Family 1 Priv. NOT ensuite

B&B per person
£26.00-£31.00 Single
£22.00-£25.00 Double

Open Jan-Dec
Dinner 1800-1900
B&B + Eve. Meal
£37.00-£46.00

B Listed Edwardian house with extensive garden in quiet residential area. Totally non-smoking.

Middledrift

85 James Street, Helensburgh, Dunbartonshire G84 9LE
Telephone: 01436 674867 Fax: 01436 679000

Detached 19th-century villa in central location. Large garden, 5 minutes' walk from sea front, 45 minutes from Glasgow and Stirling. 5 miles to Loch Lomond. Ideal touring base, off-street parking, friendly and comfortable, everyone welcome.

Mrs M K Paul
Middledrift, 85 James Street
Helensburgh
Dunbartonshire
G84 9LE
Tel: (Helensburgh)
01436 674867
Fax: 01436 679000

COMMENDED

1 Single 1 En Suite fac
1 Twin 1 Priv. NOT ensuite
1 Family 1 Pub Bath/Show

B&B per person
from £20.00 Single
from £18.50 Double

Open Jan-Dec

1860 sandstone family home of character with large established garden. Children and pets welcome.

Details of Grading and Classification are on page vi.

Key to symbols is on back flap.

STIRLING & TROSSACHS

WEST HIGHLANDS & ISLANDS, LOCH LOMOND,

HELENSBURGH continued Dunbartonshire Mrs M Richards Ravenswood, 32 Suffolk Street Helensburgh Dunbartonshire G84 9PA Tel: (Helensburgh) 01436 672112 Fax: 01436 672112	Map 1 G4	COMMENDED	2 Single 1 Twin 1 Double	2 En Suite fac 2 Priv. NOT ensuite 1 Pub Bath/Show	B&B per person £22.50-£45.00 Single £22.50-£25.00 Double	Open Jan-Dec Dinner from 1830 B&B + Eve. Meal £37.50-£60.00
			Victorian family home. Quiet location with mature gardens, close to Hill House, town centre and Loch Lomond.			
Mrs Dorothy Ross Eastbank, 10 Hanover Street Helensburgh Dunbartonshire G84 7AW Tel: (Helensburgh) 01436 673665 Fax: 01436 673665		COMMENDED Listed	1 Single 1 Twin 1 Family	1 En Suite fac 1 Pub Bath/Show	B&B per person £16.00-£18.00 Single £16.00-£21.00 Double	Open Jan-Dec
			1st floor flat conversion with all accommodation on same level. Fine views from lounge across the Clyde to Greenock. Knitting instruction available.			

HAPLAND B&B

East Abercromby Street, Helensburgh, Dunbartonshire G84 7SD
Tel: 01436 674042/01436 679243

This Victorian family home offers a warm welcome and relaxed atmosphere in comfortable surroundings. Situated five minutes walk from Helensburgh Upper Station where one can take the train to Oban and Fort William. 10 minutes' drive from Loch Lomond.

Mrs D M Smith Hapland East Abercromby Street Helensburgh Dunbartonshire G84 7SD Tel: (Helensburgh) 01436 674042/679243		COMMENDED	1 Twin 1 Double	2 En Suite fac	B&B per person £21.00-£25.00 Single £19.00-£21.00 Double	Open Jan-Dec
			Large Victorian family home in extensive grounds 10 minutes from Loch Lomond. Short walk from the Upper Station and golf course. Warm friendly atmosphere.			
INVERARAY Argyll	Map 1 F3					

CREAG DHUBH

INVERARAY, ARGYLL PA32 8XT
Telephone: 01499 302430

Small, family run Bed and Breakfast with beautiful views across Loch Fyne to the Cowal Hills. Large residents' lounge. Private car parking. Ideal area for touring.

| Mrs MacLugash
Creag Dhubh
Inveraray
Argyll
PA32 8XT
Tel: (Inveraray) 01499 302430 | | COMMENDED | 1 Twin
2 Double
1 Family | 1 En Suite fac
2 Pub Bath/Show | B&B per person
£15.00-£19.00 Double | Open Mar-Nov |
| | | | Large stone-built house with extensive garden and excellent views
over Loch Fyne. Large residents' lounge with open fire. | | | |

ISLE OF ISLAY, Argyll BALLYGRANT	Map 1

Kilmeny Farmhouse

Ballygrant, Isle of Islay, Argyll PA45 7QW
Telephone/Fax: 01496 840668

In the heart of a 300-acre beef farm, Kilmeny Farmhouse commands magnificent views of surrounding hills and glen. This family business places its emphasis on quality and personal service. Ensuite bedrooms with bath, shower etc are elegantly furnished. Public rooms are charming with a country house influence. Five-course dinner menu.

Deluxe 👑👑👑

Mrs Margaret Rozga Kilmeny Farmhouse Ballygrant Isle of Islay, Argyll PA45 7QW Tel: (Port Askaig) 01496 840668 Fax: 01496 840668	C5 **DELUXE** 👑👑👑	1 Twin 2 Double	3 En Suite fac	B&B per person to £30.00 Double	Open Jan-Dec Dinner 1900-2000 B&B + Eve. Meal £48.00-£50.00	

Traditional farmhouse on 300-acre (120ha) beef farm. Comfort, friendliness and peace. Emphasis on personal service, in a country-house atmosphere.

PORT CHARLOTTE, Isle of Islay	Map 1 B6

NERABUS

Port Charlotte, Isle of Islay PA48 7UE
Telephone and Fax: 01496 850431

House by sea, stunning views of Paps of Jura and Loch Indaal. Peaceful fields 2 miles outside Port Charlotte. Spa bath, all bedrooms ensuite, local produce for meals. B&B £17.50, Dinners £10. Peat fires. Ground-floor rooms.

Mrs P Halsall Nerabus Port Charlotte Isle of Islay, Argyll PA48 7UE Tel: (Port Charlotte) 01496 850431 Fax: 01496 850431	**COMMENDED** 👑	3 Twin	3 En Suite fac 1 Pub Bath/Show	B&B per person £16.50-£17.50 Single £17.50-£18.00 Double	Open Jan-Dec Dinner 1830-2030	

Detached house in idyllic setting, overlooking Loch Indaal to the south of the island. Ground-floor bedroom with ensuite spa bath.

HERE'S THE DIFFERENCE

STB's scheme has two distinct elements, grading and classification.

GRADING:

Measures the quality and condition of the facilities and services offered, eg, the warmth of welcome, quality of food and its presentation, condition of decor and furnishings, appearance of buildings, tidiness of grounds and gardens, condition of lighting and heating and so on.

Grading awards are: **Approved, Commended, Highly Commended, Deluxe.**

CLASSIFICATION:

Measures the range of physical facilities and services offered, eg, rooms with private bath, heating, reception, lounges, telephones and so on.

Classification awards are: **Listed to five crowns or one to five crowns.**

STIRLING & TROSSACHS

WEST HIGHLANDS & ISLANDS, LOCH LOMOND,

PORT ELLEN, Isle of Islay	Map 1 C6

Glenmachrie Farmhouse

**Mrs Rachel Whyte, Port Ellen,
Isle of Islay, Argyll PA42 7AW
Tel/Fax: 01496 302560**

Glenmachrie is a large traditional farmhouse set in a stone-walled garden by the river and surrounded by 450 acres which support Scottish Blackface Sheep, Highland ponies and Highland cattle. Furnished to a high standard Glenmachrie offers total comfort, friendly welcomes and excellent local and farm-produced food. All bedrooms, tastefully decorated, have full ensuite facilities. The dining room, set with crystal and silverware, provides the ideal setting for our delicious food which has been awarded membership to the "Taste of Scotland". Glenmachrie offers you true Highland hospitality, delicious local food and wonderful memories of an unforgettable Hebridean Holiday!

Highly Commended 🏵🏵🏵

WELCOME HOST

Glenmachrie Farmhouse (Mrs Rachel Whyte) Port Ellen Isle of Islay, Argyll PA42 7AW Tel: (Port Ellen) 01496 302560 Fax: 01496 302560	HIGHLY COMMENDED 🏵🏵🏵	3 Twin 2 Double	5 En Suite fac 1 Pub Bath/Show	B&B per person from £33.00 Single from £28.00 Double	Open Jan-Dec Dinner 1900-2000 B&B + Eve. Meal from £48.00

Farmhouse in quiet location, fine views westwards across Laggan Bay towards the Rhinns. Family-run farm using the best of Islay's larder. Private fishing for wild brown trout.

Trout-Fly Guest House Port Ellen Isle of Islay, Argyll PA42 7DF Tel: (Port Ellen) 01496 302204	COMMENDED Listed	2 Twin 1 Double	2 Limited ensuite 2 Pub Bath/Show	B&B per person £16.50-£18.50 Double	Open Jan-Dec Dinner 1800-1900

Guest house and restaurant in town centre. Convenient for ferry terminal, airport and golf course.

KILCHRENAN Argyll Mrs K Lambie Thistle-Doo Kilchrenan, by Taynuilt Argyll PA35 1HF Tel: (Kilchrenan) 01866 833339	Map 1 F2 COMMENDED 🏵🏵🏵	1 Twin 2 Double	3 En Suite fac	B&B per person £18.00-£21.00 Double	Open Jan-Dec Dinner 1800-2100 B&B + Eve. Meal £28.00-£31.00

Modern family bungalow in idyllic secluded setting overlooking Loch Awe. Home cooking.

Scotland for Golf . . .

Find out more about golf in Scotland. There's more to it than just the championship courses so get in touch with us now for information on the hidden gems of Scotland.

Write to: Information Unit, Scottish Tourist Board, 23 Ravelston Terrace, Edinburgh EH4 3EU or call: 0131-332 2433

KILLIN Perthshire	Map 1 H2						

Fairview House

MAIN STREET, KILLIN, PERTHSHIRE FK21 8UT
Telephone: 01567 820667

Muriel and *Roger Bedwell* extend a very warm Scottish welcome to their guest house in the *Heart of Scotland* where they specialise in good food in relaxing and comfortable surroundings. The picturesque village set amidst the mountains of the *Central Highlands* makes an ideal centre for touring or hillwalking.

Fairview House Main Street Killin Perthshire FK21 8UT Tel: (Killin) 01567 820667	COMMENDED 👑👑	1 Single 2 Twin 4 Double	3 En Suite fac 2 Pub Bath/Show	B&B per person £16.00-£18.00 Single £16.00-£18.00 Double	Open Jan-Dec Dinner from 1930 B&B + Eve. Meal £26.00-£28.00	

Small family run guest house specialising in home cooking.
Excellent touring centre, good walking and climbing area.

KIPPEN Stirlingshire Mrs A McCallum Sealladh Ard, Station Brae Kippen Stirlingshire Tel: (Stirling) 01786 870291	Map 1 H4	HIGHLY COMMENDED Listed	2 Twin 1 Double	1 Pub Bath/Show	B&B per person £17.50-£19.00 Double	Open Jan-Dec, exc Xmas/New Year	

Detached house on edge of village with panoramic views across the valley to the Trossachs Hills.

LOCHGOILHEAD Argyll Shore House Inn Lochgoilhead Argyll Tel: (Lochgoilhead) 01301 703340 Fax: 01301 703340	Map 1 F3	APPROVED Listed	1 Single 3 Twin 1 Double 2 Family	2 En Suite fac 2 Pub Bath/Show	B&B per person £15.00-£17.00 Single £13.00-£22.00 Double	Open Jan-Dec Dinner 1800-2100 B&B + Eve. Meal £25.00-£29.00	

Peacefully situated on the shore of Loch Goil, with open views down the loch.
Informal and friendly. Pets welcome. Bar and restaurant.

LUSS, Dunbartonshire Glenmollochan Farm per Mrs K R Wragg Luss Dunbartonshire G83 8PB Tel: (Luss) 01436 860246 Fax: 01436 860246	Map 1 G4	COMMENDED 👑👑	1 Twin 1 Double	2 En Suite fac	B&B per person £16.00-£19.50 Double	Open Easter-Oct	

Situated on working sheep farm, 2 miles (3 kms) from Luss.
Ensuite bedrooms both with superb views of Loch Lomond.

WELCOME

Whenever you are in Scotland, you can be sure of a warm welcome at your nearest Tourist Information Centre.
For guide books, maps, souvenirs, our Centres provide a service second to none – many now offer bureau-de-change facilities. And, of course, Tourist Information Centres offer free, expert advice on what to see and do, route-planning and accommodation for everyone – visitors and residents alike!

STIRLING & TROSSACHS

WEST HIGHLANDS & ISLANDS, LOCH LOMOND,

STIRLING & TROSSACHS

WEST HIGHLANDS & ISLANDS, LOCH LOMOND,

LUSS, continued Dunbartonshire	Map 1 G4

Shantron Farm

Shantron Farm, Luss, Alexandria G83 8RH
Telephone: 01389 850231 Fax: 01389 850231   **Mobile 0468 378400**

Enjoy a relaxing break in a spacious bungalow with outstanding views of Loch Lomond. Our 5,000-acre hill farm is the setting for Morag's croft in "Take the High Road" 30 minutes from Glasgow Airport. An ideal touring base and for hillwalking, fishing, watersports, golf. Large garden for guests' enjoyment.

Mrs A Lennox Shantron Farm Cottage Shantron Farm Luss, by Alexandria Dunbartonshire Tel: (Arden) 01389 850231/ 0468 378400 (mobile) Fax: 01389 850231	COMMENDED	1 Twin 1 Double 1 Family	2 En Suite fac 1 Pub Bath/Show	B&B per person £20.00-£30.00 Single £16.00-£25.00 Double	Open Mar-Nov

Cottage, in elevated position with panoramic views over Loch Lomond to the Campsie Fells. Farm is used regularly for filming of "Take the High Road".

Mrs Robertson Doune of Glen Douglas Farm Luss Dunbartonshire G83 8PD Tel: (Arrochar) 01301 702312	HIGHLY COMMENDED	1 Twin 2 Double	1 En Suite fac 1 Pub Bath/Show	B&B per person £20.00-£26.00 Single £17.00-£24.00 Double	Open Mar-Oct

18th century farmhouse on working hill sheep farm in Glen Douglas. 2 miles (3kms) from A82. Ideal for hillwalking.

Mrs J T K Short Ardallie House Luss, Loch Lomond Dunbartonshire G83 8NU Tel: (Luss) 01436 860272	COMMENDED	1 Twin 1 Double	2 Priv. NOT ensuite	B&B per person £22.00-£25.00 Single £17.00-£20.00 Double	Open Apr-Oct

Charming country house on hillside off A82 in woodland garden. Magnificent views over Loch Lomond.

MINARD, by Inveraray Argyll	Map 1 E4

Victoria House

Minard, by Inveraray PA32 8YB
Telephone: 01546 886224

Granite-faced house overlooking Loch Fyne ideal for walking, sailing and climbing. Close to Crarae Gardens, situated on A83 midway between Inveraray and Lochgilphead. Ideal overnight stop for Islay and Arran ferries.

Mrs J MacVicar Victoria House Minard, by Inveraray Argyll PA32 8YB Tel: (Minard) 01546 886224	COMMENDED	2 Single 1 Twin 1 Double	2 Pub Bath/Show	B&B per person from £17.50 Single from £15.00 Double	Open Apr-Sep

Stone-built villa in centre of village with uninterrupted views over Loch Fyne. Comfortable lounge. Off-road parking.

MUASDALE, by Tarbert Argyll Mrs MacMillan Seafield Muasdale, by Tayinloan Argyll PA29 6XD Tel: (Glenbarr) 01583 421240	Map 1 D6 COMMENDED Listed	2 Double 1 Family	1 Pub Bath/Show	B&B per person from £16.00 Single from £15.00 Double	Open Mar-Oct

House standing in its own grounds under 1 mile (2kms) from small village on west coast of Kintyre. Lovely seascapes towards islands of Gigha, Islay and Jura.

ISLE OF MULL, Argyll

BUNESSAN

Mrs Acey
Bremenvoir House
Ardtun, Bunessan
Isle of Mull, Argyll
PA67 6DH
Tel: (Fionnphort) 01681 700527

Map 1
C3

COMMENDED

1 Single	1 En Suite fac	B&B per person	Open Jan-Dec
1 Twin	1 Pub Bath/Show	from £15.00 Single	Dinner 1800-1930
1 Double		£15.00-£18.00 Double	B&B + Eve. Meal
			£23.50-£33.00

Converted farmhouse in lovely isolated location near Iona.
Evening meals specialising in local seafood and home-grown vegetables.

CRAIGNURE, Isle of Mull

Mrs Rosemarie Auld
Gorsten Farm House, Lochdon
Craignure
Isle of Mull, Argyll
Tel: (Craignure) 01680 812332

Map 1
D2

COMMENDED

1 Twin	2 En Suite fac	B&B per person	Open Apr-Oct
1 Double		£16.00-£20.00 Single	Dinner 1800-1930
		£15.00-£20.00 Double	B&B + Eve. Meal
			£26.00-£30.00

Traditional farmhouse in tranquil setting with extensive views across the
Sound of Mull to Lismore, Kerrera, Loch Linnhe, Ben Nevis and Oban.

Pennygate Lodge
Craignure
Isle of Mull, Argyll
PA65 6AY
Tel: (Craignure) 01680 812333

COMMENDED

3 Twin	4 En Suite fac	B&B per person	Open Jan-Dec
3 Double	2 Pub Bath/Show	£15.00-£28.00 Double	Dinner 1800-1930
2 Family			B&B + Eve. Meal
Suites avail			£29.00-£42.00

Former Georgian manse set in 4.5 acres (1.8ha) of landscaped garden with
magnificent views of the Sound of Mull. Ideal base for touring, near main bus
route and ferry terminal.

Redburn
Redburn, Lochdon
Craignure
Isle of Mull, Argyll
PA64 6AP
Tel: (Craignure) 01680 812370

COMMENDED

1 Twin	3 En Suite fac	B&B per person	Open Jan-Dec
2 Double		£19.00-£20.00 Single	Dinner at 1800
		£19.00-£20.00 Double	B&B + Eve. Meal
			£29.00-£31.00

Converted croft house in quiet location on lochside. 3 miles (4.8kms)
Craignure Ferry. Area for natural history enthusiasts. Home cooking.

Old Mill Cottage Guest House & Restaurant
Lochdon Head, by Craignure, Isle of Mull, Argyll PA64 6AP
Telephone: 01680 812442 Fax: 01680 812442

Situated on a sheltered sea loch 3 miles from Craignure Ferry. Our intimate
restaurant boasts a varied cuisine. A-la-carte menu includes local sea food and
Scottish beef. A beautiful location with the loch attracting a wealth of water fowl
both summer and winter. Public telephone.

Jim and Jenny Smith offer a warm welcome. **COMMENDED**

Mr & Mrs J Smith
Old Mill Cottage Guest House
& Restaurant
Lochdon, Craignure
Isle of Mull, Argyll
PA64 6AP
Tel: (Craignure) 01680 812442
Fax: 01680 812442

COMMENDED

| 1 Twin | 2 En Suite fac | B&B per person | Open Jan-Dec |
| 1 Double | | £21.50-£23.50 Double | Dinner 1800-2000 |

Centrally situated at the head of Loch Don. Bird-watchers' paradise. A wealth
of fresh local seafood and produce just for you. Non-smoking restaurant.

STIRLING & TROSSACHS

WEST HIGHLANDS & ISLANDS, LOCH LOMOND,

STIRLING & TROSSACHS

WEST HIGHLANDS & ISLANDS, LOCH LOMOND,

by CRAIGNURE, Isle of Mull	Map 1 D2		

INVERLUSSA
By Craignure, Isle of Mull, Argyll PA65 6BD
Telephone/Fax: 01680 812436
Situated close by the shores of Loch Spelve. Set in own grounds beside mountain stream. Ideal base for birdwatching, fishing, hillwalking, golfing or unwinding. Warm, spacious rooms, guests' lounge with open fire. Small, friendly establishment run by locals.
B&B from £17. Reductions for longer stays.

Helen Wilson Inverlussa Craignure Isle of Mull, Argyll PA65 6BD Tel: (Craignure) 01680 812436 Fax: 01680 812436	HIGHLY COMMENDED Listed	1 Twin 1 Double 1 Family	1 En Suite fac 1 Pub Bath/Show	B&B per person £17.00-£20.00 Single £17.00-£20.00 Double	Open Apr-Oct
		Personally run modern house in idyllic setting. Ideal base for touring Isle of Mull.			
DERVAIG, Isle of Mull Ardrioch Farm Guest House Dervaig, by Tobermory Isle of Mull, Argyll PA75 6QR Tel: (Dervaig) 01688 400264 Fax: 01688 400264	Map 1 C1 COMMENDED	1 Single 2 Twin 2 Double	2 En Suite fac 1 Pub Bath/Show	B&B per person £18.50 Single £18.50-£21.00 Double	Open Apr-Oct Dinner 1830-2000 B&B + Eve. Meal £30.00-£32.50
		Attractive cedarwood house with adjoining farm, lovely loch and hill views. Home cooking. Taste of Scotland. Inter-island cruises. Chalet annexe.			
Mr C A & Mrs H A Arnold Balmacara Dervaig Isle of Mull Argyll PA75 6QN Tel: (Dervaig) 01688 400363 Fax: 01688 400363	HIGHLY COMMENDED	2 Twin 1 Double	2 En Suite fac 1 Priv. NOT ensuite	B&B per person £25.00-£27.00 Double	Open Jan-Dec Dinner 1900-2000 B&B + Eve. Meal £36.00-£38.00
		Brand new property high above Dervaig Village. Overlooking Glen Bellart and Loch Cuin, framed by the hills and forests of North West Mull.			
Glenbellart Guest House Dervaig Isle of Mull, Argyll PA75 6QJ Tel: (Dervaig) 01688 400282	COMMENDED	1 Twin 2 Double	2 Pub Bath/Show	B&B per person £21.00-£22.00 Single £17.00-£18.00 Double	Open Easter-Oct Dinner at 1900 B&B + Eve. Meal £29.00-£34.00
		Comfortable, characterful house in centre of conservation village. Good home cooking. Ideal centre for wildlife holiday.			
Mrs Smith Achnacraig Dervaig Isle of Mull, Argyll PA75 6QW Tel: (Dervaig) 01688 400309	COMMENDED	1 Single 1 Twin 1 Double	2 Pub Bath/Show	B&B per person £16.50-£17.50 Single £16.50-£17.50 Double	Open Apr-Sep Dinner from 1930 B&B + Eve. Meal £25.50-£26.00
		Winding river, circling buzzards, stone farmhouse, stupendous views. Home-grown produce, real cooking.			

VAT is shown at 17.5%: changes in this rate may affect prices. Prices shown are for guidance only. Please send SAE with each enquiry.

FIONNPHORT, Isle of Mull	Map 1 B2

DINNER, BED AND BREAKFAST
SEAVIEW

Fionnphort, Isle of Mull PA66 6BL   Tel: 01681 700235

Traditional Scottish granite house with spectacular 'seaviews' overlooking Iona Sound. A minute's walk from Iona and Staffa ferries. Warm and comfortable. Sitting room with log fire. Well-appointed rooms. Home cooking, friendly welcome. Pub and shop nearby.

B & B from £13 per person per night. Private facilities available. Private parking.

Mrs Noddings Seaview Fionnphort Isle of Mull, Argyll PA66 6BL Tel: (Fionnphort) 01681 700235	COMMENDED	2 Twin 2 Double	1 En Suite fac 2 Pub Bath/Show	B&B per person £17.00-£20.00 Single £13.00-£19.00 Double	Open Jan-Dec Dinner 1830-1930 B&B + Eve. Meal £22.00-£29.00	

Granite-built house with views over the Sound of Iona and only a minute's walk to Iona and Staffa ferries. Friendly atmosphere. Ensuite available.

KINLOCHSPELVE, Isle of Mull	Map 1 D2					
Mrs Railton-Edwards Barrachandroman, Kinlochspelve Loch Buie Isle of Mull, Argyll PA62 6AA Tel: (Kinlochspelve) 01680 814220 Fax: 01680 814220	HIGHLY COMMENDED	2 Double	1 En Suite fac 1 Priv. NOT ensuite	B&B per person £18.00-£22.00 Double	Open Jan-Dec Dinner 1800-2200	

Luxuriously converted barn in secluded lochside location, both rooms with private facilities. Accent on fresh fish and seafood.

TOBERMORY, Isle of Mull	Map 1 C1					
Baliscate Guest House Tobermory Isle of Mull, Argyll PA75 6QA Tel: (Tobermory) 01688 302048 Fax: 01688 302666	COMMENDED	1 Twin 3 Double 1 Family	3 En Suite fac 1 Pub Bath/Show	B&B per person £20.00-£25.00 Single £17.00-£21.00 Double	Open Jan-Dec	

Set in 1.5 acres (0.6ha) of garden and woodland with magnificent views over The Sound of Mull.

Copeland House Jubilee Terrace Tobermory Isle of Mull, Argyll PA75 6PZ Tel: (Tobermory) 01688 302049	COMMENDED	1 Twin 1 Double 1 Family	3 En Suite fac	B&B per person £23.00-£25.00 Single £23.00-£25.00 Double Room only per person £20.00-£22.00	Open Jan-Dec	

Designed and built in 1993 for use as a small guest house with beautiful views over the Sound of Mull and Tobermory Bay. Close to Tobermory Harbour.

Failte Guest House Main Street Tobermory Isle of Mull, Argyll PA75 6NU Tel: (Tobermory) 01688 302495 Fax: 01688 302495	HIGHLY COMMENDED Listed	3 Twin 3 Double 1 Family	7 En Suite fac	B&B per person £25.00-£30.00 Single £20.00-£25.00 Double	Open Mar-Oct	

Scottish hospitality in comfortable guest house in prime position overlooking beautiful Tobermory Bay.

STIRLING & TROSSACHS

WEST HIGHLANDS & ISLANDS, LOCH LOMOND,

STIRLING & TROSSACHS

WEST HIGHLANDS & ISLANDS, LOCH LOMOND,

TOBERMORY, Isle of Mull continued D E McAdam Fairways Lodge Tobermory Isle of Mull, Argyll PA75 6PS Tel: (Tobermory) 01688 302238 Fax: 01688 302238	Map 1 C1	**HIGHLY COMMENDED**	1 Single 2 Twin 1 Double 1 Family	5 En Suite fac	B&B per person £27.00-£31.00 Single £27.00-£31.00 Double	Open Jan-Dec	

Situated between 3rd and 4th fairways on golf course.
Commanding view across Tobermory Bay and Sound of Mull.

Staffa Cottages Guest House Tobermory Isle of Mull, Argyll PA75 6PL Tel: (Tobermory) 01688 302464 Fax: 01688 302464		**COMMENDED**	2 Twin 2 Double	4 En Suite fac	B&B per person £20.00 Double	Open Jan-Dec Dinner from 1900 B&B + Eve. Meal £28.00-£32.00	

In quiet residential area on slopes above Tobermory with large garden.
Fine views over bay to Sound of Mull and Morvern Hills.

OBAN **Argyll** Mrs S Allister Alltnacree North Connel, by Oban Argyll PA37 1RD Tel: (Connel) 01631 710225	Map 1 E2	**HIGHLY COMMENDED** Listed	1 Twin 1 Double	2 Priv. NOT ensuite 1 Pub Bath/Show	B&B per person from £16.00 Single from £16.00 Double	Open Feb-Dec	

Modern house 7 miles north of Oban. Tranquil setting with panoramic views
from lochside garden to hills beyond. Home baking. Non-smoking.

Ardblair

Dalriach Road, Oban, Argyll PA34 5JD
Tel/Fax: 01631 562668

Oban's Leading Guest House

We're the third generation of this family-run business. We specialise in home-cooking and good old-fashioned friendly welcome and comfort. Our spacious sun-lounge and our garden have magnificent views over Oban Bay, and yet we're very central – only 3 minutes' walk from the town centre. Our safe car park takes 10 cars. We're very easy to find: just turn left half way down the hill coming into Oban, up past the tennis courts, swimming pool and there we are! We'll gladly send you a brochure, so why not phone or write to **Ian and Monika Smyth.**

AA QQQ and RAC Acclaimed

Ardblair Guest House Dalriach Road Oban Argyll PA34 5JD Tel: (Oban) 01631 562668		**COMMENDED**	2 Single 3 Twin 6 Double 3 Family Suite avail	12 En Suite fac 1 Limited ensuite 2 Pub Bath/Show	B&B per person £19.00-£22.00 Single £19.00-£22.00 Double	Open Jan-Dec Dinner from 1830 B&B + Eve. Meal £28.50-£32.00	

Personally run guest house close to town centre,
swimming pool and all amenities. Off-street parking.

| Beechgrove Guest House
Croft Road
Oban
Argyll
PA34 5JL
Tel: (Oban) 01631 566111 | COMMENDED | 1 Twin
1 Double
1 Family | 3 En Suite fac | B&B per person
from £18.00 Double | Open Mar-Oct
Dinner from 1800 | |
| Family run guest house a short walk from the harbour and shops, with pleasant views of Oban Bay and the Sound of Kerrera. |

| Briarbank Bed & Breakfast
Glencruitten Road
Oban
Argyll
PA34 4DN
Tel: (Oban) 01631 566549 | COMMENDED | 3 Double | 3 En Suite fac
1 Pub Bath/Show | B&B per person
£20.00-£22.00 Double | Open Jan-Dec
Dinner 1900-2000
B&B + Eve. Meal
from £27.50 | |
| Traditional house in large gardens with high degree of privacy yet a few minutes from ferry terminals and town. 4-poster oak bed. |

| Mrs Calderwood
The Torrans, Drummore Road
Oban
Argyll
Tel: (Oban) 01631 565342 | COMMENDED | 1 Twin
2 Double | 2 En Suite fac
1 Priv. NOT ensuite | B&B per person
£16.00-£18.00 Double | Open Jan-Dec | |
| Comfortable family home in quiet residential cul-de-sac. 1 mile (2kms) from town centre and all amenities. |

Glenara Guest House

ROCKFIELD ROAD, OBAN, ARGYLL PA34 5DQ
Telephone: 01631 563172

We offer to our guests a quality of room and breakfast (vegetarians catered for) which will ensure your return. *Glenara Guest House* is centrally situated with off-street parking. The house is individually furnished reflecting Dorothy's enthusiasm for objets d'art.
For the comfort of our guests we are a no-smoking house.

| Glenara Guest House
Rockfield Road
Oban
Argyll
PA34 5DQ
Tel: (Oban) 01631 563172 | COMMENDED | 1 Single
1 Twin
3 Double
1 Family | 3 En Suite fac
1 Priv. NOT ensuite | B&B per person
£16.00-£20.00 Single
£16.00-£22.00 Double | Open Jan-Dec | |
| Family run guest house close to the town centre and all amenities. Private parking. Non-smoking house. |

| Glenbervie Guest House
Dalriach Road
Oban
Argyll
PA34 5NL
Tel: (Oban) 01631 564770 | HIGHLY COMMENDED | 2 Single
2 Twin
2 Double
2 Family | 5 En Suite fac
1 Pub Bath/Show | B&B per person
£18.00-£20.00 Single
£18.00-£20.00 Double | Open Jan-Dec
Dinner 1830-2000 | |
| Beautifully situated overlooking Oban Bay, commanding magnificent views. 2 minutes' walk from town centre, promenade, harbour and amenities. Evening meal. Ensuite. |

| Glenroy Guest House
Rockfield Road
Oban
Argyll
PA34 5DQ
Tel: (Oban) 01631 562585 | COMMENDED | 1 Single
1 Twin
5 Double | 5 En Suite fac
3 Pub Bath/Show | B&B per person
£16.00-£17.00 Single
£16.00-£18.00 Double | Open Jan-Dec | |
| Family run guest house just off town centre. Centrally situated and convenient for all amenities. Private parking. |

Details of Grading and Classification are on page vi.

Key to symbols is on back flap.

OBAN

OBAN continued Argyll Sadie & Tam Hobbs Oakbank, Benvoulin Road Oban Argyll Tel: (Oban) 01631 563482	Map 1 E2	COMMENDED	1 Twin 1 Limited ensuite 2 Double 1 Pub Bath/Show	B&B per person £12.50-£16.50 Double	Open Jan-Dec

Small family run bed and breakfast with fine views across Kerrera to the
Isle of Mull, yet only 4 minutes' walk from town centre, harbour and promenade.

Drumriggend
DRUMRIGGEND, DRUMMORE ROAD, OBAN PA34 4JL
Telephone/Fax: 01631 563330

Drumriggend is situated in a quiet residential setting although
only 10 - 15 minutes' walk from the Town Centre. Private parking.
All bedrooms ensuite. Colour TV, central heating, welcome tray,
radio alarm, cots available. Morning call for early departure.
Dinner available by request.

AA QQQQ   **RAC Acclaimed**   **Highly Commended**

J & D Ledwidge Drumriggend, Drummore Road Oban Argyll PA34 4JL Tel: (Oban) 01631 563330 Fax: 01631 563330	HIGHLY COMMENDED	1 Twin 3 En Suite fac 1 Double 1 Family	B&B per person £16.00-£20.00 Double	Open Jan-Dec Dinner 1800-1900 B&B + Eve. Meal £22.00-£28.00

Detached house in quiet residential area. Situated on the
south side of town about 1 mile (2kms) from the centre.

Mrs B MacColl Glengorm, Dunollie Road Oban Argyll PA34 5PH Tel: (Oban) 01631 565361	COMMENDED	1 Twin 2 Pub Bath/Show 3 Double	B&B per person £15.00-£18.00 Double	Open Apr-Oct

Victorian terraced house on level ground near town centre,
convenient for restaurants, entertainments, shops and ferries.

BRACKER
Polvinister Road, Oban, Argyll PA34 5TN
Telephone/Fax: 01631 564302

Modern bungalow situated in beautiful quiet residential area
within walking distance of town (approx. 8-10 mins.) and the
golf course. All bedrooms have private facilities, TV and
tea/coffee-making. TV lounge, private parking.

Mrs C MacDonald Bracker, Polvinister Road Oban Argyll PA34 5TN Tel: (Oban) 01631 564302	COMMENDED	1 Twin 3 En Suite fac 2 Double	B&B per person £16.00-£18.00 Single £16.00-£17.00 Double	Open Mar-Nov

Modern family bungalow in secluded residential area.
Short distance from town centre and all amenities. Private parking.

Mrs MacDougall Harbour View, Shore Street Oban Argyll PA34 4LQ Tel: (Oban) 01631 563462	APPROVED	2 Twin 2 Pub Bath/Show 3 Family	B&B per person £13.00-£15.50 Single £13.00-£15.50 Double	Open Jan-Dec

Centrally situated and convenient for a level stroll to ferry, railway station and shops.

ARGYLL VILLA

Albert Road, entrance on Dalriach Road, Oban PA34 5EJ
Telephone: 01631 566897

A comfortably furnished Victorian House retaining many original features. *Argyll Villa* is a no-smoking establishment. Centrally, yet privately, situated on *Oban Hill* and close to all amenities. All rooms have colour TV, hospitality trays and panoramic views over *Oban Bay* to the *Bens of Mull*. There is a pleasant secluded garden for guests' use.

Mrs McGill Argyll Villa, Albert Road Oban Argyll PA34 5EJ Tel: (Oban) 01631 566897	COMMENDED	1 Twin 2 Double	1 En Suite fac 1 Pub Bath/Show	B&B per person £16.00-£25.00 Double	Open Jan-Dec

Victorian house. Terraced gardens with pleasant seating areas.
All rooms have panoramic views to the Bens of Mull and beyond.

Mrs MacIver Loudon, Dalriach Road Oban Argyll PA34 5EQ Tel: (Oban) 01631 563298	COMMENDED	1 Twin 2 Double	1 En Suite fac 2 Priv. NOT ensuite	B&B per person from £15.00 Double	Open Jan-Dec

Terraced Victorian villa, close to the centre of Oban,
with views over the bay towards Kerrera. Private parking.

Mrs E M MacLean Lorne View, Ardconnel Road Oban Argyll PA34 5DW Tel: (Oban) 01631 565500	COMMENDED	1 Twin 2 Double	3 Limited ensuite 1 Pub Bath/Show	B&B per person £30.00-£35.00 Single £16.00-£18.00 Double	Open Mar-Oct Dinner at 1815 B&B + Eve. Meal from £27.00

Quiet location overlooking Oban Bay. Convenient for local sports amenities
and town centre. Evening meals with advance notice except Sundays.

Mrs C McQuade Ard Struan, Croft Road Oban Argyll PA34 5JN Tel: (Oban) 01631 563689	COMMENDED	1 Twin 3 Double	4 En Suite fac	B&B per person £13.00-£20.00 Double	Open Jan-Dec Dinner from 1800

Modern, detached villa with large garden in quiet residential
area overlooking Oban Bay. Short distance from town centre.

The Old Manse Guest House Dalriach Road Oban Argyll PA34 5JE Tel: (Oban) 01631 564886	COMMENDED	1 Twin 2 Double	3 En Suite fac	B&B per person £18.00-£21.00 Double	Open Feb-Nov Dinner from 1830 B&B + Eve. Meal £27.00-£30.00

Victorian house set high above the town with fine views.
Private parking and all rooms with private facilities. Real home-cooked food.

"Dungrianach"

Deluxe

(Gaelic – 'the sunny house on the hill')
Although only a few minutes' walk from Oban ferry piers and town centre, Dungrianach sits in private woodland, right above the yacht moorings and enjoys unsurpassed views of sea and islands. Accommodation 1 twin and 1 double room, each with private facilities.
***Contact:* Mrs Elaine Robertson, 'Dungrianach', Pulpit Hill, Oban, Argyll PA34 4LX. Telephone/Fax: 01631 562840.**

Mrs E Robertson Dungrianach, Pulpit Hill Oban Argyll PA34 4LX Tel: (Oban) 01631 562840 Fax: 01631 562840	DELUXE	1 Twin 1 Double	2 En Suite fac	B&B per person £19.00-£21.00 Double	Open Apr-Sep

Secluded, in 4 acres (1.6ha) of wooded garden on top of Pulpit Hill.
Magnificent views over Oban Bay and the islands.

WEST HIGHLANDS & ISLANDS, LOCH LOMOND, STIRLING & TROSSACHS

OBAN continued Argyll	Map 1 E2

PINMACHER

Polvinister Road, Oban, Argyll PA34 5TN   Tel: 01631 563553

Comfortable bungalow in quiet part of Oban, ten minutes' walk from bus and rail stations with spacious attractive gardens and ample off-road private parking. Adjacent to golf course with open views of countryside. Open mid-March to end of October. Rooms: two double and one twin, all ensuite. Evening Meal optional – £8.

Prices from £16 B&B.

Brochure and details contact: Ruth Rodaway.

Mrs R Rodaway Pinmacher, Polvinister Road Oban Argyll PA34 5TN Tel: (Oban) 01631 563553	COMMENDED ✿✿	1 Twin 2 Double	3 En Suite fac	B&B per person £16.00-£18.00 Single £16.00-£18.00 Double	Open Mar-Oct Dinner 1900-2100

Comfortable modern bungalow quietly situated only
10 minutes' walk from town centre. Private parking.

Roseneath Guest House

DALRIACH ROAD, OBAN PA34 5EQ
Telephone: 01631 562929

Victorian house with warm and friendly atmosphere, eight minutes' walk from ferries, buses and trains, three minutes from town centre. *Roseneath* is situated in a quiet location close to swimming pool, bowling green, squash and tennis courts. Lovely views over *Oban Bay* to *Mull*. Non-smoking. Private car park.

AA QQQ   RAC Acclaimed

Roseneath Guest House Dalriach Road Oban Argyll PA34 5EQ Tel: (Oban) 01631 562929	COMMENDED ✿	2 Single 2 Twin 6 Double	6 En Suite fac 2 Limited ensuite 2 Pub Bath/Show	B&B per person £15.00-£18.00 Single £15.00-£20.00 Double	Open Jan-Dec

Personally run Victorian house in quiet area overlooking town and bay.
Near seafront and shops. Private parking. Non-smoking.

THORNLOE GUEST HOUSE

Albert Road, Oban, Argyll PA34 5JD   Tel: 01631 562879

THORNLOE is very central to all local amenities. Large cosy home-from-home Victorian house. Tea, coffee, television, ensuite for your comfort in rooms. Substantial breakfast in our dining-room which has magnificent views over to the *Islands of Kerrera and Mull*.
For something special – 4-poster bedrooms available.
Parking available.

AA QQQ   COMMENDED ✿✿   W

Thornloe Guest House Albert Road Oban Argyll PA34 5JD Tel: (Oban) 01631 562879	COMMENDED ✿✿	1 Single 2 Twin 4 Double 1 Family	7 En Suite fac 1 Priv. NOT ensuite	B&B per person £15.00-£21.00 Single £15.00-£21.00 Double	Open Feb-Dec

Completely modernised Victorian semi-detached house in centrally situated
residential area with fine views over Oban Bay towards the Isle of Mull.

Mrs Morven Wardhaugh Kathmore, Soroba Road Oban Argyll Tel: (Oban) 01631 562104	COMMENDED Listed	1 Twin 3 Double 1 Family	4 En Suite fac 1 Pub Bath/Show	B&B per person £18.00-£30.00 Single £14.00-£20.00 Double	Open Jan-Dec Dinner from 1830 B&B + Eve. Meal £22.00-£30.00

Family guest house with ample parking situated within a short walk of town centre.
Ensuite bedrooms. Evening meal by arrangement. All rooms with televisions.

by OBAN Argyll	Map 1 E2

ARDS HOUSE
Connel, by Oban, Argyll PA37 1PT
Tel: 01631 710255

Ards House is a Victorian villa situated 4 miles north of Oban on the approaches to Loch Etive with superb open views over the Firth of Lorn and Morvern Hills. An excellent base for touring Argyll and the Isles. A great place to "come home" to after a full day exploring the area or why not come for a relaxing break at anytime of the year? Members of Taste of Scotland since '93. You can be assured of good food and wine and service with a smile.

*Contact John or Jean Bowman
for more information.*

A TOTALLY NON-SMOKING HOUSE!

Ards House Connel Argyll PA37 1PT Tel: (Connel) 01631 710255	COMMENDED	3 Twin 3 Double	5 En Suite fac 1 Priv. NOT ensuite	B&B per person £25.00-£35.00 Single £21.00-£27.00 Double	Open Feb-Nov Dinner 1900-2000 B&B + Eve. Meal £32.50-£45.00	

Warm friendly atmosphere in this family run house where husband is a keen cook.
Large relaxing lounge, table licence, superb sea and sunset views.

Braeside Guest House Kilmore, by Oban Argyll PA34 4QR Tel: (Kilmore) 01631 770243	COMMENDED	1 Twin 3 Double 1 Family	4 En Suite fac 1 Priv. NOT ensuite	B&B per person £19.50-£25.50 Single £19.50-£25.50 Double	Open Feb-Nov Dinner 1830-1900 B&B + Eve. Meal £32.50-£40.00	

Modern guest house 3 miles (5kms) south of Oban on the A816.
Superb views overlooking Loch Feochan. Evening meal. Restricted licence.
Non-smoking. Private car park.

Mrs Margaret MacPherson Invercairn, Musdale Road Kilmore, by Oban Argyll PA34 4XX Tel: (Oban) 01631 770301	HIGHLY COMMENDED	1 Twin 2 Double	3 En Suite fac	B&B per person £17.00-£22.00 Double	Open Apr-Sep	

Modern bungalow in unspoilt countryside, with superb views.
4 miles (6km) from Oban.

PORT OF MENTEITH **Perthshire** Mrs Norma Erskine Inchie Farm Port of Menteith Perthshire FK8 3JZ Tel: (Port of Menteith) 01877 385233	Map 1 H3 COMMENDED	1 Twin 1 Family	1 Pub Bath/Show	B&B per person £15.00-£16.00 Double	Open Apr-Oct Dinner from 1800 B&B + Eve. Meal £25.00-£26.00	

Family farm beside Lake of Menteith. Traditional and comfortable.
Bathroom for guests' use only. Home baking. Hospitality a priority.

Details of Grading and Classification are on page vi. | Key to symbols is on back flap. |

STIRLING & TROSSACHS

WEST HIGHLANDS & ISLANDS, LOCH LOMOND,

PORT OF MENTEITH Perthshire continued	Map 1 H3

Holly Cottage
Port of Menteith, by Stirling FK8 3RA Tel: 01877 385604

Enjoy a holiday in the Trossachs bungalow in small hamlet with comfortable accommodation. Picturesque setting, views over the Lake of Menteith. Excellent base for touring and a wonderful area for fishing, walking, riding etc. The Stirling/Aberfoyle bus stops at the bungalow. Ample off-road parking for visitors.

Holly Cottage Port of Menteith by Stirling FK8 3RA Tel: (Port of Menteith) 01877 385604	COMMENDED Listed	1 Twin 1 Double	2 En Suite fac	B&B per person £18.00-£20.00 Double	Open Jan-Dec

Detached cottage with large garden, near Scotland's only "Lake".

Mrs C Tough Collymoon Pendicle Port of Menteith Perthshire FK8 3JY Tel: (Buchlyvie) 01360 850222	COMMENDED	1 Double 1 Family	1 Pub Bath/Show	B&B per person £15.00-£16.00 Double	Open Apr-Oct Dinner 1800-1900 B&B + Eve. Meal £25.00-£26.00

Family run modern bungalow in country setting surrounded by panoramic views. Home cooking a speciality. Salmon and trout fishing available.

ST CATHERINES Argyll Arnish Cottage Christian Guest House Poll Bay St Catherines Argyll PA25 8BA Tel: (Inveraray) 01499 302405	Map 1 F3 HIGHLY COMMENDED	1 Twin 2 Double	3 En Suite fac	B&B per person from £22.00 Single from £22.00 Double	Open Jan-Dec Dinner from 1900 B&B + Eve. Meal from £37.00

Family run lochside cottage in quiet conservation area. Freshly cooked local produce and seafood from the loch.

STIRLING Bannockburn Guest Lodge 24/32 Main Street Bannockburn, Stirling Stirlingshire FK7 8LY Tel: (Bannockburn) 01786 812121/816501 Fax: 01786 817628	Map 2 A4 COMMENDED Lodge	3 Twin 2 Double 1 Family	6 En Suite fac	B&B per person £24.00-£26.00 Single £19.00-£21.00 Double	Open Jan-Dec Dinner at 1800

Purpose-built 1990s facilities in a 1760s building! Ideal touring centre 1 mile (2 kms) from motorway.

Castlecroft Ballengeich Road Stirling FK8 1TN Tel: (Stirling) 01786 474933 Fax: 01786 466716	HIGHLY COMMENDED	2 Twin 3 Double 1 Family	6 En Suite fac 1 Pub Bath/Show	B&B per person £39.00-£40.00 Single £19.00-£22.00 Double	Open Jan-Dec, excl Xmas/New Year

Nestling on elevated site under Stirling Castle, this comfortable, modern house offers warm welcome. Private facilities, some suitable for disabled.

Mr and Mrs Dunbar Ravenscroft 21 Clarendon Place Stirling FK8 2QW Tel: (Stirling) 01786 473815	HIGHLY COMMENDED	2 Twin	1 En Suite fac 1 Priv. NOT ensuite	B&B per person £25.00-£30.00 Single £17.00-£20.00 Double	Open Jan-mid Dec

Traditionally furnished Victorian house, in conservation area. Close to town centre and historic sites. Non-smoking house.

Forth Guest House 23 Forth Place, Riverside Stirling FK8 1UD Tel: (Stirling) 01786 471020/ 0850 868501 (mobile) Fax: 01786 447220	**HIGHLY COMMENDED** 👑👑👑	2 Twin 2 Double 1 Family	5 En Suite fac	B&B per person £25.00-£35.00 Single £19.00-£20.00 Double	Open Jan-Dec Dinner 1900-2000 B&B + Eve. Meal £31.50-£32.50

Terraced house within easy walking distance of railway station,
town centre and swimming pool. Good location for touring.

Shalom

Manse Crescent, Stirling FK7 9AJ
Telephone: 01786 471092

Comfortable accommodation in attractive bungalow of character.
Situated in a quiet Victorian cul-de-sac 15 minutes'
walking distance from town centre. Contact Mrs R Johnson.

Mrs R Johnson Shalom, Manse Crescent Stirling FK7 9AJ Tel: (Stirling) 01786 471092	**COMMENDED** 👑	1 Single 1 Twin	1 Pub Bath/Show	B&B per person £16.00-£18.00 Single £16.00-£18.00 Double	Open Jan-Dec

Bungalow with character in quiet cul-de-sac, 3 minutes' walk to frequent
bus service, 15 minutes' walk to town centre. Off-street parking.

Mrs M Johnston West Plean House Denny Road Stirling FK7 8HA Tel: (Stirling) 01786 812208	**COMMENDED** 👑👑	1 Single 1 Double 1 Family	2 En Suite fac 1 Priv. NOT ensuite	B&B per person £25.00-£30.00 Single £20.00-£24.00 Double	Open Feb-Nov

200-year-old country house on working farm set in extensive
grounds and woodlands.Offering warm Scottish farming hospitality.

Mrs D Mailer Ashgrove, 2 Park Avenue Stirling Tel: (Stirling) 01786 472640	**HIGHLY COMMENDED** 👑👑	1 Twin 2 Double	3 En Suite fac	B&B per person £27.50 Single £22.50-£25.00 Double	Open Jan-Dec

Listed Victorian townhouse by renowned local architect.
Short walk from castle, town centre and all amenities.

Mrs E Paterson Laurinda, 66 Ochilmount Ochilview Bannockburn, Stirling FK7 8PJ Tel: (Stirling) 01786 815612	**COMMENDED** Listed	1 Double 1 Family	1 Pub Bath/Show	B&B per person £16.00-£17.00 Single £15.00-£16.00 Double	Open Jan-Dec Dinner 1800-1900 B&B + Eve. Meal £21.00-£22.00

Modern, detached villa in residential area of Bannockburn.
Ideal location for touring all main cities and tourist attractions. Parking area.

Mrs Agnes Thomson Tiroran, 45 Douglas Terrace Stirling FK7 9LW Tel: (Stirling) 01786 464655	**HIGHLY COMMENDED** 👑	1 Twin 1 Double	1 Pub Bath/Show	B&B per person £15.50-£16.00 Double	Open Apr-Oct

A warm welcome in this modern house, with easy access to the town centre.

XI Victoria Square Stirling FK8 2RA Tel: (Stirling) 01786 475545	**COMMENDED** 👑👑	1 Twin 1 Double 1 Family	2 En Suite fac 1 Priv. NOT ensuite	B&B per person £28.00-£40.00 Single from £20.00 Double	Open Jan-Dec

Victorian house with many original features situated in quiet
residential area 5 minutes' walk from town centre. Views of Stirling Castle.

Details of Grading and Classification are on page vi. | Key to symbols is on back flap. |

STRATHYRE – TARBET, by Arrochar

STRATHYRE **Perthshire** Mr & Mrs Ffinch Dochfour Strathyre Perthshire FK18 8NA Tel: (Strathyre) 01877 384256 Fax: 01877 384256	Map 1 H3	COMMENDED	1 Twin 2 Double	2 En Suite fac 1 Priv. NOT ensuite	B&B per person £16.00-£19.00 Double	Open Jan-Dec Dinner 1800-2000 B&B + Eve. Meal £23.00-£30.00	

Traditional stone-built semi-detached villa in centre of village.
Excellent views to surrounding hills. Home cooking with fresh produce.

Mr & Mrs Reid Coire Buidhe Strathyre Perthshire FK18 8NA Tel: (Strathyre) 01877 384288		APPROVED Listed	2 Single 2 Twin 2 Double 2 Family	1 En Suite fac 3 Pub Bath/Show	B&B per person from £14.00 Single £14.00-£17.00 Double	Open Jan-Dec excl Xmas Dinner from 1900 B&B + Eve. Meal £24.00-£27.00	

Personally run guest house in centre of small village offering traditional comfort.
Ideal centre for touring the West Highlands.

TARBERT, Loch Fyne **Argyll**	Map 1 E5	

Springside Bed & Breakfast

Pier Road, Tarbert, Loch Fyne, Argyll PA29 6UE
Telephone/Fax: 01880 820413

Tranquillity of traditional fisherman's cottage situated close to shore, with
excellent views over harbour entrance and five minutes' walk from
amenities in one of the most picturesque Highland fishing villages.
We cater for early and all ferry crossings on beautiful Kintyre Peninsula.
For those who prefer, vegetarian menu is available.

Mrs Marshall Springside, Pier Road Tarbert, Loch Fyne Argyll PA29 6UE Tel: (Tarbert) 01880 820413 Fax: 01880 820413	COMMENDED	1 Single 1 Twin 1 Double 2 Family	3 En Suite fac 1 Pub Bath/Show	B&B per person from £18.00 Single from £18.00 Double	Open Jan-Dec Dinner from 1800	

Traditional stone detached house, overlooking the harbour entrance,
within walking distance of village. Convenient for ferries to Islay,
Gigha, Cowal Peninsula and Arran.

Mrs Peden The Hollies Tarbert, Loch Fyne Argyll PA29 6YF Tel: (Tarbert) 01880 820742	COMMENDED	2 Twin 1 Double	2 Pub Bath/Show	B&B per person from £16.00 Single from £16.00 Double Room only per person from £13.00	Open Jan-Dec	

Comfortable accommodation in modern bungalow with open views towards
West Loch Tarbet. Convenient for ferries to Islay, Jura, Gigha, Arran,
and the Cowal Peninsula.

TARBET, by Arrochar **Dunbartonshire** Mrs E Fairfield Lochview Tarbet, by Arrochar Dunbartonshire G83 7DD Tel: (Arrochar) 01301 702200	Map 1 G3	APPROVED Listed	1 Twin 2 Double	1 Pub Bath/Show	B&B per person £15.00-£17.00 Single £14.00-£16.00 Double	Open Jan-Dec	

Georgian house on main road to west coast. Short distance
from shore of Loch Lomond. Ideal base for touring.

Mrs Kelly Bon-Etive Tarbet, by Arrochar Dunbartonshire G83 Tel: (Arrochar) 01301 702219	COMMENDED Listed	1 Twin 1 Double	1 Pub Bath/Show	B&B per person £15.50-£16.00 Double	Open Apr-Oct	

Conveniently situated in quiet cul-de-sac close to the A82,
with fine views of Loch Lomond and 'The Ben'.

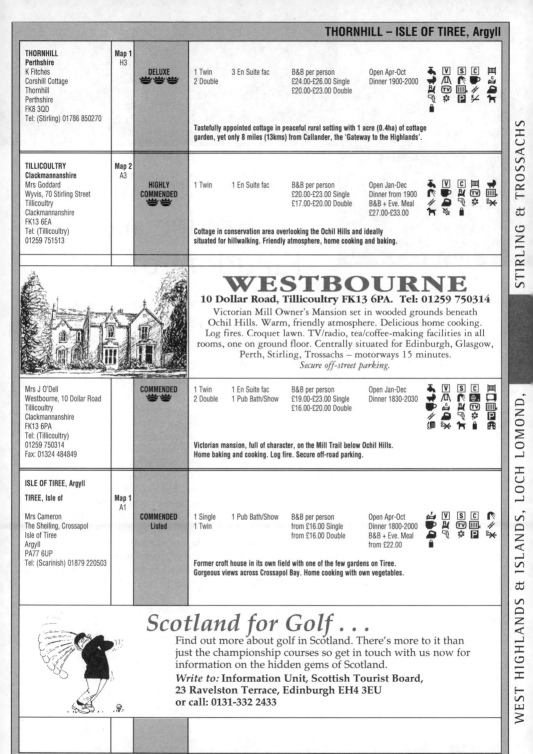

STIRLING & TROSSACHS

WEST HIGHLANDS & ISLANDS, LOCH LOMOND,

THORNHILL **Perthshire** K Fitches Corshill Cottage Thornhill Perthshire FK8 3QD Tel: (Stirling) 01786 850270	Map 1 H3 **DELUXE**	1 Twin 2 Double	3 En Suite fac	B&B per person £24.00-£26.00 Single £20.00-£23.00 Double	Open Apr-Oct Dinner 1900-2000	

Tastefully appointed cottage in peaceful rural setting with 1 acre (0.4ha) of cottage garden, yet only 8 miles (13kms) from Callander, the 'Gateway to the Highlands'.

TILLICOULTRY **Clackmannanshire** Mrs Goddard Wyvis, 70 Stirling Street Tillicoultry Clackmannanshire FK13 6EA Tel: (Tillicoultry) 01259 751513	Map 2 A3 **HIGHLY** **COMMENDED**	1 Twin	1 En Suite fac	B&B per person £20.00-£23.00 Single £17.00-£20.00 Double	Open Jan-Dec Dinner from 1900 B&B + Eve. Meal £27.00-£33.00	

Cottage in conservation area overlooking the Ochil Hills and ideally situated for hillwalking. Friendly atmosphere, home cooking and baking.

WESTBOURNE

10 Dollar Road, Tillicoultry FK13 6PA. Tel: 01259 750314

Victorian Mill Owner's Mansion set in wooded grounds beneath Ochil Hills. Warm, friendly atmosphere. Delicious home cooking. Log fires. Croquet lawn. TV/radio, tea/coffee-making facilities in all rooms, one on ground floor. Centrally situated for Edinburgh, Glasgow, Perth, Stirling, Trossachs – motorways 15 minutes.
Secure off-street parking.

Mrs J O'Dell Westbourne, 10 Dollar Road Tillicoultry Clackmannanshire FK13 6PA Tel: (Tillicoultry) 01259 750314 Fax: 01324 484849	**COMMENDED**	1 Twin 2 Double	1 En Suite fac 1 Pub Bath/Show	B&B per person £19.00-£23.00 Single £16.00-£20.00 Double	Open Jan-Dec Dinner 1830-2030	

Victorian mansion, full of character, on the Mill Trail below Ochil Hills. Home baking and cooking. Log fire. Secure off-road parking.

ISLE OF TIREE, Argyll **TIREE, Isle of** Mrs Cameron The Sheiling, Crossapol Isle of Tiree Argyll PA77 6UP Tel: (Scarinish) 01879 220503	Map 1 A1 **COMMENDED** Listed	1 Single 1 Twin	1 Pub Bath/Show	B&B per person from £16.00 Single from £16.00 Double	Open Apr-Oct Dinner 1800-2000 B&B + Eve. Meal from £22.00	

Former croft house in its own field with one of the few gardens on Tiree. Gorgeous views across Crossapol Bay. Home cooking with own vegetables.

Scotland for Golf . . .

Find out more about golf in Scotland. There's more to it than just the championship courses so get in touch with us now for information on the hidden gems of Scotland.

Write to: **Information Unit, Scottish Tourist Board, 23 Ravelston Terrace, Edinburgh EH4 3EU**
or call: 0131-332 2433

Welcome to...

Perthshire, Angus & Dundee and the Kingdom of Fife

This is an area offering plenty of contrasts: from the white-walled harbourfront houses of the East Neuk of Fife fishing villages to the windy silences of the edge of Rannoch Moor; from the pubs and upbeat nightlife of the city of Dundee to the upland tranquillity of the Angus glens. It makes a good choice if your Scottish break should have a little of everything.

That is something you will find in Perthshire itself, straddling the Highland-Lowland edge, with Perth as an important historic and commercial centre for an attractive hinterland. Here you will find excellent shopping and plenty of places nearby. Another Perthshire speciality are the little resort towns like Pitlochry or Aberfeldy, attractive places with a long tradition of catering for visitors in a Highland setting. These locations and others such as Dunkeld or Blairgowrie, make good touring centres. All of these places are especially good in autumn when the woodland colours at their best.

The old Kingdom of Fife has plenty of character. St Andrews' unique story includes its life as an academic centre (Scotland's oldest university is here), and as an important religious centre, though its cathedral is now only a ruin. To St Andrews' layers of history must be added its claim as the home of golf. Fife's story is certainly bound up with the sea, which is why the East Neuk villages, facing the Forth estuary are popular: Crail, Anstruther and their neighbours rate as some of Scotland's most attractive 'townscapes', while Anstruther's Scottish Fisheries Museum is well worth discovering.

Road and rail bridges across the Tay lead from Fife into Dundee, the 'City of Discovery'. This refers both to the many attractions here and, literally, the home of the RRS Discovery, the ship used by Captain Scott on his Antarctic expeditions.

Road and rail bridges across the Tay lead from Fife into Dundee, the 'City of Discovery'. This refers both to the many attractions here and, literally, the home of the RRS Discovery, the ship used by Captain Scott on his Antarctic expeditions. Discovery Point is one of the top attractions in Scotland and should not be missed. The city has plenty of other places of interest, including the McManus Galleries. As well as fine paintings, the history collection here tells the full story of the city's heritage of textiles, whaling and shipbuilding, journalism and jam making.

Perthshire, Angus & Dundee and the Kingdom of Fife

Angus looks both to the hills and the sea. The Angus Glens are one of Scotland's best-kept secrets.

Glens such as Isla, Prosen, Clova or Esk run far into the mountains, with motorable roads to take you truly away from it all – great places to recharge the batteries. Visit in spring when the high tops are still snow covered. Meanwhile, across the other side of the wide valley called Strathmore with its woods and farms, the sea coast has its own charms. Discover red sandstone cliffs and fine beaches, as well as fishing ports such as Arbroath, home of the local delicacy, the Arbroath smokie. (Try this fishy delight when you get here!) Between the mountains and the sea are attractions such as Glamis Castle, associated with HM Queen Elizabeth the Queen Mother, or Edzell Castle with its unique garden.

These, in turn, are reminders of more of the attractions scattered throughout the area: Blair Castle or Castle Menzies, the superb Deep Sea World at North Queensferry or the, perhaps unexpected, attraction of Scotland's Secret Bunker, a Cold War relic, tucked innocently into the rural surroundings of Fife. Many attractions open throughout the year. Surprises are guaranteed anywhere in this area.

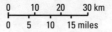

AREA TOURIST BOARD ADDRESSES

1 ANGUS AND CITY OF DUNDEE TOURIST BOARD
4 City Square
DUNDEE
DD1 3BA
Tel: 01382 434664
Fax: 01382 434665

2 KINGDOM OF FIFE TOURIST BOARD
Kingdom House
7 Hanover Court
North Street
GLENROTHES
Fife
KY7 5SB
Tel: 01592 750066
Fax: 01592 611180

3 PERTHSHIRE TOURIST BOARD
Administrative
Headquarters
Lower City Mills
West Mill Street
PERTH
PH1 5QP
Tel: 01738 627958
   01738 444144
   (Activity Line)
Fax: 01738 630416

TOURIST INFORMATION CENTRES IN SCOTLAND

ANGUS & CITY OF DUNDEE TOURIST BOARD

ARBROATH
Market Place
DD11 1HR
Tel: (01241) 872609
Jan-Dec

BRECHIN
St Ninians Place
Tel: (01356) 623050
April-Sept

CARNOUSTIE
1B High Street
Tel: (01241) 852258
April-Sept

DUNDEE &
4 City Square
DD1 3BA
Tel: (01382) 434664

FORFAR
40 East High Street
Tel: (01307) 467876
April-Sept

KIRRIEMUIR
Cumberland Close
Tel: (01575) 574097
April-Sept

MONTROSE
Bridge Street
Tel: (01674) 672000
April-Sept

KINGDOM OF FIFE TOURIST BOARD

ANSTRUTHER
Scottish Fisheries Museum
Tel: (01333) 311073
April-Sept

BURNTISLAND
4 Kirkgate
Tel: (01592) 872667
Jan-Dec

CRAIL
Museum & Heritage Centre
Marketgate
Tel: (01333) 450869
Easter-Sept

CUPAR &
The Granary, Coal Road
Tel: (01334) 652874
Easter-Sept

DUNFERMLINE &
13/15 Maygate
Tel: (01383) 720999
Jan-Dec

FORTH ROAD BRIDGE
by North Queensferry
Tel: (01383) 417759
Easter-Oct
Nov-Mar unmanned

GLENROTHES
Rothes Square
Kingdom Centre
Tel: (01592) 754954/610784
Jan-Dec

KIRKCALDY
19 Whytescauseway
Tel: (01592) 267775
Jan-Dec

LEVEN &
The Beehive, Durie Street
Tel: (01333) 429464
Jan-Dec

ST ANDREWS
70 Market Street, KY16 9NU
Tel: (01334) 472021
Jan-Dec

PERTHSHIRE TOURIST BOARD

ABERFELDY &
The Square
Tel: (01887) 820276
Jan-Dec

AUCHTERARDER
90 High Street
Tel: (01764) 663450
Jan-Dec

BLAIRGOWRIE
26 Wellmeadow
Tel: (01250) 872960
Jan-Dec

CRIEFF &
Town Hall, High Street
Tel: (01764) 652578
Jan-Dec

DUNKELD &
The Cross
Tel: (01350) 727688
Mar-Dec

KINROSS
Kinross Service Area
off Junction 6, M90
Tel: (01577) 863680
Jan-Dec

PERTH &
45 High Street, PH1 5TJ
Tel: (01738) 638353
Jan-Dec

PERTH, INVERALMOND
(A9 Western City Bypass)
Tel: (01738) 638481
Jan-Dec

PITLOCHRY &
22 Atholl Road
Tel; (01796) 472215/472751
Jan-Dec

✉ Accept written enquiries
& Disabled access

ABERDOUR Fife	Map 2 C4

HAWKCRAIG HOUSE

Hawkcraig Point, Aberdour, Fife KY3 0TZ
Telephone: 01383 860335

Old ferryman's house at water's edge overlooking Aberdour Harbour and
Inchcolm. Only 30 minutes from Edinburgh by road or rail.
Accommodation on ground floor comprises one twin (shower ensuite),
one double (bath ensuite), sitting room and conservatory.
Taste of Scotland dinners (pre-booked), residents and non-residents.
Scottish Thistle Award finalist 1996.

Mrs E Barrie Hawkcraig House Hawkcraig Point Aberdour Fife KY3 0TZ Tel: (Aberdour) 01383 860335		**DELUXE**	1 Twin 1 Double	2 En Suite fac	B&B per person £26.00-£29.00 Single £21.00-£24.00 Double	Open mid Mar-Oct Dinner 1900-2030 B&B + Eve. Meal £42.00-£45.00
			Old ferryman's house situated at water's edge overlooking Aberdour Harbour and Inchcolm Island. Steep access. Taste of Scotland member.			
ABERFELDY **Perthshire** Balnearn House Crieff Road Aberfeldy Perthshire PH15 2BJ Tel: (Aberfeldy) 01887 820431	Map 2 A1	**COMMENDED**	3 Twin 5 Double 2 Family Suite avail	10 En Suite fac 2 Priv. NOT ensuite	B&B per person from £22.50 Single £18.50-£30.00 Double	Open Apr-Oct
			Substantial stone-built house surrounded by attractive garden. Mountain view. Large car park, close to the renowned "Birks Walk".			
Fernbank House Kenmore Street Aberfeldy Perthshire PH15 2BL Tel: (Aberfeldy) 01887 820345		**HIGHLY COMMENDED**	1 Single 2 Twin 3 Double 1 Family	7 En Suite fac	B&B per person from £26.50 Single £22.50-£27.50 Double	Open Jan-Dec
			Quiet, comfortable, non-smoking Victorian country house set in own grounds with private parking. All rooms ensuite. Quality guest house.			
Mrs Malcolm Novar, 2 Home Street Aberfeldy Perthshire PH15 2AJ Tel: (Aberfeldy) 01887 820779		**COMMENDED**	1 Twin 1 Double 1 Family	2 En Suite fac 1 Priv. NOT ensuite	B&B per person £16.50-£19.00 Double	Open Apr-Oct
			Stone-built villa with attractive, well-maintained garden in residential area. Private parking. Convenient for town centre.			
Tigh'n Eilean Guest House Taybridge Drive Aberfeldy Perthshire PH15 2BP Tel: (Aberfeldy) 01887 820109		**HIGHLY COMMENDED**	1 Twin 2 Double	2 En Suite fac 1 Priv. NOT ensuite	B&B per person £17.00-£21.00 Single £18.00-£21.00 Double	Open Jan-Dec Dinner 1800-1900 B&B + Eve. Meal £29.00-£33.00
			Elegant Victorian house overlooking the river. Warm and comfortable, home cooking. One room with jacuzzi.			
by ABERFELDY **Perthshire** Mr & Mrs Bolam South Lodge, Castle Menzies Aberfeldy Perthshire PH15 2JD Tel: (Aberfeldy) 01887 820115	Map 2 A1	**HIGHLY COMMENDED** Listed	1 Twin 1 Double	2 Priv. NOT ensuite	B&B per person £16.00-£18.00 Double	Open Jan-Dec Dinner from 1900 B&B + Eve. Meal £28.00-£30.00
			Renovated and extended former lodge house, dating from 18th century. Adjacent to Castle Menzies. Spectacular views to castle and glen.			

PERTHSHIRE, ANGUS & DUNDEE   AND THE KINGDOM OF FIFE

| by ABERNETHY | Map 2 |
| Perthshire | C3 |

EASTER CLUNIE FARMHOUSE
Newburgh, Fife KY14 6EJ
Telephone: 01337 840218
19th-century comfortable centrally heated farmhouse
with panoramic views over the River Tay.
Tea and coffee-making facilities. Walled garden.
Enjoy a relaxing holiday. Close to Perth and St Andrews.

Mrs K Baird Easter Clunie Farmhouse Newburgh Fife KY14 6EJ Tel: (Newburgh) 01337 840218	COMMENDED 👑👑	2 Twin 1 Family	1 En Suite fac 2 Priv. NOT ensuite	B&B per person from £20.00 Single £15.00-£16.00 Double	Open Apr-Oct	

19th century farmhouse on working farm. Quiet setting. Splendid Victorian
walled garden. Convenient for main routes to Edinburgh and the Highlands.

ALYTH Perthshire Airlie Mount Holiday Services 2 Albert Street Alyth, Blairgowrie Perthshire PH11 8AX Tel: (Alyth) 01828 632986 Fax: 01828 632563	Map 2 C1 COMMENDED Listed	1 Single 2 Twin 2 Double 2 Family	3 En Suite fac 1 Limited ensuite 1 Priv. NOT ensuite 3 Pub Bath/Show	B&B per person from £22.00 Single from £17.00 Double Room only per person £14.00-£19.00	Open Jan-Dec Dinner 1900-2200 B&B + Eve. Meal £29.00-£35.00	

A warm welcome at this Victorian mansion, quietly located in peaceful Alyth.

Mrs Ann Ferguson Bruceton Farm Alyth, Blairgowrie Perthshire PH11 8JT Tel: (Craigton) 01575 530201	HIGHLY COMMENDED 👑👑	1 Single 1 Twin 1 Double	1 En Suite fac 2 Priv. NOT ensuite	B&B per person from £18.00 Single from £18.00 Double	Open Mar-Nov	

Secluded farmhouse, large rooms with panoramic views, within
easy reach of the picturesque glens of Perthshire and Angus.

Mrs McBain Old Stables, 2 Losset Road Alyth Perthshire PH11 8BT Tel: (Alyth) 01828 632547	HIGHLY COMMENDED 👑👑	2 Twin 1 Family	3 En Suite fac	B&B per person £17.00-£21.00 Single £17.00-£21.00 Double Room only per person £15.00-£18.00	Open Jan-Dec	

Warm and friendly welcome assured in this striking conversion of 19th century
stable. Log fireplace and sauna. Private car park close to town centre.

Mrs Jean Rimmer Lintrathen, St Ninians Road Alyth Perthshire PH11 8AR Tel: (Alyth) 01828 632785	COMMENDED Listed	1 Single 1 Double	1 Pub Bath/Show	B&B per person £14.00-£15.00 Single £14.00-£15.00 Double	Open Jan-Dec	

Modern bungalow at the edge of the town. Good touring area.
Ample car parking. Warm welcome assured from your Scottish hostess.

AMULREE Perthshire Mrs Pat Scott Tigh-na-Braan Amulree Perthshire PH8 0BZ Tel: (Amulree) 01350 725247	Map 2 A2 HIGHLY COMMENDED 👑👑	1 Twin 1 Double	2 En Suite fac	B&B per person from £19.50 Double	Open Jan-Dec Dinner 1930-2030 B&B + Eve. Meal from £30.00	

Former Victorian manse in small village surrounded by hills.
Ideal central location for touring. Non-smoking house.

PERTHSHIRE, ANGUS & DUNDEE AND THE KINGDOM OF FIFE

PERTHSHIRE, ANGUS & DUNDEE AND THE KINGDOM OF FIFE

ANSTRUTHER Fife Beaumont Lodge Guest House 43 Pittenweem Road Anstruther Fife KY10 3DT Tel: (Anstruther) 01333 310315	Map 2 D3	COMMENDED 👑👑👑	2 Twin 3 Double 1 Family	3 En Suite fac 1 Priv. NOT ensuite 1 Pub Bath/Show	B&B per person £15.00-£22.00 Single £15.00-£22.00 Double	Open Jan-Dec Dinner 1800-2000 B&B + Eve. Meal £25.00-£32.00	

Family run Guest House in the picturesque fishing village of Anstruther.
Spacious bedrooms, most ensuite.

The Hermitage Ladywalk Anstruther Fife KY10 3EX Tel: (Anstruther) 01333 310909		HIGHLY COMMENDED 👑	1 Twin 3 Double	2 Pub Bath/Show	B&B per person £20.00-£25.00 Double	Open Jan-Dec Dinner from 1900 B&B + Eve. Meal £33.50-£38.50	

19th century Listed East Neuk townhouse with secluded south-facing garden.
Comfortable accommodation furnished to a high standard. Private parking.

Mrs B Ritchie The Sheiling 32 Glenogil Gardens Anstruther Fife KY10 3ET Tel: (Anstruther) 01333 310697		COMMENDED 👑	2 Double	1 Pub Bath/Show	B&B per person £15.00-£16.00 Double	Open Apr-Oct Dinner 1800-1900 B&B + Eve. Meal £30.00-£32.00	

Pretty, white semi-detached bungalow in quiet area near harbour.
Attractive gardens. Home-made shortbread, jams and marmalade.

The Spindrift

Pittenweem Road, Anstruther, Fife KY10 3DT
Telephone and Fax: 01333 310573

Set on the western edge of Anstruther, The Spindrift has established a growing reputation for its unique brand of comfort, hospitality, freshly prepared food and service. Convenient for golf, walking, bird watching or exploring the picturesque and historic East Neuk. Please contact Eric and Moyra McFarlane for reservations.

The Spindrift Pittenweem Road Anstruther Fife KY10 3DT Tel: (Anstruther) 01333 310573 Fax: 01333 310573		HIGHLY COMMENDED 👑👑👑	2 Twin 3 Double 3 Family	8 En Suite fac	B&B per person £26.00-£30.00 Double	Open Jan-Dec Dinner 1800-1930 B&B + Eve. Meal £37.00-£42.00	

Stone-built Victorian house with wealth of original features, set in fishing village.
Short walk from town centre. Ideal touring base. Non-smoking.

ARBROATH Angus Mrs D Eaton 4 Monkbarns Drive Arbroath Angus DD11 2DS Tel: (Arbroath) 01241 879169/ 874037	Map 2 D1	COMMENDED Listed	2 Double 1 Family	2 Pub Bath/Show	B&B per person from £15.00 Single from £15.00 Double	Open Jun-Sep	

Situated in elevated position with outstanding views overlooking the River Tay.
Private parking.

Mrs S M Fergusson 6 Monkbarns Drive Arbroath Angus DD11 2DS Tel: (Arbroath) 01241 873991		COMMENDED 👑	3 Twin 1 Family	2 Pub Bath/Show	B&B per person £14.00-£15.00 Single £14.00-£15.00 Double Room only per person from £10.00	Open Apr-Sep	

Spacious family house in quiet cul-de-sac with sea views, off-road parking.
Gaelic spoken. Non-smoking.

Merlewood Guest House Elliot Place Arbroath Angus DD11 3BX Tel: (Arbroath) 01241 873076 Fax: 01241 877667		COMMENDED Listed	1 Twin 1 Double 1 Family	2 Pub Bath/Show	B&B per person £16.50-£18.50 Single £16.50 Double	Open Jan-Dec	

Family run, detached stone-built house with private parking located in residential area in west end of town, close to railway station.

Sandhutton Guest House 16 Addison Place Arbroath Angus DD11 2AX Tel: (Arbroath) 01241 872007		HIGHLY COMMENDED	2 Twin 1 Double	1 Priv. NOT ensuite 2 Pub Bath/Show	B&B per person £19.00 Single £16.00-£18.00 Double	Open Mar-Oct	

Victorian villa offering a warm welcome and comfortable non-smoking accommodation with modern facilities. Centrally located for amenities.

AUCHTERARDER **Perthshire** Mrs S Robertson Nether Coul Auchterarder Perthshire PH3 1ET Tel: (Auchterarder) 01764 663119	Map 2 B3	COMMENDED	1 Twin 1 Family	2 Priv. NOT ensuite	B&B per person £15.00-£17.00 Single £15.00-£17.00 Double	Open Jan-Dec	

Renovated stone cottage with large garden and stream. Both rooms with private facilities. Friendly atmosphere, home cooking, fresh produce.

Mrs M West, The Parsonage 111 High Street Auchterarder Perthshire PH3 1AA Tel: (Auchterarder) 01764 662392		COMMENDED	2 Twin 2 Family	1 En Suite fac 2 Pub Bath/Show	B&B per person £18.00-£22.00 Single £17.00-£20.00 Double	Open Jan-Dec	

Personally run guest house in the centre of Auchterarder. Convenient for golf courses, restaurants and all amenities. Lovely views from all bedrooms.

by AUCHTERARDER **Perthshire** Mrs Janice Scougall Raith Farm Madderty, by Crieff Perthshire PH7 3RJ Tel: (Madderty) 01764 683262	Map 2 B3	COMMENDED	2 Family	2 En Suite fac	B&B per person £18.00-£20.00 Single	Open Apr-Oct	

Traditional farmhouse situated in beautiful countryside. Convenient for touring, walking, golfing, fishing and parachuting. Children welcome.

by BALLINGRY **Fife**	Map 2 C3

NAVITIE HOUSE

Commended

Ballingry, Nr Loch Leven, Fife, KY5 8LR
Telephone: 01592 860295 Fax: 01592 869769
This period mansion, set in 4 acres of ground, offers large rooms with en-suite facilities, home cooking, sauna and excellent views over the Forth Valley. Situated 4 miles off the M90 and only 25 minutes' drive from Edinburgh. Many golf courses within a short drive.
B&B from £20 per night. Discounts for children.

Navitie House by Ballingry, nr Loch Leven Fife KY5 8LR Tel: (Ballingry) 01592 860295 Fax: 01592 869769		COMMENDED	1 Single 2 Twin 3 Double 3 Family	7 En Suite fac 2 Priv. NOT ensuite 1 Pub Bath/Show	B&B per person £24.00 Single £20.00-£22.00 Double	Open Jan-Dec Dinner 1900-2100 B&B + Eve. Meal £29.00-£31.00	

Detached 200-year-old house in its own grounds overlooking Ballingry village. Only 4 miles (6kms) from the Edinburgh to Perth motorway.

PERTHSHIRE, ANGUS & DUNDEE AND THE KINGDOM OF FIFE

Details of Grading and Classification are on page vi. | Key to symbols is on back flap. | 161

BANKFOOT **Perthshire** Mrs C McKay Blair House, Main Street Bankfoot Perthshire PH1 4AB Tel: (Bankfoot) 01738 787338	Map 2 B2	COMMENDED	1 Twin 1 Double	2 En Suite fac 2 Pub Bath/Show	B&B per person from £16.00 Double	Open Jan-Dec	
A friendly welcome at this personally-run B&B. Private parking, ideal location for touring the Perthshire area. Fishing, golfing within easy reach.							
BLACKFORD **Perthshire** Mrs R Robertson Yarrow House, Moray Street Blackford Perthshire PH4 1PY Tel: (Blackford) 01764 682358	Map 2 A3	COMMENDED	1 Single 1 Twin 1 Family	1 En Suite fac 1 Pub Bath/Show	B&B per person £15.00-£18.00 Single £15.00-£18.00 Double Room only per person £10.00-£13.00	Open Jan-Dec Dinner from 1800	
Comfortable home in the centre of village with good walks in the surrounding countryside. Convenient for the A9.							
BLAIR ATHOLL **Perthshire** Dalgreine off St Andrew's Crescent Blair Atholl Perthshire PH18 5SX Tel: (Blair Atholl) 01796 481276	Map 4 C12	COMMENDED	1 Single 2 Twin 2 Double 1 Family	2 En Suite fac 1 Priv. NOT ensuite 1 Pub Bath/Show	B&B per person £15.00-£17.00 Single £15.00-£18.00 Double	Open Jan-Dec Dinner 1830-1930 B&B + Eve. Meal £25.00-£28.00	
Well-appointed guest house, convenient for Blair Castle, Pitlochry Festival Theatre and the many local activities and attractions. Good home cooking.							
BLAIRGOWRIE **Perthshire**	Map 2 B1						

DUAN VILLA
Perth Road, Blairgowrie, Perthshire PH10 6EQ
Telephone: 01250 873053

Detached attractive Victorian villa – many original features intact – providing relaxing atmosphere to enjoy your stay in Blairgowrie.
An ideal base for sight-seeing, touring, walking, golfing, ski-ing or fishing.
There is ample parking and garden for guests' enjoyment.
Situated 10 minutes' walk from centre of town.

Mrs Adele Barrie Duan Villa, Perth Road Blairgowrie Perthshire PH10 6EQ Tel: (Blairgowrie) 01250 873053		COMMENDED	1 Twin 1 Double 1 Family	2 En Suite fac 1 Pub Bath/Show	B&B per person £14.50-£17.50 Double	Open Jan-Dec Dinner 1830-1930 B&B + Eve. Meal £23.00-£26.00	
Traditional, sandstone, detached house retaining original cornices and wood panelling. On access route to Glenshee. Evening meal by arrangement.							

Book your accommodation anywhere in Scotland the easy way – through your nearest Tourist Information Centre.

A booking fee of £2.75 is charged, and you will be asked for a small deposit.

Local bookings are usually free, or a small fee will be charged.

Glenshieling House

HATTON ROAD, BLAIRGOWRIE, PERTHSHIRE PH10 7HZ
Telephone: 01250 874605

Located away from main Balmoral Road in two acres of tranquillity.
Central heating, ensuite facilities, colour TVs. Outstanding food –
chef/owner – trained Gleneagles and France, mouth-watering choices
for breakfast and dinner, plus good wine list. Ideal touring centre,
approximately one hour – Edinburgh, Aberdeen, Glasgow.
Great golfing centre. *Access and Visa welcome.*

Glenshieling House Hatton Road, Rattray Blairgowrie Perthshire PH10 7HZ Tel: (Blairgowrie) 01250 874605	HIGHLY COMMENDED 👑👑👑	1 Single 2 Twin 2 Double 2 Family	4 En Suite fac 2 Pub Bath/Show	B&B per person £21.00-£26.50 Single £21.00-£26.50 Double	Open Jan-Dec Dinner 1800-2100 B&B + Eve. Meal £37.95-£44.45

Lovely Victorian house tranquilly set in 2 acres (0.8ha) of garden and woodland
near Blairgowrie. Chef/Proprietor trained in Gleneagles and France.

Mr & Mrs Grant Norwood House, Park Drive Blairgowrie Perthshire PH10 6PA Tel: (Blairgowrie) 01250 874146	COMMENDED 👑	1 Twin 1 Double 1 Family	1 Pub Bath/Show	B&B per person £15.00 Single £15.00 Double	Open Jan-Dec Dinner 1800-2000 B&B + Eve. Meal £21.50-£23.00

Comfortable Victorian family house in residential area. Good home cooking,
golfers, walkers and skiers welcome. Private parking. Ideal for touring Perthshire.

Duncraggan

Perth Road, Blairgowrie PH10 6EJ
Telephone: 01250 872082

Duncraggan House of character offers
peace and relaxation in comfortable and
beautiful surroundings with meals of high
standard and off-road parking. Ideally
situated for tourists, hillwalkers, golfers
and skiers alike or just relax in our acre
of garden with 9-hole putting green. Four-
poster bed in double room with private
facilities (not ensuite). NO SMOKING!

Commended 👑👑👑   AA QQQ

Mrs C McClement Duncraggan, Perth Road Blairgowrie Perthshire PH10 6EJ Tel: (Blairgowrie) 01250 872082	COMMENDED 👑👑👑	1 Single 1 Twin 1 Double	2 En Suite fac 1 Priv. NOT ensuite 2 Pub Bath/Show	B&B per person £16.00-£18.00 Single £18.00-£20.00 Double	Open Jan-mid Dec Dinner from 1900

Stone-built house of interesting design with large garden, conveniently situated
on the main Perth to Blairgowrie road. Town centre 0.5 miles (1km).

Mrs M A Stewart Broadmyre, Carsie Blairgowrie Perthshire PH10 6QW Tel: (Blairgowrie) 01250 873262	APPROVED Listed	1 Twin 1 Double 3 Family	2 Pub Bath/Show	B&B per person £14.00 Single £14.00 Double Room only per person £12.00	Open Apr-Sep Dinner 1800-2200

Friendly welcome at this motel-style accommodation with compact bedrooms,
conveniently situated 3 miles (5kms) south of Blairgowrie. Ample parking.

PERTHSHIRE, ANGUS & DUNDEE AND THE KINGDOM OF FIFE

Details of Grading and Classification are on page vi.   Key to symbols is on back flap.

by BLAIRGOWRIE **Perthshire** Mrs Shonaidh Beattie Shocarjen, The Green Burrelton, Blairgowrie Perthshire PH13 9NU Tel: (Burrelton) 01828 670223 Fax: 01828 670223	Map 2 B1	**COMMENDED** 👑👑	2 Double 1 Family	3 En Suite fac	B&B per person from £19.00 Single from £16.50 Double Room only per person £13.50–£16.00	Open Jan-Dec	
Renovated traditional house in centre of friendly village. Good touring base for Perthshire and Highlands. Perth (12 miles/19 kms) Dundee (17 miles/27 kms) Pitlochry (25 miles/40 kms) Edinburgh (50 miles/80 kms).							
Mrs M B Crichton Lunanbrae Essendy, by Blairgowrie Perthshire PH10 6RA Tel: (Essendy) 01250 884224		**HIGHLY** **COMMENDED** **Listed**	1 Twin 1 Double	2 Priv. NOT ensuite 1 Pub Bath/Show	B&B per person from £22.00 Single from £19.50 Double	Open Jan-Dec Dinner 1900-2100 B&B + Eve. Meal from £30.00	
Spacious and peacefully located bungalow with spectacular views, and large beautifully maintained garden. Ideal location for golfing, fishing, touring and walking.							
Mrs H Wightman Bankhead, Clunie Blairgowrie Perthshire PH10 6SG Tel: (Essendy) 01250 884281		**COMMENDED** 👑	1 Twin 1 Family	1 Pub Bath/Show	B&B per person from £18.00 Single from £15.00 Double	Open Jan-Dec Dinner 1830-1900 B&B + Eve. Meal £23.00	
Farmhouse on working family farm between Loch Marlee and Clunie. Ideal for touring, local fishing, golfing and skiing. All home cooking.							
BRECHIN **Angus** Mrs M Stewart Doniford, 26 Airlie Street Brechin Angus DD9 6JX Tel: (Brechin) 01356 622361	Map 4 F12	**HIGHLY** **COMMENDED** 👑👑	2 Twin	2 En Suite fac	B&B per person from £20.00 Single from £17.50 Double	Open Jan-Dec	
A traditional Scottish welcome at this villa in quiet residential area. AA QQQQ Selected. Ideal centre for touring. Formerly of Blibberhill Farm B&B. Evening meal by arrangement.							

Wood of Auldbar Farmhouse

Commended LISTED

WOOD OF AULDBAR, ABERLEMNO, BRECHIN DD9 6SZ

Telephone: 01307 830218

Award-winning farmhouse. A warm welcome awaits you at our family farm. Excellent food and accommodation. Tea facilities in all bedrooms. Smoke alarms throughout. Food Hygiene Certificate held. Ideal for touring Glens of Angus, Royal Deeside, Balmoral. Glamis within easy reach. Nature walks, bird-watching, fishing, golf; leisure centres nearby. Aberlemno Standing Stones can be viewed. Aberdeen, Dundee, St Andrews and Edinburgh all within easy reach.

B&B from £14.50. EM from £9. Reduced terms for children.

| Mrs J Stewart
Wood of Auldbar
Brechin
Angus
DD9 6SZ
Tel: (Aberlemno)
01307 830218 | **COMMENDED**
Listed | 1 Single
1 Twin
1 Family | 2 Pub Bath/Show | B&B per person
from £17.00 Single
from £14.50 Double | Open Jan-Dec
Dinner 1800-2000
B&B + Eve. Meal
from £23.50 | |
| Farmhouse with large south-facing garden on working mixed arable and stock farm in pleasant countryside. All home cooking, baking and preserves. | | | | | | |

Scotland for Golf . . .

Find out more about golf in Scotland. There's more to it than just the championship courses so get in touch with us now for information on the hidden gems of Scotland.

Write to: **Information Unit, Scottish Tourist Board, 23 Ravelston Terrace, Edinburgh EH4 3EU**
or call: 0131-332 2433

Blibberhill Farmhouse

by Brechin, Angus DD9 6TH   Telephone: 01307 830323

A warm welcome awaits you from all the family at this large 18th century farmhouse. Situated between the Angus glens and coast. Tastefully decorated and furnished. Aberdeen, Perth and St Andrews only one hour away. Glamis and Edzell Castles nearby. All home cooking and baking. Excellent children's facilities.

Special off-peak packages available.

Mrs W Stewart Blibberhill Farmhouse Brechin Angus DD9 6TH Tel: (Aberlemno) 01307 830323	**COMMENDED** ♛♛	1 Twin 1 Double 1 Family	3 En Suite fac 1 Pub Bath/Show	B&B per person £16.00-£20.00 Single £14.50-£16.50 Double	Open Jan-Dec Dinner from 1800 B&B + Eve. Meal £22.50-£24.50

Stone-built farmhouse in peaceful situation on mixed working farm.
Homemade preserves and home baking and cooking. Children welcome.

FARMHOUSE BED & BREAKFAST

TILLYGLOOM FARM, BRECHIN, ANGUS DD9 7PE
Telephone: 01356 622953

Enjoy the atmosphere of our working farm. Golf courses, country walks, nearby Angus glens and castles. TV lounge, home cooking. Prices from £13 per night B&B per person; DB&B from £19.

Contact Mrs Lorna Watson

Mrs L Watson Tillygloom Farm Brechin Angus DD9 7PE Tel: (Brechin) 01356 622953	**COMMENDED** **Listed**	1 Double 1 Family	1 Pub Bath/Show	B&B per person £14.00-£15.00 Single £13.00-£13.50 Double Room only per person £9.00-£10.00	Open Jan-Dec Dinner 1800-2000 B&B + Eve. Meal £19.00-£20.00

Friendly farmhouse welcome awaits guests at our home near Brechin.
In quiet, pleasant surroundings. Easy access to a host of local activities.

by BRECHIN **Angus** Mrs R Beatty Brathinch Farm by Brechin Angus DD9 7QX Tel: (Edzell) 01356 648292 Fax: 01356 648003	Map 4 F12	**COMMENDED** ♛	1 Twin 2 Double	2 En Suite fac 1 Priv. NOT ensuite 1 Pub Bath/Show	B&B per person £16.00-£20.00 Single £15.00-£16.00 Double Room only per person £13.00-£18.00	Open Jan-Dec

18th century farmhouse on a family run working arable farm, with large garden.
Easy access to Angus Glens.

BRIDGE OF CALLY **Perthshire** Mrs Alison J Constable Tomlea Farm Ballintuim, by Bridge of Cally, Blairgowrie Perthshire PH10 7NL Tel: (Strathardle) 01250 881383 Fax: 01250 886201	Map 2 B1	**COMMENDED** **Listed**	2 Twin	1 En Suite fac 1 Priv. NOT ensuite 2 Pub Bath/Show	B&B per person £14.00-£16.00 Single £14.00-£15.00 Double	Open Jan-Dec Dinner 1830-2000 B&B + Eve. Meal £18.00-£21.00

Working farm set in heart of Scottish glen with superb views.
Private fishing and hillwalking.

PERTHSHIRE, ANGUS & DUNDEE   AND THE KINGDOM OF FIFE

Details of Grading and Classification are on page vi.

Key to symbols is on back flap.

BURNTISLAND – CERES

BURNTISLAND
Fife
Map 2 C4

Jean & Angus Bowman
Gruinard, 148 Kinghorn Road
Burntisland
Fife
KY3 9JU
Tel: (Burntisland)
01592 873877

HIGHLY COMMENDED

1 Twin
1 Double

2 En Suite fac

B&B per person
£16.50-£25.00 Double

Open Jan-Dec
Dinner 1830-2000
B&B + Eve. Meal
from £26.50

Very well appointed traditional stone house, close to town centre.
Garden with views across the Firth of Forth.

CARNOUSTIE
Angus
Map 2 D2

PARK HOUSE
12 Park Avenue, Carnoustie, Angus DD7 7JA
Telephone: 01241 852101
Warm, luxurious bedrooms, stylish ensuite bathrooms, all with TV, radio, welcome tray and sea views. Lovely Victorian residence. Off-street parking. Walled garden, barbecue patio. Quiet seaside town, glorious beaches and world-famous Carnoustie Golf Links. Friendly, relaxed atmosphere, excellent base for golf (St Andrews nearby), coastal walk and hillwalking.

Wendy Ebblewhite
Park House, 12 Park Avenue
Carnoustie
Angus
DD7 7JA
Tel: (Carnoustie)
01241 854206/852101

HIGHLY COMMENDED

1 Single
1 Twin
2 Double

2 En Suite fac
2 Priv. NOT ensuite
1 Pub Bath/Show

B&B per person
£17.50-£30.00 Single
£17.50-£30.00 Double
Room only per person
£15.00-£20.00

Open Jan-Dec
Dinner 1800-2030
B&B + Eve. Meal
£27.00-£40.00

A detached Victorian house in its own walled garden.
Championship golf course, beach nearby. Private parking.

Mr & Mrs S Pape
The Old Manor, Panbride
Carnoustie
Angus
DD7 6JP
Tel: (Carnoustie) 01241 854804

COMMENDED

1 Double
1 Family

2 En Suite fac

B&B per person
£15.00-£20.00 Double

Open Jan-Dec

Spacious ensuite rooms in fully restored country house. Peaceful location
close to Carnoustie. Convenient for golf, beaches and Angus glens.

Mrs S M Penman
Elm Bank, 3 Camus Street
Carnoustie
Angus
DD7 7PL
Tel: (Carnoustie) 01241 852204

COMMENDED Listed

2 Family

1 Pub Bath/Show

B&B per person
from £16.00 Single
from £16.00 Double

Open Jan-Dec

A warm and friendly welcome. Centrally situated for all amenities and
within easy walking distance of golf courses and beach. Private parking.

Mrs E Watson
Balhousie Farm
Carnoustie
Angus
DD7 6LG
Tel: (Carnoustie) 01241 853533
Fax: 01241 853533

COMMENDED Listed

1 Twin
2 Double

2 Pub Bath/Show

B&B per person
from £15.00 Single

Open Jan-Dec

Traditional Victorian family farmhouse on working farm, overlooking large gardens.
Ideal for golfing and touring, close to local amenities.

CERES
Fife
Map 2 C3

Mrs M Chrisp
Scotstarvit Farm
Ceres, by Cupar
Fife
KY15 5PA
Tel: (Cupar) 01334 653591

COMMENDED

1 Twin
1 Double

1 Priv. NOT ensuite

B&B per person
£20.00-£22.00 Single
£16.00-£18.00 Double

Open Mar-Dec

Peaceful location on working farm by 16th century Scotstarvit Tower
and near Hill of Tarvit Mansion House.

	Map 2						

COMRIE
Perthshire — Map 2 A2
Mossgiel Guest House
Burrell Street
Comrie
Perthshire
PH6 2JP
Tel: (Comrie) 01764 670567/
0374 400750 (mobile)

COMMENDED

3 Twin · 4 En Suite fac · 1 Double · B&B per person £17.00-£20.00 Single £17.00-£19.00 Double £27.00-£30.00 Open Jan-Dec Dinner 1830-1930 B&B + Eve. Meal

Traditional stone-built house with modern wing on the main road in the village. Near to all amenities. Choice of home-cooked dishes. Golf packages arranged.

COUPAR ANGUS
Perthshire — Map 2 C1
Mr & Mrs Broadley
St Catherine's Croft,
14 Union Street
Coupar Angus
Perthshire
PH13 9AE
Tel: (Coupar Angus) 01828 627753

COMMENDED

1 Single · 1 Limited ensuite · 1 Twin · 1 Pub Bath/Show · 1 Family · B&B per person £16.00-£19.00 Single £16.00-£19.00 Double · Open Jan-Dec

Semi-detached stone-built property in centre of Coupar Angus. Ideal for fishing, golfing, shooting and all outdoor activities.

CRAIL
Fife — Map 2 D3
Caiplie Guest House
53 High Street
Crail
Fife
KY10 3RA
Tel: (Crail) 01333 450564

COMMENDED

1 Single · 2 Pub Bath/Show · 1 Twin · 4 Double · 1 Family · B&B per person £16.00-£18.00 Single £16.00-£18.00 Double £29.00-£31.00 · Open Mar-Nov Dinner from 1900 B&B + Eve. Meal

Compact, personally run house, former Victorian bakery, in main street of fishing village. Home cooking, fresh local produce. Taste of Scotland.

Hazelton Guest House
29 Marketgate
Crail
Fife
KY10 3TH
Tel: (Crail) 01333 450250

COMMENDED Listed

1 Single · 2 Pub Bath/Show · 2 Twin · 2 Double · 2 Family · B&B per person £16.00-£18.00 Single £16.00-£18.00 Double £31.00-£33.00 · Open Jan-Dec Dinner at 1900 B&B + Eve. Meal

In the heart of small fishing town, a friendly guest house personally run by the owners. Fresh local produce used whenever possible. Taste of Scotland.

Selcraig Guest House
47 Nethergate
Crail
Fife
KY10 3TX
Tel: (Crail) 01333 450697

COMMENDED

2 Twin · 2 Pub Bath/Show · 2 Double · 1 Family · B&B per person £23.00-£25.00 Single £18.00-£26.00 Double £31.00 · Open Jan-Dec Dinner 1800-1900 B&B + Eve. Meal

200-year-old Listed house in quiet street close to seashore. Convenient for touring the East Neuk of Fife. Non-smoking.

CRIEFF
Perthshire — Map 2 A2
The Comely Bank Guest House
32 Burrell Street
Crieff
Perthshire
PH7 4DT
Tel: (Crieff) 01764 653409

COMMENDED

1 Single · 2 En Suite fac · 1 Twin · 1 Priv. NOT ensuite · 2 Double · 2 Pub Bath/Show · 1 Family · B&B per person from £15.00 Single £16.50-£18.00 Double · Open Jan-Dec Dinner 1800-2000

Personal attention and a friendly welcome. Evening meals available and the premises are licensed.

Mrs Hancox
The Sorn, 5 Duchlage Terrace
Crieff
Perthshire
PH7 3AS
Tel: (Crieff) 01764 653516

COMMENDED Listed

1 Single · 1 Limited ensuite · 1 Twin · 1 Pub Bath/Show · 1 Family · B&B per person £12.00-£16.00 Double £19.50-£23.50 · Open Jan-Dec Dinner 1700-2000 B&B + Eve. Meal

In centre of the famous holiday town of Crieff, comfortable accommodation in traditional terraced house.

PERTHSHIRE, ANGUS & DUNDEE AND THE KINGDOM OF FIFE

PERTHSHIRE, ANGUS & DUNDEE AND THE KINGDOM OF FIFE

CRIEFF continued **Perthshire** Largybeg Perth Road Crieff Perthshire PH7 3EQ Tel: (Crieff) 01764 655860	Map 2 A2	COMMENDED ♛	1 Twin 2 Double	1 Pub Bath/Show	B&B per person £15.00 Single £15.00 Double	Open Jan-Dec	
			Modern family house, short walk from town centre and all amenities. Off-street parking. Non-smoking establishment.				
MacKenzie Lodge Broich Terrace Crieff Perthshire PH7 3BD Tel: (Crieff) 01764 653721		COMMENDED ♛♛	2 Twin 2 Double 1 Family	2 En Suite fac 2 Pub Bath/Show	B&B per person £20.00-£25.00 Single £18.00-£24.00 Double Room only per person £16.00-£20.00	Open Jan-Dec	
			Elegant Victorian "A" Listed home retaining many original features. Winner of "Warmest Welcome in Perthshire 1991". Private parking.				
Mrs Scott Concraig Farm, Muthill Road Crieff Perthshire PH7 4HH Tel: (Crieff) 01764 653237		COMMENDED Listed	1 Twin 2 Double	1 Pub Bath/Show	B&B per person £16.00-£17.00 Double	Open Apr-Oct	
			Comfortable farmhouse with spacious rooms. Peacefully situated just outside Crieff. Ideal location for golfing and touring.				
Mrs Katie Sloan Somerton House Turet Bank, Crieff Perthshire PH7 4JN Tel: (Crieff) 01764 653513 Fax: 01764 655028		COMMENDED ♛♛	1 Twin 1 Double 1 Family	3 En Suite fac	B&B per person £18.50-£20.00 Single £16.00-£18.00 Double	Open Jan-Dec	
			Friendly bed and breakfast within 15 minutes' walk of town. Ideal touring base. Home of the Turretbank Cavalier King Charles spaniels.				
Sydney Villa Guest House 57 Burrell Street Crieff Perthshire PH7 4DG Tel: (Crieff) 01764 652757		COMMENDED ♛♛	1 Twin 2 Double 1 Family	1 En Suite fac 1 Limited ensuite 2 Pub Bath/Show	B&B per person £15.00-£17.00 Single £14.00-£17.00 Double	Open Feb-Dec	
			Personally owned and run. Close to town centre and local services. Twenty-three golf courses within an hour's drive. Four-poster bed.				
CUPAR **Fife** Mrs Sonia Marston Lordscairnie Country House Cupar Fife KY15 4NN Tel: (Luthrie) 01337 870252 Fax: 01337 870252	Map 2 C3	HIGHLY COMMENDED ♛♛♛	2 Twin 1 Double	3 En Suite fac	B&B per person £25.00 Double	Open Jan-Dec Dinner 1900-2030 B&B + Eve. Meal £37.00-£40.00	
			Late Georgian house, tastefully renovated in 1995. 20 acres (8ha) of charming gardens and paddocks with thoroughbred horses and miniature cattle.				

WELCOME

Whenever you are in Scotland, you can be sure of a warm welcome at your nearest Tourist Information Centre.

For guide books, maps, souvenirs, our Centres provide a service second to none – many now offer bureau-de-change facilities. And, of course, Tourist Information Centres offer free, expert advice on what to see and do, route-planning and accommodation for everyone – visitors and residents alike!

VAT is shown at 17.5%: changes in this rate may affect prices. Prices shown are for guidance only. Please send SAE with each enquiry.

by CUPAR Fife	Map 2 C3					

TODHALL HOUSE

DAIRSIE, BY CUPAR, FIFE KY15 4RQ
Telephone and Fax: 01334 656344

An attractive listed country house overlooking the rolling farmlands of *North-East Fife,* seven miles from *St Andrews.* Ideally situated for pursuing many varied sporting activities and exploring the historic *Kingdom of Fife.* Enjoy quality accommodation and country comfort at its best. *Please call **Gill Donald** for details.*

| Mrs Gillian Donald Todhall House Dairsie, by Cupar Fife KY15 4RQ Tel: (Cupar) 01334 656344 Fax: 01334 656344 | HIGHLY COMMENDED | 1 Twin 2 Double | 3 En Suite fac | B&B per person £21.00-£27.00 Double | Open mid Mar-Oct Dinner 1830-1930 B&B + Eve. Meal £37.00-£43.00 | |

Traditional Scottish country house peacefully located in lovely scenery. Tastefully appointed bedrooms, one with 4-poster bed.

by DAIRSIE	Map 2 C3					

Easter Craigfoodie

Dairsie, Cupar, Fife KY15 4SW
Telephone: 01334 870286

Comfortable farmhouse with wonderful views over bay only 6 miles from St Andrews. Residents' lounge with TV. Ample parking. Ideal golf or touring base.

| Mrs C Scott Easter Craigfoodie Dairsie, by Cupar Fife KY15 4SW Tel: (Cupar) 01334 870286 | HIGHLY COMMENDED Listed | 1 Twin 1 Double 1 Family | 1 Pub Bath/Show | B&B per person £17.00-£19.00 Single £16.00-£17.50 Double | Open Jan-Dec | |

Traditional, Victorian farmhouse with panoramic views across Fife to Firth of Tay and Angus coast. 7 miles (11kms) from St Andrews. Ideal golf and touring base.

| DUNDEE Angus Ashley House 15 Monifieth Road Broughty Ferry, Dundee Angus DD5 2RN Tel: (Dundee) 01382 776109 | Map 2 C2 APPROVED | 1 Twin 1 Double | 2 En Suite fac | B&B per person £18.00-£20.00 Single £18.00-£20.00 Double Room only per person £13.00-£15.00 | Open Jan-Dec | |

Small family run B&B close to town centre on main bus route, ideal for golf and other amenities. Private parking.

| Errolbank Guest House 9 Dalgleish Road Dundee Angus DD4 7JN Tel: (Dundee) 01382 462118 | COMMENDED | 1 Single 2 Twin 2 Double 1 Family | 5 En Suite fac 1 Pub Bath/Show | B&B per person £16.00-£22.00 Single from £17.50 Double | Open Jan-Dec | |

Victorian villa, quiet residential area, centrally situated for touring, golf and all local amenities.

| Hillside Guest House 43 Constitution Street Dundee Angus DD3 6JH Tel: (Dundee) 01382 223443 | HIGHLY COMMENDED | 2 Single 1 Twin 1 Family | 2 En Suite fac 2 Pub Bath/Show | B&B per person £21.00-£30.00 Single £18.00-£24.00 Double | Open Jan-Dec | |

Victorian family home in quiet residential area close to city centre and all amenities. Off-street parking.

PERTHSHIRE, ANGUS & DUNDEE AND THE KINGDOM OF FIFE

DUNDEE continued **Angus** Homebank 9 Ellieslea Road West Ferry, Dundee Angus DD5 1SH Tel: (Dundee) 01382 477481	Map 2 C2	COMMENDED 👑👑	2 Twin	2 En Suite fac 1 Pub Bath/Show	B&B per person £20.00-£25.00 Single £20.00-£30.00 Double	Open Jan-Dec

Victorian mansion in own walled garden, peaceful location yet only ten minutes' walk from town centre and beaches. Within 15 minutes of Carnoustie and St Andrews golf courses.

Mrs M Laing Auchenean 177 Hamilton Street Broughty Ferry, Dundee Angus DD5 2RE Tel: (Dundee) 01382 774782		HIGHLY COMMENDED Listed	1 Single 1 Twin	1 Pub Bath/Show	B&B per person £14.50-£16.00 Single £14.50-£16.00 Double	Open Mar-Oct Dinner 1800-2000 B&B + Eve. Meal £20.00-£24.50

Detached house in quiet cul-de-sac. Residents' lounge opening on to secluded garden. Morning tea served free of charge. 5 minutes from seafront.

Mr & Mrs Mackintosh Hollies Orchard 12 Castle Roy Road Broughty Ferry Tayside DD5 2LQ Tel: (Broughty Ferry) 01382 732151		HIGHLY COMMENDED 👑	1 Single 1 Double	2 En Suite fac	B&B per person £20.00-£30.00 Single £20.00-£30.00 Double	Open Jan-Dec

Quality modern home with panoramic views over River Tay. Ensuite rooms.

Mrs E Park Dunrigh, 1 Fyne Road Broughty Ferry, Dundee Angus DD5 3JF Tel: (Dundee) 01382 778980		COMMENDED 👑	1 Single 1 Twin	1 Pub Bath/Show	B&B per person £14.00-£16.00 Single £13.00-£15.00 Double	Open Jan-Dec

Modern semi-detached house in quiet residential area.
Easy travelling distance to town centre and Discovery. Close to bus stop.

Ian Reid, The Birks 149 Arbroath Road Dundee Angus DD4 6LP Tel: (Dundee) 01382 453393		COMMENDED Listed	2 Family	2 Pub Bath/Show	B&B per person £16.00-£20.00 Single £15.00-£18.00 Double	Open Jan-Dec

Detached, stone-built house in residential area in east end of city.
Guests' car parking. On main bus route Dundee/Broughty Ferry.

Restalrig Guest House 69 Clepington Road Dundee Angus DD4 7BQ Tel: (Dundee) 01382 455412		COMMENDED 👑👑	1 Single 1 Twin 2 Family	3 En Suite fac 1 Priv. NOT ensuite	B&B per person £21.00-£23.00 Single £16.00-£18.00 Double	Open Jan-Dec

Close to ring road yet within walking distance of Dundee city centre,
this traditional stone guest house is a good base for both business and touring.

Mrs Florence Taylor Ardmoy, 359 Arbroath Road Dundee Angus DD4 7SQ Tel: (Dundee) 01382 453249		COMMENDED Listed	1 Twin 1 Double	2 Limited ensuite 1 Pub Bath/Show	B&B per person £16.00-£21.00 Single £16.00-£18.00 Double	Open Jan-Dec Dinner 1700-1900 B&B + Eve. Meal £22.00-£24.00

Spacious stone-built house in own garden on direct route to centre.
Private parking. Ideal touring base. Close to Discovery and city centre.

DUNFERMLINE **Fife** Clarke Cottage Guest House 139 Halbeath Road Dunfermline Fife KY11 4LA Tel: (Dunfermline) 01383 735935	Map 2 B4	COMMENDED 👑👑 🚶	6 Twin 3 Double	9 En Suite fac	B&B per person £23.00-£26.00 Single £21.00-£24.00 Double	Open Jan-Dec

Ensuite accommodation forming part of original Victorian house near main road and town centre. Private parking. Ideal for visiting Edinburgh and Fife.

Mrs Dunsire The Haven, 82 Pilmuir Street Dunfermline Fife KY12 0LN Tel: (Dunfermline) 01383 729039	COMMENDED Listed	2 Twin 1 Family	2 Pub Bath/Show	B&B per person £17.00-£18.00 Single £15.00 Double Room only per person £14.00	Open Jan-Dec
		Family run Victorian guest house in a central location, with many period features. Warm and friendly welcome.			
Mrs E M Fotheringham Bowleys Farm, Roscobie Dunfermline Fife KY12 0SG Tel: (Dunfermline) 01383 721056	COMMENDED	1 Twin 1 Family	1 Pub Bath/Show	B&B per person £17.00-£18.00 Single £16.00-£17.00 Double	Open Apr-Oct Dinner 1800-1900 B&B + Eve. Meal £23.00-£25.00
		Quiet, peaceful and relaxing 19th century working stock farm. Warm welcome and homebaking. 5 miles (8 kms) north of Dunfermline. Trout fishing available.			
Mrs Hooper Hillview House 9 Aberdour Road Dunfermline Fife KY11 4PB Tel: (Dunfermline) 01383 726278	COMMENDED	1 Twin 2 Double	1 Limited ensuite 2 Pub Bath/Show	B&B per person £17.00-£18.00 Single £16.00-£17.00 Double	Open Jan-Dec
		Friendly family home on the outskirts of the town. Comfortable and well-appointed rooms, some overlooking attractive rear garden.			

PITCAIRN HOUSE

82a Halbeath Road, Dunfermline, Fife KY12 7RS
Telephone: 01383 732901

Pitcairn House is a well-established family run bed and breakfast business, situated within walking distance of the town centre. Facilities include ensuite, tea and coffee, colour TV, telephone, which are provided within a very comfortable surrounding. Car parking available.

Mr H Pitcairn Pitcairn House 82a Halbeath Road Dunfermline Fife KY12 7RS Tel: (Dunfermline) 01383 732901	COMMENDED	2 Twin 1 Double	3 En Suite fac	B&B per person £23.00 Single £20.00 Double	Open Jan-Dec
		Small and friendly. Easy access to M90 and town centre. 12 miles (19 kms) from Edinburgh and good base for touring the Fife coast. All ensuite ground-floor rooms.			
DUNKELD **Perthshire** Mrs Hannah S Crozier Balmore, Perth Road Birnam, by Dunkeld Perthshire PH8 0BH Tel: (Dunkeld) 01350 728885	Map 2 B1 HIGHLY COMMENDED	1 Twin 1 Double	1 En Suite fac 1 Priv. NOT ensuite 1 Pub Bath/Show	B&B per person from £19.00 Double	Open Mar-Sep Dinner 1900-1930 B&B + Eve. Meal from £29.00
		Friendly welcome at family run house, with well-furnished accommodation in small village, just off A9. 12 miles (19kms) from Perth. Parking.			

AND THE KINGDOM OF FIFE

PERTHSHIRE, ANGUS & DUNDEE

DUNKELD continued Perthshire	Map 2 B1		

The Tap Inn
PERTH ROAD, BIRNAM, BY DUNKELD
PERTHSHIRE PH8 0AA
TELEPHONE: 01350 727699
SIX ENSUITE TWIN BEDROOMS FROM £18 PER PERSON. SATELLITE TV, TEA AND COFFEE FACILITIES, CENTRAL HEATING. FOOD AND DRINKS IN VILLAGE PUB AND BEER GARDEN WITH FRIENDLY ATMOSPHERE.

The Tap Inn Perth Road Birnam, by Dunkeld Perthshire PH8 0AA Tel: (Dunkeld) 01350 727699	APPROVED	6 Twin	6 En Suite fac	B&B per person £25.00-£28.00 Single £18.00-£20.00 Double	Open Jan-Dec Dinner 1800-2100

Family run inn situated in the old village of Birnam. Convenient for fishing, golfing and touring. Annexe bedrooms.

by DUNKELD Perthshire	Map 2 B1		

LETTER FARM
Loch of the Lowes, by Dunkeld, Perthshire PH8 0HH
Telephone: 01350 724254
This tastefully renovated farmhouse offers a warm friendly welcome to all. Ensuite facilities, kingsize beds, log fires and good home baking. The farm is central to Perthshire attractions, but exudes peace and tranquillity nestled next to Loch of the Lowes Wildlife Reserve, home of the Osprey.

Mrs Jo Andrew Letter Farm, Loch of the Lowes Dunkeld Perthshire PH8 0HH Tel: (Butterstone) 01350 724254	HIGHLY COMMENDED	1 Twin 1 Double 1 Family	3 En Suite fac	B&B per person £20.00-£25.00 Single from £20.00 Double	Open Jan-Dec

Tastefully renovated farmhouse on working farm 1.5 miles (2.5 kms) from Scottish Wildfowl Trust Reserve. 3 miles (5 kms) from Dunkeld. Peaceful location.

Mrs Jessie Mathieson The Coppers Inchmagrannachan Dunkeld Perthshire PH8 0JS Tel: (Dunkeld) 01350 727372	COMMENDED Listed	1 Twin 1 Double	1 En Suite fac 1 Pub Bath/Show	B&B per person £13.00-£17.00 Double	Open Apr-Oct Dinner from 1830 B&B + Eve. Meal from £25.00

Typical Highland welcome and home cooking in this bungalow with one ensuite bedroom. Access to fishing and golf, superb walks.

Mrs Paterson The Orchard Dalguise, by Dunkeld Perthshire PH8 0JX Tel: (Dunkeld) 01350 727446	COMMENDED	1 Twin 1 Double	2 En Suite fac	B&B per person £18.50-£24.00 Single £17.00-£19.00 Double	Open Jan-Dec Dinner 1800-1930 B&B + Eve. Meal £24.50-£27.00

Set in over two acres (0.8ha), a detached bungalow in the heart of Beatrix Potter country. Scottish produce used wherever possible.

Mrs A W Smith Stralochy Farm Spittalfield, by Murthly Perthshire PH1 4LQ Tel: (Caputh) 01738 710447	COMMENDED Listed	1 Twin 1 Double 1 Family	2 Pub Bath/Show	B&B per person £15.00-£18.00 Single £15.00 Double	Open May-Sep Dinner from 1830 B&B + Eve. Meal £22.00-£24.00

Real farmhouse hospitality on working farm overlooking the Howe of Strathmore, enjoying superb open views. Evening meals on request.

EDZELL **Angus** Mrs J Myles The Gorse, Dunlappie Road Edzell Angus DD9 7UB Tel: (Edzell) 01356 648207 Fax: 01356 648265	**Map 4** F12	COMMENDED ♔	1 Single 2 Twin	2 Pub Bath/Show	B&B per person £14.00-£15.00 Single £14.00-£15.00 Double	Open Jan-Dec	

Quietly situated opposite golf course with open views of hills to rear.
Home baking and a warm welcome. A non-smoking house.

FALKLAND **Fife** Mrs A Heather Ladieburn Cottage, High Street Falkland Fife KY15 7BZ Tel: (Falkland) 01337 857016	**Map 2** C3	COMMENDED ♔ ♔ ♔	1 Twin 1 Family	2 En Suite fac	B&B per person £20.00-£25.00 Single £18.00-£20.00 Double	Open Jan-Dec Dinner 1800-2000 B&B + Eve. Meal £25.00-£30.00	

19th century house in centre of village opposite the historic Falkland Palace.
Both bedrooms overlook the palace and have ensuite facilities. Dinner available.

Mrs Sarah G McGregor Templelands Farm Falkland Fife KY15 7DE Tel: (Falkland) 01337 857383		COMMENDED ♔	1 Double 1 Family	2 Pub Bath/Show	B&B per person from £18.00 Single from £15.00 Double	Open Apr-Oct Dinner from 1900 B&B + Eve. Meal £22.00-£23.00	

Farmhouse on side of Lomond Hills with superb views over Howe of Fife.
Home cooking using fresh local produce. 20 miles (32 kms) from St Andrews.
Convenient for touring.

FEARNAN, by Kenmore **Perthshire** Mrs E Clapham Easter Auchtar by Aberfeldy Perthshire PH15 2PG Tel: (Kenmore) 01887 830316 Fax: 01887 830380	**Map 2** A1	COMMENDED ♔ ♔ ♔	1 Twin 1 Double 1 Family	3 En Suite fac	B&B per person from £21.00 Double	Open Mar-Dec	

Converted 19th century farm buildings in two acres (0.8ha) of garden. Close to
Loch Tay. Ideal location for riding, golf, boating, fishing, water sports and skiing.

FORFAR **Angus**	**Map 2** D1	

Farmhouse Bed & Breakfast
WEST MAINS OF TURIN, FORFAR DD8 2TE
Telephone: 01307 830229 Fax: 01307 830229

Family run stock farm has a panoramic view over Rescobie Loch. Warm
welcome awaits you. Good home cooking and baking ensures guests have
an enjoyable stay. Ideal area for golfing (20 mins from Carnoustie),
hillwalking, horse-riding, visiting Castles, National Trust properties and
gardens. Snooker for evening entertainment.

Mrs C Jolly West Mains of Turin Rescobie, Forfar Angus DD8 2TE Tel: (Aberlemno) 01307 830229	COMMENDED ♔ ♔	1 Single 1 Double 1 Family	1 En Suite fac 1 Priv. NOT ensuite 1 Pub Bath/Show	B&B per person £15.00-£18.00 Single £15.00-£18.00 Double	Open Mar-Oct Dinner 1800-1830 B&B + Eve. Meal £24.00-£28.00	

Farmhouse on working stock farm, 4 miles (6 kms) east of Forfar.
In elevated position with panoramic views southwards over Rescobie Loch.

PERTHSHIRE, ANGUS & DUNDEE　　AND THE KINGDOM OF FIFE

FORFAR continued Angus	Map 2 D1				

WEMYSS FARM

Montrose Road, Forfar DD8 2TB   Tel/Fax: Forfar 01307 462887

Situated 2½ miles along the B9113, our 190-acre farm has a wide variety of animals. Glamis Castle nearby. Many other castles etc. within easy reach. Ideal touring base for Glens, Dundee (12 miles), Perth, St Andrews, Aberdeen, Edinburgh, Balmoral, Deeside and East Coast resorts. Hillwalking, shooting, golf and fishing nearby. Children welcome.

A warm welcome awaits!

Mrs D Lindsay Wemyss Farm, Montrose Road Forfar Angus DD8 2TB Tel: (Forfar) 01307 462887 Fax: 01307 462887	COMMENDED Listed	1 Double 1 Family	2 Pub Bath/Show	B&B per person from £18.00 Single from £15.00 Double Room only per person from £12.00	Open Jan-Dec Dinner 1800-1930 B&B + Eve. Meal from £24.00

Family farmhouse on working farm. Centrally situated for touring Angus and east coast. Home cooking and baking. Children welcome.

by FORFAR Angus	Map 2 D1				
Mrs Kirby Glencoul House Justinhaugh, by Forfar Angus DD8 3SF Tel: (Foreside) 01307 860248	COMMENDED Listed	1 Twin 1 Family	2 Pub Bath/Show	B&B per person £14.00-£16.00 Single £14.00-£16.00 Double Room only per person £12.00-£14.00	Open Jan-Nov Dinner 1800-2000 B&B + Eve. Meal £21.50-£23.50

Former Customs House on South Esk. Fishing available. Quiet and peaceful. Close to glens of Clova and Isla. Close to Forfar, Kirriemuir and Brechin.

Mrs J McKenzie Quarrybank Cottage Balgavies, by Forfar Angus DD8 2TF Tel: (Aberlemno) 01307 830303 Fax: 01307 830414	HIGHLY COMMENDED	1 Single 2 Double	1 En Suite fac 1 Limited ensuite 1 Priv. NOT ensuite 1 Pub Bath/Show	B&B per person £22.50-£25.00 Single £20.00-£22.00 Double	Open Mar-Oct Dinner 1900-2100 B&B + Eve. Meal £30.00-£32.00

Family home in peaceful rural location, 4.5 miles (7km) east of Forfar. Woodland garden. Private parking. Imaginative home cooking using local produce.

Mr & Mrs R Milne Redroofs Balgavies, by Forfar Angus DD8 2TN Tel: (Aberlemno) 01307 830268 Fax: 01307 830268	COMMENDED	2 Double 1 Family	1 En Suite fac 2 Pub Bath/Show	B&B per person £15.00-£17.50 Single £15.00 Double	Open Jan-Dec

Large bungalow in woodland area. Ideal central base for outdoor activities. Children and pets welcome. Private parking.

FINAVON FARMHOUSE

Finavon, by Forfar, Angus DD8 3PX
Telephone: 01307 850269

A warm welcome awaits friends both old and new, in comfort and ease let the Romes cosset you, with good food to tempt taste buds and a large garden to view.
Let our Finavon Farmhouse be your next holiday venue.

Mrs L Rome Finavon Farmhouse Finavon, by Forfar Angus DD8 3PX Tel: (Finavon) 01307 850269	HIGHLY COMMENDED	2 Twin 1 Double	3 En Suite fac	B&B per person £17.50-£23.50 Single £17.50-£18.50 Double Room only per person £14.00-£20.00	Open Feb-Nov Dinner 1830-2000 B&B + Eve. Meal £26.00-£32.00

Warm welcome assured in this modern house in extensive secluded grounds at foot of Finavon Hill. Offers excellent facilities. Good base for touring.

VAT is shown at 17.5%: changes in this rate may affect prices. Prices shown are for guidance only. Please send SAE with each enquiry.

FORTINGALL **Perthshire** Mrs Tulloch Fendoch Fortingall Perthshire PH15 2LL Tel: (Kenmore) 01887 830322	Map 2 A1	COMMENDED ♛♛	1 Twin 1 Double 1 Family	2 En Suite fac 1 Priv. NOT ensuite 1 Pub Bath/Show	B&B per person £15.00-£17.00 Double	Open Jan-Dec Dinner 1800-2200 B&B + Eve. Meal £25.00-£27.00

A warm welcome and home cooking at this house, in quiet attractive village at foot of Glen Lyon. An ideal base for touring and outdoor activities.

FREUCHIE **Fife** Mrs J Duncan Little Freuchie Farm Freuchie, by Falkland Fife KY15 7HU Tel: (Falkland) 01337 857372	Map 2 C3	COMMENDED ♛	1 Twin 1 Family	2 Pub Bath/Show	B&B per person £16.00-£18.00 Double	Open Mar-Nov

Spacious, 19th century farmhouse in own gardens. Panoramic views. Centrally situated for walking, golf and historic Falkland. St. Andrews 18 miles. Home baking.

GLAMIS **Angus** Mrs G Jarron Hatton of Ogilvy Glamis, Forfar Angus DD8 1UH Tel: (Glamis) 01307 840229 Fax: 01307 840229	Map 2 C1	HIGHLY COMMENDED ♛♛	1 Twin	1 En Suite fac	B&B per person from £17.00 Double	Open Apr-Oct

Ideal base for touring Angus and Glamis Castle. A warm welcome awaits at this traditional farmhouse on mixed farm. Ideal base for the Angus glens, folk museum and many castles.

GLENISLA **Perthshire** Mrs M Clark Purgavie Farm Glenisla, by Kirriemuir Angus DD8 5HZ Tel: (Lintrathen) 01575 560213/ 0860 392794 (mobile) Fax: 01575 560213	Map 4 D12	HIGHLY COMMENDED ♛♛♛	1 Twin 2 Family	2 En Suite fac 1 Priv. NOT ensuite	B&B per person £20.00-£22.00 Single £16.00-£18.00 Double Room only per person £11.00-£13.00	Open Jan-Dec Dinner from 1800

19th century house on working farm, with views over Strathmore Valley. Glamis Castle, 7 miles (13 kms), Kirriemuir 6 miles (11 kms). Scottish cooking.

S J Evans Glenmarkie Farmhouse Glenisla Perthshire PH11 8QB Tel: (Glenisla) 01575 582341 Fax: 01575 582341		COMMENDED ♛♛	1 Twin 2 Double	1 En Suite fac 1 Pub Bath/Show	B&B per person to £18.00 Single to £18.00 Double	Open Jan-Dec Dinner 1800-2200 B&B + Eve. Meal £30.00-£31.00

Family run farmhouse deep in picturesque Glenisla. Home cooking. Ideal for all outdoor pursuits. Own stables. Hacking/trekking in small groups.

WELCOME

Whenever you are in Scotland, you can be sure of a warm welcome at your nearest Tourist Information Centre.

For guide books, maps, souvenirs, our Centres provide a service second to none – many now offer bureau-de-change facilities. And, of course, Tourist Information Centres offer free, expert advice on what to see and do, route-planning and accommodation for everyone – visitors and residents alike!

PERTHSHIRE, ANGUS & DUNDEE   AND THE KINGDOM OF FIFE

GUARDBRIDGE, by St Andrews Fife	Map 2 D2	

"The Larches"

7 River Terrace, Guardbridge, by St Andrews KY16 0XA
Telephone: 01334 838008   Fax: 01334 838008

Guardbridge is situated on the A919 between St Andrews (3 miles) and Dundee (6 miles). Convenient for golf, riding, beautiful countryside and beaches. Rooms ensuite or private bathroom, colour TV, tea/coffee facilities. Centrally heated throughout. Residents' lounge always available. VCR with large selection of films plus satellite TV. Early breakfast on request with comprehensive menu. *Every home comfort*

The Larches
7 River Terrace
Guardbridge, by St Andrews
Fife
KY16 0XA
Tel: (Guardbridge)
01334 838008
Fax: 01334 838008

COMMENDED

1 Twin   2 Pub Bath/Show
1 Double
1 Family

B&B per person
£18.00-£22.00 Single
£16.00-£18.00 Double

Open Jan-Dec

A former memorial hall, now converted into a family home, near centre of Guardbridge and R.A.F. Leuchars. 4 miles (6 kms) from St. Andrews.

INVERKEITHING
Fife
The Roods, Mrs Marley
16 Bannerman Avenue
Inverkeithing
Fife
KY11 1NG
Tel: (Inverkeithing)
01383 415049
Fax: 01383 415049

Map 2
B4

HIGHLY COMMENDED

1 Twin   2 En Suite fac
1 Double

B&B per person
£18.00-£25.00 Single
£18.00-£25.00 Double

Open Jan-Dec
Dinner 1900-2000
B&B + Eve. Meal
£30.00-£37.00

**Quietly secluded family home. Close to rail station and M90.
Well-appointed bedrooms offering mini office and fax facilities.**

KILLIECRANKIE
Perthshire
Mrs E Goodfellow
Tighdornie, Aldclune
Killiecrankie
Perthshire
PH16 5LR
Tel: (Pitlochry) 01796 473276

Map 4
C12

COMMENDED

1 Twin   3 En Suite fac
1 Double
1 Family

B&B per person
£20.00-£22.00 Double

Open Jan-Dec

**Modern house on outskirts of Killiecrankie, ideal location for outdoor pursuits.
Ample parking. Lovely scenery.**

KINGSBARNS
Fife
Mr Peter Erskine
Cambo House
Kingsbarns, by St Andrews
Fife
KY16 8QD
Tel: (Crail) 01333 450313
Fax: 01333 450987

Map 2
D3

HIGHLY COMMENDED

1 Twin   1 En Suite fac
2 Double   2 Priv. NOT ensuite

B&B per person
£35.00-£55.00 Single
£35.00-£45.00 Double

Open Jan-Dec
Dinner 1800-2000

**Elegant Victorian mansion on wooded coastal estate, close to St Andrews
with handsome four poster bed in principal guest bedroom.**

Mrs Farida Hay
Kingsbarns Bed & Breakfast
3 Main Street
Kingsbarns
Fife
KY16 8SL
Tel: (Boarhills) 01334 880234

COMMENDED

1 Twin   3 En Suite fac
2 Double

B&B per person
£25.00-£28.00 Single
£18.50-£19.00 Double

Open Mar-Oct

**Family run, 6 miles (10 kms) from St Andrews. Off-street parking and
only 0.5 mile (1 km) from the beach. Wide choice of golf courses.**

| KINLOCH RANNOCH | Map 1 |
| Perthshire | H1 |

BUNRANNOCH HOUSE

Kinloch Rannoch, Perthshire PH16 5QB
Tel: 01882 632407

Lovely Victorian house set in 2 acres of grounds on the outskirts of Kinloch Rannoch. A warm welcome awaits you, together with a complimentary tea tray of home cooking on arrival. Comfortable accommodation includes 3 double, 2 twin and 2 family rooms, most en-suite. All rooms have uninterrupted Highland views and tea/coffee-making facilities. Fire Certificate.

Fishing, walking, cycling, birdwatching, boating and horse-riding provide ample choice. Log fires and good cooking. B&B FROM £16.00.

Bunrannoch House Kinloch Rannoch Pitlochry Perthshire PH16 5QB Tel: (Kinloch Rannoch) 01882 632407	COMMENDED	1 Single 1 Twin 3 Double 2 Family	5 En Suite fac 2 Pub Bath/Show	B&B per person £16.00-£18.00 Single £16.00-£18.00 Double	Open Jan-Dec, excl Xmas/New Year Dinner 1900-2130 B&B + Eve. Meal £30.00-£32.00	

With supreme hospitality Jenny welcomes you into her warm, friendly home, a former shooting lodge. Taste of Scotland home cooking with local produce.

Mrs Steffen Cuilmore Cottage Kinloch Rannoch Perthshire PH16 5QB Tel: (Kinloch Rannoch) 01882 632218 Fax: 01882 632218	DELUXE	1 Twin 1 Double	2 Priv. NOT ensuite	B&B per person £25.00-£26.00 Double	Open Feb-Oct Dinner 1900-2100 B&B + Eve. Meal £50.00-£55.00	

Traditional, cosy 18th century croft. Best of local produce, own fruit and vegetables, home baking. Taste of Scotland special award winner.

| KINROSS | Map 2 |
| Perthshire | B3 |

Mrs A Bell Hillview House, Gairneybank Kinross Tel: (Kinross) 01577 863802	COMMENDED Listed	1 Twin 2 Double	1 En Suite fac 2 Pub Bath/Show	B&B per person £16.00-£17.00 Single £15.00-£17.00 Double	Open Mar-Nov	

Modern detached house, with large garden overlooking open countryside, yet close to the motorway and only 2 miles (3 kms) from Kinross. Homemade bread and jams.

The Innkeeper's Cottage

32 MUIRS, KINROSS KY13 7AS
Telephone and Fax: 01577 862270

Commended
Listed

This cottage dates back to the *Battle of Waterloo* and is the home of the *Keeper of the Inn*. It has been welcoming guests for many years by offering good, clean, comfortable accommodation in small but cosy country-style rooms. This is complemented by fresh homecooked country fayre provided at the Inn opposite.

The Innkeeper Innkeeper's Cottage 32 Muirs, Kinross Kinross-shire KY13 7AS Tel: (Kinross) 01577 862270 Fax: 01577 862270	COMMENDED Listed	1 Twin 2 Double	1 Pub Bath/Show	B&B per person £25.00-£30.00 Single £12.00-£17.50 Double	Open Jan-Dec Dinner 1700-2100	

This idyllic cottage is the home of the keeper of the Inn opposite and has been welcoming guests for years.

Details of Grading and Classification are on page vi.

Key to symbols is on back flap.

PERTHSHIRE, ANGUS & DUNDEE AND THE KINGDOM OF FIFE

PERTHSHIRE, ANGUS & DUNDEE AND THE KINGDOM OF FIFE

KINROSS continued **Perthshire** Mrs Lawrie 68 Muirs Kinross KY13 7AU Tel: (Kinross) 01577 864799	Map 2 B3	COMMENDED	1 Twin 2 Double	2 En Suite fac 1 Pub Bath/Show	B&B per person £17.00-£25.00 Double	Open Jan-Dec	

Large, modern family house in quiet close with off-street parking. Town centre and all facilities within easy walking distance.

THE MUIRS INN

49 MUIRS, KINROSS KY13 7AU
Telephone: 01577 862270
Commended

A quaint Scottish Country Inn – at its best. Offering traditional en-suite bedroom comfort and value for money with award nominated home-cooked country cuisine served at sensible prices in its popular "Maltings" restaurant plus a connoisseur's choice of Scottish Wines, Real Ales and Malt Whiskies in addition to the Inn's own branded beers and ciders.

Situated in the Historical Town of Kinross, this well-appointed Inn is great for sporting and touring holidays with all Scotland's cities and 120 golf courses within driving distance plus local trout fishing on Loch Leven or walking and pony trekking in the surrounding hills. It's ideal for leisure or pleasure and The Inn is *Really* – Simply Something Special.

The Muirs Inn Kinross 49 Muirs Kinross KY13 7AU Tel: (Kinross) 01577 862270 Fax: 01577 862270		COMMENDED	2 Twin 3 Double	5 En Suite fac	B&B per person £35.00-£40.00 Single £25.00-£30.00 Double	Open Jan-Dec Dinner 1700-2100 B&B + Eve. Meal £45.00-£50.00	

Scottish country inn. Award nominated restaurant. Simply something special.

by KINROSS **Perthshire** Agnes Shand Schiehallion Crook of Devon, by Kinross Kinross-shire KY13 7UL Tel: (Fossoway) 01577 840356	Map 2 B3	COMMENDED	1 Twin 1 Double 1 Family	1 Priv. NOT ensuite 2 Pub Bath/Show	B&B per person £15.00-£17.00 Single £15.00-£17.00 Double Room only per person £11.00	Open Jan-Dec	

On the outskirts of the village, a peaceful situation, family home with comfortable rooms. Non-smokers preferred.

KIRKCALDY **Fife** Mrs B Linton Norview, 59 Normand Road Dysart, Kirkcaldy Fife KY1 2XP Tel: (Kirkcaldy) 01592 652804	Map 2 C4	APPROVED Listed	1 Single 1 Twin 1 Family	2 Pub Bath/Show	B&B per person £12.00-£15.00 Single £12.00-£15.00 Double Room only per person £10.00-£13.00	Open Jan-Dec	

Personally run bed and breakfast on main tourist route. Ideal for touring Fife. Golf courses and other amenities close by.

Sam & Lesley Millar Gamekeeper's Cottage Balbirnie Park Markinch Fife KY7 6JU Tel: (Kirkcaldy) 01592 612742		COMMENDED	1 Double 1 Family	1 En Suite fac 1 Priv. NOT ensuite	B&B per person £16.50-£18.50 Single £16.50-£18.50 Double	Open Jan-Dec Dinner 1700-2100 B&B + Eve. Meal £24.50-£26.50	

A warm welcome awaits at our little slice of heaven. Set in peaceful woodland, Gamekeeper's is truly an enchanted cottage. Great home cooking and hospitality.

KIRKMICHAEL Perthshire Mr & Mrs Mills Ardlebrig Kirkmichael Perthshire PH10 7NY Tel: (Strathardle) 01250 881350	Map 4 D12	**COMMENDED** 👑	1 Single 1 Twin 1 Family	1 Pub Bath/Show	B&B per person £14.00 Single £14.00 Double	Open Jan-Dec Dinner 1800-2100 B&B + Eve. Meal £20.00	
			Family run B&B, set amid the scenic splendour of Perthshire, offering quality home cooking.				

KIRRIEMUIR Angus Mrs J Lindsay Crepto, Kinnordy Place Kirriemuir Angus DD8 4JW Tel: (Kirriemuir) 01575 572746	Map 2 C1	**COMMENDED** Listed	1 Single 1 Twin 1 Double	2 Pub Bath/Show	B&B per person £14.50-£15.50 Single £14.50-£15.50 Double	Open Jan-Dec	
			Modern house in quiet cul-de-sac. 10 minutes' walk from centre of town. Gateway to Angus glens.				

Mrs M Marchant The Welton of Kingoldrum Kirriemuir Angus DD8 5HY Tel: (Kirriemuir) 01575 574743 Fax: 01575 574743		**COMMENDED** 👑👑👑	1 Twin 2 Double	3 En Suite fac	B&B per person £20.00-£22.00 Single £16.00-£19.00 Double Room only per person £10.00-£12.00	Open Jan-Dec Dinner 1830-2130 B&B + Eve. Meal £26.00-£28.50	
			Self-contained flat on working hill farm. Situated in an Angus glen with panoramic views. Access to local hills.				

LASSODIE, by Dunfermline Fife Mr N. Woolley Loch Fitty Cottage Lassodie, by Dunfermline Fife KY12 0SP Tel: (Kelty) 01383 831081	Map 2 B4	**COMMENDED** Listed	1 Double 1 Family	1 En Suite fac 1 Priv. NOT ensuite	B&B per person £18.00-£20.00 Single £16.00-£17.00 Double	Open Jan-Dec	
			Rural roadside location, with large natural garden, yet close to all local amenities and major attractions. Children welcome.				

LAWERS Perthshire Mr & Mrs Jolly Lower Duallin Croft Lawers, Loch Tayside Perthshire PH15 2NZ Tel: (Killin) 01567 820353	Map 1 H1	**COMMENDED** 👑👑👑	1 Single 1 Twin 1 Double	3 En Suite fac 1 Pub Bath/Show	B&B per person from £14.00 Single from £14.00 Double	Open Jan-Dec Dinner 1700-2000	
			Custom-built whitewashed croft. Fantastic views over Loch Tay and Ben Lawers. Ideal for fishing, hillwalking, wild flowers and birdwatching.				

LEUCHARS, by St Andrews Fife Mrs Stilwell Hillpark House, 96 Main Street Leuchars Fife KY16 0HF Tel: (St Andrews) 01334 839280 Fax: 01334 839280	Map 2 D2	**HIGHLY COMMENDED** 👑👑👑	1 Double 1 Family	2 En Suite fac 1 Pub Bath/Show	B&B per person £22.00-£25.00 Single £19.50-£21.50 Double	Open Jan-Dec Dinner 1900-2100 B&B + Eve. Meal £28.50-£34.00	
			Elegant Victorian sandstone property, situated halfway between St Andrews and Dundee. Recent refurbishment offers modern comfort, retaining original features.				

LEVEN Fife Mrs Pamela MacDonald Dunclutha, 16 Victoria Road Leven, Fife KY8 4EX Tel: (Leven) 01333 425515 Fax: 01333 422311	Map 2 C3	**COMMENDED** 👑👑	1 Twin 1 Double 2 Family	3 En Suite fac 1 Priv. NOT ensuite	B&B per person £18.00-£24.00 Double	Open Jan-Dec	
			Victorian former manse. 2 mins level walk from centre of Leven. Good base for golfing enthusiasts.				

PERTHSHIRE, ANGUS & DUNDEE AND THE KINGDOM OF FIFE

PERTHSHIRE, ANGUS & DUNDEE AND THE KINGDOM OF FIFE

LUNAN, by Montrose **Angus** Mrs A MacKintosh Lunan Lodge Lunan, by Montrose Angus DD10 9TG Tel: (Inverkeilor) 01241 830267 Fax: 01241 830435	Map 2 E1	COMMENDED	2 Twin 1 Family	2 Pub Bath/Show	B&B per person to £20.00 Single from £16.00 Double	Open Apr-Oct	
			Warm welcome at modernised 18th century manse, in quiet countryside overlooking Lunan Bay. 15 mins walk from sea. 4 miles (5 kms) Montrose and Bird Sanctuary.				
LUNCARTY, by Perth **Perthshire** Mrs Haddow Ordie House Luncarty, Perth Perthshire PH1 4PR Tel: (Stanley) 01738 828471	Map 2 B2	COMMENDED	1 Twin 2 Double	2 En Suite fac 1 Limited ensuite 1 Pub Bath/Show	B&B per person £17.00-£18.00 Single £15.00-£16.00 Double	Open Jan-Dec Dinner 1700-1830	
			Traditional Scottish hospitality in friendly, family home. Ideal touring base.				
MARKINCH **Fife** Mrs C Craig Shythrum Farm Markinch, by Glenrothes Fife KY7 6HB Tel: (Glenrothes) 01592 758372	Map 2 C3	COMMENDED	1 Twin 1 Family	1 En Suite fac 1 Pub Bath/Show	B&B per person £16.00-£18.00 Single £16.00-£18.00 Double	Open mid Jan- mid Dec Dinner from 1800 B&B + Eve. Meal from £23.00	
			Working farm adjacent to coaching route used by Mary Queen of Scots. Balgonie Castle 0.5 miles (1km), Falkland Palace 5 miles (8kms), Glenrothes 2 miles (3kms).				
MEIGLE **Perthshire** Ray & May Eskdale Stripside, Longleys Meigle Perthshire PH12 8QX Tel: (Meigle) 01828 640388	Map 2 C1	HIGHLY COMMENDED	1 Twin 2 Double	3 En Suite fac	B&B per person £22.50 Single £17.50 Double	Open Jan-Dec Dinner at 1900 B&B + Eve. Meal £26.50	
			Renovated farmhouse with a ground-floor bedroom, set back from the A94. Open rural views. Registered cattery.				
MILNATHORT, by Kinross **Kinross-shire** Mr & Mrs Cameron Warroch Lodge Milnathort Kinross-shire KY13 7RS Tel: (Kinross) 01577 863779	Map 2 B3	COMMENDED	2 Twin	1 En Suite fac 1 Priv. NOT ensuite 1 Pub Bath/Show	B&B per person £17.00 Single £17.00 Double	Open Jan-Dec	
			Period lodge house set in attractive countryside. Located 4 miles (6 kms) from Junction 6 of M90, with easy access to major towns.				
MONTROSE **Angus** The Limes Guest House 15 King Street Montrose Angus DD10 8NL Tel: (Montrose) 01674 677236 Fax: 01674 677236	Map 4 F12	COMMENDED	2 Single 4 Twin 4 Double 2 Family	4 En Suite fac 4 Limited ensuite 2 Priv. NOT ensuite 3 Pub Bath/Show	B&B per person from £18.00 Single from £16.50 Double Room only per person from £15.00	Open Jan-Dec Dinner from 1800	
			Family run, centrally situated in quiet, residential part of town. A few minutes' walk from the centre, railway station and beach. Private parking.				
Mrs P H Massuch The Station House Farnell, by Brechin Angus DD9 6UH Tel: (Farnell) 01674 820208		COMMENDED	3 Twin	1 En Suite fac 2 Pub Bath/Show	B&B per person to £17.50 Single to £27.50 Double	Open Jan-Dec Dinner 1700-2000	
			Pleasant rural setting in large grounds. Minutes from numerous activities. Spacious accommodation. Large car park. Dog kennels. Shooting and fishing can be arranged.				

Oaklands Guest House 10 Rossie Island Road Montrose Angus DD10 9NN Tel: (Montrose) 01674 672018 Fax: 01674 672018		COMMENDED 👑👑	1 Single 3 Twin 2 Double 1 Family	7 En Suite fac	B&B per person from £20.00 Single from £16.50 Double	Open Jan-Dec

Ensuite facilities available at this comfortable family house, within walking distance of Montrose town centre. Parking. Boat fishing available.

Mrs A Ruxton Muirshade of Gallery Farm Montrose Angus DD10 9JU Tel: (Northwaterbridge) 01674 840209		COMMENDED 👑👑	1 Twin 2 Double	2 En Suite fac 1 Priv. NOT ensuite 1 Pub Bath/Show	B&B per person from £16.00 Double	Open Apr-Oct Dinner 1800-1930 B&B + Eve. Meal from £25.00

Farmhouse on working stock and cereal farm, 5 miles (8 kms) from Montrose and sandy beaches. Ideal for touring coast and Angus glens. Home baking.

Mrs M Scott Fairfield, 24 The Mall Montrose Angus DD10 8NW Tel: (Montrose) 01674 676386		COMMENDED Listed	2 Twin 1 Double	1 Pub Bath/Show	B&B per person from £16.00 Single from £15.00 Double	Open Jan-Dec

Detached Georgian house, centrally situated in residential area, with ample street parking. Secure cycle parking. All rooms with washbasin, TV and tea-making facilities.

NEWBURGH **Fife** Mrs Barbara Baird Ninewells Farm Woodriffe Road Newburgh Fife KY14 6EY Tel: (Newburgh) 01337 840307 Fax: 01337 840307	Map 2 C2	HIGHLY COMMENDED Listed	1 Twin 1 Double 1 Family	1 Priv. NOT ensuite 2 Pub Bath/Show	B&B per person £20.00-£25.00 Single £16.00-£22.00 Double	Open Apr-Oct

Traditional farmhouse on operational arable/stock farm. Elevated position with panoramic views of Tay Valley. Convenient for Edinburgh, Perth and many golf courses.

Mrs A Duff Hillview, 46 Scotland Terrace Newburgh Fife KY14 6AR Tel: (Newburgh) 01337 840570		COMMENDED Listed	1 Twin 1 Double	1 Pub Bath/Show	B&B per person £13.00-£15.00 Double	Open Apr-Sep

Family home in quiet residential area of Fife village. Ideal centre for touring. In the Tay Valley between Perth and St Andrews.

NEWMILLS **Fife** Mrs P McFarlane Langlees Farm Newmills, by Culross Fife KY12 8HA Tel: (Newmills) 01383 881152	Map 2 B4	COMMENDED Listed	1 Single 1 Twin	1 Pub Bath/Show	B&B per person to £15.00 Single to £15.00 Double	Open Jan-Dec Dinner 1700-2000 B&B + Eve. Meal to £22.00

Family B&B on working farm. Large garden. Lovely local walks. Children welcome. Ideal touring base for central Scotland.

by NEWPORT-ON-TAY **Fife** Forgan House Forgan Newport-on-Tay Fife DD6 8RB Tel: (Newport-on-Tay) 01382 542760 Fax: 01382 542760	Map 2 D2	HIGHLY COMMENDED 👑👑👑	2 Twin 2 Double	3 En Suite fac 1 Priv. NOT ensuite	B&B per person from £30.00 Single from £25.00 Double	Open Jan-Dec Dinner 1900-2000 B&B + Eve. Meal from £42.50

Georgian country house set in 5 acres (2ha) of grounds and gardens located between Dundee and St Andrews.

AND THE KINGDOM OF FIFE

PERTHSHIRE, ANGUS & DUNDEE

PERTHSHIRE, ANGUS & DUNDEE AND THE KINGDOM OF FIFE

PEAT INN Fife Mrs I Grant West Mains Farm Peat Inn Fife KY15 5LF Tel: (Peat Inn) 01334 840313	Map 2 D3	COMMENDED Listed	1 Twin 1 Double	1 Pub Bath/Show	B&B per person £14.00-£15.00 Double	Open Apr-Oct	

Home baking on mixed farm with open views of countryside. Good base for touring Fife fishing villages. 7 miles (11kms) from St Andrews.

PERTH	Map 2 B2

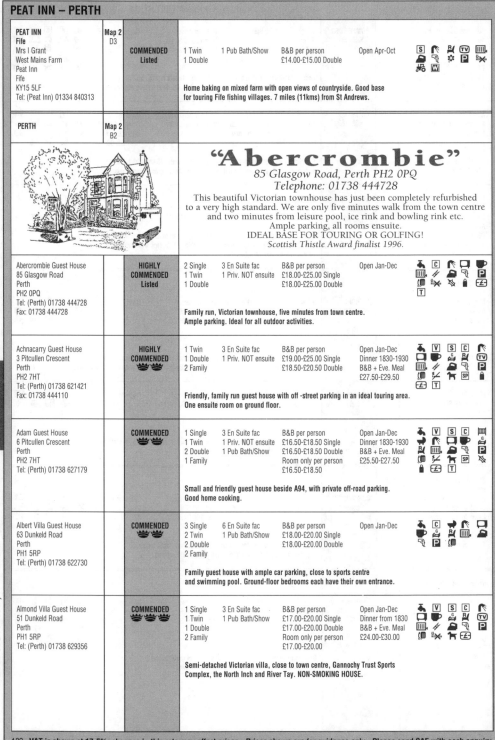

"Abercrombie"

85 Glasgow Road, Perth PH2 0PQ
Telephone: 01738 444728

This beautiful Victorian townhouse has just been completely refurbished to a very high standard. We are only five minutes walk from the town centre and two minutes from leisure pool, ice rink and bowling rink etc.
Ample parking, all rooms ensuite.
IDEAL BASE FOR TOURING OR GOLFING!
Scottish Thistle Award finalist 1996.

Abercrombie Guest House 85 Glasgow Road Perth PH2 0PQ Tel: (Perth) 01738 444728 Fax: 01738 444728	HIGHLY COMMENDED Listed	2 Single 1 Twin 1 Double	3 En Suite fac 1 Priv. NOT ensuite	B&B per person £18.00-£25.00 Single £18.00-£25.00 Double	Open Jan-Dec	

Family run, Victorian townhouse, five minutes from town centre. Ample parking. Ideal for all outdoor activities.

Achnacarry Guest House 3 Pitcullen Crescent Perth PH2 7HT Tel: (Perth) 01738 621421 Fax: 01738 444110	HIGHLY COMMENDED	1 Twin 1 Double 2 Family	3 En Suite fac 1 Priv. NOT ensuite	B&B per person £19.00-£25.00 Single £18.50-£20.50 Double	Open Jan-Dec Dinner 1830-1930 B&B + Eve. Meal £27.50-£29.50	

Friendly, family run guest house with off-street parking in an ideal touring area. One ensuite room on ground floor.

Adam Guest House 6 Pitcullen Crescent Perth PH2 7HT Tel: (Perth) 01738 627179	COMMENDED	1 Single 1 Twin 2 Double 1 Family	3 En Suite fac 1 Priv. NOT ensuite 1 Pub Bath/Show	B&B per person £16.50-£18.50 Single £16.50-£18.50 Double Room only per person £16.50-£18.50	Open Jan-Dec Dinner 1830-1930 B&B + Eve. Meal £25.50-£27.50	

Small and friendly guest house beside A94, with private off-road parking. Good home cooking.

Albert Villa Guest House 63 Dunkeld Road Perth PH1 5RP Tel: (Perth) 01738 622730	COMMENDED	3 Single 2 Twin 2 Double 2 Family	6 En Suite fac 1 Pub Bath/Show	B&B per person £18.00-£20.00 Single £18.00-£20.00 Double	Open Jan-Dec	

Family guest house with ample car parking, close to sports centre and swimming pool. Ground-floor bedrooms each have their own entrance.

Almond Villa Guest House 51 Dunkeld Road Perth PH1 5RP Tel: (Perth) 01738 629356	COMMENDED	1 Single 1 Twin 1 Double 2 Family	3 En Suite fac 1 Pub Bath/Show	B&B per person £17.00-£20.00 Single £17.00-£20.00 Double Room only per person £17.00-£20.00	Open Jan-Dec Dinner from 1830 B&B + Eve. Meal £24.00-£30.00	

Semi-detached Victorian villa, close to town centre, Gannochy Trust Sports Complex, the North Inch and River Tay. NON-SMOKING HOUSE.

Alpine Guest House 7 Strathview Terrace Perth PH2 7HY Tel: (Perth) 01738 637687	COMMENDED 👑👑👑	1 Single 1 Twin 2 Double 1 Family	4 En Suite fac 1 Pub Bath/Show	B&B per person £18.00-£20.00 Single £20.00-£22.00 Double	Open Jan-Dec Dinner 1800-2000 B&B + Eve. Meal £26.00-£30.00

Personally run, situated on main A94 tourist route with easy access to town centre and surrounding area. Large private car park.

Ardfern House 15 Pitcullen Crescent Perth PH2 7HT Tel: (Perth) 01738 637031	COMMENDED 👑	1 Twin 1 Double 1 Family	2 En Suite fac 1 Priv. NOT ensuite 1 Pub Bath/Show	B&B per person £16.00-£20.00 Single £15.00-£18.00 Double	Open Jan-Dec Dinner 1800-1830 B&B + Eve. Meal £24.00-£27.00

Victorian semi-villa on outskirts of city within easy access to all amenities. Non-smoking throughout. Off-road parking.

Arisaig Guest House 4 Pitcullen Crescent Perth PH2 7HT Tel: (Perth) 01738 628240 Fax: 01738 628240	HIGHLY COMMENDED 👑👑	1 Single 1 Twin 1 Double 2 Family	4 En Suite fac 1 Priv. NOT ensuite	B&B per person £16.00-£19.00 Single £17.50-£19.50 Double Room only per person from £15.00	Open Jan-Dec

Comfortable, family run guest house, with off-street parking. Close to city's many facilities. Local touring base. Ground-floor bedroom.

Auld Manse Guest House Pitcullen Crescent Perth PH2 7HT Tel: (Perth) 01738 629187	COMMENDED 👑	1 Single 1 Twin 2 Double 1 Family	2 En Suite fac 1 Pub Bath/Show	B&B per person £16.00 Single £16.00-£18.00 Double	Open Jan-Dec Dinner from 1830 B&B + Eve. Meal £25.00-£26.00

Former church manse, now family run guest house. On main A94, 10 minutes' walk to city centre, 1 mile (2 kms) from Scone Palace. Private parking.

Beechgrove Guest House Dundee Road Perth PH2 7AD Tel: (Perth) 01738 636147	HIGHLY COMMENDED 👑👑	1 Single 2 Twin 2 Double 1 Family	6 En Suite fac	B&B per person from £25.00 Single £20.00-£27.50 Double	Open Jan-Dec

Listed building and former manse set in extensive grounds. Peaceful and quiet, yet only a few minutes' walk from the city centre. 1 annexe room.

St Leonard's House

4 St Leonard's Bank, Perth, Perthshire PH2 8EB
Telephone/Fax: 01738 440144 or 627874

Relax in friendly atmosphere and good quality accommodation. Quiet location facing park, near shops, bus, rail, own parking. Perth is a lovely city with art gallery, museum, ice rink, leisure centre, golf etc. An excellent centre for touring Perthshire with its magnificent scenery.
Totally non-smoking.

Mrs Anne Campbell St Leonard's House 4 St Leonard's Bank Perth Perthshire PH2 8EB Tel: (Perth) 01738 627874 Fax: 01738 627874	COMMENDED 👑👑	3 Twin 1 Double 1 Family	4 En Suite fac 1 Priv. NOT ensuite	B&B per person £20.00-£22.00 Single £17.00-£19.00 Double	Open Jan-Dec Dinner 1800-1930 B&B + Eve. Meal £26.00-£28.00

Traditional stone house in quiet central location. Two minutes' walk from railway station. Ideal touring centre. Private parking.

PERTHSHIRE, ANGUS & DUNDEE AND THE KINGDOM OF FIFE

Details of Grading and Classification are on page vi. | Key to symbols is on back flap. | 183

PERTHSHIRE, ANGUS & DUNDEE AND THE KINGDOM OF FIFE

PERTH continued	Map 2 B2	

Clark Kimberley
57-59 Dunkeld Road, Perth PH1 5RP
Tel: 01738 637406   Fax: 01738 643983
Ian and Kathryn Sayer offer a warm, friendly welcome to guests of their Bed and Breakfast establishment. All rooms have ensuite/private facilities and are clean, comfortable and well-equipped. It is an ideal base from which to explore Perthshire and the surrounding areas.
Totally Non-Smoking.   **AA Recommended QQQ**

Clark Kimberley 57-59 Dunkeld Road Perth PH1 5RP Tel: (Perth) 01738 637406 Fax: 01738 643983	COMMENDED	1 Single 2 Double 4 Family	6 En Suite fac 1 Priv. NOT ensuite	B&B per person £18.00-£25.00 Single £17.00-£19.00 Double	Open Jan-Dec
Detached house on main Inverness road out of the city. City centre within walking distance. Private parking. Non-smoking house.					
Clunie Guest House 12 Pitcullen Crescent Perth PH2 7HT Tel: (Perth) 01738 623625	COMMENDED	1 Single 1 Twin 2 Double 3 Family	7 En Suite fac	B&B per person from £18.00 Single from £18.00 Double	Open Jan-Dec Dinner from 1800 B&B + Eve. Meal from £27.00
Personally run in residential part of town. Easy access to town centre and on main bus route.					
The Darroch Guest House 9 Pitcullen Crescent Perth PH2 7HT Tel: (Perth) 01738 636893	COMMENDED	2 Single 1 Twin 1 Double 2 Family	3 En Suite fac 1 Pub Bath/Show	B&B per person £15.00-£16.50 Single £15.00-£18.50 Double	Open Jan-Dec Dinner at 1830 B&B + Eve. Meal £22.50-£26.00
Semi-detached, Victorian villa, easily found on main A94 tourist route. Double-glazed throughout. Extensive breakfast menu. Off-street parking.					
Mrs V Harding Rhodes Villa, 75 Dunkeld Road Perth PH1 5RP Tel: (Perth) 01738 628466	COMMENDED	1 Single 2 Twin 1 Double	4 En Suite fac	B&B per person £16.50-£18.50 Single £16.50-£18.50 Double	Open Jan-Dec Dinner 1700-1930 B&B + Eve. Meal £23.00-£25.00
Personal attention and a friendly welcome. Close to amenities with private parking. Enroute to the north. Ideally situated for touring.					
Hazeldene Guest House Pitcullen Crescent Perth PH2 7HP Tel: (Perth) 01738 623550	COMMENDED	1 Single 1 Twin 2 Double 1 Family	5 En Suite fac	B&B per person £20.00-£24.00 Single £17.00-£22.00 Double	Open Jan-Dec
Family run guest house, on main tourist route to north east but near to city centre. Private car parking available.					
Iona Guest House 2 Pitcullen Crescent Perth PH2 7HT Tel: (Perth) 01738 627261	COMMENDED	2 Single 1 Twin 1 Double 1 Family	2 En Suite fac 2 Pub Bath/Show	B&B per person £15.00-£18.00 Single £15.00-£19.00 Double	Open Jan-Dec Dinner 1800-1930 B&B + Eve. Meal £23.00-£27.00
In residential area, 10 minutes from the town centre with private parking. Over 30 golf courses within 30 miles (48 kms) radius.					
Kinnaird Guest House 5 Marshall Place Perth PH2 8AH Tel: (Perth) 01738 628021/ 630685 Fax: 01738 444056	HIGHLY COMMENDED	1 Single 4 Twin 2 Double	7 En Suite fac	B&B per person from £20.00 Single from £20.00 Double	Open Jan-Dec Dinner from 1800
Georgian house, centrally situated overlooking park. Private parking. Short walk to town centre and convenient for railway and bus stations.					

Kinnoull Guest House 5 Pitcullen Crescent Perth PH2 7HT Tel: (Perth) 01738 634165	COMMENDED 👑👑👑	1 Twin 2 Double 1 Family	4 En Suite fac	B&B per person £20.00-£25.00 Single £15.00-£20.00 Double Room only per person £12.00-£17.00	Open Jan-Dec Dinner 1800-1900 B&B + Eve. Meal £23.00-£28.00

Family run guest house on main tourist route north (A94), within easy reach of city centre. Private facilities for all bedrooms.

Mr & Mrs Livingstone Westview, 49 Dunkeld Road Perth PH1 5RP Tel: (Perth) 01738 627787 Fax: 01738 627787	COMMENDED 👑👑👑	1 Twin 2 Double	3 En Suite fac 1 Pub Bath/Show	B&B per person from £18.00 Double	Open Jan-Dec Dinner 1800-2100

Townhouse in easy walking distance of town centre, on A9 with private parking. All rooms with colour TV, twin let as single.

Mr & Mrs McNicol Abbotsford, 23 James Street Perth PH2 8LX Tel: (Perth) 01738 635219	COMMENDED Listed	1 Single 2 Twin 3 Family	6 Limited ensuite	B&B per person £15.00-£17.00 Single £14.00-£16.00 Double	Open Jan-Dec

Victorian villa, in quiet residential area, a few minutes' walk from the town centre, station and bus station. All rooms have shower and colour TV.

Clifton House

36 Glasgow Road, Perth PH2 0PB
Telephone: 01738 621997

A delightful Victorian house situated on the outskirts of the city centre, in an elevated position affording views across the city from all rooms. Accommodation is very tastefully furnished and your hosts Colin and Margaret assure you of a very warm welcome and a very comfortable stay.

Mr & Mrs Moreland Clifton House 36 Glasgow Road Perth Perthshire PH2 0PB Tel: (Perth) 01738 621997	COMMENDED 👑👑	1 Single 1 Double 1 Family	2 En Suite fac 1 Priv. NOT ensuite	B&B per person £16.00-£19.00 Single £16.00-£19.00 Double	Open Jan-Dec

Delightful Victorian house, within easy walking distance of town centre. Ample private parking. Ideal location for all leisure facilities.

Mr & Mrs Napier Lindally 10-12 North William Street Perth PH1 5PT Tel: (Perth) 01738 636728 Fax: 01738 636728	APPROVED Listed	2 Twin 2 Double 1 Family	1 Pub Bath/Show	B&B per person £14.00-£16.00 Single £14.00-£16.00 Double Room only per person £12.00-£14.00	Open Jan-Dec Dinner 1800-1900 B&B + Eve. Meal £18.00-£22.00

Family home situated centrally in Perth, only minutes walk from all amenities. Evening meal also available.

Park Lane Guest House 17 Marshall Place Perth PH2 8AG Tel: (Perth) 01738 637218 Fax: 01738 643519	HIGHLY COMMENDED 👑👑	1 Single 2 Twin 2 Double 1 Family	6 En Suite fac	B&B per person £20.00-£23.00 Single £20.00-£23.00 Double	Open Jan-Dec

Georgian house overlooking park next to city centre. All ensuite rooms, private car park. Walking distance to golf course, restaurants and all amenities.

Pitcullen Guest House 17 Pitcullen Crescent Perth PH2 7HT Tel: (Perth) 01738 626506/ 0378 742928(mobile) Fax: 01738 628265	COMMENDED 👑👑	1 Single 4 Twin 1 Double	5 En Suite fac 1 Priv. NOT ensuite 1 Pub Bath/Show	B&B per person from £22.50 Single from £19.00 Double	Open Jan-Dec

Personally run and conveniently situated on A94 tourist route. Only 5 minutes from City Centre. Private parking.

Details of Grading and Classification are on page vi. | Key to symbols is on back flap. | 185

PERTHSHIRE, ANGUS & DUNDEE AND THE KINGDOM OF FIFE

PERTHSHIRE, ANGUS & DUNDEE AND THE KINGDOM OF FIFE

	Map	Award	Rooms	Bath	Price	Open
PERTH continued Mr & Mrs Reid Ballabeg, 14 Keir Street Bridgend Perth PH2 7HJ Tel: (Perth) 01738 620434	Map 2 B2	COMMENDED	1 Single 1 Double 1 Family	1 Pub Bath/Show	B&B per person £16.00-£19.00 Single £16.00-£19.00 Double	Open Jan-Dec

Friendly, family run house in quiet street off A94. Evening snacks available in rooms. 10 minutes from the city centre.

| Mrs P Smith
Beeches, 2 Comely Bank
Perth
PH2 7HU
Tel: (Perth) 01738 624486 | | COMMENDED | 2 Single
1 Twin
1 Double | 3 En Suite fac
2 Pub Bath/Show | B&B per person
£17.00-£20.00 Single
£17.00-£20.00 Double | Open Jan-Dec
Dinner 1800-1900
B&B + Eve. Meal
£25.00-£28.00 |

Semi-detached villa with ample car parking, conveniently situated on A94 tourist route.

| Tigh Mhorag Guest House
69 Dunkeld Road
Perth
PH1 5RP
Tel: (Perth) 01738 622902 | | COMMENDED | 2 Single
2 Twin
2 Double | 3 En Suite fac
1 Pub Bath/Show | B&B per person
£15.00-£18.00 Single
£17.00 Double
Room only per person
£11.00-£13.00 | Open Jan-Dec
Dinner from 1800 |

Family run guest house with well-kept garden to rear, and convenient for town centre.

| Mrs Angela Young
Inchview, 25 Marshall Place
Perth
PH2 8AG
Tel: (Perth) 01738 629610 | | APPROVED
Listed | 1 Single
1 Double
1 Family | 2 En Suite fac
1 Limited ensuite
2 Pub Bath/Show | B&B per person
£15.00-£16.00 Single
£15.00-£16.00 Double | Open Jan-Dec |

Centrally situated overlooking South Inch Park.
Winner of Perth's Best Floral Display 1991.

| **by PERTH**
Mr and Mrs Iain Comrie
Lismore, 1 Rorrie Terrace
Methven, by Perth
PH1 3PL
Tel: (Methven) 01738 840441 | Map 2
B2 | COMMENDED
Listed | 1 Twin
1 Double | 1 Pub Bath/Show | B&B per person
£13.50-£17.50 Single
£12.50-£14.50 Double | Open Dec-Oct |

Comfortable home in quiet residential area of village,
6 miles (10 kms) from Perth. Good base for touring.

TOPHEAD FARM
TULLYBELTON, STANLEY, BY PERTH PH1 4PT
Telephone and Fax: 01738 828259

Enjoy the panoramic views from the verandah of this farmhouse which is tastefully furnished. Superking beds in two of the three comfortable bedrooms. Guests can relax in the lounge and enjoy breakfasts with a difference. A good centre for touring, fishing and walking. Glasgow, Edinburgh and St. Andrews *1 hour away* with Dundee, Pitlochry and Crieff *30 minutes away*. **Come on and spoil yourselves!** No smoking.

| Mrs Dorothy Dow
Tophead Farm, Tullybelton
Stanley, by Perth
Perthshire
PH1 4PT
Tel: (Stanley) 01738 828259
Fax: 01738 828259 | | HIGHLY
COMMENDED | 1 Twin
1 Double
1 Family | 1 En Suite fac
1 Priv. NOT ensuite
1 Pub Bath/Show | B&B per person
from £16.00 Single
from £16.00 Double | Open Jan-Dec |

A very warm Scottish welcome in this traditional farmhouse on 200-acre (80ha) dairy farm. Perth 4 miles (6 kms). Extensive views over rural Perthshire.

| Mrs A Guthrie
Newmill Farm
Stanley, Perth
Perthshire
PH1 4QD
Tel: (Stanley) 01738 828281 | | COMMENDED | 1 Twin
2 Double | 3 En Suite fac
2 Pub Bath/Show | B&B per person
£18.00-£20.00 Single
£18.00-£19.00 Double | Open Feb-Oct
Dinner 1800-1900
B&B + Eve. Meal
£30.00-£32.00 |

Traditional farmhouse on 330 acre (133ha) arable farm. Convenient for the A9, 6 miles (10 kms) from Perth. Suitable for fishing and other outdoor pursuits.

| Mrs Howden
Stanley Farm
Stanley
Perthshire
PH1 4QQ
Tel: (Stanley) 01738 828334 | COMMENDED | 1 Double
1 Family | 2 Pub Bath/Show | B&B per person
£17.00-£19.00 Single
£14.00-£16.00 Double | Open Apr-Oct
Dinner 1900-2030
B&B + Eve. Meal
£22.00-£25.00 | |

Friendly, family farmhouse central for touring Perthshire. Home cooking and baking. Children especially welcome.

HUNTINGTOWER HOUSE
Crieff Road, Perth PH1 3JJ   Tel: 01738 624681

This is a charming country house with a large secluded garden, near Perth. There is easy access to main routes throughout Scotland, and so is an excellent stop for touring holidays or business. There is ample parking for cars and a friendly welcome is assured.

| Mrs H Lindsay
Huntingtower House
Crieff Road
by Perth
Perthshire
PH1 3JJ
Tel: (Perth) 01738 624681 | COMMENDED | 2 Twin
1 Double | 1 Pub Bath/Show | B&B per person
£15.00-£17.00 Double | Open Jan-Dec | |

Detached Victorian house with ¾ acre (0.3ha) secluded garden. Convenient for touring with easy access to the A85 and A9 and other main routes.

| Mrs D McFarlane
Letham Farm
Bankfoot
Perthshire
PH1 4EF
Tel: (Bankfoot) 01738 787322 | COMMENDED | 1 Twin
1 Double
1 Family | 2 Pub Bath/Show | B&B per person
£17.00-£18.00 Single
£14.00-£15.00 Double | Open Mar-Nov
Dinner from 1830
B&B + Eve. Meal
£24.00-£25.00 | |

300-acre (121ha) arable and raspberry farm in beautiful countryside, yet only 10 minutes from Perth. Warm welcome and home cooking.

| Mrs M Niven
Braeknowe
Tibbermore
Perthshire
PH1 1QJ
Tel: (Perth) 01738 840295 | HIGHLY COMMENDED Listed | 1 Twin
1 Double | 1 Pub Bath/Show | B&B per person
£15.00-£17.00 Single
£15.00-£17.00 Double | Open May-Oct | |

Modern bungalow with conservatory in quiet setting, yet with easy access to major roads. 5 miles (8 kms) west of city centre.

Avonlea
Highly Commended

At Pitmurthly Farm, Redgorton, near Luncarty, by Perth PH1 3HX Tel: 01738 828363   Fax: 01738 828053

Comfortable farmhouse with peaceful garden 4 miles north of Perth (off A9). Bedrooms tastefully furnished, comfortable beds and lovely views. Spacious lounge and dining room for guests. An ideal location for touring Perthshire or for relaxing. Walking, golf, fishing, and good restaurants nearby. River Tay 2 miles. *En-suite available. Ample safe parking. Open all year.*
Highly commended. Contact Mrs C Smith.

| Mrs C Smith, Avonlea
at Pitmurthly Farm, Redgorton
by Luncarty, by Perth
Perthshire
PH1 3HX
Tel: (Perth) 01738 828363
Fax: 01738 828053 | HIGHLY COMMENDED | 1 Single
1 Twin
1 Double | 1 En Suite fac
1 Pub Bath/Show | B&B per person
£16.00-£19.00 Single
£15.00-£19.00 Double | Open Jan-Dec | |

Traditional Scottish hospitality at this comfortable farmhouse, set in peaceful countryside 5 minutes from historic Perth. Ideal for touring, golf and walking.

Details of Grading and Classification are on page vi. | Key to symbols is on back flap. | 187

PITLOCHRY

PITLOCHRY **Perthshire** Mrs S A Anderson Silver Howe, Perth Road Pitlochry Perthshire PH16 5LY Tel: (Pitlochry) 01796 472181	Map 2 A1	**HIGHLY COMMENDED**	2 Twin 2 Double	4 En Suite fac	B&B per person £25.00 Single £20.00 Double	Open Jan-Dec	

Detached modern bungalow on town outskirts with large south-facing garden and outlook to Tummel Valley.

Mrs Beattie Cresta, 15 Lettoch Terrace Pitlochry Perthshire PH16 5BA Tel: (Pitlochry) 01796 472204	**COMMENDED** Listed	1 Single 1 Twin 1 Double	1 Pub Bath/Show	B&B per person to £15.00 Single to £15.00 Double	Open Apr-Oct	

A friendly welcome in this B&B in a quiet central part of Pitlochry. Ideal location for touring Perthshire.

Buttonboss Lodge 27 Atholl Road Pitlochry Perthshire PH16 5BX Tel: (Pitlochry) 01796 472065	**COMMENDED**	2 Single 3 Twin 4 Double	4 En Suite fac 1 Pub Bath/Show	B&B per person £15.00-£16.00 Single £15.00-£19.00 Double	Open Jan-Dec	

Traditional Victorian house in centre of Pitlochry. Within walking distance of all facilities. Private parking.

Carra Beag Guest House 16 Toberargan Road Pitlochry Perthshire PH16 5HG Tel: (Pitlochry) 01796 472835	**APPROVED**	1 Single 3 Twin 4 Double 2 Family	9 En Suite fac 1 Pub Bath/Show	B&B per person £21.00-£29.00 Single £21.00-£29.00 Double	Open Jan-Dec Dinner 1800-1830 B&B + Eve. Meal £28.50-£41.00	

Quiet and relaxing, centrally situated with commanding views and ample parking. Putting green. One ensuite annexe.

Craigroyston House

2 LOWER OAKFIELD, PITLOCHRY PH16 5HQ
Telephone/Fax: 01796 472053

A Victorian Country House set in own grounds with views of the surrounding hills. Centrally situated, there is direct pedestrian access to the town centre.

★ All rooms have private facilities and are equipped to a high standard.
★ Colour TV, welcome tray, central heating.
★ Residents' lounge.
★ Dining room with separate tables.
★ Safe private parking.

AA SELECTED QQQQ

Bed & Breakfast from £18 per person.

Craigroyston House 2 Lower Oakfield Pitlochry, Perthshire PH16 5HQ Tel/Fax: (Pitlochry) 01796 472053	**HIGHLY COMMENDED**	3 Twin 3 Double 2 Family	8 En Suite fac	B&B per person £18.00-£27.00 Double	Open Jan-Dec	

Family run Victorian villa near town centre, with large garden overlooking wooded hills. 10 minutes' walk from theatre.

Dalshian House Old Perth Road Pitlochry Perthshire PH16 5JS Tel: (Pitlochry) 01796 472173	**COMMENDED**	1 Twin 4 Double 2 Family	7 En Suite fac	B&B per person £20.50-£24.00 Single £20.50-£24.00 Double	Open Feb-Dec Dinner 1830-2000 B&B + Eve. Meal £31.00-£34.50	

A warm welcome at this Listed property situated on outskirts of Pitlochry. Set in picturesque parkland.

Derrybeg Guest House

18 Lower Oakfield, Pitlochry PH16 5DS
Telephone: 01796 472070

Both of DERRYBEG's adjoining buildings are set in a quiet location only a few minutes' walk from the town centre, enjoying magnificent views of the Vale of Atholl. The resident proprietors, Derek and Marion Stephenson, ensure only the finest hospitality, comfort, and good home cooking.

HIGHLY COMMENDED 👑👑👑

- All bedrooms with private facilities.
- Colour television and welcome tea/coffee tray in all bedrooms.
- Open all year for B&B or DB&B. Unlicensed, but guests welcome to supply own table wine.
- Full central heating throughout.
- Comfortable lounge and dining room.
- Food Hygiene Excellent Award.
- Ample parking in the grounds.
- Leisure activities can easily be arranged, i.e. theatre bookings, golf, fishing, pony-trekking, etc.

Colour brochure/tariff and details of weekly reductions available on request.

Derrybeg Guest House 18 Lower Oakfield Pitlochry Perthshire PH16 5DS Tel: (Pitlochry) 01796 472070	**HIGHLY COMMENDED** 👑👑👑	2 Single 2 Twin 6 Double 1 Family	11 En Suite fac	B&B per person £17.00-£25.00 Single £17.00-£25.00 Double Room only per person £12.00-£25.00	Open Jan-Nov Dinner 1815-1845 B&B + Eve. Meal £29.00-£38.00	

Privately owned, detached house, with large south-facing garden, in quiet, but central location. Elevated position overlooking Tummel Valley. 3 annexe rooms.

DUNDARAVE HOUSE

Dundarave is the ideal place to stay, with its peaceful ambience, the best of home-cooked food and pleasant ensuite rooms, all with colour TV and tea/coffee-making facilities. The comfortable lounge is open all day.

For your overnight stay or longer please contact your hosts:
Mae and Bob Collier.

AA SELECTED QQQQ
STB HIGHLY COMMENDED 👑👑👑

STRATHVIEW TERRACE, PITLOCHRY PH16 5AT
Telephone: 01796 473109

Dundarave House Strathview Terrace Pitlochry Perthshire PH16 5AT Tel: (Pitlochry) 01796 473109	**HIGHLY COMMENDED** 👑👑👑	2 Single 2 Twin 2 Double 1 Family	5 En Suite fac 2 Pub Bath/Show	B&B per person £22.00-£26.00 Single £22.00-£26.00 Double	Open Mar-Oct Dinner 1800-1900 B&B + Eve. Meal £35.00-£39.00	

Charming Victorian house, quiet location and stunning views, close to centre of Pitlochry. Ground-floor room. Personal, attentive service.

Mrs Miller Dunreen, 8 Lettoch Terrace Pitlochry Perthshire PH16 5BA Tel: (Pitlochry) 01796 472974	**COMMENDED** Listed	2 Double	1 Pub Bath/Show	B&B per person from £14.50 Single from £14.50 Double	Open Mar-Oct	

A warm welcome awaits in a comfortable house in a quiet residential area. Private parking. Convenient for town centre. Ideal location for touring.

| PITLOCHRY continued Perthshire | Map 2 A1 | | | |

KINNAIRD HOUSE
Kirkmichael Road, Pitlochry, Perthshire PH16 5JL
Telephone: 01796 472843

On a peaceful hillside in the beautiful Vale of Atholl, KINNAIRD HOUSE commands superb views. All rooms are ensuite and are furnished and decorated to a very high standard with every comfort in mind. Come and enjoy the friendly, relaxed atmosphere.
We are recommended for our healthy hearty breakfasts!

| Mr & Mrs A Norris Kinnaird House Kirkmichael Road Pitlochry Perthshire PH16 5JL Tel: (Pitlochry) 01796 472843 | HIGHLY COMMENDED 👑👑 | 1 Twin 2 Double | 3 En Suite fac | B&B per person £18.00-£25.00 Double | Open Jan-Dec |

Detached Victorian villa in rural setting 1.5 miles (2.5 kms) from the town. Superb views of the surrounding countryside.

| Mrs Spaven Wester Knockfarrie Knockfarrie Road Pitlochry Perthshire PH16 5DN Tel: (Pitlochry) 01796 472020 | HIGHLY COMMENDED 👑👑 | 1 Twin 2 Double | 3 En Suite fac | B&B per person £18.00-£25.00 Double | Open Apr-Nov |

Victorian house, elegantly furnished, in quiet location. Open views across Strathtummel and the hills beyond.

COMAR HOUSE
Strathview Terrace, Pitlochry PH16 5AT
Tel: 01796 473531   Fax: 01796 473811

A beautiful stone-built house with turret overlooking Pitlochry. It is ideally situated for touring. There are many distilleries, castles, gardens, sporting and outdoor activities within the surrounding area.
A warm and friendly welcome awaits you from *Isabel and Bill Watson.*
Open: April to October.

| Mr & Mrs W Watson Comar House Strathview Terrace Pitlochry Perthshire PH16 5AT Tel: (Pitlochry) 01796 473531 Fax: 01796 473811 | HIGHLY COMMENDED 👑👑 | 1 Single 3 Twin 1 Double 1 Family | 4 En Suite fac 1 Pub Bath/Show | B&B per person £16.00-£22.00 Single £16.00-£22.00 Double | Open Apr-Oct |

A friendly welcome in this elegant, turreted, period house, standing high above town with panoramic views.

| Mrs Ann Williamson Lynedoch, 9 Lettoch Terrace Pitlochry Perthshire PH16 5BA Tel: (Pitlochry) 01796 472119 | COMMENDED Listed | 1 Twin 2 Double | 2 Pub Bath/Show | B&B per person £15.00 Single £15.00 Double | Open Mar-Oct |

Accommodation in house and adjoining annexe. In quiet residential area. Convenient for all amenities near the centre of Pitlochry.

| ST ANDREWS Fife Mrs M Allan 2 King Street St Andrews Fife KY16 8JQ Tel: (St Andrews) 01334 476326 | Map 2 D2 APPROVED Listed | 1 Twin 1 Double | 2 Priv. NOT ensuite 1 Pub Bath/Show | B&B per person £14.00-£16.00 Double | Open Jan-Dec |

Friendly welcome awaits. Quiet. Fairly central. Within walking distance of town centre and its many amenities.

Aslar Guest House 120 North Street St Andrews Fife KY16 9AF Tel: (St Andrews) 01334 473460 Fax: 01334 477540	**HIGHLY COMMENDED**	1 Single 2 Twin 2 Double	5 En Suite fac	B&B per person £24.00-£27.00 Single £24.00-£27.00 Double Room only per person £20.00-£22.00	Open Jan-Dec

Victorian, family run terraced house furnished to a high standard. Centrally situated for shops, golf courses, restaurants and cultural pursuits. All rooms ensuite.

Bellcraig Guest House 8 Murray Park St Andrews Fife KY16 9AW Tel: (St Andrews) 01334 472962 Fax: 01334 472962	**COMMENDED**	2 Twin 2 Double 1 Family	5 En Suite fac 1 Pub Bath/Show	B&B per person £17.00-£26.00 Double	Open Jan-Dec

Well-appointed guest house. Ideal base for golfing parties, situated a few minutes' walk from the famous Old Course in the heart of historic St Andrews.

Cleveden House 3 Murray Place St Andrews Fife KY16 9AP Tel: (St Andrews) 01334 474212	**COMMENDED**	2 Single 2 Twin 1 Double 1 Family	4 En Suite fac 1 Priv. NOT ensuite 1 Pub Bath/Show	B&B per person £17.00-£25.00 Single £17.00-£25.00 Double	Open Jan-Dec

Personally run guest house, five minutes' walk from the Old Course, beaches and town centre. Large lounge where tea, coffee and home baking served.

Mrs M Coull Abbey Cottage, Abbey Walk St Andrews Fife KY16 9LB Tel: (St Andrews) 01334 473727	**COMMENDED**	1 Twin 1 Double 1 Family	1 En Suite fac 1 Limited ensuite 1 Priv. NOT ensuite	B&B per person £16.00-£18.00 Single £16.00-£18.00 Double	Open Jan-Dec

18th century Listed property with walled cottage garden. Close to centre of St Andrews with its beaches, golf, university and historical buildings.

Craigmore Guest House 3 Murray Park St Andrews Fife KY16 9AW Tel: (St Andrews) 01334 472142 Fax: 01334 477963	**HIGHLY COMMENDED**	1 Twin 3 Double 2 Family	6 En Suite fac	B&B per person £20.00-£40.00 Single £20.00-£25.00 Double	Open Jan-Dec

Long-established, very well appointed, traditional stone guest house in centre of St. Andrews. Only minutes from town centre, beaches and Old Course.

Mrs E L Finlay 2 Kilrymont Place St Andrews Fife KY16 8DH Tel: (St Andrews) 01334 475478	**COMMENDED** Listed	1 Twin 1 Double	1 Priv. NOT ensuite	B&B per person £20.00-£22.00 Single £17.00-£19.00 Double Room only per person £14.00-£16.00	Open Jan-Dec

Modern, semi-detached house in quiet residential area. Ideal touring base and convenient for town centre, golf courses and beaches.

Glenderran Guest House 9 Murray Park St Andrews Fife KY16 9AW Tel: (St Andrews) 01334 477951 Fax: 01334 477908	**HIGHLY COMMENDED**	2 Single 1 Twin 2 Double	3 En Suite fac 2 Priv. NOT ensuite	B&B per person £20.00-£26.00 Single £20.00-£26.00 Double	Open Jan-Dec

Tastefully refurbished, Victorian townhouse retaining some original features. Warm and comfortable atmosphere. Non-smoking throughout.

PERTHSHIRE, ANGUS & DUNDEE AND THE KINGDOM OF FIFE

PERTHSHIRE, ANGUS & DUNDEE AND THE KINGDOM OF FIFE

	Map 2					
ST ANDREWS continued **Fife** Mrs Hart Braeside House 25 Nelson Street St Andrews Fife KY16 8AJ Tel: (St Andrews) 01334 472698	D2	COMMENDED ♛♛	1 Twin 1 Double	2 En Suite fac	B&B per person £16.00-£20.00 Single £16.00-£20.00 Double	Open Jan-Dec

Detached house with parking near the centre of St Andrews. Both rooms ensuite.

---

4 Cairnsden Gardens

St Andrews KY16 8SQ
Telephone: 01334 472433

Spacious modern bungalow in very quiet area.
Good home cooking. Comfortable lounge with TV.
Lots of parking space.

Mrs Lily Mason 4 Cairnsden Gardens St Andrews Fife KY16 8SQ Tel: (St Andrews) 01334 472433	COMMENDED Listed	1 Twin 1 Double	2 Pub Bath/Show	B&B per person £18.00-£25.00 Single £15.00-£20.00 Double	Open Jan-Dec

Comfortable, personally run bed and breakfast, in quiet residential area
with private parking. Ideal base for touring Fife and its many golf courses.

Mrs I Methven Ardmore, 1 Drumcarrow Road St Andrews Fife KY16 8SE Tel: (St Andrews) 01334 474574	COMMENDED Listed	2 Twin	1 Pub Bath/Show	B&B per person £13.00-£15.00 Double	Open Jan-Dec

Family house in quiet residential area within walking distance of town centre.
Convenient for all amenities.

Number Ten Guest House 10 Hope Street St Andrews Fife KY16 9HJ Tel: (St Andrews) 01334 474601	COMMENDED ♛♛	3 Single 1 Twin 3 Double 3 Family	10 En Suite fac	B&B per person £25.00-£28.00 Single £25.00-£28.00 Double	Open Feb-Dec

Elegant Georgian terraced house, quietly situated but only minutes
from the town centre and beach. All rooms with private facilities.
Old Course 5 minutes' walk.

Mrs J Pumford Linton, 16 Hepburn Gardens St Andrews Fife KY16 9DD Tel: (St Andrews) 01334 474673	HIGHLY COMMENDED ♛♛	1 Twin 1 Double	1 En Suite fac 1 Priv. NOT ensuite	B&B per person £18.00-£21.00 Double	Open Apr-Oct

Spacious Edwardian house, with open views to parkland and beyond. Within a
short walk of the town and golf courses. Private parking. Non-smoking house.

Mrs V Rhind Hazlehead, 16 Lindsay Gardens St Andrews Fife KY16 8XB Tel: (St Andrews) 01334 475677	COMMENDED Listed	1 Double 1 Family	1 Pub Bath/Show	B&B per person £18.00-£24.00 Single £14.50-£16.50 Double	Open Jan-Dec Dinner 1800-2000 B&B + Eve. Meal £22.50-£25.00

Modern detached villa in quiet residential area, 1 mile (2kms) from town centre.
Easy parking. Home cooking.

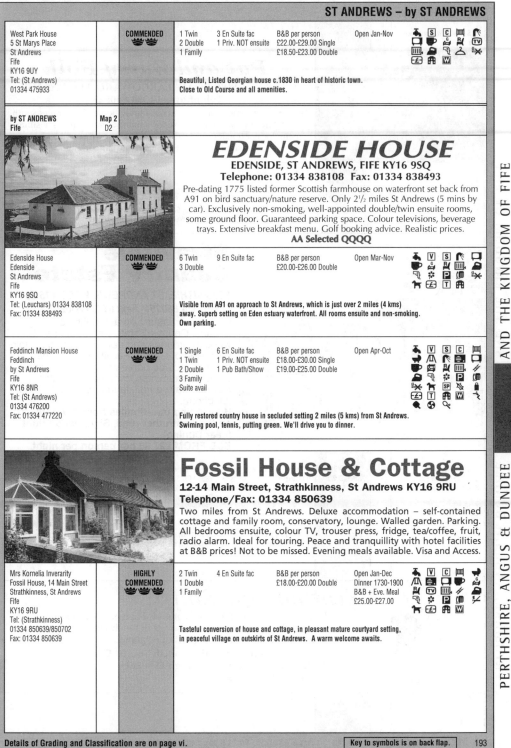

| West Park House
5 St Marys Place
St Andrews
Fife
KY16 9UY
Tel: (St Andrews)
01334 475933 | COMMENDED | 1 Twin
2 Double
1 Family | 3 En Suite fac
1 Priv. NOT ensuite | B&B per person
£22.00-£29.00 Single
£18.50-£23.00 Double | Open Jan-Nov |

Beautiful, Listed Georgian house c.1830 in heart of historic town.
Close to Old Course and all amenities.

| by ST ANDREWS
Fife | Map 2
D2 | | | | |

EDENSIDE HOUSE
EDENSIDE, ST ANDREWS, FIFE KY16 9SQ
Telephone: 01334 838108 Fax: 01334 838493

Pre-dating 1775 listed former Scottish farmhouse on waterfront set back from A91 on bird sanctuary/nature reserve. Only 2½ miles St Andrews (5 mins by car). Exclusively non-smoking, well-appointed double/twin ensuite rooms, some ground floor. Guaranteed parking space. Colour televisions, beverage trays. Extensive breakfast menu. Golf booking advice. Realistic prices.

AA Selected QQQQ

| Edenside House
Edenside
St Andrews
Fife
KY16 9SQ
Tel: (Leuchars) 01334 838108
Fax: 01334 838493 | COMMENDED | 6 Twin
3 Double | 9 En Suite fac | B&B per person
£20.00-£26.00 Double | Open Mar-Nov |

Visible from A91 on approach to St Andrews, which is just over 2 miles (4 kms) away. Superb setting on Eden estuary waterfront. All rooms ensuite and non-smoking. Own parking.

| Feddinch Mansion House
Feddinch
by St Andrews
Fife
KY16 8NR
Tel: (St Andrews)
01334 476200
Fax: 01334 477220 | COMMENDED | 1 Single
1 Twin
2 Double
3 Family
Suite avail | 6 En Suite fac
1 Priv. NOT ensuite
1 Pub Bath/Show | B&B per person
£18.00-£30.00 Single
£19.00-£25.00 Double | Open Apr-Oct |

Fully restored country house in secluded setting 2 miles (5 kms) from St Andrews. Swiming pool, tennis, putting green. We'll drive you to dinner.

Fossil House & Cottage
12-14 Main Street, Strathkinness, St Andrews KY16 9RU
Telephone/Fax: 01334 850639

Two miles from St Andrews. Deluxe accommodation – self-contained cottage and family room, conservatory, lounge. Walled garden. Parking. All bedrooms ensuite, colour TV, trouser press, fridge, tea/coffee, fruit, radio alarm. Ideal for touring. Peace and tranquillity with hotel facilities at B&B prices! Not to be missed. Evening meals available. Visa and Access.

| Mrs Kornelia Inverarity
Fossil House, 14 Main Street
Strathkinness, St Andrews
Fife
KY16 9RU
Tel: (Strathkinness)
01334 850639/850702
Fax: 01334 850639 | HIGHLY
COMMENDED | 2 Twin
1 Double
1 Family | 4 En Suite fac | B&B per person
£18.00-£20.00 Double | Open Jan-Dec
Dinner 1730-1900
B&B + Eve. Meal
£25.00-£27.00 |

Tasteful conversion of house and cottage, in pleasant mature courtyard setting, in peaceful village on outskirts of St Andrews. A warm welcome awaits.

PERTHSHIRE, ANGUS & DUNDEE AND THE KINGDOM OF FIFE

PERTHSHIRE, ANGUS & DUNDEE AND THE KINGDOM OF FIFE

by ST ANDREWS continued Fife	Map 2 D2

Pat and Barry Poll

8 ST ANDREWS ROAD, LARGOWARD, FIFE KY9 1HZ
Telephone: 01334 840523

A warm welcome awaits you at our family home, seven miles south of St Andrews. An ideal centre for numerous golf courses, visiting many local attractions or just relaxing in our garden. All bedrooms are on the ground floor. Private car parking.

B L Poll 8 St Andrews Road Largoward Fife KY9 1HZ Tel: (Peat Inn) 01334 840523	COMMENDED Listed	1 Twin 1 Double	1 Pub Bath/Show	B&B per person £17.00-£19.00 Single £15.00-£18.00 Double	Open Feb-Dec

Comfortable accommodation in small village. Garden and parking. Just 7 miles (11 kms) from St Andrews and close to the attractive East Neuk fishing villages.

Stravithie Country Estate

STRAVITHIE, ST ANDREWS, FIFE KY16 8LT
Tel: 01334 880251 Fax: 01334 880297

Bed and Breakfast on a beautiful old Scottish Country Estate with 30 acres of wooded grounds and gardens. Rooms within east wing of Castle. Facilities within the grounds include horse-riding, trout-fishing, open-air badminton, table-tennis, putting, golf-net, nature trail, launderette and telephone.
How to find us – 3 miles from St Andrews on the Anstruther road. Signpost on right (near Dunino).
B&B FROM £27.50 per person per night.

Stravithie House Stravithie Country Estate St Andrews Fife KY16 8LT Tel: (St Andrews) 01334 880251 Fax: 01334 880297	COMMENDED	2 Twin 1 Double	3 En Suite fac	B&B per person £30.00-£32.50 Single £27.50-£30.00 Double Room only per person £19.50-£22.00	Open Mar-Dec Dinner 1800-2000 B&B + Eve. Meal £35.00-£45.00

19th century mansion house in 30 acres (12ha) of peaceful grounds with nature walks, trout stream, riding, badminton, putting etc. St Andrews 3 miles (5 kms).

Scotland for Golf . . .

Find out more about golf in Scotland. There's more to it than just the championship courses so get in touch with us now for information on the hidden gems of Scotland.

Write to: **Information Unit, Scottish Tourist Board, 23 Ravelston Terrace, Edinburgh EH4 3EU or call: 0131-332 2433**

ST FILLANS Perthshire Mrs Russell Clachbheo St Fillans Perthshire PH6 2NG Tel: (St Fillans) 01764 685228	Map 1 H2	COMMENDED Listed	1 Twin 2 Double	1 Limited ensuite 2 Priv. NOT ensuite	B&B per person £17.00-£18.00 Single £15.00-£17.00 Double	Open Mar-Nov	

Situated high above St Fillans commanding excellent views of the loch.
Private facilities available.

ST MONANS Fife Miss M Aitken Inverforth, 20 Braehead St Monans Fife KY10 2AN Tel: (St Monans) 01333 730205	Map 2 D3	COMMENDED Listed	2 Twin 1 Double	1 Pub Bath/Show	B&B per person £16.00-£17.50 Single £16.00-£17.50 Double	Open mid May- mid Oct	

Overlooking the harbour in this attractive small fishing village,
a Victorian house with spacious bedrooms. Home baking.

NEWARK HOUSE

St Monans, Fife KY10 2DB   Tel: 01333 730027

Newark House is a traditional Fife farmhouse in a secluded
coastal location enjoying splendid sea views. It is ideally
situated for the golfer with St Andrews only 20 mins drive,
and for the non-golfer with an abundance of local
heritage, walks, bird-watching and local amenities.

Mrs Carol Thomson Newark House St Monans Fife KY10 2DB Tel: (St Monans) 01333 730027	COMMENDED Listed	1 Single 1 Double 1 Family	2 En Suite fac 1 Pub Bath/Show	B&B per person £17.00-£20.00 Single £15.00-£17.00 Double	Open Apr-Oct Dinner 1800-1930	

Traditional Fife farmhouse in secluded location beside the sea and ruins of
Newark Castle. Golf, walks, bird-watching and an abundance of local heritage.

SCONE, by Perth Perthshire	Map 2 B2

"ACUSHLA"

80 Angus Road, Scone, Perth PH2 6RB
Telephone: 01738 552885 Fax: 01738 552010

Detached comfortable friendly family home 2 miles north from Perth in quiet
historic country village close to all Highland amenities including Scone Palace.
Restaurant 5 minutes' walk away. Ample parking space. Dundee and
St Andrews ½ hour, Edinburgh, Glasgow 1 hour, Aberdeen 1½ hours,
Inverness 2 hours' drive away. The gateway to the Highlands.

Mrs Sue White Acushla, 80 Angus Road Scone, by Perth Perthshire PH2 6RB Tel: (Perth) 01738 552885 Fax: 01738 552010	COMMENDED	1 Twin 1 Family	2 Priv. NOT ensuite 2 Pub Bath/Show	B&B per person £15.00-£17.00 Single £16.00-£18.00 Double	Open Jan-Dec	

Detached house with warm and friendly atmosphere. On main bus route.
2 miles (3kms) from Perth. Plenty of parking available.

PERTHSHIRE, ANGUS & DUNDEE   AND THE KINGDOM OF FIFE

SCOTLANDWELL, by Kinross
Kinross-shire
Mrs S M Wardell
6 Bankfoot Park
Scotlandwell, by Kinross
Kinross-shire
KY13 7JP
Tel: (Scotlandwell)
01592 840515

Map 2
C3

COMMENDED

2 Twin | 1 Priv. NOT ensuite | B&B per person | Open Jan-Dec
| 1 Pub Bath/Show | £18.00 Single
| | £18.00 Double

Family home near Loch Leven. Easy access to Lomond Hills and Fife Coast. Bee-keeping, gliding, fishing, bird-watching and country parks.

TUMMEL BRIDGE
Perthshire
Mrs Sheena Forsythe
Heatherbank
Tummel Bridge
Perthshire
PH16 5NX
Tel: (Tummel Bridge)
01882 634324

Map 2
A1

COMMENDED
Listed

1 Single | 1 En Suite fac | B&B per person | Open Mar-Oct
1 Twin | 1 Pub Bath/Show | to £15.00 Single
1 Double | | from £15.00 Double

Modern detached bungalow in village in area renowned for its mountain and loch views. One ensuite bedroom. Good area for touring, golf and fishing.

Grampian Highlands, Aberdeen and the North East Coast

This is one of the most characterful areas in all of Scotland. It runs down from the high granites of the Cairngorm mountains down to a superb coastline. Between are high hills and wooded farmlands, river valleys and little towns, as well as Aberdeen, Scotland's third largest city, lying between the mouths of the Rivers Dee and Don.

As a major Scottish centre, Aberdeen offers plenty for visitors: museums, art gallery, leisure centres, theatre, arts centre and, given the city's preoccupation with flowers, splendid parks, including Europe's largest glasshouse, the Winter Gardens in the Duthie Park. Children are also very well catered for with one of Scotland's largest funfairs and also the Satrosphere, a hands-on science discovery centre, among the many attractions. There is also a superb choice of accommodation and places to eat and drink.

Aberdeen is the gateway to Royal Deeside. This attractive area gained its fame through association with the royal family and their holiday home at Balmoral. However, there is plenty more to enjoy along the valley of the River Dee, including walking, climbing and nature interest, as well as castles and a distillery, the Royal Lochnagar.

All rivers lead to the sea – and no visit here is complete without sampling the coastline.

Malt whisky distilling is most strongly associated with the valley of the River Spey, within easy reach over the hills from the Dee. On Speyside, signposts guide you round the unique Malt Whisky Trail – more distilleries (and the Speyside Cooperage) to visit, as well as very attractive scenery of river-valley birch and pine, with high moors as a backdrop. (Most of the distilleries are open to visitors all year.) Yet another river valley is also worth discovering: the River Don also has many enthusiasts and leads past places like Kildrummy Castle, one of the finest of Scotland's mediaeval ruins, and also Kildrummy Castle Gardens. The birchwoods of the Dee, Don and the lower Spey in particular are a photographer's delight in autumn.

All rivers lead to the sea – and no visit here is complete without sampling the coastline. Find long empty beaches at places like Cruden Bay (superb golf as well) or Lossiemouth or awesome rocks and cliffs at the Bullers of Buchan near Peterhead or at many points on the Moray Firth coast. (Look for puffins, too.) There is also wildlife interest in plenty at the Loch of Strathbeg, a wintering ground of international importance for geese. Or discover photogenic little villages tucked below the cliffs at places like Pennan or Gardenstown. Birdwatchers will enjoy the seabird colonies in late spring, as well as the geese in winter.

Some more of the area's major attractions outside Aberdeen include Duff House, set within parkland in the attractive little coastal town of Banff.

This country house gallery is an outstation of the National Gallery of Scotland. Scotland's Lighthouse Museum at Kinnaird Head in Fraserburgh should also not be missed. It features not only a fascinating portrait of the traditions of two centuries of lighthouse keeping but also a tour of Kinnaird Lighthouse itself, on top of a 16th century castle. Both places open all year. There is lots more to see, notably another local speciality – castles. The best of them are on the Castle Trail which takes in everything from ancient fortresses evolving into grand homes through the centuries, such as Fyvie, to elegant mansions like Haddo House. Lots of variety in city, countryside or coast.

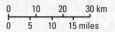

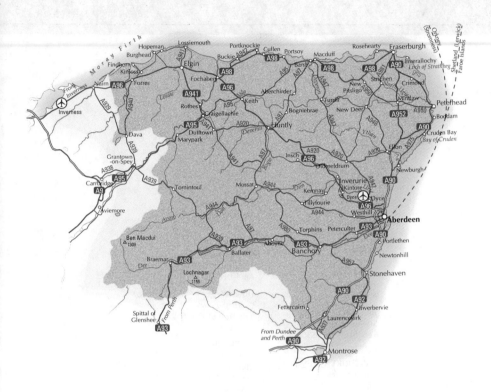

AREA TOURIST BOARD ADDRESSES

ABERDEEN AND GRAMPIAN TOURIST BOARD
Migvie House
North Silver Street
ABERDEEN
AB10 1RJ
Tel: 01224 632727
Fax: 01224 848805

TOURIST INFORMATION CENTRES IN SCOTLAND

ABERDEEN AND GRAMPIAN TOURIST BOARD

ABERDEEN ♿
St Nicholas House
Broad Street
AB9 1DE
Tel: (01224) 632727
Jan-Dec

ABOYNE
The Square
Tel: (013398) 86060
Easter-Oct

ALFORD ♿
Railway Museum
Station Yard
Tel: (019755) 62052
April-Oct

BALLATER
Station Square
Tel: (013397) 55306
Easter-end Oct

BANCHORY ♿
Bridge Street
AB31 3SX
Tel: (01330) 822000
Jan-Dec

BANFF
Collie Lodge
AB45 1AU
Tel: (01261) 812419
April-Oct

BRAEMAR ♿
The Mews
Mar Road
Tel: (013397) 41600
Jan-Dec

CRATHIE
Car Park
Balmoral Castle
Tel: (013397) 42414
Easter-Oct

DUFFTOWN
Clock Tower
The Square
Tel: (01340) 820501
April-Oct

ELGIN
17 High Street
IV30 1EG
Tel: (01343) 542666
Jan-Dec

FORRES
116 High Street
Tel: (01309) 672938
April-Oct

FRASERBURGH
Saltoun Square
Tel: (01346) 518315
April-Oct

HUNTLY ♿
9a The Square
Tel: (01466) 792255
April-Oct

INVERURIE
Town Hall
Market Place
Tel: (01467) 620600
April-Oct

STONEHAVEN
66 Allardice Street
Tel: (01569) 762806
Easter-End Oct

TOMINTOUL
The Square
Tel: (01807) 580285
April-Oct

 Accept written enquiries
♿ Disabled access

ABERCHIRDER, by Huntly
Banffshire
Mrs E Gregor
Skeibhill Farm
Aberchirder
Banffshire
AB54 7TT
Tel: (Aberchirder)
01466 780301

Map 4 F8

COMMENDED Listed

2 Family | 1 Pub Bath/Show

B&B per person
£12.50-£13.00 Single
£12.50-£13.00 Double
Room only per person
£9.00-£10.00

Open Jan-Dec
Dinner 1800-2000
B&B + Eve. Meal
£17.00-£18.00

Home cooking and baking on friendly working family farm. Close to Castle and Whisky Trails. 8 miles (13 kms) from Banff, 11 miles (17 kms) from Huntly.

ABERDEEN
Abbotswell Guest House
28 Abbotswell Crescent
Aberdeen
AB1 5AR
Tel: (Aberdeen) 01224 871788
Fax: 01224 891257

Map 4 G10

COMMENDED Listed

3 Single   3 En Suite fac
2 Twin   3 Pub Bath/Show
4 Double
1 Family

B&B per person
£20.00-£30.00 Single
£16.00-£25.00 Double

Open Jan-Dec
Dinner at 1800
B&B + Eve. Meal
£30.00-£40.00

Recently modernised bungalow with garden. Close to industrial estate and only 1.5 miles (2.5 kms) from city centre.

Aberdeen Nicoll's Guest House
63 Springbank Terrace
Aberdeen
AB1 2JZ
Tel: (Aberdeen) 01224 572867
Fax: 01224 572867

COMMENDED Listed

4 Twin   2 En Suite fac
2 Family 2 Pub Bath/Show

B&B per person
£20.00-£28.00 Single
£16.00-£22.00 Double

Open Jan-Dec

Family run, granite terraced guest house. Centrally located within ¼ mile (½ km) of city centre shops, 1 mile (2 kms) from Duthie Park.

Aldersyde Guest House
138 Bon Accord Street
Aberdeen
AB1 2TX
Tel: (Aberdeen) 01224 580012

COMMENDED Listed

2 Twin   2 Pub Bath/Show
1 Double
2 Family

B&B per person
£20.00-£22.00 Single
£15.00-£17.00 Double

Open Jan-Dec

Early Victorian family house with many original features. Quietly situated, but convenient for city centre.

Antrim Guest House
157 Crown Street
Aberdeen AB11 6HT
Tel: (Aberdeen) 01224 590987
Fax: 01224 575826

APPROVED Listed

3 Single   3 Pub Bath/Show
3 Twin
1 Family

B&B per person
£20.00-£22.00 Single
£14.00-£15.00 Double

Open Jan-Dec

Situated close to city centre, railway and bus stations. Private parking.

Balvenie Guest House
9 St Swithin Street
Aberdeen
AB1 6XB
Tel: (Aberdeen) 01224 322559
Fax: 01224 322773

APPROVED Listed

2 Single   2 Pub Bath/Show
2 Twin
1 Double

B&B per person
£18.00-£22.00 Single
£14.00-£16.00 Double

Open Jan-Dec
Dinner 1800-2030

Late Victorian granite-built house in residential area in West End, close to city centre. Parking. Convenient for local and the airport buses.

Bimini
69 Constitution Street
Aberdeen
AB2 1ET
Tel: (Aberdeen) 01224 646912
Fax: 01224 646912

COMMENDED

1 Single   2 Pub Bath/Show
4 Twin
1 Double
1 Family

B&B per person
£18.00-£24.00 Single
£18.00-£25.00 Double

Open Jan-Dec

Personally run guest house. In residential area close to centre and all local amenities. Car park to rear.

WELCOME

Whenever you are in Scotland, you can be sure of a warm welcome at your nearest Tourist Information Centre.

For guide books, maps, souvenirs, our Centres provide a service second to none – many now offer bureau-de-change facilities. And, of course, Tourist Information Centres offer free, expert advice on what to see and do, route-planning and accommodation for everyone – visitors and residents alike!

ABERDEEN AND THE NORTH EAST COAST

GRAMPIAN HIGHLANDS,

ABERDEEN continued	**Map 4 G10**	**COMMENDED** ♔♔	2 Twin 3 Double 2 Family	6 En Suite fac 1 Pub Bath/Show	B&B per person £25.00-£27.00 Single £20.00-£22.00 Double	Open Jan-Dec	

Fourways Guest House
435 Great Western Road
Aberdeen
AB1 6NJ
Tel: (Aberdeen) 01224 310218

Centrally situated in residential area of city.
On main tourist route for Royal Deeside.

FURAIN GUEST HOUSE

North Deeside Road, Peterculter, Aberdeen AB14 0QN
Telephone: 01224 732189

FURAIN GUEST HOUSE, on the A93, 8 miles west of Aberdeen centre, close to several historic castles and convenient for touring some of the most beautiful countryside in the UK. We give a full Scottish breakfast with choice, special diets catered for.

		COMMENDED ♔♔	1 Single 3 Twin 2 Double 2 Family	8 En Suite fac 1 Pub Bath/Show	B&B per person £27.00-£31.00 Single £19.00-£21.00 Double	Open Jan-Dec Dinner 1900-2100 B&B + Eve. Meal £27.00-£39.00	

Furain Guest House
92 North Deeside Road
Peterculter
Aberdeen
AB14 0QN
Tel: (Aberdeen) 01224 732189

Late Victorian house built of red granite. Family run. Convenient for town,
Royal Deeside and the Castle Trail. Private car parking.

		COMMENDED Listed	2 Single 1 Twin 1 Double	2 Pub Bath/Show	B&B per person £18.00-£23.00 Single £15.00-£17.00 Double	Open Jan-Dec	

Greyholme
35 Springbank Terrace
Aberdeen
AB1 2LR
Tel: (Aberdeen) 01224 587081
Fax: 01224 212287

Personally run guest house close to city centre and all amenities.
Near to main bus routes. Safe off-street parking available.

		COMMENDED Listed	2 Single 2 Twin 1 Double 2 Family	4 En Suite fac 3 Priv. NOT ensuite	B&B per person £20.00-£25.00 Single £18.00-£20.00 Double	Open Jan-Dec	

Hamilton Guest House
22 Hamilton Place
Aberdeen
AB15 2BH
Tel: (Aberdeen) 01224 644619

Elegant Victorian family home in quiet residential area,
yet handy for city centre and all amenities.

		COMMENDED Listed	2 Single 1 Double 2 Family	1 Limited ensuite 1 Pub Bath/Show	B&B per person £20.00-£26.00 Single £15.00-£19.00 Double	Open Jan-Dec	

Kingswood House
422 Great Western Road
Aberdeen
AB1 6NQ
Tel: (Aberdeen) 01224 323368

Granite-built Victorian townhouse, personally run and situated
a short distance from town centre. On main bus route.

		COMMENDED ♔	1 Single 3 Twin 1 Double 1 Family	1 En Suite fac 2 Pub Bath/Show	B&B per person from £19.00 Single from £15.00 Double	Open Jan-Dec	

Klibreck Guest House
410 Great Western Road
Aberdeen
AB1 6NR
Tel: (Aberdeen) 01224 316115

Granite building, corner site in residential area in city's West End.
On main bus route to city centre and Royal Deeside. Off-road parking.

		COMMENDED ♔	1 Single 1 Twin 1 Family	2 Pub Bath/Show	B&B per person £16.00-£19.00 Single £15.00-£18.00 Double	Open Jan-Dec	

Mrs Margaret Laing
20 Louisville Avenue
Aberdeen
AB1 6TX
Tel: (Aberdeen) 01224 319812

Terraced granite house in quiet residential area 2 miles (3 kms) from city centre.
Close to main Inverness, Braemar and Perth roads.

Royal Crown Guest House 111 Crown Street Aberdeen AB1 2HH Tel: (Aberdeen) 01224 586461 Fax: 01224 586461	COMMENDED Listed	2 Single 2 Twin 2 Double 2 Family	2 En Suite fac 3 Limited ensuite 2 Pub Bath/Show	B&B per person £20.00-£30.00 Single £15.00-£24.00 Double	Open Jan-Dec	
		Traditional granite townhouse, centrally situated within walking distance of all amenities. Car parking.				

Scottish Agricultural College

CRAIBSTONE ESTATE, BUCKSBURN, ABERDEEN AB21 9TR
Telephone: 01224 711195   Fax: 01224 711298

Craibstone Estate, situated in quiet rural location within large woodland estate only five miles from Aberdeen. An excellent base for touring the North-East of Scotland, playing the many golf courses or just relaxing in our tranquil environment. Whatever your needs we will give you a warm welcome at Craibstone.

Scottish Agricultural College Crabstone Estate Bucksburn, Aberdeen AB21 9TR Tel: (Aberdeen) 01224 711195 Fax: 01224 711298	APPROVED	79 Single 34 Twin	60 En Suite fac 6 Pub Bath/Show	B&B per person £18.00-£27.00 Single £16.00-£24.00 Double	Open mid March- mid-???? Dinner 1730-1900 B&B + Eve. Meal £23.50-£34.50	
		Halls of Residence, set in extensive country park on outskirts of Aberdeen, with easy access to all amenities. Sutton Hall Approved 3 crown, Mackie and Hunter Halls Approved 1 crown.				
Stonegrange Guest House 253 Stoneywood Road Bucksburn, Aberdeen AB2 9JS Tel: (Aberdeen) 01224 716151	APPROVED	2 Single 1 Twin 2 Double 1 Family	2 En Suite fac 3 Pub Bath/Show	B&B per person £14.00-£18.00 Single £14.00 Double	Open Jan-Dec Dinner 1700-2100	
		Family run guest house with easy access to Aberdeen Airport and all local and city amenities. Friendly welcome assured.				
Strathboyne Guest House 26 Abergeldie Terrace Aberdeen AB1 6EE Tel: (Aberdeen) 01224 593400	COMMENDED	1 Single 1 Twin 2 Double 1 Family	4 En Suite fac 1 Pub Bath/Show	B&B per person £20.00-£26.00 Single £18.00-£20.00 Double	Open Jan-Dec Dinner 1750-1800 B&B + Eve. Meal £26.00-£34.00	
		Semi-detached house in residential area, close to local park. Breakfast menu and evening dinner. Near bus route and 10 minutes' walk to city centre.				
University of Aberdeen Conference Office Regent Walk Old Aberdeen Tel: (Aberdeen) 01224 272664 Fax: 01224 276246	COMMENDED	1169 Single 22 Twin	143 En Suite fac 172 Pub Bath/Show	B&B per person £23.90-£39.50 Single £34.15 Double	Open Jan-Dec Dinner 1800-1930 B&B + Eve. Meal £32.30-£52.65	
		Recently opened accommodation on university campus all ensuited with access to all facilities.				

St ELMO

64 HILTON DRIVE, ABERDEEN AB24 4NP
Telephone: 01224 483065   Mobile: 0585 849776
e.mail k.watt@aberdeen.ac.uk.

This clean, comfortable, smoke-free family accommodation is ideal for guests looking for a small, quiet place to stay, but yet on a city centre bus route, close to airport, university and hospital. Each room has self-catering facilities (microwave, fridge, etc). CTV. *Special weekly rates.* On/off-street car parking available.

Mrs A Watt St Elmo, 64 Hilton Drive Aberdeen AB24 4NP Tel: (Aberdeen) 01224 483065/ 0585 849776 (mobile)	COMMENDED Listed	2 Twin 1 Double	1 Pub Bath/Show	B&B per person £17.00-£21.00 Single £14.00-£15.00 Double	Open Jan-Dec	
		Detached bungalow in residential area with frequent bus service. City centre 2 miles (3kms). No smoking.				

Details of Grading and Classification are on page vi. | Key to symbols is on back flap. | 205

by ABERDEEN	Map 4 G10						
Patricia A Allen 3 Greystone Place Newtonhill Kincardineshire AB3 2PW Tel: (Newtonhill) 01569 730391		APPROVED Listed	2 Family	2 Pub Bath/Show	B&B per person £15.00-£21.00 Single £14.00-£15.00 Double	Open Jan-Dec Dinner 1830-2000 B&B + Eve. Meal £20.00-£22.50	

A friendly welcome awaits at this comfortable semi-detached house, set in coastal village 10 miles from Aberdeen. Evening meals by arrangement.

| Mrs Goudriaan Blackdog Heights Bridge of Don, Aberdeen Aberdeenshire AB23 8BT Tel: (Aberdeen) 01224 704287 | | COMMENDED Listed | 2 Single 1 Twin 1 Double | 1 Pub Bath/Show | B&B per person £16.00-£18.00 Single £15.00-£17.00 Double Room only per person £15.00-£16.00 | Open Jan-Dec | |

Large modern bungalow in own grounds 5 miles (8kms) from Aberdeen, 2 miles (3kms) from Exhibition Centre. Handy for main A92 and near the beach.

| **ABERLOUR** **Banffshire** Mrs E J Mitchell Roys Croft Aberlour Banffshire AB38 9NR Tel: (Aberlour) 01340 871408 | Map 4 D8 | COMMENDED | 1 Single 1 Twin 1 Double | 1 En Suite fac 1 Pub Bath/Show | B&B per person £15.00-£19.00 Single £13.50-£17.50 Double Room only per person £12.50-£15.50 | Open Jan-Dec | |

Small working croft in the heart of the Whisky Trail near the delightful village of Charlestown of Aberlour in Speyside.

| **ABOYNE** **Aberdeenshire** | Map 4 F11 | | | | | | |

ARBOR LODGE

Ballater Road, Aboyne AB34 5HY
Telephone: 013398 86951

ARBOR LODGE is a large luxury home set in a woodland garden in the picturesque village of Aboyne. All bedrooms have ensuite bathrooms, tea-making facilities and television. Ideally located for touring Royal Deeside. Activities include golf, fishing, bowling, tennis, gliding, water skiing, swimming, squash and hillwalking.

| Arbor Lodge Ballater Road Aboyne Aberdeenshire, AB34 5HY Tel: (Aboyne) 013398 86951 Fax: 013398 86951 | | DELUXE | 3 Twin | 3 En Suite fac | B&B per person £25.00-£27.00 Single £24.00 Double | Open Mar-Oct | |

A newly built, spacious house of character with large landscaped garden, front and rear. Near centre of village. All bedrooms ensuite.

ALLTDINNIE

Birse, Aboyne, Aberdeenshire AB34 5ES
Telephone: 013398 86323

Delightful country house set in secluded grounds close to Aboyne. Whether you want to explore the Castle Trail, Whisky Trail, hillwalk or play our golf courses, assistance is on hand with routes planned and tee times arranged. Alternatively relax and enjoy warm Scottish hospitality.

| Mrs Eileen Barton Alltdinnie, Birse Aboyne Aberdeenshire AB34 5ES Tel: (Aboyne) 013398 86323 | | HIGHLY COMMENDED | 1 Single 1 Twin 1 Double | 2 Priv. NOT ensuite 1 Pub Bath/Show | B&B per person £22.00-£24.00 Single £22.00-£24.00 Double | Open Apr-Oct Dinner 1900-2000 B&B + Eve. Meal £36.00-£42.00 | |

Historic, Victorian country house, peacefully located with large attractive gardens. Owners can arrange a variety of 2/3 night packages. Ideal situation for "Castle and Whisky Trails ".

Phyllis & Michael Ingham Struan Hall, Ballater Road Aboyne Aberdeenshire AB34 5HY Tel: (Aboyne) 013398 87241 Fax: 013398 87241	**DELUXE**	2 Twin 1 Double	3 En Suite fac	B&B per person £22.00-£24.00 Double	Open Mar-Oct

A warm and friendly welcome at this family home set in
2 acres (0.8ha) of woodland garden. Peaceful but central location.

BIRKWOOD LODGE
Gordon Crescent, Aboyne AB34 5HJ
Telephone/Fax: 013398 86347

Experience genuine Scottish hospitality in this lovely Victorian home. Enjoy good food prepared daily from the excellent choice of local produce. Quietly situated, Birkwood Lodge has an uninterrupted view South over the village green where the Highland Games are held. Salmon fishing to let. Wonderful golf courses within easy reach.

Mrs E L Thorburn Birkwood Lodge Gordon Crescent Aboyne Aberdeenshire AB34 5HJ Tel: (Aboyne) 013398 86347 Fax: 013398 86347	**HIGHLY COMMENDED**	2 Twin 1 Double	2 En Suite fac 1 Priv. NOT ensuite	B&B per person £23.50-£30.00 Single from £23.50 Double	Open Jan-Dec Dinner 1900-2030 B&B + Eve. Meal £40.00-£47.50

Personal attention, fresh country produce and a high standard of comfort, combine to provide a memorable experience of Royal Deeside.

ALFORD **Aberdeenshire** Mrs S M Blackman Dunvegan, 26 Gordon Road Alford Aberdeenshire AB33 8AL Tel: (Alford) 019755 63077	Map 4 F10	**COMMENDED** Listed	1 Twin 1 Double	1 Pub Bath/Show	B&B per person £15.00-£17.00 Single from £15.00 Double	Open Jan-Dec

Detached, refurbished bungalow in village of Alford with private parking. Close to Transport Museum. Ideally situated for Whisky and Castle Trails.

Mrs Iris Henderson 13 Montgarrie Road Alford Aberdeenshire AB33 8AE Tel: (Alford) 019755 62159	**COMMENDED** Listed	1 Twin 1 Double	1 Pub Bath/Show	B&B per person to £15.00 Single to £14.00 Double	Open Mar-Oct

Friendly welcome in comfortable accommodation. Within walking distance of local park, museums and village amenities.

by ALFORD **Aberdeenshire** Mrs C E Braiden Macbrae Lodge Mongarrie, Alford Aberdeenshire AB33 8AX Tel: (Alford) 019755 63421	Map 4 F10	**COMMENDED**	1 Twin 1 Double 1 Family	2 Pub Bath/Show	B&B per person £16.00 Single £16.00 Double	Open Jan-Dec

In quiet position, with lovely views of open countryside. Comfortable accommodation and home-baking. Ideal for Castle and Whisky Trails.

BALLATER **Aberdeenshire** Averill Chalmers Bank House, Station Square Ballater Tel: (Ballater) 013397 55996 Fax: 013397 55996	Map 4 E11	**HIGHLY COMMENDED**	1 Twin 1 Double 2 Family	4 En Suite fac	B&B per person £25.00 Single £19.50 Double	Open Jan-Dec

Central, convenient to all amenities. Recently refurbished, family run, offering excellent views over village and Royal Deeside beyond.

ABERDEEN AND THE NORTH EAST COAST

GRAMPIAN HIGHLANDS,

Details of Grading and Classification are on page vi.

Key to symbols is on back flap.

BALLATER continued **Aberdeenshire** Mrs A P Henchie Morven Lodge 29 Braemar Road Ballater Aberdeenshire AB35 5RQ Tel: (Ballater) 013397 55373	**Map 4** E11	COMMENDED 👑👑	1 Twin 2 Double	1 Priv. NOT ensuite 2 Pub Bath/Show	B&B per person from £16.00 Double	Open May-Oct	

Former rectory situated close to the town centre.
Convenient base for touring Deeside.

Moorside Guest House
BRAEMAR ROAD, BALLATER AB35 5RL
TELEPHONE/FAX: 013397 55492

A warm welcome awaits you at this former manse near the village centre. All bedrooms have ensuite facilities, colour TV, tea/coffee-makers and electric blankets. Residents' lounge and separate dining room where excellent breakfasts are served. Off-street parking. Ideal centre for hillwalking, golf and touring Royal Deeside.

Moorside Guest House Braemar Road Ballater Aberdeenshire AB35 5RL Tel: (Ballater) 013397 55492 Fax: 013397 55492	COMMENDED 👑👑	3 Twin 3 Double 3 Family	9 En Suite fac	B&B per person £21.00-£26.00 Single £18.00-£20.00 Double	Open Mar-Nov

Friendly, personally run guest house. All rooms ensuite, TVs and courtesy trays.
Large garden and car park. Excellent restaurants nearby.

Netherley Guest House 2 Netherley Place Ballater Aberdeenshire AB35 5QE Tel: (Ballater) 013397 55792 Fax: 01339 881231	COMMENDED 👑👑	2 Single 2 Twin 2 Double 3 Family	4 En Suite fac 2 Pub Bath/Show	B&B per person £18.00-£20.00 Single £16.00-£20.00 Double Room only per person £15.00-£19.00	Open Jan-Dec Dinner from 1830 B&B + Eve. Meal £28.00-£32.00

Family run guest house in a quiet location in the centre of a renowned village.
Close to shops and amenities.

by BALLATER **Aberdeenshire**	**Map 4** E11

MIGVIE HOUSE
By Tarland, Aboyne, Aberdeenshire AB34 4XL
Telephone/Fax: 013398 81313

We are just off the beaten track, tucked into the south-facing slopes of Royal Deeside, with its romantic castles, distilleries and numerous sporting pursuits. The culmination of a perfect day could end at our peaceful old farmhouse, with antiques, wood fires and mountain views amidst a small Highland estate.

C Luffman Migvie House, Tarland Aboyne Aberdeenshire AB34 4XL Tel: (Tarland) 013398 81313 Fax: 013398 81313	HIGHLY COMMENDED 👑👑👑	2 Twin 1 Double	3 En Suite fac	B&B per person £20.00-£25.00 Single £18.00-£20.00 Double	Open Jan-Dec Dinner 1900-2000 B&B + Eve. Meal £28.00-£35.00

Traditional stone farmhouse lovingly restored. Tucked into
south-facing slopes of Royal Deeside. Evening meals.

BANCHORY **Kincardineshire** Kathleen Balsamo Towerbank House 93 High Street Banchory Kincardineshire AB31 3XT Tel: (Banchory) 01330 824798/ 822657	**Map 4** F11	HIGHLY COMMENDED 👑👑	2 Twin	2 En Suite fac	B&B per person from £20.00 Single from £17.00 Double	Open Jan-Dec	
				Centrally situated Victorian house, south-facing with splendid views towards the Deeside hills.			
Mrs Hampson The Old Police House 3 Bridge Street Banchory Kincardineshire AB31 5SX Tel: (Banchory) 01330 824000		HIGHLY COMMENDED 👑👑	1 Twin 1 Double	2 En Suite fac	B&B per person from £20.00 Single from £18.00 Double	Open Jan-Dec	
				Banchory's original Police Station and Prison. House of great character and warmth. Centrally located and close to all amenities.			

The Old West Manse
71 Station Road, Banchory, Kincardineshire AB31 5UD
Telephone/Fax: 01330 822202

Luxuriously refurbished Victorian manse set in the heart of Royal Deeside
amidst the famous *Castle* and *Whisky* trails. Deluxe accommodation,
tastefully designed by Laura Ashley and furnished to the very highest
standard. Expansive gardens and ample private parking. Golf and fishing
by prior arrangement. A real *Home-from-Home* experience.

Mr & Mrs Taylor The Old West Manse B&B 71 Station Road Banchory Kincardineshire AB31 5UD Tel/Fax: (Banchory) 01330 822202	DELUXE 👑👑	2 Twin 1 Double	2 En Suite fac 1 Priv. NOT ensuite	B&B per person £26.00-£32.00 Single £20.00-£24.00 Double Room only per person £20.00-£27.00	Open Jan-Dec	
			Former manse. A real home-from-home experience in a relaxed and informal atmosphere. Fine views over River Dee and hills beyond.			
Village Guest House 83 High Street Banchory Kincardineshire AB31 3TJ Tel: (Banchory) 01330 823307	HIGHLY COMMENDED Listed	1 Twin 2 Double 1 Family Suites avail	1 Priv. NOT ensuite 3 Pub Bath/Show	B&B per person £19.00-£22.50 Single £19.00-£22.50 Double Room only per person £18.00-£20.00	Open Jan-Dec Dinner 1900-2000 B&B + Eve. Meal £29.00-£32.50	
			Charming Victorian house in centre of Royal Deeside village. Warm Scottish welcome, finished with a taste of tartan.			

ABERDEEN AND THE NORTH EAST COAST, GRAMPIAN HIGHLANDS

by BANCHORY Kincardineshire Mrs P Law Monthammock Farm Durris, by Banchory Kincardineshire AB31 3DX Tel: (Drumoak) 01330 811421	Map 4 F11	COMMENDED	1 Twin 1 Double	1 En Suite fac 1 Priv. NOT ensuite 1 Pub Bath/Show	B&B per person to £22.00 Single to £18.00 Double	Open Jan-Dec Dinner 1800-1930 B&B + Eve. Meal £30.00-£32.00	

Tranquillity and a warm welcome at this sympathetically converted steading, with spectacular views over Deeside.

Mrs Irene Taylor Wester Knockhill, Strachan Banchory Kincardineshire AB31 6LL Tel: (Banchory) 01330 824328	HIGHLY COMMENDED	1 Twin 2 Double	2 En Suite fac 1 Priv. NOT ensuite	B&B per person £20.00-£27.50 Double	Open Feb-Nov	

Spacious modernised house on small farm. Large garden bounded by a stream. Peaceful setting in beautiful Royal Deeside.

BANFF Dorothy & Alec Clark Montcoffer House, Montcoffer Banff AB45 3LJ Tel: (Banff) 01261 812979	Map 4 F7	APPROVED	1 Single 1 Double 1 Family	2 En Suite fac 1 Priv. NOT ensuite	B&B per person £16.00 Single £16.00 Double	Open Jan-Dec Dinner 1800-2000

Listed 17th century mansion, overlooking Deveron Valley. Ideal centre for walking, golf, fishing, Castle and Whisky trails.

The Trinity and Alvah Manse Castle Street Banff AB45 1DH Tel: (Banff) 01261 812244	COMMENDED Listed	1 Twin 2 Double	2 Priv. NOT ensuite 1 Pub Bath/Show	B&B per person from £17.50 Single £15.00-£17.50 Double	Open Jan-Dec Dinner 1800-2000 B&B + Eve. Meal £21.00-£24.00	

Former manse near town centre, stylishly renovated to a high standard. International owners with number of languages spoken.

MORAYHILL
Bellevue Road, Banff AB45 1BJ
Telephone: 01261 815956

This comfortable family home is situated in Banff, an historic coastal town with many fine buildings including Duff House, a Country House Gallery. There are many good golf courses including Duff House Royal close by. The castle and coastal trails are also within easy reach.

Mrs Wilkie Morayhill, Bellevue Road Banff AB45 1BJ Tel: (Banff) 01261 815956	COMMENDED	2 Twin 1 Double	2 En Suite fac 1 Pub Bath/Show	B&B per person from £15.00 Single from £15.00 Double	Open Jan-Dec

Large Victorian house, centrally situated for town, golf and fishing. Warm and friendly welcome assured.

by BANFF Mrs C Elrick Mains of Blackton, King Edward Banff AB45 3NJ Tel: (King Edward) 01888 551205	Map 4 F7	APPROVED	1 Twin 1 Double 1 Family	1 En Suite fac 1 Pub Bath/Show	B&B per person £21.50-£27.00 Single £13.50-£19.00 Double	Open Apr-Sep Dinner 1830-2030

120-acre (48ha) farm in quiet countryside. Local activities include golf, fishing and country walks. Home baking. Extended Georgian farmhouse with some original furnishings.

BRAEMAR
Aberdeenshire
Clunie Lodge
Clunie Bank Road
Braemar
Aberdeenshire
AB35 5YP
Tel: (Braemar) 013397 41330

Map 4
D11

COMMENDED

1 Twin 3 En Suite fac
2 Double 1 Priv. NOT ensuite
2 Family 1 Pub Bath/Show

B&B per person
£16.50-£18.00 Double

Open Dec-Oct
Dinner 1800-2000
B&B + Eve. Meal
£28.00-£30.00

Family run, Victorian, former manse in the centre of Braemar. Home cooking.
5-day midweek break. Ideal for skiing and hillwalking.

Cranford Guest House &
    Wishing Well Restaurant
15 Glenshee Road
Braemar
Aberdeenshire
AB35 5YQ
Tel: (Braemar) 013397 41675

COMMENDED

2 Twin 3 En Suite fac
2 Double 1 Priv. NOT ensuite

B&B per person
from £18.00 Double

Open Jan-Oct
Dinner 1800-2030

Traditional B&B with the best of local Scottish produce and homebaking,
tastefully served in our licensed restaurant from 6.00pm.

Mrs A E MacKinnon
Birchwood, Chapel Brae
Braemar
AB35 5YT
Tel: (Braemar) 013397 41599
Fax: 013397 41440

COMMENDED

1 Single 2 Pub Bath/Show
1 Double
1 Family

B&B per person
£17.50-£18.50 Single
£16.00-£18.00 Double
Room only per person
£16.00-£18.00

Open Jan-Dec

Traditional, stone-built, detached house with large garden, in
peaceful location on edge of village and local nature reserve.

Schiehallion House
Glenshee Road
Braemar
Aberdeenshire
AB35 5YQ
Tel: (Braemar) 013397 41679

COMMENDED

1 Single 5 En Suite fac
3 Twin 1 Pub Bath/Show
3 Double
2 Family

B&B per person
from £18.50 Single
£17.50-£19.50 Double

Open Jan-Oct
Dinner from 1900
B&B + Eve. Meal
£30.00-£32.00

Comfortable, tastefully decorated, Victorian house at gateway to Royal Deeside.
Offering personal service, home cooking, log fires. Some annexed rooms.

BUCKIE
Banffshire
Mrs Marion McKay
Rhiconich, 11 Highfield Road
Buckie
Banffshire
AB56 1BE
Tel: (Buckie) 01542 831465

Map 4
E7

COMMENDED
Listed

2 Twin 1 Pub Bath/Show
1 Double

B&B per person
from £15.00 Single
from £15.00 Double

Open Jan-Dec

Modern detached bungalow in quiet residential area on the outskirts of town.

Mrs Norma Pirie
Rosemount,
62 East Church Street
Buckie
Banffshire
AB56 1ER
Tel: (Buckie) 01542 833434

HIGHLY
COMMENDED

2 Twin 2 En Suite fac
1 Double 1 Priv. NOT ensuite

B&B per person
£17.50-£20.00 Double

Open Jan-Dec

Modernised Victorian detached house, centrally situated
overlooking harbour. Ideal for fishing and golf.

DUFFTOWN
Banffshire
Jennifer & Robin Longhurst
Tullich House
Dufftown
Banffshire
AB55 3JT
Tel: (Dufftown) 01340 821008

Map 4
E9

HIGHLY
COMMENDED
Listed

2 Twin 1 Pub Bath/Show

B&B per person
to £20.00 Single
to £17.50 Double

Open Jan-Dec
Dinner 1900-2100
B&B + Eve. Meal
to £27.50

Tastefully restored period country house, in peaceful rural
setting about 2 miles (3 kms) from Dufftown. Innovative cuisine.

ABERDEEN AND THE NORTH EAST COAST

GRAMPIAN HIGHLANDS,

Details of Grading and Classification are on page vi.

Key to symbols is on back flap.

ABERDEEN AND THE NORTH EAST COAST, GRAMPIAN HIGHLANDS,

DUFFTOWN continued
Banffshire
Mrs E MacMillan
Davaar, Church Street
Dufftown, Keith
Banffshire
AB55 4AR
Tel: (Dufftown) 01340 820464

Map 4
E9

COMMENDED
Listed

1 Twin 2 En Suite fac
2 Double 1 Pub Bath/Show

B&B per person
£13.50-£16.50 Double

Open Jan-Dec
Dinner 1800-2000
B&B + Eve. Meal
from £24.50

Comfortable and personally run accommodation. Close to Whisky
and Castle Trails. Traditional Scottish home baking.

Mrs Lynn Morrison
Nashville, 8a Balvenie Street
Dufftown, Keith
Banffshire
AB55 4AB
Tel: (Dufftown) 01340 820553

COMMENDED

1 Twin 1 Pub Bath/Show
1 Double
1 Family

B&B per person
£12.00-£14.00 Single
£12.00-£14.00 Double

Open Jan-Dec

Family run home in town centre. Convenient for Whisky Trail.
A warm welcome awaits you.

Mrs Mary M Robertson
11 Conval Street
Dufftown, Keith
Banffshire
AB55 4AE
Tel: (Dufftown) 01340 820818

COMMENDED

1 Twin 1 Pub Bath/Show
1 Double

B&B per person
£13.00-£14.00 Double

Open Jan-Dec
Dinner 1800-2000
B&B + Eve. Meal
£20.00-£21.00

Warm welcome at quiet modern bungalow, off main street
18 miles (29 kms) south of Elgin. On Whisky Trail.

Tannochbrae Guest House
& Restaurant
22 Fife Street
Dufftown, Keith
Banffshire
AB55 4AL
Tel: (Dufftown) 01340 820541

COMMENDED

1 Single 5 En Suite fac
1 Twin
1 Double
2 Family

B&B per person
£16.50-£20.00 Single
£16.50-£20.00 Double

Open Jan-Dec
Dinner 1800-2100
B&B + Eve. Meal
£26.50-£30.00

Personally run restaurant and guest house in the centre of Dufftown. Scottish
chef specialises in local fare. Ideal for Speyside Way and the famous Whisky Trail.

ELGIN
Moray
Mrs C.C. Ann Cartmell
The Croft, 10 Institution Road
Elgin
Moray
IV30 1QX
Tel: (Elgin) 01343 546004

Map 4
D8

HIGHLY
COMMENDED

1 Single 1 En Suite fac
1 Double 1 Pub Bath/Show
1 Family

B&B per person
from £18.00 Single
£18.00-£21.00 Double

Open Jan-Dec

A friendly, family run Victorian townhouse, in quiet residential area, within
walking distance of local amenities. Large comfortable rooms totally refurbished.

The Lodge Guest House
20 Duff Avenue
Elgin
Moray
IV30 1QS
Tel: (Elgin) 01343 549981

HIGHLY
COMMENDED

4 Single 8 En Suite fac
2 Twin
1 Double
1 Family

B&B per person
£17.00-£23.00 Single
£17.00-£19.00 Double

Open Jan-Dec

Recently refurbished Listed villa in extensive grounds with private parking.
Quietly situated but convenient for all amenities.

Mrs Anne Munn
Carronvale
18 South Guildry Street
Elgin
Moray
IV30 1QN
Tel: (Elgin) 01343 546864

APPROVED

1 Twin 1 Pub Bath/Show
2 Double

B&B per person
£17.00-£20.00 Single
£14.00-£16.00 Double

Open Jan-Dec
Dinner 1830-1930
B&B + Eve. Meal
£22.50-£28.50

Victorian townhouse partly given over to form art gallery.
Non-smokers only. Close to town centre.

VAT is shown at 17.5%: changes in this rate may affect prices. Prices shown are for guidance only. Please send SAE with each enquiry.

Southbank Guest House 36 Academy Street Elgin Moray IV30 1LP Tel: (Elgin) 01343 547132		COMMENDED	2 Single 2 Twin 3 Double 4 Family	5 En Suite fac 3 Pub Bath/Show	B&B per person £17.00-£23.00 Single £16.00-£20.00 Double	Open Jan-Dec Dinner from 1800 B&B + Eve. Meal £21.50-£25.50

Family run, Georgian detached house in quiet residential street.
5 minutes' walk from railway station and town centre.

by ELGIN Moray	Map 4 D8

ARDGYE HOUSE
Elgin, Moray IV30 3UP   Tel/Fax: 01343 850618

ARDGYE HOUSE is a spacious mansion house set in 150 acres, situated close to main Aberdeen to Inverness road (3.5 miles west of Elgin). Superb accommodation in quiet surroundings. Central position ideal for beaches, golf, riding, fishing, castles and distilleries.

For full details contact Carol and Alistair McInnes.

Ardgye House Elgin Moray IV30 3UP Tel: (Alves) 01343 850618 Fax: 01343 850618		HIGHLY COMMENDED	1 Single 2 Twin 3 Double 3 Family	4 En Suite fac 2 Limited ensuite 3 Priv. NOT ensuite	B&B per person £16.00-£20.00 Single £16.00-£18.00 Double	Open Jan-Dec

Gracious Edwardian mansion in own extensive grounds easily accessible from A96. 3 miles (5 kms) from Elgin. Private facilities available.

ELLON Aberdeenshire Ashlea House 58 Station Road Ellon Aberdeenshire AB41 9AL Tel: (Ellon) 01358 720263	Map 4 G9	COMMENDED	2 Twin	1 Pub Bath/Show	B&B per person £14.00-£15.00 Double	Open Jan-Dec

Delightful family run Victorian house, close to local amenities.
Handy for Castle and Whisky Trails.

by ELLON Aberdeenshire Mrs I Jamieson Mains of Leask Slains, by Ellon Aberdeenshire AB41 8LA Tel: (Auchleuchries) 01358 711242	Map 4 G9	COMMENDED Listed	1 Twin 1 Double	1 Pub Bath/Show	B&B per person from £15.00 Single from £13.50 Double	Open May-Sep

Comfortable accommodation on working farm, near coast, with easy access to beaches, golf courses and Castle Trail. Ideal touring base.

FINDHORN Moray Mrs E Cowie Heath House Findhorn Moray IV36 0YY Tel: (Findhorn) 01309 691082 Fax: 01309 691082	Map 4 C7	HIGHLY COMMENDED Listed	1 Twin 2 Double	1 En Suite fac 1 Pub Bath/Show	B&B per person £18.00-£20.00 Double	Open Feb-Oct

Modern house in secluded setting on outskirts of Findhorn close to beach.
Warm and friendly welcome.

by FOCHABERS Moray Mrs Mary K Shand Castlehill Cottage, Blackdam Fochabers Moray IV32 7LJ Tel: (Fochabers) 01343 820761	Map 4 E8	COMMENDED	1 Twin 1 Family	2 Pub Bath/Show	B&B per person from £14.00 Single from £12.00 Double Room only per person from £9.00	Open Jan-Dec

Family cottage set back from A96, with own flower garden
and ample parking. 6 miles (10 kms) east of Elgin.

Details of Grading and Classification are on page vi.   Key to symbols is on back flap.   213

ABERDEEN AND THE NORTH EAST COAST, GRAMPIAN HIGHLANDS,

FORDYCE Banffshire	Map 4 F7		

ACADEMY HOUSE

School Road, Fordyce, Banffshire AB45 2SJ Tel: 01261 842743

Situated close to the Moray Firth, Academy House is an ideal base for visitors who wish to explore the secrets of the coast or the treasures of Grampian and the near Highlands. Step inside the former headmaster's house and experience the warmth and hospitality of a beautifully restored family home.

Mrs Leith Academy House, School Road Fordyce Banffshire AB45 2SJ · Tel: (Portsoy) 01261 842743	DELUXE Listed	1 Twin 2 Double	2 Pub Bath/Show	B&B per person £18.00-£20.00 Single £15.00-£18.00 Double	Open Jan-Dec Dinner 1900-2030 B&B + Eve. Meal £25.00-£30.00
		Scottish hospitality in stylish country home set in beautiful conservation village. Quality cooking with local produce. Well located for touring.			

FORRES Moray Mrs Catherine M Bain Springfield, Croft Road Forres Moray IV36 0JS Tel: (Forres) 01309 676965 Fax: 01309 673376	Map 4 C8 HIGHLY COMMENDED 👑👑	1 Double 1 Family	2 En Suite fac	B&B per person £18.00-£22.00 Single to £17.50 Double	Open Jan-Dec
		Large, comfortable, modern home set in own grounds. Non-smoking house.			

Mrs Jacqueline S Banks April Rise, 16 Forbes Road Forres Moray IV36 0HP Tel: (Forres) 01309 674066	COMMENDED Listed	1 Single 1 Twin 1 Family	2 En Suite fac 1 Pub Bath/Show	B&B per person from £16.50 Single £14.50-£16.50 Double	Open Jan-Dec Dinner 1800-1900 B&B + Eve. Meal £21.00-£23.50
		Traditional Scottish hospitality in friendly family home. Ideal touring base.			

Mrs Barbara MacDonald Morven, Caroline Street Forres Moray IV36 0AN Tel: (Forres) 01309 673788 Fax: 01309 673788	COMMENDED 👑👑	2 Twin	1 Priv. NOT ensuite 2 Pub Bath/Show	B&B per person £16.00-£18.00 Single £16.00-£18.00 Double	Open Jan-Dec
		Bed and Breakfast in a warm friendly family atmosphere, with all conveniences.			

Mr and Mrs B MacDonald The Pines, Victoria Road Forres Moray IV36 0BN Tel: (Forres) 01309 673810	COMMENDED 👑👑	1 Twin 1 Family	1 En Suite fac 1 Priv. NOT ensuite	B&B per person £15.00-£18.00 Single £15.00-£18.50 Double	Open Jan-Dec
		Traditional Victorian terraced house, original features throughout. Convenient for town amenities.			

Mrs L Ross Tormhor Guest House 11 High Street Forres Moray IV36 0BU Tel: (Forres) 01309 673837	COMMENDED 👑👑	1 Twin 2 Double	1 En Suite fac 2 Pub Bath/Show	B&B per person from £16.00 Single from £14.00 Double Room only per person from £11.00	Open Apr-Oct
		Relax in pleasant, comfortable surroundings, overlooking prize-winning gardens. Friendly service and full Scottish breakfast.			

VAT is shown at 17.5%: changes in this rate may affect prices. Prices shown are for guidance only. Please send SAE with each enquiry.

by FORRES **Moray** Mrs Flora Barclay Moss-Side Farm, Rafford Forres Moray IV36 0SL Tel: (Forres) 01309 672954	Map 4 C8	COMMENDED Listed	1 Twin 1 Double 1 Family	1 Pub Bath/Show	B&B per person £13.00 Single £13.00 Double Room only per person £9.00	Open May-Sep `Dinner 1900-2000 B&B + Eve. Meal from £23.00

Traditional farmhouse with modern extension set in 28 acres (11ha) on the outskirts of Forres. Ideal for golf, fishing and walking.

Mrs Angela Fowler Invercairn House, Brodie Forres Moray IV36 0TD Tel: (Brodie) 01309 641261		COMMENDED	2 Single 2 Twin 1 Family	2 Pub Bath/Show	B&B per person £13.00-£16.00 Single £13.00-£16.00 Double	Open Jan-Dec Dinner 1800-2100 B&B + Eve. Meal from £19.50

Intriguing, former Victorian railway station adjacent to Brodie Castle. Excellent touring base. Local produce, deliciously prepared. Warm, comfortable and friendly atmosphere.

FRASERBURGH **Aberdeenshire** Mrs M Greig Clifton House 131 Charlotte Street Fraserburgh Aberdeenshire AB43 9LS Tel: (Fraserburgh) 01346 518365	Map 4 G7	COMMENDED	2 Single 1 Double 1 Family	1 En Suite fac 1 Limited ensuite 2 Pub Bath/Show	B&B per person from £16.00 Single from £15.00 Double	Open Jan-Dec

Family run guest house in centre of Fraserburgh. Near shopping facilities and all amenities. On main bus routes.

FYVIE **Aberdeenshire** Mrs M Wyness Meikle Camaloun Fyvie Aberdeenshire AB53 8JY Tel: (Fyvie) 01651 891319	Map 4 G9	COMMENDED	1 Twin 1 Double	1 En Suite fac 1 Priv. NOT ensuite	B&B per person from £25.00 Single £20.00-£22.00 Double	Open Mar-Nov

Large comfortable farmhouse, with inviting garden and superb views over rolling farmland. Ideal for Whisky and Castle Trails. Close to Fyvie Castle.

GAMRIE **Banffshire** Lucy R Smith Bankhead Croft Gamrie Banffshire Tel: (Gardenstown) 01261 851584	Map 4 G7	COMMENDED	1 Twin 1 Double 1 Family	2 En Suite fac 1 Priv. NOT ensuite 1 Pub Bath/Show	B&B per person £15.00-£17.00 Single from £16.50 Double Room only per person from £12.00	Open Jan-Dec Dinner 1800-2100 B&B + Eve. Meal £24.00-£24.50

Modern country cottage in peaceful surroundings. 2 miles (3 kms) from coast. 6 miles (10 kms) east of Banff. Home cooking. Large caravan available.

GARDENSTOWN **Banffshire** Mrs Broom The Old Bank House 69 Strait Path Gardenstown Banffshire AB45 3ZQ Tel: (Banff) 01261 851497 Fax: 01261 851497	Map 4 G7	APPROVED Listed	1 Twin 1 Family	2 Priv. NOT ensuite 1 Pub Bath/Show	B&B per person £15.00-£17.00 Double	Open Jan-Dec

A former fisherman's cottage, it boasts fine sea views from attic rooms, and much photographed scene from the front door. With steep stairs not suitable for disabilities.

Mrs P Duncan Palace Farm Gamrie, by Banff Banffshire AB45 3HS Tel: (Gardenstown) 01261 851261		COMMENDED	1 Twin 1 Double 1 Family	2 En Suite fac 1 Priv. NOT ensuite 1 Pub Bath/Show	B&B per person £17.00-£19.00 Single £18.00 Double	Open Mar-Nov Dinner 1830-2100

Warm welcome in family farmhouse only 2 miles (3 kms) from the sea. Excellent home cooking.

ABERDEEN AND THE NORTH EAST COAST, GRAMPIAN HIGHLANDS,

Details of Grading and Classification are on page vi.

Key to symbols is on back flap.

by GARMOUTH	Map 4
Moray	E7

COMMENDED

Mrs Lorna Smith
Gladhill Farm
Garmouth, Fochabers
Moray
IV32 7NN
Tel: (Spey Bay) 01343 870331

1 Single 2 Pub Bath/Show
1 Twin
1 Family

B&B per person
from £15.00 Single
£14.00 Double

Open May-Sep
Dinner from 1830
B&B + Eve. Meal
from £21.00

Traditional Scottish hospitality in friendly farmhouse. Ideal touring base.

GLENLIVET	Map 4
Banffshire	D9

Roadside Cottage

Tomnavoulin, Glenlivet, Ballindalloch, Banffshire AB37 9JL
Telephone: 01807 590486
Awake to bird-song, the aroma of a traditional breakfast, a stunning view from your window. Every guest is a VIP in this land of moor and hills, rivers and ski-slopes, birds and wildlife – and whisky! This is the good life! Scotvec Certificate of Excellence.
Member of Pride of Moray.

HIGHLY COMMENDED Listed

Mrs Rita Marks
Roadside Cottage, Tomnavoulin
Glenlivet, Ballindalloch
Banffshire
AB37 9JL
Tel: (Glenlivet) 01807 590486

1 Single 1 Pub Bath/Show
1 Double
1 Family

B&B per person
£14.00-£17.00 Single
£14.00-£17.00 Double

Open Jan-Dec
exc Xmas
Dinner 1800-2200
B&B + Eve. Meal
£20.00-£24.00

Traditional, stone-built Highland cottage tastefully restored to modern standards.
Children and pets welcome.

HUNTLY	Map 4
Aberdeenshire	F9

COMMENDED

Mr & Mrs D Calcraft
Braeside, Provost Street
Huntly
Aberdeenshire
AB54 5BB
Tel: (Huntly) 01466 793825

1 Single 1 En Suite fac
1 Twin   1 Pub Bath/Show
1 Double

B&B per person
from £15.00 Single
£15.00-£18.00 Double

Open Jan-Dec

Modern detached house with private parking in quiet location.
Close to town centre, railway station and all amenities.

COMMENDED

Dunedin Guest House
17 Bogie Street
Huntly
Aberdeenshire
AB54 5DX
Tel: (Huntly) 01466 794162

4 Twin   6 En Suite fac
1 Double
1 Family

B&B per person
£23.00 Single
£18.50 Double

Open Jan-Dec

Totally refurbished guest house in quiet street close to town centre.
Ample parking. On Castle and Whisky Trails.

COMMENDED

Mrs Manson
Greenmount, 43 Gordon Street
Huntly
Aberdeenshire
AB54 5EQ
Tel: (Huntly) 01466 792482

2 Single 4 En Suite fac
4 Twin   1 Priv. NOT ensuite
2 Family 1 Pub Bath/Show

B&B per person
£15.00-£20.00 Single
£15.00-£18.00 Double

Open Jan-Dec,
ex Xmas/New Year
Dinner 1800-1900
B&B + Eve. Meal
£24.00-£29.00

c.1854 townhouse with annexe. Friendly personal attention, laundry room,
private parking. In town centre but quiet. On Castle and Whisky Trails.

COMMENDED

Mrs R M Thomson
Southview, Victoria Road
Huntly
Aberdeenshire
AB54 5AH
Tel: (Huntly) 01466 792456

2 Twin   2 Pub Bath/Show
1 Double
1 Family

B&B per person
£14.00 Single
£14.00 Double

Open Jan-Dec
Dinner 1700-1800

Detached Victorian house in quiet residential area close to town centre.
Overlooking the bowling green.

by HUNTLY **Aberdeenshire** Mrs A J Morrison Haddoch Farm Huntly Aberdeenshire AB54 4SL Tel: (Rothiemay) 01466 711217	Map 4 F9	**COMMENDED** Listed	1 Double 1 Family	2 Pub Bath/Show	B&B per person £14.00-£15.00 Single £13.00-£14.00 Double	Open Apr-Sep Dinner 1800-2000 B&B + Eve. Meal £18.00-£20.00	

Mixed stock/arable farm near River Deveron, on B9022, 3 miles (5 kms) from Huntly and 15 miles (24 kms) from coast. Fine views of countryside. Home cooking.

Paula Ross Yonder Bognie Forgue, by Huntly Aberdeenshire AB54 6BR Tel: (Forgue) 01466 730375		**COMMENDED**	2 Double	1 Pub Bath/Show	B&B per person £14.00-£15.00 Single £13.50-£14.00 Double	Open Jan-Dec Dinner at 1800 B&B + Eve. Meal £20.00-£22.50	

Traditional family farmhouse on mixed 152-acre (62ha) farm. 7 miles (11 kms) from Huntly, 12 miles (19 kms) from Banff on A97. French and Italian spoken.

INVERURIE **Aberdeenshire** Mrs Black Breaslann, Old Chapel Road Inverurie Aberdeenshire AB51 4QN Tel: (Inverurie) 01467 621608 Fax: 01467 621608	Map 4 G9	**COMMENDED**	5 Twin	5 En Suite fac 1 Pub Bath/Show	B&B per person £20.00-£22.00 Single £15.00-£18.00 Double	Open Jan-Dec	

Modern comfortable bungalow with attractive gardens and off-street parking. 10 minutes' walk from town centre.

Mrs E Harper Broadsea, Burnhervie Inverurie Aberdeenshire AB51 5LB Tel: (Pitcaple) 01467 681386		**COMMENDED**	1 Double	1 En Suite fac	B&B per person £16.00-£18.00 Double	Open Jan-Dec Dinner 1800-1930 B&B + Eve. Meal £24.00-£26.00	

Accommodation of a high standard on this family farm of 200 acres (81ha). Inverurie 5 miles. Aberdeen 20 miles. Bennachie is very close by.

Mrs Milne Earlsmohr, 85 High Street Inverurie Aberdeenshire AB51 3QJ Tel: (Inverurie) 01467 620606		**COMMENDED** Listed	1 Single 1 Double 1 Family	1 Pub Bath/Show	B&B per person £16.00 Single £16.00 Double	Open Jan-Dec	

Detached Edwardian granite-built house with own garden, situated ½ mile (0.8km) from town centre. Non-smoking.

JOHNSHAVEN **Kincardineshire** Mrs Margaret Gibson Ellington, Station Place Johnshaven Kincardineshire DD10 0JD Tel: (Johnshaven) 01561 362756	Map 4 G12	**COMMENDED**	1 Twin 1 Double	2 En Suite fac	B&B per person from £17.00 Single from £17.00 Double	Open Jan-Dec	

New family home, quietly situated in fishing village of Johnshaven. Bedrooms ensuite. One ground-floor bedroom. Off-road parking.

by KEITH **Banffshire** Mrs Eileen Fleming Chapelhill Croft, Grange Keith Banffshire AB55 3LQ Tel: (Grange) 01542 870302	Map 4 E8	**COMMENDED** Listed	1 Twin 1 Double	1 En Suite fac 1 Pub Bath/Show	B&B per person £13.00-£16.00 Double	Open Jan-Dec Dinner 1730-2000 B&B + Eve. Meal £21.50-£24.50	

Warm, friendly welcome on working croft. Guests welcome to participate in running of the croft. Home cooking.

Details of Grading and Classification are on page vi.	Key to symbols is on back flap.	217

ABERDEEN AND THE NORTH EAST COAST

GRAMPIAN HIGHLANDS,

by KEITH continued **Banffshire** Mrs Jean Jackson The Haughs Farm Keith Banffshire AB55 3QN Tel: (Keith) 01542 882238	Map 4 E8	COMMENDED 👑👑👑	2 Twin 2 Double	3 En Suite fac 1 Priv. NOT ensuite	B&B per person £15.50-£19.50 Double	Open Apr-Oct Dinner 1800-1900 B&B + Eve. Meal £26.50-£28.50
			Traditional farmhouse on 165-acre (67ha) farm near town, just off main road. On Whisky Trail. Many local sports including golf available at numerous courses.			
KEMNAY **Aberdeenshire** Julie Dainty Backhill of Burnhervie Country Homestay, Kemnay Aberdeenshire AB51 5JT Tel: (Kemnay) 01467 642139	Map 4 F10	HIGHLY COMMENDED Listed	1 Twin 1 Double	2 Priv. NOT ensuite 1 Pub Bath/Show	B&B per person £25.00-£28.00 Single £25.00-£28.00 Double	Open Apr-Sep
			Beautifully restored Victorian farmhouse with stylish, very comfortable accommodation. Set beside the River Don, with large garden. A wonderfully tranquil haven.			
LOSSIEMOUTH **Moray** Jean & Gordon Cox Mormond, Prospect Terrace Lossiemouth Moray IV31 6JS Tel: (Lossiemouth) 01343 813143	Map 4 D7	HIGHLY COMMENDED 👑	1 Twin 2 Double	2 Pub Bath/Show	B&B per person £14.50-£20.00 Single £14.50-£15.00 Double	Open Jan-Nov
			Traditional villa in quiet residential area, with outstanding view across Moray Firth. Close to all amenities. Friendly, happy atmosphere.			
Mrs Marjorie MacKenzie Moray View, 1 Seatown Road Lossiemouth Moray IV31 6JL Tel: (Lossiemouth) 01343 813915		COMMENDED 👑	1 Twin 2 Double	2 Pub Bath/Show	B&B per person to £18.00 Single to £15.00 Double	Open Jan-Dec
			350-year-old house of character immediately on sea front, overlooking harbour and beach. Convenient for town centre and all amenities.			
Mrs Jean R McPherson Skerry Lodge, Stotfield Road Lossiemouth Moray IV31 6QR Tel: (Lossiemouth) 01343 814981		COMMENDED 👑👑	1 Twin 2 Double	1 En Suite fac 1 Pub Bath/Show	B&B per person £14.00-£16.00 Single £14.00-£16.00 Double Room only per person £12.00-£14.00	Open Jan-Dec
			Traditional, family-run establishment, with friendly atmosphere. Situated on seafront with magnificent views of Moray Firth. No smoking. Residents' lounge.			
Mrs Anne Main Letchworth Lodge Dunbar Street Lossiemouth Moray IV31 6AN Tel: (Lossiemouth) 01343 812132		COMMENDED Listed	2 Twin 1 Double	1 Pub Bath/Show	B&B per person £14.00-£15.50 Double	Open Jan-Dec
			Traditional family run guest house with friendly atmosphere. Convenient for championship golf course, beach and town.			
Mrs Jennifer I Toye 45 St Gerardines Road Lossiemouth Moray IV31 6JX Tel: (Lossiemouth) 01343 812276		COMMENDED 👑	1 Twin 1 Double	1 Pub Bath/Show	B&B per person £14.00-£18.00 Double	Open Apr-Oct
			Modern detached bungalow with large garden in residential area on south side of town centre. Within walking distance of beach, golf and bowling.			

MACDUFF
Banffshire
Mr G C Brittain
50 Duff Street
Macduff
Banffshire
AB44 1LQ
Tel: (Macduff) 01261 832920

Map 4
F7

COMMENDED

2 Twin   2 En Suite fac   B&B per person   Open Mar-Oct
1 Family   1 Priv. NOT ensuite   £15.00-£17.50 Single
  1 Pub Bath/Show   £15.00-£17.50 Double

Situated in harbour town. Central for golfing, fishing, sailing, bowls,
as well as places of interest. Golfing parties catered for, including transport.

Mrs Kathleen Greig
11 Gellymill Street
Macduff
Banffshire
AB44 1TN
Tel: (Macduff) 01261 833314

COMMENDED
Listed

1 Twin   1 Pub Bath/Show   B&B per person   Open Jan-Dec
1 Double   from £13.00 Single   Dinner 1930-2000
   from £12.00 Double   B&B + Eve. Meal
   £18.00-£20.00

Comfortable family home in quiet street, near to harbour in small fishing town.
Home cooking and baking.

METHLICK
Aberdeenshire
Mrs C Staff
Sunnybrae Farm, Gight
Methlick, Ellon
Aberdeenshire
AB41 0JA
Tel: (Methlick) 01651 806456

Map 4
G9

APPROVED

1 Single   2 En Suite fac   B&B per person   Open Jan-Dec
1 Twin   1 Pub Bath/Show   £17.00-£20.00 Single
1 Double   £17.00-£20.00 Double

Comfortable accommodation on a working farm, in a quiet peaceful location
with superb views. Close to castle and whisky trails.

NEWMACHAR
Aberdeenshire
Mrs V Horne
7 Reisque Avenue
Newmachar, Aberdeen
AB21 0PP
Tel: (Newmachar)
01651 862384

Map 4
G10

COMMENDED
Listed

1 Twin   1 Pub Bath/Show   B&B per person   Open Jan-Dec
1 Double   £14.00-£15.00 Single
   £12.50-£14.00 Double
   Room only per person
   £10.00

Semi-detached house in quiet location, in village 10 miles (16 kms)
North of Aberdeen. Warm welcome assured.

OLD DEER, by Peterhead
Aberdeenshire
Mrs Rhind
Old Deer Bank House
6 Abbey Street, Old Deer
Aberdeenshire
AB42 8LN
Tel: (Mintlaw) 01771 623463

Map 4
G8

COMMENDED

1 Twin   2 En Suite fac   B&B per person   Open Jan-Dec
1 Double   £17.00-£18.00 Single
   £17.00-£18.00 Double

Originally village bank, now comfortable family home, tastefully refurbished.
In centre of quiet historic village. Close to Aden Country Park.

OLDMELDRUM
Aberdeenshire

Map 4
G9

CROMLET HILL
SOUTH ROAD, OLDMELDRUM, ABERDEENSHIRE AB51 0AB
Telephone: 01651 872315   Fax: 01651 872164

A superb Listed building overlooking *Bennachie* and the *Grampian Hills*
beyond. Recently restored, the original features are retained inside and
out and the house is furnished in sympathetic and luxurious style. Set
in beautiful secluded gardens including a large Victorian conservatory.
Private parking. Aberdeen City Centre 30 minutes.

John Page
Cromlet Hill, South Road
Oldmeldrum
Aberdeenshire
AB51 0AB
Tel: (Oldmeldrum)
01651 872315
Fax: 01651 872164

DELUXE

1 Twin   3 En Suite fac   B&B per person   Open Jan-Dec
1 Double   £24.00-£35.00 Single   Dinner from 1930
1 Family   £20.00-£30.00 Double   B&B + Eve. Meal
   £35.00-£50.00

Spacious, elegant, Listed Georgian mansion, in large secluded
gardens within conservation area. Airport 20 minutes.

Details of Grading and Classification are on page vi.

Key to symbols is on back flap.

OLD RAYNE – STONEHAVEN

Left margin: ABERDEEN AND THE NORTH EAST COAST, GRAMPIAN HIGHLANDS,

Location / Contact	Map	Grading	Rooms	Facilities	Prices	Opening
OLD RAYNE **Aberdeenshire** Mill Croft Guest House Old Rayne, by Inverurie Aberdeenshire AB52 6RY Tel: (Old Rayne) 01464 851210	Map 4 G9	HIGHLY COMMENDED	1 Twin 1 Double 1 Family	2 En Suite fac 1 Priv. NOT ensuite	B&B per person £16.00-£18.00 Single £16.00-£18.00 Double B&B + Eve. Meal £23.00-£25.00	Open Jan-Dec Dinner 1830-1930

Friendly welcome at working croft with excellent views over Grampian countryside. On Castle Trail. Residential woodcraft courses.

| **PETERHEAD** **Aberdeenshire** Carrick Guest House 16 Merchant Street Peterhead Aberdeenshire AB42 6DU Tel: (Peterhead) 01779 470610 Fax: 01779 470610 | Map 4 H8 | COMMENDED | 2 Single 3 Twin 2 Family | 7 En Suite fac | B&B per person £17.00-£25.00 Single £17.00-£20.00 Double | Open Jan-Dec |

Comfortable accommodation, centrally situated for all amenities. Two minutes' walk from main shopping centre, harbour and beach.

| **ST CYRUS** **Kincardineshire** Mrs A Coates Burnmouth St Cyrus Kincardineshire DD10 0DL Tel: (St Cyrus) 01674 850430 | Map 4 G12 | COMMENDED Listed | 1 Single 1 Twin 2 Double 1 Family | 2 En Suite fac 1 Priv. NOT ensuite 2 Pub Bath/Show | B&B per person £17.00-£18.00 Single £16.00-£17.00 Double Room only per person £14.00 | Open Mar-Oct Dinner 1800-2000 |

In small hamlet overlooking the sea, 7 miles (11 kms) North of Montrose. Fishing can be arranged, good base for touring.

| Mrs Alison Williamson Kirkside Bothy St Cyrus Nature Reserve St Cyrus Kincardineshire DD10 0AQ Tel: (Montrose) 01674 830780 | | COMMENDED Listed | 3 Twin 1 Family | 4 En Suite fac | B&B per person £18.00 Single £18.00 Double | Open Jan-Dec |

Stone-built 19th century former fishing station, converted to provide ensuite bedroom accommodation. In peaceful location overlooking St Cyrus Nature Reserve and sandy beach.

| **STONEHAVEN** **Kincardineshire** Arduthie House Ann Street Stonehaven Kincardineshire AB3 2DA Tel: (Stonehaven) 01569 762381 Fax: 01569 762381 | Map 4 G11 | COMMENDED | 1 Twin 1 Double 2 Family | 3 En Suite fac 1 Pub Bath/Show | B&B per person £18.00-£20.00 Single £17.00-£20.00 Double | Open Jan-Dec Dinner at 1830 |

Detached Victorian house with large attractive garden, situated in the centre of Stonehaven. Spacious guests' lounge on first floor.

| Mrs V Craib Car-Lyn-Vale Rickarton, by Stonehaven Kincardineshire AB39 3TD Tel: (Stonehaven) 01569 762406 | | HIGHLY COMMENDED | 1 Twin 2 Double | 3 En Suite fac | B&B per person £20.00-£25.00 Single £17.50-£19.50 Double | Open Apr-Oct |

Friendly B&B. Non-smoking. 10 minutes from Stonehaven in rural setting. Ensuite facilities. Ample, safe parking, in spacious grounds.

| Mrs E M Duguid Dunnottar Mains Farm Stonehaven Kincardineshire AB3 2TL Tel: (Stonehaven) 01569 762621 Fax: 01569 762621 | | COMMENDED Listed | 1 Double 1 Family | 1 Pub Bath/Show | B&B per person £16.00-£17.00 Double | Open Apr-Oct |

Traditional farmhouse welcome at this working farm, overlooking Dunnottar Castle on the coast.

VAT is shown at 17.5%: changes in this rate may affect prices. Prices shown are for guidance only. Please send SAE with each enquiry.

Mrs A Paton Woodside of Grasslaw Stonehaven Kincardineshire AB3 2XQ Tel: (Stonehaven) 01569 763799		COMMENDED 👑 👑	2 Twin 1 Double 1 Family	4 En Suite fac	B&B per person £19.00-£21.00 Single £17.00-£19.50 Double	Open Jan-Dec	

Modern bungalow in rural setting, yet within easy access to main routes and Deeside. Ample parking. All rooms ensuite. Warm welcome assured.

Windsor Grove Guest House Fetteresso Stonehaven Kincardine AB39 3UT Tel: (Stonehaven) 01569 766299/764257 Fax: 01569 766221		COMMENDED 👑 👑	1 Twin 1 Double 1 Family	3 En Suite fac	B&B per person to £19.00 Single to £17.50 Double	Open Jan-Dec	

Family run, modern house, 1.5 miles (2.5 kms) from Stonehaven. In quiet country location. Easy access to A94. Ample safe off-road parking.

STRATHDON **Aberdeenshire** Mrs E Ogg Farmhouse Bed & Breakfast Buchaam Holiday Properties Buchaam Farm Strathdon Aberdeenshire AB36 8TN Tel: (Strathdon) 019756 51238 Fax: 019756 51238	**Map 4** **E10**	COMMENDED Listed	1 Twin 1 Double 1 Family	2 Pub Bath/Show	B&B per person £14.00 Double	Open May-Oct	

Large farmhouse on 600-acre (243ha) mixed farm with sporting facilities, including badminton, table tennis and putting green. Free river fishing.

by TOMINTOUL **Banffshire** Irene Duffus Auchriachan Farmhouse, Mains of Auchriachan Tomintoul Ballindalloch, Banffshire AB37 9EQ Tel: (Tomintoul) 01807 580416	**Map 4** **D10**	COMMENDED 👑 👑	1 Twin 1 Double 1 Family	2 En Suite fac	B&B per person £14.00-£16.00 Double	Open Jan-Dec	

Traditional farmhouse 1 mile (2 kms) from Tomintoul centre. Ideal for skiing holiday.

Mrs Anne Shearer Croughly Farm Tomintoul, Ballindalloch Banffshire AB37 9EN Tel: (Tomintoul) 01807 580476		COMMENDED 👑 👑	1 Double 1 Family	1 En Suite fac 1 Priv. NOT ensuite	B&B per person £17.00 Single £14.00-£15.00 Double	Open Apr-Oct	

18th century Listed farmhouse, overlooking the River Conglass with stunning views of the Cairngorms. 2 miles (3 kms) from Tomintoul.

Mrs Elma Turner Findron Farm, Braemar Road Tomintoul Banffshire AB37 9ER Tel: (Tomintoul) 01807 580382		HIGHLY COMMENDED 👑 👑 👑	2 Double 1 Family	2 En Suite fac 1 Priv. NOT ensuite	B&B per person £14.00-£17.00 Single £14.00-£17.00 Double	Open Jan-Dec Dinner 1800-1930 B&B + Eve. Meal £19.00-£25.00	

Comfortable farmhouse with a warm and friendly welcome, situated 1 mile (2 kms) from Tomintoul. Ensuite and private bathrooms.

by TURRIFF **Aberdeenshire** Mrs C R M Roebuck Lendrum Farm, Birkenhills by Turriff Aberdeenshire AB53 8HA Tel: (Cuminestown) 01888 544285	**Map 4** **F8**	COMMENDED 👑 👑	1 Twin 1 Family	1 En Suite fac 1 Pub Bath/Show	B&B per person £17.00-£20.00 Single £17.00-£20.00 Double Room only per person £15.00-£16.00	Open Jan-Dec	

Historic working farm in Buchan countryside. Near picturesque coast, castles, gardens, distilleries. Warm welcome, comfortable, good food, peaceful.

ABERDEEN AND THE NORTH EAST COAST

GRAMPIAN HIGHLANDS,

Details of Grading and Classification are on page vi.

Key to symbols is on back flap.

Welcome to...

The Highlands and Skye

The largest loch by water volume (Loch Ness), the highest mountain (Ben Nevis), the most westerly place on mainland Britain (Ardnamurchan Point), the most spectacular mountain range (the Cuillins of Skye): superlatives abound in the Highlands and Skye.

Though the scenery is grand and wild, the sense of remoteness is tempered by excellent communications and transport links by road, rail and air. (Inverness Airport, for example, has direct London flights, while Skye now has its own bridge.) This in turn means that distance is no deterrent for that early spring break or autumn holiday, when the landscapes have that special sparkle. Besides, the Highlands' increasing resident population, as more and more escape to the unspoilt northlands, means an even better choice of accommodation and more places to eat than ever before.

The area is also big enough to have its own scenic variety, from the soaring crags of Glen Coe, looming over the main road, to the wide-open rolling moors of Caithness in the north, where the sense of space and sky is inspiring. Then there are the old pinewoods of upper Speyside, with the Cairngorms in the background; the long reaches of the Great Glen, whose most famous loch hides a monster mystery; the sunny shores of the inner Moray Firth around the resort of Nairn with its fine golf courses, and the glorious vistas to the Small Isles from the 'Road to the Isles' between Fort William and Mallaig (even better by rail). From the big glens such as Cannich and Affric on the backbone of Scotland, to the ancient sandstones from which the Torridon mountains are shaped, the north and west offer unmatched scenic spectacle, dramatic at every season.

Though the scenery is grand, there are also substantial towns with everything for the visitor. Inverness is often called the capital of the Highlands and is a natural gateway and route centre to the north.

Though the scenery is grand, there are also substantial towns with everything for the visitor. Inverness is often called the capital of the Highlands and is a natural gateway and route centre to the north. At the other end of the Great Glen, Fort William, in the shadow of Ben Nevis, is another busy location with an excellent range of tourist facilities. The eastern seaboard has a string of attractive towns, for example, picturesque Dornoch with its cathedral and famous golf course, while, further north, Wick and Thurso are other major centres.

In these towns and in other places there is plenty to entertain the visitor.

You can ride a steam railway from Aviemore to Boat of Garten, or walk a treetop trail at the Landmark Centre at Carrbridge. You can explore the Norse connection at the Northlands Viking Centre beyond Wick, pan for gold near Helmsdale, or discover the life of the crofters on Skye. There are boat trips to see dolphins, four-wheel drive safaris in Speyside, self-guided tape tours of the attractive little burgh of Cromarty in Easter Ross, and a glorious garden at Inverewe which is in the same latitude as Leningrad – but a lot milder thanks to the Gulf Stream. All this and mountains, too! The Highlands and Skye are nearer than you think.

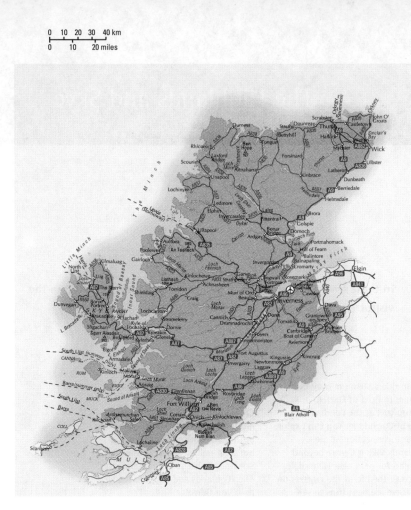

AREA TOURIST BOARD ADDRESSES

THE HIGHLANDS OF SCOTLAND TOURIST BOARD
Information Centre
Grampian Road
AVIEMORE
Inverness-shire
PH22 1PP
Tel: 0990 143070
Fax: 01479 811063

TOURIST INFORMATION CENTRES IN SCOTLAND

THE HIGHLANDS OF SCOTLAND TOURIST BOARD

AVIEMORE ♿ ✉
Grampian Road
Inverness-shire
PH22 1PP
Tel: (01479) 810363
Jan-Dec

BALLACHULISH
Argyll
Tel: (01855) 811296
April-Oct

BETTYHILL ♿
Clachan
Sutherland
Tel: (01641) 521342
April-end Sept

BROADFORD
Isle of Skye
Tel: (01471) 822361
April-Oct

CARRBRIDGE
Main Street
Inverness-shire
Tel: (01479) 841630
May-Sept

DAVIOT WOOD
A9 by Inverness
Tel: (01463) 772203
April-Oct

DORNOCH ✉
The Square
Sutherland
IV25 3SD
Tel: (01862) 810400
Jan-Dec

DURNESS ♿
Sango
Sutherland
Tel: (01971) 511259
April-end Oct

FORT AUGUSTUS
Car Park
Inverness-shire
Tel: (01320) 366367
April-Oct

FORT WILLIAM ♿ ✉
Cameron Square
Inverness-shire
PH33 6AJ
Tel: (01397) 703781
Jan-Dec

GAIRLOCH ♿ ✉
Auchtercairn
Ross-shire
Tel: (01445) 712130
Jan-Dec

GLENSHIEL
Shiel Bridge
Ross-shire
Tel: (01599) 511264
April-Oct

GRANTOWN ON SPEY
High Street
Morayshire
Tel: (01479) 872773
April-Oct

HELMSDALE
Coupar Park
Sutherland
Tel (01431) 821640
Apr-end Sep

INVERNESS ✉
Castle Wynd
IV2 3BJ
Tel: (01463) 234353
Jan-Dec

JOHN O'GROATS
County Road
Caithness
Tel: (01955) 611373
April-Oct

KILCHOAN
Argyll
Tel: (01972) 510222
April-Oct

KINGUSSIE
King Street
Inverness-shire
Tel: (01540) 661297
May-Sept

KYLE OF LOCHALSH
Car Park
Inverness-shire
Tel: (01599) 534276
April-Oct

LAIRG ♿
Sutherland
Tel: (01549) 402160
April-Oct

LOCHCARRON ♿
Main Street
Ross-shire
Tel: (01520) 722357
Easter-Oct

LOCHINVER ♿
Main Street
Sutherland
Tel: (01571) 844330
April-Oct

MALLAIG
Inverness-shire
Tel: (01687) 462170
April-Oct

NAIRN
62 King Street
Nairnshire
Tel: (01667) 452753
April-Oct

NORTH KESSOCK ♿ ✉
Ross-shire
Tel: (01463) 731505
Jan-Dec

PORTREE ✉
Meall House
Isle of Skye
IV51 9BZ
Tel: (01478) 612137
Jan-Dec

RALIA
A9 North by Newtonmore
Inverness-shire
Tel: (01540) 673253
Jan-Dec

SPEAN BRIDGE
Inverness-shire
Tel: (01397) 712576
April-Oct

STRATHPEFFER ♿
The Square
Ross-shire
Tel: (01997) 421415
April-Nov

STRONTIAN
Argyll
Tel: (01967) 402131
April-Oct

THURSO
Riverside
Tel: (01847) 892371
April-Oct

UIG
Ferry Terminal
Isle of Skye
Tel: (01470) 542404
April-Oct

ULLAPOOL
Argyle Street
Ross-shire
Tel: (01854) 612135
April-Nov

WICK ✉
Whitechapel Road
Caithness
KW1 4EA
Tel: (01955) 602596
Jan-Dec

✉   Accept written enquiries
♿   Disabled access

THE HIGHLANDS & SKYE

ACHARACLE Argyll	Map 3 F12		

BELMONT
Acharacle, Ardnamurchan, Argyll PH36 4JT
Telephone: 01967 431266

Good food and a warm welcome await you at Belmont, a converted manse overlooking Loch Shiel and the Moidart Hills. This family run establishment is the ideal centre for exploring the unspoilt Ardnamurchan Peninsula, with its abundant wildlife, excellent beaches and numerous walks. Ensuite facilities. Children welcome.

Mrs C L Learmouth Belmont Acharacle, Ardnamurchan Argyll PH36 4JT Tel: (Salen) 01967 431266	COMMENDED 👑👑	1 Single 1 Twin 1 Double	2 En Suite fac 1 Priv. NOT ensuite	B&B per person £16.00-£19.00 Single £16.00-£19.00 Double	Open Jan-Dec Dinner 1800-2100 B&B + Eve. Meal £27.00-£30.00	

Former manse, overlooking Loch Shiel towards hills of Moidart. Good home cooking.

ALNESS Ross-shire Mrs Dorothy MacDougall Averon Bank Cottage Ardross Road Alness Ross-shire IV17 0QA Tel: (Alness) 01349 882392	Map 4 B7 COMMENDED 👑👑	3 Twin	3 En Suite fac	B&B per person to £18.00 Single £16.00-£18.00 Double	Open Jan-Dec	

Detached cottage in small cul-de-sac, on the outskirts
of the village, with private garden area.

ARDNAMURCHAN Argyll	Map 3 E12		

Feorag House
Glenborrodale, Acharacle, Argyll PH36 4JP
Telephone: 01972 500248

Feorag House, a haven of comfort, peace, warmth, good food and good friends located in the village of Glenborrodale on the Ardnamurchan Peninsula, the most westerly point of mainland Britain. Set amongst 13 acres of private grounds and only 50 yards from the secluded shoreline, the house enjoys breathtaking views from all ensuite rooms. The excellent cuisine is a sheer delight using mostly local produce. Most activities are readily available with fishing, walking, stalking, sailing and golf all close by. Wildlife abounds from otters, seals and porpoise to pinemartens, wildcats, red deer and golden eagles.

The perfect relaxing holiday.

Feorag House Glenborrodale Acharacle Argyll PH36 4JP Tel: (Glenborrodale) 01972 500248	DELUXE 👑👑👑	1 Twin 2 Double	3 En Suite fac	B&B per person £29.00-£39.00 Single £29.00-£39.00 Double	Open Jan-Dec Dinner 1930-2100 B&B + Eve. Meal £49.00-£59.00	

Delightful country house on shores of Loch Sunart. Peace and tranquillity,
warm and friendly atmosphere with imaginative cuisine. Ideal central location
for exploring Ardnamurchan.

ARISAIG **Inverness-shire** Kinloid Farm Guest House Kinloid, Kilmartin Arisaig Inverness-shire PH39 4NS Tel: (Arisaig) 01687 450366 Fax: 01687 450366	**Map 3** F11	COMMENDED	1 Twin 2 Double	3 En Suite fac 1 Pub Bath/Show	B&B per person from £20.00 Double	Open Apr-Oct Dinner at 1830	

Bungalow-style farmhouse on working farm about 0.5 miles (1 km) from the village. Magnificent sea and mountain views.

Old Library Lodge & Restaurant Arisaig Inverness-shire PH39 Tel: (Arisaig) 01687 450651 Fax: 01687 450219		HIGHLY COMMENDED	1 Twin 5 Double	6 En Suite fac	B&B per person from £42.00 Single from £32.00 Double	Open Apr-Nov Dinner 1830-2130	

Family run restaurant with rooms, specialising in fresh local produce, and home-made bread. Magnificent views to Inner Hebrides. In 'Good Hotel Guide'.

AULTBEA **Ross-shire** Cartmel Guest House Birchburn Road Aultbea Ross-shire IV22 2HZ Tel: (Aultbea) 01445 731375	**Map 3** F6	COMMENDED	2 Twin 2 Double	2 En Suite fac 1 Pub Bath/Show	B&B per person £22.00-£25.00 Single £16.00-£19.00 Double	Open Jan-Dec Dinner from 1830 B&B + Eve. Meal from £28.00	

Comfortable bungalow guest house set in 1.5 acres (0.6ha) of mature garden. Personally run. Vegetarians very welcome. Regret no smoking.

Mrs A MacLennan Sandale, 5 Pier Road Aultbea Ross-shire IV22 2JQ Tel: (Aultbea) 01445 731336		COMMENDED	1 Double 2 Family	3 En Suite fac	B&B per person from £15.00 Single from £15.00 Double	Open Mar-Nov Dinner 1800-2000 B&B + Eve. Meal from £25.00	

House with sun lounge and views over Loch Ewe, set in a colourful garden. Traditional Scottish hospitality. Good home cooking.

Mrs P MacRae Cove View, Mellon Charles Aultbea Ross-shire Tel: (Aultbea) 01445 731351		COMMENDED Listed	1 Single 1 Twin 1 Double	2 Priv. NOT ensuite 2 Pub Bath/Show	B&B per person £15.50 Single £15.00 Double	Open Jan-Dec Dinner 1800-1900	

Cottage in quiet crofting area, 3 miles (5kms) from village of Aultbea. Views out over Loch Ewe.

Mellondale Guest House 47 Mellon Charles Aultbea Ross-shire IV22 2JL Tel: (Aultbea) 01445 731326		HIGHLY COMMENDED	2 Twin 2 Double	4 En Suite fac 2 Pub Bath/Show	B&B per person £17.00-£21.00 Single £17.00-£21.00 Double	Open Feb-Nov Dinner from 1830 B&B + Eve. Meal £26.00-£30.00	

Modern family guest house set in 4 acres (1.6ha), with views of Loch Ewe. 9 miles (14.4 kms) from Inverewe Gardens. Ideal walking centre.

AVIEMORE **Inverness-shire** A'Anside Guest House off Grampian Road (North end) Aviemore Inverness-shire PH22 1QD Tel: (Aviemore) 01479 810871	**Map 4** C10	COMMENDED	1 Twin 2 Double 2 Family	5 En Suite fac	B&B per person £18.00-£21.00 Double	Open Jan-Dec	

Modern bungalow sitting above the town. Stunning views over the town to the Cairngorm Mountains. Most rooms ensuite facilities.

Ardlogie Guest House Dalfaber Road Aviemore Inverness-shire PH22 1PU Tel: (Aviemore) 01479 810747		COMMENDED Listed	1 Twin 4 Double	4 En Suite fac 1 Priv. NOT ensuite	B&B per person £17.00-£19.00 Double	Open Jan-Dec	

Semi-detached house in quiet road, 5 minutes' walk from centre with its many facilities. Ideal for skiing, walking and touring.

THE HIGHLANDS & SKYE

Details of Grading and Classification are on page vi.

Key to symbols is on back flap.

THE HIGHLANDS & SKYE

	Map 4 C10						
AVIEMORE continued **Inverness-shire** Mr R Bruce Hame, Dalfaber Road Aviemore Inverness-shire PH22 1PY Tel: (Aviemore) 01479 810822/ 0836 560174 (mobile)		COMMENDED ♛	1 Twin 2 Double	1 Pub Bath/Show	B&B per person £15.00-£20.00 Single £14.00-£16.00 Double	Open Jan-Dec	

Traditional Scottish hospitality in friendly home, situated in quiet location but only 5 minutes' walk from all amenities.

Mrs Burgon Ardenlea, 13 Craig-na-Gower Aviemore Inverness-shire PH22 1RW Tel: (Aviemore) 01479 811738		COMMENDED Listed	1 Twin 1 Double	2 En Suite fac	B&B per person £16.00-£20.00 Single £13.50-£15.50 Double	Open Jan-Dec	

Traditional Scottish hospitality in friendly family home. Ideal base for touring beautiful Strathspey.

Cairngorm Guest House Grampian Road Aviemore Inverness-shire PH22 1RP Tel: (Aviemore) 01479 810630 Fax: 01479 810630		COMMENDED ♛ ♛	3 Twin 5 Double 1 Family	9 En Suite fac	B&B per person from £20.00 Single £16.00-£20.00 Double	Open Jan-Dec	

Detached stone villa, within 5 minutes' walk of the centre and 10 minutes from bus and rail stations.

Mr and Mrs S Carruthers Iona, 18 Morlich Place Aviemore Inverness-shire PH22 1TH Tel: (Aviemore) 01479 810941 Fax: 01479 811583		COMMENDED ♛ ♛	2 Twin 1 Double	1 En Suite fac 1 Pub Bath/Show	B&B per person £16.50-£18.50 Single £14.50-£16.50 Double	Open Jan-Dec, exc Xmas	

Friendly bed and breakfast in new house, situated towards the north end of the village, at the end of a quiet cul-de-sac. Facilities for outdoor activities.

Mrs E Clark Sonas, 19 Muirton Aviemore Inverness-shire PH22 1SF Tel: (Aviemore) 01479 810409		HIGHLY COMMENDED Listed	1 Twin 2 Double	2 Pub Bath/Show	B&B per person from £17.50 Single from £15.50 Double	Open Jan-Dec excl Xmas/New Year	

Modern detached bungalow in quiet residential area of village. All bedrooms have washbasins, colour TVs and tea/coffee-making facilities.

Mrs A M Ferguson Cairn Eilrig, Glenmore Aviemore Inverness-shire PH22 1QU Tel: (Cairngorm) 01479 861223		COMMENDED Listed	1 Twin 1 Family	1 Pub Bath/Show	B&B per person from £13.00 Double	Open Jan-Dec	

Bungalow situated in Glenmore Forest Park with superb open views of the Cairngorms. Warm Highland hospitality guaranteed. Ski lifts 2 miles (3 kms).

Ms D J Harris Junipers, 5 Dell Mhor Aviemore Inverness-shire PH22 1QW Tel: (Aviemore) 01479 810405/ 0589 923807		COMMENDED Listed	1 Single 1 Double 1 Family	1 En Suite fac 1 Pub Bath/Show	B&B per person £14.00-£16.00 Single £13.50-£14.50 Double	Open Jan-Dec	

Comfortable home with large sun room and Alpine garden, midway between Aviemore and Coylumbridge.

Book your accommodation anywhere in Scotland the easy way – through your nearest Tourist Information Centre.

A booking fee of £2.75 is charged, and you will be asked for a small deposit.

Local bookings are usually free, or a small fee will be charged.

KINAPOL GUEST HOUSE
Dalfaber Road, Aviemore, Inverness-shire PH22 1PY
Tel/Fax: 01479 810513   **Commended** 👑

Small modern guest house in quiet situation, only 5 minutes' walk to station, buses and centre of Aviemore. All bedrooms have H&C, electric blankets, tea/coffee trays etc., and most have views of Cairngorm Mountains. Large bright guests' lounge with TV and hot drinks trolley. Large garden with access to river. Drying cupboard and ski store. Mountain bikes for hire. Reduced rates for week bookings and continental breakfasts. ***Major credit cards accepted***

Kinapol Guest House Dalfaber Road Aviemore Inverness-shire PH22 1PY Tel: (Aviemore) 01479 810513 Fax: 01479 810513	COMMENDED 👑	1 Twin 3 Double 1 Family	2 Pub Bath/Show	B&B per person £15.00-£20.00 Single £14.00-£15.00 Double	Open Jan-Dec	

Friendly welcome at modern house, set in large garden with views of Cairngorms.
Quiet location but only 5 minutes' walk to the town centre.

Lynwilg House Aviemore Inverness-shire PH22 1PZ Tel: (Aviemore) 01479 811685	HIGHLY COMMENDED 👑👑👑	1 Single 1 Twin 2 Double	3 En Suite fac 1 Priv. NOT ensuite	B&B per person £25.00-£35.00 Single £25.00-£35.00 Double	Open Jan-Nov Dinner 1900-2000 B&B + Eve. Meal £40.00-£55.00	

1930s country house set in 4 acres (1.6ha) of landscaped gardens overlooking
the Cairngorms, approximately 1 mile (2 kms) south of Aviemore.

Ravenscraig Guest House Aviemore Inverness-shire PH22 1RP Tel: (Aviemore) 01479 810278	COMMENDED 👑👑	1 Single 4 Twin 5 Double 2 Family	12 En Suite fac	B&B per person £18.00-£22.00 Single £18.00-£22.00 Double Room only per person £15.00-£19.00	Open Jan-Dec	

Situated on edge of village, within a few minutes' walk of Aviemore centre.
All rooms ensuite. Some ground-floor annexe accommodation.

BADACHRO **Ross-shire** Mrs D Moore Hazel Cottage, Leacnasaide Badachro, Gairloch Ross-shire Tel: (Badachro) 01445 741300	Map 3 F7 COMMENDED 👑👑	1 Twin 2 Double	2 En Suite fac 1 Priv. NOT ensuite	B&B per person £17.00-£18.00 Double	Open May-Sep	

Modern detached house with garden. On quiet wooded road.
Badachro 1 mile (2 kms), 4 miles (6 kms) Gairloch.

Mr & Mrs G Willey Harbour View Badachro Ross-shire IV21 2AA Tel: (Badachro) 01445 741316	COMMENDED 👑👑	2 Double 1 Family	3 En Suite fac 1 Pub Bath/Show	B&B per person £17.00-£19.00 Double	Open Mar-Oct Dinner at 1900 B&B + Eve. Meal £26.00-£28.00	

With superb views over Badachro Bay, this extended fisherman's cottage,
having small rooms and coombed ceilings, retains its original period charm.

THE HIGHLANDS & SKYE

BALLACHULISH Argyll	Map 1 F1

Craiglinnhe Guest House

BALLACHULISH, ARGYLL PA39 4JX   Tel/Fax: 01855 811270

Craiglinnhe, situated close to the water's edge amidst magnificent scenery, provides an excellent touring base for the Western Highlands. Set in beautiful gardens, this small, personally managed guest house offers traditional Scottish hospitality in extremely well-appointed accommodation. An ideal setting in which to relax and unwind.

Brochure on request.   Commended ♕♕♕

Craiglinnhe Guest House Ballachulish Argyll PA39 4JX Tel: (Ballachulish) 01855 811270 Fax: 01855 811270	COMMENDED ♕♕♕ 🚶	3 Twin 3 Double	6 En Suite fac	B&B per person £19.00-£21.00 Double	Open Dec-Oct Dinner from 1900 B&B + Eve. Meal £28.00-£31.00

Family run guest house overlooking Loch Linnhe and the mountains beyond. Hillwalking and mountaineering in the area. Good centre for touring.

FERN VILLA GUEST HOUSE

Loanfern, Ballachulish, Argyll PA39 4JE
Telephone: 01855 811393 Fax: 01855 811727

Non-smoking. All rooms ensuite. A warm welcome awaits you in this fine Highland house situated in the lochside village only one mile from Glencoe. The perfect base for walking, climbing or touring in the West Highlands. Quality accommodation, food and wine. D,B&B weekly rate £196. B&B from £17-£20 per person per night. **AA Selected QQQQ**

Fern Villa Guest House Ballachulish Argyll PA39 4JE Tel: (Ballachulish) 01855 811393 Fax: 01855 811727	COMMENDED ♕♕♕	2 Twin 3 Double	5 En Suite fac	B&B per person £17.00-£20.00 Double	Open Jan-Dec Dinner from 1900 B&B + Eve. Meal £27.00-£30.00

Granite-built house in lochside village amidst spectacular scenery, convenient for Fort William. Excellent touring base. Table licence.

Lyn-Leven Guest House Ballachulish Argyll PA39 4JP Tel: (Ballachulish) 01855 811392 Fax: 01855 811600	COMMENDED ♕♕♕	4 Twin 3 Double 1 Family	8 En Suite fac 1 Pub Bath/Show	B&B per person £22.00-£25.00 Single £18.00-£19.50 Double	Open Jan-Dec Dinner from 1830 B&B + Eve. Meal £27.00-£29.50

Family run modern guest house in Ballachulish village and overlooking Loch Leven. All home cooking.

Mr & Mrs M MacAskill Park View, 18 Park Road Ballachulish Argyll PA39 4JS Tel: (Ballachulish) 01855 811560	COMMENDED ♕	1 Twin 2 Double	2 Pub Bath/Show	B&B per person from £12.50 Double	Open Jan-Dec

Family house in quiet residential situation, overlooking a small park. Convenient for Glencoe and Fort William.

Ballachulish Home Farm

Highly Commended

BALLACHULISH, ARGYLL PA39 4JX

A warm welcome awaits you at our modern farmhouse, situated on an elevated site amid naturally wooded parkland, giving a sense of peace and quietness. Accommodation includes three double rooms, all en-suite, bright spacious lounge, separate dining room and drying facilities. Very central for touring West Highlands.

For details contact Mrs J McLauchlan. Tel: 01855 811792.

Joan McLauchlan Ballachulish Home Farm Ballachulish Argyll PA39 4JX Tel: (Ballachulish) 01855 811792		HIGHLY COMMENDED	1 Twin 3 En Suite fac B&B per person Open Jan-Oct 2 Double from £20.00 Double **New, traditional-style farmhouse, situated on an elevated site amid naturally wooded parkland, giving a sense of peace and quietness. Open view across Loch Leven.**
Mrs J Watt Riverside House Ballachulish Argyll PA39 4JE Tel: (Ballachulish) 01855 811473		COMMENDED	1 Twin 1 En Suite fac B&B per person Open Mar-Oct 2 Double 2 Pub Bath/Show from £14.00 Double **Modern family house, in quiet location in centre of village. 1 mile from Glencoe, 15 miles (24 kms) from Fort William.**
BALMACARA **Ross-shire** Mrs A Gordon Ashgrove, Balmacara Square Balmacara, by Kyle of Lochalsh Ross-shire IV40 8DJ Tel: (Balmacara) 01599 566259	**Map 3** F9	COMMENDED	1 Twin 3 En Suite fac B&B per person Open Mar-Nov 1 Double £16.00-£19.00 Double 1 Family **Traditional village cottage, off main road to Skye. 3 miles (5 kms) from Kyle of Lochalsh and the new Skye Bridge.**
Mrs M McGlennon Sgurr-Mor Lodge, Reraig Balmacara, by Kyle of Lochalsh Ross-shire IV40 8DH Tel: (Balmacara) 01599 566242		HIGHLY COMMENDED	1 Twin 2 En Suite fac B&B per person Open Jan-Dec 1 Double from £25.00 Double **Modern Highland lodge, with large south-facing garden, overlooking Loch Alsh, towards Skye. All rooms with private facilities. Parking.**

Old Post Office House

Balmacara, by Kyle of Lochalsh IV40 8DH
Telephone: 01599 566200 Fax: 01599 555322

Our comfortable family home has successfully operated as a guest house for eleven years. We are open all year, offering the good and simple comforts to travellers. Situated on the village street beside shops, pub, restaurant, petrol station and opposite the jetty into Loch Alsh!

Miss Anne F McGlennon Old Post Office House Balmacara by Kyle of Lochalsh Tel: (Balmacara) 01599 566200 Fax: 01599 555322		COMMENDED Listed	2 Twin 2 Pub Bath/Show B&B per person Open Jan-Dec 1 Double £15.00-£20.00 Double **Modernised and renovated former post office situated on shores of Loch Alsh. With fine views southwards to Kylerhea and Isle of Skye.**

THE HIGHLANDS & SKYE

	Map 4 A8						
BEAULY **Inverness-shire** George & Pat Borland Knoydart, Windhill Beauly Inverness-shire IV4 7AS Tel: (Inverness) 01463 782353		HIGHLY COMMENDED 👑👑 🚶	1 Twin 2 Double	3 En Suite fac 1 Pub Bath/Show	B&B per person from £22.00 Single from £18.00 Double	Open Easter-Sep	

Luxurious modern home set in beautiful rural area. Ideally situated for touring. Warm welcome assured.

| Mrs C Munro
Wester Moniack Farm
Kirkhill, by Inverness
Inverness-shire
IV5 7PQ
Tel: (Drumchardine)
01463 831237 | | COMMENDED Listed | 1 Double
1 Family | 1 Pub Bath/Show | B&B per person
£14.00-£15.00 Single
£14.00-£15.00 Double | Open Jan-Dec
Dinner 1830-2000
B&B + Eve. Meal
£21.00-£23.00 | |

Farmhouse with family atmosphere in a peaceful setting, next to Castle and Winery. Conveniently situated for Inverness and touring the Highlands.

| Mrs M Ritchie
Rheindown Farm
Beauly
Inverness-shire
IV4 7AB
Tel: (Beauly) 01463 782461 | | COMMENDED 👑 | 1 Double
1 Family | 1 Pub Bath/Show | B&B per person
£14.00-£15.00 Single
£14.00-£15.00 Double | Open Apr-Oct | |

Farmhouse on working farm, in elevated position overlooking Beauly and the Firth beyond. Home cooking.

| **BOAT OF GARTEN**
Inverness-shire
Avingormack Guest House
Boat of Garten
Inverness-shire
PH24 3BT
Tel: (Boat of Garten)
01479 831614 | Map 4 C10 | HIGHLY COMMENDED 👑👑👑 | 1 Twin
2 Double
1 Family | 2 En Suite fac
2 Pub Bath/Show | B&B per person
£19.50-£21.00 Double | Open Jan-Dec
Dinner 1900-2000
B&B + Eve. Meal
from £33.00 | |

Converted farmhouse with panoramic mountain views in rural location. Award-winning traditional and vegetarian cuisine.

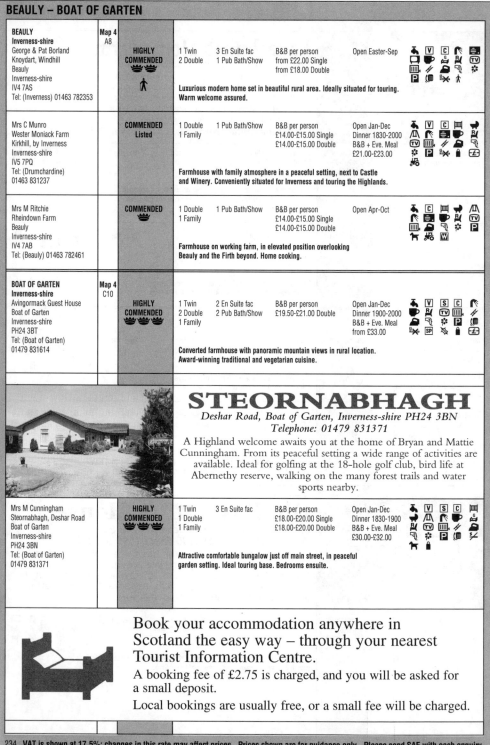

STEORNABHAGH

Deshar Road, Boat of Garten, Inverness-shire PH24 3BN
Telephone: 01479 831371

A Highland welcome awaits you at the home of Bryan and Mattie Cunningham. From its peaceful setting a wide range of activities are available. Ideal for golfing at the 18-hole golf club, bird life at Abernethy reserve, walking on the many forest trails and water sports nearby.

| Mrs M Cunningham
Steornabhagh, Deshar Road
Boat of Garten
Inverness-shire
PH24 3BN
Tel: (Boat of Garten)
01479 831371 | | HIGHLY COMMENDED 👑👑👑 | 1 Twin
1 Double
1 Family | 3 En Suite fac | B&B per person
£18.00-£20.00 Single
£18.00-£20.00 Double | Open Jan-Dec
Dinner 1830-1900
B&B + Eve. Meal
£30.00-£32.00 | |

Attractive comfortable bungalow just off main street, in peaceful garden setting. Ideal touring base. Bedrooms ensuite.

Book your accommodation anywhere in Scotland the easy way – through your nearest Tourist Information Centre.

A booking fee of £2.75 is charged, and you will be asked for a small deposit.

Local bookings are usually free, or a small fee will be charged.

"LOCHEIL"

BOAT OF GARTEN, INVERNESS-SHIRE PH24 3BX
Telephone: 01479 831603

John and Barbara Davison offer all-year Bed and Breakfast accommodation in their comfortable home 1 mile from the "Osprey Village" on the A95 road midway between Aviemore and Grantown-on-Spey. Dinners and packed lunches on prior notice. Residents' CTV lounge. 1-acre garden, ample parking. *Brochure on request.*

Mrs B A Davison Locheil Boat of Garten Inverness-shire PH24 3BX Tel: (Boat of Garten) 01479 831603	COMMENDED 👑	2 Single 1 Twin 1 Double	1 Pub Bath/Show	B&B per person £14.00-£15.50 Single £14.00-£15.50 Double	Open Jan-Dec Dinner from 1900 B&B + Eve. Meal £23.00-£24.50	

Stone-built house with new guest sitting room. Comfortable bed and breakfast accommodation. Evening meals and packed lunches by arrangement. Sorry no pets.

Granlea Guest House Boat of Garten Inverness-shire PH24 3BN Tel: (Boat of Garten) 01479 831601	COMMENDED 👑👑👑	1 Twin 2 Double 1 Family	2 En Suite fac 1 Pub Bath/Show	B&B per person £16.00-£17.00 Single £16.00-£18.00 Double	Open Jan-Dec Dinner 1830-2000	

Stone built Edwardian house, in village centre, close to Osprey reserve and golf course. Ideal touring base.

GLENSANDA

Mullingarroch, Boat of Garten, Inverness-shire PH24 3BY
Telephone: 01479 831494

Modern custom-built home designed with comfort in mind. Bright spacious TV lounge with open fire to relax in after enjoying the many amenities the area offers. Ideal base for touring, angling, golfing, bird-watching, ski-ing, off-road driving and more. All bedrooms have ensuite shower room, heating, tea/coffee tray.

Mrs S Lyons Glensanda Street of Kincardine Boat of Garten Inverness-shire PH24 3BY Tel: (Boat of Garten) 01479 831494	HIGHLY COMMENDED 👑👑	1 Twin 2 Double	3 En Suite fac	B&B per person £18.00-£19.00 Single £18.00-£19.00 Double	Open Jan-Dec	

Modern bungalow with views of Cairngorms on B970. 7 miles (11 kms) Aviemore, 1 mile (2 kms) Boat of Garten. All rooms ensuite.

MOORFIELD HOUSE

Deshar Road, Boat of Garten, Inverness-shire PH24 3BN
Telephone: 01479 831646

Quietly situated in the village. Moorfield is a Victorian House, AA/RAC acclaimed. Warm comfortable rooms all with private facilities, TV, tea/coffee makers. Licensed hospitality bar in cosy residents' lounge. Private parking. Traditional home-cooked dinners. Within easy reach of most Highland attractions, suited to those seeking peace and tranquillity.

Moorfield House Deshar Road Boat of Garten Inverness-shire PH24 3BN Tel: (Boat of Garten) 01479 831646	COMMENDED 👑👑👑	1 Single 1 Twin 1 Double 1 Family	3 En Suite fac 1 Priv. NOT ensuite	B&B per person £22.00 Single £19.00 Double	Open Jan-Dec Dinner 1830-1900 B&B + Eve. Meal £29.00	

Personally run hotel in centre of peaceful Highland village. Ideally situated for walking, golfing, fishing, etc. Home cooking.

(side margin) **THE HIGHLANDS & SKYE**

THE HIGHLANDS & SKYE

BOAT OF GARTEN continued **Inverness-shire** Ryvoan Guest House Kinchurdy Road Boat of Garten Inverness-shire PH24 3BP Tel: (Boat of Garten) 01479 831654	Map 4 C10	HIGHLY COMMENDED	1 Twin 1 Double 1 Family	2 En Suite fac 2 Pub Bath/Show	B&B per person from £18.00 Double	Open Jan-Dec Dinner at 1900 B&B + Eve. Meal from £31.00

Victorian house set in mature woodland, with period accommodation and modern facilities. Near RSPB reserve, golf club and Cairngorms.

BRORA **Sutherland** Mrs J Ballantyne Clynelish Farm Brora Sutherland KW9 6LR Tel: (Brora) 01408 621265 Fax: 01408 621265	Map 4 C6	COMMENDED	1 Twin 1 Double 1 Family	2 En Suite fac 1 Priv. NOT ensuite	B&B per person £16.00-£19.00 Double	Open Mar-Oct

Family home, on working farm, in rural setting about a mile (2 kms) from Brora and beaches.

Tigh Fada

Golf Road, Brora, Sutherland KW9 6QS   Tel/Fax: 01408 621332

Scots couple John and Ishbel have a warm, comfortable non-smoking home in peaceful situation overlooking their 4-hole pitch and putt, croquet green. Garden gate to golf course and sandy beach. Complimentary evening cup and home baking by peat fire. Highland hospitality at its best – try it!   *(Great breakfasts too)*

John & Ishbel Clarkson Tigh Fada, Golf Road Brora Sutherland KW9 6QS Tel: (Brora) 01408 621332 Fax: 01408 621332	COMMENDED	2 Twin 1 Double	1 En Suite fac 2 Priv. NOT ensuite	B&B per person £16.00-£20.00 Double	Open Jan-Dec

Fine sea views and peat fires, home baking and a real Highland welcome. Ideal halfway house between Inverness and John O'Groats.

Mrs M Cooper Lynwood, Golf Road Brora Sutherland KW9 6QS Tel: (Brora) 01408 621226 Fax: 01408 621226	HIGHLY COMMENDED	2 Twin 1 Double 1 Family	3 En Suite fac 1 Pub Bath/Show	B&B per person £22.00-£25.00 Single £17.00-£20.00 Double	Open Mar-Dec Dinner 1900-2000 B&B + Eve. Meal £27.00-£30.00

Family home in substantial Edwardian house, in its own grounds overlooking Brora harbour. Home cooking. Annexe garden room available on ground floor.

CANNICH **Inverness-shire**	Map 3 H9

Kerrow House

Cannich, Strathglass, Inverness-shire IV4 7NA
Telephone: 01456 415243 Fax: 01456 415425

Magnificent country house offering warm hospitality. Comfortable stylish rooms with private facilities. Wine and dine in licensed restaurant enjoying superb cuisine. Relax in peaceful family atmosphere of beautiful house and grounds. Also self-catering. Open all year and close to Glens of Affric and Cannich. Prices from £15 to £30.

Mr & Mrs Doyle Kerrow House Cannich, Strathglass Inverness-shire IV4 7NA Tel: (Cannich) 01456 415243 Fax: 01456 415425	COMMENDED	1 Twin 1 Double 1 Family	3 Priv. NOT ensuite	B&B per person £15.00-£30.00 Single £15.00-£20.00 Double	Open Jan-Dec Dinner 1900-2130 B&B + Eve. Meal £30.00-£40.00

Large country house, 200 years old with many period features. Set in wooded grounds on banks of River Glass. Bedrooms with own bathrooms.

CARRBRIDGE Inverness-shire	Map 4 C9

Craigellachie House

Main Street, Carrbridge, Inverness-shire PH23 3AS
Telephone: 01479 841641

Set in the centre of the beautiful Highland village of Carrbridge. Craigellachie House offers a warm welcome. Comfortable residents' lounge with open fire and beautiful dining room where food of a high standard is served. Ideally situated for exploring the Highlands or participating in a wide range of outdoor activities.

Craigellachie House Main Street Carrbridge Inverness-shire PH23 3AS Tel: (Carrbridge) 01479 841641	COMMENDED	1 Single 2 Twin 2 Double 2 Family	3 En Suite fac 2 Pub Bath/Show	B&B per person £15.00-£23.00 Single £15.00-£18.00 Double	Open Jan-Dec Dinner 1900-2000 B&B + Eve. Meal £25.00-£28.00

Warm comfortable hospitality assured. Ample parking. Centre of village.
Ideal base for holiday activities. Dinners available using fresh Scottish produce.

M A King Finiskaig, 4 Rowan Park Carrbridge Inverness-shire PH23 3AE Tel: (Aviemore) 01479 841349	COMMENDED Listed	1 Twin 1 Double	1 Pub Bath/Show	B&B per person from £16.00 Single £14.00-£16.00 Double Room only per person from £10.00	Open Jan-Dec

Friendly B&B in modern house in picturesque Highland village.
Ideal base for touring Strathspey.

Mrs F Ritchie Pine View, Carr Road Carrbridge Inverness-shire PH23 3AB Tel: (Carrbridge) 01479 841217	COMMENDED Listed	1 Twin 1 Double 1 Family	1 Pub Bath/Show	B&B per person £15.00 Single £14.00 Double	Open Jan-Dec

Victorian house in quiet residential area of Carrbridge.
Convenient for touring. Aviemore 7 miles (11 kms).

CASTLETOWN, by Thurso Caithness	Map 4 D3

GARTH HOUSE

Castletown, Caithness KW14 8SL   Tel: 01847 821429

Garth House is over 250 years old. This comfortable family home has been carefully restored by the present owners. It is situated between Wick and Thurso near Dunnet Bay and Dunnet Head, Britain's most northerly mainland point. There is a large garden for guests' enjoyment, also an outdoor model railway.   *Open January to December.*

Mr & Mrs P Garfield Garth House Castletown Caithness KW14 8SL Tel: (Castletown) 01847 821429	HIGHLY COMMENDED	1 Twin 1 Double	1 En Suite fac 1 Priv. NOT ensuite	B&B per person from £18.00 Single from £18.00 Double	Open Jan-Dec

Large stone-built house dated 1727. Lovingly restored, this "gentleman's seat"
welcomes you in comfort and style. Garden railway.

THE HIGHLANDS & SKYE

CAWDOR – CORPACH, by Fort William

CAWDOR
Inverness-shire
Mrs Jennifer MacLeod
Dallaschyle
Cawdor
Nairn
IV12 5XS
Tel: (Croy) 01667 493422

Map 4
C8

COMMENDED
Listed

| 1 Double | 1 Pub Bath/Show | B&B per person to £22.00 Single to £16.00 Double | Open Apr-Nov |
| 1 Family | | | |

Spacious modern house, in peaceful woodland setting, with large garden.
Close to Cawdor Castle and Culloden Moor.

Mrs Mhairi Munro
Limegrove
Cawdor
Nairn
IV12 5RA
Tel: (Cawdor) 01667 404307

COMMENDED
Listed

| 1 Twin | 1 En Suite fac | B&B per person from £15.00 Single | Open Jan-Dec |
| 2 Double | 1 Pub Bath/Show | from £15.00 Double | |

Highland welcome. Comfortable accommodation in picturesque
conservation village of Cawdor. Short walk to Cawdor Castle.

CONON BRIDGE
Ross-shire
Mrs C Morrison
Dun Eistein, Alcaig
Conon Bridge, by Dingwall
Ross-shire
IV7 8HS
Tel: (Dingwall) 01349 862210

Map 4
A8

COMMENDED

| 1 Double | 1 En Suite fac | B&B per person from £21.00 Single | Open Apr-Oct |
| 1 Family | 1 Priv. NOT ensuite | from £15.00 Double | |

Highland cottage on country road with views of Ben Wyvis from garden.
11 miles (18 kms) north of Inverness. Non-smoking.

CONTIN
Ross-shire
Mrs A Dale
Larchfield, Craigdarroch Drive
Contin
Ross-shire
IV14 9EL
Tel: (Strathpeffer)
01997 421157

Map 4
A8

HIGHLY
COMMENDED

1 Twin	2 En Suite fac	B&B per person £16.00-£18.00 Double	Open Jan-Dec
1 Double	1 Priv. NOT ensuite		
1 Family			

A warm welcome awaits at this modern house set in
country surroundings and furnished to a high standard.

CORPACH, by Fort William
Inverness-shire
R Cumming
Travee
Corpach, by Fort William
Inverness-shire
PH33 7LR
Tel: (Corpach) 01397 772380
Fax: 01397 772380

Map 3
H12

COMMENDED

| 1 Twin | 2 Pub Bath/Show | B&B per person from £19.00 Single | Open Jan-Dec |
| 2 Double | | from £15.00 Double | |

Friendly welcoming, family home, 4 miles (6 kms) from Fort William,
with super views over Loch Linnhe and Ben Nevis.

Mrs McCallum
The Neuk
Corpach, by Fort William
Inverness-shire
PH33 7LR
Tel: (Corpach) 01397 772244

COMMENDED

2 Twin	3 En Suite fac	B&B per person £20.00-£30.00 Single	Open Jan-Dec
1 Family		£16.00-£22.00 Double	Dinner 1730-1900
			B&B + Eve. Meal £24.00-£38.00

Detached villa on the Mallaig road (A830). View of Ben Nevis across Loch Linnhe.
Evening meal and home cooking.

Mrs MacPhee
Tangasdale
Corpach, by Fort William
Inverness-shire
PH33 7LT
Tel: (Corpach) 01397 772591

COMMENDED

| 2 Family | 1 Pub Bath/Show | B&B per person from £13.50 Double | Open Jan-Dec |

Modern bungalow with all rooms on the ground floor,
close to the canal and Neptune's Staircase.

Mrs Wynne
Heston
Corpach, by Fort William
Inverness-shire
PH33 7LT
Tel: (Fort William)
01397 772425

COMMENDED

| 1 Twin | 2 En Suite fac | B&B per person £20.00-£22.00 Single | Open Mar-Oct |
| 1 Double | 1 Pub Bath/Show | £16.00-£18.00 Double | |

Modern family home with magnificent views across Loch Linnhe.
4 miles (6 kms) from Fort William.

VAT is shown at 17.5%: changes in this rate may affect prices. Prices shown are for guidance only. Please send SAE with each enquiry.

CROMARTY **Ross-shire** Mrs F Ricketts Beechfield House 4 Urquhart Court Cromarty Ross-shire IV11 8YD Tel: (Cromarty) 01381 600308	Map 4 B7	HIGHLY COMMENDED ♛♛♛	2 Twin 1 Double	2 En Suite fac 1 Priv. NOT ensuite	B&B per person £17.00-£25.00 Single £17.00-£20.00 Double	Open Jan-Dec	

Large modern house, built with the guests' comfort in mind.
Off-street parking. On the outskirts of town.

CULLODEN MOOR **Inverness-shire** Mrs P Alexander Ballagan Farm Culloden Moor, by Inverness Inverness-shire IV1 2EL Tel: (Culloden) 01463 790213	Map 4 B8	COMMENDED Listed	1 Twin 1 Family	1 Pub Bath/Show	B&B per person £15.00-£16.00 Double	Open Apr-Oct Dinner 1830-1930	

Farmhouse on working cattle farm in rural location 8 miles (13 kms)
south east of Inverness. Culloden Battlefield and Clava Cairns are nearby.

Mrs E M C Alexander Culdoich Farm Culloden Moor, by Inverness Inverness-shire IV1 2EP Tel: (Culloden) 01463 790268		COMMENDED ♛	1 Double 1 Family	1 Pub Bath/Show	B&B per person from £16.00 Double	Open May-Oct Dinner from 1900 B&B + Eve. Meal from £26.00	

18th century farmhouse on mixed arable and livestock farm, on hillside near
Culloden Battlefield and Clava Stones. Home baking and cooking.

Mrs R MacKay Leanach Farm Culloden Moor, by Inverness Inverness-shire IV1 2EJ Tel: (Culloden) 01463 791027		COMMENDED ♛♛♛	2 Twin 1 Double	3 En Suite fac	B&B per person £18.00-£19.00 Double Room only per person £15.00-£16.00	Open Jan-Dec Dinner 1800-1830 B&B + Eve. Meal £28.00-£29.50	

Large family farmhouse on 400-acre (162ha) sheep and cattle farm.
5 miles (9 kms) from Inverness, near Culloden Battlefield.

Mrs M MacLean Woodside of Culloden Westhill, Inverness Inverness-shire IV1 2BP Tel: (Culloden) 01463 790242		HIGHLY COMMENDED ♛♛♛	2 Twin 1 Double	3 En Suite fac	B&B per person from £20.00 Single from £18.00 Double	Open Feb-Nov Dinner from 1830 B&B + Eve. Meal from £27.00	

Working farm overlooking Moray Firth, close to Culloden Battlefield and
3 miles (5 kms) east of Inverness. Specialist in sheepdog trials.

by CULLODEN MOOR **Inverness-shire** Mrs T M Honnor Westhill House, Westhill by Inverness IV1 2BP Tel: (Culloden) 01463 793225 Fax: 01463 792503	Map 4 B8	COMMENDED ♛	2 Twin	2 En Suite fac	B&B per person £16.00-£18.00 Double	Open Mar-Oct	

Modern family home, own grounds, open countryside. 1 mile (2 kms) Culloden
Battlefield. 4 miles (6 kms) Inverness. Two rooms, one in annexe. Warm welcome.

Book your accommodation anywhere in Scotland the easy way – through your nearest Tourist Information Centre.

A booking fee of £2.75 is charged, and you will be asked for a small deposit.

Local bookings are usually free, or a small fee will be charged.

THE HIGHLANDS & SKYE

THE HIGHLANDS & SKYE

DALCROSS, by Inverness Inverness-shire	Map 4 B8

Easter Dalziel Farmhouse

Easter Dalziel Farm, Dalcross, Inverness IV1 2JL
Telephone and Fax: 01667 462213

This Scottish farming family offers true Highland hospitality on 200-acre stock/arable farm 7 miles east of Inverness, between A96 and B9039. Delightful early Victorian farmhouse in superb central location with panoramic views. Many recommendations including Elizabeth Gundrey's S.O.T.B.T. and the Best Bed and Breakfast.

AA QQQ RECOMMENDED

Mrs Pottie
Easter Dalziel Farm
Dalcross
Inverness-shire
IV1 2JL
Tel: (Ardersier) 01667 462213
Fax: 01667 462213

HIGHLY COMMENDED

1 Twin   2 Pub Bath/Show
2 Double

B&B per person
£15.00-£18.00 Double
Room only per person
£13.00-£16.00

Open Jan-Dec
Dinner from 1900
B&B + Eve. Meal
£26.00-£29.00

Victorian farmhouse, on stock/arable farm. Friendly atmosphere. Log fire in lounge and home baking. Inverness 7 mls (11 kms). Culloden 5 mls (8 kms).

DAVIOT
Inverness-shire
M MacLeod
Chalna
Daviot
Inverness-shire
IV1 2XQ
Tel: (Daviot) 01463 772239

Map 4 B9

COMMENDED

1 Twin   1 En Suite fac
1 Double   1 Pub Bath/Show
1 Family

B&B per person
£18.00-£20.00 Single
£15.50-£18.50 Double

Open Mar-Oct

Modern, detached, stone-built villa, in extensive grounds in rural setting.
7 miles (11 kms) south of Inverness. Fishing available.

DIABAIG
Ross-shire
Mrs B J Peacock
Upper Diabaig
Torridon, Achnasheen
Ross-shire
IV22 2HE
Tel: (Diabaig) 01445 790227

Map 3 F8

COMMENDED

2 Twin   1 En Suite fac
1 Double   1 Pub Bath/Show

B&B per person
from £15.00 Double

Open Apr-Sep
Dinner from 1900
B&B + Eve. Meal
from £27.50

Dramatic drive by Torridon Hills to modern house on working croft.
Traditional Scottish hospitality. Warm and comfortable. Good home cooking.

Miss I A Ross
3 Diabaig
Torridon, Achnasheen
Ross-shire
IV22 2HE
Tel: (Diabaig) 01445 790240/
790268

COMMENDED
Listed

1 Single   1 Priv. NOT ensuite
1 Twin   1 Pub Bath/Show
1 Double

B&B per person
£13.00-£13.50 Single
£13.00-£13.50 Double
Room only per person
£9.00

Open Jan-Dec
Dinner 1900-2130
B&B + Eve. Meal
£23.00-£23.50

Modern bungalow in village of Diabaig, looking out over bay to surrounding hills.
Ideal for boat and fishing trips, walking and climbing in Torridon Mountains.

DINGWALL
Ross-shire
Mrs M Duffus
18 Millcraig Road
Dingwall
Ross-shire
IV15 9PS
Tel: (Dingwall) 01349 862194

Map 4 A8

COMMENDED

1 Twin   2 Pub Bath/Show
1 Double

B&B per person
to £13.50 Double

Open Apr-Oct

With a warm welcome, home bakes and a cheerful smile
you soon join the ranks of Mabel's extended family. Non-smoking throughout.

DORES
Inverness-shire
Mrs J Morrison
Beinn Dhearg, Torr Gardens
Dores
Inverness-shire
IV1 2TS
Tel: (Dores) 01463 751336

Map 4 B9

COMMENDED

1 Twin   3 En Suite fac
1 Double   1 Pub Bath/Show
1 Family

B&B per person
£16.50-£19.00 Double

Open Jan-Dec

Modern, spacious house, in quiet setting 100yds (91m) from Loch Ness,
8 miles (13 kms) south of Inverness. Wonderful views across the loch.
All ensuite. Private parking.

DORNIE, by Kyle of Lochalsh Ross-shire	Map 3 G9

Tigh Tasgaidh

Dornie, Kyle of Lochalsh, Ross-shire IV40 8EH
Telephone: 01599 555242

The old bank house, situated in Dornie village. Overlooking Loch Long with views of the Isle of Skye and the Cuillins. Ideal centre for walking or touring. Comfortable non-smoking accommodation, bedrooms with private facilities, central heating, colour TV, tea and coffee-making facilities.

Mrs Clayton Tigh Tasgaidh Dornie, by Kyle of Lochalsh Ross-shire IV40 8EH Tel: (Dornie) 01599 555242	COMMENDED 👑👑	1 Twin 2 Double	3 En Suite fac 1 Pub Bath/Show	B&B per person £15.00-£18.00 Double	Open Feb-Nov	

Detached house standing in its own grounds overlooking Loch Long. In a quiet residential area but near main Inverness-Skye road. Non-smoking.

Castle View

Upper Ardelve, By Dornie, Kyle of Lochalsh IV40 8EY
Telephone: 01599 555453

The countryside surrounding Eilean Donan Castle is of exceptional beauty and grandeur with magnificent mountain, loch and forest scenery. Rich in wildlife, the area offers fascinating rewards for observant nature lovers. There are otters, seals, wild goats and deer, whilst overhead may be seen buzzards, falcons and the magnificent Golden Eagle.

Rosemary McClelland Castle View, Upper Ardelve Dornie, by Kyle of Lochalsh Ross-shire IV40 8EY Tel: (Dornie) 01599 555453	COMMENDED 👑👑	1 Twin 2 Double	3 En Suite fac	B&B per person to £18.00 Double	Open Jan-Dec Dinner 1900-2000 B&B + Eve. Meal to £26.00	

Warm welcome assured in new croft house with breathtaking views to Eilean Donan Castle, Loch Duich and the Sisters of Kintail.

Mrs Peterkin Sealladh-mara Dornie, by Kyle of Lochalsh Ross-shire IV40 Tel: (Dornie) 01599 555296	COMMENDED Listed	1 Twin 1 Double 1 Family	1 Pub Bath/Show	B&B per person £14.00 Single £14.00 Double	Open Jan-Dec Dinner 1800-2030	

Modern family home, looking over Loch Duich and Eilean Donan Castle towards Kintail mountains. Handy for touring to Skye and Wester Ross. Ideal for walking.

DORNOCH Sutherland	Map 4 B6

HIGHFIELD

Evelix Road, Dornoch, Sutherland IV25 3HR
Telephone and Fax: 01862 810909

Highfield is a large, comfortable, non-smoking house standing in an acre of ground, with beautiful southerly views, yet only a few hundred yards from the centre of Dornoch. Our renowned hospitality, high standards of service and informal atmosphere ensure guests return year after year to golf, explore or just relax.

Mrs J Dooley Highfield, Evelix Road Dornoch Sutherland IV25 3HR Tel: (Dornoch) 01862 810909 Fax: 01862 810909	DELUXE 👑👑👑	1 Twin 2 Double	3 En Suite fac	B&B per person £22.00-£24.00 Double	Open Jan-Dec	

A modern house at edge of this picturesque golfing town – a warm welcome assured in this very comfortable family home.

THE HIGHLANDS & SKYE

THE HIGHLANDS & SKYE

DORNOCH continued **Sutherland** Mrs E A Dunlop Cluaine, Evelix Dornoch Sutherland IV25 3RD Tel: (Dornoch) 01862 810276	Map 4 B6	COMMENDED	1 Twin 1 Family	1 En Suite fac 1 Priv. NOT ensuite	B&B per person £17.00-£21.00 Single £16.00-£19.00 Double	Open May-Oct	

Personally run B&B with ground-floor rooms, set in 3 acres (1.2ha) of woodland and gardens. Ideal base for touring. Beaches and golf courses nearby.

Mrs B Fraser Khuzistan, 9 Poles Road Dornoch Sutherland IV25 3HP Tel: (Dornoch) 01862 810552	HIGHLY COMMENDED	1 Twin 2 Double	1 En Suite fac 2 Priv. NOT ensuite	B&B per person £17.00-£19.00 Double	Open Apr-Oct	

Friendly, family run modern home (including a ground-floor room) with excellent garden area. Off-road parking available.

ACHANDEAN

The Meadows, Off Castle Close, Dornoch, Sutherland IV25 3SF
Telephone/Fax: 01862 810413
Comfortable, spacious bungalow of character, situated on
Right-Hand Side of Town Centre, off Castle Close, very
central to shops, beach and championship golf course.
Loch Fleet Nature Reserve is nearby. Ideal for touring the
Highlands, walks, etc. This picturesque little town has a
13th-century cathedral amongst its attractions.

Mrs Audrey Hellier Achandean, The Meadows off Castle Close Dornoch Sutherland IV25 3SF Tel: (Dornoch) 01862 810413 Fax: 01862 810413	COMMENDED	1 Twin 2 Double	2 En Suite fac 1 Priv. NOT ensuite	B&B per person £18.00-£22.00 Double	Open Jan-Dec Dinner 1830-1930

Bungalow set one road back from cathedral town centre on right-hand side.
Ideal touring base with off-road parking in this central quiet location.

PARFOUR

Rowan Crescent, Dornoch IV25 3QP
Telephone/Fax: 01862 810955
Modern family home. Situated close to Royal Dornoch
Golf Club and miles of sandy beaches. Guest lounge,
private parking. Activity holidays, *Golf* tee times
arranged for Brora, Tain, Dornoch, Golspie.
Walking guide available for daily scenic walking.

Mrs S Young Parfour, Rowan Crescent Dornoch Sutherland IV25 3QP Tel: (Dornoch) 01862 810955 Fax: 01862 810955	HIGHLY COMMENDED	1 Twin 2 Double	3 En Suite fac	B&B per person £20.00-£35.00 Single £18.50-£22.00 Double	Open Jan-Dec

Homely, modern bungalow. Convenient for town centre, golf course and beach.
Private parking.

BY DORNOCH **Sutherland** Mrs D Fraser Corven, Station Road Embo, by Dornoch Sutherland IV25 3PT Tel: (Dornoch) 01862 810128	Map 4 B6	COMMENDED Listed	1 Twin 2 Double	1 En Suite fac 1 Pub Bath/Show	B&B per person £14.00-£16.00 Single £14.00-£16.00 Double	Open Feb-Nov

Small-detached bungalow with fine views across the bay to hills beyond.
Sandy beaches and golf courses nearby. Non-smoking throughout.

DRUMBEG **Sutherland** Taigh Druimbeag, Mrs M Waud Drumbeg Sutherland IV27 4NW Tel: (Drumbeg) 01571 833209	Map 3 G4	COMMENDED 👑👑👑	1 Twin 2 Double	3 En Suite fac	B&B per person from £22.50 Single from £22.50 Double	Open Easter Mon-Oct Dinner at 1900 B&B + Eve. Meal from £35.00	

In house-party style, Ron and Margaret provide a warm welcome, convivial company. Fresh veg, self-indulgent puddings. Wonderfully peaceful situation.

DRUMNADROCHIT **Inverness-shire** Mrs Tina Beet Heatherlea, Balmacaan Road Drumnadrochit Inverness-shire IV3 6UR Tel: (Drumnadrochit) 01456 450561	Map 4 A9	HIGHLY COMMENDED Listed	1 Twin 2 Double	1 En Suite fac 1 Pub Bath/Show	B&B per person from £13.00 Double	Open Jan-Dec	

Modern family home in popular Highland village close to Loch Ness.
Good views to loch and hills. Inverness 14 miles (22 kms).

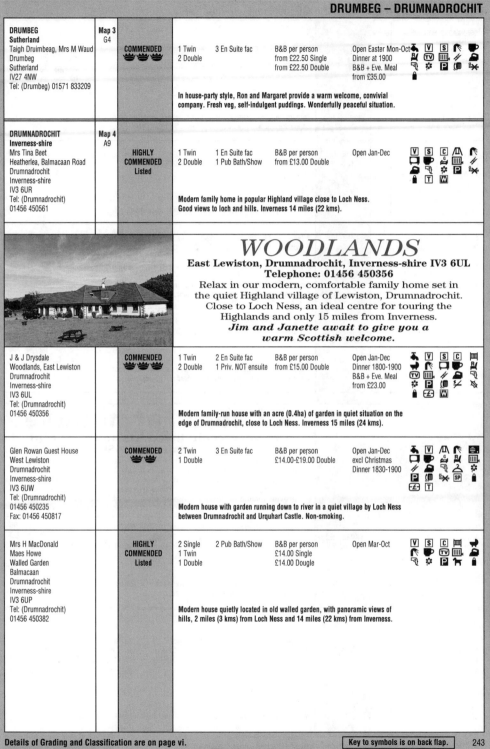

WOODLANDS
East Lewiston, Drumnadrochit, Inverness-shire IV3 6UL
Telephone: 01456 450356
Relax in our modern, comfortable family home set in
the quiet Highland village of Lewiston, Drumnadrochit.
Close to Loch Ness, an ideal centre for touring the
Highlands and only 15 miles from Inverness.
*Jim and Janette await to give you a
warm Scottish welcome.*

J & J Drysdale Woodlands, East Lewiston Drumnadrochit Inverness-shire IV3 6UL Tel: (Drumnadrochit) 01456 450356	COMMENDED 👑👑👑	1 Twin 2 Double	2 En Suite fac 1 Priv. NOT ensuite	B&B per person from £15.00 Double	Open Jan-Dec Dinner 1800-1900 B&B + Eve. Meal from £23.00	

Modern family-run house with an acre (0.4ha) of garden in quiet situation on the
edge of Drumnadrochit, close to Loch Ness. Inverness 15 miles (24 kms).

Glen Rowan Guest House West Lewiston Drumnadrochit Inverness-shire IV3 6UW Tel: (Drumnadrochit) 01456 450235 Fax: 01456 450817	COMMENDED 👑👑	2 Twin 1 Double	3 En Suite fac	B&B per person £14.00-£19.00 Double	Open Jan-Dec excl Christmas Dinner 1830-1900	

Modern house with garden running down to river in a quiet village by Loch Ness
between Drumnadrochit and Urquhart Castle. Non-smoking.

Mrs H MacDonald Maes Howe Walled Garden Balmacaan Drumnadrochit Inverness-shire IV3 6UP Tel: (Drumnadrochit) 01456 450382	HIGHLY COMMENDED Listed	2 Single 1 Twin 1 Double	2 Pub Bath/Show	B&B per person £14.00 Single £14.00 Dougle	Open Mar-Oct	

Modern house quietly located in old walled garden, with panoramic views of
hills, 2 miles (3 kms) from Loch Ness and 14 miles (22 kms) from Inverness.

THE HIGHLANDS & SKYE

THE HIGHLANDS & SKYE

DRUMNADROCHIT continued
Inverness-shire
Capt and Mrs A D
  MacDonald-Haig
Borlum Farm
Drumnadrochit
Inverness-shire
IV3 6XN
Tel: (Drumnadrochit)
01456 450358
Fax: 01456 450358

Map 4
A9

COMMENDED

1 Twin
3 Double
1 Family

2 En Suite fac
2 Pub Bath/Show

B&B per person
from £19.00 Double

Open Jan-Dec

Comfortable country house with many period features, welcomes non-smokers.
On working farm with fine views of Loch Ness. Riding available.

Mrs E Paterson
Allanmore Farm
Drumnadrochit
Inverness-shire
IV3 6XE
Tel: (Drumnadrochit)
01456 450247

COMMENDED
Listed

1 Twin
2 Double

1 Pub Bath/Show

B&B per person
£13.50-£14.00 Double

Open Apr-Oct

16th century farmhouse on stock and arable farm in peaceful setting.

Sandra & Bill Silke
Westwood, Lower Balmacaan
Drumnadrochit
Inverness-shire
IV3 6UL
Tel: (Drumnadrochit)
01456 450826

COMMENDED
Listed

2 Twin
1 Double

2 En Suite fac
1 Pub Bath/Show

B&B per person
£13.00-£19.00 Double

Open Jan-Dec
Dinner 1800-2030
B&B + Eve. Meal
£22.00-£28.00

Modern centrally heated bungalow. Quiet location in popular
Highland village near Loch Ness and Glen Affric.

Mrs Caroline Urquhart
Drumbuie Farm, Drumbuie
Drumnadrochit
Inverness-shire
IV3 6XP
Tel: (Drumnadrochit)
01456 450634

HIGHLY
COMMENDED

1 Twin
2 Double

3 En Suite fac

B&B per person
£15.00-£18.00 Double

Open Jan-Dec
Dinner 1900-2000
B&B + Eve. Meal
£25.00-£28.00

Modern farmhouse, with all rooms ensuite, on an elevated site overlooking
Loch Ness and surrounding farmland. Own herd of Highland cattle.

Kilmore Farmhouse
Drumnadrochit, Inverness-shire IV3 6UH
Telephone: 01456 450524

Modern, luxury custom-built family run farmhouse peacefully situated at
walking distance from Loch Ness. An ideal base for hillwalking and touring
the Highlands. All rooms are ground-floor and tastefully decorated. Guests'
lounge with log fire. A friendly and warm welcome and home cooking
provides value for money. Evening meal available. See Highland cattle.
Non-smoking.   *Major credit cards accepted*

Mrs M Van Loon
Kilmore Farmhouse
Drumnadrochit
Inverness-shire
IV3 6UH
Tel: (Drumnadrochit)
01456 450524

HIGHLY
COMMENDED

1 Twin
2 Double

3 En Suite fac

B&B per person
£14.00-£18.00 Double
Room only per person
£12.00-£16.00

Open Jan-Dec
Dinner 1830-1930
B&B + Eve. Meal
£22.00-£26.00

Modern farmhouse peacefully situated with splendid views of surrounding hills.
Site of Special Scientific Interest. Highland cattle.

DULNAIN BRIDGE
by Grantown-on-Spey
Inverness-shire
Rosegrove Guest House
Skye of Curr
Dulnain Bridge
by Grantown-on-Spey
Inverness-shire
PH26 3PA
Tel: (Dulnain Bridge)
01479 851335

Map 4
C9

COMMENDED

1 Single
2 Twin
2 Double
1 Family

3 En Suite fac
3 Pub Bath/Show

B&B per person
£15.00-£18.00 Single
£15.00-£18.00 Double

Open Jan-Dec
Dinner 1830-1930
B&B + Eve. Meal
£24.00-£27.00

Modern house, personally run. Home cooking. A short distance from Dulnain Bridge.

DUNBEATH **Caithness** Mrs M MacDonald Tormore Farm Dunbeath Caithness KW6 6EH Tel: (Dunbeath) 01593 731240	Map 4 D4	COMMENDED Listed	1 Twin 1 Double 1 Family	1 Pub Bath/Show	B&B per person £13.00-£14.00 Single £13.00-£14.00 Double	Open May-Sep Dinner 1800-2130 B&B + Eve. Meal £19.00-£22.00	

Warm Highland hospitality on this traditional working farm.
Dinner available on request. One ground-floor bedroom.

DUNDONNELL **Ross-shire** Mr & Mrs P Hayball The Old Schoolhouse, Badcaul Dundonnell Ross-shire IV23 2QY Tel: (Dundonnell) 01854 633311 Fax: 01854 633311	Map 3 G7	HIGHLY COMMENDED	1 Twin 1 Double	1 Pub Bath/Show	B&B per person £15.00-£17.00 Single £13.00-£15.00 Double	Open Mar-Nov Dinner at 1900 B&B + Eve. Meal £23.00-£28.00	

Traditional stone-built house on Little Loch Broom near An Teallach.
Warm welcome and home cooking.

Mrs A Ross 4 Camusnagaul Dundonnell Ross-shire IV23 2QT Tel: (Dundonnell) 01854 633237		HIGHLY COMMENDED	1 Twin 1 Double 1 Family	1 Pub Bath/Show	B&B per person £14.00-£14.50 Double	Open Jan-Dec	

Ideal for walkers and climbers, being close to the An Teallach mountain range.
Warm welcome assured on working croft.

DURNESS **Sutherland** Port-na-Con Guest House Loch Eriboll by Altnaharra, Lairg Sutherland IV27 4UN Tel: (Durness) 01971 511367 Fax: 01971 511367	Map 4 A3	HIGHLY COMMENDED	1 Twin 2 Double 1 Family	1 En Suite fac 1 Priv. NOT ensuite 1 Pub Bath/Show	B&B per person £16.50-£19.00 Double	Open Apr-Oct Dinner 1900-2100 B&B + Eve. Meal £27.50-£30.00	

A warm friendly atmosphere. Home-cooked food of a high standard, sensible wine
list and a superb waterside location in this remote area. Teeming with wildlife.

DUROR **Argyll** Mrs F C Worthington Lagnaha Farm Duror of Appin Argyll PA38 4BS Tel: (Duror) 01631 740207 Fax: 01631 740207	Map 1 E1	COMMENDED	1 Single 2 Double	1 En Suite fac 1 Pub Bath/Show	B&B per person £15.00-£20.00 Single £15.00-£20.00 Double Room only per person £15.00-£20.00	Open Easter-October	

Traditional Listed 19th century farmhouse 6 miles (10 kms) from Glencoe.
An ideal base for touring Appin and the West of Scotland.

FORT AUGUSTUS **Inverness-shire** Mairi MacIver Fort Augustus Abbey Fort Augustus Inverness-shire PH32 4BD Tel: (Fort Augustus) 01320 366233 Fax: 01320 366228	Map 4 A10	APPROVED Listed	12 Single 13 Twin 4 Family	8 Pub Bath/Show	B&B per person £15.00 Single £15.00 Double Room only per person £12.00	Open Jan-Dec Dinner 1730-2000 B&B + Eve. Meal £21.00-£27.00	

A unique experience staying at a Benedictine Abbey. Set in magnificent
grounds by Loch Ness. Fascinating Heritage Exhibition open to the public.

J G Nairn Appin, Inverness Road Fort Augustus Inverness-shire PH32 4DH Tel: (Fort Augustus) 01320 366541		COMMENDED	1 Twin 2 Double	1 En Suite fac 1 Pub Bath/Show	B&B per person £13.00-£17.00 Double	Open Apr-Oct	

Detached modern bungalow on the edge of a small village.
Ideal base for touring the Highlands.

THE HIGHLANDS & SKYE

Details of Grading and Classification are on page vi.

Key to symbols is on back flap.

THE HIGHLANDS & SKYE

FORT AUGUSTUS continued **Inverness-shire** Mrs L H Service Sonas Fort Augustus Inverness-shire PH32 4DH Tel: (Fort Augustus) 01320 366291	Map 4 A10	**HIGHLY COMMENDED** 👑👑👑	1 Twin 1 Double 1 Family	3 En Suite fac	B&B per person from £13.00 Double	Open Jan-Dec	

Modern house in elevated position on the northern edge of the village, with excellent views of surrounding hills.

FORT WILLIAM **Inverness-shire**	Map 3 H12

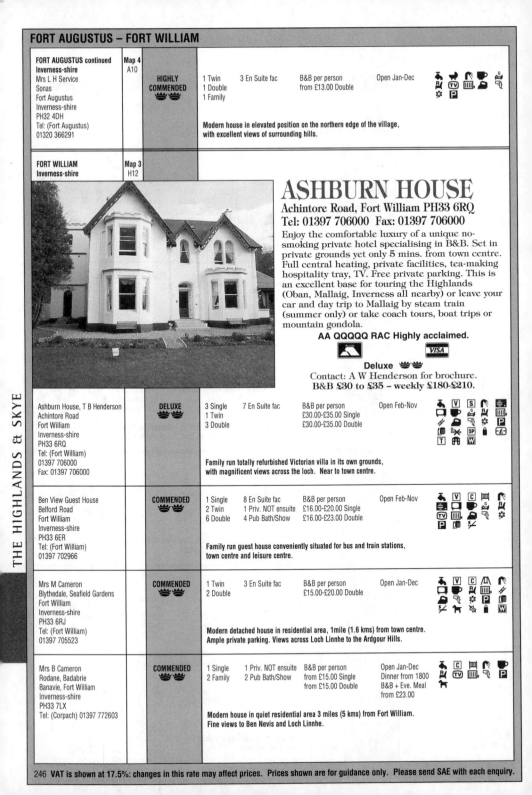

ASHBURN HOUSE
Achintore Road, Fort William PH33 6RQ
Tel: 01397 706000 Fax: 01397 706000

Enjoy the comfortable luxury of a unique no-smoking private hotel specialising in B&B. Set in private grounds yet only 5 mins. from town centre. Full central heating, private facilities, tea-making hospitality tray, TV. Free private parking. This is an excellent base for touring the Highlands (Oban, Mallaig, Inverness all nearby) or leave your car and day trip to Mallaig by steam train (summer only) or take coach tours, boat trips or mountain gondola.

AA QQQQQ RAC Highly acclaimed.

VISA

Deluxe 👑👑
Contact: A W Henderson for brochure.
B&B £30 to £35 – weekly £180-£210.

Ashburn House, T B Henderson Achintore Road Fort William Inverness-shire PH33 6RQ Tel: (Fort William) 01397 706000 Fax: 01397 706000	**DELUXE** 👑👑	3 Single 1 Twin 3 Double	7 En Suite fac	B&B per person £30.00-£35.00 Single £30.00-£35.00 Double	Open Feb-Nov	

Family run totally refurbished Victorian villa in its own grounds, with magnificent views across the loch. Near to town centre.

Ben View Guest House Belford Road Fort William Inverness-shire PH33 6ER Tel: (Fort William) 01397 702966	**COMMENDED** 👑👑	1 Single 2 Twin 6 Double	8 En Suite fac 1 Priv. NOT ensuite 4 Pub Bath/Show	B&B per person £16.00-£20.00 Single £16.00-£23.00 Double	Open Feb-Nov	

Family run guest house conveniently situated for bus and train stations, town centre and leisure centre.

Mrs M Cameron Blythedale, Seafield Gardens Fort William Inverness-shire PH33 6RJ Tel: (Fort William) 01397 705523	**COMMENDED** 👑👑	1 Twin 2 Double	3 En Suite fac	B&B per person £15.00-£20.00 Double	Open Jan-Dec	

Modern detached house in residential area, 1mile (1.6 kms) from town centre. Ample private parking. Views across Loch Linnhe to the Ardgour Hills.

Mrs B Cameron Rodane, Badabrie Banavie, Fort William Inverness-shire PH33 7LX Tel: (Corpach) 01397 772603	**COMMENDED** 👑👑	1 Single 2 Family	1 Priv. NOT ensuite 2 Pub Bath/Show	B&B per person from £15.00 Single from £15.00 Double	Open Jan-Dec Dinner from 1800 B&B + Eve. Meal from £23.00	

Modern house in quiet residential area 3 miles (5 kms) from Fort William. Fine views to Ben Nevis and Loch Linnhe.

Mrs N Cameron Bardnaclavan 17 Sutherland Avenue Fort William Inverness-shire PH33 6JS Tel: (Fort William) 01397 704678	COMMENDED Listed	1 Single 1 Twin 1 Family	1 Pub Bath/Show	B&B per person £15.00-£17.00 Single £14.00-£15.00 Double	Open Easter-Oct

Family home affording splendid views over Loch Linnhe.
1 mile (2 kms) from town centre. Non-smoking.

THE GRANGE
Grange Road, Fort William, Inverness-shire PH33 6JF
Telephone: 01397 705516

Overlooking Loch Linnhe, set in its own grounds, a 10-minute walk from the town centre, restaurants and shore front. Offering exceptional Bed and Breakfast in a refurbished Victorian townhouse with a friendly atmosphere. Luxury bedrooms all with private facilities, some with loch views. Large, varied breakfast menu.
No smoking!   *Winner of 1996 Scottish Thistle Award.*

Mrs J Campbell The Grange, Grange Road Fort William Inverness-shire PH33 6JF Tel: (Fort William) 01397 705516	DELUXE	3 Double	3 En Suite fac	B&B per person £28.00-£33.00 Double	Open Apr-Oct

Late Victorian house sympathetically renovated within easy walking
distance of Fort William (10 minutes). Views over Loch Linnhe. Private parking.

Mrs Fiona Campbell Leasona Torlundy, Fort William Inverness-shire PH33 6SW Tel: (Fort William) 01397 704661	COMMENDED	1 Twin 2 Double	2 En Suite fac 1 Priv. NOT ensuite	B&B per person £13.00-£17.00 Double	Open Jan-Dec

Modern family home in super glen setting, views to Ben Nevis.
Ideal base for hillwalking, bird-watching, pony trekking and Aonach Mor.

Mrs F A Cook Melantee, Achintore Road Fort William Inverness-shire PH33 6RW Tel: (Fort William) 01397 705329	COMMENDED	1 Single 1 Twin 1 Double 1 Family	2 Pub Bath/Show	B&B per person £13.50-£15.00 Single £11.00-£12.00 Double Room only per person £13.50-£15.00	Open Jan-Dec

Bungalow 1.5 miles (3 kms) from town centre, overlooking the shores of
Loch Linnhe and the Ardgour hills and on the main A82 road.

Craig Nevis Guest House Belford Road Fort William Inverness-shire PH33 6BU Tel: (Fort William) 01397 702023	COMMENDED	1 Twin 3 Double 2 Family	2 En Suite fac 2 Pub Bath/Show	B&B per person £15.00-£18.00 Single £14.00-£20.00 Double	Open Jan-Dec

Personally run guest house. Short distance from town centre,
swimming pool and all amenities.

Crolinnhe Grange Road Fort William Inverness-shire PH33 6JF Tel: (Fort William) 01397 702709	DELUXE	1 Twin 4 Double	3 En Suite fac 1 Priv. NOT ensuite 1 Pub Bath/Show	B&B per person £28.00-£35.00 Single £28.00-£35.00 Double	Open Mar-Nov

Family run detached Victorian villa c.1880, refurbished to a high standard.
Friendly and welcoming atmosphere. Large colourful garden. Superb views.
Scottish Thistle Award Finalist 1996.

THE HIGHLANDS & SKYE

FORT WILLIAM continued **Inverness-shire** Distillery House Glenlochy Distillery North Road Fort William Inverness-shire PH33 6LH Tel: (Fort William) 01397 700103/702980	**Map 3** **H12**	**HIGHLY** **COMMENDED** 👑👑👑	1 Single 2 Twin 3 Double 1 Family	7 En Suite fac	B&B per person from £20.00 Single from £20.00 Double	Open Jan-Dec	

Distillery house at old Glenlochy Distillery in Fort William. Beside A82, the road to the Isles and Ben Nevis. Short distance from the town centre.

VORINGFOSS

5 Stirling Place, Fort William PH33 6UW   Tel: 01397 704062

Highland hospitality at its best for those who prefer a quiet situation within one mile of the town centre. Landscaped garden affords panoramic views to surrounding hills. An ideal centre from which to explore the West Highlands. Private parking and easy access to local bus route. Special diets catered for.

Mr & Mrs Fraser Voringfoss, 5 Stirling Place Fort William Inverness-shire PH33 6UW Tel: (Fort William) 01397 704062	**HIGHLY** **COMMENDED** 👑👑👑	1 Twin 2 Double	3 En Suite fac 2 Pub Bath/Show	B&B per person £16.00-£30.00 Single £16.00-£26.00 Double	Open Jan-Dec	

Modern family home in quiet residential area 1 mile (2 kms) from town centre. On main bus route.

Glenlochy Guest House

Nevis Bridge, Fort William
Inverness-shire PH33 6PF
Telephone: 01397 702909

This comfortable, family-run guest house is situated in its own spacious grounds, overlooking the River Nevis close to Ben Nevis, 3/4 mile from town centre. It is an ideal base for touring. Eight of the 10 rooms are ensuite. Colour TV and tea/coffee facilities in all rooms. Private parking.

For brochure and details contact Mrs MacBeth.

Glenlochy Guest House Nevis Bridge Fort William Inverness-shire PH33 6PF Tel: (Fort William) 01397 702909	**COMMENDED** 👑👑	4 Twin 4 Double 2 Family	8 En Suite fac 1 Pub Bath/Show	B&B per person £16.00-£23.00 Single £14.00-£23.00 Double	Open Jan-Dec	

Detached house with garden situated at Nevis Bridge, midway between Ben Nevis and the town centre. 0.5 miles (1 km) to railway station. 2 annexe rooms.

Glen Shiel Guest House Achintore Road Fort William Inverness-shire PH33 6RW Tel: (Fort William) 01397 702271	COMMENDED 👑 👑	1 Twin 3 Double	3 En Suite fac 2 Pub Bath/Show	B&B per person £15.00-£19.00 Double	Open Apr-Oct	

Modern house on the outskirts of the town with excellent views over Loch Linnhe. Good touring base.

Guisachan House Alma Road Fort William Inverness-shire PH33 6HA Tel: (Fort William) 01397 703797/704447	COMMENDED 👑 👑 👑	2 Single 5 Twin 6 Double 3 Family	15 En Suite fac 1 Priv. NOT ensuite	B&B per person £18.00-£28.00 Single £18.00-£27.00 Double	Open Jan-Dec Dinner from 1830 B&B + Eve. Meal from £27.00	

Family run establishment within easy walking distance of town centre, rail and bus stations. Home cooking. Some annexe accommodation.

Westhaven

Achintore Road, Fort William PH33 6RW Tel: 01397 705500

Magnificent situation overlooking Loch Linnhe and surrounding hills.
Spacious ensuite rooms are furnished to highest standards with colour TV
and hospitality tray and each has its own stunning loch view.
There is a comfortable residents' lounge, pleasant garden and ample parking.
Perfect base for touring.

Open all year **HIGHLY COMMENDED** 👑 👑

Mrs E Hamill Westhaven, Achintore Road Fort William Inverness-shire PH33 6RW Tel: (Fort William) 01397 705500	HIGHLY COMMENDED 👑 👑	1 Twin 2 Double	3 En Suite fac	B&B per person £18.00-£23.00 Double	Open Jan-Dec	

Modern detached house overlooking Loch Linnhe with all facilities and ample parking. Town centre 1.5 miles (2.4 kms).

Hillview Guest House Achintore Road Fort William Inverness-shire PH33 6RW Tel: (Fort William) 01397 704349	COMMENDED 👑 👑	1 Single 1 Twin 3 Double 1 Family	4 En Suite fac 1 Pub Bath/Show	B&B per person £17.00-£19.00 Single £16.00-£19.00 Double	Open Jan-Dec	

Family run guest house overlooking Loch Linnhe and about 1.5 miles (2.5kms) from Fort William.

Lochan Cottage Guest House Lochyside, by Fort William Inverness-shire PH33 Tel: (Fort William) 01397 702695	COMMENDED 👑 👑 👑	1 Twin 5 Double	6 En Suite fac	B&B per person £17.00-£22.00 Double	Open Jan-Dec Dinner from 1900 B&B + Eve. Meal £26.00-£31.00	

Friendly guest house in quiet location, Fort William 2 miles (3 kms). Large garden with views of Ben Nevis and Aonach Mor. German, Dutch and French spoken.

Lochiel Villa Guest House Achintore Road Fort William Inverness-shire PH33 6RQ Tel: (Fort William) 01397 703616	COMMENDED 👑 👑	1 Twin 6 Double 1 Family	3 En Suite fac 3 Pub Bath/Show	B&B per person £15.00-£24.00 Double	Open Mar-Nov	

Granite semi-villa with open views over Loch Linnhe. 500 yards (450m) from town centre.

THE HIGHLANDS & SKYE

Details of Grading and Classification are on page vi.

Key to symbols is on back flap.

| FORT WILLIAM continued
Inverness-shire | Map 3
H12 | | | |

LOCHVIEW GUEST HOUSE

Heathercroft Road, Fort William PH33 6RE
Telephone/Fax: 01397 703149

Lochview is situated on the hillside above the town in a quiet location with panoramic views over Loch Linnhe and the Ardgour Hills. All bedrooms are tastefully decorated and have private facilities, colour TV and tea/coffee facilities. There is a large garden and private parking.

Lochview Guest House Heathercroft, off Argyll Terrace Fort William Inverness-shire PH33 6RE Tel: (Fort William) 01397 703149 Fax: 01397 703149	COMMENDED	1 Single 2 Twin 5 Double	8 En Suite fac	B&B per person £25.00-£30.00 Single £18.00-£21.00 Double	Open Apr-Oct	
		Situated on a hillside above the town giving panoramic views over Loch Linnhe and the Ardgour Hills. Non-smoking house.				
Wilma & Jim McCourt 6 Caberfeidh, Fassifern Road Fort William Inverness-shire PH33 6BE Tel: (Fort William) 01397 703756	COMMENDED	1 Double 2 Family	1 En Suite fac 1 Pub Bath/Show	B&B per person £14.00-£20.00 Double	Open Jan-Dec	
		Semi-detached family house, very close to town centre, railway station and all amenities.				
Mrs T MacDonald Dorlin, Cameron Road Fort William Inverness-shire PH33 6LJ Tel: (Fort William) 01397 702016	COMMENDED	2 Double	2 En Suite fac	B&B per person £17.00-£20.00 Double	Open Jan-Dec	
		Modern bungalow in elevated position in quiet residential area close to town centre. Fine views over Loch Linnhe.				
Mrs Mary MacLean Innishfree Lochyside, by Fort William Inverness-shire PH33 7NX Tel: (Fort William) 01397 705471	HIGHLY COMMENDED	1 Double 1 Family	2 En Suite fac	B&B per person from £17.00 Double	Open Jan-Nov	
		Modern family home, with open outlook towards Ben Nevis and Aonach Mor. Open all year. Private parking.				
Mrs J MacLeod Rustic View Lochyside, by Fort William Inverness-shire PH33 7NX Tel: (Fort William) 01397 704709	HIGHLY COMMENDED	2 Double	2 En Suite fac	B&B per person £20.00-£30.00 Single £17.00-£20.00 Double	Open Apr-Oct	
		Modern family home in large garden. Short way from town centre and all amenities. Panoramic mountain views.				

Scotland for Golf . . .

Find out more about golf in Scotland. There's more to it than just the championship courses so get in touch with us now for information on the hidden gems of Scotland.

Write to: **Information Unit, Scottish Tourist Board,
23 Ravelston Terrace, Edinburgh EH4 3EU
or call: 0131-332 2433**

THE HIGHLANDS & SKYE

Heather & Charles Moore Abrach House 4 Caithness Place Fort William Inverness-shire PH33 6JP Tel: (Fort William) 01397 702535	COMMENDED 💧	1 Single 1 Double 1 Family	2 En Suite fac 1 Priv. NOT ensuite 2 Pub Bath/Show	B&B per person £15.00-£20.00 Single £15.00-£25.00 Double	Open Jan-Oct

Modern house in elevated position with excellent views
over Fort William and surrounding hills and loch.

V Moreland Dalbreac, Mallaig Road Corpach, by Fort William Inverness-shire PH33 7JR Tel: (Corpach) 01397 772309	COMMENDED 💧💧	1 Twin 2 Double	2 En Suite fac 1 Priv. NOT ensuite	B&B per person £15.00-£18.00 Double	Open Apr-Oct

Bungalow on the Road to the Isles. Homely atmosphere.
Evening meal on request. Home cooking and baking. Ample car parking.

Catriona Ann Morrison Torlinnhe, Achintore Road Fort William Inverness-shire PH33 6RN Tel: (Fort William) 01397 702583	COMMENDED 💧💧	1 Single 1 Twin 2 Double 2 Family	5 En Suite fac 1 Priv. NOT ensuite	B&B per person £15.00-£20.00 Single £15.00-£20.00 Double	Open Jan-Dec

Friendly family run guest house with ample car parking situated 1 mile
south of the town centre. Views of Loch Linnhe and the hills beyond.

Orchy Villa Guest House Alma Road Fort William Inverness-shire PH33 6HA Tel: (Fort William) 01397 702445 Fax: 01397 702445	COMMENDED 💧	1 Twin 2 Double 1 Family	4 Pub Bath/Show	B&B per person £13.00-£16.00 Single £13.00-£16.00 Double	Open Jan-Dec

Personally run quiet house close to town centre, swimming pool and leisure centre.
Short distance to bus and railway station. Panoramic views.

Rhu Mhor Guest House Alma Road Fort William Inverness-shire PH33 6BP Tel: (Fort William) 01397 702213	COMMENDED Listed	3 Twin 3 Double 1 Family	2 Pub Bath/Show	B&B per person £17.00-£17.50 Single £17.00-£17.50 Double	Open Apr-Oct Dinner from 1900 B&B + Eve. Meal £27.00-£28.00

Large family house with extensive wild garden in quiet area above town.
Short distance from town centre and all amenities.

G Ross Dalkeith, Belford Road Fort William Inverness-shire PH33 6BU Tel: (Fort William) 01397 704140	COMMENDED 💧💧	1 Twin 4 Double	3 En Suite fac 2 Pub Bath/Show	B&B per person £16.00-£28.00 Double	Open Apr-Oct

Detached stone-built villa, convenient for leisure centre, bus and rail stations.
Ample private parking.

Mrs Varley Ardmory, Victoria Road Fort William Inverness-shire PH33 6BH Tel: (Fort William) 01397 705943	COMMENDED 💧💧	1 Twin 2 Double	3 En Suite fac 1 Pub Bath/Show	B&B per person £16.00-£22.00 Double	Open Jan-Dec

Modern family home in quiet residential street.
Short walk from town centre and all amenities.

THE HIGHLANDS & SKYE

Details of Grading and Classification are on page vi.

Key to symbols is on back flap.

FORT WILLIAM – by FORT WILLIAM

FORT WILLIAM continued
Inverness-shire
Mrs Walker
Viewfield House, Alma Road
Fort William
Inverness-shire
PH33 6HD
Tel: (Fort William)
01397 704763

Map 3 H12

COMMENDED

3 Family | 2 En Suite fac / 1 Priv. NOT ensuite / 1 Pub Bath/Show

B&B per person
£16.00-£25.00 Single
£15.00-£19.00 Double

Open Jan-Dec

Family house in elevated location set above Fort William yet within walking distance of town centre. Private parking available.

Mrs Wiseman
17 Mossfield Drive, Lochyside
Fort William
Inverness-shire
PH33 7PE
Tel: (Fort William)
01397 703502

COMMENDED Listed

1 Single / 1 Twin / 1 Double | 1 En Suite fac / 1 Pub Bath/Show

B&B per person
£15.00-£18.00 Single
£15.00-£18.00 Double
Room only per person
£13.00-£15.00

Open Apr-Oct

Modern bungalow set in quiet residential area 2.5 miles (4 kms) outside Fort William. Restaurants and hotels nearby.

---

by FORT WILLIAM
Inverness-shire
Mrs Cameron
Strone Farm, by Muirshearlich
Banavie, Fort William
Inverness-shire
PH33 7PB
Tel: (Spean Bridge)
01397 712773

Map 3 H12

COMMENDED

2 Double | 2 En Suite fac

B&B per person
£20.00-£25.00 Single
from £18.00 Double
B&B + Eve. Meal
£27.00-£28.00

Open Jan-Sep
Dinner from 1900

Farmhouse on working farm overlooking the Caledonian Canal with panoramic views of Ben Nevis. 7 miles (12 kms) north of Fort William. Dinner by arrangement.

Mrs Davie
Carinbrook
Banavie, by Fort William
Inverness-shire
PH33 7LX
Tel: (Corpach) 01397 772318

COMMENDED

1 Single / 1 Twin / 3 Double | 3 En Suite fac / 2 Priv. NOT ensuite / 2 Pub Bath/Show

B&B per person
from £18.00 Single
from £18.00 Double
B&B + Eve. Meal
from £27.00

Open Jan-Nov
Dinner 1900-1930

Modern family house, 4 miles (6 kms) from Fort William. Excellent views of Ben Nevis, Fort William and Loch Linnhe.

Mrs B Grieve
Nevis View, 14 Farrow Drive
Corpach, by Fort William
Inverness-shire
PH33 7JW
Tel: (Corpach) 01397 772447/
0589 535036 (mobile)
Fax: 01397 772800

COMMENDED Listed

1 Single / 1 Double / 1 Family | 3 Priv. NOT ensuite / 2 Pub Bath/Show

B&B per person
£18.00-£20.00 Single
£14.00-£15.00 Double

Open Jan-Dec
Dinner 1800-1900

Family home in quiet residential estate. Views of Ben Nevis and Loch Eil. Home cooking. No-smoking house. Vegetarian and vegan diets catered for.

Mrs McInnes
Taormina
Banavie, by Fort William
Inverness-shire
PH33 7LY
Tel: (Corpach) 01397 772217

COMMENDED

1 Single / 1 Twin / 1 Double | 2 Pub Bath/Show

B&B per person
£14.00-£14.50 Single
£14.00-£14.50 Double

Open Mar-Oct

Modern bungalow quietly situated off "Road to the Isles". Restaurant and railway nearby. Caledonian Canal 50 metres, Fort William 3 miles (5 kms).

Mrs M Maclachlan

10 Guisach Terrace, Corpach, Fort William
Inverness-shire PH33 7JN   Téléphone: 01397 772785

Open all year! 1 twin, 2 double, 1 ensuite. B&B single £17-£19.50; twin/double £16-£19.50. We are situated in the village of Corpach, 3 miles from Fort William. All rooms have H&C and tea/coffee-making facilities. TV lounge for residents' exclusive use. Parking.
A warm welcome and hearty breakfast awaits you.

Mrs Mary Maclachlan 10 Guisach Terrace Corpach, Fort William Inverness-shire PH33 7JN Tel: (Corpach) 01397 772785	COMMENDED 👑👑👑	1 Twin 2 Double	1 En Suite fac 1 Pub Bath/Show	B&B per person £17.00-£19.50 Single £16.00-£19.00 Double	Open Jan-Dec	

Family home in quiet village, 5 miles (8 kms) from Fort William on Mallaig road.
Good base for touring.

Mrs I MacLean Grianan, 4 Lochiel Crescent Banavie, Fort William Inverness-shire PH33 7LZ Tel: (Corpach) 01397 772659	COMMENDED 👑	3 Double	1 Pub Bath/Show	B&B per person £13.50-£15.00 Double	Open Apr-Oct	

Modern detached bungalow in a quiet residential area near to Neptune's
Staircase on the Caledonian Canal. Fine views towards Ben Nevis.

CLINTWOOD

23 HILLVIEW DRIVE, CORPACH, FORT WILLIAM PH33 7LS
TELEPHONE: 01397 772680

Let us welcome you to our home, a modern villa situated 4 miles from town. We enjoy magnificent views of Ben Nevis and surrounding mountains. All bedrooms are tastefully furnished and have private facilities, central heating, TV, welcome tray. The breakfast room looks onto a pleasant garden as does the guests' lounge.

Mrs McLeod Clintwood, 23 Hillview Drive Corpach, by Fort William Inverness-shire PH33 7LS Tel: (Corpach) 01397 772680	HIGHLY COMMENDED 👑👑	1 Twin 2 Double	3 En Suite fac	B&B per person from £22.00 Double	Open Apr-Oct	

A warm Highland welcome in this attractively appointed modern
villa in village of Corpach. Fort William 4 miles (6kms).

Mansefield Guest House Corpach, Fort William Inverness-shire PH33 7LT Tel: (Corpach) 01397 772262	COMMENDED 👑👑	1 Twin 2 Double 2 Family	2 En Suite fac 2 Pub Bath/Show	B&B per person £20.00-£23.50 Single £17.00-£20.50 Double	Open Jan-Dec Dinner from 1900 B&B + Eve. Meal £28.50-£32.00	

Victorian house with its own garden. 3 miles (5kms) from Fort William,
on the Road to the Isles. Home cooking and preserves, fresh produce.

BE SURE TO CHOOSE THE SCOTTISH TOURIST BOARD'S SIGN OF QUALITY

by FORT WILLIAM continued Inverness-shire	Map 3 H12

TORBEAG HOUSE

Muirshearlich, Banavie, By Fort William PH33 7PB
Telephone/Fax: 01397 772412

This elegant country house must surely occupy one of the most stunning locations in Scotland with magnificent views of *Ben Nevis* and the *Great Glen*. Here you will find a warm welcome, peace and tranquillity, luxurious accommodation and good food, including home-made bread and preserves etc, all in beautiful surroundings.

TAIGH TORBEAG COMHAIR BEINN NIMHEIS
(House on the little hill opposite the Hill of Heaven)

Further details from
GLADYS or KEN WHYTE

Torbeag House
Muirshearlich, Banavie
Fort William
Inverness-shire
PH33 7PB
Tel: (Corpach) 01397 772412
Fax: 01397 772412.

DELUXE

1 Twin
2 Double

2 En Suite fac
1 Priv. NOT ensuite

B&B per person
£20.00-£32.00 Double

Open Jan-Dec
Dinner from 1930
B&B + Eve. Meal
£36.00-£48.00

Spacious, modern country home in secluded setting 5.5 miles (9 kms) from Fort William and magnificent views of Ben Nevis. Warm welcome, log fire, home baking.

FOYERS
Inverness-shire
Foyers Bay House
Lower Foyers
Inverness-shire
IV1 2YB
Tel: (Gorthleck) 01456 486624
Fax: 01456 486337

Map 4
A10

COMMENDED

2 Twin
1 Double

3 En Suite fac

B&B per person
£23.00-£33.00 Single
£18.00-£23.00 Double

Open Jan-Dec
Dinner 1900-2000
B&B + Eve. Meal
£26.00-£41.00

Friendly welcome at modernised Victorian house overlooking Loch Ness and set in 4 acres (1.6ha) of ground. 500 yards (460m) from Falls of Foyers.

GAIRLOCH
Ross-shire
Lynn Bennett-MacKenzie
Croit Mo Sheanair, 29 Strath
Gairloch
Ross-shire
IV21 2DA
Tel: (Gairloch) 01445 712389

Map 3
F7

COMMENDED

2 Twin
1 Double

1 En Suite fac
1 Pub Bath/Show

B&B per person
£14.50-£18.50 Double

Open Jan-Dec
excl Xmas/New Year

Modern house on edge of Gairloch village, looking out over bay towards Skye.
Home baking.

Birchwood Guest House
Gairloch
Ross-shire
IV21 2AH
Tel: (Gairloch) 01445 712011

COMMENDED

3 Twin
2 Double
1 Family

6 En Suite fac
1 Pub Bath/Show

B&B per person
£19.00-£24.00 Single
£19.00-£24.00 Double

Open Apr-Oct

Personally run, completely refurbished house in elevated position affording excellent views over harbour. All rooms with ensuite facilities.

Charleston Guest House
Gairloch
Ross-shire
IV21 2AH
Tel: (Gairloch) 01445 712497

COMMENDED

2 Single
2 Twin
2 Double
3 Family

2 Pub Bath/Show

B&B per person
£16.50-£17.00 Single
£16.50-£17.00 Double

Open Apr-Oct
Dinner from 1900
B&B + Eve. Meal
from £24.00

Large 18th century house, situated on sea-loch overlooking Gairloch harbour.
Personally run, all home cooking. Children and pets welcome.

| Fran Cree
Rua Reidh Lighthouse Hostel
Melvaig, Gairloch
IV21 2EA
Tel: (Gairloch) 01445 771263
Fax: 01445 771263 | **APPROVED**
Listed | 1 Twin
2 Double
4 Family | 3 En Suite fac
2 Pub Bath/Show | B&B per person
£11.00-£16.00 Double
Room only per person
£7.00-£12.00 | Open Jan-Dec
Dinner 1800-2000
B&B + Eve. Meal
£19.00-£24.00 |
| | | **Situated on remote peninsula in NW Highlands, offering a holiday out of the ordinary. Friendly relaxed atmosphere.** | | | |

| John & Barbara Hitchon
Tomatin Cottage
52 Lonemore
Gairloch
Ross-shire
Tel: (Gairloch) 01445 712355 | **HIGHLY COMMENDED** | 2 Twin | 2 Priv. NOT ensuite | B&B per person
£17.00-£22.00 Double | Open Jan-Dec
Dinner from 1900
B&B + Eve. Meal
£28.00-£34.00 |
| | | **A warm welcome and good food await you at this comfortable no-smoking house with wonderful views to the Isle of Skye and the Torridon mountains.** | | | |

| Horisdale House
Strath
Gairloch
Ross-shire
IV21 2DA
Tel: (Gairloch) 01445 712151 | **HIGHLY COMMENDED** | 2 Single
1 Twin
1 Double | 2 Priv. NOT ensuite
1 Pub Bath/Show | B&B per person
to £20.00 Single
to £19.00 Double | Open May-Sep
Dinner from 1900
B&B + Eve. Meal
from £32.00 |
| | | **Modern detached house with attractive garden and excellent views. Home cooking with emphasis on fresh produce. Regret no pets allowed.** | | | |

| Kerrysdale House
Gairloch
Ross-shire
IV21 2AL
Tel: (Gairloch) 01445 712292 | **COMMENDED** | 1 Twin
2 Double | 2 En Suite fac
1 Priv. NOT ensuite | B&B per person
£18.00-£26.00 Single
£18.00-£23.00 Double | Open Feb-Nov |
| | | **18th century farmhouse recently refurbished and tastefully decorated. Modern comforts in a peaceful setting. 1 mile (2 kms) south of Gairloch.** | | | |

DUISARY

24 Strath, Gairloch, Ross-shire IV21 2DA   Tel: 01445 712252

Duisary, a modernised traditional croft house on the outskirts of the village, provides true Highland hospitality. All bedrooms have central heating, wash-hand basin and tea-making facilities. One bedroom ensuite. Two public bathrooms. Here one can relax and enjoy some of Scotland's finest scenery. Spectacular views of the sea, Skye and Torridon Hills, Inverewe Gardens 6 miles, golf course 1 mile. Fishing and walking opportunities.   *B&B from £15.*

| Miss I MacKenzie
Duisary, 24 Strath
Gairloch
Ross-shire
IV21 2DA
Tel: (Gairloch) 01445 712252 | **COMMENDED** | 1 Twin
1 Double
1 Family | 1 En Suite fac
2 Pub Bath/Show | B&B per person
from £15.00 Single
from £15.00 Double | Open Apr-Oct |
| | | **Traditional stone-built croft house on edge of village, with fine views across Gairloch to the hills of Torridon.** | | | |

| The Mountain Restaurant
& Lodge
Strath Square
Gairloch
Ross-shire
IV21 2BX
Tel: (Gairloch) 01445 712316 | **COMMENDED**
Listed | 1 Twin
2 Double | 3 En Suite fac | B&B per person
£19.95-£28.50 Double | Open Mar-Oct, Dec
Dinner 1830-2100 |
| | | **In Gairloch's main square, with views across the bay. Daytime coffee shop, dinners by candlelight in an informal atmosphere.** | | | |

| GARVE | Map 4 |
| Ross-shire | A8 |

MRS HAZEL HAYTON

Birch Cottage, Station Road, Garve, Ross-shire IV23 2PS
Telephone: 01997 414237
Comfortable, friendly accommodation. Ideal base for touring and walking. All rooms ensuite, TV, tea-making. Guest lounge, garden, patio, parking.
Open all year.   **Welcome Host Certificate Holder**

Mrs Hayton Birch Cottage, Station Road Garve Ross-shire IV23 2PS Tel: (Garve) 01997 414237	**HIGHLY COMMENDED**	1 Twin 3 En Suite fac 1 Double 1 Pub Bath/Show 1 Family	B&B per person £15.00-£16.00 Single £13.50-£14.00 Double	Open Jan-Dec

Traditional Highland cottage en route to Gairloch/Ullapool. Refurbished to a high standard. Garve railway station 50 metres. 2 annexe bedrooms.

| GLENCOE | Map 1 |
| Argyll | F1 |

Dorrington Lodge 6 Tighphuirst Glencoe Argyll PA39 4HN Tel: (Ballachulish) 01855 811653	**COMMENDED**	2 Twin 3 En Suite fac 3 Double 2 Pub Bath/Show	B&B per person £14.00-£18.00 Double	Open Feb-Oct, Xmas/New Year Dinner from 1900 B&B + Eve. Meal £24.00-£28.00

Comfortable, modern house just off main road, with excellent views over Loch Leven. Home-cooked meals using quality local produce. No smoking.

Dunire Guest House Glencoe Argyll PA39 4HS Tel: (Ballachulish) 01855 811305	**COMMENDED**	2 Twin 4 En Suite fac 3 Double 2 Pub Bath/Show	B&B per person £14.00-£18.50 Double	Open 28th Dec-Oct

Modern bungalow in centre of Glencoe Village.
Ideal base for touring, climbing and hillwalking.

SCORRYBREAC GUEST HOUSE

GLENCOE, ARGYLL PA39 4HT
Telephone: 01855 811354
Scorrybreac is a comfortable well-appointed guest house in beautiful woodland surroundings managed by the resident owners. We are a no-smoking establishment. It is an ideal base for exploring the Glencoe and Ben Nevis area or for a shorter stay on a more extended tour of the Highlands.

Scorrybreac Guest House Glencoe Argyll PA39 4HT Tel: (Ballachulish) 01855 811354	**COMMENDED**	3 Twin 5 En Suite fac 3 Double 1 Priv. NOT ensuite	B&B per person £16.00-£28.00 Single £14.00-£20.00 Double	Open Dec-Oct Dinner 1830-1900 B&B + Eve. Meal £26.50-£32.50

Modern single-storey house with large garden overlooking Loch Leven.
In a quiet secluded situation on the edge of the village with local forest walks.

GLENCOE
STRATHLACHLAN – THE GLENCOE GUEST HOUSE
Upper Carnoch, Glencoe PA39 4HT   Tel: 01855 811244

A family run guest house in a quiet, peaceful, riverside setting. Spectacular mountain views. Comfortable ensuite rooms with TVs and tea and coffee-making facilities. Central heating. Pleasant residents' lounge. Drying room. An ideal location for touring and sightseeing the beautiful West Coast or local walking, climbing and skiing.

Strathlachlan The Glencoe Guest House Upper Carnoch Glencoe Argyll PA39 4HT Tel: (Ballachulish) 01855 811244 Fax: 01855 811244		**COMMENDED** 👑👑	2 Twin 2 Double 2 Family	4 En Suite fac 1 Pub Bath/Show	B&B per person £16.00-£19.00 Single £14.00-£19.00 Double	Open Jan-Dec

Quiet peaceful riverside setting on edge of village. Magnificent views. Ideal base for touring and for mountain sports. Family run.

by GLENSHIEL **Ross-shire** Duich House Letterfearn Glenshiel Ross-shire IV40 8HS Tel: (Dornie) 01599 555259/ 555333 Fax: 01599 555259	Map 3 G10	**HIGHLY COMMENDED** 👑👑👑	2 Double	2 Priv. NOT ensuite	B&B per person £30.00-£40.00 Single £20.00-£30.00 Double	Open Jan-Dec Dinner from 1930

Listed Country house overlooking Loch Duich with magnificent views to Five Sisters of Kintail.

GLEN URQUHART **Inverness-shire** Mrs Patricia Moir Cragaig Glen Urquhart Inverness-shire IV3 6TN Tel: (Glen Urquhart) 01456 476246	Map 4 A9	**COMMENDED** 👑	2 Twin 1 Double	2 Pub Bath/Show	B&B per person from £15.00 Single £14.00-£16.00 Double	Open Apr-Sep

Set in its own attractive gardens, 5.5m (9 kms) from Drumnadrochit. Cragaig overlooks Loch Meiklie and is convenient for Glen Affric, Strathglass and Loch Ness.

GOLSPIE **Sutherland** Mrs N Grant Deo Greine Farm, Backies Golspie Sutherland KW10 6SE Tel: (Golspie) 01408 633106	Map 4 B6	**COMMENDED** 👑👑👑	2 Twin 1 Double 1 Family	3 En Suite fac 1 Priv. NOT ensuite	B&B per person from £18.00 Double	Open Apr-Oct Dinner from 1800 B&B + Eve. Meal from £28.00

Crofting farmhouse, situated in hills behind Golspie, in an elevated position overlooking surrounding countryside.

Scotland for Golf . . .

Find out more about golf in Scotland. There's more to it than just the championship courses so get in touch with us now for information on the hidden gems of Scotland.

Write to: **Information Unit, Scottish Tourist Board, 23 Ravelston Terrace, Edinburgh EH4 3EU** or call: **0131-332 2433**

THE HIGHLANDS & SKYE

Details of Grading and Classification are on page vi.

Key to symbols is on back flap.

GRANTOWN-ON-SPEY Moray	Map 4 C9	

Ardconnel House

Woodlands Terrace, Grantown-on-Spey,
Moray PH26 3JU   Tel/Fax: 01479 872104
DELUXE 👑👑👑 AA QQQQQ PREMIER SELECTED

Ardconnel House is situated at the southern fringe of
Grantown-on-Spey opposite Lochan, Forest and Hills;
the charming town centre and world-famous River Spey
are just a short walk. The house is beautifully furnished
throughout; there is a spacious sitting room with log fire
and all bedrooms have ensuite private facilities and are
extremely comfortable being equipped with quality
beds, colour televisions, welcome trays and hairdryers.
Excellent home cooking using fresh local produce is
complemented by an interesting selection of modestly
priced wines.
Deluxe accommodation at a realistic price.
Colour brochure available on request –
please call 01479 872104.

Ardconnel House Woodlands Terrace Grantown-on-Spey Moray PH26 3JU Tel: (Grantown-on-Spey) 01479 872104 Fax: 01479 872104	DELUXE 👑👑👑	1 Twin 4 Double 1 Family	6 En Suite fac	B&B per person £32.00 Single £25.00-£33.00 Double	Open Mar-Oct Dinner from 1900 B&B + Eve. Meal £42.00-£50.00

Splendid Victorian villa with ample private car parking, all rooms ensuite.
No smoking throughout. Superb 4-poster room. Taste of Scotland selected member.

Brooklynn Grant Road Grantown-on-Spey Moray PH26 3LA Tel: (Grantown-on-Spey) 01479 873113	COMMENDED 👑👑	1 Single 1 Twin 4 Double	2 En Suite fac 1 Pub Bath/Show	B&B per person £16.50-£19.50 Single £16.50-£19.50 Double	Open Apr-Sep

Attractive villa and garden in quiet area within easy walking distance of town,
woods and river. Many personal touches, evening meal by arrangement.

Crann Tara Guest House High Street Grantown-on-Spey Moray PH26 3EN Tel: (Grantown-on-Spey) 01479 872197	COMMENDED 👑	1 Single 1 Twin 3 Family	2 Pub Bath/Show	B&B per person £15.00-£16.00 Single £15.00-£16.00 Double Room only per person £14.00-£15.00	Open Jan-Dec Dinner from 1830 B&B + Eve. Meal £24.00-£25.00

19th century townhouse, recently modernised and personally run. Near River Spey,
with rod storage and drying room. Cycle hire and repair. Off-street car parking.
Dinner available.

THE HIGHLANDS & SKYE

Scottish TOURIST BOARD COMMENDED

FOR QUALITY
GO GRADED

Culdearn House

WOODLANDS TERRACE
GRANTOWN-ON-SPEY PH26 3JU
TEL: 01479 872106   FAX: 01479 873641

Elegant Country House offering house party atmosphere and warm welcome from the Scottish hosts Isobel and Alasdair Little who provide freshly prepared food and modestly priced wines. All guest rooms have ensuite private facilities with colour TV, radio, hairdryer and welcome tray. Culdearn House has been modernised and decorated with sympathy to offer a high standard of comfort. Ideal location for fishing, golf, riding, walking, bird-watching and visiting castles and historic sites. Log fires in season. 3 and 7 day breaks available from £120; all rates include dinner.

AA Premier selected RAC Highly Acclaimed.
Taste of Scotland selected members.
"AA Guest House of the Year" 1995
"RAC Hotel of the Year" 1996
Please contact Isobel and Alasdair Little for reservations.

Culdearn House Woodlands Terrace Grantown-on-Spey Moray PH26 3JU Tel: (Grantown-on-Spey) 01479 872106 Fax: 01479 873641	DELUXE ♛♛♛	1 Single 3 Twin 5 Double	9 En Suite fac	Open Mar-Oct Dinner 1845-1930 B&B + Eve. Meal £40.00-£55.00	

Elegant Victorian house, retaining many original features. Warm and friendly atmosphere. All rooms ensuite facilities. Taste of Scotland member.

Bank House

1 The Square, Grantown-on-Spey, Moray PH26 3HG
Telephone: 01479 873256

Centrally situated for Inverness, Elgin, Forres, Nairn and Aviemore. Large comfortable heated rooms with colour TV, tea/coffee facilities and armchairs – 3 rooms (family, twin, single). Full Scottish breakfast. Private bathroom available at extra charge. Five minutes' walk from the renowned River Spey and golf course.

Mrs Helen Hunter Bank House, 1 The Square Grantown-on-Spey Moray PH26 3HG Tel: (Grantown-on-Spey) 01479 873256	COMMENDED Listed	1 Single 1 Twin 1 Family	1 Priv. NOT ensuite 1 Pub Bath/Show	B&B per person £15.00-£18.00 Single £15.00-£17.00 Double	Open Jan-Dec	

Former Bank Manager's flat offering very spacious comfortable accommodation. Ideal touring base.

WELCOME

Whenever you are in Scotland, you can be sure of a warm welcome at your nearest Tourist Information Centre.
For guide books, maps, souvenirs, our Centres provide a service second to none – many now offer bureau-de-change facilities. And, of course, Tourist Information Centres offer free, expert advice on what to see and do, route-planning and accommodation for everyone – visitors and residents alike!

THE HIGHLANDS & SKYE

Details of Grading and Classification are on page vi.

Key to symbols is on back flap.

KINROSS HOUSE

Woodside Avenue, Grantown-on-Spey PH26 3JR
Tel: 01479 872042 Fax: 01479 873504

Kinross House sits on a quiet and pretty avenue an easy stroll from pinewoods and river, and from the centre of this delightful country town.

David and Katherine Elder provide Highland hospitality and comfort at its very best in their smoke-free house.

- Bedrooms are bright, warm and restful with many thoughtful little extras.
- One bedroom is suitable for ambulant disabled guests.
- Delicious dinner carefully planned and freshly prepared with quality ingredients.
- David wears his McIntosh kilt to serve dinner.
- Interesting selection of wines and Speyside Malts.

Kinross Guest House
Woodside Avenue
Grantown-on-Spey
Moray
PH26 3JR
Tel: (Grantown-on-Spey)
01479 872042
Fax: 01479 873504

HIGHLY COMMENDED

2 Single
2 Twin
1 Double
1 Family

5 En Suite fac
2 Pub Bath/Show

B&B per person
£21.00-£29.00 Single
£23.00-£26.00 Double

Open Apr-Oct
Dinner from 1900
B&B + Eve. Meal
£33.50-£41.50

Attractive Victorian villa in peaceful residential area. Welcoming and relaxed atmosphere with your Scottish hosts. No-smoking house.

Miss Fenella Palmer
Fearna House, Old Spey Bridge
Grantown-on-Spey
Moray
PH26 3NQ
Tel: (Grantown-on-Spey)
01479 872016

COMMENDED

2 Twin
1 Double

2 En Suite fac
1 Priv. NOT ensuite

B&B per person
from £20.00 Single
from £17.00 Double

Open Jan-Dec
Dinner 1830-2000
B&B + Eve. Meal
£27.00-£30.00

19th century country house situated 1 mile (2 kms) from town, overlooking the River Spey to the hills beyond. Dinner by arrangement.

Parkburn Guest House
High Street
Grantown-on-Spey
Moray
PH26 3EN
Tel: (Grantown-on-Spey)
01479 873116

COMMENDED

1 Single
2 Twin
2 Double

2 En Suite fac
1 Pub Bath/Show

B&B per person
from £18.00 Single
from £16.00 Double

Open Jan-Dec

Semi detached Victorian villa standing back from main road with ample parking available. Fishing and fishing tuition can be arranged.

The Pines
Woodside Avenue
Grantown-on-Spey
Moray
PH26 3JR
Tel: (Grantown-on-Spey)
01479 872092
Fax: 01479 872092

COMMENDED

1 Single
3 Twin
2 Double
3 Family

5 En Suite fac
2 Pub Bath/Show

B&B per person
£16.50-£22.00 Single
£16.50-£22.00 Double

Open Mar-Oct
Dinner from 1830
B&B + Eve. Meal
from £26.50

Family run, situated on edge of pine wood, only 0.5 miles (1 km) from town centre. All home cooking. Dogs welcome.

Rossmor Guest House
Woodlands Terrace
Grantown-on-Spey
Moray
PH26 3JU
Tel: (Grantown-on-Spey)
01479 872201

COMMENDED

2 Twin
3 Double
1 Family

6 En Suite fac

B&B per person
£20.00-£22.00 Single
£20.00-£22.00 Double

Open Jan-Dec

Spacious Victorian detached house with original features and large garden. A warm welcome. Parking. Panoramic views. No smoking throughout.

THE HIGHLANDS & SKYE

HALKIRK **Caithness** Mrs M Banks Glenlivet, Fairview Halkirk Caithness KW12 6XF Tel: (Halkirk) 01847 831302	**Map 4** D3	COMMENDED	1 Single 2 Twin 1 Double	2 Pub Bath/Show	B&B per person £13.00 Single £13.00 Double	Open Jan-Dec	

Modern house on outskirts of the village, close to river
and 6 miles (10 kms) south of Thurso.

Sandy & Jessie Waters The Bungalow Banachmore Farm Harpsdale, Halkirk Caithness KW12 6UN Tel: (Westerdale) 01847 841216		HIGHLY COMMENDED	1 Twin 1 Double 1 Family	3 En Suite fac 1 Pub Bath/Show	B&B per person from £17.00 Single from £17.00 Double	Open Jan-Dec Dinner 1830-2000	

Modern detached house on a working farm in a quiet rural setting,
¾ mile (1.5 kms) from salmon fishing on River Thurso. All rooms ensuite.

HELMSDALE **Sutherland** Mrs S Blance Broomhill House Helmsdale Sutherland KW8 6JS Tel: (Helmsdale) 01431 821259 Fax: 01431 821259	**Map 4** C5	COMMENDED	1 Twin 1 Double	2 En Suite fac 1 Pub Bath/Show	B&B per person £16.00-£19.00 Double	Open Apr-Oct Dinner 1700-1900 B&B + Eve. Meal £25.00-£28.00	

Victorian, stone-built house with turret. Magnificent
panoramic view over Helmsdale to the sea.

Mrs E McAngus Glebe House, Sutherland Street Helmsdale Sutherland KW8 6LQ Tel: (Helmsdale) 01431 821682		COMMENDED	1 Twin 1 Double	2 En Suite fac 1 Pub Bath/Show	B&B per person from £16.00 Double	Open Jan-Dec	

Detached traditional stone-built house, in quiet cul-de-sac with parking at rear.
Both rooms ensuite.

Mrs M C Polson Torbuie, Navidale Helmsdale Sutherland KW8 6JS Tel: (Helmsdale) 01431 821424		HIGHLY COMMENDED	2 Double	2 En Suite fac	B&B per person £15.00-£18.00 Single £15.00-£17.00 Double	Open Apr-Oct	

Well-appointed house with superb views overlooking sea. Good base for touring.

INSH **Inverness-shire** Ian & Pamela Grant Greenfield Croft Insh Inverness-shire PH21 1NT Tel: (Kingussie) 01540 661010	**Map 4** C10	HIGHLY COMMENDED	1 Twin 2 Double	3 En Suite fac	B&B per person from £18.00 Single from £15.00 Double	Open Jan-Dec Dinner from 1900 B&B + Eve. Meal from £25.50	

Newly built house on a working croft in quiet Highland village with superb views.
Home cooking, log fire, all rooms with ensuite facilities.

INVERGARRY **Inverness-shire** Mr & Mrs Buswell 1/2/3 Nursery Cottages Invergarry Inverness-shire PH35 4HL Tel: (Invergarry) 01809 501297	**Map 3** H11	COMMENDED	1 Single 1 Double 1 Family	1 Priv. NOT ensuite 2 Pub Bath/Show	B&B per person £14.00-£17.00 Single £14.00-£17.00 Double	Open Jan-Dec Dinner 1800-1900	

Mid 19th century homely cottage. 7 miles (11 kms) south of Fort Augustus.
Centrally located for touring the Highlands.

THE HIGHLANDS & SKYE

THE HIGHLANDS & SKYE

| INVERGARRY continued
Inverness-shire | Map 3
H11 | | |

FOREST LODGE

South Laggan, Invergarry, by Spean Bridge
Inverness-shire PH34 4EA. Telephone: 01809 501219

Staying one night or more, Ian and Janet Shearer's comfortable home offers pleasant ensuite accommodation, relaxed surroundings and home cooking served with friendly attention. Forest Lodge is conveniently situated in the centre of the Great Glen and is ideal for touring or participating in outdoor pursuits.

Forest Lodge Guest House South Laggan Invergarry, by Spean Bridge Inverness-shire PH34 4EA Tel: (Invergarry) 01809 501219	COMMENDED 👑👑👑	2 Twin 3 Double 2 Family	6 En Suite fac 1 Priv. NOT ensuite	B&B per person £15.00-£18.00 Double	Open Jan-Dec Dinner from 1930 B&B + Eve. Meal £26.00-£29.00

Family run guest house in the heart of the Great Glen where Caledonian Canal joins Lochs Lochy and Oich. Ideal centre for outdoor activities.

Drynachan Cottage

INVERGARRY, INVERNESS-SHIRE PH35 4HL
Telephone: 01809 501225

Seventeeth-century Highland cottage, visited by *Bonnie Prince Charlie* in 1746, idyllically situated on the shores of Loch Oich. Comfortable accommodation with open fire and home cooking. Large garden with many birds. Access to Great Glen Cycle Track. Ideal for hillwalking, ski-ing, cycling and touring. Cycle store and drying area.

Ms Caroline Francis Drynachan Cottage Invergarry Inverness-shire PH35 4HL Tel: (Invergarry) 01809 501225	COMMENDED 👑👑	1 Twin 1 Double 1 Family	1 En Suite fac 1 Pub Bath/Show	B&B per person £14.00-£18.00 Single £13.00-£18.00 Double	Open Jan-Dec Dinner 1900-1930 B&B + Eve. Meal £23.00-£28.00

Historic Highland cottage, recently renovated, centrally situated in the Great Glen, 25 miles north of Fort William, log fire, home cooking.

Mrs H Fraser Ardfriseal, Mandally Road Invergarry Inverness-shire PH35 4HP Tel: (Invergarry) 01809 501281	COMMENDED 👑	1 Twin 2 Double	1 Pub Bath/Show	B&B per person from £19.00 Single from £15.00 Double	Open May-Oct

Modern family home in secluded area with magnificent views of surrounding hills. 1 mile (2 kms) from Invergarry.

Mrs F I Jamieson Lilac Cottage, South Laggan Spean Bridge Inverness-shire PH34 4EA Tel: (Invergarry) 01809 501410	COMMENDED Listed	1 Twin 2 Double	1 Pub Bath/Show	B&B per person from £14.00 Single from £14.00 Double	Open Jan-Dec Dinner 1900-2000

Modernised 100-year-old croft house convenient for touring West of Scotland. Evening meal and home cooking.

WELCOME

Whenever you are in Scotland, you can be sure of a warm welcome at your nearest Tourist Information Centre.

For guide books, maps, souvenirs, our Centres provide a service second to none – many now offer bureau-de-change facilities. And, of course, Tourist Information Centres offer free, expert advice on what to see and do, route-planning and accommodation for everyone – visitors and residents alike!

North Laggan Farmhouse
by Spean Bridge, Inverness PH34 4EB
Telephone: 01809 501335

Overlooking the Caledonian Canal and Loch Oich, set ½ mile off A82, 2 miles south of Invergarry amidst sheep-farming country. A completely modernised croft house which retains much of its original character. Two comfortable bed/sitting rooms. Home-made bread, good food and individual attention guaranteed.

Mrs Waugh
North Laggan Farmhouse
by Invergarry
Inverness-shire
PH34 4EB
Tel: (Invergarry)
01809 501335

COMMENDED
Listed

1 Twin
1 Family

1 Pub Bath/Show

B&B per person
£18.50 Single
Room only per person
£14.50

Open May-Sep
Dinner from 1900
B&B + Eve. Meal
from £24.00

In peaceful open countryside overlooking the Caledonian Canal and Loch Oich.
Warm welcome, home-made bread and good home cooking. Non-smoking home.

INVERGORDON
Ross-shire
Craigaron Guest House
17 Saltburn
Invergordon
Ross-shire
IV18 0JX
Tel: (Invergordon)
01349 853640

Map 4
B7

COMMENDED

1 Single
3 Twin
1 Double

3 En Suite fac
1 Pub Bath/Show

B&B per person
from £20.00 Single
from £17.00 Double
Room only per person
from £14.00

Open Jan-Dec
Dinner 1900-1930
B&B + Eve. Meal
£27.00-£36.00

19th century converted fisherman's cottage overlooking the sea.
Five minute drive from town centre.

INVERMORISTON
Inverness-shire
Mr & Mrs M Douglas
Burnside, Dalcataig
Glenmoriston
Inverness-shire
IV3 6YG
Tel: (Glenmoriston)
01320 351262

Map 4
A10

COMMENDED

1 Single
1 Twin
1 Double

2 En Suite fac
1 Priv. NOT ensuite

B&B per person
£15.00-£18.00 Single
£15.00-£18.00 Double

Open Apr-Oct

Warm Highland hospitality at this modern bungalow 1 mile (2kms) from
Invermoriston and near Loch Ness. Peace and tranquillity with birdsong.

Mrs I Greig
Georgeston
Invermoriston
Inverness-shire
IV3 6YA
Tel: (Glenmoriston)
01320 351264

COMMENDED

1 Twin
2 Double

1 En Suite fac
1 Pub Bath/Show

B&B per person
£13.00-£16.00 Double

Open Jan-Dec

Detached bungalow on outskirts of village and just off main road.
Ample parking and nice views.

INVERNESS

Aberfeldy Lodge Guest House
11 Southside Road
Inverness
IV2 3BG
Tel: (Inverness) 01463 231120

Map 4
B8

COMMENDED

3 Twin
3 Double
3 Family

9 En Suite fac

B&B per person
£19.00-£25.00 Double

Open Jan-Dec
Dinner 1800-1830
B&B + Eve. Meal
£31.50-£37.50

Substantial detached house with large garden in quiet residential area.
Close to town centre and convenient for bus and railway stations. Private parking.

Abermar Guest House
25 Fairfield Road
Inverness
IV3 5QD
Tel: (Inverness) 01463 239019

APPROVED

5 Single
2 Twin
2 Double
2 Family

3 En Suite fac
2 Limited ensuite
3 Pub Bath/Show

B&B per person
£16.00-£17.00 Single
£16.00-£17.00 Double

Open Jan-Dec

Detached house situated in a residential area. 5 minutes' walk from the town centre.
Convenient base for touring the Highlands. Private parking.

THE HIGHLANDS & SKYE

THE HIGHLANDS & SKYE

INVERNESS continued	Map 4 B8						
Ach Aluinn Guest House 27 Fairfield Road Inverness IV3 5QD Tel: (Inverness) 01463 230127	COMMENDED ♔♔	1 Single 2 Twin 2 Family	4 En Suite fac 1 Priv. NOT ensuite	B&B per person £16.00-£20.00 Single £16.00-£20.00 Double	Open Jan-Dec		

Newly refurbished, detached, Victorian house with private parking in quiet residential road. 10 minutes' walk from town centre. All rooms ensuite.

| Mrs C D Aird Pitfarrane, 57 Crown Street Inverness IV2 3AY Tel: (Inverness) 01463 239338 | COMMENDED ♔♔ | 2 Twin 1 Double 1 Family | 1 En Suite fac 3 Limited ensuite 1 Pub Bath/Show | B&B per person £16.00-£18.00 Double | Open Jan-Dec | | |

End-terraced house in quiet residential area within 10 minutes' walk from town centre. Some private parking.

Atherstone Guest House

42 Fairfield Road, Inverness IV3 5QD
Telephone: 01463 240240

Enjoy a warm Highland welcome at this Victorian home just minutes from town centre. Ensuite rooms, central heating, tea/coffee trays and parking. The friendly atmosphere and personal attention from Alex and Jenny Liddell make Atherstone the ideal place to relax after a day touring Loch Ness and the Highlands.

| Atherstone Guest House 42 Fairfield Road Inverness IV3 5QD Tel: (Inverness) 01463 240240 | COMMENDED ♔♔ | 1 Single 1 Double 1 Family | 3 En Suite fac | B&B per person £16.00-£18.00 Single £16.00-£18.00 Double Room only per person £16.00 | Open Jan-Dec | | |

Attractively decorated and comfortably furnished with a homely atmosphere. All rooms ensuite. Private parking.

| Atholdene House 20 Southside Road Inverness IV2 3BG Tel: (Inverness) 01463 233565 | COMMENDED ♔♔♔ | 1 Single 4 Twin 3 Double 1 Family | 7 En Suite fac 1 Pub Bath/Show | B&B per person £22.00-£37.00 Single £18.00-£23.00 Double | Open Jan-Dec Dinner 1800-1900 B&B + Eve. Meal £28.00-£47.00 | | |

Late Victorian stone villa, modernised throughout with ample parking. Short walk from bus and railway stations.

| Mrs E Balnave, Burnbank 43 Montague Row Inverness IV3 5DX Tel: (Macdhui) 01463 712637 | COMMENDED Listed | 1 Single 1 Twin | 2 Limited ensuite 1 Pub Bath/Show | B&B per person £12.50-£15.00 Single £12.50-£15.00 Double | Open Apr-Sep | | |

Warm friendly welcome assured in this centrally located family run B&B. Ideal base for touring.

| Mrs Boynton 12 Annfield Road Inverness IV2 3HX Tel: (Inverness) 01463 233188 | COMMENDED ♔ | 1 Double 1 Family | 1 Pub Bath/Show | B&B per person £13.50 Double | Open Jan-Dec | | |

Family run house in quiet residential area within easy walking distance of town centre. Home baking and preserves.

| Braemore Guest House 1 Victoria Drive Inverness IV2 3QB Tel: (Inverness) 01463 243318 | DELUXE ♔♔ | 1 Twin 2 Double | 3 En Suite fac | B&B per person £30.00-£35.00 Single £22.00-£30.00 Double | Open Jan-Dec | | |

Attractive Victorian house furnished with fine antiques. Quiet location. Walking distance of town centre. No smoking.

Mr & Mrs J Campbell St Vincents 12A Diriebught Road Inverness IV2 3QW Tel: (Inverness) 01463 224717	COMMENDED	1 Twin 1 Double 1 Family	2 En Suite fac 1 Priv. NOT ensuite	B&B per person £16.00-£18.00 Double Room only per person £14.00-£16.00	Open Jan-Dec
Newly built modern spacious family house in quiet residential area. Close to town centre and all amenities. Private parking.					

Mrs Carson-Duff Cambeth Lodge 49 Fairfield Road Inverness IV3 5QP Tel: (Inverness) 01463 231764	COMMENDED	2 Twin 1 Family	1 En Suite fac 1 Pub Bath/Show	B&B per person £13.50-£17.50 Double	Open Jan-Dec Dinner from 1800
Victorian, stone building with private parking in quiet residential area. 10 minutes' walk to town centre.					

Mrs Elizabeth Chisholm Carbisdale, 43 Charles Street Inverness IV2 3AH Tel: (Inverness) 01463 225689 Fax: 01463 225689	HIGHLY COMMENDED	1 Twin 2 Double	2 Pub Bath/Show	B&B per person from £14.00 Single from £14.00 Double	Open Jan-Dec
Terraced family home furnished to high standard. Warm welcome. Close to town centre, and easy walk from rail station.					

Clisham House 43 Fairfield Road Inverness IV3 5QP Tel: (Inverness) 01463 239965 Fax: 01463 239965	COMMENDED	2 Double 2 Family	4 En Suite fac	B&B per person from £21.00 Single from £21.00 Double	Open Jan-Dec
Large detached townhouse with interior woodwork of character. Ample parking. Within walking distance of town centre.					

The Cottage 6a Bruce Gardens Inverness IV3 5EN Tel: (Inverness) 01463 240253 Fax: 01463 233836	DELUXE	1 Twin 1 Double	2 En Suite fac	B&B per person £35.00 Single £21.00 Double	Open Apr-Sep Dinner at 1845 B&B + Eve. Meal £34.00-£36.00
Modern cottage in traditional style, close to town centre, river walks and theatre.					

Craigside Lodge 4 Gordon Terrace Inverness IV2 3HD Tel: (Inverness) 01463 231576 Fax: 01463 713409	COMMENDED	3 Twin 3 Double	6 En Suite fac	B&B per person from £20.00 Single from £19.00 Double	Open Jan-Dec
Detached Victorian house set in quiet elevated position. Outstanding views of castle, river and town. Within a 5-minute walk of town centre.					

Mrs A Davidson 37 Ballifeary Lane Inverness IV3 5PH Tel: (Inverness) 01463 237637	COMMENDED	1 Twin 2 Double	3 En Suite fac	B&B per person £15.00-£20.00 Double	Open Jan-Dec
Modern family home in quiet area, within walking distance of town centre and all amenities. Close to Eden Court Theatre.					

Dionard Guest House 39 Old Edinburgh Road Inverness IV2 3HJ Tel: (Inverness) 01463 233557	HIGHLY COMMENDED	1 Twin 2 Double	3 En Suite fac	B&B per person £18.00-£22.00 Double	Open Jan-Dec
Victorian house with modern extension, ½ mile (1 km) from town centre. Car parking available.					

Mrs I Donald Kerrisdale, 4 Muirfield Road Inverness IV2 4AY Tel: (Inverness) 01463 235489	HIGHLY COMMENDED	1 Twin 1 Double 1 Family	1 En Suite fac 1 Pub Bath/Show	B&B per person from £17.00 Double	Open Jan-Dec Dinner at 1800 B&B + Eve. Meal from £26.00
Spacious Victorian house with large garden, situated in quiet residential area within walking distance of the town centre. Home cooking.					

Details of Grading and Classification are on page vi.   Key to symbols is on back flap.

THE HIGHLANDS & SKYE

INVERNESS continued	Map 4 B8		

Clach Mhuilinn
7 HARRIS ROAD INVERNESS IV2 3LS TEL: 01463 237059 FAX: 01463 242092

Let us welcome you to our no-smoking detached house in a quiet, residential area 20 minutes' stroll from Inverness centre. Stay a while and unwind, enjoying delicious breakfasts overlooking the lovely garden. Explore the beautiful Highlands, returning nightly to your comfortable room. Bar meals available nearby.
Contact: Mrs Jacqi Elmslie.

Mrs J R Elmslie
Clach Mhuilinn, 7 Harris Road
Inverness
IV2 3LS
Tel: (Inverness) 01463 237059
Fax: 01463 242092

HIGHLY COMMENDED

1 Single / 1 Twin / 1 Double
1 En Suite fac / 1 Priv. NOT ensuite / 1 Pub Bath/Show
B&B per person £19.00-£23.00 Single / £19.00-£23.00 Double
Open Mar-Nov

Modern, non-smoking family home in residential area with attractive garden and off-street parking.

Felstead Guest House
18 Ness Bank
Inverness
IV2 4SF
Tel: (Inverness) 01463 231634

COMMENDED

3 Single / 2 Double / 3 Family
4 En Suite fac / 2 Pub Bath/Show
B&B per person £18.00-£25.00 Single / £20.00-£28.00 Double
Open Jan-Dec

Listed Georgian townhouse overlooking River Ness. Eden Court Theatre, museum and restaurants all within easy walking distance. Some private parking available.

Mrs June Fiddes
The Tilt, Old Perth Road
Inverness
IV2 3UT
Tel: (Inverness) 01463 225352

COMMENDED

1 Single / 1 Twin / 1 Family
1 Pub Bath/Show
B&B per person from £14.00 Single / from £13.00 Double
Open Jan-Dec

Family home within short distance of A9, town centre and all amenities. Convenient for Raigmore Hospital. Strictly non-smoking. Vegetarian menus.

Mr & Mrs W Y Findlay
Mary Ann Villa
Mary Ann Court
Ardross Place
Inverness
IV3 5BZ
Tel: (Inverness) 01463 230187

COMMENDED Listed

1 Single / 1 Twin / 1 Family
1 Pub Bath/Show
B&B per person £14.00-£17.00 Single / £14.00-£17.00 Double / Room only per person £12.00-£15.00
Open Jan-Dec

Family run house in quiet secluded area very close to town centre.

Mr Ian Frew & Mrs Kay Frew
Cottinch House
1 Southside Place
Inverness
Inverness-shire
IV2 3JO
Tel: (Machdui) 01463 225261

APPROVED Listed

1 Twin / 1 Double / 1 Family
3 Priv. NOT ensuite / 1 Pub Bath/Show
B&B per person £14.00-£16.00 Double / Room only per person £10.00-£12.00
Open Jan-Dec

Conveniently situated near town centre, and all amenities.

Sunnyholm
12 MAYFIELD ROAD, INVERNESS IV2 4AE
Telephone: 01463 231336
This well-appointed, traditionally built Scottish bungalow of the early 1930s is situated in a large, mature, secluded garden in a very pleasant, residential area and has ample private parking. It is within 6-7 minutes walking distance of the Town Centre, Castle, Tourist Information Centre Office and other essential holiday amenities.

Mrs Agnes Gordon
Sunnyholm, 12 Mayfield Road
Inverness
IV2 4AE
Tel: (Inverness) 01463 231336

COMMENDED

2 Twin / 2 Double
4 En Suite fac
B&B per person £20.00-£25.00 Single / £17.00-£19.00 Double
Open Jan-Dec

Bungalow situated in quiet residential area close to town centre and castle. All bedrooms ensuite. Private car park.

Neil & Margaret Hart Melrose Villa 35 Kenneth Street Inverness IV3 5DH Tel: (Inverness) 01463 233745	COMMENDED Listed	3 Single 3 Double 3 Family	6 En Suite fac 1 Pub Bath/Show	B&B per person £15.00-£20.00 Single £12.00-£20.00 Double	Open Jan-Dec	

Family run guest house within a few minutes' walk of the town centre. Warm and friendly atmosphere. Vegetarian breakfast available.

TAMARUE

70A Ballifeary Road, Inverness IV3 5PF
Tel: 01463 239724

Comfortable accommodation in excellent residential location near to riverside walks, golf courses, Loch Ness cruises, sports and aqua centres and Eden Court Theatre. Long-established reputation for cleanliness and attractive surroundings. Ample private parking.   **Totally non-smoking house!**

Mrs Joan Hendry Tamarue, 70A Ballifeary Road Inverness IV3 5PF Tel: (Inverness) 01463 239724	COMMENDED	1 Twin 2 Double	1 Priv. NOT ensuite 1 Pub Bath/Show	B&B per person £12.50-£18.00 Double	Open Apr-Oct	

Situated in quiet residential area, close to town centre, River Ness, golf course and Eden Court Theatre. Off-street parking.

Mrs Helen Kennedy Kendon, 9 Old Mill Lane Inverness IV2 3XP Tel: (Inverness) 01463 238215	COMMENDED	1 Twin 2 Double	3 En Suite fac	B&B per person £18.00-£20.00 Double	Open Mar-Nov	

Modern bungalow. A family home in quiet residential area. 1 mile (2 kms) from town centre, easy access from A9. All bedrooms ensuite.

Larchfield House 14/15 Ness Bank Inverness IV2 4SF Tel: (Inverness) 01463 233874 Fax: 01463 711600	APPROVED	3 Single 6 Twin 5 Double 3 Family	8 En Suite fac 3 Limited ensuite 3 Priv. NOT ensuite 3 Pub Bath/Show	B&B per person £20.00-£25.00 Single £20.00-£25.00 Double	Open Jan-Dec	

Personally run, on east bank of River Ness. Close to town centre. Open fire in lounge.

Millwood House

36 Old Mill Road, Inverness IV2 3HR
Tel: 01463 237254 Fax: 01463 719400
e-mail: millwood@sigma96.demon.co.uk
www url:
http://www.sigma96.demon.co.uk/millwood/millwood.htm

Millwood House stands in a large, beautiful secluded garden. Close by is the town of Inverness. Come and stay awhile enjoying our warm hospitality. Each bedroom has an individual charm with every comfort to make your stay with us a truly memorable one. Breakfast at Millwood House is special, with a splendid choice, to be enjoyed in the dining room overlooking the lovely garden. The sitting room with an open fire is cosy, being furnished with antiques, garden flowers and lots of books to browse. A perfect base for touring the spectacular scenery of the Highlands. Private parking. Please call Gillian or Bill Lee for further information.   AA QQQQ

Gillian & Bill Lee Millwood House 36 Old Mill Road Inverness IV2 3HR Tel: (Inverness) 01463 237254 Fax: 01463 719400	DELUXE	1 Twin 1 Double	1 En Suite fac 1 Priv. NOT ensuite 1 Pub Bath/Show	B&B per person from £23.00 Double	Open Jan-Dec	

A warm friendly welcome in comfortable family home. Large secluded garden, in pleasant residential area close to town centre.

THE HIGHLANDS & SKYE

INVERNESS

INVERNESS continued	Map 4 B8					
Mrs MacCuish 1 Caulfield Park Inverness IV1 2GB Tel: (Inverness) 01463 792882	HIGHLY COMMENDED	1 Twin 1 Double	1 En Suite fac 1 Pub Bath/Show	B&B per person £15.00-£17.00 Double	Open May-Sep	
		Modern detached house with large garden on eastern outskirts of Inverness. 3 miles (5 kms) from Culloden Battlefield. Private parking.				
Mrs L M MacDonald Baemore, 48 Fairfield Road Inverness IV3 5QD Tel: (Inverness) 01463 234095	COMMENDED	1 Twin 1 Family	1 Pub Bath/Show	B&B per person £13.00-£15.00 Double	Open Apr-Sep	
		Highland hospitality in friendly family home. Short walk to town centre.				
Mrs C MacDonald An Airidh, 65 Fairfield Road Inverness IV3 5LH Tel: (Inverness) 01463 240673	COMMENDED Listed	1 Twin 1 Double 1 Family	1 Priv. NOT ensuite 2 Pub Bath/Show	B&B per person £14.00-£16.00 Single £13.00-£15.00 Double	Open Nov-Sep Dinner 1830-2000	
		Family home in quiet residential area. Short walking distance from town centre and all amenities.				
Ms H M M MacGregor Abbotsford, 7 Fairfield Road Inverness Inverness-shire IV3 5QA Tel: (Inverness) 01463 238412	COMMENDED	1 Twin 1 Family	2 En Suite fac	B&B per person £18.00-£20.00 Single £18.00-£20.00 Double Room only per person £15.00-£17.00	Open Jan-Dec	
		Small and friendly guest house within easy walking distance of city centre. Off-road parking available.				
Mrs Margaret MacGruer 62 Old Edinburgh Road Inverness Inverness-shire IV2 3PG Tel: (Inverness) 01463 238892	HIGHLY COMMENDED	1 Double 1 Family	1 Pub Bath/Show	B&B per person to £16.00 Double	Open Feb-Nov	
		Detached house standing in its own grounds in a quiet residential area but only 0.5 miles (1 km) from the town centre.				
Mr & Mrs MacKay 50 Fairfield Road Inverness IV3 5QW Tel: (Inverness) 01463 712623	COMMENDED	1 Twin 1 Double 1 Family	2 En Suite fac 1 Pub Bath/Show	B&B per person £15.00-£18.00 Double	Open Jan-Dec	
		Victorian, corner, terraced house in residential area. Ten minutes' walk to town centre and railway station.				
Mrs A MacKenzie Braehead, 5 Crown Circus Inverness IV2 3NH Tel: (Inverness) 01463 224222	COMMENDED	1 Single 1 Double 1 Family	2 Pub Bath/Show	B&B per person from £16.00 Single from £15.00 Double	Open Jan-Dec	
		Traditional stone-built Victorian villa in residential area of Inverness with easy access to town centre and all amenities. Non-smoking.				

SCOTTISH TOURIST BOARD
QUALITY COMMENDATIONS ARE:

Deluxe – An EXCELLENT quality standard
Highly Commended – A VERY GOOD quality standard
Commended – A GOOD quality standard
Approved – An ADEQUATE quality standard

VAT is shown at 17.5%: changes in this rate may affect prices.   Prices shown are for guidance only.   Please send SAE with each enquiry.

Trafford Bank

96 Fairfield Road, Inverness IV3 5LL   Tel: 01463 241414
e-mail: traff@pop.cali.co.uk
URL http://www.ibmpcug.co.uk/~ecs/guest/trafford/trafford.html

Visiting the Highlands? Why not stay with the McKenzies at their home in a quiet residential area of Inverness? We offer superior, spacious accommodation with ensuite facilities, complimentary fresh fruit and flowers in all rooms. Gourmet Scottish breakfasts. Ample private parking. Close to town centre. Ideal touring base.

Mr & Mrs McKenzie
Trafford Bank
96 Fairfield Road
Inverness
IV3 5LL
Tel: (Inverness) 01463 241414

COMMENDED

1 Twin   5 En Suite fac
4 Double

B&B per person
from £27.50 Single
from £20.00 Double

Open Jan-Dec
Dinner 1900-2000
B&B + Eve. Meal
from £32.50

Spacious Victorian house convenient for the town centre. Traditional comfort and hospitality. Good food.

Mrs Nicola McKinnie
Furan Cottage
100 Old Edinburgh Road
Inverness
IV2 3HT
Tel: (Inverness) 01463 712094

COMMENDED
Listed

1 Single   2 Limited ensuite
1 Double   2 Pub Bath/Show
1 Family

B&B per person
£14.00-£16.00 Single
£14.00-£16.00 Double

Open Jan-Dec
Dinner 1800-2000
B&B + Eve. Meal
£24.00-£26.00

Family home on main road, 1 mile (2 kms) from town centre. Home-cooked evening meals provided. Private parking. No-smoking house.

Mrs A MacKinnon
6 Broadstone Park
Inverness
IV2 3LA
Tel: (Inverness) 01463 221506

COMMENDED

1 Single   3 En Suite fac
1 Twin   1 Pub Bath/Show
1 Family

B&B per person
£18.00-£24.00 Single
£18.00-£23.00 Double

Open Jan-Dec

Semi-detached house in quiet residential road, 5 minutes' walk from town centre, bus and railway station. Off-road parking.

Iain & Fiona MacNeil
Willow Cottage
1 Muirfield Road
Inverness
IV2 4AY
Tel: (Machdui) 01463 221653

HIGHLY
COMMENDED

1 Twin   1 En Suite fac
1 Double   1 Priv. NOT ensuite

B&B per person
from £20.00 Single
£16.00-£18.00 Double

Open Easter-Oct

Friendly family run cottage-style house with garden. Private parking and near to town centre.

Mrs U Moffat
Lorne House, 40 Crown Drive
Inverness
IV2 3QG
Tel: (Inverness) 01463 236271

HIGHLY
COMMENDED

1 Double   1 En Suite fac
1 Family   1 Priv. NOT ensuite
            1 Pub Bath/Show

B&B per person
£17.00-£25.00 Double

Open Jan-Dec

Victorian detached house in quiet residential area, close to town centre and railway station. Guest car parking. Private and ensuite facilities.

Select your holiday accommodation with confidence,

Scottish TOURIST BOARD — DELUXE
Scottish TOURIST BOARD — HIGHLY COMMENDED
Scottish TOURIST BOARD — COMMENDED
Scottish TOURIST BOARD — APPROVED

use The Scottish Tourist Board's Grading and Classification Scheme

THE HIGHLANDS & SKYE

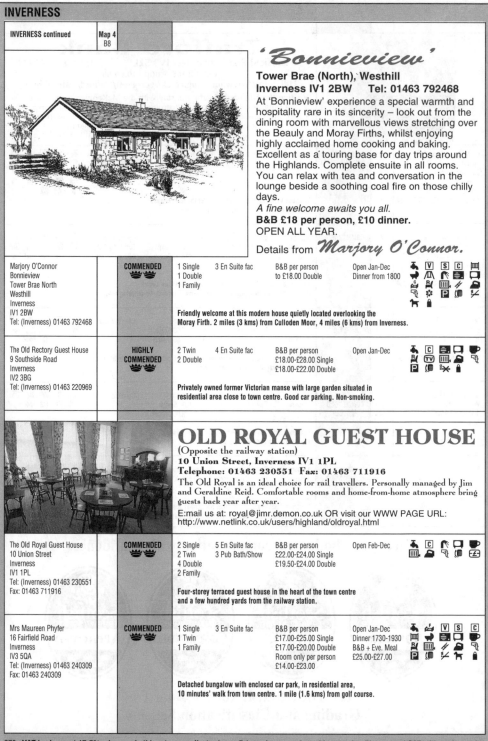

| INVERNESS continued | Map 4 B8 | | | |

'Bonnieview'

Tower Brae (North), Westhill
Inverness IV1 2BW   Tel: 01463 792468

At 'Bonnieview' experience a special warmth and hospitality rare in its sincerity – look out from the dining room with marvellous views stretching over the Beauly and Moray Firths, whilst enjoying highly acclaimed home cooking and baking. Excellent as a touring base for day trips around the Highlands. Complete ensuite in all rooms. You can relax with tea and conversation in the lounge beside a soothing coal fire on those chilly days.
A fine welcome awaits you all.
B&B £18 per person, £10 dinner.
OPEN ALL YEAR.

Details from *Marjory O'Connor.*

Marjory O'Connor Bonnieview Tower Brae North Westhill Inverness IV1 2BW Tel: (Inverness) 01463 792468	COMMENDED	1 Single 1 Double 1 Family	3 En Suite fac	B&B per person to £18.00 Double	Open Jan-Dec Dinner from 1800
		Friendly welcome at this modern house quietly located overlooking the Moray Firth. 2 miles (3 kms) from Culloden Moor, 4 miles (6 kms) from Inverness.			
The Old Rectory Guest House 9 Southside Road Inverness IV2 3BG Tel: (Inverness) 01463 220969	HIGHLY COMMENDED	2 Twin 2 Double	4 En Suite fac	B&B per person £18.00-£28.00 Single £18.00-£22.00 Double	Open Jan-Dec
		Privately owned former Victorian manse with large garden situated in residential area close to town centre. Good car parking. Non-smoking.			

OLD ROYAL GUEST HOUSE

(Opposite the railway station)
10 Union Street, Inverness IV1 1PL
Telephone: 01463 230551 Fax: 01463 711916

The Old Royal is an ideal choice for rail travellers. Personally managed by Jim and Geraldine Reid. Comfortable rooms and home-from-home atmosphere bring guests back year after year.

E:mail us at: royal@jimr.demon.co.uk OR visit our WWW PAGE URL: http://www.netlink.co.uk/users/highland/oldroyal.html

The Old Royal Guest House 10 Union Street Inverness IV1 1PL Tel: (Inverness) 01463 230551 Fax: 01463 711916	COMMENDED	2 Single 2 Twin 4 Double 2 Family	5 En Suite fac 3 Pub Bath/Show	B&B per person £22.00-£24.00 Single £19.50-£24.00 Double	Open Feb-Dec
		Four-storey terraced guest house in the heart of the town centre and a few hundred yards from the railway station.			
Mrs Maureen Phyfer 16 Fairfield Road Inverness IV3 5QA Tel: (Inverness) 01463 240309 Fax: 01463 240309	COMMENDED	1 Single 1 Twin 1 Family	3 En Suite fac	B&B per person £17.00-£25.00 Single £17.00-£20.00 Double Room only per person £14.00-£23.00	Open Jan-Dec Dinner 1730-1930 B&B + Eve. Meal £25.00-£27.00
		Detached bungalow with enclosed car park, in residential area, 10 minutes' walk from town centre. 1 mile (1.6 kms) from golf course.			

Pine Guest House 60 Telford Street Inverness IV3 5LE Tel: (Inverness) 01463 233032 Fax: 01463 233032	COMMENDED 👑👑	3 Single 3 Family	2 En Suite fac 1 Limited ensuite 1 Pub Bath/Show	B&B per person from £17.00 Single from £16.00 Double	Open Jan-Dec Dinner 1800-1900 B&B + Eve. Meal from £26.00	
		Detached townhouse ½ mile (800 metres) from centre of Inverness and on main bus route. Private parking available.				
Mr Reid 99 Kenneth Street Inverness IV3 5QQ Tel: (Inverness) 01463 235397	COMMENDED 👑👑	1 Single 2 Double 2 Family	2 En Suite fac 1 Priv. NOT ensuite 1 Pub Bath/Show	B&B per person £16.00-£18.00 Single £13.50-£16.50 Double Room only per person £12.00-£16.00	Open Jan-Dec	
		Scottish hospitality in friendly family home. 10 minutes' walk from town centre.				
Mrs M Shields Ardgowan, 45 Fairfield Road Inverness IV3 5QP Tel: (Inverness) 01463 236489	COMMENDED 👑👑	1 Twin 1 Family	1 En Suite fac 1 Pub Bath/Show	B&B per person from £16.00 Single from £15.50 Double	Open Jan-Dec	
		A large semi-detached house with spacious rooms within a few minutes' walk of the town centre.				

LYNDON

50 Telford Street, Inverness IV3 5LE
Telephone: 01463 232551

Centrally situated with a high standard of comfortable accommodation, 10 minutes' walk from town centre. Fully equipped, spacious rooms including satellite TV. Personal, friendly service is assured, as is a warm welcome.

Donna Smith Lyndon B+B, 50 Telford Street Inverness IV3 5LE Tel: (Inverness) 01463 232551	COMMENDED 👑	1 Twin 1 Double 1 Family	1 Limited ensuite 1 Pub Bath/Show	B&B per person £12.00-£15.00 Double	Open Jan-Dec	
		Comfortable home, a short distance from the town centre. Most rooms on ground floor.				
Mrs J Wilson Cairnsmore, 41 Charles Street Inverness IV2 3AH Tel: (Inverness) 01463 233485	HIGHLY COMMENDED Listed	1 Twin 2 Double	1 Pub Bath/Show	B&B per person from £15.00 Double	Open Jan-Dec	
		Terraced house in quiet residential area, renovated to a high standard, close to shops, town centre, rail and bus station.				
Mr L H Zeffert Bruar Cottage 11 Mayfield Road Inverness IV2 4AE Tel: (Machdui) 01463 713949	COMMENDED 👑👑	2 Twin	1 Priv. NOT ensuite	B&B per person £16.00-£20.00 Single £14.00-£18.00 Double	Open Jan-Dec	
		Comfortable family home in residential area, short walk to town centre. Non-smoking.				
by INVERNESS Mrs M Mansfield 3a Resaurie Smithton, by Inverness Inverness-shire IV1 2NH Tel: (Inverness) 01463 791714	Map 4 B8 COMMENDED 👑👑	1 Twin 2 Double	1 En Suite fac 1 Pub Bath/Show	B&B per person £15.00-£19.00 Double	Open Jan-Dec Dinner 1800-2000 B&B + Eve. Meal £27.00-£31.00	
		Modern house set in quiet residential area 4 miles (6 kms) from Inverness with panoramic views across the Moray Firth. Warm and friendly stay assured. Non-smoking.				

THE HIGHLANDS & SKYE

by INVERNESS continued

Map 4 B8

Mrs Alison Parsons
Ballindarroch House
Aldourie, Inverness
Inverness-shire
IV1 2DL
Tel: (Dores) 01463 751348

COMMENDED

1 Single	1 Priv. NOT ensuite	B&B per person	Open Jan-Dec
2 Twin	2 Pub Bath/Show	£18.00-£25.00 Single	
1 Double		£18.00-£25.00 Double	

Unique country house in 10 acres (4ha) of woodland gardens near Loch Ness and Caledonian Canal. 10 minutes drive from Inverness.

Mrs Effie Rowan
Laimrig
Upper Myrtlefield, Nairnside
Inverness
IV1 2BX
Tel: (Inverness) 01463 793464

HIGHLY COMMENDED

1 Twin	3 En Suite fac	B&B per person	Open Jan-Dec
2 Double		from £20.00 Single	
		from £18.00 Double	

Modern family house with large garden 4 miles (6 kms) from Inverness town centre. Extensive views over Moray Firth to Black Isle. Private parking.

LAGGAN VIEW

Ness Castle Fishings, Dores Road, By Inverness IV1 2DH
Telephone: 01463 235996 Fax: 01463 711552

Attractive centrally heated spacious house surrounded by beautiful garden in rural setting with scenic views of Ness Valley. Only 3 miles from town centre on B862. Walks nearby through woods and by river. Varied evening meal menu using local produce at a time to suit.

Mrs Elizabeth Saggers
Laggan View
Ness Castle Fishings
Dores Road, by Inverness
Inverness-shire
IV1 2DH
Tel: (Inverness) 01463 235996
Fax: 01463 711552

COMMENDED

1 Twin	2 En Suite fac	B&B per person	Open Jan-Dec
1 Double	1 Priv. NOT ensuite	from £18.00 Single	Dinner 1800-2100
1 Family		from £18.00 Double	B&B + Eve. Meal from £27.00

Quiet secluded house in countryside with magnificient views.
Close to Inverness, ideal base for touring the Highlands.

Sky House
Upper Cullernie
Balloch, by Inverness
Inverness-shire
IV1 2HU
Tel: (Inverness) 01463 792582
Fax: 01463 792582

COMMENDED

1 Twin	2 En Suite fac	B&B per person	Open Jan-Dec
1 Family		£18.00-£24.00 Double	Dinner from 1930
			B&B + Eve. Meal £28.00-£34.00

A friendly and relaxed welcome at this modern house with superb views over Moray Firth to Black Isle. 4 miles (6 kms) from Inverness. Non-smoking throughout.

JOHN O'GROATS
Caithness

Map 4 E2

Mrs Barton
Bencorragh House
Upper Gills, Canisbay
Caithness
KW1 4YB
Tel: (John O'Groats)
01955 611449

COMMENDED

1 Twin	4 En Suite fac	B&B per person	Open Apr-Oct
2 Double		£20.00-£24.00 Single	Dinner 1800-2030
1 Family		£17.00-£19.00 Double	

A working croft in grounds of 10 acres (4ha). All rooms ensuite.
Large conservatory and comfortable lounge. Angling holidays a speciality.

Caber-feidh Guest House
John O'Groats
Caithness
KW1 4YR
Tel: (John O'Groats)
01955 611219

APPROVED Listed

4 Single	3 En Suite fac	B&B per person	Open Jan-Dec
3 Twin	3 Pub Bath/Show	£14.50-£15.50 Single	Dinner 1830-2000
2 Double		£13.50-£14.50 Double	B&B + Eve. Meal £19.00-£20.00
3 Family			

Centrally situated in John O' Groats and 2 miles (3 kms) from Duncansby Head. It is well situated for exploring the north east.

VAT is shown at 17.5%: changes in this rate may affect prices. Prices shown are for guidance only. Please send SAE with each enquiry.

Mrs J Sinclair Swona View John O'Groats Caithness KW1 4YS Tel: (John O'Groats) 01955 611297		COMMENDED 👑👑	1 Twin 2 Double	1 En Suite fac 2 Pub Bath/Show	B&B per person £14.00-£17.00 Double	Open Apr-Oct
Comfortable modern bungalow with fine views across Pentland Firth to Orkney.						

by JOHN O'GROATS Caithness Mrs C G Manson Post Office Canisbay Caithness KW1 4YH Tel: (John O'Groats) 01955 611213 Fax: 01955 611213	Map 4 E2	COMMENDED 👑👑	1 Twin 2 Double	1 En Suite fac 2 Limited ensuite 1 Pub Bath/Show	B&B per person £18.00-£20.00 Single £18.50-£20.50 Double	Open Apr-Sep
100-year-old Post Office house. Panoramic views of Pentland Firth, close to John O'Groats and Orkney Ferries. Personally run. Extensive breakfast menu.						

KILCHOAN, by Ardnamurchan Argyll Mr and Mrs R Thompson Far View, Mingary Pier Road Kilchoan, Acharacle Argyll PH36 4LH Tel: (Kilchoan) 01972 510357	Map 1 C1	HIGHLY COMMENDED 👑👑👑	1 Twin 2 Double	2 En Suite fac 1 Priv. NOT ensuite	B&B per person £22.00-£33.00 Double	Open Mar-Nov Dinner at 1930 B&B + Eve. Meal £30.00-£41.00
Residents' lounge with open fire, private suite available, imaginative home cooking, table licence, near Mull ferry.						

KILTARLITY Inverness-shire J E & S M Cartlidge Badgers Walk Culmill IV4 7HP Tel: (Kiltarlity) 01463 741311	Map 4 A9	COMMENDED 👑👑	2 Single 1 Double	1 En Suite fac 2 Priv. NOT ensuite 1 Pub Bath/Show	B&B per person £12.50-£16.50 Single £12.50-£16.50 Double	Open Apr-Oct Dinner 1830-1930 B&B + Eve. Meal £19.00-£23.00
Peaceful tranquil setting in natural woodland. Excellent base for touring, golfing and fishing. Emphasis on home-grown produce.						

BROOMHILL

Kiltarlity, Beauly, Inverness-shire IV4 7JH
Telephone: 01463 741447

Former Edwardian manse retaining its original character, set in peaceful countryside 11 miles from Inverness and 8 miles from Loch Ness. Large, warm, comfortable rooms. Traditional home cooking with dinners and packed lunches if required. Pleasant walks in all directions through farmland, woodland and forest.

Mrs Eunice Ramsden Broomhill Kiltarlity, Beauly Inverness-shire IV4 7JH Tel: (Kiltarlity) 01463 741447		COMMENDED Listed	1 Twin 1 Double	1 Pub Bath/Show	B&B per person £11.00-£12.50 Single £11.00-£12.50 Double	Open Jan-Dec Dinner 1800-1900 B&B + Eve. Meal £17.50
Large country house set in own grounds amongst open countryside. 11 miles (18 kms) from Inverness. Totally non-smoking. Packed lunches and evening meals available.						

THE HIGHLANDS & SKYE

Details of Grading and Classification are on page vi. | Key to symbols is on back flap. |

KINCRAIG, by Kingussie Inverness-shire	Map 4 C10

Braeriach Guest House
Kincraig, By Kingussie, Inverness-shire PH21 1QA
Telephone: 01540 651369

Braeriach Guest House sits on the banks of the River Spey with superb views of the Cairngorm Mountains beyond. Ideal base for walking, bird-watching, fishing, golf and exploring. Comfy en-suite rooms with river views. Imaginative freshly prepared 3-course dinners. Peaceful surroundings and a warm welcome.

Braeriach Guest House Kincraig, by Kingussie Inverness-shire PH21 1OA Tel: (Kincraig) 01540 651369	COMMENDED	1 Twin 2 Double 1 Family	4 En Suite fac	B&B per person from £22.00 Single £18.00-£22.00 Double	Open Jan-Dec Dinner 1900-1930
Former manse situated on the banks of the River Spey with picturesque garden extending to private jetty. Dinners available using home-grown vegetables and free-range eggs.					
Grampian View Kincraig Inverness-shire PH21 1NA Tel: (Kincraig) 01540 651383	COMMENDED	1 Single 2 Twin 2 Double	4 En Suite fac 1 Priv. NOT ensuite	B&B per person from £17.00 Single from £17.00 Double	Open Jan-Dec
Family run Victorian house, with original fireplaces and woodwork, offering bed and breakfast with a touch of elegance. Ideal touring base.					
Insh Hall Lodge Kincraig Kingussie Inverness-shire PH21 1NU Tel: (Kincraig) 01540 651272 Fax: 01540 651208	COMMENDED Listed	6 Twin 3 Double 6 Family	15 En Suite fac	B&B per person £20.50-£21.00 Single £15.50-£16.00 Double	Open Jan-Dec Dinner 1800-2200 B&B + Eve. Meal £27.50-£28.00
Comfortable ensuite accommodation 100 yards (90m) from Loch Insh. Sauna, Minigym, TV lounges. Central for visitor attractions. Licensed restaurant. Watersports and winter skiing.					
Insh House Guest House Kincraig Inverness-shire PH21 1NU Tel: (Kincraig) 01540 651377	COMMENDED	2 Single 1 Twin 1 Double 1 Family	2 En Suite fac 1 Pub Bath/Show	B&B per person £16.00-£20.00 Single £16.00-£20.00 Double	Open Jan-Dec Dinner at 1900 B&B + Eve. Meal £25.00-£30.00
Fine example of a Telford House in 2 acres (0.8ha) of secluded grounds. Close to Loch Insh, 10 minutes to Aviemore. Skiing, watersports, riding and gliding.					
Mrs V MacLeod Carn Ban, by Loch Insh Kincraig Inverness-shire PH21 1NU Tel: (Kincraig) 01540 651313	COMMENDED	1 Twin 1 Family	1 Pub Bath/Show	B&B per person from £16.00 Single £14.50-£16.00 Double	Open Jan-Dec
Traditional Scottish hospitality in modern house on shores of Loch Insh.					
March House Guest House Feshiebridge Kincraig Inverness-shire PH21 1NG Tel: (Kincraig) 01540 651388 Fax: 01540 651388	HIGHLY COMMENDED	3 Twin 2 Double 1 Family	5 En Suite fac 1 Priv. NOT ensuite	B&B per person £20.00-£25.00 Single £18.00-£20.00 Double	Open Dec-Oct Dinner from 1900
Peaceful location in beautiful Glenfeshie. Personally run, relaxing atmosphere. Emphasis on fresh food served in our new spacious conservatory looking to the mountains. Taste of Scotland.					

THE HIGHLANDS & SKYE

Kirkbeag

KINCRAIG, KINGUSSIE, INVERNESS-SHIRE PH21 1ND
Telephone: 01540 651298

Enjoy a Highland Welcome and home cooking in our comfortable family home, located on the B9152, 1 mile north of Kincraig Village. Ideal for watersports, walking, touring, bird-watching, skiing, or learning to woodturn, carve or silversmith. Children welcome. Regret no pets.
B&B from £15.50 per person per night. Dinners by arrangement.
Full details from Sheila Paisley.

Mr & Mrs J Paisley Kirkbeag, Milehead Kincraig Inverness-shire PH21 1ND Tel: (Kincraig) 01540 651298	COMMENDED Listed	1 Twin 1 Double	2 Pub Bath/Show	B&B per person £15.50-£20.00 Single £15.50-£17.50 Double	Open Jan-Dec Dinner 1800-2000 B&B + Eve. Meal £25.00-£26.50	

19th century church, converted to family home. Spiral staircase and craft workshop.
Craft courses available. Aviemore 5 miles (8 kms). Smokers welcome.

KINGUSSIE **Inverness-shire** Avondale Guest House Newtonmore Road Kingussie Inverness-shire PH21 1HF Tel: (Kingussie) 01540 661731 Fax: 01540 661731	Map 4 B11 HIGHLY COMMENDED	1 Single 2 Twin 4 Double	5 En Suite fac 1 Pub Bath/Show	B&B per person £18.00-£21.00 Single £18.00-£21.00 Double	Open Jan-Dec Dinner 1900-1930 B&B + Eve. Meal £27.00-£30.00	

Stone-built house with own large garden near centre of village.
Friendly atmosphere, ample parking. Skiing and fishing can be arranged.

Bhuna Monadh

85 High Street, Kingussie, Inverness-shire PH21 1HX
Telephone: 01540 661186/0385 931345

A warm welcome awaits you at Bhuna Monadh (pronounced voo-na-mona) which means foot of the mountain. This listed building is situated in the village of Kingussie in the heart of the Highlands. Relax in spacious, comfortable rooms and enjoy good home cooking.

J Gibson Bhuna Monadh, 85 High Street Kingussie Inverness-shire PH21 1HX Tel: (Kingussie) 01540 661186/ 0385 931345 (mobile)	COMMENDED	2 Family	2 En Suite fac	B&B per person £16.00-£18.00 Single £16.00-£18.00 Double	Open Jan-Dec Dinner from 1900 B&B + Eve. Meal from £26.50	

This recently refurbished Listed building offers comfortable accommodation
in spacious bedrooms with ensuite bathrooms, TV and hot drink facilities.

Homewood Lodge Newtonmore Road Kingussie Inverness-shire PH21 1HD Tel: (Kingussie) 01540 661507	COMMENDED	1 Twin 1 Double 2 Family	4 En Suite fac	B&B per person £15.00-£18.00 Double	Open Jan-Dec Dinner from 1900 B&B + Eve. Meal £22.00-£25.00	

Friendly guest house on edge of village. Views to Cairngorm mountains.
Ideal base for touring area.

Mrs Jarratt St Helens, Ardbroilach Road Kingussie Inverness-shire PH21 1JX Tel: (Kingussie) 01540 661430	HIGHLY COMMENDED	1 Twin 2 Double	2 En Suite fac 1 Priv. NOT ensuite	B&B per person £18.00-£20.00 Double	Open Jan-Dec	

Elegant stone-built house c.1895 in elevated position with large secluded
gardens and excellent views over village and Cairngorm mountains beyond.

THE HIGHLANDS & SKYE

THE HIGHLANDS & SKYE

KINGUSSIE continued Inverness-shire	Map 4 B11

GLENGARRY

Highly Commended
♛♛

East Terrace, Kingussie, Inverness-shire PH21 1JS
Telephone: 01540 661386

Beautifully situated in its own grounds, this high-quality establishment, with an enviable reputation, is ideally suited to the discerning visitor. The perfect base for summer and winter pursuits. Well-appointed bedrooms, private off-road parking and a tranquil setting.
For brochure and details contact: Mel and Ann Short, Proprietors.

Mr & Mrs M B Short Glengarry, East Terrace Kingussie Inverness-shire PH21 1JS Tel: (Kingussie) 01540 661386	HIGHLY COMMENDED ♛♛	2 Single 2 Double	1 En Suite fac 1 Pub Bath/Show	B&B per person £17.00-£20.00 Single £17.00-£20.00 Double	Open Jan-Dec Dinner at 1900 B&B + Eve. Meal £26.00-£29.00

Stone-built house c.1900 with large garden and summer house, in quiet residential area, only a few minutes' walk from centre of Kingussie. No smoking throughout.

KINLOCHBERVIE **Sutherland** Old School Restaurant & Guest House Inshegra Kinlochbervie Sutherland IV27 4RH Tel: (Kinlochbervie) 01971 521383	Map 3 H3 COMMENDED ♛♛♛	1 Single 3 Twin 1 Double 1 Family	4 En Suite fac 1 Pub Bath/Show	B&B per person £18.00-£26.00 Single £18.00-£26.00 Double	Open Jan-Dec Dinner 1800-2030

Restaurant with comfortable rooms in converted bungalow and bothy.
Superb views of sea and surrounding countryside. All annexe accommodation.

KINLOCHEWE **Ross-shire** Mrs E Forrest Cromasaig, Torridon Road Kinlochewe Ross-shire Tel: (Kinlochewe) 01445 760234 Fax: 01445 760234	Map 3 G8 COMMENDED Listed	1 Twin 1 Double 1 Family	1 Pub Bath/Show	B&B per person £16.00-£17.00 Single £16.00-£17.00 Double B&B + Eve. Meal £25.00-£27.00	Open Jan-Dec Dinner 1800-2000

Warm hospitality from climbing hosts. Refurbished croft cottage with log fire, drying facilities. At foot of Beinn Eighe – transport available. Non-smoking throughout.

KINLOCHLEVEN **Argyll** Mrs Robertson Edencoille, Garbhien Road Kinlochleven Argyll PA40 4SE Tel: (Kinlochleven) 01855 831358	Map 3 H12 COMMENDED ♛	3 Twin 1 Family	2 Pub Bath/Show	B&B per person £18.00-£25.00 Single £15.00-£16.00 Double	Open Jan-Dec Dinner 1800-2100 B&B + Eve. Meal £23.00-£25.00

Family home on scenic road from Glencoe.
Central for walking, climbing and skiing in the Lochaber area.

Scotland for Golf . . .

Find out more about golf in Scotland. There's more to it than just the championship courses so get in touch with us now for information on the hidden gems of Scotland.

Write to: **Information Unit, Scottish Tourist Board, 23 Ravelston Terrace, Edinburgh EH4 3EU**
or call: 0131-332 2433

KISHORN Ross-shire	Map 3 F9

M. Moyes

1 Achintraid, Kishorn, Ross-shire IV54 8XB
Telephone: 01520 733224 Fax: 01520 733232

Very comfortable family home on edge of Loch Kishorn, ideal base for walking or touring, large upstairs residents' lounge with patio overlooking 'Bealach na Ba' and the Cuillins of Skye. We provide a full Scottish breakfast and good home cooking using the best of fine Highland produce.
Ample parking. Central heating.

Mrs M Moyes 1 Achintraid Kishorn Ross-shire IV54 8XB Tel: (Kishorn) 01520 733224 Fax: 01520 733232	COMMENDED 👑👑👑	1 Twin 1 Double	2 En Suite fac	B&B per person £20.00-£25.00 Single £18.00 Double	Open Jan-Dec Dinner 1800-2000 B&B + Eve. Meal £30.00

Friendly, comfortable, ensuite accommodation. Large upstairs lounge with patio, looking towards Bealach na Ba. Ideal base for walks and touring.

Mrs P Van Hinsbergh Craigellachie, Achintraid Kishorn Ross-shire IV54 8XB Tel: (Kishorn) 01520 733253	COMMENDED 👑	1 Twin 1 Double	2 En Suite fac	B&B per person £15.00-£18.00 Single £15.00-£18.00 Double Room only per person £12.00-£15.00	Open Apr-Sep Dinner 1800-2000 B&B + Eve. Meal £25.00-£28.00

Situated on the shore of Loch Kishorn with superb views towards the Applecross Mountains. High standard of home cooking with local produce.

KYLE OF LOCHALSH Inverness-shire	Map 3 F9

Old Schoolhouse
Licensed Restaurant

Tigh Fasgaidh, Erbusaig, By Kyle, Ross-shire IV40 8BB
Telephone and Fax: 01599 534369

Idyllically situated on the outskirts of Erbusaig, this former schoolhouse offers high standards of comfort in accommodation with its spacious ensuite bedrooms. The charming restaurant provides a relaxed atmosphere for fine dining from the à la carte menu. Taste of Scotland recommended. Three miles from Kyle, four miles from Plockton.

Mr & Mrs Cumine The Old Schoolhouse Licensed Restaurant Erbusaig, Kyle of Lochalsh Ross-shire IV40 8BB Tel: (Kyle) 01599 534369 Fax: 01599 534369	COMMENDED 👑👑👑	1 Twin 2 Double	3 En Suite fac	B&B per person £25.00-£35.00 Single £19.00-£25.00 Double	Open Apr-Oct Dinner 1900-2230

Restaurant with ensuite accommodation, 3 miles (5 kms) from Skye Bridge at Kyle of Lochalsh, 4 miles (6 kms) from Plockton.

Mrs F Murchison Achomraich, Main Street Kyle of Lochalsh Ross-shire IV40 8DA Tel: (Kyle) 01599 534210	APPROVED Listed	1 Twin 2 Double	1 Pub Bath/Show	B&B per person £14.00-£16.00 Single £14.00-£16.00 Double	Open Apr-Sep

Traditional Scottish hospitality in friendly family home. Ideal base for touring Skye and Wester Ross. Walking distance from station.

KYLESKU Sutherland	Map 3 H4				
Mrs C Evans The Ridge, Unapool Croft Road Kylesku, by Lairg Sutherland IV27 4HW Tel: (Scourie) 01971 502226	HIGHLY COMMENDED 👑	1 Twin 1 Double	1 Pub Bath/Show	B&B per person from £16.50 Double	Open Jan-Dec Dinner 1900-1930 B&B + Eve. Meal £28.00

Tranquillity, superb views and home cooking in this small and friendly house. Ideal centre for walking and sightseeing.

THE HIGHLANDS & SKYE

Details of Grading and Classification are on page vi. | Key to symbols is on back flap. | 277

THE HIGHLANDS & SKYE

KYLESKU continued Sutherland	Map 3 H4	

Non-Smokers' Sanctuary 🚭

"Linne Mhuirich", Unapool Croft Road, KYLESKU via Lairg, Sutherland IV27 4HW   Tel: 01971 502227

Fiona and Diarmid MacAulay welcome non-smokers to their modern crofthouse, "Taste of Scotland" recommended. Their guests return year after year for the peace, comfort and attention, wonderful views and excellent food. Varied and interesting menus: local fish, seafood, pâtés, soups, casseroles, vegetarian dishes, delicious home baking. 1 twin has private bathroom.

EARLY BOOKING ESSENTIAL

Mrs F MacAulay Linne Mhuirich Unapool Croft Road Kylesku, via Lairg Sutherland IV27 4HW Tel: (Scourie) 01971 502227	COMMENDED 👑👑	1 Twin 1 Double	1 Priv. NOT ensuite 1 Pub Bath/Show	B&B per person £25.00 Single £17.50-£20.50 Double	Open May-Oct Dinner at 1930 B&B + Eve. Meal £28.00-£31.00

Friendly and attentive Taste of Scotland recommended croft house.
Peacefully situated near Kylesku Bridge. Directions for walks provided.

Newton Lodge Newton Kylesku Sutherland IV27 4HW Tel: (Scourie) 01971 502070	HIGHLY COMMENDED 👑👑👑	3 Twin 4 Double	7 En Suite fac	B&B per person £24.50-£26.00 Double	Open Apr-Oct Dinner 1900-1930

A large, modern comfortable house surrounded by an inspiring panorama of
mountains and lochs. Ample car parking available. Vegetarians catered for.

LAIDE Ross-shire	Map 3 F6	

'CUL NA MARA'

Highly Commended 👑👑

Sand Passage, Laide, Ross-shire IV22 2ND
Telephone: 01445 731295

A stay at "Cul Na Mara" (*Gaelic – Song of the sea*) is an enjoyable experience. Superior bed and breakfast accommodation. Guest rooms fully ensuite and fitted with colour television. Private dining room – fully laid out garden overlooking the Minch. Private parking. *Early booking advisable*.

Bill Hart Cul na Mara, Sand Passage Laide Ross-shire IV22 2ND Tel: (Aultbea) 01445 731295	HIGHLY COMMENDED 👑👑	1 Double 1 Family	2 En Suite fac	B&B per person from £19.00 Double	Open Jan-Dec Dinner from 1900

Modern Highland home in quiet crofting area. Excellent sandy beaches nearby.
Home cooking, with emphasis on fresh produce. Evening high tea available.

Mrs A MacIver The Sheiling Achgarve, Laide Ross-shire IV22 2NS Tel: (Aultbea) 01445 731487	HIGHLY COMMENDED 👑👑👑	1 Twin 1 Double	2 En Suite fac	B&B per person from £16.50 Single	Open Apr-Sept Dinner 1800-1900 B&B + Eve. Meal from £26.50

Recently built bungalow and finished to a high standard in small crofting
community on Gruinard Bay. Fine views. Ideal base for touring Wester Ross.

Old Smiddy Guest House Laide Ross-shire Tel: (Aultbea) 01445 731425 Fax: 01445 731425	HIGHLY COMMENDED 👑👑👑	1 Double 1 Family	1 En Suite fac 1 Priv. NOT ensuite	B&B per person £20.00-£26.00 Single £20.00-£26.00 Double	Open Feb-Nov Dinner 1900-1930 B&B + Eve. Meal £34.00-£42.00

Enjoy a West Highland experience with your Highland hosts
in their delightful cottage. Private fishing on 18 lochs.

LAIRG **Sutherland** Mrs M K Fraser Ambleside, Lochside Lairg Sutherland IV27 4EG Tel: (Lairg) 01549 402130	Map 4 A6	COMMENDED	1 Twin 2 Double	3 En Suite fac	B&B per person £15.50-£17.00 Double	Open Apr-Oct	

Modern personally run bed and breakfast, comfortable and well-furnished, centrally situated in quiet location with private parking.

Mrs B M Paterson Strathwin Lairg Sutherland IV27 4AZ Tel: (Lairg) 01549 402487	COMMENDED	1 Double 1 Family	1 Pub Bath/Show	B&B per person £13.50-£14.00 Single £13.50-£14.00 Double	Open Apr-Sep	

Modern bungalow in quiet location overlooking Little Loch Shin. Parking adjacent.

Margaret Walker Park House Lairg Sutherland IV27 4AU Tel: (Lairg) 01549 402208 Fax: 01549 402208	COMMENDED	1 Twin 1 Double 1 Family	3 En Suite fac	B&B per person £21.00-£33.00 Single £18.00-£23.00 Double	Open Jan-Dec Dinner from 1900 B&B + Eve. Meal £32.00-£35.00	

A warm welcome awaits you in this Victorian-style house overlooking Loch Shin. Friendly and relaxed atmosphere. Emphasis on home cooking.

LOCHCARRON **Ross-shire**	Map 3 G9

Kinloch House
Lochcarron, Ross-shire IV54 8YS
Telephone: 01520 722417

This lovely former manse allows us to offer the best in comfort as a base for exploring our spectacularly beautiful and varied region, including Skye, Glenelg, Torridon and the Applecross Peninsula. Fine walks and numerous restaurants nearby.
Come for a night and wish you had booked for a week.

Susan Duncan Kinloch House Lochcarron Ross-shire IV54 8YS Tel: (Lochcarron) 01520 722417	COMMENDED	1 Double 1 Family	2 En Suite fac	B&B per person to £30.00 Single from £20.00 Double	Open Apr-Oct

Spacious Victorian house by golf course, near sea loch and village. All rooms ensuite. Breakfasts to suit your taste.

Ms M F Innes Aultsigh, Croft Road Lochcarron Ross-shire IV54 8YA Tel: (Lochcarron) 01520 722558	COMMENDED Listed	1 Twin 2 Double	2 Pub Bath/Show	B&B per person from £16.00 Single £15.00-£16.00 Double	Open Jan-Dec

Detached modern bungalow in elevated position, with magnificent panoramic views of Loch Carron and hills.

Mrs L Leckie Clisham, Main Street Lochcarron Ross-shire Tel: (Lochcarron) 01520 722610	COMMENDED	1 Twin 2 Double	2 Pub Bath/Show	B&B per person from £16.00 Single from £14.00 Double	Open Jan-Dec Dinner 1830-1930 B&B + Eve. Meal from £22.00

Friendly, family run guest house with views over Loch Carron. Tearoom available with home baking. Parking opposite.

THE HIGHLANDS & SKYE

THE HIGHLANDS & SKYE

	Map 3						

LOCHCARRON continued
Ross-shire
Mrs C Michael
Castle Cottage, Main Street
Lochcarron
Ross-shire
IV54 8YB
Tel: (Lochcarron) 01520 722564

Map 3 G9 — COMMENDED

1 Twin / 2 Double — 1 En Suite fac / 1 Pub Bath/Show — B&B per person £15.00-£18.00 Single £15.00-£18.00 Double — Open Jan-Dec

Modernised detached house in village centre with fine views across Loch Carron from all rooms.

LOCHINVER
Sutherland
Ann H Brown
Suilven, Badnaban
Lochinver
Sutherland
IV27 4LR
Tel: (Lochinver) 01571 844358

Map 3 G5 — COMMENDED

1 Twin / 1 Double — 1 Pub Bath/Show — B&B per person £21.00 Single £16.00 Double — Open Jan-Dec Dinner 1830-2000 B&B + Eve. Meal £27.00

Bungalow with superb views across the Minch. Mrs Brown prides herself on her home cooking. Boat trips and sea angling. Dinner available.

Mrs M Garner
Veyatie, 66 Baddidarroch
Lochinver
Sutherland
IV27 4LP
Tel: (Lochinver) 01571 844424

HIGHLY COMMENDED

2 Twin / 1 Double — 2 En Suite fac / 1 Priv. NOT ensuite — B&B per person £20.00-£23.00 Double — Open Apr-Oct

Spacious modern bungalow in secluded situation. Facing south with magnificent views across the harbour to Suilven. Private parking on site.

Mrs J McBain
Davar
Lochinver
Sutherland
IV27 4LJ
Tel: (Lochinver) 01571 844501

HIGHLY COMMENDED

1 Twin / 2 Double — 3 En Suite fac — B&B per person £18.00-£21.00 Double — Open Apr-Sep

Modern family run house overlooking Lochinver Bay, with range of comfortable facilities. Private parking on site.

Mrs J Matheson
Polcraig
Lochinver
Sutherland
IV27 4LD
Tel: (Lochinver) 01571 844429

COMMENDED

2 Twin / 1 Double — 2 En Suite fac / 1 Pub Bath/Show — B&B per person £15.00-£20.00 Double — Open Apr-Oct

Modern family run home in quiet situation, with views to Lochinver Bay. Ample car parking on site.

Mr & Mrs A Munro
Ardglas
Lochinver
Sutherland
IV27 4LJ
Tel: (Lochinver) 01571 844257
Fax: 01571 844632

COMMENDED

1 Single / 1 Twin / 4 Double / 2 Family — 3 Pub Bath/Show — B&B per person £13.00-£15.00 Single £13.00-£15.00 Double — Open Jan-Dec

Set above this popular fishing village with spectacular harbour, sea and mountain views. Homely atmosphere. Private parking.

LOCH MAREE
Ross-shire
Mrs I Grant
Garbhaig House
Loch Maree, by Achnasheen
Ross-shire
IV22 2HW
Tel: (Gairloch) 01445 712412

Map 3 F7 — COMMENDED

1 Double / 2 Family — 2 Pub Bath/Show — B&B per person from £14.00 Single from £14.00 Double — Open Jan-Dec Dinner 1830-1900

Modernised, detached bungalow on working croft with fine views over Loch Maree to hills beyond. Warm welcome with plain home cooking.

The Old Mill Highland Lodge
Talladale
Loch Maree
Ross-shire
IV22 2HL
Tel: (Kinlochewe) 01445 760271

HIGHLY COMMENDED

4 Twin / 2 Double — 5 En Suite fac / 1 Priv. NOT ensuite — B&B per person £25.00-£32.00 Double — Open Jan-Dec Dinner from 1930 B&B + Eve. Meal £36.00-£48.50

Beside a mountain stream sits this imaginative conversion of an old horsemill. Comfortable house with an accent on good food, wine and tranquillity.

VAT is shown at 17.5%: changes in this rate may affect prices. Prices shown are for guidance only. Please send SAE with each enquiry.

MALLAIG **Inverness-shire** Mrs C King Seaview Mallaig Inverness-shire PH41 4QS Tel: (Mallaig) 01687 462059	**Map 3** F11	APPROVED Listed	1 Twin 1 Double 1 Family	2 Pub Bath/Show	B&B per person £13.00-£18.00 Single £13.00-£15.00 Double	Open Jan-Dec

Situated in the centre of the village overlooking the harbour. Convenient for railway station and ferry terminal. Television in each bedroom.

Mr A Lewis Quarterdeck, East Bay Mallaig Inverness-shire PH41 4QR Tel: (Mallaig) 01687 462880 Fax: 01687 462604	APPROVED 🏅🏅🏅	1 Twin 1 Double	2 En Suite fac	B&B per person £12.00-£17.00 Single £11.00-£15.00 Double	Open Apr-Sep

View the fishing harbour activities from your bedroom and lounge windows and watch the sun go down over the Cullins of Skye.

Springbank Guest House East Bay Mallaig Inverness-shire PH41 4QF Tel: (Mallaig) 01687 462459	APPROVED 🏅	1 Single 1 Twin 1 Double 1 Family	2 Pub Bath/Show	B&B per person £13.00-£16.00 Single £13.00-£16.00 Double Dinner 1900-2000 B&B + Eve. Meal £20.50-£23.50	Open Jan-Dec

On the waterfront with view of working harbour. Evening meal by arrangement.

Western Isles Guest House East Bay Mallaig Inverness-shire PH41 4QG Tel: (Mallaig) 01687 462320 Fax: 01687 462320	COMMENDED 🏅	1 Single 1 Double 1 Family	3 Pub Bath/Show	B&B per person £15.00-£17.00 Single £15.00-£17.00 Double Dinner 1800-1930 B&B + Eve. Meal £25.00	Open Jan-Nov

Modern house overlooking the harbour and fishing boats, well situated for ferries to the islands. 4 miles (6 kms) from renowned Morar sands.

MELVICH **Sutherland**	**Map 4** C3

The Shieling Guest House
MELVICH, SUTHERLAND, KW14 7YJ
Telephone: 01641 531256   Fax: 01641 531356
Guests return annually to this high-quality accommodation with emphasis on comfort, huge choice breakfast and Taste-of-Scotland dinners by arrangement. Two beautifully furnished lounges and separate dining room exclusively for guests' use, ensure privacy or company. Born in Sutherland, Joan and Hugh guarantee genuine native hospitality. Spectacular views! Perfect peace!
Chosen by Which? Good B&B Guide.

Mrs Joan Campbell The Shieling Guest House Melvich Sutherland KW14 7YJ Tel: (Melvich) 01641 531256 Fax: 01641 531356	HIGHLY COMMENDED 🏅🏅🏅	1 Twin 2 Double	3 En Suite fac	B&B per person £20.00-£24.00 Double Dinner at 1830 B&B + Eve. Meal to £37.50	Open Apr-Oct

Genuine Highland hospitality, home-cooked meals, varied breakfast choice. Spectacular views over bay. Picture window in coffee lounge, separate TV lounge. Taste of Scotland.

Tigh-na-Clash Guest House (Mrs Joan Ritchie) Melvich Sutherland KW14 7YJ Tel: (Melvich) 01641 531262 Fax: 01641 531262	COMMENDED 🏅🏅🏅	2 Single 2 Twin 4 Double	4 En Suite fac 2 Pub Bath/Show	B&B per person £17.00-£21.50 Single £17.00-£21.50 Double Dinner 1700-2030	Open Apr-Oct

Personally run Guest House, pub and restaurant complex. Ideal for touring north coast and overnight stop for Orkney Isles.

THE HIGHLANDS & SKYE

THE HIGHLANDS & SKYE

MORAR **Inverness-shire** Mrs C A Finch Glenancross Morar, Mallaig Inverness-shire PH40 4PD Tel: (Arisaig) 01687 450294	Map 3 F11	APPROVED	1 Twin	1 En Suite fac	B&B per person from £13.00 Double	Open Jan-Dec Dinner from 1800 B&B + Eve. Meal from £18.00	
			Small family run bed and breakfast in quiet rural situation near to Morar Sands and Arisaig. Owners keen riders, nearby trekking centre.				
Sunset Morar, by Mallaig Inverness-shire PH40 4PA Tel: (Mallaig) 01687 462259		APPROVED	1 Twin 1 Double 2 Family	1 Pub Bath/Show	B&B per person £12.50-£16.00 Single £12.50-£15.00 Double	Open Jan-Dec Dinner 1900-2100 B&B + Eve. Meal £19.50-£23.00	
			Small family house in West Highland village, very close to the renowned Morar Sands. Mallaig 3 miles (5 kms) with ferries to Skye and Small Isles.				
MUIR OF ORD **Ross-shire** Mrs W A Keir Monadh Liath, Ord Wood Muir-of-Ord Ross-shire IV6 7XS Tel: (Muir of Ord) 01463 870587	Map 4 A8	COMMENDED	2 Twin 1 Double	1 Pub Bath/Show	B&B per person from £14.50 Double	Open Jan-Dec	
			In quiet residential area, on the outskirts of the town, large modern house set in extensive gardens. Ample parking available.				
NAIRN Duchally Guest House Wellington Road Nairn IV12 4RE Tel: (Nairn) 01667 453003	Map 4 C8	COMMENDED	4 Single 2 Twin 2 Double 4 Family	5 En Suite fac 6 Priv. NOT ensuite 3 Pub Bath/Show	B&B per person £17.50-£25.00 Single £17.50-£25.00 Double	Open Jan-Dec Dinner 1730-1830 B&B + Eve. Meal £25.00-£32.50	
			Large family run guest house, convenient for town centre, golf courses and beaches. Off-street parking.				
Mrs H Fraser Sandown House Sandown Farm Lane Nairn IV12 5NE Tel: (Nairn) 01667 454745		COMMENDED Listed	1 Single 1 Twin 1 Family	2 Pub Bath/Show	B&B per person £12.00-£16.00 Single £12.00-£16.00 Double	Open Jan-Nov Dinner from 1800	
			19th century house in rural area with heated pool in summer. Overlooking Moray Firth and close to beach and golf course. 1 mile (2 kms) to town centre.				
Glen Lyon Lodge Waverley Road Nairn IV12 4RH Tel: (Nairn) 01667 452780		COMMENDED	1 Single 2 Twin 1 Double 2 Family	6 En Suite fac 1 Pub Bath/Show	B&B per person £18.00-£21.00 Single £18.00-£21.00 Double	Open Jan-Dec Dinner 1830-1900 B&B + Eve. Meal £26.00-£29.00	
			Friendly welcome in family run guest house. Close to town centre and ten minutes from beach.				
Mrs P Hudson & Mr Maxwell Durham House 4 Academy Street Nairn Inverness-shire IV12 4RJ Tel: (Nairn) 01667 452345		COMMENDED	1 Twin 1 Double 1 Family	2 En Suite fac 2 Pub Bath/Show	B&B per person £17.00-£20.00 Double	Open Jan-Dec Dinner 1800-1930 B&B + Eve. Meal £27.00-£30.00	
			19th century elegant villa, set in its own grounds, with off-street parking. Extensive home baking and cooking.				

by NAIRN Mr & Mrs G Pearson Brightmony Farm House Auldearn Nairn IV12 5PP Tel: (Nairn) 01667 455550	Map 4 C8	COMMENDED Listed	1 Twin 2 Double	1 Pub Bath/Show	B&B per person £15.00 Single £14.00 Double	Open Mar-Nov	

A listed, Georgian farmhouse, large bedrooms, log fire, peaceful and relaxed, superb views over Moray Firth.

NETHY BRIDGE **Inverness-shire** Linda Renton Aspen Lodge Nethy Bridge Inverness-shire PH25 3DA Tel: (Nethy Bridge) 01479 821042 Fax: 01479 821042	Map 4 C10	COMMENDED Listed	1 Twin 1 Double	1 En Suite fac 1 Priv. NOT ensuite	B&B per person from £18.50 Single from £18.50 Double	Open Jan-Dec	

Situated in the heart of picturesque Nethybridge. Ideal base for Strathspey. Walking, bird-watching and touring beautiful Strathspey.

NEWTONMORE **Inverness-shire** Nicola Drucquer Eagle View, Perth Road Newtonmore Inverness-shire PH20 1AP Tel: (Newtonmore) 01540 673675 Fax: 01540 673675	Map 4 B11	COMMENDED	2 Twin 2 Double	3 En Suite fac 1 Priv. NOT ensuite	B&B per person £17.00-£20.00 Single £15.00-£18.00 Double	Open Jan-Dec Dinner from 1900	

Traditional stone-built house with large garden and ample parking. Warm and friendly atmosphere, situated near centre of village. Non-smoking house.

BEN-Y-GLOE

Fort William Road, Newtonmore, Inverness-shire PH20 1DG
Telephone and Fax: 01540 673633
Celia and John would like to welcome you to their family home.
An attractive spacious house set in its own grounds, centrally situated
for all amenities and ideal for touring the Highlands. Ground-floor
bedrooms with private facilities, tea-coffee, colour TV, own keys,
TV lounge and delicious cooked breakfasts. £17 per person.

Celia Ferrie Ben-y-Gloe, Fort William Road Newtonmore Inverness-shire PH20 1DG Tel: (Newtonmore) 01540 673633 Fax: 01540 673633		COMMENDED	1 Twin 2 Double	3 En Suite fac	B&B per person from £17.00 Single from £17.00 Double	Open Jan-Dec	

Traditional Scottish hospitality in friendly Bed & Breakfast. Within walking distance of all village amenities and ideal touring base for Spey Valley.

Glenquoich Guest House Glen Road Newtonmore Inverness-shire Tel: (Newtonmore) 01540 673461 Fax: 01540 673007		COMMENDED	1 Single 1 Twin 2 Double 1 Family	1 En Suite fac 2 Pub Bath/Show	B&B per person £16.00-£18.00 Single £17.00-£20.00 Double	Open Jan-Dec	

Victorian house of character near centre of village. Friendly welcome, open fires.

Mrs M Johnston Ardnabruach, Glen Road Newtonmore Inverness-shire PH20 1DZ Tel: (Newtonmore) 01540 673339		COMMENDED Listed	1 Single 1 Twin 1 Double	1 Pub Bath/Show	B&B per person from £13.50 Single from £13.50 Double Room only per person from £10.00	Open Jan-Dec	

Set in own grounds, our friendly relaxed Victorian home offers you Highland hospitality and personal attention. Beautiful location overlooking village.

Details of Grading and Classification are on page vi.

Key to symbols is on back flap.

THE HIGHLANDS & SKYE

NEWTONMORE continued **Inverness-shire** Mrs K Main Craigellachie House Main Street Newtonmore Inverness-shire PH20 1DA Tel: (Newtonmore) 01540 673360	**Map 4** **B11**	COMMENDED	1 Double 1 Family	1 Pub Bath/Show	B&B per person £16.00-£18.00 Single £15.00-£17.00 Double	Open Jan-Dec, exc Xmas Dinner 1830-2000 B&B + Eve. Meal from £23.00

Oldest house in Newtonmore offering comfortable accommodation in family home.
Vegetarians catered for.

WOODCLIFFE

Laggan Road, Newtonmore   Telephone: 01540 673839

In quiet surroundings on the edge of a small Highland village, we offer you a warm welcome in our comfortable home with an open coal fire. Unrivalled opportunities for all outdoor activities in this beautiful area. Wonderful centre for touring or just relaxing.

Mrs A Morrison Woodcliffe, Laggan Road Newtonmore Inverness-shire PH20 1DG Tel: (Newtonmore) 01540 673839	COMMENDED Listed	·1 Double 1 Family	1 En Suite fac 1 Pub Bath/Show	B&B per person £14.00-£16.00 Single £14.00-£16.00 Double	Open Jan-Dec

Stone-built house on edge of quiet Highland village. Comfortable stay
assured in this welcoming family home. Garden nursery business in grounds.

Dorothy Muir Greenways, Golf Course Road Newtonmore Inverness-shire PH20 1AT Tel: (Newtonmore) 01540 673325	COMMENDED	1 Single 1 Twin 1 Double	1 Pub Bath/Show	B&B per person to £13.00 Single to £13.00 Double	Open Jan-Dec

Friendly welcome to our cosy, traditional, stone-built home. Central yet
in a wooded garden overlooking golf course and mountains. Ideal touring base.

NORTH KESSOCK **Ross-shire** Mrs N Bonthrone 37 Drumsmittal Road North Kessock Ross-shire IV1 1XF Tel: (Kessock) 01463 731777	**Map 4** **B8** HIGHLY COMMENDED Listed	1 Single 1 Double	1 Pub Bath/Show	B&B per person £14.00-£15.00 Single £14.00-£15.00 Double	Open Jan-Dec excl Xmas

Modern family home in quiet residential area on the Black Isle.
Convenient for A9. Close to Inverness. Off-street parking.

Mrs Grigor Redfield Farm North Kessock Ross-shire IV1 1XD Tel: (Munlochy) 01463 811228	COMMENDED	1 Twin 1 Double	1 En Suite fac 1 Priv. NOT ensuite 2 Pub Bath/Show	B&B per person from £16.00 Double	Open Jan-Dec Dinner 1900-2000 B&B + Eve. Meal from £48.00

On mixed working farm, 4 miles (7 kms) north of Inverness,
large family farmhouse. Home baking.

Mr & Mrs R S Prentice Kilda, 3 Bellfield Drive North Kessock Ross-shire IV1 1XT Tel: (Kessock) 01463 731567	COMMENDED Listed	1 Single 1 Twin 1 Double	1 Pub Bath/Show	B&B per person £15.00 Single £14.00 Double	Open May-Sep

Situated right on the seafront with uninterrupted views across the Beauly Firth.
Dolphin-viewing from the property.

ONICH, by Fort William Inverness-shire	Map 3 G12

Camus House Lochside Lodge

Onich, by Fort William, Inverness-shire PH33 6RY
Telephone: 01855 821200

In extensive lochside gardens, midway between Ben Nevis and Glencoe. Ideal base for touring, walking, mountain-biking, climbing and ski-ing. Open from January to November. Most rooms are ensuite with central heating and teasmaid. We provide excellent cooking, friendly service and are licensed.
DB&B £33-£42. Weekly £196 - £275. Brochure available.

| Camus House
Lochside Lodge
Onich
Inverness-shire
PH33 6RY
Tel: (Onich) 01855 821200 | COMMENDED | 2 Twin
3 Double
2 Family | 6 En Suite fac
1 Pub Bath/Show | B&B per person
£18.00-£27.50 Single
£18.00-£27.50 Double | Open Jan-Nov
Dinner to 1915
B&B + Eve. Meal
to £42.00 | |

Large well-appointed house, comfortably furnished, superb views of the sea loch and hills. Fort William 10 miles (16 kms), Glencoe 5 miles (8 kms).

| Mr Collins
Tom-na-Creige
North Ballachulish
Onich
Inverness-shire
PH33 6RY
Tel: (Onich) 01855 821405 | COMMENDED | 1 Twin
1 Double | 2 En Suite fac | B&B per person
£16.50-£18.50 Double | Open Jan-Dec | |

Modern comfortable ensuite accommodation with inspiring views over Loch Linnhe.

| Mrs J McLean
Forester's Bungalow, Inchree
Onich
Inverness-shire
PH33 6SE
Tel: (Onich) 01855 821285 | COMMENDED | 2 Twin
1 Family | 1 Pub Bath/Show | B&B per person
£14.00-£15.00 Double | Open Apr-Oct
Dinner 1830-1930
B&B + Eve. Meal
from £21.00 | |

Detached cottage in secluded setting 0.5 miles (1 km) from the main road and near the Corran Ferry. Good base for forest walks or for touring.

| Mrs M MacLean
Janika, Bunree
Onich
Inverness-shire
PH33 6SE
Tel: (Onich) 01855 821359 | COMMENDED | 1 Twin
1 Double | 1 Pub Bath/Show | B&B per person
from £15.00 Double | Open Apr-Oct | |

Family house on 5-acre (2ha) croft, running down to the shores of Loch Linnhe at the Corran Narrows. 8 miles (13 kms) from Fort William.

| PLOCKTON
Ross-shire
Mrs Cameron
2 Frithard Road
Plockton
Ross-shire
IV52 8TQ
Tel: (Plockton) 01599 544226 | Map 3
F9

COMMENDED | 2 Double
1 Family | 1 En Suite fac
2 Priv. NOT ensuite
2 Pub Bath/Show | B&B per person
£15.00-£20.00 Single
£15.00-£18.00 Double | Open Jan-Dec | |

Semi-detached house, comfortable warm and quiet. Ideal for all ages. Situated near village and loch. Ground-floor rooms.

THE HIGHLANDS & SKYE

LOOK FOR THE SIGNS OF THE WELCOME HOSTS

Welcome Host

They will provide a traditional Scottish welcome and quality service throughout your stay.

Details of Grading and Classification are on page vi.

Key to symbols is on back flap.

THE HIGHLANDS & SKYE (side margin)

| PLOCKTON continued | Map 3 |
| Ross-shire | F9 |

TOMACS

FRITHARD, PLOCKTON, ROSS-SHIRE IV52 8TQ
Telephone: 01599 544321

We are situated at the far end of Plockton, five minutes' walk
from the hotels and shops. Our comfortable family home has
spectacular views of *Loch Carron* and the *Applecross Hills*.
Plockton is renowned for its scenery and won the
Scottish Tourism Oscar for *Best Village for Tourism 1994.*

Mrs Janet Mackenzie Jones	**COMMENDED**	1 Twin	1 En Suite fac	B&B per person	Open Jan-Dec
Tomacs, Frithard		2 Double	1 Priv. NOT ensuite	£15.00-£16.00 Double	
Plockton			1 Pub Bath/Show		
Ross-shire					
IV52 8TQ					
Tel: (Plockton) 01599 544321					

Comfortable family home in quiet location in village of Plockton.

An-Caladh

25 Harbour Street, Plockton, Ross-shire IV52 8TN
Telephone: 01599 544356

Traditional white-washed Highland cottage overlooking Plockton
Bay. Centrally heated throughout. Relax and enjoy the breathtaking
views from our garden opening onto the shore. Ideal base for
hillwalking, this year we are offering evening wildlife or sea angling
trips in our own D.O.T. licensed vessel. Special rates for residents.

Mrs MacAulay Rowe	**COMMENDED**	1 Twin	2 En Suite fac	B&B per person	Open Jan-Dec
An Caladh, 25 Harbour Street		2 Double	1 Priv. NOT ensuite	from £16.00 Double	
Plockton				Room only per person	
Ross-shire				from £12.00	
IV52 8TN					
Tel: (Plockton) 01599 544356					

Traditional cottage, family run, overlooking the bay in peaceful conservation
village. Boat trips and guided tours of Hamish Macbeth country.

THE SHIELING

PLOCKTON, ROSS-SHIRE IV52 8TL   Tel: 01599 544282

Comfortable, family home centrally situated in Plockton, *1994
Winner of the Tourist Village of the Year* and featured in BBC's
Hamish MacBeth. Panoramic views over Loch Carron from our
spacious residents' lounge, within walking distance of hotels.
Ideal base for touring and walking.
Recommended by the Which? Good Bed & Breakfast Guide.

Mrs Jane MacDonald	**COMMENDED**	1 Twin	1 En Suite fac	B&B per person	Open Apr-Oct
The Shieling		2 Double	1 Pub Bath/Show	from £15.00 Double	
Plockton					
Ross-shire					
IV52 8TL					
Tel: (Plockton) 01599 544282					

Family home with a beautiful view over Loch Carron.
Short walk to shops and hotels. Ideal centre for touring and walking.

Ann MacKenzie	**COMMENDED**	3 Double	2 En Suite fac	B&B per person	Open Jan-Dec
Heron's Flight			1 Priv. NOT ensuite	from £16.00 Double	
Plockton					
Ross-shire					
IV52 8TL					
Tel: (Plockton) 01599 544220					
Fax: 01599 544220					

Traditional Highland hospitality in friendly family
home on shores of Loch Carron. Car parking.

Mrs L Wilson Cherrytrees Duirinish, by Plockton Tel: (Plockton) 01599 544402		COMMENDED	1 Twin 1 Double 1 Family	3 En Suite fac	B&B per person £16.00-£20.00 Single £16.00-£20.00 Double Room only per person £14.00-£18.00	Open Apr-Nov	

Highland hospitality in friendly family home.
Panoramic views to Applecross and Cuillins.

POOLEWE **Ross-shire** Mrs K MacDonald Benlair, Near Cove Poolewe Ross-shire IV22 2LS Tel: (Poolewe) 01445 781354	Map 3 F7	COMMENDED	2 Twin	2 En Suite fac	B&B per person from £20.00 Single from £20.00 Double	Open Apr-Oct	

Family run cottage in tranquil setting with superb views over the sea,
200 yards (190m) from sandy beach, near village of Cove.

Mrs R MacIver Creagard, 2 Naast Poolewe Ross-shire Tel: (Poolewe) 01445 781389		COMMENDED Listed	1 Single 1 Twin 2 Double	1 Pub Bath/Show	B&B per person £11.50-£13.00 Single £11.50-£13.00 Double	Open Apr-Oct Dinner 1800-1900 B&B + Eve. Meal £20.00-£21.50	

Modern croft house overlooking Loch Ewe and the Munros beyond.
Dinner and lounge available. 6 miles (10 kms) from Inverewe Gardens.

Mrs M MacLeod Bruach Ard, Inverasdale Poolewe Ross-shire Tel: (Poolewe) 01445 781214		COMMENDED	1 Twin 2 Double	3 En Suite fac	B&B per person £17.50-£19.50 Single £17.50-£19.50 Double	Open Apr-Nov Dinner 1900-1930 B&B + Eve. Meal £27.50-£29.50	

Modern family home in elevated position with superb views over Loch Ewe.
Evening meals featuring local seafood available.

REDBURN, by Belivat **Inverness-shire** Jill Jones Redburn House Redburn, Belivat Nairn IV12 5JE Tel: (Dunphail) 01309 651323 Fax: 01309 651323	Map 4 C8	HIGHLY COMMENDED Listed	1 Double 1 Family	1 Pub Bath/Show	B&B per person £22.00-£24.00 Single £17.50-£20.00 Double	Open Apr-Oct	

Large comfortable family house in Nairnshire countryside, just off A939,
8 miles (12 kms) south of Nairn. Ample private parking. Kennels available.

SCOURIE **Sutherland** Mrs Jana MacDonald Cnoc-Aluinn Scourie Sutherland Tel: (Scourie) 01971 502024 Fax: 01971 502024	Map 3 H4	HIGHLY COMMENDED	2 Double 1 Family	3 En Suite fac	B&B per person £18.00-£25.00 Double Room only per person from £15.00	Open Mar-Oct Dinner 1900-2000	

Modern, purpose-built guest house with superb views over the Minch. All home cooking.

Scourie Lodge Scourie Sutherland IV27 4SX Tel: (Scourie) 01971 502248		HIGHLY COMMENDED Listed	1 Twin 2 Double	2 Pub Bath/Show	B&B per person £18.50-£25.50 Single £17.50-£19.50 Double	Open Mar-Oct Dinner 1800-1930 B&B + Eve. Meal £30.00-£38.00	

Beautifully situated on Scourie Bay. Ideal for the north west of Scotland.
Comfortable accommodation. We welcome children. No smoking.

Mrs Sarah Thomson Braeval, Scourie More Scourie Sutherland IV27 4TG Tel: (Scourie) 01971 502076		COMMENDED Listed	1 Twin 2 Double	2 Pub Bath/Show	B&B per person £13.00-£16.00 Single from £13.00 Double	Open May-Sep	

Modern bungalow set up above this typical west coast Highland village.
Fine views of Scourie Bay and Handa Island in the distance.

THE HIGHLANDS & SKYE

Details of Grading and Classification are on page vi.

Key to symbols is on back flap.

THE HIGHLANDS & SKYE

SHIELDAIG **Ross-shire** Mrs M C Calcott Tigh Fada, 117 Doireaonar Shieldaig, Strathcarron Ross-shire IV54 8XH Tel: (Shieldaig) 01520 755248	**Map 3** F8	**COMMENDED** Listed	1 Twin 1 Double 1 Family	2 Pub Bath/Show	B&B per person from £13.50 Double	Open Jan-Dec Dinner from 1900 B&B + Eve. Meal from £21.50

Centrally heated accommodation on working croft, specialising in Hebridean and Angora wool. Evening meal and home baking.

INNIS MHOR

COMMENDED

Ardheslaig, Nr Shieldaig, Strathcarron
Ross-shire IV54 8XH Tel/Fax: 01520 755339

This comfortable, family home is located near Shieldaig on the scenic coastal road round the Applecross Peninsula and next to the shore of Loch Torridon. Ideally situated for touring the West Coast, climbing, walking, fishing, nature watching or just relaxing amid the breathtaking scenery.

Details from Chris and Erica Sermon.

Mr & Mrs C Sermon Innis Mhor, Ardheslaig Shieldaig Ross-shire IV54 8XH Tel: (Shieldaig) 01520 755339 Fax: 01520 755339		**COMMENDED**	2 Single 1 Twin 2 Double	2 Pub Bath/Show	B&B per person £16.50-£17.50 Single £14.50-£16.50 Double	Open Jan-Dec exc Xmas Dinner 1900-2000 B&B + Eve. Meal £24.50-£27.50

Comfortable family home peacefully located overlooking Loch Torridon and the Applecross Peninsula. Private parking. Ideal for fishing, walking and climbing.

ISLE OF SKYE, Inverness-shire **ARDVASAR, Sleat,** **Isle of Skye** Mrs Barton Hazelwood Ardvasar, Sleat Isle of Skye, Inverness-shire IV45 8RS Tel: (Ardvasar) 01471 844200	**Map 3** E11	**COMMENDED** Listed	1 Twin 1 Double	1 Pub Bath/Show	B&B per person £16.00-£17.00 Double	Open Jan-Dec

Modern family home in village of Ardvasar, overlooking Sound of Sleat. Very convenient for ferry to Mallaig.

BERNISDALE, by Portree **Isle of Skye** Mrs D MacLeod Benview House Bernisdale, by Portree Isle of Skye, Inverness-shire IV51 9NS Tel: (Skeabost Bridge) 01470 532208	**Map 3** D8	**COMMENDED**	1 Single 2 Family	2 Pub Bath/Show	B&B per person from £15.00 Single from £15.00 Double	Open Apr-Oct Dinner from 1830 B&B + Eve. Meal from £24.00

Warm welcome at detached house in quiet area of Bernisdale township with views of Loch Snizort. Central for touring Skye.

BROADFORD, Isle of Skye Mrs J Donaldson Fairwinds, Elgol Road Broadford Isle of Skye, Inverness-shire IV49 9AB Tel: (Broadford) 01471 822270	**Map 3** E10	**HIGHLY** **COMMENDED**	1 Twin 2 Double	3 En Suite fac	B&B per person £17.00-£19.00 Double	Open Mar-Oct

Peacefully situated bungalow in extensive garden overlooking Broadford River and the mountains. Bicycles for hire.

ASHGROVE

11 Black Park, Broadford, Isle of Skye IV49 9AE
Telephone: 01471 822327

Comfortable accommodation in three-bedroomed bungalow. Two bedrooms with WHB, one bedroom with WHB, shower and toilet en-suite. Colour TV lounge, tea-making facilities. Cot available. Seven miles from Skye Bridge. Turn off main road at Lime Park/Black Park junction.

From £13 to £18 per person.   **Commended**

Mrs M Fletcher Ashgrove, 11 Black Park Broadford Isle of Skye, Inverness-shire IV49 9AE Tel: (Broadford) 01471 822327	COMMENDED	1 Twin 1 Double 1 Family	1 En Suite fac 1 Pub Bath/Show	B&B per person £13.00-£18.00 Double	Open Jan-Dec
		Modern bungalow with fine views of sea and mountains.			
Mrs M A B Macgregor Langdale House Waterloo, Breakish Isle of Skye, Inverness-shire IV42 8QE Tel: (Broadford) 01471 822376	COMMENDED	1 Twin 2 Double	3 En Suite fac	B&B per person £20.00 Double	Open Mar-Nov Dinner 1900-2000 B&B + Eve. Meal £35.00
		Superb views of sea and mountains from most rooms. Nature watch. Vegetarian and Coeliac food by arrangement.			

Ptarmigan

Broadford, Isle of Skye IV49 9AQ
Telephone: 01471 822744 Fax: 01471 822745

A warm welcome awaits you at Ptarmigan. Ensuite bedrooms on ground floor with panoramic views across Broadford Bay. 15 metres from seashore. Ideal bird/otter-watching – binoculars supplied. Excellent base for touring Skye and S.W. Ross-shire. Minutes walk from pubs/restaurants. Ample parking.

Mrs D MacPhie Ptarmigan Broadford Isle of Skye, Inverness-shire IV49 9AQ Tel: (Broadford) 01471 822744 Fax: 01471 822745	HIGHLY COMMENDED	1 Twin 2 Double	3 En Suite fac 1 Pub Bath/Show	B&B per person £20.00-£25.00 Double	Open Jan-Dec
		Modern family home on seashore of Broadford Bay. Panoramic views across islands to mainland.			
Mrs Robertson Tigh a Croisean, 4 Black Park Broadford Isle of Skye, Inverness-shire IV49 9AE Tel: (Broadford) 01471 822338	HIGHLY COMMENDED	1 Twin 2 Double	3 En Suite fac 1 Pub Bath/Show	B&B per person £18.00-£22.00 Double	Open Apr-Sep
		Comfortable family home in quiet location in Broadford village. All rooms with private facilities.			
Mrs M Robertson Earsary, 7-8 Harrapool Broadford Isle of Skye, Inverness-shire IV49 9AQ Tel: (Broadford) 01471 822697	HIGHLY COMMENDED	1 Twin 1 Double 1 Family	3 En Suite fac	B&B per person £20.00-£25.00 Single £16.00-£20.00 Double	Open Jan-Dec Dinner 1730-1900
		Modern house with high standard of accommodation on working croft. Panoramic views over Broadford Bay.			
Mrs D Robertson Westside, Elgol Road Broadford Isle of Skye, Inverness-shire IV49 9AB Tel: (Broadford) 01471 822320	HIGHLY COMMENDED	1 Single 1 Twin 1 Double	3 En Suite fac 1 Pub Bath/Show	B&B per person £18.00-£20.00 Single £18.00-£20.00 Double	Open Jan-Dec
		A warm welcome and good food at this modern bungalow in a quiet lane, with views across to Beinn Na Cailleach.			

THE HIGHLANDS & SKYE

Details of Grading and Classification are on page vi. | Key to symbols is on back flap. | 289

BROADFORD, Isle of Skye continued Mrs Scott Tigh-na-Mara Lower Harrapool, Broadford Isle of Skye, Inverness-shire IV49 9AB Tel: (Broadford) 01471 822475	Map 3 E10	**COMMENDED** 👑👑	1 Family	1 Priv. NOT ensuite 1 Pub Bath/Show	B&B per person £17.00-£18.00 Double Room only per person £15.00-£16.00	Open Apr-Oct	

Family room in 150-year-old cottage on the sea shore.
8 miles (12 kms) from Skye Bridge. Own sitting room.

Highly Commended
👑👑👑

CORRY LODGE

LIVERAS, BROADFORD, ISLE OF SKYE IV49 9AA
Telephone: 01471 822235   Fax: 01471 822318

This is a comfortable 18th-century family house situated on the outskirts of Broadford. Ideal centre for touring the Isle of Skye. Ample parking, large garden. *Brochure available.*

Home of the Liveras Fold of Highland Cattle.

Talisker Award for Highest Quality Accommodation (1994).

Jane Wilcken Corry Lodge, Liveras Broadford Isle of Skye, Inverness-shire IV49 9AA Tel: (Broadford) 01471 822235 Fax: 01471 822318		**HIGHLY COMMENDED** 👑👑👑	2 Twin 2 Double	4 En Suite fac	B&B per person £25.00-£30.00 Double B&B + Eve. Meal £40.00-£45.50	Open Mar-Oct Dinner 1930-2000	

Late 18th century shooting lodge, totally restored to its former splendour on 80-acre (32ha) estate stretching to the shoreline.

by BROADFORD, Isle of Skye Mrs Flora A MacLeod Hazelwood Cottage, Heaste by Broadford Isle of Skye, Inverness-shire IV42 8QF Tel: (Broadford) 01471 822294	Map 3 E10	**COMMENDED** 👑	1 Twin 2 Double	2 En Suite fac 1 Pub Bath/Show	B&B per person £16.00-£20.00 Double	Open Apr-Nov	

Modern bungalow on working croft, with panoramic views over Loch Eishort towards the hills of Knoydart.

DUNVEGAN, Isle of Skye Mrs A E Gracie Silverdale, 14 Skinidin Dunvegan Isle of Skye, Inverness-shire IV55 8ZS Tel: (Dunvegan) 01470 521251 Fax: 01470 521251	Map 3 D9	**HIGHLY COMMENDED** 👑👑	1 Twin 1 Double 1 Family	2 En Suite fac 1 Priv. NOT ensuite 1 Pub Bath/Show	B&B per person from £16.00 Double	Open Jan-Dec	

Modern house with superb views over Loch Dunvegan. Decor and furnishings to a high standard. Acclaimed restaurant nearby.

Mrs MacDonald Herebost Dunvegan Isle of Skye, Inverness-shire IV55 8GZ Tel: (Dunvegan) 01470 521255		**COMMENDED** 👑👑	1 Twin 2 Double	1 En Suite fac 1 Priv. NOT ensuite 1 Pub Bath/Show	B&B per person £14.00-£18.00 Double	Open Apr-Oct	

Modern bungalow on working sheep farm situated just off the Dunvegan Road with views to the south. Supper in the lounge in the evening.

by ELGOL, Isle of Skye Strathaird House by Elgol Isle of Skye, Inverness-shire IV49 9AX Tel: (Loch Scavaig) 01471 866269/ 01444 452990 (off season)	Map 3 E10	**APPROVED** Listed	2 Single 1 Double 4 Family	4 Pub Bath/Show	B&B per person £17.10-£26.00 Single £15.30-£24.00 Double B&B + Eve. Meal £27.80-£38.50	Open Apr-Sep Dinner 1900-2000	

Family run guest house in own extensive grounds with views of sea and Cuillins.
10 miles (16 kms) west of Broadford.

GLENDALE, Isle of Skye	Map 3 C8						
Mrs Kernachan 4 Lephin Glendale Isle of Skye, Inverness-shire IV55 8WJ Tel: (Glendale) 01470 511376 Fax: 01470 511376		COMMENDED Listed	2 Twin 1 Double	1 Pub Bath/Show	B&B per person from £14.50 Double	Open Jan-Dec Dinner 1830-2000 B&B + Eve. Meal from £22.50	

Situated with views across Glendale to Outer Hebrides, a quiet and beautiful part of north west Skye. Evening meal available. Vegetarians catered for.

ISLEORNSAY, Isle of Skye	Map 3 F10

Mrs F A Macdonald

6 Duisdale Beag, Isleornsay, Isle of Skye IV43 8QU
Telephone: 01471 833230

We are situated on a working croft in an elevated location overlooking the sea and just a 10-minute walk from the local hotel which serves restaurant and bar meals. This is a peaceful area with beautiful mountain views. Enjoy Highland hospitality where Gaelic is spoken.
No-smoking throughout.

Mrs MacDonald 6 Duisdale Beag Isleornsay, Sleat Isle of Skye, Inverness-shire Tel: (Isle Ornsay) 01471 833230	COMMENDED	1 Twin 2 Double	2 En Suite fac 2 Pub Bath/Show	B&B per person £15.00-£20.00 Single £15.00-£18.00 Double	Open Mar-Sep

Modern bungalow in elevated position in small country village overlooking the sea. Gaelic spoken.

KENSALEYRE, by Portree Isle of Skye	Map 3 D8						
Corran Guest House Eyre Kensaleyre, by Portree Isle of Skye, Inverness-shire IV51 9XE Tel: (Skeabost Bridge) 01470 532311		COMMENDED	1 Single 1 Double 2 Family	1 En Suite fac 3 Priv. NOT ensuite 3 Pub Bath/Show	B&B per person £18.00-£20.00 Single £18.00-£20.00 Double	Open Jan-Dec Dinner at 1900 B&B + Eve. Meal £28.00-£30.00	

In a small country village overlooking Loch Snizort, 6 miles (10kms) from Portree and from Uig ferry terminal. Extensive gardens with lovely views.

KILMUIR, by Uig Isle of Skye	Map 3 D9

Kilmuir House

Kilmuir
Near Uig
Isle of Skye
IV51 9YN
Tel: 01470 542262

Lovely old manse in large walled garden overlooking Loch Snizort and Outer Hebrides. Furnished with antiques and centrally heated throughout, we offer excellent home cooking using local produce and our own free-range eggs. Kilmuir is steeped in history and Gaelic culture and tradition is still much in evidence here.

Mrs S Phelps Kilmuir House Kilmuir, by Uig Isle of Skye, Inverness-shire IV51 9YN Tel: (Uig) 01470 542262	COMMENDED Listed	1 Twin 1 Double 1 Family	2 Pub Bath/Show	B&B per person £15.00-£16.00 Double	Open Jan-Dec Dinner 1900-2000 B&B + Eve. Meal £24.00-£25.00

Former manse in superb situation overlooking loch to Outer Isles. Warm hospitality and high standard of home cooking using fresh local produce.

THE HIGHLANDS & SKYE

LUIB, by Broadford **Isle of Skye** Mrs Dobson Luib House Luib, by Broadford Isle of Skye, Inverness-shire IV49 9AN Tel: (Broadford) 01471 822724	Map 3 E9	COMMENDED 👑👑👑	1 Twin 1 Double	2 En Suite fac 1 Pub Bath/Show	B&B per person £13.00–£17.00 Double	Open Jan-Dec Dinner 2000-2100 B&B + Eve. Meal £22.00–£26.00	

Detached modernised house on a working croft with Highland cattle,
overlooking Loch Ainort and on main road from Broadford to Portree.

ORD, Sleat, Isle of Skye Mrs B La Trobe Fiordhem Ord Isle of Skye, Inverness-shire IV44 8RN Tel: (Tarskavaig) 01471 855226	Map 3 E10	COMMENDED 👑👑👑	1 Twin 3 Double	3 En Suite fac 1 Pub Bath/Show	B&B per person £25.00–£30.00 Single £22.00–£26.00 Double	Open Easter-Oct Dinner 1830-1930 B&B + Eve. Meal £30.00–£40.00	

Unique stone cottage, 20 feet (6m) from lochside. Breathtaking
views of Cuillins and the Small Isles. Location of distinction.

PORTREE, Isle of Skye Elizabeth MacDonald 25 Urquhart Place Portree Isle of Skye, Inverness-shire IV51 9HS Tel: (Portree) 01478 612374	Map 3 E9	COMMENDED 👑👑	1 Single 1 Twin 1 Double	1 En Suite fac 2 Priv. NOT ensuite 1 Pub Bath/Show	B&B per person £15.00 Single £13.00–£16.00 Double	Open Apr-Oct	

Traditional Highland hospitality in friendly family home.
1 mile (1.6 kms) from town centre. Gaelic spoken.

AN-AIRIDH

6 FISHERFIELD, PORTREE, ISLE OF SKYE IV51 9EU
Telephone: 01478 612250
The house is situated off the main road within 10 minutes walking distance
from Portree overlooking the bay. Accommodation comprises 2 single rooms
(£18 pp) with H/C facilities, one double (£20 pp) with ensuite facilities, one twin
with ensuite facilities, also two family rooms (£22 pp) with ensuite facilities.
Open all year.

Mrs MacLeod An Airidh, Viewfield Road Portree Isle of Skye, Inverness-shire IV51 9EU Tel: (Portree) 01478 612250	APPROVED 👑👑	2 Single 1 Twin 1 Double 2 Family	4 En Suite fac 2 Priv. NOT ensuite 1 Pub Bath/Show	B&B per person £18.00 Single £20.00–£22.00 Double	Open Jan-Dec Dinner from 1800

Modern guest house on edge of Portree overlooking the bay towards
Ben Tianavaig and Raasay. Excellent base for exploring Skye.

Mrs McPhie Balloch, Viewfield Road Portree, Isle of Skye Inverness-shire, IV51 9ES Tel: (Portree) 01478 612093	HIGHLY COMMENDED 👑👑👑	1 Single 1 Twin 2 Double	4 En Suite fac	B&B per person £18.00–£21.00 Single £18.00–£21.00 Double	Open Mar-Dec

Large comfortable house in own garden on edge of Portree. All rooms ensuite.

Mrs E Nicolson Almondbank, Viewfield Road Portree, Isle of Skye Inverness-shire, IV51 9EU Tel: (Portree) 01478 612696 Fax: 01478 613114	HIGHLY COMMENDED 👑👑👑	2 Twin 2 Double	3 En Suite fac 1 Priv. NOT ensuite	B&B per person £21.00–£26.50 Double	Open Jan-Dec Dinner from 1800 B&B + Eve. Meal to £39.00

Modern house on the outskirts of Portree. Well-appointed
lounge and dining room with panoramic views of Portree Bay.

The Shielings Guest House Torvaig Portree Isle of Skye, Inverness-shire IV51 9HU Tel: (Portree) 01478 613024	COMMENDED 👑👑	1 Twin 3 Double	4 En Suite fac	B&B per person £16.00–£22.00 Double	Open Jan-Dec excl Xmas/New Year Dinner at 1900 B&B + Eve. Meal £25.00–£31.00

Converted croft cottage with superb views. Situated just
2 miles (3 kms) outside Portree. Home cooking and a
warm homely atmosphere.

THE HIGHLANDS & SKYE

Mrs P M Thorpe Jacamar, Achachork Road Portree Isle of Skye, Inverness-shire IV51 9HT Tel: (Portree) 01478 612274	COMMENDED ♛	1 Double 1 Family	1 En Suite fac 1 Pub Bath/Show	B&B per person £16.00-£17.00 Single £15.00-£18.00 Double	Open Jan-Dec Dinner 1830-1930 B&B + Eve. Meal £23.50-£26.50	
Modern bungalow, with open outlook beyond Portree towards the Cuillins. Portree 2.5 miles (4 kms).						

by PORTREE, Isle of Skye	Map 3 E9

Tianavaig Bed & Breakfast

1/7 Camastianavaig Braes, by Portree, Isle of Skye IV51 9LQ
Telephone: 01478 650325

Tianavaig is situated in a wild, beautiful rural seashore location. The sea and mountain views are magnificent. Scenic walks. Abundant wildlife are all around. Tianavaig is a very comfortable modern home offering pretty bedrooms with tea facilities. A cosy peaceful guest lounge with log fire, maps and guide books. Approximately 5 miles to Portree.

Nevelee Corry Tianavaig, 1/7 Camastianavaig Braes, by Portree Isle of Skye, Inverness-shire IV51 9LQ Tel: (Sligachan) 01478 650325	COMMENDED Listed	2 Double 1 Family	1 En Suite fac 1 Pub Bath/Show	B&B per person to £16.00 Single from £15.00 Double	Open Jan-Dec ex Xmas	
A pretty rural location by the seashore, magnificent sea and mountain views. Guest lounge with log fire. Portree 5 miles (8 kms).						

STAFFIN, Isle of Skye	Map 3 E8					
Mrs M McDonald Ben Edra, 1 Maligar Staffin, by Portree Isle of Skye, Inverness-shire IV51 9JF Tel: (Staffin) 01470 562291	COMMENDED Listed	1 Twin 1 Family	1 Pub Bath/Show	B&B per person £15.00-£16.00 Single £13.00-£14.00 Double	Open Apr-Oct Dinner 1800-2000 B&B + Eve. Meal £22.00-£24.00	
Traditional working croft house. Warm island welcome, home baking, cooking. Peat fires. Superb views of the Storr. Salmon/trout fishing available.						

Mrs Katie M MacLeod 10 Digg Staffin Isle of Skye, Inverness-shire Tel: (Staffin) 01470 562276	COMMENDED Listed	1 Twin 2 Double	1 Pub Bath/Show	B&B per person from £14.00 Double	Open Mar-Oct
Traditional Highland hospitality on working croft. Home baking provided in a friendly warm atmosphere.					

TEANGUE, Sleat, Isle of Skye	Map 3 F10					
B & J Shaw Alltan House Ferindonald, Sleat Isle of Skye, Inverness-shire IV44 8RQ Tel: (Ardvasar) 01471 844342	COMMENDED Listed	1 Twin 2 Double	2 Pub Bath/Show	B&B per person from £15.00 Double	Open Mar-Nov	
Modern house in elevated position offering panoramic views over the Sound of Sleat to the mountains of Knoydart, 4 miles (6 kms) from Armadale ferry.						

TREASLANE, Isle of Skye	Map 3 D8					
Auchendinny Guest House Treaslane Skeabost Bridge Isle of Skye, Inverness-shire IV51 9NX Tel: (Skeabost Bridge) 01470 532470	HIGHLY COMMENDED ♛♛♛ ♿	2 Twin 4 Double 1 Family	7 En Suite fac	B&B per person £17.00-£23.00 Double	Open Mar-Oct Dinner from 1900 B&B + Eve. Meal £29.00-£35.00	
On A850 Dunvegan Road 8.5 miles (14 kms) from Portree. Peaceful lochside setting, beautiful views.						

THE HIGHLANDS & SKYE

THE HIGHLANDS & SKYE

TREASLANE, Isle of Skye **continued** Mrs M Cameron Hillcroft, 2 Treaslane by Portree Isle of Skye, Inverness-shire IV51 9NX Tel: (Edinbane) 01470 582304	Map 3 D8	HIGHLY COMMENDED ♔♔	2 Double	1 En Suite fac 1 Priv. NOT ensuite	B&B per person £15.00-£22.00 Double	Open Mar-Nov	

Friendly welcome at modernised house on working croft overlooking
Loch Snizort. On A850 9 miles (14 kms) north of Portree.

UIG, Isle of Skye Mrs Anne Morrison Braeholm Uig Isle of Skye, Inverness-shire IV51 9XX Tel: (Uig) 01470 542396 Fax: 01470 542396	Map 3 D8	COMMENDED ♔	1 Twin 1 Double	1 Pub Bath/Show	B&B per person £15.50-£16.50 Double	Open Jan-Dec	

Traditional cottage at water's edge. Approximately 100 metres to Uig ferry.
Home cooking and baking provided in a friendly warm setting.

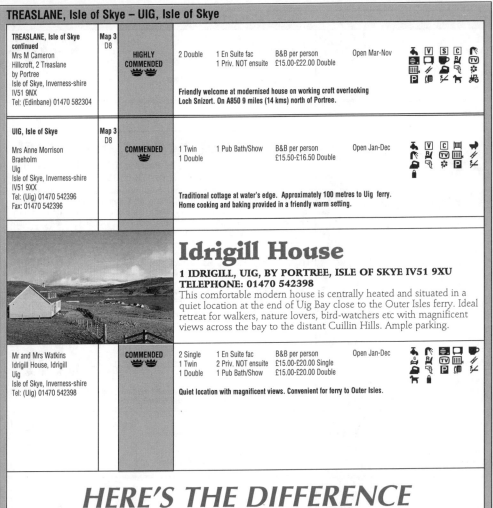

Idrigill House

1 IDRIGILL, UIG, BY PORTREE, ISLE OF SKYE IV51 9XU
TELEPHONE: 01470 542398

This comfortable modern house is centrally heated and situated in a
quiet location at the end of Uig Bay close to the Outer Isles ferry. Ideal
retreat for walkers, nature lovers, bird-watchers etc with magnificent
views across the bay to the distant Cuillin Hills. Ample parking.

Mr and Mrs Watkins Idrigill House, Idrigill Uig Isle of Skye, Inverness-shire Tel: (Uig) 01470 542398	COMMENDED ♔♔	2 Single 1 Twin 1 Double	1 En Suite fac 2 Priv. NOT ensuite 1 Pub Bath/Show	B&B per person £15.00-£20.00 Single £15.00-£20.00 Double	Open Jan-Dec

Quiet location with magnificent views. Convenient for ferry to Outer Isles.

HERE'S THE DIFFERENCE

STB's scheme has two distinct elements, grading and classification.

GRADING:

Measures the quality and condition of the facilities and services offered, eg, the warmth
of welcome, quality of food and its presentation, condition of decor and furnishings,
appearance of buildings, tidiness of grounds and gardens, condition of lighting and
heating and so on.

Grading awards are: **Approved, Commended, Highly Commended, Deluxe.**

CLASSIFICATION:

Measures the range of physical facilities and services offered, eg, rooms with private
bath, heating, reception, lounges, telephones and so on.

Classification awards are: **Listed to five crowns or one to five crowns.**

SPEAN BRIDGE Inverness-shire	Map 3 H12	

Barbagianni Guest House
Spean Bridge PH34 4EU   Telephone: 01397 712437

This is a family run guest house, situated in its own grounds, overlooking Ben Nevis mountain range on outskirts of Spean Bridge. Ideal base for touring. Central heating, tea/coffee facilities, (all rooms with private facilities). Comfortable lounge with TV. Home cooking. Parking.

Barbagianni Guest House Tirindrish Spean Bridge Inverness-shire PH34 4EU Tel: (Spean Bridge) 01397 712437	HIGHLY COMMENDED	1 Single 1 Twin 5 Double	6 En Suite fac 1 Priv. NOT ensuite	B&B per person £17.00-£18.00 Single £17.00-£18.00 Double	Open Mar- 20 Oct Dinner from 1930 B&B + Eve. Meal £32.00
		Detached modern house of interesting design, in its own grounds with excellent views over Ben Nevis and beyond. Friendly atmosphere, home baking. Dinner is at 7.30pm.			
Mrs M Cairns Invergloy House, Invergloy Spean Bridge Inverness-shire PH34 4DY Tel: (Spean Bridge) 01397 712681	HIGHLY COMMENDED	3 Twin	3 En Suite fac 1 Pub Bath/Show	B&B per person £18.00-£19.00 Double	Open Jan-Dec Dinner from 1930 B&B + Eve. Meal £28.50-£30.00
		A warm welcome is offered in our peaceful country home, in 50 acres (20ha) of woodland estate. Access to lochside.			
Coinachan Spean Bridge Inverness-shire Tel: (Spean Bridge) 01397 712417	COMMENDED	1 Twin 2 Double	3 En Suite fac	B&B per person £17.50-£19.50 Double	Open Jan-Dec Dinner 1930-2030 B&B + Eve. Meal £30.00-£32.00
		A warm welcome at this comfortable cottage, tastefully renovated in peaceful location yet convenient for the A82. Excellent views of the Commando Memorial.			
Coire Glas Guest House Roy Bridge Road Spean Bridge Inverness-shire PH34 4EU Tel: (Spean Bridge) 01397 712272	COMMENDED	1 Single 4 Twin 4 Double 2 Family	8 En Suite fac 1 Pub Bath/Show	B&B per person £14.00-£23.00 Single £14.00-£18.00 Double	Open Jan-Oct Dinner 1900-2000 B&B + Eve. Meal £24.00-£38.00
		Family run guest house set back from A86 tourist route, only 6 miles (9 kms) from Aonach Mor gondola station. Views of the Ben Nevis mountain range.			
Distant Hills Guest House Spean Bridge Inverness-shire PH34 4EU Tel: (Spean Bridge) 01397 712452	HIGHLY COMMENDED	4 Twin 3 Double	7 En Suite fac 1 Pub Bath/Show	B&B per person £21.00 Single £16.00 Double	Open Feb-Oct Dinner 1700-2030 B&B + Eve. Meal £26.00
		Modern bungalow at edge of quiet village. Friendly and personal attention. Excellent views of Aonach Mor, ideally situated for touring and skiing.			
Inverour Guest House Spean Bridge Inverness-shire PH34 4EU Tel: (Spean Bridge) 01397 712218	COMMENDED	2 Single 2 Twin 3 Double	3 En Suite fac 2 Pub Bath/Show	B&B per person from £15.00 Single from £15.00 Double	Open Jan-Dec excl Xmas Dinner 1900-2000 B&B + Eve. Meal from £27.00
		Comfortable, homely atmosphere. Situated in an ideal centre for touring the west of Scotland.			
Mrs L MacGregor Achnabobane Farmhouse Spean Bridge Inverness-shire PH34 4EX Tel: (Spean Bridge) 01397 712565/712342 Fax: 01397 712342	COMMENDED	1 Twin 3 Double 2 Family	3 En Suite fac 2 Pub Bath/Show	B&B per person £15.00-£30.00 Single £15.00-£25.00 Double	Open Apr-Mar, excl Nov Dinner 1830-1930 B&B + Eve. Meal £25.00-£35.00
		Traditional farmhouse in quiet location with magnificent views of Ben Nevis and Nevis Range. 2 miles south of Spean Bridge. Small collection of traditional Scottish rare breeds of animal.			

THE HIGHLANDS & SKYE

Details of Grading and Classification are on page vi.   Key to symbols is on back flap.

THE HIGHLANDS & SKYE

| SPEAN BRIDGE continued
Inverness-shire | Map 3
H12 |

Old Pines

Restaurant with Rooms, Spean Bridge, Inverness-shire PH34 4EG
Telephone: 01397 712324 Fax: 01397 712433

Quiet situation. Breathtaking views of Aonach Mor and Ben Nevis. Ideal base for touring the West Highlands. Happy family home with a relaxing, informal atmosphere, pretty ensuite bedrooms, flowers, books and log fires. Outstanding dinners in a magical setting.
Contact: Bill and Sukie Barber   *"A Very Special Place"*

| Old Pines,
Restaurant with Rooms
Spean Bridge
Inverness-shire
PH34 4EG
Tel: (Spean Bridge)
01397 712324
Fax: 01397 712433 | HIGHLY
COMMENDED | 2 Single
2 Twin
2 Double
2 Family
Suite avail | 7 En Suite fac
1 Priv. NOT ensuite | B&B per person
£25.00-£45.00 Single
£20.00-£35.00 Double | Open Jan-Dec
Dinner from 2000
B&B + Eve. Meal
£40.00-£65.00 |

"Best Small Hotel in Britain 1994" – Judith Chalmers Holiday Care Awards. Winner of the 1995 "Taste of Scotland Classic Scotch Lamb Challenge".

| Smiddy House
Spean Bridge
Inverness-shire
PH34 4EU
Tel: (Spean Bridge)
01397 712335 | COMMENDED | 1 Twin
2 Double
1 Family | 4 En Suite fac | B&B per person
£21.00 Single
£16.00 Double | Open Jan-Dec
Dinner 1900-2100
B&B + Eve. Meal
from £26.00 |

Completely refurbished family run house at the centre of this small Highland village, ideal for touring, walking and skiing.

| Peter & Jean Wilson
Tirindrish House
Spean Bridge
Inverness-shire
PH34 4EU
Tel: (Spean Bridge)
01397 712398
Fax: 01397 712398 | COMMENDED | 1 Twin
1 Double
1 Family | 1 En Suite fac
2 Priv. NOT ensuite | B&B per person
£16.00-£25.00 Single
£16.00-£18.00 Double
Room only per person
£14.00-£16.00 | Open Apr-Oct
Dinner 1900-2000
B&B + Eve. Meal
£26.00-£28.00 |

Historic Highland house, dating from Jacobite times, in extensive grounds. 10 miles (16 kms) from Fort William.

| STRATHCARRON
Ross-shire | Map 3
G9 |

"THE SHIELING"

Achintee, Strathcarron, Ross-shire IV54 8YX
Telephone: 01520 722364

Only minutes from a railway station, surrounded by spectacular scenery, a comfortable base for many leisure activities, particularly hillwalking and climbing. Central for day trips to such places as Skye and Inverewe Gardens.

| Mrs J Levy
The Shieling, Achintee
Strathcarron
Ross-shire
IV54 8YX
Tel: (Lochcarron)
01520 722364 | COMMENDED
Listed | 1 Single
2 Twin | 1 En Suite fac
1 Pub Bath/Show | B&B per person
from £15.00 Single
£15.00-£18.00 Double | Open Apr-Oct |

Welcoming, family home in beautiful West Highland area. Close to station on Kyle line. 2 twins and small single. Evening meal by arrangement. Non-smoking.

| STRATHPEFFER
Ross-shire
Mrs G P Cameron
White Lodge
Strathpeffer
Ross-shire
IV14 9AL
Tel: (Strathpeffer)
01997 421730 | Map 4
A8

HIGHLY
COMMENDED | 1 Twin
1 Double | 2 En Suite fac | B&B per person
£25.00 Single
£18.00-£19.00 Double | Open Apr-Sep
Dinner 1830-1930 |

'B' Listed 18th century lodge overlooking charming square of small Highland spa village.

Mrs Derbyshire Inver Lodge Strathpeffer Ross-shire IV14 9DL Tel: (Strathpeffer) 01997 421392	COMMENDED ♛	1 Twin 1 Family	2 Pub Bath/Show	B&B per person £18.00-£21.00 Single £15.00 Double	Open Mar-Dec Dinner 1930-2030 B&B + Eve. Meal £25.50-£31.50	

Stone-built family home in lovely Highland spa town.
Dinner available using quality local produce. Open wood fire.

Gardenside Guest House
STRATHPEFFER, ROSS-SHIRE IV14 9BJ
Telephone: 01997 421242   Fax: 01997 421242
The Guest House is located on the south-west side of the
village of Strathpeffer surrounded by woodland and fields.
The accommodation consists of six letting rooms, four with ensuite
facilities. All bedrooms are equipped with tea and coffee-making
facilities. A guests' lounge with TV is available to residents.
NON-SMOKING ESTABLISHMENT

Gardenside Guest House Strathpeffer Ross-shire IV14 9BJ Tel: (Strathpeffer) 01997 421242	COMMENDED ♛♛♛	2 Twin 4 Double	4 En Suite fac 1 Pub Bath/Show	B&B per person £15.00-£18.00 Double	Open Apr-Nov Dinner 1830-2000 B&B + Eve. Meal £25.00-£28.00	

Friendly welcome at family run guest house in spa village.
Good walking country and touring base. 21 miles (32 kms) from Inverness.

Mrs J MacDonald Scoraig, 8 Kinnettas Square Strathpeffer Ross-shire IV14 9BD Tel: (Strathpeffer) 01997 421847	COMMENDED Listed	1 Single 1 Twin 1 Double 1 Family	1 En Suite fac 1 Priv. NOT ensuite 2 Pub Bath/Show	B&B per person £13.00-£14.00 Single £13.00-£15.00 Double	Open Jan-Dec Dinner 1800-2000 B&B + Eve. Meal £20.00-£22.00	

Comfortable personally run B&B, situated in quiet residential area close to
village centre. Ideal touring base, home cooking, dinner by arrangement.
Private parking.

CRAIGVAR
THE SQUARE, STRATHPEFFER IV14 9DL   Tel: 01997 421622
Beautifully situated overlooking the square in this charming Victorian spa
village. This distinctive Georgian House offers superb luxury facilities.
★ All rooms have colour TV, tea/coffee facilities, direct-dial telephone.
★ All bedrooms have attractive ensuite bathrooms.
★ Four-poster bedroom/open fires.
★ Excellent parking.
★ Ideal touring base.

Mrs M Scott Craigvar, The Square Strathpeffer Ross-shire IV14 9DL Tel: (Strathpeffer) 01997 421622	DELUXE ♛♛	1 Single 1 Twin 1 Double	3 En Suite fac	B&B per person from £21.00 Single £16.50-£21.00 Double	Open Apr-Oct	

Beautifully situated overlooking the square in charming spa village, this
distinctive Georgian house offers attractive ensuite rooms. 4-poster bed.

STRATHY POINT **Sutherland** Mrs P MacAskill Sharvedda Strathy Point, by Thurso Sutherland KW14 7RY Tel: (Strathy) 01641 541311	Map 4 B3 HIGHLY COMMENDED ♛	1 Twin 1 Double	1 Pub Bath/Show	B&B per person £20.00 Single from £16.00 Double	Open Apr-Oct Dinner 1800-2030 B&B + Eve. Meal £26.00	

Modern family home with views to sea and open croft land.
Evening meals available. Home baking.

THE HIGHLANDS & SKYE

Details of Grading and Classification are on page vi. | Key to symbols is on back flap. |

THE HIGHLANDS & SKYE

STROMEFERRY
Ross-shire
Mrs P Davey
Soluis Mu Thuath
Braeintra, Achmore
Stromeferry
Ross-shire
IV53 8UN
Tel: (Stromeferry)
01599 577219

Map 3 F9

COMMENDED ♛

2 Twin / 1 Double / 1 Family — 4 En Suite fac — B&B per person £16.00-£18.00 Single / £16.00-£18.00 Double — Open Feb-Nov

Purpose-built by owners set amidst quiet countryside.
Excellent centre for Skye, Applecross and Torridon. No smoking.

STRONTIAN
Argyll

Map 1 E1

Kinloch House

Strontian, Acharacle, Argyll PH36 4HZ   Tel: 01967 402138

New bungalow set in 13 acres. Magnificent position overlooking Loch Sunart and surrounding mountains. Close to village of Strontian. Ideal centre for exploring an area of outstanding natural beauty with abundant wildlife. All rooms with ensuite facilities.

Special rates for 3 and 5-night Spring, Autumn and Winter Breaks.

Mrs C Frith
Kinloch House
Strontian, Acharacle
Argyll
PH36 4HZ
Tel: (Strontian) 01967 402138

HIGHLY COMMENDED ♛♛

1 Twin / 2 Double — 3 En Suite fac — B&B per person £15.00-£20.00 Double — Open Jan-Nov

New bungalow in superb location overlooking Loch Sunart
to the mountains beyond. Evening meal by prior arrangement.

Mrs D MacPherson
Struan, 19 Anaheilt
Strontian
Argyll
PH36 4JA
Tel: (Strontian) 01967 402057

COMMENDED ♛

1 Single / 1 Twin / 1 Double — 3 En Suite fac — B&B per person £15.00-£17.00 Single / £15.00-£17.00 Double — Open Apr-Oct

Modern bungalow with ground-floor bedrooms in working croft
in peaceful glen about half a mile (1 km) from the lochside. Friendly welcome.

TAIN
Ross-shire
Mrs Anderson
Rosslyn, 2 Moss Road
Tain
Ross-shire
IV19 1HQ
Tel: (Tain) 01862 892697

Map 4 B7

COMMENDED ♛

1 Twin / 1 Family — 2 En Suite fac / 1 Pub Bath/Show — B&B per person from £15.00 Single / from £15.00 Double — Open Mar-Nov

Comfortable, personally run B&B close to town centre.
Ideal base for touring the Highlands. Private parking.

Golf View Guest House
13 Knockbreck Road
Tain
Ross-shire
Tel: (Tain) 01862 892856
Fax: 01862 892856

HIGHLY COMMENDED ♛♛

3 Twin / 1 Double / 1 Family — 3 En Suite fac / 1 Pub Bath/Show — B&B per person £18.00-£25.00 Single / £16.00-£22.00 Double — Open Jan-Dec

Secluded Victorian house with panoramic views over golf course and
across the Dornoch Firth. Centrally situated in Scotland's oldest Royal Burgh.

Mrs M MacLean
23 Moss Road
Tain
Ross-shire
IV19 1HH
Tel: (Tain) 01862 894087

COMMENDED ♛

1 Twin / 1 Double — 2 En Suite fac / 2 Pub Bath/Show — B&B per person £15.00 Single / £15.00-£16.00 Double — Open Jan-Dec

Comfortable family-run home in quiet location. Log-burning stove in lounge
and a warm welcome assured. Tea, coffee and home baking on arrival.

Mrs K M Roberts
Carringtons, Morangie Road
Tain
Ross-shire
IV19 1PY
Tel: (Tain) 01862 892635

COMMENDED ♛♛

1 Double / 2 Family — 1 En Suite fac / 1 Limited ensuite / 2 Pub Bath/Show — B&B per person from £15.00 Single / from £15.00 Double — Open Jan-Dec

Detached family home on the outskirts of Tain overlooking the sea.
Close to town centre and golf course.

Mrs Shirley Ross Dunbíus, Morangie Road Tain Ross-shire Tel: (Tain) 01862 893010 Fax: 01862 893010		**COMMENDED** ♛ ♛	1 Twin 2 Family	3 En Suite fac	B&B per person from £18.00 Single from £16.00 Double	Open Jan-Dec

Comfortable modern family home with friendly Highland hosts.
Ample off-road parking available.

THURSO **Caithness** Mrs J Falconer, Murray House 1 Campbell Street Thurso Caithness KW14 7HD Tel: (Thurso) 01847 895759	Map 4 D3	**HIGHLY** **COMMENDED** ♛ ♛	1 Single 1 Twin 1 Double 1 Family	2 En Suite fac 2 Pub Bath/Show	B&B per person £16.00-£22.00 Single £15.00-£20.00 Double	Open Jan-Dec

Set in the centre of the town, a warm welcome and comfortable stay
are assured in this refurbished 19th century townhouse. Private parking.

Mrs M Fisher Carlingwark, 5 Mears Place Thurso Caithness KW14 7EW Tel: (Thurso) 01847 894124		**HIGHLY** **COMMENDED** ♛	1 Single 1 Twin 1 Double	2 Pub Bath/Show	B&B per person £15.00-£16.00 Single £15.00-£16.00 Double	Open May-Sep

Modern detached bungalow with enclosed landscaped garden in quiet cul-de-sac.
Well-furnished and comfortable, friendly family home. Evening cup of tea and
home baking.

Mrs Henderson Kerrera, 12 Rose Street Thurso Caithness KW14 7HH Tel: (Thurso) 01847 895127		**COMMENDED** ♛	2 Twin	1 Pub Bath/Show	B&B per person £15.00-£16.00 Single £15.00-£16.00 Double	Open Feb-Nov

A warm welcome awaits you in this comfortable family home,
quiet location in centre of town, convenient for railway station.

Mrs McDonald Seaview Farm, Hill of Forss Thurso Caithness KW14 7XQ Tel: (Thurso) 01847 892315		**COMMENDED** Listed	1 Twin 2 Double	1 Pub Bath/Show	B&B per person £14.00-£16.00 Single £14.00-£15.00 Double	Open Jan-Dec

Working farm, warm welcome and home bakes, display of
Highland dancing and trophies. Two miles (3 kms) from Orkney ferry.

Mrs Murray 1 Granville Crescent Thurso Caithness KW14 7NP Tel: (Thurso) 01847 892993		**COMMENDED** ♛ ♛	2 Twin	1 En Suite fac 1 Priv. NOT ensuite 1 Pub Bath/Show	B&B per person £18.00-£20.00 Single £15.00-£16.50 Double	Open Jan-Dec

Quietly situated, yet within easy reach of station and all facilities.
All ground-floor rooms, one ensuite, one with private bathroom.

Mrs M Sinclair Shinval, Glengolly Thurso Caithness KW14 7XN Tel: (Thurso) 01847 894306		**COMMENDED** ♛ ♛	1 Twin 1 Double 1 Family	1 En Suite fac 1 Priv. NOT ensuite 2 Pub Bath/Show	B&B per person £14.50-£18.00 Single £14.50-£18.00 Double Room only per person £12.00-£16.00	Open Jan-Dec

Family home in quiet rural setting. 2 miles (3 kms) from Thurso.
Extensive countryside views.

Mrs E Taylor Oldfield Park Thurso Caithness KW14 8RE Tel: (Thurso) 01847 893637		**COMMENDED** Listed	1 Twin 2 Double	1 En Suite fac 1 Pub Bath/Show	B&B per person £15.00-£22.00 Single £15.00-£22.00 Double	Open May-Sep

Comfortable B&B set back from main road, large garden,
ample private parking, short walk from town centre.

Mrs D Thomson Annandale 2 Rendel Govan Road Thurso Caithness KW14 7EP Tel: (Thurso) 01847 893942		**COMMENDED** ♛	2 Twin 1 Double	2 Pub Bath/Show	B&B per person £15.00-£16.50 Double	Open May-Sep

Comfortable B&B situated in quiet residential area.
Ideal base for touring north coast and convenient for Orkney ferry.

THE HIGHLANDS & SKYE

Details of Grading and Classification are on page vi.

Key to symbols is on back flap.

THE HIGHLANDS & SKYE

| TORRIDON | Map 3 |
| Ross-shire | G8 |

BEN DAMPH LODGE

TORRIDON, ROSS-SHIRE IV22 2EY
Telephone: 01445 791251   Fax: 01445 791296

BEN DAMPH LODGE is a former stable block to the
Loch Torridon Hotel.
New spacious, budget accommodation with all
modern facilities. Prices from £7.50 per person.
***New Bistro** open all day plus bar.*
Petrol and Craft Shop.

Ben Damph Lodge Torridon Ross-shire IV22 2EY Tel: (Torridon) 01445 791251/ 791242 Fax: 01445 791296	COMMENDED Lodge	14 Family	14 En Suite fac	B&B per person £26.50-£43.25 Single £26.50 Double Room only per person from £7.50	Open Jan-Dec Dinner 1830-2030

Comfortable lodge accommodation in the midst of Torridon Mountains,
restaurant and bar close by.

| ULLAPOOL | Map 3 |
| Ross-shire | G6 |

Ardvreck Guest House

Morefield Brae, Ullapool IV26 2TH
Telephone and Fax: 01854 612028

Spacious and well-appointed accommodation. All rooms ensuite with
television and tea/coffee facilities, rural setting with spectacular views of sea,
mountains, and Ullapool. Durness on the North Coast (75 miles) can be
reached in a day as can the famous Inverewe Gardens (55 miles south)
B&B from £20.00   *Contact Mrs Stockall*

Ardvreck Guest House Morefield Brae Ullapool Ross-shire IV26 2TH Tel: (Ullapool) 01854 612028/ 612561 Fax: 01854 612028	HIGHLY COMMENDED	2 Single 2 Twin 4 Double 2 Family	10 En Suite fac	B&B per person £20.00-£24.00 Single £20.00-£24.00 Double Room only per person £18.00-£22.00	Open Mar-Nov

Quiet secluded guest house with spectacular views over Loch Broom.
All rooms ensuite. Ullapool 1.5 miles (2.5 kms).

Mrs I Boa Ardale, Market Street Ullapool Ross-shire Tel: (Ullapool) 01854 612220	COMMENDED	1 Twin 2 Double	1 En Suite fac 1 Pub Bath/Show	B&B per person from £14.00 Double	Open Mar-Oct

Modern bungalow in tree-lined avenue. Close to town centre and all amenities.
Car parking available. Gaelic spoken.

Mrs E Campbell Clisham, 56 Rhue Ullapool Ross-shire IV26 2TJ Tel: (Ullapool) 01854 612498/ (except Sunday)	COMMENDED	2 Family	1 Pub Bath/Show	B&B per person £13.50-£14.00 Double	Open May-Oct

Small working croft peacefully situated in elevated position,
giving superb views over Loch Broom. 3 miles (5 kms) north of Ullapool.

Mrs F Campbell Corrieshalloch House Fasnagrianach Loch Broom, by Ullapool Ross-shire IV23 2RU Tel: (Lochbroom) 01854 655204 Fax: 01854 655204	COMMENDED	1 Twin 2 Double	1 En Suite fac 1 Pub Bath/Show	B&B per person £14.00-£16.00 Single £14.00-£16.00 Double B&B + Eve. Meal £23.00-£25.00	Open Jan-Dec Dinner 1830-1930

New house on a small working croft in attractive countryside setting.
Home cooking using quality local produce and home-grown vegetables.

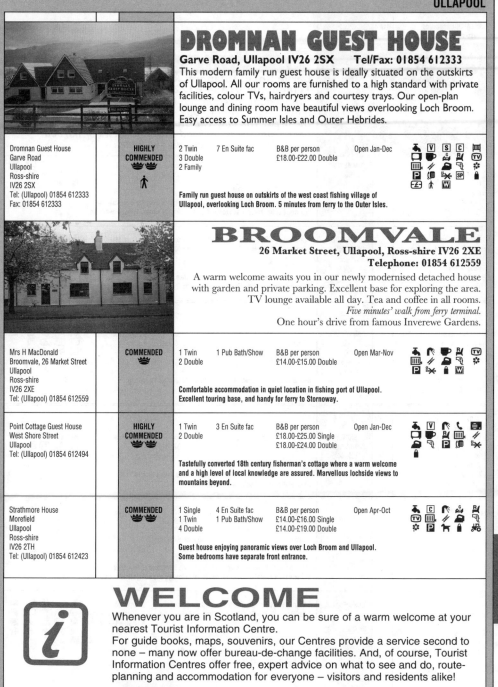

DROMNAN GUEST HOUSE

Garve Road, Ullapool IV26 2SX   Tel/Fax: 01854 612333

This modern family run guest house is ideally situated on the outskirts of Ullapool. All our rooms are furnished to a high standard with private facilities, colour TVs, hairdryers and courtesy trays. Our open-plan lounge and dining room have beautiful views overlooking Loch Broom. Easy access to Summer Isles and Outer Hebrides.

Dromnan Guest House Garve Road Ullapool Ross-shire IV26 2SX Tel: (Ullapool) 01854 612333 Fax: 01854 612333	HIGHLY COMMENDED	2 Twin 3 Double 2 Family	7 En Suite fac	B&B per person £18.00-£22.00 Double	Open Jan-Dec

Family run guest house on outskirts of the west coast fishing village of Ullapool, overlooking Loch Broom. 5 minutes from ferry to the Outer Isles.

BROOMVALE

26 Market Street, Ullapool, Ross-shire IV26 2XE
Telephone: 01854 612559

A warm welcome awaits you in our newly modernised detached house with garden and private parking. Excellent base for exploring the area. TV lounge available all day. Tea and coffee in all rooms.
Five minutes' walk from ferry terminal.
One hour's drive from famous Inverewe Gardens.

Mrs H MacDonald Broomvale, 26 Market Street Ullapool Ross-shire IV26 2XE Tel: (Ullapool) 01854 612559	COMMENDED	1 Twin 2 Double	1 Pub Bath/Show	B&B per person £14.00-£15.00 Double	Open Mar-Nov

Comfortable accommodation in quiet location in fishing port of Ullapool. Excellent touring base, and handy for ferry to Stornoway.

Point Cottage Guest House West Shore Street Ullapool Tel: (Ullapool) 01854 612494	HIGHLY COMMENDED	1 Twin 2 Double	3 En Suite fac	B&B per person £18.00-£25.00 Single £18.00-£24.00 Double	Open Jan-Dec

Tastefully converted 18th century fisherman's cottage where a warm welcome and a high level of local knowledge are assured. Marvellous lochside views to mountains beyond.

Strathmore House Morefield Ullapool Ross-shire IV26 2TH Tel: (Ullapool) 01854 612423	COMMENDED	1 Single 1 Twin 4 Double	4 En Suite fac 1 Pub Bath/Show	B&B per person £14.00-£16.00 Single £14.00-£19.00 Double	Open Apr-Oct

Guest house enjoying panoramic views over Loch Broom and Ullapool. Some bedrooms have separate front entrance.

WELCOME

Whenever you are in Scotland, you can be sure of a warm welcome at your nearest Tourist Information Centre.

For guide books, maps, souvenirs, our Centres provide a service second to none – many now offer bureau-de-change facilities. And, of course, Tourist Information Centres offer free, expert advice on what to see and do, route-planning and accommodation for everyone – visitors and residents alike!

THE HIGHLANDS & SKYE

THE HIGHLANDS & SKYE

ULLAPOOL continued Ross-shire	Map 3 G6		

The Bungalow

Garve Road, Ullapool, Ross-shire IV26 2SX
Telephone: 01854 612233

Family home overlooking Loch Broom and surrounding hills. ¼ mile from village. Excellent base for exploring the area. The only two-storey bungalow in Ullapool set back from the main road with fine views of harbour and village. Ample parking available.

Mrs C Sykes The Bungalow, Garve Road Ullapool Ross-shire IV26 2SX Tel: (Ullapool) 01854 612233	COMMENDED ♛	1 Twin 1 Double	2 Priv. NOT ensuite	B&B per person £14.00-£15.00 Double	Open May-Sep
The only two-storey "Bungalow" in Ullapool, set back from the main road, with fine views of the harbour and town. ¼ mile (0.5km) to centre. Parking available.					
Mrs J Urquhart Ardlair, Morefield Ullapool Ross-shire IV26 2TH Tel: (Ullapool) 01854 612087	COMMENDED ♛♛	1 Double 2 Family	2 En Suite fac 1 Pub Bath/Show	B&B per person £14.00-£17.00 Double	Open May-Oct
Purpose-built modern house in elevated position, giving excellent views over Loch Broom. Under 2 miles (3 kms) north of Ullapool.					
by ULLAPOOL Ross-shire Mrs M Mackenzie Torran, Loggie Lochbroom, Ullapool Ross-shire IV23 2SG Tel: (Lochbroom) 01854 655227	Map 3 G6 COMMENDED ♛	1 Twin 1 Double	1 Pub Bath/Show	B&B per person £15.00-£16.00 Double	Open Mar-Nov
New bungalow in peaceful lochside setting. Ideal base for touring, walking, bird-watching and fishing.					
WICK **Caithness** Mrs Bremner The Clachan, South Road Wick Caithness KW1 5NH Tel: (Wick) 01955 605384	Map 4 E3 HIGHLY COMMENDED ♛♛	1 Twin 2 Double	3 En Suite fac	B&B per person £20.00-£25.00 Single £18.00-£20.00 Double	Open Jan-Dec
Family run recently refurbished, detached house dating back to 1938 on quiet main street with off-street parking.					
Mrs Coghill Dunelm, 7 Sinclair Terrace Wick Caithness KW1 5AD Tel: (Wick) 01955 602120/ 605791	APPROVED ♛♛	1 Single 1 Twin 1 Double 1 Family	1 En Suite fac 3 Limited ensuite 2 Pub Bath/Show	B&B per person from £15.00 Single from £15.00 Double Room only per person from £13.00	Open Jan-Dec
Stone terraced Listed building, 5 minutes' walk from town centre, harbour, bus and railway stations. Large, comfortable lounge and separate breakfast room.					
Mrs C Gunn Hebron, 25 Beaufoy Street Wick Caithness KW1 5QG Tel: (Wick) 01955 603515	COMMENDED ♛	1 Twin 1 Family	1 Limited ensuite 2 Pub Bath/Show	B&B per person from £15.00 Double	Open Mar-Oct Dinner 1700-2000 B&B + Eve. Meal from £23.00
Stone-built house in quiet residential area within easy walking distance of town centre.					

Mrs S Gunn Papigoe Cottage, Papigoe Wick Caithness KW1 4RD Tel: (Wick) 01955 603363	APPROVED Listed	1 Twin 1 Double 1 Family	2 Pub Bath/Show	B&B per person £13.50 Single £13.50 Double	Open Jan-Dec Dinner 1900-2030	

A warm welcome is assured as you are treated as one of the family in this modest bungalow. Mrs Gunn is knowledgeable on this historic area.

GREENVOE
George Street, Wick, Caithness KW1 4DE
Telephone: 01955 603942

Detached house in peaceful situation in large garden close to town centre with panoramic views over Wick River. Supper of sandwiches and home baking provided in evening at no extra charge, bath robes also provided. Private parking, convenient for bus and railway station. 30 minutes to Orkney Ferry.

Mr & Mrs J Johnston Greenvoe, George Street Wick Caithness Tel: (Wick) 01955 603942	HIGHLY COMMENDED Listed	1 Single 1 Twin 1 Double	2 Pub Bath/Show	B&B per person £14.00 Single £14.00 Double	Open Jan-Dec	

A large modern comfortable house, 0.5 miles (1 km) from town centre. A non-smoking establishment. Private parking.

Mr A Stewart Bilbster House Wick Caithness KW1 5TB Tel: (Watten) 01955 621212	COMMENDED	1 Twin 2 Double	2 En Suite fac 1 Pub Bath/Show	B&B per person £14.50-£15.50 Single £14.50-£15.50 Double	Open Apr-Sep	

Listed country house dating from late 1700s set in 5 acres (2ha) of grounds. Traditionally furnished.

Mrs P Weir Warrington, Thurso Road Wick KW1 5LE Tel: (Wick) 01955 604138	COMMENDED Listed	1 Single 2 Double	1 Pub Bath/Show	B&B per person from £15.00 Single from £15.00 Double	Open Jan-Dec	

A warm welcome awaits you at this detached Edwardian villa. Convenient for bus and train stations. Ideal base for exploring Caithness and beyond.

Select your holiday accommodation with confidence,

use The Scottish Tourist Board's
Grading and Classification Scheme

THE HIGHLANDS & SKYE

Outer Islands

The Outer Islands are for people looking for a totally different experience – for a sense of being outside Britain and seeing a different culture.

They are for discriminating visitors, for those who enjoy wild places and a glimpse of the past and who appreciate that distinct character and a strong heritage are precious in this modern age. They are also for those who enjoy adventure and fun. The three island groupings – the Western Isles, Orkney and Shetland differ from each other, though Orkney and Shetland share a common Norse heritage. All three have good links by ferry and by air. Late spring in the islands is a particular delight, with rare northern wild flowers and spectacular seabird colonies adding to the sense of being somewhere different.

The Western Isles are the stronghold of the Gael, though everyone speaks English as well. Some of the finest sandy beaches in Britain can be found here, mostly on the west side of the islands, along with the characteristic machair – shell-sand on which a rich sward of wild flowers grows. There are some spectacular ancient monuments as well, notably the famous Calanais (Callanish) Standing Stones – Scotland's Stonehenge. You can glimpse more recent ways of life at the Black House at Arnol, an old-style restored croft house and there are a variety of other visitor centres portraying the heritage of the Gael. However, it is the pace of life, set in a distinct landscape and culture which will make the deepest impression.

Older than Stonehenge, the Standing Stones of Callanish on Lewis in the Western Isles are one of the many ancient sites scattered throughout the Outer Islands.

Orkney is a scattering of green islands, relatively fertile, with a strong sense of community and also more prehistoric sites to the square mile than anywhere else in Britain. Skara Brae, a 5000 year old Stone Age village and Maes Howe, a unique burial chamber probably pillaged by the Vikings, are just two of them. There are wildlife sites galore, especially seabirds, notably on the rugged island of Hoy.

Orkney's strong naval tradition is portrayed in a brilliant museum at Lyness on Hoy, overlooking the former naval anchorage at Scapa Flow. The highest vertical sea-cliff in Britain is also on Hoy and is just another surprise, as is the superb Norman work in St Magnus Cathedral in Kirkwall. However, the friendliness of the people should not be surprising – that is common in these Outer Island communities.

Outer Islands

Shetland is another cluster of islands, bound together like Orkney by an excellent network of inter-island ferries. Below the horizon, out of sight of the Scottish mainland, Shetland has the strongest sense of somewhere different.

Here the Scandinavian influence is strongest. Nowhere is more than 3 miles (5 km) from the sea. Magnificent seascapes and seabird colonies, from Sumburgh Head in the south to Hermaness in the north, are a speciality. There are brochs (circular defensive towers) and other early sites, as well as a croft museum, castles, and the main town of Lerwick to explore. June in these northern latitudes is a special time. This is the land of the 'simmer (summer) dim' – where the short night brings only twilight, leaving even more daylight hours to enjoy the stark beauty of the place.

Scale:
```
0    25   50   75   100 km
0         25        50 miles
```

Map labels:
UNST
YELL
SHETLAND
FOULA
Lerwick
From Norway
From Faroe Islands
FAIR ISLE
WESTRAY
NORTH RONALDSAY
ROUSAY
SANDAY
Stromness
Kirkwall
ORKNEY
HOY
SOUTH RONALDSAY
Burwick
Scrabster
John O'Groats
Thurso
Stornoway
Callanish
LEWIS
A857
ST KILDA
HARRIS
Tarbert
SCALPAY
Leverburgh
Ullapool
Otternish
NORTH UIST
Lochmaddy
Uig
BENBECULA
SOUTH UIST
Sconser
Kyle of Lochalsh
Inverness
Lochboisdale
Kyleakin
BARRA
Castlebay
(Summer only)
(Summer only)
Mallaig
Oban
ABERDEEN

AREA TOURIST BOARD ADDRESSES

1 ORKNEY TOURIST BOARD
6 Broad Street
KIRKWALL
Orkney
KW15 1NX
Tel: 01856 872856
Fax: 01856 875056

2 WESTERN ISLES TOURIST BOARD
26 Cromwell Street
Stornoway
Isle of Lewis
HS1 2DD
Tel: 01851 703088
Fax: 01851 705244

3 SHETLAND TOURIST BOARD
Market Cross
LERWICK
Shetland
ZE1 0LU
Tel: 01595 693434
Fax: 01595 695807

Outer Islands

**TOURIST INFORMATION
CENTRES IN SCOTLAND**

**ORKNEY TOURIST
BOARD**

KIRKWALL
6 Broad Street, KW15 1DH
Tel: (01856) 872856
Jan-Dec

STROMNESS
Ferry Terminal Building
The Pier Head
Tel: (01856) 850716
Jan-Dec

**WESTERN ISLES
TOURIST BOARD**

CASTLEBAY
Main Street
Isle of Barra
Tel: (01871) 810336
Easter-Oct

LOCHBOISDALE
Pier Road
Isle of South Uist
Tel: (01878) 700286
Easter-Oct

LOCHMADDY
Pier Road
Isle of North Uist
Tel: (01876) 500321
Easter-Oct

STORNOWAY
26 Cromwell Street
Isle of Lewis
Tel: (01851) 703088
Jan-Dec

TARBERT
Pier Road
Isle of Harris
Tel: (01859) 502011
Easter-Oct

**SHETLAND ISLANDS
TOURISM**

LERWICK
The Market Cross
Shetland, ZE1 0LU
Tel: (01595) 693434
Jan-Dec

 Accept written enquiries
  Disabled access

ISLE OF BENBECULA, Western Isles

LINICLATE

Inchyra Guest House
Liniclate
Benbecula
Western Isles
HS7 5PY
Tel: (Benbecula) 01870 602176

Map 3
B8

COMMENDED
👑👑👑

2 Single	8 En Suite fac	B&B per person	Open Jan-Dec
4 Twin		to £27.00 Single	Dinner 1800-2000
2 Double		to £21.00 Double	B&B + Eve. Meal
			£31.00-£37.00

Family run guest house, on working croft on main Lochmaddy to Lochboisdale road, about 6 miles (10 kms) from Benbecula Airport. Annexe accommodation.

TORLUM, Isle of Benbecula

Mrs Gretta Campbell
Borve
5 Torlum
Benbecula, Western Isles
HS7 5PP
Tel: (Benbecula) 01870 602685

Map 3
B8

HIGHLY
COMMENDED
👑👑👑

2 Twin	2 En Suite fac	B&B per person	Open Jan-Dec
1 Double	1 Pub Bath/Show	£16.00-£18.00 Single	Dinner 1800-1900
1 Family		£16.00-£18.00 Double	B&B + Eve. Meal
			£26.00-£28.00

Modern family home on working croft. Remains of Borve Castle on croft. Near sandy beaches, hotel and leisure centre.

ISLE OF HARRIS, Western Isles

LEVERBURGH

Mrs C MacKenzie
Garryknowe, Ferry Road
Leverburgh
Harris, Western Isles
PA83 3UA
Tel: (Leverburgh)
01859 520520246

Map 3
C7

COMMENDED
👑👑

1 Twin	1 En Suite fac	B&B per person	Open Apr-Oct
2 Double	2 Pub Bath/Show	from £15.00 Single	Dinner 1800-2000
		£15.00-£18.00 Double	B&B + Eve. Meal
			£24.00-£27.00

Renovated house in the township of Leverburgh. Near sea and passenger ferry to Uist. 21 miles (34 kms) from Tarbert.

TARBERT, Isle of Harris

Allan Cottage Guest House
Tarbert
Harris, Western Isles
HS3 3DJ
Tel: (Harris) 01859 502146

Map 3
C6

HIGHLY
COMMENDED
👑👑👑

1 Twin	2 En Suite fac	B&B per person	Open Apr-Sep
2 Double	1 Priv. NOT ensuite	£25.00-£26.00 Double	Dinner from 1900
			B&B + Eve. Meal
			£41.00-£42.00

Recently converted Old Harris Telephone Exchange, offering very high standard of comfort and cuisine.

Mrs A Morrison
Hillcrest
West Tarbert
Harris, Western Isles
HS3 3AH
Tel: (Harris) 01859 502119

HIGHLY
COMMENDED
👑👑

1 Twin	1 En Suite fac	B&B per person	Open Apr-Nov
1 Double	2 Pub Bath/Show	from £15.00 Single	Dinner from 1900
1 Family		from £15.00 Double	B&B + Eve. Meal
			from £24.00

Modern croft house in elevated position with fine view over West Loch Tarbert. About 1 mile (2 kms) from ferry terminal.

Mrs J M Morrison
Avalon, 12 Westside
Tarbert
Harris, Western Isles
HS3 3BG
Tel: (Harris) 01859 502334

HIGHLY
COMMENDED
👑👑👑
🚶

2 Twin	2 En Suite fac	B&B per person	Open Jan-Dec
1 Double	1 Pub Bath/Show	from £15.00 Single	Dinner 1800-1900
		from £15.00 Double	B&B + Eve. Meal
			from £23.00

New house on working croft with magnificent view over West Loch Tarbert. Ideal for hillwalking, fishing and bird-watching.

Flora Morrison
Tigh na Mara
Tarbert
Harris, Western Isles
Tel: (Harris) 01859 502270

COMMENDED
👑

1 Single	1 Pub Bath/Show	B&B per person	Open Jan-Dec
1 Twin		£15.00-£16.00 Single	Dinner from 1830
1 Family		£15.00-£16.00 Double	B&B + Eve. Meal
			£25.00-£26.00

Detached house with scenic views over East Loch Tarbert. Only about 500 metres from ferry terminal. Ideal centre for touring Harris.

OUTER ISLANDS

ISLE OF LEWIS, Western Isles **ACHMORE** Mrs W Golder Lochview, 35b Achmore Achmore Lewis, Western Isles PA86 9DU Tel: (Crossbost) 01851 860205	Map 3 D5	COMMENDED ♔	1 Twin 2 Double	2 Pub Bath/Show	B&B per person to £15.00 Single to £15.00 Double	Open Jan-Dec Dinner 1800-1900 B&B + Eve. Meal to £23.00	

Detached bungalow in a rural location overlooking Loch Achmore. Callanish Standing Stones about 5 miles (8 kms). Good touring centre for west coast.

AIGNISH, Point, Isle of Lewis Mrs L G MacDonald Ceol-Na-Mara, 1A Aignish Point Lewis, Western Isles HS2 0PB Tel: (Garrabost) 01851 870339	Map 3 E4	COMMENDED ♔	1 Twin 1 Double 1 Family	2 Pub Bath/Show	B&B per person £17.00 Single £15.00 Double	Open Jan-Dec Dinner 1830-2000 B&B + Eve. Meal £23.50-£25.50	

Comfortable modern home in pleasant rural Stornoway across the causeway on the Eye Peninsula. Home cooking and baking.

BACK, Isle of Lewis Mrs M Fraser Seaside Villa Back Lewis, Western Isles PA86 Tel: (Back) 01851 820208	Map 3 E4	HIGHLY COMMENDED ♔♔♔	1 Twin 2 Double	3 En Suite fac 1 Pub Bath/Show	B&B per person from £18.00 Single from £17.00 Double	Open Jan-Dec Dinner from 1800	

Modern house on working croft, friendly atmosphere with home baking and cooking, 7 miles (11 kms) from Stornoway. Lovely sea views.

CALLANISH, Isle of Lewis Eshcol Guest House 21 Breascleit Callanish Lewis, Western Isles HS2 9ED Tel: (Callanish) 01851 621357	Map 3 D4	HIGHLY COMMENDED ♔♔♔	2 Twin 1 Double	2 En Suite fac 1 Priv. NOT ensuite	B&B per person £23.00-£25.00 Single £23.00-£25.00 Double	Open Jan-Dec Dinner 1700-1900 B&B + Eve. Meal from £39.00	

Modern detached house with superb views. Near to Callanish Standing Stones and Carloway Broch. Ensuite facilites. Brochure available.

Catherine Morrison 27 Callanish Callanish, Lewis Western Isles, HS2 9DY Tel: (Callanish) 01851 621392		COMMENDED ♔♔	1 Twin 1 Double	1 Priv. NOT ensuite 1 Pub Bath/Show	B&B per person from £17.00 Double	Open Mar-Sep	

Comfortable accommodation on working croft close to the standing stones and overlooking the sea loch.

STORNOWAY, Isle of Lewis Mrs A C MacLeod Ravenswood 12 Matheson Road Stornoway Lewis, Western Isles HS87 2LR Tel: (Stornoway) 01851 702673	Map 3 D4	HIGHLY COMMENDED ♔♔♔	1 Single 1 Twin 1 Double	2 En Suite fac 1 Pub Bath/Show	B&B per person £18.00-£20.00 Single £18.00-£20.00 Double	Open Jan-Dec	

Turn of the century villa in a quiet area of Stornoway yet a short stroll to the harbour and town centre. Private parking.

ISLE OF NORTH UIST, Western Isles **BERNERAY** D A McKillop Burnside Croft Berneray North Uist, Western Isles Tel: (Berneray) 01876 540235 Fax: 01876 540235	Map 3 B7	COMMENDED ♔♔♔	1 Twin 2 Double	2 En Suite fac 1 Priv. NOT ensuite	B&B per person £20.00-£24.00 Single £20.00-£24.00 Double Room only per person £16.00-£18.00	Open Jan-Dec Dinner 1800-2030 B&B + Eve. Meal £26.00-£32.00	

A fine example of traditional Highland hospitality. You quickly become one of the family enjoying Gloria's good food and Don Alick's wide-ranging conversation.

OUTER ISLANDS

OUTER ISLANDS

GRIMSAY, Isle of North Uist Mrs C MacLeod Glendale, 7 Kallin Grimsay North Uist, Western Isles HS6 5HY Tel: (Benbecula) 01870 602029	Map 3 B8	COMMENDED 👑 👑	2 Twin 1 Double	2 En Suite fac 1 Priv. NOT ensuite	B&B per person from £18.00 Single from £15.00 Double	Open Jan-Dec Dinner 1900-2000 B&B + Eve. Meal from £27.00
			Modern house in quiet position overlooking the harbour. Views over the Minch and to the hills of South Uist. All rooms with private facilities.			
LOCHMADDY, Isle of North Uist Stag Lodge Lochmaddy Isle of North Uist, Western Isles Tel: (Lochmaddy) 01876 500364 Fax: 01876 500417	Map 3 B8	COMMENDED 👑 👑 👑	2 Twin 2 Double 1 Family	4 En Suite fac 1 Priv. NOT ensuite 1 Pub Bath/Show	B&B per person £18.00-£25.00 Single £18.00-£25.00 Double	Open Jan-Dec Dinner 1800-2130 B&B + Eve. Meal £27.00-£40.00
			Newly converted from two houses to form one, convenient for ferry. Ideal for fishing and walking holidays. Car hire available.			
SOLLAS, Isle of North Uist Mrs Lexy Pillans Creagan Fois, Claddach Valley Malaclate North Uist, Western Isles HS6 5BX Tel: (Sollas) 01876 560204	Map 3 B7	COMMENDED 👑 👑	1 Twin 1 Double 1 Family	3 En Suite fac	B&B per person from £16.00 Double	Open Jan-Dec Dinner 1900-2000 B&B + Eve. Meal from £26.00
			Recently built bungalow with panoramic view overlooking Tidal Strand to Vallay. Peaceful location which is near RSPB reserve.			
ORKNEY **BIRSAY** Mrs Clouston Primrose Cottage Birsay Orkney KW17 2NB Tel: (Birsay) 01856 721384	Map 5 B10	COMMENDED 👑 👑	1 Single 1 Twin 1 Double	2 En Suite fac 1 Pub Bath/Show	B&B per person £13.00-£18.00 Single £13.00-£18.00 Double	Open Jan-Dec Dinner 1800-2000 B&B + Eve. Meal £19.00-£24.00
			In quiet location overlooking Marwick Bay, close to RSPB reserves. Local produce used whenever possible, fresh fish and shellfish. Reduced rates for longer stays.			
DOUNBY, Orkney Mr & Mrs D Paice Dounby House Dounby Orkney KW17 2HT Tel: (Harray) 01856 771535	Map 5 B11	COMMENDED 👑 👑	1 Twin 2 Double	1 En Suite fac 1 Pub Bath/Show	B&B per person £15.00 Single £15.00 Double	Open Feb-Nov Dinner from 1800 B&B + Eve. Meal from £23.00
			Family run Victorian house in quiet village 17 miles (27 kms) from Kirkwall, 9 miles (14 kms) from Stromness. Specialises in bird-watching holidays.			
EVIE, Orkney Woodwick House Evie Orkney KW17 2PQ Tel: (Evie) 01856 751330 Fax: 01856 751383	Map 5 B10	COMMENDED 👑 👑 👑	1 Single 1 Twin 2 Double 1 Family Suites avail	3 En Suite fac 2 Pub Bath/Show	B&B per person £28.00-£36.00 Single £20.00-£33.00 Double	Open Jan-Dec Dinner 1900-2030 B&B + Eve. Meal £33.50-£48.00
			Peace and seclusion in idyllic surroundings. 12 acres (5ha) of wooded grounds with views to the islands. Imaginative fresh food.			

KIRKWALL, Orkney	Map 5 B11						
Mrs M Flett Briar Lea, 10 Dundas Crescent Kirkwall Orkney KW15 1JQ Tel: (Kirkwall) 01856 872747		COMMENDED Listed	2 Single 2 Twin	2 Pub Bath/Show	B&B per person £15.00-£17.00 Single £15.00-£17.00 Double Room only per person £13.00-£15.00	Open Jan-Dec	

19th century stone-built house retaining many original features with large walled garden. Residential area with easy access to town centre.

| Sanderlay Guest House
2 Viewfield Drive
Kirkwall
Orkney
KW15 1RB
Tel: (Kirkwall) 01856 872343
Fax: 01856 876350 | | COMMENDED
👑👑 | 1 Single
1 Twin
2 Double
2 Family | 4 En Suite fac
1 Pub Bath/Show | B&B per person
£13.00-£21.00 Single
£13.00-£19.00 Double
Room only per person
£10.00-£18.00 | Open Jan-Dec | |

Comfortable modern house in quiet residential area on outskirts of town. Some ensuite and 3 self-contained family units.

| Mrs Tonge
Orkrest, Annfield Crescent
Kirkwall
Orkney
KW15 1NS
Tel: (Kirkwall) 01856 872172 | | COMMENDED
👑 | 2 Twin
1 Double | 1 Pub Bath/Show | B&B per person
from £15.00 Single
from £15.00 Double | Open Apr-Oct | |

Modern house within walking distance of town centre. Ground-floor rooms. Lovely views over the harbour to the North Islands.

ORPHIR, Orkney	Map 5 B11						
Mrs Kathy Tait Westrow Lodge Orphir Orkney KW17 2RB Tel: (Orphir) 01856 811360		HIGHLY COMMENDED 👑👑	2 Double	2 En Suite fac	B&B per person £20.00-£22.00 Single £20.00-£22.00 Double Room only per person £20.00-£22.00	Open Jan-Dec	

New bed and breakfast facility located between Kirkwall and Stromness, 0.5 mile (1 km) from Houton ferry. Spectacular views of Scapa Flow and surrounding countryside.

RENDALL, Orkney	Map 5 B11						
Mrs I Sinclair Riff Rendall Orkney KW17 2PB Tel: (Finstown) 01856 761541		COMMENDED 👑	1 Twin 1 Double	2 Pub Bath/Show	B&B per person £12.00-£13.00 Single £12.00-£13.00 Double	Open Jan-Dec Dinner 1900-2000 B&B + Eve. Meal £18.00-£19.00	

A fine example of Orcadian hospitality. Mrs Sinclair, in her farmhouse by the shore, treats you as one of the family. 4 miles to Rousay ferry.

ST MARGARET'S HOPE, Orkney	Map 4 E1						
Mrs M Cromarty The Anchorage St Margaret's Hope Orkney KW17 2SN Tel: (St Margaret's Hope) 01856 831456		HIGHLY COMMENDED 👑👑👑	2 Single 1 Twin 1 Double	4 En Suite fac 2 Pub Bath/Show	B&B per person £18.00-£20.00 Single £18.00-£20.00 Double Room only per person £16.00-£18.00	Open Jan-Dec Dinner 1800-2100	

Listed 19th century, traditional, stone-built house, fully refurbished, overlooking St Margaret's Hope Bay. Seafood on request.

| Mrs Gunn
Bellevue House
St Margaret's Hope
Orkney
KW17 2TL
Tel: (St Margaret's Hope)
01856 831294 | | HIGHLY
COMMENDED
👑👑 | 1 Double
1 Family | 1 Priv. NOT ensuite
2 Pub Bath/Show | B&B per person
£13.00-£15.00 Single
£13.00-£15.00 Double | Open Jan-Dec
Dinner 1800-2100 | |

Stone-built family home dating from 1886 with splendid views of surrounding countryside including Scottish mainland.

OUTER ISLANDS

Details of Grading and Classification are on page vi.

Key to symbols is on back flap.

OUTER ISLANDS

STENNESS, Orkney Mrs MacKay Upper Nist House Stenness Orkney KW16 3HE Tel: (Finstown) 01856 761378	Map 5 B11	COMMENDED Listed	1 Twin 1 Family	1 Pub Bath/Show	B&B per person £13.00-£15.00 Single £13.00-£15.00 Double	Open Apr-Oct
Situated in open countryside midway between Kirkwall and Stromness. Ideal base for exploring Orkney's mainland, and for trips to the other islands.						
STROMNESS, Orkney Mrs V Hourston 15 John Street Stromness Orkney KW16 3AD Tel: (Stromness) 01856 850642/851250	Map 5 B11	COMMENDED Listed	2 Single 1 Twin 1 Double 1 Family	1 En Suite fac 1 Pub Bath/Show	B&B per person £15.00-£17.00 Single £15.00-£17.00 Double	Open Jan-Dec
In quiet situation above harbour, convenient for ferry terminal and shops. Wide choice at breakfast. Rooms with colour TV, tea and coffee and many accessories.						
Alison M Shearer Thira, Innertown Stromness Orkney KW16 3YP Tel: (Kinghouse) 01856 851181		COMMENDED	2 Single 2 Double	4 En Suite fac	B&B per person to £23.00 Single to £23.00 Double Room only per person to £21.00	Open Feb-Nov Dinner 1800-1900 B&B + Eve. Meal to £31.00
Situated in a quiet location 2 miles from Stromness, unrivalled views of Hoy Sound. Home cooking with fresh produce. All rooms ensuite. Private parking.						
Mrs S Thomas Stenigar, Ness Road Stromness Orkney KW16 3DW Tel: (Stromness) 01856 850438		COMMENDED	2 Twin 1 Double	2 En Suite fac 1 Priv. NOT ensuite	B&B per person £25.00 Single £18.00-£25.00 Double Room only per person £15.00-£20.00	Open Apr-Oct Dinner 1800-2100
Rambling historic house with bags of character. Comfortable lounge with sea views to Hoy. Golf course and yacht club nearby.						
Mrs M Tulloch Olnadale, Innertown Stromness Orkney KW16 3JW Tel: (Stromness) 01856 850418		COMMENDED Listed	1 Twin 2 Double	1 En Suite fac 1 Pub Bath/Show	B&B per person from £16.00 Single £15.00-£16.00 Double	Open Jan-Dec
Modern house in quiet road on edge of town, with panoramic views of Hoy Sound. short walk to town and harbour. Good base for touring Orkney.						
SHETLAND **LERWICK** Carradale Guest House 36 King Harald Street Lerwick Shetland ZE1 0EQ Tel: (Lerwick) 01595 692251	Map 5 G5	COMMENDED	2 Single 1 Twin 1 Double	1 En Suite fac 2 Pub Bath/Show	B&B per person £19.00-£23.00 Single £18.00-£20.00 Double	Open Jan-Dec Dinner 1830-1900 B&B + Eve. Meal £23.00-£29.00
Victorian, semi-detached villa retained as a family home. Ground-floor ensuite single room.						
NORTH MAINLAND, Shetland Mrs E Wood Westayre Muckle Roe, Brae Shetland Tel: (Brae) 01806 522368	Map 5 F3	HIGHLY COMMENDED	1 Twin	1 En Suite fac	B&B per person £15.00-£17.00 Double	Open Mar-Dec Dinner 1800-1900 B&B + Eve. Meal £24.00-£25.00
Warm welcome on working croft. Magnificent cliff scenery. Clean sandy beaches. Bird-watching a stone's throw away. Peaceful.						

OUT SKERRIES, Shetland	Map 5 H3	COMMENDED ♛	1 Single 1 Twin 1 Double	2 Pub Bath/Show	B&B per person £14.00 Single £14.00 Double Room only per person £10.00	Open Jan-Dec Dinner 1800-2100 B&B + Eve. Meal £21.00	

Mrs K Johnson
Rocklea, East Isle
Out Skerries
Shetland
ZE2 9AS
Tel: (Out Skerries)
01806 515228

Family run, fully modernised house close to the pier.
Bird-watching, seal-watching and sea fishing available.

SCALLOWAY, Shetland	Map 5 F5						

Broch House

Upper Scalloway, Scalloway, Shetland ZE1 0UP
Telephone: 01595 880767 Fax: 01595 880731

Three twin rooms with ensuite facilities, colour TV and
tea-making facilities. Residents' lounge.
Within 15 minutes of Lerwick. Near local bus route.

Broch House Guest House
Upper Scalloway
Scalloway
Shetland
ZE1 0UP
Tel: (Scalloway) 01595 880767
Fax: 01595 880731

COMMENDED ♛♛
3 Twin 3 En Suite fac B&B per person to £19.00 Single to £17.00 Double Open Jan-Dec

Modern house in elevated position with excellent views over Scalloway.
All rooms ensuite facilities.

UNST, Island of Map 5 G1
Miss F Wilson
Barns, New-Gord
Westing, Unst
Shetland
ZE2 9DW
Tel: (Uyeasound)
01957 755249

COMMENDED Listed
4 Twin 3 Pub Bath/Show B&B per person £16.00-£17.00 Single £16.00-£17.00 Double Open Jan-Dec Dinner 1800-2000 B&B + Eve. Meal £22.00-£23.00

Comfortable family house with magnificent coastal views. Ideal for bird-watching,
local fishing and walking. French spoken. 2 annexe rooms.

ISLE OF SOUTH UIST, Western Isles Map 3 B10
LOCHBOISDALE
Patricia Murray
Brae Lea House
Lochboisdale
Isle of South Uist
Western Isles
HS8 5TH
Tel: (Lochboisdale)
01878 700497
Fax: 01878 700497

COMMENDED ♛♛
1 Single 1 Twin 2 Double 1 Family 5 En Suite fac 2 Pub Bath/Show B&B per person £20.00-£25.00 Single £20.00-£25.00 Double Room only per person £15.00-£20.00 Open Jan-Dec Dinner 1830-2130 B&B + Eve. Meal £28.00-£32.00

Modern bungalow with full ensuite facilities. Quietly situated at edge of village.
Well situated for ferry.

OUTER ISLANDS

Dundonnell

1 bothy, living/sleeping area, sleeps up to 12,
£2.35-£4.20
Badrallach Bothy, Croft No. 9, Badrallach,
Dundonnell, Ross-shire, IV23 2QP

Edinburgh

2 double, 7 family, £12.00-£18.00 double
Kinnaird Christian Hostel,
Frances Kinnaird House,
14 Coates Crescent, Edinburgh, EH3 7AG
Tel: 0131 225 3608

3 family, 5 pub bath/show,
B&B per person £8.50-£10.00 single
Drifters Backpackers Hostel,
7 Lower Gilmore Place,
Edinburgh, EH3 9NY   Tel: 0131 229 2436

Glencoe

1 house, 2 bunkhouses, 4 bedrms (grd flr
avail), sleeps 1-60, total sleeping capacity 60,
min let 1 night, £5.50-£7.00 per night,
Jan-Dec
H MacColl, Leacantuim Farm Bunkhouses,
Glencoe, Argyll, PA39 4HX
Tel: (Ballachulish) 01855811 256

Grantown-on-Spey

1 hostel, 2 pub rms, 9 bedrms (grd flr avail),
sleeps 27, min let 1 night,
£8.00-£12.00 per night, Jan-Dec
Sue Redfearn, The Strathspey Estate Office,
Heathfield, Grantown-on-Spey,
Moray, PH26 3LG
Tel: (Grantown-on-Spey) 01479 872529
Fax: 01479 873452

Kincraig, by Kingussie

1 hostel, 2 pub rms, 12 bedrms (grd flr avail),
sleeps 36, min let 1 night, £8.00 per night,
Jan-Dec
The Warden, Badenoch Christian Centre,
Kincraig, Inverness-shire, PH21 1NA
Tel: (Kincraig) 01540 651373
Fax: 01540 651373

Kingussie

1 self catering hostel, sleeps 34,
£8.00 per person per night, Jan-Dec
Mr W and Mrs J Petrie, 68 High Street,
Kingussie, Inverness-shire, PH12 1HZ
Tel: 01450 661334

1 twin, 2 double, 2 priv. NOT ensuite,
2 pub bath/show, B&B per person
£15.00-£17.00 double, room only
per person to £12.00, Jan-Dec
Graham Christie, Dunmhor House,
67 High Street, Kingussie,
Inverness-shire, PH21 1HX
Tekl: 01540 661809

Lerwick

1 hostel, 5 pub rms, 10 bedrms (grd flr avail),
sleeps 64, min let 1 night,
£5.85-£6.95 per person per night, Apr-Oct
Islesburgh Youth Hostel, Islesburgh House,
King Harald Street, Lerwick,
Shetland, ZE1 0EQ
Tel: (Lerwick) 01595 692114

Lochmaddy

1 outdoor activity centre,
5 bedrms (grd flr avail), sleeps 20,
from £6.00 per person per night, Jan-Dec
Niall Johnson, Uist Outdoor Centre,
Cearn Dusgaidh, Lochmaddy,
North Uist, Western Isles
Tel: (Lochmaddy) 01876 500480

Nethy Bridge

1 hostel, 4 pub rms, 15 bedrms (grd flr avail),
sleeps 8-59, min let weekend,
£6.50-£9.50 per person per night, Jan-Dec
Richard Eccles, Nethy House, Nethy Bridge,
Inverness-shire, PH25 3DP
Tel: (Nethy Bridge) 01479 821370
Fax: 01479 821370.

Onich, by Fort William

1 bunkhouse, 1 pub rm,
3 bedrms (grd flr avail), sleeps 25,
min let 1 night, £6.00 per night, Jan-Dec
Inchree Bunkhouse, Onich, Fort William,
Inverness-shire, PH33 6SD
Tel: (Onich) 01855 821287
Fax: 01855 821287

Perth

1 halls of residence, 1 pub rm, 62 bedrms,
sleeps 64, min let 1-2 nights,
£10.00 per person per night,
college recess periods in Oct, Easter, Summer
Mrs K Soutar, Residence Manager,
Perth College, Crieff Road, Perth, PH1 2NX
Tel: (Perth) 01738 621171 ext 223
(day)/622192
Fax: 01738 631364

Portree

1 independent hostel, 1 pub rm, 5 bedrms
(grd flr avail), sleeps 6, min let 1 night,
£8.50-£9.50 per night, Jan-Dec
Portree Backpackers Hostel, Dunvegan Road,
Portree, IV51 9HQ
Tel: (Portree) 01478 613641

Sleat

1 bunkhouse, 2 pub rms, 2 bedrms, sleeps 10,
£5.00-£6.00 per person per night, Jan-Dec
Peter MacDonald, Sleat Bunkhouse,
The Glede, Kilmore, Isle of Skye
Tel: (Ardvasar) 01471 844440/01471 844272

Ullapool

3 twin, 5 family, 3 en suite fac,
5 pub bath/show, room only per person
£8.00-£10.00, Jan-Dec
West House Hostel, West Argyle Street,
Ullapool, Ross-shire, IV26 2TY

The Scottish Tourist Board, in conjunction with the English and Wales Tourist Boards, operates a national accessible scheme that identifies, acknowledges and promotes those accommodation establishments that meet the needs of visitors with disabilities.

The three categories of accessibility, drawn up in close consultation with specialist organisations concerned with the needs of people with disabilities, are:

CATEGORY 1	CATEGORY 2	CATEGORY 3
Unassisted wheelchair access for residents	Assisted wheelchair access for residents	Access for residents with mobility difficulties

Category 1

Airlie Mount Holiday Services
2 Albert Street
Alyth
Blairgowrie
PH11 8AX

Ardgarth Guest House
1 St Mary's Place
Portobello
Edinburgh
EH15 2QF

Mrs Borrett
Cruachan
Dalmally
Argyll
PA33 1AA

Rowantree Guest House
38 Main Street
Glenluce
Newton Stewart
Wigtownshire
DG8 0PS

The Courtyard Restaurant
Eaglesfield, by Lockerbie
Dumfriesshire
DG11 3PQ

Westwood House
Houndwood
By St Abbs
Berwickshire
TD14 5TP

Category 2

Auchendinny Guest House
Treaslane
Skeabost Bridge
Isle of Skye
Inverness-shire
IV51 9NX

Mill Croft Guest House
Lawrence Road
Old Rayne, Insch
Aberdeenshire
AB5 6RY

Mrs C A Murphy
Orchard House
298 Annan Road
Dumfries
DG1 3JE

Old Pines Restaurant with Rooms
by Spean Bridge
Inverness-shire
PH34 4EG

Category 3

Aaron Glen Guest House
7 Nivensknowe Road
Loanhead
Midlothian
EH20 9AU

Arden House
Newtonmore Road
Kingussie
Inverness-shire
PH21 1HE

Avalon
12 West Side
Tarbert
Harris, Western Isles
HS3 3BG

Averon Guest House
44 Gilmore Place
Edinburgh
EH3 9NQ

Avondale Guest House
Newtonmore Road
Kingussie
Inverness-shire
PH21 1HF

Birchtree Cottage
1 Barnton Grove
Edinburgh
EH4 6EQ

Blackton Farm
King Edward
Banffshire
AB45 3NJ

Dromnan Guest House
Garve Road
Ullapool
Ross-shire
IV26 2SX

Farmers Inn
Main Street
Clarencefield
Dumfriesshire
DG4 4NF

Innis Mhor
Ardheslaig
Strathcarron
Ross-shire
IV54 8XH

Kinross House Guest
House
Woodside Avenue
Grantown-on-Spey
Moray
PH26 3JR

Lindsay Guest House
108 Polwarth Terrace
Edinburgh
EH11 1NN

Mr D Barclay
Burnock Water
Haywood Road
Moffat
Dumfriesshire
DG10 9BU

Mrs Bennett
Mossfiel
Doune Road
Dunblane
Perthshire
FK15 9ND

Mrs Fife
Beehive Cottage
Kingston
North Berwick
East Lothian
EH39 5JE

Clarke Cottage Guest
House
139 Halbeath Road
Dunfermline
Fife
KY11 4LA

Craiglinnhe Guest House
Ballachulish
Argyll
PA39 4JX

Mrs I Knight
Hopefield House
Main Street
Gullane
East Lothian
EH31 2DP

Mrs M Cooper
Lynwood, Golf Road
Brora
Sutherland

Mrs P j Borland
Knoydart
Windhill
Beauly
Inverness-shire
IV4 7AS

Priory Lodge
8 The Loan
South Queensferry
West Lothian
EH30 9NS

The Priory
Bracklinn Road
Callander
Perthshire
FK17 8EH

Index of Establishment Locations

Use this index to find which section of this book a location appears in

The Scottish Tourist Board produces a series of four accommodation guides to help you choose your holiday accommodation. The most comprehensive guides on the market, they give details of facilities, price, location and every establishment in them carries a quality assurance award from the Scottish Tourist Board.

SCOTLAND: HOTELS & GUEST HOUSES 1997 £9.50
(incl. p&p)

Over 1,600 places to stay in Scotland, from luxury town and country hotels to budget-priced guest houses. Details of prices and facilities, with location maps. Completely revised each year.
Full colour throughout.

SCOTLAND: BED & BREAKFAST 1997 £6.50
(incl. p&p)

Over 1,500 Bed & Breakfast establishments throughout Scotland offering inexpensive accomodation. The perfect way to enjoy a budget trip and meet Scottish folk in their own homes. Details of prices and facilities, with location maps. Completely revised each year.

SCOTLAND: CAMPING & CARAVAN PARKS 1997 £4.50
(incl. p&p)

Over 200 parks detailed with prices, available facilities and lots of other useful information. Parks inspected by the British Holiday Parks Grading Scheme. Also includes caravan holiday homes for hire. Location maps. Completely revised each year.

SCOTLAND: SELF CATERING 1997 £7.00
(incl. p&p)

Over 1,200 cottages, apartments and chalets to let – many in scenic areas. Details of prices and facilities, with location maps. Completely revised each year. Full colour throughout.

You can order any of the above by filling in the coupon or by telephone.

ORDER FORM ON
NEXT PAGE

PUBLICATIONS ORDER FORM

Mail Order

Please tick the publications you would like, cut out this section and send it with your cheque, postal order (made payable to Scottish Tourist Board) or credit card details to:

Scottish Tourist Board, FREEPOST, Dunoon, Argyll PA23 8PQ

Scotland: Hotels & Guest Houses 1997 _____**£9.50**
(incl. P&P) ◼

Scotland: Bed & Breakfast 1997 _____**£6.50**
(incl. P&P) ◼

Scotland: Camping & Caravan Parks 1997_____**£4.50**
(incl. P&P) ◼

Scotland: Self Catering 1997 _____**£7.00**
(incl. P&P) ◼

BLOCK CAPITALS PLEASE:

NAME (Mr/Mrs/Ms) _____

ADDRESS _____

_____

POST CODE_____ TELEPHONE NO. _____

TOTAL REMITTANCE ENCLOSED £_____

PLEASE CHARGE MY *VISA/ACCESS ACCOUNT (*delete as appropriate)

| Card No. | | Expiry Date | |

Signature _____

Date _____

Telephone Orders

To order BY PHONE: simply ring 0990 511 511 (national call rate) quoting the books you would like and give your credit card details.